Eliminating Racism

Profiles in Controversy

PERSPECTIVES IN SOCIAL PSYCHOLOGY

A Series of Texts and Monographs • Edited by Elliot Aronson

A Continuation Order Plan is available for this series. A continuation order will bring
delivery of each new volume immediately upon publication. Volumes are billed only
upon actual shipment. For further information please contact the publisher.

Eliminating Racism

Profiles in Controversy

Edited by
Phyllis A. Katz
Institute for Research on Social Problems
Boulder, Colorado

and
Dalmas A. Taylor
Wayne State University
Detroit, Michigan

Published under the auspices of the Society for the
Psychological Study of Social Issues

Plenum Press • New York and London

Library of Congress Cataloging in Publication Data

Eliminating racism: profiles in controversy / edited by Phyllis A. Katz and Dalmas
   A. Taylor.
     p.   cm.—(Perspectives in social psychology)
   Includes bibliographies and index.
   ISBN 0-306-42631-5
   1. Racism—United States. 2. United States—Race relations. I. Katz, Phyllis A. II.
Taylor, Dalmas A. (Dalmas Arnold), 1933-   . III. Series.
E184.A1E39 1988   87-32172
305.8′00973—dc19   CIP

© 1988 Plenum Press, New York
A Division of Plenum Publishing Corporation
233 Spring Street, New York, N.Y. 10013

Printed in the United States of America

This book is dedicated to our children

Martin J. Katz
Margaret E. Katz
Monique M. Taylor
Carla E. Taylor and
Courtney A. Taylor

whose world will hopefully be made better by
applications of its contents

Contributors

David J. Armor, National Policy Analysts, 5006 Klingle Street, Washington, DC 20016

Elliot Aronson, Adlai E. Stevenson College, University of California, Santa Cruz, California 95064

Lawrence Bobo, Department of Sociology, University of Wisconsin, Madison, Wisconsin 53706

Marilynn B. Brewer, Department of Psychology, University of California, Los Angeles, California 90024

Stuart W. Cook, Department of Psychology and Institute for Behavioral Science, University of Colorado, Boulder, Colorado 80309

Harold B. Gerard, Department of Psychology, University of California, Los Angeles, California 90024

Ira Glasser, American Civil Liberties Union, 132 West 43rd Street, New York, New York 10036

Nathan Glazer, Graduate School of Education, Harvard University, Cambridge, Massachusetts 92138

Alex Gonzalez, Department of Psychology, California State University, Cedar at Shay, Fresno, California 93740

Willis D. Hawley, Office of the Dean of Education, Peabody College, Vanderbilt University, Nashville, Tennessee 37203

James M. Jones, Department of Psychology, University of Delaware, Newark, Delaware 19716

Phyllis A. Katz, Institute for Research on Social Problems, 520 Pearl Street, Boulder, Colorado 80302

Norman Miller, Department of Psychology, University of Southern California, Los Angeles, California 90007

Don T. Nakanishi, Graduate School of Education, University of California, Los Angeles, California 90024

Thomas F. Pettigrew, Board of Studies in Psychology, Adlai E. Stevenson College, University of California, Santa Cruz, California 95064, and Psychology Subfaculty, University of Amsterdam, Weesperplein 8, 1018 XA Amsterdam, The Netherlands

Albert Ramirez, Department of Psychology, University of Colorado, Boulder, Colorado 80309-0345

Pamela Trotman Reid, Department of Psychology, University of Tennessee at Chattanooga, Chattanooga, Tennessee 37403

David O. Sears, College of Letters and Sciences, University of California, Los Angeles, California 90024

Mark A. Smylie, School of Education, University of Illinois, Chicago, Illinois 60680

Dalmas A. Taylor, College of Liberal Arts, Wayne State University, Detroit, Michigan 48202

Harry C. Triandis, Department of Psychology, University of Illinois, Champaign, Illinois 61820

Joseph E. Trimble, Department of Psychology, Western Washington University, Bellingham, Washington 98225

Prologue

This is an important book. As the months of 1987 wind down, our country is embroiled in an ongoing debate about the appropriateness of Judge Robert Bork for the United States Supreme Court. Regardless of the debate's outcome—readers of this book will know, and may someday find irrelevant, the sordid details—far more is at stake than the candidacy of a single individual. Rather, it is our country's attitudes toward and treatment of minority groups, the poor, the powerless, the elderly, the many stigmatized victims of American society. During the decade of the 80s, under the presidency of Ronald Reagan, our nation has taken small but significant steps backward, away from a visionary posture of social concern and responsibility toward a zero-sum mentality that justifies support for our most affluent citizens at the expense of the less powerful. Racism has been part of the American fabric since our nation's founding. Now, abetted by the recidivist policies of the Reagan administration, racism and its other ugly "ism" cousins are in danger of becoming fashionable.

Thus this book is important because it is timely. There is more, however. Guided by the skillful hand of its two distinguished editors and coauthors, Phyllis Katz and Dalmas Taylor, the book adds several new chapters to the continuing story of racism. It is a complex and interesting story, with surprising twists and turns. *Brown v. Board of Education*, the landmark 1954 Supreme Court ruling movingly described by Linda Brown Smith in her foreword, changed the law of the land. But although it legislated equality, it could not legislate an end to racism. Nor could it result in a set of policies that would ensure racial harmony or even a clear reduction in intragroup and intergroup conflict. Even as one important door was flung open, others were shut.

Building on Phyllis Katz's 1976 edited volume on racism, as well as the work of noted social scientists—many of whom have served as contributors to the present collection—this book examines continuing theoretical controversies; the continuing existence of racism directed at groups other than blacks; and the social, psychological, and political consequences of various policy initiatives and opportunities. The resulting portrait of racism is rich, complex, and filled with nuances. There are few simple truths to be found in the pages of this book.

Finally, a word about the organization that has sponsored this book. The Society for the Psychological Study of Social Issues (SPSSI) is a 50-year-old organization of social scientists, committed to applying social science wisdom to the analysis and redress of social problems and issues. The work of SPSSI, as represented by the many books we have sponsored over the years, has consistently combined attention to the subtlety and complexity of social science knowledge with the determination to apply what we know to pressing social problems. *Eliminating Racism: Profiles in Controversy* is very much in the spirit of this SPSSI tradition. It is therefore with great pleasure and pride that SPSSI has sponsored this book, and that I personally urge you to read it for yourself.

Jeffrey Z. Rubin
President, 1987–1988
Society for Psychological
Study of Social Issues

September, 1987

Foreword

The chapters presented here provide the reader with an awareness of the divergent views of what constitutes racism and frameworks for reducing it. This book points out that the dialogue and research on this subject since the mid-1970s have yielded increased controversy over the theories, foundation, and continued existence of racism. Ironically, what we viewed in the 1954 *Brown* decision and the Civil Rights Act of 1964 as the beginning of the end of racism turned out to be the beginning of confusion over the course of action to ensure societal acceptance of political mandates. Hence, the title of this book captures the essence of the emotional core of any forum for examining racism, past and present.

One of the most controversial forums has been that of education, beginning with the U.S. Supreme Court's 1954 ruling in *Brown v. Board of Education*. Behind every event that has spawned controversy is a profile in courage. It was not a simple decision for the players in the scenario of the *Brown v. Board of Education* case to step forward and present themselves as evidence of discrimination. Black parents supported by black organizations viewed this legal action as a chance for equal opportunity. Yet, the 1950s were a time when black communities were pained by the thought that bigotry and institutional racism would forever stand in the way of their achieving equality.

Because the foundation of racism and discrimination appeared to be rooted in the American system of slavery, it was somehow believed that with the end of that system would come the end of unequal treatment. Unfortunately, the reconstruction period of America's history started court-ruled separation. Black people of that time were concerned with basic survival because with freedom came no civil rights, no political rights, nor any rights to be educated in the nation's public schools.

Black people attempted to win these rights through the legal system. The 1876, *U.S. v. Reese* and *U.S. v. Cruikshank*, the civil rights cases of 1883, and finally *Plessy v. Ferguson* in 1896 were all U.S. Supreme Court decisions that further impaired efforts to equalize a system that was inherently unequal.

Without fanfare, race relations began to change on a day when this country was still posting signs reading, "Whites Only." On a balmy day in the fall of 1951 in the quiet Kansas town of Topeka, a mild-mannered black man took his 7-year-old daughter by the hand and walked briskly four blocks from their home to the all-white Sumner School and tried without success to enroll her. The child of whom I speak was me, Linda Carol Brown, and the man was my father, the late Reverend Oliver Leon Brown.

Black parents in Topeka felt that the day of trying to enroll their children in the school nearest their home was long overdue. Many were the evenings when my father would arrive home to find my mother almost in tears because I would get only halfway to the school bus stop, which was a seven-block walk from my home. I could make only half the walk because the cold would get too bitter for a small child to bear. I can still remember starting that bitter walk, and the terrible cold that would cause my tears to freeze on my face. I would return home running as fast as I could back through the busy and dangerous railroad yards of the Rock Island Railroad. Through the railroad yards was the only route I could take to reach a very busy avenue that I had to cross to catch the school bus that would carry me some two miles across town to the all-black Monroe public school. These were the circumstances that so angered black parents.

My father pondered, "Why should my child have to cross dangerous railroad tracks and face unbearable winter weather waiting for a badly overcrowded school bus to carry her two miles across town, when there is a school only four blocks from our home? Why must I have to spend time trying to explain to my child that she cannot go to the same school with her neighborhood playmates, who are predominantly white, Indian, and Hispanic, because her skin is black?"

In the face of discouragement, my father, along with 11 other parents, met with the local NAACP and its lawyer, Charles S. Scott, to examine the school situation in Topeka. After trying enrollment and being turned down, a suit was filed in federal court in February 1951.

In Topeka, the issue was not so much integrating public schools to improve the quality of instruction as it was the inaccessibility of the neighborhood schools. Black people were able to live all over town but could not send their children to the schools closest to their home.

During the local court battle, there was a very definite division in the black community. There were those who felt this action was long overdue and still another faction that expressed concern about upsetting the balance of things, which they feared could lead to job loss and threats of violence.

Once again, black parents in Topeka were alarmed because of the prospects for resegregation in the city schools. Although the local board of education developed guidelines with regard to open enrollment that would supposedly keep it from affecting racial balance adversely, black parents remained uneasy. Because of this concern, several local black attorneys began examining records of the Topeka school system. On close scrutiny, they found that there appeared to be several schools with student populations that could easily become resegregated if left unquestioned. Reopening the original *Brown* case gave us an avenue, in Topeka, for placing the school system and its policies under a legal microscope. Thirty-two years after the original *Brown* decision, the reopened case was presented in federal court in October, 1986.

Minorities, the handicapped, and females nationwide must continue exercising their right to legal checks and balances with regard to equal educational opportunity. Continued resistance to desegregating schools is symbolic; it illustrates that America was founded on principles that did not include its minority population. Therefore, it must be fought even by blacks convinced that the educational merit of integrated schools is overstated, misconceived, or simply untrue. For quite literally, the right—whether exercised or not—of black children or any children to attend integrated public schools is a right crucial not only to the success of individual people but to the survival of this country. The majority of our population is growing older, and the young families giving birth to new generations are predominantly black and Hispanic.

The local school board, which somehow believed itself to be above reproach, mailed threatening letters to black teachers, challenging their right to continued employment depending on the outcome of the *Brown* case.

After the unsuccessful attempts in federal court, an appeal was made to the U.S. Supreme Court under the guidance of the NAACP legal staff, specifically the now Honorable Justice Thurgood Marshall. At the Supreme Court level, the case was consolidated with similar cases and argued in terms of the psychological damage brought about by segregation in public education. Experts from the psychological community were called in to testify about whether segregation, in fact, did serve to break a youngster's morale and to block the development of the strong positive self-concept so essential to educational progress.

I don't think my father ever got discouraged. He was the type of man who really had the stamina for going ahead, but at this particular time, neither my parents nor I knew how far-reaching the outcome of the suit would become.

I inherited much of the recognition that might have gone to my father, had it not been for his untimely death in 1961 at the age of 42. If he had lived, I am sure that he would have become a strong civil rights activist in the movement of the 1960s. Little did he know, years ago, that, when he stepped off the witness stand, he was stepping into the pages of history.

Sometimes, I wonder if we really did the nation and its children a favor by taking this case to the Supreme Court. I know that it was the right thing for my father to do then, but after more than 30 years, we find that the Court's ruling remains unfulfilled.

There is still *de facto* segregation throughout much of the United States. It is not that the schools are not equally physically equipped; the problem lies in the physical makeup of the inner city. The housing patterns are still causing predominantly black schools in certain areas. We witness every day the problem of urban renewal: the building of low-income housing in a neighborhood that is already 90% black, thereby making the school in that neighborhood 99% black.

In June 1978, the *Bakke* decision served as a red flag for black America because it brought to light the truth of racism, and discrimination in our society has been so pervasive that none, regardless of educational attainment, wealth, or position, have managed to escape its impact.

The experience in the *Brown* case taught us that blame is an exercise in futility unless accompanied by evidence and action. *Plessy v. Ferguson* was to blame; public schools subscribed to that doctrine, which placed the evidence needed to take action right in front of our faces. The issues are more complex now; a perfect example is *Brown III*, the reopening of the 1954 case, filed in 1979 on behalf of my children and six other families in Topeka. In this instance, attorneys examined more subtle forms of educational discrimination and its effects if left unchallenged. In 1979, the Topeka Board of Education successfully voted to institute an open enrollment policy, lifting past neighborhood boundary restrictions. On request, to be approved by school officials, students could attend any school within the governance of the Topeka Board of Education.

Most of the equality in this country has been legislated or court-ordered, for example, through *Brown v. Board or Education* (1954), the Civil Rights Act of 1964, Title IX, and Public Law 94-14. We are at a crossroads initiated by another era of forced change. According to experts, there are three forces that cause people to change. Change occurs when people hurt, become bored with mediocrity, or discover mutually acceptable goals. All of these forces are at work now.

Efforts to counter racism and discrimination may or may not always be successful, but fighting for survival is never a "no-win" policy.

LINDA BROWN SMITH

Contents

I.   THEORETICAL CONTROVERSIES

A. INTEGRATION VERSUS PLURALISM

3

B. Symbolic versus Realistic Group Conflict

4

5

Lawrence Bobo

II. RACISM TOWARD BLACKS: HOW GENERALIZABLE?

6

James M. Jones

7

8

9

10

Pamela Trotman Reid

III. SOCIAL POLICY

A. DESEGREGATION

11

Harold B. Gerard

12

Stuart W. Cook

B. BUSING

13

David J. Armor

14

Willis D. Hawley and Mark A. Smylie

C. Intergroup Conflict

15

Desegregation, Jigsaw, and the Mexican-American Experience 301
Elliot Aronson and Alex Gonzalez

16

Contact and Cooperation: When Do They Work? 315
Marilynn B. Brewer and Norman Miller

D. Affirmative Action

17

The Future of Preferential Affirmative Action 329
Nathan Glazer

18

Affirmative Action and the Legacy of Racial Injustice 341
Ira Glasser

19

Conclusion 359
Dalmas A. Taylor and Phyllis A. Katz

Introduction

Phyllis A. Katz and Dalmas A. Taylor

More than 10 years ago, the Society for the Psychological Study of Social Issues (SPSSI) published a manuscript about racism. That book, edited by one of the present editors (Katz, 1976), focused on both the origins and the possible solutions to the problem of white racism toward blacks. The various authors reviewed the pertinent social science literature. Since then, much appears to have changed, and the present volume originated in order to gauge and document what has transpired since the mid-1970s. Differing ways of viewing the problem of racism are apparent in a variety of realms, including research, theory, emotional tone, and the sociopolitical context. The purpose of this volume, then, is to describe some of these changes, to discuss their interrelationships, and to assess the current state of the field.

Three compelling trends have occurred in race research over the past decade. The first and most striking one is the proliferation of controversies with regard to earlier ideas and concepts. In 1975, most social scientists believed that a variety of remedies (such as desegregation and affirmative action) would be effective in reducing racist attitudes and behavior. These expectations arose from earlier theoretical positions and were in accord with the political climate of the 1960s. Hopefulness was evident, combined with optimism that progress would continue to be made in reducing white racism and elevating the economic and social status of minorities. The increased interest in racism research (e.g., Katz, 1976) was concomitant with the legislative and judicial progress generated by the civil rights movement.

The picture appears to be quite different now. The momentum generated by the civil rights movement appears to have slowed (or some would say reversed; e.g., Marable, 1984); the political climate has changed from optimism to retrenchment; and social scientists have been busily debating about the theoretical and empirical underpinnings of such previously accepted notions as the "contact" hypothesis and affirmative action. There are now at least two sides to every issue pertinent to the question of how best to reduce racism. Although the goal has presumably not changed, the most salient characteristic since the mid-1970s has been the emergence of controversy regarding the effectiveness of previously espoused solutions.

For this reason, the present editors decided to use the theme of controversy as our

PHYLLIS A. KATZ • Institute for Research on Social Problems, 520 Pearl Street, Boulder, Colorado 80302.   DALMAS A. TAYLOR • College of Liberal Arts, Wayne State University, Detroit, Michigan 48202.

major organizational framework. A dialectical approach seemed to best capture the flavor of what has transpired. Toward this end, we have selected areas where contradictory positions have emerged and have chosen a number of distinguished protagonists to delineate their positions.

In one sense, the theme of controversy or paradox has been present from the very beginnings of scientific research on racism. The reader will note, for example, that many of the chapter authors refer to the seminal work of Gunnar Myrdal. In 1944, Myrdal addressed the paradox that was (and perhaps still is) at the root of American racism, namely, the dilemma of reconciling prejudice and discrimination (particularly against blacks) with the espoused American ideals of equality and justice. In 1944, Myrdal remarked that, with regard to race relations, "America is continuously struggling for its soul" (p. 4). Both the prejudice and the guilt may be, to borrow from Rap Brown, as American as apple pie. How this ambivalent "dilemma" has been enacted has varied with each historical period, but it remains with us, nevertheless. The concept of *symbolic racism* (discussed in the ensuing chapters by Sears and by Bobo) suggests that we may be witnessing yet another transformation of this dilemma to a more subtle level. From our current vantage point, we seek to explain and understand why controversy has increased since the mid-1970s, relative to the previous decade. It may be the case, however, that the absence of controversy in the late 1960s and early 1970s was the exception.

A second important trend in research over the past decade has been the increase in the number of minority group theorists and investigators (cf. Boykin, Franklin, & Yates, 1979). Before the mid-1970s, most studies about racism were conducted by white males. This circumstance, of course, was not essentially different from that in other fields, as academia was then primarily a white and largely male world. Although particularly paradoxical with regard to the study of racism, a perspective other than a white one was largely absent from the scholarly literature.[1] The recent increase in ethnic diversity among investigators, then, brings with it both welcome and needed change. Since the mid-1970s, minority group researchers have contributed new and significant perspectives to the field, both in the promulgation of new theories and in the interpretations of older ones. We have attempted to reflect this change in this book.

A third significant trend also merits attention. The overwhelming majority of studies about racism conducted through the early 1970s were concerned primarily with racism toward blacks. Since the mid-1970s, considerably more attention has been devoted to the effects of racism on other minority groups, including Hispanic Americans, Asian Americans, and native Americans. Concurrently, there has been a related proliferation of work dealing with sexism that was initially generated by the women's movement. This trend undoubtedly reflects the increased consciousness on the part of all groups that have experienced discrimination and economic disadvantage.

Much of this newer work builds on earlier theories about racism toward blacks. The question of how much similarity there is between blacks and other disadvantaged groups is itself an issue of controversy, however. Many investigators believe that the underlying mechanisms of ingroup–outgroup processes are analogous for all oppressed ethnic minority groups.[2] Nevertheless, each group has its own unique history and has experienced

---

[1] Although the work of two black psychologists (Kenneth and Mamie Clark) was extremely important in the *Brown v. Board of Education* desegregation decision, it should be noted that the other signers of the Social Science Statement that influenced the Court (discussed at length in Stuart Cook's chapter) were white.

[2] The term *ethnic minority group* is used to convey the broad range of culturally diverse populations that have suffered discrimination at the hands of whites. The dynamics, however, in most instances, could refer to women even though women do not, as a group, constitute a statistical minority. The issue of the parallels between racism and sexism has been dealt with recently in a Society for the Psychological Study of Social Issues (SPSSI) volume edited by Smith and Stewart (1983).

different patterns of discrimination. These effects have not always been comparable. As Nakanishi notes in Chapter 8, for example, discrimination against Japanese-Americans has not resulted in the academic achievement decrements associated with other minorities but has had other negative impacts. The assessment of racism's effects, then, clearly need to be broadened. It follows that various techniques for reducing racism and sexism may also differ for particular groups.

The generalizability of research on white racism toward blacks is essentially an empirical question, and one that has theoretical ramifications as well. It is dealt with by a number of authors in the succeeding chapters. Glazer, for example, espouses a position against the general utility of affirmative action programs but suggests that they should be used for blacks because of the profound social and historical antecedents uniquely associated with racism toward blacks. Pettigrew (Chapter 2) and Jones (Chapter 6) also comment on the particularly pernicious and devastating effects of white racism toward blacks. On the other hand, Ramirez, Nakanishi, and Trimble point to the unique aspects of racism toward Hispanic, Asian Pacific, and native Americans, respectively in Chapters 7, 8, and 9. Reid (Chapter 10) also cautions us not to "lump" gender groups within minorities together because of the often differential effects of racism on males and females within each group.

To summarize, there have been three prominent trends in racism research over the past decade. These include a proliferation of controversy with regard to both theory and remediation techniques, an increase in minority investigators, and a broadened focus on a variety of minority groups in addition to blacks. This book, then, has been organized so as to reflect these trends. The focus is on controversy, the ethnic and gender composition of the book's authors is varied, and the relation between racism toward blacks and that toward other minority groups is specifically considered.

ORIGINS AND POSSIBLE EFFECTS OF RECENT CONTROVERSIES

The questions can be raised: Why do social scientists today seem so embroiled in debates with one another in contrast to the mid-1970s? Why has controversy been the hallmark since then, and what are the implications for future research and public policy?

There appear to be at least three possible explanations underlying the proliferation of divergent views. The first has to do with the nature of cumulative social science data. Generally, as a field matures and more data are collected, methodology becomes more varied, and complexity and conflicting results become more evident. This trend appears to be relevant to our understanding of both school desegregation effects (dealt with in Chapter 11 and 12) and the current status of the "contact" hypothesis. This hypothesis, originally postulated by Allport (1954), suggests that an increase in intergroup interaction will result in improved race relations under certain specified conditions. Tests of the contact hypothesis have generally been positive in laboratory-controlled conditions. In field studies, however, the data have been much less consistent. This disparity has led some investigators (e.g., Gerard in Chapter 11) to question the theoretical underpinnings of the hypothesis itself and other researchers (e.g., Cook, Chapter 12; Aronson & Gonzalez, Chapter 15) to conclude that this very inconsistency can, in fact, be explained on the basis of the theory; that is, negative results occur where basic prerequisites have not been met. As more research is conducted, then, some data will appear to be in accordance with and some to contradict existing theory. In one sense, then, the presence of controversy may simply be reflecting the more mature state of the field.

A second factor that may be related to divergence is that earlier theoretical explanations may gradually become outdated and may need to be revised and/or supplanted. This trend may be involved in conceptualizations about white prejudice. Since the mid-1960s, decreased societal tolerance of verbal expressions of bigotry has made overt prejudice much less acceptable and infrequent. Some have argued (e.g.,Bobo, Chapter 5) that these changes are profound and that white attitudes that impact negatively on blacks reflect group interest motives and/or ideals about individualism rather than racism. In contrast, Sears and his colleagues have argued (see Chapter 4) that the underlying processes remain similar even though the forms have changed. Thus, although responses and societal norms have changed considerably, whether theories that explain contemporary intergroup attitudes and behavior need to be revised is itself a controversial issue.

This factor may also be relevant to the contact hypothesis. Several disappointing reviews of school desegregation research led some investigators to conclude that Allport's theory was wrong. Despite this possibility, the extensive citation of Allport's work suggests that his concepts remain very much with us. Thus, although the field may be ripe for new theoretical positions, it appears that varying interpretations of data relevant to our long-standing theories are generating much of the controversy.

A third explanation for the increased controversy has less to do with science and more to do with the political backdrop. Although social scientists can influence policy, their values are, in turn, also affected by the existing political climate. Since 1981, we have had a conservative administration for which civil rights enforcement has not been a high priority, and by which many earlier gains and goals are being publicly questioned. Certain positions that might have been difficult to state in the mid-1970s are more fashionable now. The effects (both actual and potential) of this change in political climate on the status of minority groups and women have been chilling. Such a dramatic political change affects individuals and groups (including social scientists) in profound ways, by altering the rate and direction of social change processes.

The processes of social change are extremely complex (Katz, 1974; Lauer, 1973; McGrath, 1983), and what emerges most clearly is that it is a constant process that is rarely if ever, unidirectional. A comparison of the varying actions of national administrations demonstrates vividly how profoundly the prevailing political climate can affect the course of social change (Taylor, 1984b). Governmental influence is evident both in the research enterprise itself and in its effects on general public opinion.

With regard to research, the political climate influences the kinds of support given (or not given) to social scientists in both direct and indirect ways. For example, the current administration has attempted (although not always successfully) to reduce overall funding levels for social science research and social issues research (such as racism and sexism) in particular. Some readers may recall that the mission statement at the National Institutes of Mental Health was altered briefly in the early 1980s so as to exclude social research and the study of outgroup discrimination as being relevant to mental health. In contrast, the 1960s and the early 1970s witnessed an increase in the support of these types of scientific efforts.

Governmental action (or inaction) also affects public attitudes in complicated ways. Although some have argued that the actions of the current administration merely reflect the country's conservative mandate, a myriad of public opinion surveys do not support this contention. If anything, in the race relations area, more people support strategies such as affirmative action more strongly now than they did in the mid-1970s (Ferguson & Rogers, 1986).

Nevertheless, people of color are experiencing lowered economic and social status as a result of current government policies (see Jones, 1985). This phenomenon itself interacts with public attitudes. Myrdal's work (1944) suggests, for example, that white attitudes toward blacks will become more negative as the status of blacks deteriorates; thus deterioration further compounds the problem of intergroup relations. In an early methodological note, Myrdal attempted to clarify the "vicious circle" of what was then referred to as "the

Negro problem." Basically, he argued that white prejudice was determined in part by black economic and social status. According to Myrdal, the lowering of black status indices, such as wages, housing, and education, increases white prejudice (which consequently keeps the indices low), whereas the raising of these indices reduces white prejudice. Thus, perception of steady improvement should have positive effects for people of color and intergroup relations, and actions that cause backsliding should have negative repercussions that may go beyond any specific actions.

If this "vicious circle" concept has any validity, the failure of some earlier governmental economic programs to make a dent in hard-core black unemployment (see Murray, 1984), combined with the present administration's attempts to reduce such social programs, does not augur well for the next decade of civil rights progress. Present economic indicators demonstrate a number of declines. Current estimates show, for example, that 86% of black youth live in poverty; one out of every six blacks will be arrested before he or she reaches the age of 19; and unemployment among black youth is up as high as 52% in some areas (Jones, 1986). Moreover, since reaching a peak in the mid-1970s, the number of black college students and faculty has declined considerably (Staples, 1986). Such statistics would appear to some to be a good reason to increase governmental efforts to ameliorate these problems. Paradoxically, however, current efforts appear to be in the opposite direction. Poverty programs are being cut. The Civil Rights Commission no longer sees its mission as the enforcement of civil rights. The Equal Employment Opportunity Commission has significantly diminished its enforcement of affirmative action cases. Job training programs have been drastically reduced and so on. Statistics such as these do not, of course, tell the whole story (as the following chapters will demonstrate). Nevertheless, such declines demonstrate how social movements can lose popular momentum and how the political matrix can strongly influence what is considered acceptable public policy.

It should be noted that the formulation of government policies (even decisions to cut back programs) often relies on social science statistics, but these are often used selectively as justification. As an example, one of the social science treatises currently in vogue is a book by Charles Murray entitled *Losing Ground: American Social Policy, 1950–1980* (1984). In a peculiar twist of logic, Murray made the argument (now widely accepted among many government policymakers) that the amount of money that government spends on economic programs has no effect on poverty (and consequently, on the disproportionate number of minority individuals included in the poverty category). Despite a number of critiques (e.g., Corcoran, Duncan, Gurin, & Gurin, 1985; Ellwood & Summers, 1984; Jencks, 1985) that note multiple deficiencies in Murray's argument (including the fact that most government entitlement programs included in the analysis were aimed at middle-class groups), the book continues to be used as a justification for current policy change. Without going into a detailed critique of Murray's work, we merely wish to point out that reliance on social science by policymakers is still fashionable—it is simply more selective and more in keeping with prevailing ideology.

To summarize, in the field of race relations, the decade from 1975 to 1985 witnessed considerable intellectual controversy, loss of momentum for civil rights progress, and declines in many economic and social indicators for blacks or other oppressed groups. The co-occurrence of these factors is not coincidental.

A final general question can be raised, namely, how the trends since the mid-1970s have affected the tenor of social science research and its relation to public policy. It appears to us that one of the most pervasive effects of this controversy is an increase in intellectual confusion. This lack of faith in any clear-cut course of remedial action may be placing social scientists in a conceptually chaotic situation that seriously undermines their motivation for advocacy in this most significant arena.

It is interesting to note the discrepancy that exists between the present lack of white interest in American racism, on the one hand, and the unanimity of outspoken condemnation of racist practices in South Africa, on the other. More blatant forms of racism, particularly those that occur elsewhere, are apparently easier to deal with. This circumstance is reminiscent of the status of civil rights when the "problem" was perceived to be solely in the South. It is also easy for whites to forget that it was not so long ago that these more virulent forms of racism (e.g., genocide, slavery, and apartheid) were an integral part of the U.S. social structure, and their effects are still very much with us. Perhaps Myrdal's explication of the American "dilemma" did not go far enough; the dilemma may include pathological denial. It may be particularly imperative, therefore, that social scientists extricate themselves from their current controversies so that their knowledge can be used more effectively.

THE MANY FACES OF RACISM

We have chosen not to begin this chapter with the customary definitions on the assumption that the term *racism* has many common meanings by now. Nevertheless, it is of interest to trace the history of its usage and to note some of the different ways in which the authors in this book use (or do not use) the term.

In the 1937 edition of Webster's unabridged dictionary, the word *racism* was not even included. By 1949, however, it had clearly entered into the lexicon, probably because of the racist philosophy of Nazi Germany. In the 1949 edition of *Webster's Intercollegiate Dictionary*, the term is defined as the "assumption of inherent racial superiority or the purity and superiority of certain races and consequent discrimination against other races." There are several interesting features in this definition. First, it subsumes both a belief system and the behavior that derives from it. Second, the belief system is based on "inherent" and presumably biologically based differences. A more recent dictionary definition (Webster, 1983) is somewhat similar: "A belief that race is the primary determinant of human traits and capacities and that racial differences produce an inherent superiority of a particular race." Note again the emphasis on biological differences, but the more current definition talks only about the belief system and not the ensuing behavior.

Although the authors in this book differ considerably in their usage of the term *racism,* none would currently define it in this way. Although views about genetic inferiority have not disappeared from public attitudes, some of the authors in this book (e.g., Jones and Sears) make the point that beliefs in underlying biological differences as a justification for discriminatory behavior are becoming increasingly untenable.

One of the present authors (Katz, 1976) previously defined racism rather broadly as "the unequal treatment of individuals because of their membership in a particular group," thereby stressing the behavioral component. The other author (Taylor, 1984a) has also emphasized the behavioral aspects in an attempt to distinguish the concept of *racism* from the concept of *prejudice.* Taylor defines racism as "the cumulative effects of individuals, institutions, and cultures that result in the oppression of ethnic minorities." Although prejudice and discrimination may often be components of racism, they need not be. Taylor's definition focuses on social structure and processes and the manner in which they influence individual behavior rather than the reverse. Conceptually, separating the constructs of racism and prejudice clarifies the fact that attitudes do not always lead to particular behaviors and that certain behaviors can have the same devastating effects, with or without an attitudinal component. This separation made it easier for people to focus on the concept of *institutional racism,* where consequences are negative even though the intent might not be malevolent.

As Sears correctly notes, the term *racism* is more perjorative than some of its synonyms. Nevertheless, it has been in wide usage for at least 15 years and appears to have more connotative power than other terms. To be called *discriminating*, for example, might be viewed as a positive attribute, particularly if no reference is made to what is being discriminated against. The use of *racist* as an adjective leaves no doubt about its valence.

Many specific facets of racism are discussed in this book. A very comprehensive treatment of the term is found in Jones's chapter. He notes that there are three types of racism: individual, institutional, and cultural. The definition of *individual racism* has a great deal of overlap with that of *prejudice* because it refers to individual attitudes. Jones argues that cultural racism is the most pernicious form and perhaps the hardest one to eradicate; he is referring to negative evaluations by whites of black cultural values. These values have historical roots in both African culture and mechanisms used by blacks to cope with oppression. Although Ramirez does not specifically use the term *cultural racism*, the phenomenon he speaks about (i.e., devaluation of culturally different Hispanic values and modes of behavior) appears to be another example of the construct. Reid, in her chapter, reviews a number of definitions of *racism*, including Chesler's (1976), which refers to "acts of institutional procedures which help create or perpetuate sets of advantages or privileges for whites and exclusions or deprivations for minority groups." In this definition, Chesler included both individual discriminatory behavior and institutional racism. Reid points out that Chesler added a proviso, namely, "an ideology of explicit or implicit superiority or advantage of one racial group over another, plus the institutional power to implement that ideology in social operations." Thus, for Chesler, racism is a combination of beliefs and behavior patterns, combined with the power to enact these beliefs.

Sears contrasts "old-fashioned racism" with "symbolic racism"; both types refer to the individual level. In contrast to earlier expressed negative attitudes, symbolic racism is a combination of antiblack affect combined with certain white American Protestant values, such as strong beliefs in individualism and consequent aversion to government help programs. Symbolic racism is typically measured by a person's antipathy to black militancy and to public policies regarding busing, affirmative action, and welfare. Sears's focus on white devaluation of other groups' values seems also to have some overlap with cultural racism.

A number of the authors do not use the term *racism* at all, preferring instead such synonyms as "inequality" (Triandis), "discrimination" (Pettigrew; Trimble), "prejudice" (Bobo; Aronson & Gonzalez), "intergroup conflict" (Brewer & Miller and others), and "racial injustice" (Glasser). Many of the authors who do not specifically use the term, however, do deal specifically with its effects (e.g., segregation and diminished educational and economic opportunities).

Although we have clearly not imposed any uniformity of definition on our contributors, the chapters themselves demonstrate the many variegated aspects of racism. Whether one prefers to focus on the individual, institutional, cultural, old-fashioned, or symbolic variety, we agree with Sears that racism is "deeply ingrained throughout Western culture" and has represented a "major complex of national and cultural beliefs for nearly five centuries." The only point we would add to this observation is that such beliefs have also been typically combined with discriminatory behavior patterns.

OTHER GENERAL ISSUES ADDRESSED

Paralleling the rise in intellectual controversy, we have found a paradox in societal behavior over the past few years. On the one hand, there has been considerable legisla-

tive and judicial progress in the civil rights area, combined with an improvement in public attitudes toward egalitarian goals. On the one hand, there also appears to be increased opposition to specific policies that might be effective in reaching these goals. As Glasser notes, the principles are no longer in doubt, but implementation of these principles has proved to be more difficult than was originally anticipated. The reasons underlying this paradox are explored by a number of contributors (e.g., Sears, Bobo, and Glasser), who offer such explanations as changing mores, transformation of attitude expression, group interest motivations, and the loss of moral consensus. Clearly, the political matrix discussed above also affects this seemingly contradictory public behavior.

A second issue, related to our previous discussion about the meaning of racism, has to do with the historical biases that researchers have brought to the scientific enterprise. For many years, liberal behavioral scientists developed conceptualizations that may have been more reflective of their own ideologies than of the harsh realities of the problems they were dealing with. Most of these theories were promulgated when psychology was largely an all-white, male discipline. One example is the intense preoccupation with attitudes and the widely held (but no longer tenable) assumption that white attitudes needed to be changed first to ameliorate intergroup tensions. How such white bias still affects policy is exemplified by a desegregation study commissioned by the U.S. Civil Rights Commission, with no minority members on the advisory council (*New York Times*, October 30, 1985). As more blacks and other minorities have entered into the behavioral sciences, theories and research paradigms have taken on a different character. There is more talk now, for example, about racism and less about prejudice, and behavioral change is now being researched more than attitude change.

A final issue that is dealt with by several authors concerns the philosophical underpinnings of egalitarian goals. What would a utopian, egalitarian society be like? The image of a "melting pot" has long been a part of our heritage, but as Pettigrew points out, it has always been a myth and, in recent years, not a very popular one at that, particularly for minorities. A closer look at the symbolic aspects of this image reveals why this may be so. Metaphorically, it refers to commonalities among different groups. In actuality, however, the term *melting pot* is synonymous (according to *Roget's Thesaurus*) with *crucible* and *cauldron*. A crucible is a utensil that gives off intense heat and makes all things the same by destroying their original properties. The experience of the Jews in Hitler's ovens is a grim and concrete reminder of what too much melting might do. Even with the cauldron image, where only some of the properties are changed, not everyone wants to be a part of a soup that may be tasteless to start with.

Alternatives to the melting-pot theme include pluralism and varying degrees of cultural assimilation (discussed by both Pettigrew and Triandis). The whole issue of what kind of integration is desirable may be more a white issue than a minority one and may reflect the white bias noted above. As Marable (1984) noted, "It is not a case of wanting integration or separation, it is a case of wanting freedom, justice, and equality" (p. 62). If we need another image, perhaps a salad bowl would be a better update for the melting-pot metaphor. Here, the individual parts retain their distinctive characteristics even while they blend well with each other. (See Taylor, 1974, for a more extensive discussion of this version of pluralism.)

ORGANIZATION OF THIS BOOK

This book is divided into three parts, each dealing with differing areas of controversy. The first section (Chapters 2 through 5) deals with two kinds of theoretical controversies. The chapters by Pettigrew and Triandis, respectively, address what the appropriate

goals of an egalitarian society should be. Although the format here was originally intended to be a dialectical one, based on these authors' previous writings (i.e., integration vs. pluralism), in actuality the final products are not as contradictory as the editors originally envisioned, in part because Pettigrew has changed some of his earlier ideas on the subject. In this book, he does not take the stance that integration is the preferred goal; rather, he attempts to demonstrate that integration is not the opposite of pluralism in most instances and that the perception that they are opposites is politically based. He argues that we have never been a nation that fully espoused either the melting-pot view (particularly for blacks) or complete pluralism (as some degree of assimilation has always been part of our society). He goes on to suggest that the controversy has particular salience for blacks and for black–white relations, which he views as qualitatively different from other interethnic group relations because of the distinctive and deeply entrenched quality of antiblack discrimination. Because of this, he argues, remedies that raised the status of European immigrants cannot be expected to be effective for blacks.

In a somewhat more optimistic tone, Triandis suggests that pluralism (as distinct from monism) is a feasible goal, and he advocates a four-pronged strategy to achieve what he calls "additive multiculturalism." Although he recognizes the interactional problems that come about because of societal heterogeneity, he suggests that techniques be implemented to train whites to appreciate nonmainstream cultures and to interact effectively with many different kinds of people. Triandis is against current attempts at integration that disregard cultural differences. He further argues against the possibility that economically dependent groups can be successfully integrated without first achieving sufficient political power.

The second set of papers, by Sears and by Bobo, are more clearly in opposition to each other in interpreting current data on racial attitudes. Sears explicates the concept of symbolic racism, originally introduced to explain the political role and the changing form of white racism. Symbolic racism is conceptualized as antiblack affect combined with the perception that blacks are violating such American Protestant ethical values as self-reliance and individualism. The construct is measured by attitudes that deny the role of discrimination, which perceive blacks (and presumably other minority groups) as pushing too hard, and which are resentful of programs perceived as "reverse discrimination" toward whites. According to Sears, whites today (because of social desirability effects) much less frequently express negative stereotypes or opposition to interracial contact and equal access, but symbolic racism measures are more predictive of actual behavior. He maintains that direct personal racial threat has little effect on white attitudes (e.g., whites may be against busing programs even when their own children are not involved). In this chapter, Sears further discusses ways in which the symbolic racism construct is being refined.

Bobo differs considerably in his interpretation of symbolic racism. In Chapter 5, he attempts to clarify the distinctive psychological significance of group conflict (a position he has espoused) and prejudice in racial attitudes. He does not see these as mutually exclusive, although he focuses on the role of group conflict. Group conflict is not inevitable despite considerable inequality in economic and political power. Group conflict motives, when present, are reflected in perceptions of incompatible group interests, concern about relative group standing, and threats to group interests. Additionally, the dominant group is typically the major cultural determiner, and its ideology is used to justify its privileged status. According to Bobo, these group conflict and ideological variables contribute more to understanding the paradox referred to earlier (i.e., improved attitudes but resistance to implementation) than does symbolic racism. At the very least, he believes that the two interpretations are equally viable.

The second section of the book (Chapters 6 through 10) deals with the varying forms

of racism experienced by different groups, including blacks, Hispanics, Asian Americans, and native Americans. The final chapter in this section, by Reid, deals with the similarities and differences between racism and sexism and the specific problems experienced by black women, who are affected by both. As previously noted, each of these articles deals both with the unique aspects of discrimination toward each group and compares this with the literature on racism toward blacks.

The first chapter in Part II, by Jones, delineates his theory about levels of racism toward blacks. As previously noted, Jones maintains that there are three levels: individual, institutional, and cultural. Each one is associated with differing kinds of problems for the target group as well as differing kinds of remedies. For individual racism (which he differentiates further into the dominative, aversive, and symbolic varieties), attitude change and interracial contact have been the most widely used remediation strategies. Institutional racism is more complicated and pernicious, requiring, according to Jones, remedies such as affirmative action programs. Institutional racism is itself embedded in the larger problem of cultural racism, which Jones views as the most pervasive and difficult one to deal with because it attacks the foundation of black culture, either by ignoring that there is such a thing, or by denigrating those values that have emerged as blacks have learned to adapt to an oppressive and stigmatizing environment. According to Jones, white attitudes toward black culture (including its African origins) place blacks at risk because they often have to choose between keeping their heritage or making it in the white system (which often means denying that heritage).

Ramirez, in Chapter 7, touches on a comparable problem for Hispanics, namely, the issue of being different in what he views as a culturally monolithic society. Compounding the problem for Hispanics, according to Ramirez, is the relative lack of awareness of Hispanics as victims of prejudice. Even among social scientists, Ramirez argues, the topic is rarely addressed. As is true for blacks, the value orientations of Hispanics are viewed by whites in a pejorative way, and considerable victim-blaming occurs. As a result, many Hispanics have internalized these beliefs, and this internalization often reflects itself in low levels of self-esteem and motivation. Ramirez makes the point that earlier research comparing Hispanics with Anglos was biased because it used measures that were not culturally equivalent for the two groups. One of the particular problems faced by Hispanics is Anglo prejudice toward their accented speech, which generalizes to other attributes as well. (One wonders why whites have negative attitudes toward Spanish accents while regarding French ones as "cute.") Ramirez finds some parallels here to attitudes toward black English. He advocates equal social power and influence between groups as a remedy and cites as an example the beneficial results that occurred in high schools with Chicano rather than Anglo administrators.

In Chapter 8, Nakanishi focuses on the effects of a unique experience in the lives of Japanese-Americans: the internment that occurred in World War II, in which 120,000 individuals were imprisoned simply because of their Japanese heritage. It took this group 20 years to respond politically to this experience, and Nakanishi feels that this response was influenced by the black power movement of the 1960s, which increased the group consciousness of all people of color. The organized political action that took place (and still is taking place) has had beneficial effects for the Japanese-American community, including legislative changes, monetary reparations, and a general increase in political involvement. Nakanishi also talks about the erroneous belief that Japanese-Americans have totally overcome their pejorative racial status and are unaffected by discrimination. Nakanishi believes that the view that Japanese-Americans are the "model minority" has undermined assistance attempts and represents an "ironic twist to the 'victim-blaming' perspective."

Trimble deals in Chapter 9 with the unique problems of racism experienced by

American Indians. In a historical account, he traces the different phases of Euro-Americans' treatment of Indians, beginning with positive reactions by the first explorers and the subsequent negative stereotypes associated with the "bad" Indian. The policies of the federal government have varied widely for 200 years and have included genocide, isolationism, paternalism, and the denial of basic civil rights. In 1830, as more and more Indian land was claimed by whites, Indians were forced to leave their ancestral homes, in violation of earlier treaties made with the government, and it was not until 1948 that all Indians were granted full citizenship. Contemporary results of racism toward Indians include high poverty levels, low achievement and low self-esteem of Indian students, inadequate law enforcement, and the persistence of negative stereotypes. Racism toward Indians has been exacerbated by stereotypes perpetuated in "western" movies, which tend to show Indians in subordinate roles, to show little respect for tribal customs, and to underestimate within-group diversity. Additionally, according to Trimble, the news media tend to portray caricatures of Indians and to show them as if they were all living in the past. Trimble notes that researchers contribute to negative bias by focusing almost exclusively on negative attributes, such as alcoholism and other self-destructive behavior, while ignoring other aspects of Indian life.

The final chapter in this section, by Reid, compares the processes of racism and sexism and looks at their joint effects on black women. Although the processes and effects of racism and sexism show some important similarities, Reid points out some important differences as well. Unlike racism (at least on an individual level), sexism is not regarded as pathological, and its causes have not usually been explained by intrapersonal theories. Sexism is not viewed as a typically American problem, whereas racism usually is, according to Reid. Moreover, males and females are more intertwined in the socialization process than are members of different racial groups. Finally, women can theoretically become a dominant force in society because of their numbers, whereas minority groups cannot. Like some of the other authors in this section, Reid points to bias in research on racism and sexism (including choice of topics, subject selection, interpretation of results, and publication decisions) because research standards and norms are generally decided by white men. In her article, Reid pays particular attention to how the forces of racism and sexism have combined to make black women one of the most economically and racially disadvantaged groups. She points out the fact that the "consequences of racism have not always been gender-blind." In tracing the history of the treatment of black women in this country, she notes that black women were often treated differently during slavery than were black men, because they were subjected to sexual victimization by white men in addition to other oppressions. In the early stages of the civil rights movement, black women were often treated in sexist ways by black men as well as by white ones. According to Reid, the conflicting demands of racial and gender identity have posed unique problems for black women. As an example, standards of physical attractiveness, which play a significant role in female identity, are all determined by whites. She suggests that more research be targeted specifically on the special needs of black women, a recommendation that probably applies equally well to other groups discussed in this section. Although Reid's is the only chapter in this portion of the book that deals with differential racism toward males and females within the same group, this issue may be equally germane to other ethnic minority groups.

The third and final section of this volume is concerned with controversies with regard to four specific remedies that have been offered to reduce both individual and institutional racism: school desegregation, busing to achieve this desegregation, the use of specific contact techniques, and affirmative action. Although we chose contributors whose previous writing appeared to place them on divergent sides of these issues, the reader will note that, in some instances, the polarity is not extreme.

In one sense, the first six chapters of this section all deal with differing facets of the same issue: school desegregation and its implementation on both the societal and the classroom level. The first two chapters in this section focus primarily on interpretations of data relevant to the contact hypothesis in school desegregation, as well as on their relationship to the social science statement offered in the landmark *Brown v. Board of Education of Topeka, Kansas* decision, which ruled that *de jure* segregation of schools was unconstitutional. These two chapters are the only nonoriginal material in the volume.

Gerard raises the question of whether the social science community misled the U.S. Supreme Court with regard to the expected psychological and social benefits of school desegregation. According to Gerard, the conditions associated with successful attitude change as a result of contact (e.g., authority endorsement and absence of competition) usually cannot be met in school situations. He argues that longitudinal data show a widening gap in academic achievement between blacks and whites, thus making it impossible to attain equal status, one of the major conditions for favorable outcomes. He cites both his own large study and those of others to show that stereotypes have persisted rather than dissolved over time and that self-segregation is widespread in classrooms. Because academic performance did not improve, attitudes did not become more positive, and the self-esteem of black students diminished after desegregation, he believes there is little evidence to support the original hypotheses. As a result, Gerard argues, social scientists have lost credibility.

Cook, one of the original signers of the previously referred to Social Science Statement, believes that Gerard has presented a misleading picture of overall findings and has distorted the historical record concerning the impact of and the information contained in the Social Science Statement presented to the Supreme Court in 1954. According to Cook, it is important to understand that what was under review in the *Brown v. Board of Education* case was *de jure* segregation (i.e., segregation mandated by the southern courts) and not *de facto* segregation (more typical elsewhere and caused by residential patterns). The statement reviewed the literature available through 1954 on the effects of *de jure* segregation on blacks and concluded that it contributed to black students' belief that their status was inferior to whites. Cook maintains that this was an accurate assessment of existing evidence. He notes that, at that time, busing was used for segregation purposes, and that it was not until 1971, in the *Swann v. Charlotte* case, that busing was used as a remedy for desegregating schools. Thus, the whole busing issue did not affect the statement. In addition to his attempt to clarify what the statement did or did not say, Cook maintains that Gerard's reading of the evidence is incorrect, and that, when taken cumulatively, the evidence is positive.

Chapters 13 and 14 look specifically at the effects of busing, and once again, we find divergent interpretations of this body of evidence. Armor evaluates three issues with regard to the busing controversy: (a) the use of racial balance formulas, (b) the efficacy of mandatory busing and the "white flight" phenomenon, and (c) the expansion of remedies that include both a city and its surrounding suburbs (where white flight has taken them). He notes that the original *Brown* decision did not contain anything about remedies, and that mandatory busing violates the nonracial assignment approach taken in the earlier decisions. Armor believes that the courts had come full circle in the 1970s by replacing mandatory racial segregation with a system of mandatory racial integration. He raises the question of whether remedies such as busing to achieve racial balance are aggravating rather than alleviating school segregation and presents data that show that mandatory busing results in a very high proportion of whites (50% in Seattle and Los Angeles) leaving the district, in effect making desegregation impossible. Although plans that encompass the suburbs could solve this problem, the U.S. Supreme Court reversed Detroit's attempt to include the suburbs, and such consolidation plans have generally not been upheld since 1979. Armor concludes, then, that mandatory busing programs have hindered desegregation and suggests instead that we replace them with voluntary options and modified voucher-type programs to achieve interdistrict voluntary desegregation.

Hawley and Smylie disagree with Armor's rationale and conclusion on a number of counts. They begin with the assumption (in contrast to Gerard) that school desegregation benefits those who experience it, both by increasing learning opportunities and by preparing children to live in an integrated society. Learning for minorities is increased in desegregated schools for a variety of reasons: higher and more diverse peer levels, increased teacher expectations and training, and more financial resources. These authors also suggest that the potential costs of desegregation (e.g., time and energy lost in riding the bus, financial costs, and loss of parent involvement) have not been shown to affect student behavior very much. Moreover, protests by whites are usually short-lived and not typical, despite the media coverage where incidents occur. Although Hawley and Smylie, too, discuss the "white flight" issue, they note that it is not constant but that it is the greatest from the year before to two years after desegregation occurs. They point out that the reason that voluntary desegregation results in less white flight is that less desegregation is achieved in voluntary programs. To believe that voluntary programs work is, according to these authors, wish fulfillment. They also note that legal mandates to desegregate schools do not occur in a vacuum but are based on findings of discrimination. It should be noted that both the Armor and the Hawley and Smylie chapters present extremely cogent arguments for differing ways to implement the same goal and, thus, are reflective of the controversy we spoke of earlier.

The subsequent two chapters (15 and 16) direct our attention to the more molecular aspects of the desegregation issue, namely, how classrooms can be better organized to achieve the desired results. Aronson and Gonzalez begin their chapter by noting the basic incompatibility of the typical American classroom with the conditions needed for favorable contact effects. As previously noted, these include equal status contact, pursuit of common goals, and institutional support. According to these authors, the pursuit of common goals is the condition least likely to be fulfilled because classrooms are typically highly competitive, and this competition has the effect of emphasizing preexisting differences in ability. They go on to describe an ingenious, yet easily applicable, classroom technique that forces cooperative learning behavior called the *jigsaw technique*. In this procedure, the class is divided into small (six-person) interracial groups in which each component of a lesson is mastered by one person. Cooperation with each person is necessary in order for the whole group to learn the lesson, and this requirement dramatically changes the reinforcement contingencies typically experienced by students. Findings in classrooms using the jigsaw technique reveal almost consistently positive effects in these groups, including more liking for groupmates and school in general, increases in self-esteem, reduction of negative ethnic stereotypes, and increases in minority academic performance. This technique appears to be particularly effective with Hispanic students. The very positive findings associated with the jigsaw procedure contrast with the inconsistent trends obtained in many reviews of desegregation research. These authors would argue that the success of this technique rests on the fact that, in microcosm, it reflects most accurately what the social scientists stated to the U.S. Supreme Court in 1954: Equal status and cooperation are produced by interdependence.

Brewer and Miller, in Chapter 16, focus our attention on yet another important aspect of desegregation: whether improvement in intergroup relations (such as was found by Aronson & Gonzalez) generalizes beyond the immediate contact situation. These authors present us with a fine-grained analysis of what techniques work to achieve this goal. They note that three types of generalization can be achieved: category-based (where more positive attitudes are expressed toward a group), differentiated (where intergroup perceptions become more complex), and decategorization (where social group categories are not attended to and reactions to individuals are personalized). In the first type, the distinctiveness of the category is salient, and this distinctiveness may undermine positive effects in the long run. The second type, the differentiated type of generalization, is achieved by exposing people to diversity within other groups and focusing their attention on distinctive information. In the third type, decategorization, the category information is replaced by individualistic information, which may be totally unrelated to the social category. In the view of these authors, the typical desegregation situation tends to emphasize category-based interaction, whereas it should be designed so as to eliminate the salience of social categories. These authors argue that the use of cooperative learning strategies may not, by themselves, be able to accomplish this goal. They recommend two additional stipulations: (a) that the group be interpersonal rather than task-oriented, and (b) that the selection of group members be perceived as independent of social group categories. Data are presented to substantiate these recommendations for maximizing the probability of generalized positive effects from intergroup contact.

The last two authors, who take opposing viewpoints, are Glazer and Glasser, and their field of battle concerns the use of affirmative action strategies as remedies for institutional racism. Glazer, in Chapter 17, distinguishes first between seeking out applicants from people of color for various positions and the use of "statistical targets," that is, goals and timetables for hiring a specified number of such applicants. A good summary of the underlying philosophical assumptions underlying these positions is presented. There are many people who oppose the use of "quotas" because they feel that they contradict other ideals regarding color-blindness. Glazer notes that the use of goals has not been strongly enforced under the present administration. This appears to be a rather mild way of stating what has transpired, according to the editors. The current administration has gone on record as being against such goals, arguing (against evidence to the contrary, which Glazer presents) that they have not worked. Moreover, the current administration has also joined in court action with many groups seeking to set aside court-imposed affirmative action plans, including instances in which unions have had a clear history of discriminatory practices. This action constitutes more than "lack of enforcement." Glazer takes the position that preferential affirmative-action programs have had positive effects, particularly for blacks, but that dropping such federal requirements for most other people of color and for women would have little effect because procedures that require preference have become institutionalized, particularly in higher education.[3] He concludes that we should do away with affirmative action for some groups and limit the time used for affirmative action purposes for others.

A forceful argument in favor of affirmative action is presented by Glasser, the only author in the volume who is not a social scientist (he is the Executive Director of the American Civil Liberties Union). In the next to last chapter of the book, Glasser outlines the moral case for affirmative action and describes what he views as the loss of the general moral consensus regarding the implementation of racial equality. He notes that no remedy is more controversial than affirmative action and that it has three aspects that require differentiation. The first is court action imposed as a legal remedy to correct

[3]The editors feel that, because Glasser's chapter deals only with affirmative action programs for blacks and not women or other minorities, some of Professor Glazer's opinions, particularly those concerning the effects on women, are not responded to in this book, and that there are contradictory opinions on this issue (cf. Kahn & Robbins, 1985). It should be noted that Harvard University, which Professor Glazer refers to as having institutionalized affirmative action plans, has only a 5% female tenured faculty rate (J. Williams, 1985, personal communication), so perhaps these plans have not had much impact to begin with.

existing discriminatory practices, Glasser argues that, in the face of persistent discrimination, it is neither unreasonable nor unusual for a court to order its end and to measure compliance with a reasonable goal and timetable. In fact, according to Glasser, not applying such remedies in the face of persistent discrimination and exclusion is immoral. The second way of conceptualizing affirmative action is as compensatory opportunity programs, such as the G.I. Bill, which gave various employment and educational preferences to all veterans without their having to prove that they had been personally disadvantaged by military service. Although the moral principle underlying compensatory opportunity for people of color is now under attack, Glasser asks why such programs shouldn't be justifiable on behalf of blacks who were more pervasively disadvantaged by government actions than veterans. A third aspect of affirmative action involves efforts to achieve fair and visible representations for people of color. This component is an argument for affirmative action but is not itself affirmative action.

Glasser goes on to discuss the various criticisms that have been leveled at the affirmative action concept. One is that it lowers standards and undermines the merit system. Glasser argues that preferences have always been given on criteria other than merit (e.g., seniority and children of alumni) and that rules should be the same for blacks as they have always been for whites. A second criticism involves the notion that preference toward a black person would unjustly exclude a white person. Glasser considers this not "reverse discrimination" but a redressing of the fact that, for centuries, less qualified whites were employed while more qualified blacks were not. A final criticism frequently made against affirmative action is that such remedies damage blacks (and presumably other peoples of color as well). Here, Glasser argues that it was discrimination and not the effort to end it that damaged blacks. In contrast to the previous chapter, Glasser believes that doing away with affirmative action would be harmful, but he does agree with Glazer that affirmative action should be a temporary remedy, comparable to the use of chemotherapy in treating cancer.

The final chapter, by the editors, represents an attempt to synthesize the varied information and views presented and to extrapolate from these to assess what future trends in research and social policy on racism might look like.

CONCLUSIONS

As the reader can tell from this brief review of the chapters, the views and interpretations presented in this book are provocative and represent a broad spectrum of positions with regard to remedies for racism. The readers will undoubtedly come to their own conclusions about which ones are the most cogent and persuasive. Our aim here was to focus on current controversial issues, and we think that our contributors have done an excellent job in this regard.

REFERENCES

Allport, G. (1954). *The nature of prejudice.* Reading, MA: Addison-Wesley.
Boykin, A. W., Franklin, A. J., & Yates, J. F. (1979). *Research directions of black psychologists.* New York: Russell Sage Foundation.
Chesler, M. A. (1976). Contemporary sociological theories of racism. In P. A. Katz (Ed.), *Towards the elimination of racism.* New York: Pergamon Press.
Corcoran, M., Duncan, G. J., Gurin, G., & Gurin, P. (1985). Myth and reality: The causes of and persistence of poverty. *Journal of Policy Analysis and Management,* 4(4), 516–536.
Ellwood, D. T., & Summers, L. A. (1984, December). *Poverty in America: Is welfare the answer or the*

problem? Paper presented at the conference on Poverty and Policy: Retrospect and Prospects, Williamsburg, VA (Preliminary—not for quotation).

Ferguson, T., & Rogers, J. (1986, May). The myth of America's turn to the right. *Atlantic,* pp. 43–53.

Jencks, C. (1985). How poor are the poor? *New York Review of Books, 32,* 41–49.

Jones, J. M. (1985). Racism: A cultural analysis of the problem. In J. F. Dovidio & S. L. Gaertner (Eds.), *Prejudice and discrimination and racism: Theory and research.* New York: Academic Press.

Jones, K. M. (1986, March). The black male in jeopardy. *Crisis, 93*(3), 137–164.

Kahn, E. D., & Robbins, L. (Eds.). (1985). Sex discrimination in academe. *Journal of Social Issues, 41*(4), 1–187.

Katz, D. (1974). Factors affecting social change: A social psychological interpretation. *Journal of Social Issues, 30*(3), 159–180.

Katz, D. (1983). Factors affecting social change: A social psychological interpretation. *Journal of Social Issues, 39*(4), 25–44.

Katz, P. A. (1976). *Towards the elimination of racism.* New York: Pergamon Press.

Lauer, R. H. (1973). *Perspectives on social change.* Boston: Allyn & Bacon.

Marable, M. (1984). *Race, reform and rebellion: The second reconstruction in black America 1945–1982.* Jackson, MS: University Press of Mississippi.

McGrath, J. E. (1983). Looking ahead by looking backwards: Some recurrent themes about social change. *Journal of Social Issues, 39*(4), 225–239.

Murray, C. (1984). *Losing ground: American social policy, 1950–1980.* New York: Basic Books.

Myrdal, G. (1944). *An American dilemma.* New York: Harper & Row.

Pear, R. (1985, October 30). Advisor to U.S. desegregation study quits, saying it's biased. *New York Times,* p. 10.

Smith, A., & Stewart, A. J. (Eds.). (1983). Racism and sexism in black women's lives. *Journal of Social Issues, 39*(3), 1–158.

Staples, B. (1986, April 27). The dwindling black presence on campus. *New York Times Magazine,* pp. 46–62.

Taylor, D. A. (1974). Should we integrate organizations? In H. L. Fromkin & J. J. Sherwood (Eds.), *Integrating the organization: A social psychological analysis.* Glencoe, IL: Free Press.

Taylor, D. A. (1984a). Race prejudice, discrimination, and racism. In A. Kahn, E. Donnerstein, & M. Donnerstein (Eds.), *Social psychology.* Dubuque, IA: Wm. C. Brown.

Taylor, D. A. (1984b, June). Towards the promised land. *Psychology Today,* 46–48.

I

THEORETICAL CONTROVERSIES

A. Integration versus Pluralism

2

Integration and Pluralism

Thomas F. Pettigrew

Integration is often presented today as the logical opposite of pluralism. This confusion presents a pointed example of how muddled conceptualization has become in the intergroup area. This chapter contends that this confusion has largely political origins. First, we provide a few essential definitions. Then we discuss the myths that have developed on both sides of the political debate and present the case for the uniqueness of black–white relations in the United States. Finally, the chapter closes with a synthesis of this perspective, and its implications for American race relations.

BASIC DEFINITIONS

The useful figure from Berry (1984; Figure 1) contrasts *integration* with three related concepts. The term differs from *assimilation* in its concern for maintaining cultural identity and characteristics, and from *separation* in its concern for furthering intergroup relations. Yet, integration shares with assimilation a focus on intergroup ties, and with separation a focus on cultural survival. In short, integration represents something more than *desegregation*, simply the ending of formal group separation; and it is the diametric opposite of *marginalization*, the loss of both intragroup and intergroup inclusion and identification.

Seen in this light, integration is necessarily a dynamic set of social processes that allow a trade-off between intragroup identity and intergroup bonds. These social-psychological processes distinguish integration from mere desegregation by facilitating this complex trade-off between in-group and out-group concerns. Importantly shaped by social structure, such processes must involve human interaction. And an array of social-psychological ideas, from the intergroup contact hypothesis (Allport, 1954) to network theory (Granovetter, 1985), have been used to specify these processes. More formally, then, *integration* can be defined as intergroup interaction that involves social processes that facilitate both intragroup integrity and intergroup relations.

Two key varieties of *pluralism* must be delineated before it can be distinguished from

THOMAS F. PETTIGREW • Board of Studies in Psychology, Adlai E. Stevenson College, University of California, Santa Cruz, California 95064 and Psychology Subfaculty, University of Amsterdam, Weesperplein 8, 1018 XA Amsterdam, The Netherlands.

Are positive relations valued and sought?	Are cultural identity and customs to be retained?	
	Yes	No
Yes	Integration	Assimilation
No	Separation	Marginalization

FIGURE 1. Berry's model of intergroup relations. (Adapted from Berry, 1984, p. 12.)

integration: structural and cultural.[1] *Structural pluralism* refers to a national society in which various groups, each with a psychological sense of its own historical peoplehood, maintain some structural separation from each other in intimate primary group relationships and in certain aspects of institutional life (Gordon, 1978). Such separation allows, but does not ensure, *cultural pluralism*, the perpetuation of various groups' distinctive cultural patterns.

Obviously, complete structural pluralism is antithetical by definition to integration. But American institutions do not approach such a restrictive situation save for the notable racial exceptions of blacks in ghettos and native Americans on reservations. Varying degrees of structural pluralism exists among white ethnicities, but it persists in rigorous form only in isolated situations. The typically high intermarriage rates between white ethnicities is a revealing indicator of the extensive erosion of structural barriers between these groups in American society today.

Cultural pluralism is even less prevalent. It is evinced in its purest form largely among first-generation Americans. Except for its more intense varieties, cultural pluralism rarely conflicts with integration. Indeed, as Figure 1 suggests, integration has the potential of enhancing as well as blending cultural traditions. In short, integration can occur—and in practice, has occurred—in the United States together with varying degrees of both structural and cultural pluralism.

But as Popper emphasized (1976), it is the facts and theories—not words and their meanings—that "must be taken seriously" (p. 19). These formal definitions are misleading unless placed in the referent contexts in which these common concepts are typically used. *Assimilation* and *pluralism* are concepts used in North America largely in reference to *national* groups that have arrived over the past 150 years with distinctively non-Anglo cultures. *Integration* is a concept shaped by black–white relations in the United States to refer to inclusion processes for a *racial* group that has a unique history of rigorous exclusion. Some of the confusion over these terms has arisen from a failure to grasp their formal properties. But far more of the confusion stems from a misreading of the intergroup facts of late-twentieth-century American life.

TWO MYTHS

Much has been made during this century of America as a melting pot, as the ultimate assimilator and blender of races, creeds, cultures, and nationalities. Though the idea had

[1]As Yinger (1985) demonstrated, two additional perspectives can also be distinguished: psychological and biological. Consistent with the analysis advanced in this paper, recent work on American ethnicity has uncovered evidence that the phenomenon is increasingly a matter of personal identification, more than it is a matter of actual ancestral roots. Alba and Chamlin (1983) found, for example, that a large and increasing proportion of white Americans identify with only one ethnic group but are, in fact, of mixed ethnic origin.

been voiced earlier, the term derives from Israel Zangwill's 1908 drama. Its currency at the turn of the century was not accidental, of course. Unity among an enormous variety of peoples was the national concern—as it has often been in American history. Thus, though the melting-pot metaphor was clearly erroneous at its conception, it was a highly functional myth for the society. Following the Parsons (1955) and White (1961) insight that ideological contentions reveal a society's principal social strains, one can trace American concern about unity throughout the twentieth century by noting the popularity of this persistent metaphor. Even when it became apparent by the 1940s and 1950s that it was an exaggeration, it was ingeniously bolstered by the concept of a *triple melting pot*. Kennedy (1944) introduced the term after studying intermarriage trends in New Haven from 1870 through 1940, trends that revealed cross-ethnic marriages largely within, but not across, the three principal religious groups. Herberg (1955) popularized the concept in his volume, *Protestant-Catholic-Jews*, which significantly became a best-selling book in the 1950s.

One decade later, however, the melting-pot contention came under heavy attack. Indeed, it was widely vilified as a deceitful component of a wider dominant ideology of Anglo-dominated assimilation that obscured the cultural distinctiveness and contributions of ethnic groups. Again, the timing suggests that the 1960s—with its civil rights movement and demands for black inclusion—caused the ideological emphasis of white thought to shift dramatically, because new strains were felt from black protests for profound structural and cultural changes.

Several interrelated aspects of this reversal deserve mention. Note that the debate, from the myth's origins and continuation to its rejection, was largely political and was carried on by Catholic and Jewish Americans themselves. It is ironic that this trend in ideological emphasis was the exact reverse of the actual intergroup patterns of the United States. In Zangwill's time, interethnic, interreligious, and interracial marriages were rare; today, such marriages are all increasing markedly—with the revealing exception of black–white marriages. But the shift in position accurately reflects the strains in the position of the non-Protestant ethnicities themselves: first, to win acceptance in a competitive society dominated by Protestants, and then, once ensconced in American society, to win rights of distinctive cultural expression and practice.

The sharply drawn terms of the issue—assimilation versus pluralism—reflected the perceptions and needs of *white* groups, not those of black Americans. Blacks were far from Zangwill's view. Only with black incursions into white preserves in the 1960s did the debate reflect the black presence: *integration* versus pluralism. We have noted the fallacy behind equating assimilation with integration, a fallacy rooted in the notion that black Americans are just another ethnicity struggling for power and privilege with other groups. Yet, this new ideological perspective, fueled by threat, took root quickly in the early days of the civil rights movement. Glazer's article in *Commentary*, entitled "Negroes and Jews: The New Challenge to Pluralism" (1964), cogently presented the emerging ideology of threat. And *Beyond the Melting Pot*, Glazer's best-selling book coauthored with now-Senator Daniel P. Moynihan, provided the new view a wide audience and intellectual legitimization (Glazer & Moynihan, 1963). Later, the proponents of this and related positions labeled themselves the "new conservatives."

More recently, critics have countered the renewed emphasis on ethnicity as divisive, inegalitarian, and even racist in its effects (Morgan, 1981; Steinberg, 1981). By substituting "cultural" for "opportunity" explanations, the ideological emphasis on pluralism can obscure the racially discriminatory structures that remain in place in American society. Steinberg (1981) was especially direct:

> Indeed, black intellectuals and leaders have had good reason to balk at the pluralist doctrine. As a group, blacks have always experienced the bitter side of pluralism, and

ideological justifications for maintaining ethnic boundaries carried insidious overtones of racial segregation. . . . Just as ethnic groups have class reasons for tearing down ethnic barriers ahead of them, they also have class reasons for raising ethnic barriers behind them. Thus, it is not uncommon for ethnic groups to invoke democratic principles to combat the ethnic exclusivity of more privileged groups, but to turn around and cite pluralistic principles in defense of their own discriminatory practices. (pp. 255, 258)

As often happens in politically charged debates, a countermyth to the melting-pot conception began to take shape in the 1960s. At least as invalid as what it proposed to replace, the new myth of *complete pluralism* does justice to neither the complexity nor the subtlety of intergroup relations in the United States in the 1980s (Pettigrew, Franklin, & Mack, 1971). In "a nation of immigrants," assimilation is not the opposite of but a part of the same social processes as pluralism. The two conceptually separate phenomena are, in reality, inseparable parts of the same ball of wax, called *American society*. In such a society, claims of complete pluralism are even more absurd than the melting-pot metaphor.

The inseparability of assimilation and pluralism becomes clear when we think of group changes longitudinally. Greeley (1969) proposed an interesting, if speculative, six-step paradigm for the American acculturation and assimilation process that illustrates its interwoven quality with pluralism across time. Observe how assimilation predominates in several of Greeley's steps, pluralism in others, both together in the hopeful sixth step—but all within a single, continuous set of group processes:

1. *Cultural shock* among the new arrivals
2. *Organization and self-consciousness*—and sometimes the actual initiation of a sense of nationalism for "the old country"
3. *Assimilation of the elite*
4. *Militancy*, led by the elite and made possible by the accumulation of at least a modicum of power
5. *Self-hatred and antimilitancy*, articulated most strongly again by the group's elite in reaction to the previous stage
6. *Emerging adjustment*, signifying an easy acceptance of both the ethnic and the "American" identities as completely compatible

Like the Netherlands' complex structural arrangements and "rules of the game" between religious, political, cultural, and racial groups (Goudsblom, 1967), the United States has evolved its own characteristic intergroup structural arrangements and rules. Gordon's useful distinction between *cultural* and *structural* can be applied once more. Behavioral and cultural assimilation—or, more simply, *acculturation*—is the process of learning the manners and style of the society. Structural assimilation—or, more simply, *assimilation*—is the large-scale entrance into cliques, clubs, and institutions of the host society (Gordon, 1964). Once again, acculturation can occur without significant assimilation.

Gordon (1964) maintained that modern American society is best characterized by mass acculturation side by side with only moderate assimilation. But evidence by Alba and others suggests that this assessment understates the degree of "ethnic melting" existent today. Using national survey data on white Roman Catholic Americans, Alba (1976) found "extensive and increasing social assimilation" even by 1963 (p. 1045). Expanding Kennedy's earlier results (1944), Alba's respondents reported higher rates of intermarriage and interethnic ancestry with each generation in the United States. Even larger percentages had "close friends" from other groups. And these trends now extended to Protestants and Jews as well as other Catholic ethnicities. Alba (1981) believed that these data signal the "twilight of ethnicity among American Catholics of European ancestry." He concluded that social assimilation has proceeded much further than many acknowledge. While reports of the death of ethnic communities were premature, contrary reports of their continued vitality are greatly exaggerated. (p. 1045)

But such widespread social assimilation does not characterize black America. Alba's data (1976) reveal the distinctiveness of the black case. His white Roman Catholic sample reported considerable closeness to Protestants (19% had a Protestant relative and 37% a Protestant close friend) and moderate closeness to Jews (of those in areas with significant Jewish population, 5% had a Jewish relative and 25% a Jewish close friend). But virtually none (2 out of 1,346 respondents) had a black relative and fewer than 5% had a close black friend. This striking difference highlights a major, though often ignored, point: American black–white relations are qualitatively, not simply quantitatively, different from ethnic relations.

BLACK AMERICAN UNIQUENESS

Black Americans constitute a unique minority not only in the United States but in the world at large. Two broad and related aspects of American race relations characterize this unique status: (a) black Americans experience a special type of marginality, and (b) antiblack discrimination alone reflects the confluence of race, slavery, and segregation.

BLACKS EXPERIENCE A SPECIAL TYPE OF MARGINALITY IN AMERICAN SOCIETY

Black American marginality uniquely combines a long history of being simultaneously an integral part and on the outside of the society. The anthropologist Ruth Landes insightfully noted in 1955 that

our ugliest racism has never seriously questioned the Americanism of Negroes. They "belong" here, unlike Negroes living in Britain, France, . . . unlike American Indians, Orientals, and Mexicans in the Southwest. (p. 1254)

Indeed, black Americans perceive themselves and are perceived as "belonging" to American society. They are neither immigrants nor aliens. Nor are they a colonized people in the full sense. Their arrival in Virginia in 1619 predates all but Indian Americans and the earliest British settlers. They are centuries removed from their homelands; and they are the one group in the United States that did not choose to come to the New World. The tragedy of American racial history, then, is that black people were both accepted as belonging and yet racially denied their full rights as citizens. Repeated attempts from both ends of the political spectrum to characterize this special form of marginality as simply that of immigrant groups in general (e.g., Glazer & Moynihan, 1963) or of colonized peoples in general (Blauner, 1972) fail to capture the depth of the black problem. In contrast to most colonized peoples, for example, black Americans lack a population majority, a prior territorial claim, and a group history and culture sharply separated from the dominant group. They are both a part of and apart from the wider American society in a way unparalleled by other minority groups.

The black dilemma of being both within and without is most clearly illustrated in the cultural domain (Jones, 1972). Black Americans have an important and distinctive subculture. But this subculture differs from those of national ethnicities in two critical respects. First, it was shaped not in another part of the world but in North America for over 3½ centuries. Second, the black subculture does not receive the recognition routinely granted most national ethnic subcultures; indeed, many whites even reject the idea of its existence. This lack of recognition persists in spite of the fact that blacks have contributed far beyond their numbers distinctive elements to the wider culture of the United States and the Western world more generally. Yet, blacks also share a language, a religion, and a broad national culture with other Americans.

In a significant way, European immigrants over the past century and blacks faced opposite cultural problems. The new Europeans were seen as not "American" enough; the dominant pressure on them was to give up their strange and threatening ways and to assimilate. Blacks were Americans of a lower caste; the dominant pressure on them was to "stay in their place" and *not* to attempt assimilation into the mainstream culture of the privileged. As Lieberson (1980) stated the case:

> The emphasis called for blacks to remain in their station whereas for immigrants it was on their ability to leave their old-world traits and become as much as possible like the older white settlers. . . . For the new immigrant groups, it was a question of their potential *ability* rather than whether it was *appropriate*. . . . [Thus,] the *assimilation* issue was central to the concerns of dominant whites in dealing with the new immigrant groups,· whereas for blacks it was a matter of *place* and *appropriateness*. (p. 35, original italics)

The force of this special situation for blacks can be readily appreciated when comparisons are made with the nation's second largest minority: Mexican-Americans (Chicanos). A distinctive Chicano subculture is widely perceived; and, like the criticism that immigrant groups over the past century have typically endured, Chicanos are often criticized for being too culturally different and not "American" enough. Moreover, although blacks are both seen and see themselves as thoroughly "American," an array of factors make group and national identities difficult for Chicanos. Consider (a) their great diversity across region, generation, and social class; (b) the accessibility of the Mexican border, wich keeps the old country vividly in view and makes it possible for new immigrants to try out America and easily return; (c) the extent and recency of their massive migration to the city; (d) the difficulty inherent in dealing with American authorities after years of bruising encounters with them along the troubled U.S.–Mexican border; and (e) their possession of a world language other than English. Small wonder that Mexican-Americans have an unusually slow rate of acquiring U.S. citizenship and sharp disagreements over a common group label. Note, too, that in most of these regards, the situation of Chicanos more closely resembles earlier white ethnic situations than those of black Americans.

The point to emphasize, then, is that the marginal status of black people in modern America differs in kind from the marginal status of other minorities. Save for West Indian migrants, blacks do not experience the traditional pull between another nation's culture and American culture, for which the assimilation and pluralism concepts were specifically fashioned. Nor do they face charges of being "un-American" and not belonging. Their marginal position is more complex, and the use of theory and concepts developed for the immigrant experience obscures more than it enlightens. Blacks' marginalization is created by their being a long-term, integral component of American society while, at the same time, being denied the privileges that otherwise accrue to such a central position.

Antiblack Discrimination Alone Reflects the Confluence of Race, Slavery, and Segregation

Many American groups have suffered discrimination in various forms. But once again, the phenomenon for blacks is different, made so by their being the only group to experience the confluence of race, slavery, and segregation. It is race, as socially defined by British tradition, that defines black Americans. Based on this distinction, black Americans endured two full centuries of chattel slavery and another century of legalized and enforced segregation. The United States is still struggling to this day to remove this legacy of the past. Direct vestiges of these systems remain deeply entrenched throughout American social structure, most notably in urban residential segregation and racial intermarriage.

The incisive research of Lieberson (1963, 1980) reveals the special character of anti-black discrimination in comparison with that historically faced by the new European ethnic groups. Consider education. The southern concentration of blacks, combined with the vastly better educational opportunities in the North available to "the new Euro-peans," generated a substantial disadvantage for blacks. In 1900, Lieberson (1980, p. 157) noted, 90% of blacks lived in the South, compared to only 5% of the new immigrants; and southern schools spent about one fourth as many funds per pupil and stayed open two thirds as long as schools in the prosperous North. Yet, even within the North during this period, blacks fell behind the new arrivals. Part of this growing educational discrepancy can be traced to the differential selection of who came to the North: although no govern-mental restrictions applied to black citizens, educational requirements were made more stringent for immigrants. And though they had earlier shown at least as much motivation to stay in school, blacks began to fall behind educationally because of more limited economic means and fewer occupational incentives for further schooling.

As part of the same process, blacks fell behind white ethnic groups occupationally. Lieberson (1980) traced their contrasting occupational paths during the twentieth cen-tury. The gap between them especially widened following World War II. Earlier social analyses stressed black gains during the 1940s. But Lieberson revealed how the now not-so-new Europeans demonstrated far more dramatic advances during these years. Several factors were involved. By the 1940s, young ethnic cohorts were rapidly improving their educational levels. Moreover, large-scale European immigration ceased, whereas black migration from the South rose sharply.

Most important, far more intense discrimination against blacks restrained their par-ticipation in the nation's economic expansion at all levels. Even among the eminent recorded in *Who's Who*, blacks have lagged behind new European groups and, until recent decades, could attain prominence only in the segregated black world (Lieberson & Carter, 1979). A principal reason for this marked discrepancy highlights once again the significant cultural contrast between the groups:

> A major difference between the new Europeans and blacks stems from the cultural position of the groups. What was distinctively black in the arts was not particularly appreciated by the larger white-dominated society in the sense of attaching much esteem or prestige to black culture. By contrast, the European immigrant groups, although highly despised, did have some members who were able to use their "high culture" as a pathway to distinction since it was considered part of western tradition. This also meant that whites from these groups could break into a national network whereas blacks could not. One is reminded of the fact that most all of the white ethnic groups were able to generate ethnic cooking that was attractive to others whereas this was not the case for blacks. (Lieberson & Carter, 1979, p. 363)

At the blue-collar level, labor unions provided ethnic whites with protections gener-ally not available to blacks. Actually, in many areas of employment, unions joined with management to exclude blacks from all but the most menial jobs. The effects of such active exclusion became vividly obvious by 1940 in the linkage between education and jobs. In Lieberson's words (1980), ethnic workers

> do massively better than what blacks with comparable educational levels are able to attain. This must in no small way be due to the much more severe discrimination against blacks. (p. 359)

The educational and occupational handicaps of blacks are heightened by housing segregation unmatched in its intensity by that for any other American group. Lieberson (1963) investigated residential separation of blacks and ethnic groups from 1910 to 1950 across 10 large northern cities. In 1910, before mass black in-migration, black–white housing segregation indices were not sharply different from those for new Europeans and native whites. But the 1910–1920 period witnessed highly divergent trends. As black separation rose rapidly, that of the new ethnics dropped significantly. By 1950, the housing segregation of blacks had increased further, whereas that of white ethnic groups had decreased further. Such a significant discrepancy in residential segregation not only acts as a causal variable that affects life chances and choices but also reflects the significantly lower "standing of blacks relative to the new European ethnic groups" (Lieberson, 1980, p. 11).

These housing differences continue today. Throughout the 1960s and 1970s, urban blacks were residentially segregated from their fellow Americans far more extensively than any other urban ethnic or racial group. In 1960, seven out of every eight (87%) nonwhite families living in nonwhite blocks of central cities would have had to move to a white block before a racially random pattern would be attained. By 1970, this index of housing segregation for central cities with large black populations had slipped to 84%, and by 1980, to 78% (Farley, 1984, p. 35; Sorenson, Taeuber, & Hollingworth, 1975; Taeuber & Taeuber, 1965). But although urban residential segregation by race eased slightly between 1970 and 1980 in many central cities (such as Dallas, Houston, Oakland, and Jacksonville), it did not decline in all (Cleveland, Newark, Philadelphia, St. Louis, and Washington; Farley, 1984, p. 35). Even at the accelerated rate of desegregation in the 1970s, random residential patterns of blacks and whites would not be approximated in the United States until 2110. A strong case can be made that this residential separation of black from white Americans is the bedrock structural foundation of modern discrimination in the United States (Pettigrew, 1975, 1986).

New York City's 1960 residential patterns are illustrative. Kantrowitz (1969) showed that six new European groups averaged segregation indices of 40.8 from each other as compared with 80.1 from blacks. In Chicago, the Taeubers (1965) demonstrated how Puerto Ricans were able to disperse more in one generation than blacks had managed throughout the twentieth century. They also showed that little of this imposed housing segregation can be attributed to economic factors. And until recently, the black middle class has been almost as victimized by this massive discriminatory pattern as the black working class (Logan & Schneider, 1984; Taeuber & Taeuber, 1965).

Racial intermarriage presents the most persuasive evidence of any domain that black–white relations are qualitatively different from those of white nationalities. We have noted how interethnic rates of marriage have steadily climbed over the past two generations. By contrast, black–white intermarriage rates in the United States rank among the lowest in the Western world. Indeed, until struck down by the U.S. Supreme Court in 1967 as unconstitutional, many states still had laws against such marriages. Though undoubtedly an undercount, the 1980 U.S. Census listed only 166,000 black–white married couples out of a national total of 48,765,000: one third of 1% (Simpson & Yinger, 1985, p. 298).

Survey data provide a crude index of the special depth of this phenomenon in American thinking. In 1968, Gallup asked probability samples of citizens of 13 Western nations if they approved or disapproved "of marriage between whites and non-whites/blacks?" Table 1 provides the striking results. Rivaled only by the British, Americans disapproved far more than the samples of any other nation tested (Erskine, 1973). Nor have these attitudes eased significantly in recent years. Table 2 shows the rising percentage of white Americans who oppose racial intermarriage laws. Observe, however,

TABLE 1. Approval of Interracial Marriage in 13 Western Nations (1968)[a]

Gallup survey question: "Do you approve or disapprove of marriage between whites and non-whites/blacks?"

	Percentage		
	Approve	Disapprove	No opinion
Sweden	67	21	12
France	62	25	13
Finland	58	34	8
The Netherlands	51	23	26
Switzerland	50	35	15
Greece	50	36	14
Austria	39	53	8
Canada	36	53	11
Norway	35	44	21
West Germany	35	47	18
Uruguay	30	44	26
Great Britain	29	57	14
United States	20	72	8

[a] From "The Polls: Interracial Socializing" by H. Erskine, 1973, *Public Opinion Quarterly*, 37, 292–294. Copyright 1973 by *Public Opinion Quarterly*. Reprinted by permission.

that the basic shift occurred between 1963 and 1972, probably influenced by the fact that the high court had ruled out such laws in 1967. But change has since slowed considerably, with a third in 1982 still either in favor of such laws or undecided, despite their unconstitutionality.

Some politically conservative writers ignore this clear uniqueness of the black American case. Glib analogies have been drawn in recent decades in both popular and technical literatures between blacks and white immigrant groups, between blacks and Hispanic groups, and between blacks and Asian Americans (e.g., Kristol, 1966). We have noted numerous difficulties with these analogies. Additional problems with them are identified in Chapters 6 through 10 of this book. The point is that, if one can effectively deny the unique experience of black Americans, then it is possible to argue that they have neither special problems nor special claims for remedy on American society and can be treated in the same manner as any other groups who may have suffered other forms of discrimination in the United States.[2]

Put bluntly, then, the real controversy lurking behind the integration versus pluralism arguments concerns the special status of black Americans. From such data as those presented above, many specialists argue that three centuries of slavery and legalized racial segregation have created unique structural, cultural, and psychological barriers to democratic relations between black and white Americans. Such a central contention marks the classic work of Gunnar Myrdal (1944) right up to the bulk of work today (e.g., Jones, 1972; Lieberson, 1980; Pettigrew, in press). And like all uncomfortable contentions of social science that conflict with the political milieu, this conclusion is under current attack. Yet, the lesson seems clear. Remedies that successfully raised the status of the

---

[2]A popular case in point involves the argument that the post–World War II progress of Chinese- and Japanese-Americans "proves" that *racial* prejudice and discrimination as such cannot be involved in black problems. Lieberson (1980) provided a thorough refutation of this loose reasoning; he stressed such differences as the level of hostility, the degree of threat and competition, and the social contexts of the groups' positions in American society.

TABLE 2. Longitudinal Trend in Percentage of U.S. Whites Who Reject Racial Intermarriage Law[a]

	1963	1970	1972	1973	1974	1975	1976	1977	1980	1982
Percentage "no" to: "Do you think there should be laws against marriages between blacks and whites?"	36	48	61	61	64	60	66	71	68	68

[a] Adapted from Kluegel & Smith (1986), Table 7.1.

new Europeans cannot be expected to be as effective for blacks. One major reason is simply that the forms of the barriers against the groups are so different. But another reason is simply the change in time and American society. Lieberson (1980) wrote:

> If the content of the issues raised by blacks currently is different from that raised by the South-Central-Eastern Europeans, in essence this is because society itself is different. Because the latter groups have met their needs in earlier periods with different forms of change—for example, Social Security, job benefits, unionization, growth of public higher education—the expectation should not be that these will provide workable solutions for people decades later who are just beginning to reach out with their political potential. (p. 119)

In sum, black Americans represent a unique minority: a long-standing, highly acculturated group that truly "belongs," yet one with sharp boundaries characterized by extremely low rates of residential contact and intermarriage with other Americans. Thus, the uniqueness of the black American case argues for extreme caution in applying to blacks the assimilation and pluralism models developed for white ethnic groups.

IMPLICATIONS FOR BLACK–WHITE RELATIONS

Several implications for black–white relations can be drawn from this analysis. Pitting assimilation against pluralism as if they were necessarily rival and competing processes makes little sense for white ethnic groups. Pitting integration against pluralism for black Americans makes even less sense. First, it confuses assimilation with integration. Second, it imposes the terms of a popular debate for white ethnicities on the radically different experience of black Americans. Third, at the root of the muddled debate is the overgeneralization of white ethnic concerns to the position of black Americans. This is not to imply that there are no similarities whatsoever between the ethnic and the black situations.[3] But it is to say that the group boundaries between blacks and whites have proved far more impenetrable than any other intergroup boundaries in American society. Indeed, this difference is qualitatively, not simply quantitatively, distinct—as is vividly demonstrated in the data on racial segregation in housing and racial intermarriage.

Herein lies the unique feature of black American claims for a remedy on America society, a feature obscured both within and outside social science. The special black claim is not historical *per se*—that they are the only group on these shores to have endured both slavery and legalized segregation. Historical claims alone to special remedy are tenuous

[3]Thus, some generational differences among blacks in northern cities resemble those of ethnic groups earlier (Lieberson, 1973, 1978). Yet, even here, cautious interpretations are required. These results "may be seen as an argument to view the black situation in the North as simply analogous to that faced by European and Asian immigrants and their descendents. Nothing could be further from the truth than such a gross and oversimplified view" (Lieberson, 1973, p. 564).

at best—as demonstrated by conflicting historical claims heard throughout the world. Rather, it is a structural claim of special barriers to full citizenship that actively continue to operate in present-day American society. As seen in housing discrimination, these barriers stem from the special American experience of black people and are not qualitatively comparable with those faced by other groups. This is not to deny the extent or seriousness of the discrimination that has marked the experience of many other groups in American life. But it is to assert that the special claim of black Americans to the elimination of the society's uniquely antiblack structural restraints will continue to be obscured as long as our conceptualization of the problem confuses it with the contrasting claims of other groups.

REFERENCES

Alba, R. D. (1976). Social assimilation among American Catholic national-origin groups. *American Sociological Review, 41*, 1030–1046.

Alba, R. D. (1981). The twilight of ethnicity among American Catholics of European ancestry. *Annals, 454*, 86–97.

Alba, R. D., & Chamlin, M. B. (1983). A preliminary examination of ethnic identification among whites. *American Sociological Review, 48*, 240–247.

Allport, G. W. (1954). *The nature of prejudice*. Reading, MA: Addison-Wesley.

Berry, J. W. (1984). Cultural relations in plural societies: Alternatives to segregation and their sociopsychological implications. In N. Miller & M. B. Brewer (Eds.), *Groups in contact: The psychology of desegregation*. New York: Academic Press.

Blauner, R. (1972). *Racial oppression in America*. New York: Harper & Row.

Erskine, H. (1973). The polls: Interracial socializing. *Public Opinion Quarterly, 37*, 284–294.

Farley, R. (1984). *Blacks and whites: Narrowing the gap?* Cambridge: Harvard University Press.

Glazer, N. (1964, December). Negroes and Jews: The new challenge to pluralism. *Commentary, 38*, 29–34.

Glazer, N., & Moynihan, D. P. (1963). *Beyond the melting pot: The Negroes, Puerto Ricans, Jews, Italians, and Irish of New York City*. Cambridge: MIT and Harvard University Presses.

Gordon, M. (1964). *Assimilation in American life*. New York: Oxford University Press.

Gordon, M. (1978). *Human nature, class, and ethnicity*. New York: Oxford University Press.

Goudsblom, J. (1967). *Dutch society*. New York: Random House.

Granovetter, M. (1985). *The microstructure of school desegregation*. Unpublished paper. Sociology Department, State University of New York, Stony Brook.

Greeley, A. M. (1969). *Why can't they be like us?* New York: Institute of Human Relations Press.

Herberg, W. (1955) *Protestant-Catholic-Jews*. New York: Doubleday.

Jones, J. M. (1972). *Prejudice and racism*. Reading, MA: Addison-Wesley.

Kantrowitz, N. (1969). Ethnic and racial segregation in the New York metropolis, 1960. *American Journal of Sociology, 74*, 685–695.

Kennedy, R. J. (1944). Single or triple melting pot? *American Journal of Sociology, 49*, 331–339.

Kluegel, J. R., & Smith, E. R. (1986). *Thinking about inequality*. Chicago: University of Chicago Press.

Kristol, I. (1966). The Negro is like the immigrant yesterday. *New York Times Magazine*, pp. 50–51, 124–142.

Landes, R. (1955). Biracialism in American society: A comparative view. *American Anthropologist, 57*, 1253–1263.

Lieberson, S. (1963). *Ethnic patterns in American cities*. New York: Free Press.

Lieberson, S. (1963). Generational differences among blacks in the North. *American Journal of Sociology, 79*, 550–565.

Lieberson, S. (1978). Reconsideration of the income differences found between migrants and northern-born blacks. *American Journal of Sociology, 83*, 940–966.

Lieberson, S. (1980). *A piece of the pie: Blacks and white immigrants since 1880*. Berkeley: University of California Press.

Lieberson, S., & Carter, D. K. (1979). Making it in America: Differences between eminent blacks and white ethnic groups. *American Sociological Review, 44*, 347–366.

Logan, J. R., & Schneider, M. (1984). Racial segregation and racial change in American suburbs, 1970–1980. *American Journal of Sociology, 89*, 874–888.

Morgan, G. D. (1981). *America without ethnicity*. Port Washington, NY: Kennikat (National Universities Publications).

Myrdal, G. (1944). *An American dilemma*. New York: Harper & Row.

Parsons, T. (1955). Social strains in America. In D. Bell (Ed.), *The new American right*. New York: Criterion Books.

Pettigrew, T. F. (Ed.). (1975). *Racial discrimination in the United States*. New York: Harper & Row.

Pettigrew, T. F. (in press). *Modern racism: American Black–white relations since the 1960s*. Cambridge, MA: Harvard University Press.

Pettigrew, T. F., Franklin, J. H., & Mack, R. W. (1971). *Ethnicity in·American life*. New York: Anti-Defamation League.

Popper, K. R. (1976). *Unended quest: An intellectual autobiography*. La Salle, IL: Open Court Publishing.

Simpson, G., & Yinger, M. (1985). *Racial and cultural minorities* (5th ed.). New York: Plenum Press.

Sorenson, A., Taeuber, K. E., & Hollingworth, L. G. (1975). Indices of racial residential segregation for 109 cities in the United States. *Sociological Focus, 8*, 125–142.

Steinberg, S. (1981). *The ethnic myth: Race, ethnicity, and class in America*. New York: Atheneum.

Taeuber, K. E., & Taeuber, A. F. (1965). *Negroes in cities*. Chicago: Aldine.

White, W. (1961). *Beyond conformity*. New York: Free Press.

Yinger, J. M. (1985). Ethnicity. *Annual Review of Sociology, 11*, 151–180.

3

The Future of Pluralism Revisited

Harry C. Triandis

This chapter explores the future of pluralism from the point of view of social psychology. It examines social-psychological principles relevant to achieving a society that accommodates a variety of cultural groups and at the same time reduces intergroup conflict.

DEFINITIONS

Pluralism, in contrast to *monism*, was first used by philosophers to deal with the questions: "How many things are there in the world?" and "How many kinds of things are there in the world?" When translated to societal issues, these questions become one: "How many kinds of cultures can coexist in a given society?"

Culture is here defined as the human-made part of the environment. This includes not only the material part of the environment (objective culture) but also the way the human-made part of the environment is perceived (subjective culture). As people live in different environments, which provide them with different schedules of reinforcement, they develop distinct points of view about the way the environment is structured. For example, some learn that planning is a useful activity, and others that it is a waste of time.

Society is here defined as the collective body of persons composing a community as citizens of civil government. Thus, within the United States, we have more than 200 million persons who are subjects of one government, but these persons may have very different subjective cultures. The environment of the economically depressed ghetto is very different from the environment of the affluent suburb. Furthermore, historical factors and migrations are antecedents of major aspects of the heterogeneity of American society.

Assimilation refers to a policy of making each cultural group adopt the culture of the mainstream. *Integration* refers to the policy of coordinating the goals of each cultural group, but allowing each group to maintain its culture. There is some evidence suggesting that integration is to be preferred. Murphy (1961, 1965) reported fewer breakdowns

This is a revised and updated version of my presidential address to the Society for the Psychological Study of Social Issues, Division 9 of APA, presented in September 1976 and published in 1976 in the *Journal of Social Issues, 32,* 179–208.

HARRY C. TRIANDIS • Department of Psychology, University of Illinois, Champaign, Illinois 61820.

and psychiatric hospitalizations among immigrant groups, per capita, in countries with an integration policy (e.g., Canada) than in countries with an assimilation (melting-pot) policy, such as the United States.

Berry (1984) discussed integration as the condition in which both the cultural identity of each cultural group is maintained and positive relations between the two groups are valued. He contrasted this condition with assimilation (where the former is not true), segregation (where the latter is not true), and deculturation (where neither is true). He reviewed data that show the integration is the preferred policy (Berry, Kalin, & Taylor, 1976) and is associated with good mental health for both cultural groups.

This chapter advocates *additive multiculturalism,* a concept defined in detail later on. Such a construct is consistent with societal creativity. History tells us that creativity is maximal when thesis and antithesis are in clear view (Simonton, 1975). A homogeneous society will inevitably become stale, static, and unlikely to survive in a fast-changing environment. Heterogeneity means interpersonal conflict, but there are ways to teach people to deal with it, and when people are trained so they can deal with heterogeneity (Landis & Brislin, 1983) one has an exciting, creative, well-adjusted-to-its-environment kind of society, with productive conflict (Deutsch, 1969).

THEORETICAL ANALYSIS

To address the question, "How are people of different cultural backgrounds to coexist in a given society?" we need to look at a prototypical relationship—a dyad consisting of one individual from Culture A and one individual from Culture B. What is the meaning of a good relationship within this dyad? Exchange theorists (Homans, 1974; Thibaut & Kelley, 1959) have given us some guidelines: A good relationship is one in which the rewards exceed the costs.

Rewards are transfers of resources from one person to another. Thus, if O gives P love or status or a service or a gift or some information or some money, O transfers a reward to P (Foa & Foa, 1974). A cost is incurred when a resource is taken away or denied, or when a person is forced to behave in a way that precludes obtaining the benefits that an alternative behavior provides. Thus, if O takes away money (say, steals) or denies status (say, by insulting P), there is a cost for P.

A complication arises from the fact that it is not so much the absolute size of the resource exchange itself as the meaning of the exchange that determines if it is a reward or a cost. The meaning of the exchange depends on at least two variables: (a) expectations and (b) the perceived antecedents and consequences of the exchange. For example, if P expects to receive a gift worth $10 and instead receives a gift worth $1,000, the surprise, embarrassment, and activity required to understand the event may make this event more like a cost than a reward, even though the amount of the resource that was transferred is 100 times greater than expected.

Expectations in the form of stereotypes, implicit personality theories, attribution habits, and strategies for perceptual selectivity provide further complications. A behavior may be perceived very differently when it is associated with a person of a particular race or social class from when it is associated with another person. In short, preexisting good or bad relationships between two people or two groups tend to engender self-fulfilling prophesies.

In other words, a *good relationship* means that the interactions between P and O are consistent with their expectations and do not involve antecedents or consequences that are perceived to be costly in the future or implying a negative meaning for the exchange.

The second complication concerns the perceived antecedents of the behavior. Here, we can borrow from attribution theory, which shows, among other things, that the meaning of a behavior is a function of the attributions we make about it. P explains O's behavior to herself or himself in terms of perceived antecedents or consequences. For example, P may attribute the strange behavior of O's giving a $1,000 gift to O's attempt to bribe her or him, or to pressure that O received from others to make this gift, or to the intrinsic pleasure that O might experience from making the gift, and so on. Each of these perceived causes or antecedents results in a different meaning for the behavior. P may feel that the gift is a *cost* if he or she sees it as a bribe. On the other hand, P may see it as a reward if he or she sees it as a consequence of O's deriving pleasure from making it.

The perceived consequences of the exchange may be associated with different probabilities and values for different cultural groups. Obviously, $100 given to a person who has insufficient funds for the next meal is more valuable than $100 given to a millionaire. Similarly, an interaction that increases status with a person who has low self-esteem will be more valuable than one with an arrogant individual. Generally, the economists are correct in considering relationships between prices and supply and demand. When a resource is abundant, its value is low; when it is scarce, its value is high.

Foa and Foa (1974) assembled much evidence supporting the hypothesis that particularistic exchanges, such as exchanges of love, status, and services, are more valuable than universalistic exchanges, such as exchanges of money, information, or goods. This is true at least in highly developed, technological societies, where generally there is considerable affluence, stores are full of goods, and libraries and the mass media disseminate more information than we really care to have. By contrast, these societies do not have well-developed systems for exchanges of love, status, and services. One often gets more of these particularistic exchanges in a traditional society, such as an Indian village, where, with the exception of the lowest castes, the majority have status given to them by virtue of caste membership, the extended families can be sources of much exchange of love (though also of hate), and very complex systems of interdependence result in a lot of services being given—for cooking, shopping, laundry, education, social events, and so on. For example, even in today's relatively modern India, an important marriage is celebrated over a period of a month or so, with relatives coming from all over the country to participate in the celebration. For American tastes, that much celebrating and the receipt of that much status and service from so many relatives would be overwhelming, but many Indians find it a memorable experience that they would not like to be without. The point of my argument is simple: Modern technological society, although giving to most people certain kinds of resources (e.g., goods), is depriving them of others (e.g., status). Thus, the values of particularistic exchanges are particularly high in modern technological societies.

APPLICATIONS TO INTERGROUP RELATIONS

Now, let us examine the relationships among different groups within a heterogeneous society. One of the realities of different subjective cultures is that they result in different expectations and different perceptions of antecedents or consequences of interactions. Thus, the greater the heterogeneity within a given society, the greater the probability that interactions will be costly. As the interactions become more and more costly and less rewarding, as we move from consideration of relatively different groups interacting with each other, we are seeing an increase of the conditions of alienation. This argument might imply that heterogeneity is undesirable. But this is not the case if we use other criteria to judge the society. For example, creativity has been found to be maximal where there is political fragmentation and instability (Simonton, 1975). The great civilizations of the past have been characterized by heterogeneity (Naroll, Benjamin, Fohl, Fried, Hildreth, & Schaefer, 1971). Thus, rather than banishing heterogeneity, we must discover ways to harness it. We must discover how to make optimal use of it.

Much of the discussion that follows focuses on black–white relations. A parallel discussion for native Americans, Spanish-speaking Americans, white ethnics, and Eskimos could have been provided. In principle, relationships between old and young, men and women, straights and gays, and numerous other such contrast groups can be analyzed in the same way, and the analysis will lead to similar conclusions. The black–white conflict is then prototypical of the others, and it is the one conflict whose reduction can serve as a prototype for the reduction of the other conflicts. Although the discussion focuses on blacks, it is equally applicable to the other "unmeltable ethnics" (Novak, 1972).

Heterogeneity is likely to lead to conflict within a society, particularly when it involves a physically visible division of majority and minority groups, as is the case with racial distinctions in the United States. Historical and cultural antecedents of interracial relationships in this country have resulted in situations in which the rewards received by the white majority from exploitation of the black minority have been constantly greater than the costs. For the blacks, there has been enough hope and enough improvement in social standing to place increasingly larger segments of the black community in situations where their rewards exceed their costs; however, this improvement does not imply that all is well. Many blacks still feel outside the mainstream of American life, and there is a substantial group within the black community whose costs are greater than its rewards. This heterogeneity within the black community has not been emphasized enough; yet, it has major implications for the issues of pluralism, integration, and racial harmony.

Our research on black and white subjective cultures (Triandis, 1976) suggests that, overall, the similarities of black and white subjective cultures are much more overwhelming than the differences. Yet, some segments of the black community—namely, unemployed males who live in ghettos—look at the world around them in a manner that is very different from the way other samples of blacks look at the world. Specifically, our data suggest that the black unemployed see their environment as chaotic; they do not trust other people, institutions, and other blacks who "have made it." This syndrome, which we called *ecosystem distrust,* is a natural outcome of an environment in which extreme poverty, discrimination, rejection, and unpredictability are the defining characteristics. Let us not make the mistake of blaming the victim; the blame must be placed on the environment of this group of people.

One must recognize, however, that, in many cases, the behavior of people with ecosystem distrust must be changed, because it fails to take advantage of opportunities offered in the environment. After all, environments often change. Ecosystem distrust may develop in one environment as a perfectly natural outgrowth of that environment and may then persist in all sorts of other environments. This phenomenon is somewhat parallel to Solomon and Wynn's dogs, which, once shocked in a particular box after a particular signal, persisted in jumping out of the box as soon as the signal was presented, long after the shock was turned off. Thus, those samples that learn to be helpless in some environments persist in their helplessness (Seligman, 1975) even when the environment has changed. Such situations require intervention.

Although our data show that the black unemployed male who lives in a ghetto is extreme in ecosystem distrust, we find traces of this syndrome in other black groups. Other research (Schuman & Hatchett, 1974) also finds alienation in the black community. Such alienation is a direct outcome of the poor relationships between blacks and the dominant group. It probably also applies to Amerindians, Eskimos in Alaska, and other groups that have cultures that are still quite different from the culture of the majority.

To understand this alienation better, let us look at the social exchanges between minority and majority groups in terms of our theoretical scheme. Take a black, Amerindian, or Eskimo who is very poor, and consider that person's exchanges with the majority culture. Minority members are denied the most valuable particularistic resources of status or services. Instead, they receive mostly money, goods, or information. By contrast, the majority receives from the minority some services, in the form of activities of servants, waiters, bus drivers, garbage collectors, and so on, and some status, in the form of being elected by them to important positions in society, such as mayor, governor, senator, or president, and in some cases even love—admiration and imitation. In other words, the exchange is definitely in favor of the majority; they receive the valuable resources, and they give the less valuable resources.[1]

Homans (1974) pointed out that when one person (O) receives less from the interaction with another (P) than P does from interaction with O, then P has *power*. It has long been known that whites have the resources and the power. What we need to know, however, is precisely how much of a difference this difference in power makes. Of course, this is very difficult to determine, but estimates do exist. Specifically, Dowdall (1974) estimated gains and losses by examining family income, unemployment rates, and occupational status levels of blacks and whites with equivalent demographic characteristics: age, sex, education, and so on. He found little evidence of a change in the white-gain–black-loss picture over the preceding few years[2] and quoted Thurow's (1969) computation that whites gain somewhere between $5 and $15 billion per year (in 1960 dollar values) that is lost by blacks as a result of differential wage structures, job discrimination, and so on. This amount would translate into $20 to $60 billion in 1984 dollars. Even if we accept Otis Dudley Duncan's analysis (cited in Mosteller & Moynihan, 1972) that the black–white income gap is due only 40% to job discrimination, with 46% due to particular techniques of child rearing in black families and 14% due to poor schooling, we would still conclude that between $2 and $6 billion (in 1960 dollar values—close to $20 billion today) constitute losses sustained by blacks or gains obtained by whites. The picture is even more bleak if we recognize that these white gains are realized to a large extent by those whites who are most privileged, as employers are among those who gain most from wage differentials.

All this discussion concerns the least valuable resource: money. In the case of the most valuable resources, such a status, the situation is undoubtedly much more unequal, unfair, and offensive to the black minority. We cannot estimate the cost of the disrespect

---

[1]Foa and Foa (1974) made the point that, in industrial societies, exchanges of status, love, and service are particularly valuable because those exchanges require time. Time is a scarce commodity in such societies. In less developed countries, money, goods, and information are relatively more valuable than in developed countries. The relative devaluation of money in the United States can be seen by examining wages. It is very difficult to get anyone to work for $3 per hour, whereas in most of the underdeveloped world, that is an "excellent" wage. Paradoxically, the low value of money holds also in the black ghetto, only more so. Triandis (1976), during a 5-year research project that required many interactions with both middle-class and ghetto blacks, noted that a small sum of money would motivate the middle class but not the ghetto black. It is as if the small sum can do little for someone who is in a depressed condition, whereas it can provide benefits for someone who is already living comfortably. Furthermore, money can do little to overcome the lack of status of the ghetto dweller, unless the quantity of money is *very* substantial.

[2]The latest statistics are as follows: the mean incomes of white men ($15,626), black men ($10,557), white women ($7,176), and black women ($7,297) show little difference for the women because black women work longer hours than white women. The black men still earn only 67% of the amount white men earn. If we limit the statistics to fully employed men, the percentage was 69% for 1971 and 71% for 1981. Thus, whereas black women moved from 77% to parity, black men moved from 62% to 71%. It is an improvement, but the picture has not changed very much. (The latest statistics were supplied by Francine Blau, in a personal communication. See also F. Blau & M. Ferber, 1986).

by the police, the low self-esteem engendered by our educational system, the relative lack of high-status models on the black horizon, and so on. We can only guess that these costs are substantial.

Of course, inequality is inconsistent with the dominant American ideology. As Myrdal (1944) pointed out, the *American Dilemma* is that the ideology includes the "all men are created equal" notion; yet, inequality is clear and present. How do humans deal with such cognitive inconsistencies? Although we do not have to accept all aspects of cognitive dissonance theory, there is enough support for the notion that Western people strive toward consistency (Abelson, Aronson, McGuire, Newcomb, Rosenberg, & Tennenbaum, 1968) for us to know that such inconsistencies lead to some form of cognitive work. Abelson (1959) pointed out that individuals can handle inconsistency in different ways. Mechanisms that might be used by the majority include the following:

1. They can stop thinking, and undoubtedly, many members of the majority have adopted this way out. Many people are annoyed when somebody brings up these inconsistencies, as that forces them out of their preferred mode of functioning.
2. They can bolster one cognition. "Why," they would say, "all Americans are equal, there is no inequality; exploitation talk is a Communist plot to disgrace this great country."
3. They can differentiate. Here, the subject might say, "The American creed refers to people like me. People who are very different in skin color, beliefs, and so on are not in the set. In fact, they are inferior and must be taken care of, protected, given welfare." Noblesse oblige!
4. Still another way to deal with the inconsistency is to transcend it: "It is true that there is inequality, but I am at the bottom of some hierarchies, too. It is a fact of life; if you live in a society you are unequal sometime. We are all equally unequal, so we are equal!"

Consider now the effect of exploitation on the minority. Here, too, there is a discrepancy between what one expects to receive from a relationship and what one does receive. In equity theory (Berkowitz & Walster, 1976), the perceiver sees her or his own inputs and outcomes and compares them to the inputs and outcomes of the other. Inputs include efforts to have a good social relationship, skills, status, and other resources that a person brings to the relationship. Outcomes include both the costs and the rewards that one experiences from a relationship. Positive outcomes occur when rewards exceed costs. Minority members regard as costs the facts that members of their group have been exploited in the past while contributing to the economic development of this continent, have (as in the case of Amerindians) given up their lands and their way of life, and have signed treaties that have not been observed.

What about the rewards? Participation in a modern state can be a reward. But in the case of the minorities, this also involves being paid less, being excluded from important jobs, and being an underdog in most power relationships. When the minority members compare themselves with the majority, they see large costs and small rewards. Hence, the relationship is seen as grossly inequitable. How can equity be restored? One can stop thinking, but that is unlikely if one is severely injured by the inequity. One can bolster some element, such as exaggerating the benefits received from the relationship. Undoubtedly, many blacks, described as Uncle Toms, do just that. One can differentiate and think of the self as unworthy of comparison with the majority other. Thus, many blacks accept the views of the majority concerning themselves; they think of themselves as inferior. It is interesting to note that, in the research of Marx (1967) and of Schuman and Hatchett (1974), the more educated the blacks, the more alienated they felt. Being educated makes it much less probable that they will accept the notion that they are inferior.

Finally, one can transcend the inequity by believing that inequity is a normal state of affairs.

Cognitive solutions to inequity are likely to occur among people who are introspective. But those who are more pragmatic must *act* to restore equity. How can this be done? Clearly, by decreasing one's costs and/or increasing one's rewards.

Not all minority members are in a state of inequity, and not all who are in state of inequity will choose the same means to restore equity. But it is useful to explore what people can do in such situations. To decrease costs, minority group members can sometimes give less of value to the majority. This option can take many forms, including producing less, cooperating less, revealing less, and giving less status. Behaviors that the majority interprets as laziness, irresponsibility, uncooperativeness, hostility, and so on might be due to efforts by the minority to reduce costs and to pursue its self-interest. The increasing difficulties of white researchers in getting information from such samples [X (Clark), 1973] is another example of such cost-reduction efforts.

As for increases in rewards, taking away from the majority group status, money, information, or services can sometimes be rewarding. Some behavior that the majority considers antisocial or criminal might be seen as an effort to reduce inequity. For example, a black adolescent who snatches away the purse of a white old lady may be viewed as taking away a resource and as restoring equity.

Foa and Donnenwerth (1971) made the important point that, for some blacks, violence may constitute one of the very few available means of obtaining status. A similar point has been made about some sections of the Italian lower class, both here and abroad. Lewis (1966), in his discussion of the culture of poverty, made the distinction between cultural groups that are poor in monetary terms and those that are also poor in their ability to provide social support. It is when both kinds of poverty are present that Lewis described the situation as a "culture of poverty." This distinction is important because it is not poverty in universalistic resources such as money, but poverty in particularistic resources such as love and status that is really important. Many unemployed minority-group members have neither. Unemployed majority-group members may lack money, but they often have institutions that maintain interpersonal support systems; they thus escape from the culture of poverty. In any case, it is useful to emphasize the rather different situation of the unemployed blacks and the fact that many undesirable behaviors, such as reliance on drugs and violence, are the outcome of their particular condition. The greater vulnerability to mental illness among blacks, women, and the less educated (Kessler, Price, & Wortman, 1985) has been traced to the quality of the social support systems available to them. To acquire and maintain a social support network, one needs resources (e.g., ability to give good advice, status, or money). It is not surprising that resource-deprived segments of the population are more vulnerable to a range of ills, physical (hypertension and ulcers), mental (psychoses), and social (high homicide, divorce, desertion, wife beating, child abuse, crime, and delinquency). Naroll (1983) assembled an impressive set of facts from around the world indicating that weak primary groups and social support networks are linked to the above-mentioned personal and social problems.

The situation of unemployed blacks is also very different from the situation of other minority groups. The most important difference is that centuries of slavery altered the social fabric of the black community so that the patterns of interdependence characteristic of traditional societies were severely weakened. A characteristic of many European or Asian groups that migrated to this country was that they had strong norms, imposed sanctions on those who broke them, and had a system of interdependence that included both rights and obligations. Slavery broke up the African social system and created an intrinsically anomic social situation. Thus, the black case as extremely different and in no sense comparable to the Chinese or eastern European immigration to this country. Those who dismiss this argument on the grounds that slavery has been dead for more than 100 years simply show their narrow time perspective. One hundred years is an insignificant period of time on the scale of cultural evolution. Historians find strong connections between events that took place thousands of years ago and the present. We tend to be too impressed by superficial changes in technology and to forget the extent to which our fundamental, unquestioned, and unchallenged assumptions and our values reflect events that occurred 2,000 years ago in the eastern Mediterranean. For example, the concepts of male superiority, property values, democracy, and freedom have a long history.

To judge blacks against the standards created by the eastern European or Asian migrations is to ignore essential distinctions. Violence and other natural manifestations of the existing inequitable social relationships are condemned with attributions to dispositional characteristics, and we forget the importance of situational variables. This is a problem that has been clarified by studies of human attribution tendencies (Jones, Kanouse, Kelley, Nisbett, Valins, & Weiner, 1972). Humans have a tendency to make dispositional attributions for negative behavior when the actor is disliked (Nisbett, Caputo, Legant, & Marecek, 1973). Research on intergroup relations, for example, shows that in-groups perceive positive actions by in-group members as being due to dispositional and negative actions as being due to situational factors; conversely, they attribute positive actions of out-groups to situational and negative actions to dispositional factors. The data come from India (Taylor & Jaggi, 1974) and the Arab-Israeli conflict (Heradveit, 1979). The phenomenon is so reliable that it can be used as an index of the goodness of relations between in-group and out-group. For instance, in Singapore, the Chinese–Malay relationship is so good, and economic development is perceived so clearly as a superordinate goal (Sherif, 1968), that the phenomenon is not observed (Ward & Hewstone, 1985).

There is no doubt that criminal behaviors are undesirable from the point of view of both the minority and the majority groups. The majority group sometimes suffers directly; the minority group is even more often the target of aggression by frustrated members of its own group and also sustains a loss of status because the behavior of some minority group members is socially undesirable. But the way to stop these unfortunate actions is not to increase the number of police. As Lewin observed long ago, social systems tend to reach quasi-stationary equilibria. An equilibrium that is maintained by large police forces involves, by its very nature, large forces on the minority group side. Guerrilla warfare is a real possibility if we choose repression rather than reconciliation.

The only way to stop such unfortunate behaviors is to restore equity. To restore equity, we need to close the status gap. The status gap is great because there are real differences in education, income, and socially desirable behavior between some black subgroups and other blacks.

Illinois Studies of the Economically Disadvantaged

A three-phased study was designed to develop training materials for white supervisors and black hard-core-unemployed workers. In Phase I, the major variations in the perception of the social environment among blacks and whites were determined (Triandis, 1976). In Phase II, we constructed training materials, called *culture assimilators*, to train white supervisors and black hard-core workers. In Phase III, we attempted to show that the training had beneficial effects and improved the interaction between blacks and whites (Weldon, Carlston, Rissman, Slobodin, & Triandis, 1975).

We selected samples of (a) white middle-class college females; (b) white lower-class high-school males; (c) black lower-class high-school males; and (d) black lower-class, hard-core-unemployed males. These samples were strategically selected for an examination of the limits of variation of black and white subjective cultures; the first and last samples differed in age, sex, race, and social class, and the two other samples were as similar as possible, except that they differed in race.

We asked these samples to make a large number of judgments, 5,600 to be exact, involving different kinds of social stimuli.

These data were subjected to Tucker's three-mode factor analysis (1966). This technique gives the patterns of consistency revealed by the answers of the respondents across different modes. For example, with respondents reacting to 100 or so roles on 20 or so behaviors, it is possible to obtain patterns of consistency across roles, across behaviors, and across respondents. One finds that some roles involving interracial relations and hostile behaviors are used by the subjects quite frequently. But even more interestingly, one looks for patterns of consistency across subjects; some subjects give responses that are quite similar to responses given by still other subjects. By means of discriminant-function analysis, it is then possible to find out if the groupings of subjects as selected for study are strongly related to the subject-points-of-view that emerge from the factor analysis.

Hypotheses derived from the previous study were then tested with a broader sample of respondents. We studied 240 persons, making sure that half of these respondents were black and half white; one third middle class, one third working-class, and one third hard-core-unemployed; one half females and the other half males; and one half young (18–25) and the other half older (35–45). With 10 persons in each cell of this 24-cell design, we were able to do multivariate analyses of variance to confirm some of these hypotheses.

What emerged from these studies? First and most striking was the tremendous heterogeneity of the black samples. What emerged was a black majority that was very much like the white majority, looking at the social environment in more or less the same terms as the whites. They had the same beliefs, the same aspirations. But then, there was a black minority that may have constituted something like 10% of all blacks and that was very different.

The black hard-core sample was different from the other samples. As we looked at their answers on the various instruments, the impression was clear. They saw the eco-system as unreliable and unpredictable, other people as untrustworthy, behavior as haphazardly connected with outcomes, black professionals as exploiters, and the establishment as exploitive.

These findings converge with conclusions derived by entirely different methods. Thus, Ley (1974), a social geographer, used a variety of methods, including participant observations, to study a section of Philadelphia's black ghetto. He reported that the environment was of "unrelieved uncertainty" (p. 159), involving much internal competition, a "jungle" in the words of some of the residents, with maximum potential hostility needing maximum defensiveness for survival, and characterized by "exploitative anarchy" (p. 285).

This was the environment that had been created by discrimination and prejudice, in which the black community were the victims. Almost anyone placed in such an environment would react with ecosystem distrust, though there are a few unusual individuals— orchids in the jungle, as Ley called them—who do not exhibit such distrust. Turner and Wilson (1976) also concluded that the most disaffected blacks are young, urban, low-SES males.

THEORETICAL INTERPRETATION

It seems probable that differences in subjective culture emerge from differences in the availability of resources, in the presence of the historical, economic, and cultural factors suggested earlier. Clearly, whites have more resources than blacks, and the black hard-core-unemployed have fewer resources than most blacks. The effect of extreme lack of resources, in addition to interpersonal competition, hostility, and distrust, must be an attempt to make the few available resources stretch as much as possible. This can be done by finding novel ways to obtain gratification. Behavior is selected that results in greater emphasis on immediate gratification. The lack of resources also means that the total level of reinforcements received might be considerably lower. After all, a parent who has money can reward children in numerous ways not available to a parent without money, who is forced to use physical punishment, which Skinner (1953) showed to be less effective than positive reinforcement. Reliance on punishment could have the effect of socializing children much less, thus increasing the probability of delinquency. Low levels of reinforcement also have the effect of providing little cognitive connection between what one does and one's outcomes, leading to the expectation of external control of reinforcement. Less imposition of social norms, leading, in turn, to lower levels of normative clarity and less satisfaction with the total social situation, and leading finally to antiestablishment attitudes. Finally, low levels of reinforcement may lead to a defensive self-esteem, which involves cognitive distortions that increase the virtues of the available resources and devalue the unavailable resources. In short, it is fair to say that, when a society allows a large gap in levels of reinforcement, it is likely that there will emerge an unusual subjective culture, some features of which are likely to be undesirable.

Thus, the historically established patterns of economic exploitation, reinforced by cultural mores, institutional racism, and other features of the society, have created a particular ecosystem for the hard-core-unemployed, particularly if they are black. The subjective culture of this group is a natural outcome of this ecosystem. The ecosystem is not of their own creation. They are responding to it. Actually, our data suggest that they are responding adaptively. For example, they are more resigned to crime and other undesirable features of their environment than are people outside that environment, a reaction that is adaptive in the sense that they find living in that environment more tolerable. This does not mean that the environment is acceptable, only that it involves the realization that there is not much that can be done about it.

ON THE CONSEQUENCES OF INEQUALITY

Inequality is not a new problem, nor is it a purely American dilemma. The history of the world is full of examples of exploitation. The association of wage differentials with sex, age, and ethnic groups has also had a long history. There are major problems of societal integration in India, in South America, and in Africa. But what is novel in the United States is that we have the ideology and the resources to make progress toward the elimination of inequality. In a study by Hofstede (1980), a factor called *power distance* differentiated the 50+ countries of this investigation. Countries high in this factor were those with considerable inequality (the Philippines, Mexico, Venezuela, and India), and those low tended to be central and northern European. Naroll's analysis of social ills (1983) has indicated that Norway is the "model country."[3] The United States, in these studies, is somewhere in the middle and on the "good" side of most dimensions but, of course, a long way from being the model country.

---

[3]Naroll used several indexes derived from UN statistics and other sources, including physical health, mental health, brotherhood, progress, peace, order, and variety and quality of life. According to these indexes, Norway scored best on physical health, was equal to several countries on peace and order and was also best on variety and on quality of life. Spain was tops on the mental health index; Luxembourg on brotherhood; and the United States on the progress index. By averaging across the indexes, Naroll concluded that Norway had the best profile.

Inequality leads to large differences in subjective culture (at least for some subgroups), which lead to undesirable behaviors by some members of these subgroups, which lead to projection of these undesirable behaviors to all members of the minority group by majority members. Inequality increases the probability of crime by members of the subgroups that are most deprived; then, the majority blames the whole minority group for the increased crime, not just those subgroups. Hence, the majority gives less status to the minority and justifies the inequality on the grounds of the lower morality of the minority group. Inequality thus creates a feedback that results in the reinforcement of inequality.

INTEGRATION AS A REMEDY

The major prevailing view is that integration is a remedy for this situation. When people use the word *integration* today, they mean merely putting people together, hoping that one group will become assimilated.[4] One overoptimistic view is that if we "integrate" (i.e., put blacks and whites together in) our schools, industries, and neighborhoods, we will have instant harmony. I now believe that we have not explored enough other alternatives. Let me first state why integration, in the form of putting people together, is not the remedy. The evidence from integration studies is that to merely put people together in a room, without creating conditions of interdependence, superordinate goals, and superordinate normative regulators and associated sanctions for their implementation (Sherif, 1968), has little effect and can be counterproductive (Brewer & Kramer, 1985).

In a variety of situations around the world, mere contact has increased prejudice (Amir, 1976). This is perhaps too strong a statement, but it is consistent with the data *when the status differences are large.* Contact does generate prejudice, even among professionals who ought to know better. Consider, as an example, the stereotypes of professional personnel working for the Bureau of Indian Affairs (Hennigh, 1975). Teachers, nurses, and physicians working in Alaska had much more negative stereotypes of Eskimos than those having little contact. Urban Indians who work among economically deprived rural samples often feel that the "peasants are intolerably backward," whereas those with little contact have a positive, though romantic, view.

Amir's review (1969, 1976) of the contact literature shows contact to be beneficial only under particular specified conditions. Equal-status contact is helpful; contact when holding superordinate goals, contact that receives institutional support, contact between cultural groups that are similar on dimensions other than status (such as on values), and contact under conditions of pleasurable stimulation (such as in camps, at concerts, or on trips) can lead to improved attitudes. However, when such conditions do not hold, contact can lead to more prejudice. Unequal-status contact, mutually exclusive goals leading to zero-sum relationships, contact that is opposed by institutional norms, contact between groups that have very different subjective cultures, and contact under conditions of failure, anxiety, or distress can all lead to increased prejudice. The data reviews by Gerard (see Chapter 11) and by Brewer and Miller (see Chapter 16) concur with this pessimistic view of mere contact.

When there is a difference between two groups, A and B, on an attribute that is

[4]The majority of the contributors to the debate about bilingualism in editorials and letters to the editor express assimilationist points of view. Among the frequent comparisons are Quebec and Belgium. Although with respect to black culture the extreme assimilationist position is usually not taken, the implication that blacks who are psychologically white are "good" can be found in many of these editorials. In fact, the Triandis (1976) data indicate that the black middle class is already psychologically white. The cultural differences in subjective culture are observed only in the case of those blacks who live in ghettos.

related to status—for example, income, housing, or education—contact is likely to make the difference more salient. Stereotypes develop when such differences are made salient (Campbell, 1967). Furthermore, in societies such as the United States, where there is an egalitarian ideology, the status inequality becomes even more salient. People have to explain in inequality to themselves, so they generate cognitions that justify the inequality. For example, they may develop the stereotype *lazy* to explain observed differences in income.

In my studies of stereotypes of Greeks and Americans that were in contact with each other (Triandis & Vassiliou, 1967; Vassiliou, Triandis, Vassiliou, & McGuire, 1972), the Americans devalued the Greeks on the dimensions of efficiency, skill, and competence in getting things done, and the Greeks devalued the Americans on the dimension of interpersonal warmth. In fact, both groups seemed to have an implicit personality theory in which work competence was negatively correlated with social competence, as measured by charm, warmth, and friendliness. Thus, each group appeared to observe the difference in the standard of living and translated it by means of its own implicit theory: the Americans said that the Greeks were high in social competence and low in work competence, and the Greeks said the same about themselves and saw the Americans as high in work competence, but low in social competence.

A similar situation is likely to prevail in black–white contact. Contact in situations of unequal status is likely to generate prejudice rather than to reduce it because some prejudice emerges as a *justification* of the status gap.

A SPECIFIC PROPOSAL

Rather than integration, as it is conceived of by the popular press, we need *additive multiculturalism*. The idea was suggested by Lambert's discussion (1973) of additive and subtractive bilingualism. Lambert argued that an English-Canadian who learns French adds to her or his capacities; when a French-Canadian learns English, there is danger of assimilation into the vast North American culture and the loss of French identity. Whites who learn about black subjective culture and learn to appreciate the positive features of black culture become enriched. Asking blacks to become culturally white is subtractive multiculturalism. As Taylor (1974) wrote, perhaps too strongly, integration as advocated today is a white idea about how blacks would become psychologically white. That conception is subtractive multiculturalism. The way to reduce conflict is not for one side to lose what the other side gains, but for both sides to gain.

Some of the negative features of American society—including anxiety over achievement, which results in much "Type A behavior" and a third of a million deaths from heart attacks each year—might be reduced if we adopt a more relaxed outlook, often found among blacks. Perhaps we should contemplate whether our crime, pollution, suicide, and divorce rates are where they should be. In any case, we need to understand the feelings associated with each kind of multiculturalism. Desirable pluralism permits everyone to have additive multiculturalist experiences. Ideally, pluralism involves enjoyment of our ability to switch from one cultural system to another. There is a real sense of accomplishment associated with having the skill to shift cultures. The balanced bilingual-bicultural person—or even more, the multicultural person—gets kicks out of life that are simply not available to the monolingual-monocultural person. There is a thrill associated with having the competence to master different environments, to be successful in different settings. The person who delights in different social settings, different ideologies, and different life-styles simply gets more out of life. There are now effective ways to train people to appreciate other cultures (Brislin & Pedersen, 1976; Landis & Brislin, 1983). We must use these procedures in our schools to broaden the perspective of most students.

At the simplest level, we find this broadening in the appreciation of different foods. Contrast the meat-and-potatoes diet of some people with the diet of those who have the means to explore the multinational cuisine of a large city. The ability to appreciate the full range of music produced in different parts of the world is another example. But food and music appreciation are not as difficult to learn as the subtle ways of human interaction, and particularly intimacy. To be able to become intimate[5] with many kinds of people who are very different is a great accomplishment. This should be the goal of a good education, and the essential step forward to a pluralist society.

A good education also means an education that is adjusted to the needs of the minority as well as to the majority groups. Castañada, James, and Robbins (1974) outlined some of the ways in which schools must change to provide the best learning environments for Latin-background, black, and native American children. Castañada, for instance, pointed out that teachers frequently punish behaviors that are learned in the child's home, thus making the school environment noxious. The Spanish-American emphasis on family, the personalization of interpersonal relations, the clear-cut sex-role differentiation, and so on create a particular way of thinking, feeling, and learning. A teacher who is not aware of these cultural influences can easily lose contact with a child. For example, the teaching of a Spanish-background child may be improved if the teacher sits close to the child, touches a lot, hugs, smiles, uses older children to teach younger children, involves the children in group activities, sends work to the child's home so the parents can get involved, arranges for Mexican foods to be cooked in class, teaches Spanish songs to all children, and so on. Similarly, if monocultural American children understood why native Americans have values stressing harmony with nature rather than its conquest, a present rather than a future time orientation, giving one's money away rather than saving it, respect for age rather than emphasis on youth, such children would broaden their perspective. The dominant American culture will profit from the inclusion of such conceptions in its repertoire of values: Harmony with nature is much more conducive to the respect that ecology imposes on technology in the postindustrial era; respect for old age may be much more functional in a nation where the majority is old, as it will be soon; a present orientation may be more realistic in a society that can no longer afford to grow rapidly because of energy and resource limitations; and so on. The majority culture can be enriched by considering the viewpoints of the several minority cultures that exist in America rather than trying to force these minorities to adopt a monocultural, impoverished, provincial viewpoint that may, in the long run, reduce creativity and the chances of effective adjustment in a fast-changing world.

Such goals are equally viable for minority and majority members provided we respect each other's cultural identity. We must not ask blacks to become culturally white. We must not ask them to lose their identity. Integration in the form of becoming like us implies by definition that their culture is inferior. Rather, what we want is to find more common superordinate goals and methods of interdependence that give self-respect to all. We need to be creative if we are to discover such methods.

Tom Pettigrew (1969) asked whether we should be racially separate or together. He suggested that we must move toward a "true integration," in which the races are together but each has autonomy. Taylor (1974) disagreed with Pettigrew's position. Taylor has argued that dependent people cannot be integrated in an egalitarian society. Integration, he argued, can imply loss of identity and inferiority. He insisted that only after

---

[5]By *intimate*, we meant here the development of mutual trust and appreciation of the basic quality of humanity that each has and a tolerance for whatever differences are observed.

power is equalized can we have racial justice. Similarly, Ron Katanga stated: "We can't be independent unless we have something to offer; we can live with whites interdependently once we have black power" (cited by Pettigrew in Epps, 1974). Taylor (1974) was optimistic and gave us some examples of power shifting to blacks: In Atlanta the NAACP agreed to the busing of only 3,000 instead of 30,000 students in exchange for 9 out of 17 administrative positions in the school system, including the positions of superintendent and assistant superintendent of instruction. The argument was that power could lead to decisions that would improve the quality of education of the black children of Atlanta, and that was better than mere integration. Taylor (personal communication, 1976) was also impressed by discussions among administrators of the Massachusetts Institute of Technology about transferring a substantial portion of the MIT group life insurance from a white-controlled to two black-controlled insurance companies. His argument was that only when the power gap between the races is made much smaller is contact likely to lead to harmony. Thus, as a first step toward pluralism, he visualized what he called "empowerment strategies" for blacks to acquire power. He also emphasized the importance of institutional racism, much more than individual prejudice, as a barrier to pluralism.

There is much to recommend Taylor's position. Mere integration, as advocated today, will not lead to additive multiculturalism. To reach additive multiculturalism, a four-pronged strategy is required.

1. *There is an urgent need for programs that guarantee jobs to every American who is capable of working.* Our data show the largest gap in subjective culture not between blacks and whites but between unemployed blacks and employed blacks. Current estimates of unemployment rates among young black males exceed 50%. This is a totally unacceptable rate. A program of guaranteed jobs for those who can work, negative income tax for those who earn too little, job-supportive services (such as public nurseries), and welfare payments for the old and disabled may eventually cost less than the $200 billion spent on various forms of welfare ("Progress against Poverty," 1976). Such a program can benefit both whites and blacks (though blacks will be helped proportionately more), the costs can be diffused through the income tax structure, and it is consistent with the dominant values of this society: it would put people to work (Rothbart, 1976). I would add one more most important benefit: It would create the preconditions for successful contact. Given the importance of having a job within the American status system, the elimination of the unequal rates of unemployment via elimination of most unemployment would immediately reduce one of the important dissimilarities that make successful interracial contact difficult.

Our evidence (Triandis, 1976), as well as that of Feldman (1974), suggests that working-class blacks are very similar in their subjective cultures to working-class whites; the discrepancies in subjective culture occur among the unemployed. Thus, by eliminating this category, we would move toward another precondition of successful contact. Finally, by integrating the unemployed into the economy, we would create some commitment to the successful operation of the whole economic system, as well as to a variety of superordinate goals.

For the guaranteed-jobs plan to have the desired effects, however, these jobs must be identified not as government-jobs-specially-made-to-take-care-of-the-unemployment-problem, but as legitimate jobs. This means that a variety of avenues toward full employment must be created simultaneously: stimulation of the private sector, identification of activities that have national priority (such as conservation projects), job training, and other programs. A productivity and motivation analysis relevant to the above is needed to ensure that this plan will not constitute an impractical ideological statement. During the last century, in the industrialized world, people moved from the 70+-hour work week to the 38-hour week, and from a 50-year life expectancy to 70+. Thus, the total number of hours worked by people during a lifetime has changed. Furthermore, increasingly, sections of the society are supported by other sections. This circumstance has had a demotivating effect. Specifically, Lévy-Leboyer (1984) analyzed the number of hours worked when life expectancy was in the 50-to-60 range and what it is now. She found that people spent about 30% of their life working whereas now they spend 10% of their life working. As this change has taken place, more and more people have moved toward the elimination of effort (e.g., labor-saving appliances are widely used). As work becomes less important, people become demotivated to work. Survival can now occur without work.

Demotivation for work is accompanied by an increase in leisure activities. Generally, physical activities are prestigeful only if they occur for no pay (e.g., athletic activities). This shift of values and behaviors results in a society where a few people work hard and derive their identities from their work, and the majority either work with little satisfaction in that activity or do not work at all, being supported by other segments of the society. We need to rethink what our current policies do to self-esteem and individual identity. To what extent are our high divorce, crime, and mental illness rates related to our employment policies?

2. *Blacks and other minorities must seek power.* They need to develop a flexible, imaginative approach to acquiring it. To get power, they need resources. They do have one important resource: a common fate. If they manage to communicate within each community the importance of concerted action for improving their position in American society, they will be able to engage in balance-or-power politics and thus to acquire more resources than they now have.

The primary thrust here must be political. It requires voter registration and long-term planning to place blacks in positions of power. The black caucus in the House of Representatives has already achieved some power. Some congressional committees are chaired by blacks. This achievement has not resulted in major changes because the economy has been under pressure and the anticipated deficits have been large. However, it is the kind of development that will eventually lead to power, and to shifts in resources.

The most important next steps are job training and job creation, as well as efforts to improve the education and skills of minorities. Such efforts would be consistent with the previous recommendation, as well as essential for minorities to increase their power.

3. *To learn about another culture, one must be secure in one's own identity. The essence of additive multiculturalism is that those who have a firm identity—the well-established mainstream of America—must do the learning.* And they should learn not only about blacks, but also about Spanish-speakers, native Americans, and other ethnic minorities that exist in significant numbers in the United States. To be educated in this country should mean that one is able to have good, effective, and intimate relationships with the 10 or more important cultural groups that exist here. Specifically, whites must learn to interact effectively with blacks. Right now, given the status of blacks and whites in this country, whites have no good reasons to learn how to get along with blacks. Unlike the American who, if he or she is to visit Paris, should learn a bit of French, whites have little motivation to learn how to get along with blacks.

Note that I am emphasizing that learning to get along means learning new interaction skills. But this is exactly what additive pluralism is all about. It is being able to get along not only with one's own group but also with other groups. New techniques for culture learning (Albert, 1983; Brislin & Pedersen, 1976; Landis, Day, McGrew, Thomas, & Miller, 1976; Seelye, 1975; Triandis, 1975, 1976) are becoming available. These techniques can train people to engage in interactions—where the rewards exceed the cost for both persons—with a large variety of ethnic groups. By extension, some of these techniques can be used to improve relationships between men and women, old and young, and so on.

For example, the culture assimilator has been an effective technique for cross-cultural training (Triandis, 1976). It consists of a sample of several hundred "episodes" that portray interaction between members of the majority and the minority. Trainees from the majority are asked to make attributions, presented in multiple-choice format, about the causes of the behavior of the minority member in the particular episode. As they select each attribution, they are asked to turn to a specific page, where they receive feedback. When they select the incorrect attribution, they are told to "try again." When they select the correct attribution, they are told why it is correct and are given specific cultural information that explains the minority point of view. "Correct" is here determined empirically. In preparing assimilators, researchers present episodes and attributions of the kind mentioned above to samples of minority and majority members, who select the attribution they believe to be correct. When there is a significant difference in the frequency of choice of attribution by the minority and majority samples, that information is used to select episodes and attributions to be included in the training. Evaluations of the effectiveness of such training have indicated that it improves intergroup relations (see Albert, 1983, for a review).

In short, whenever the life experiences of a group are sufficiently different from the experiences of another group, the gap in subjective cultures requires an effort to reduce misunderstandings. Each group must learn more about the perspective of the other groups than happens now.

4. *The techniques of fostering cooperation in schools developed by Aronson and the Johnsons* (see Chapter 15) *must be adopted by most American schools.*

The key element in both of these techniques is to foster interdependence and cooperation within the schoolroom. By giving to different pupils materials that they must teach to the other students in order to do well in school themselves, or by creating common goals for groups of pupils who receive the same grade, one can improve interpersonal relations in the classroom.

WE NEED MORE RESEARCH

Consider a theoretical model that describes black–white contact. There might be n dimensions on which two groups might be different. In the case of assimilated blacks, n tends to be close to zero; they differ little from whites. In the case of blacks with ecosystem distrust, n may be a very large number.

Now consider m dimensions specifying the conditions under which contact is likely to lead to "successful" interpersonal relationships, that is, relationships in which the rewards exceed the costs of *both* blacks and whites. It is likely that, in work relationships (one of the m dimensions), this would be the case, whereas in other relationships, it may not be the case.

One of the research projects urgently needed is one that specifies how the n dimensions of differences are related to the m dimensions of successful contact. For example, a difference in trust in the American system of government may have strong implications for cooperation between a white and a black person in a business venture, whereas it may have little relevance to an intimate relationship; conversely, a difference in trust in the reliability of friends may have little significance in a relationship that is specified by a written contract but very large significance for an intimate relationship. We need to develop a much greater understanding of how differences in subjective culture between blacks and whites have implications for some interpersonal relationships but not for others.

There is already enough research to indicate that acceptance in formal settings is more likely than acceptance in informal settings (Goldstein & Davis, 1973; Pettigrew, 1969; Triandis & Davis, 1965). We also know that, when superordinate goals can be made salient, when contact receives institutional support, and when contact is associated with pleasurable events, it is more likely to lead to successful interpersonal relationships. In short, we already know some of the m dimensions. But there may be others that we still need to discover.

On the antecedent side of the coin, we know that certain characteristics of the groups in contact help to predispose them to successful interpersonal relationships. When two groups have similar status and know each other's subjective cultures, there is a high probability of successful interpersonal relationships in those social situations that induce cooperation. This is not so when people are of different status or do not know each others' subjective culture.

It follows from this discussion that contact without the preconditions of similarity in status, knowledge of the other group's subjective culture, and similarity of goals may have undesirable consequences. Yet, much of the current thinking on integration proposes exactly that kind of contact.

In addition, we must learn a great deal more than we know now about successful intergroup contact. The aim should be to create in the shortest time the largest number of what we defined above as "successful interpersonal relationships." We must become an experimenting society (Campbell, 1969). As research on this topic gives usable answers, we may be able to create a new group of professionals—applied social psychologists— whose job it would be to counsel people on how to achieve successful interpersonal relationships in the shortest time. Such people might be called *human relations catalysts*. In situations where people with different subjective cultures must interact, they would act as consultants to provide the kind of training and perspective needed to establish a successful interpersonal relationship. The human relations catalysts would know what skills, knowledge, and attitudes are needed to be successful in particular job settings, in schools, or in community activities. We already know much about this kind of problem (Brislin & Pederson, 1976; Landis & Brislin, 1983), but we still have too many research gaps to be able to train such professionals well today.

A VISION OF THE FUTURE

What kind of society would emerge from such activities? It would be one in which people would have more choices, and their choices would be more acceptable to others. Few situations are more confining than unemployment. The unemployed person is forced to seek other avenues to gain status or income; crime is a common one. Yet, unemployment is often imposed by outside circumstances rather than a matter of free choice. Furthermore, a person with a steady job can seek better housing and better schools. This does not mean that all blacks will want to live in white neighborhoods. Nor does it mean that all will want to send their children to integrated schools. But note the large difference between having to be segregated and *deciding* to be segregated. Increasing the number of times when people decide to adopt a particular life-style rather than having the life-style imposed on them via ideology, legal action, or economic pressure, seems desirable.

Some blacks will go to all-black schools, some will work in all-black companies, and some will live in all-black neighborhoods, but they will do so as a matter of free choice. The catalysts, who will often be black, after careful examination of each case might conclude that the integration of a particular individual is premature or unlikely to lead to successful interpersonal relationships. They would so advise a client, giving reasons for that advice. Then the client might voluntarily choose to go to an all-black school. Hopefully, over time, fewer and fewer persons would receive such advice. My emphasis is on dealing with individuals and recognizing that there are individual differences. The law should give everyone the right to integrate, but it may not be to everybody's advantage to exercise this right immediately. A child with low self-esteem who is placed in a school where failure is guaranteed is not served well.

One of the ways in which the catalysts might operate would be the analysis of the subjective culture of various groups of clients in relation to the known subjective cultures of various mainstream groups. Then, by identifying the smallest existing gaps in subjective culture, they would advise their clients about the right move and would train these clients to be successful in the new social setting in which they will have to work, live, or learn. Broadening the clients' perspective concerning various subjective cultures seems to be an effective way to train them for intercultural behavior (Triandis, 1976). It does increase cognitive complexity and makes people more flexible in different kinds of social environments (Triandis, 1975). The catalysts would keep constantly abreast of changes in the subjective culture, job requirements, specially needed skills, and so on of different job settings and would advise their clients to move into those situations in which the clients are likely to be most successful.

Finally, we need to learn to value different life-styles and to assign equal status to them, even though they are different. Just as a Nobel prize winner in physics is different from a Nobel prize winner in literature, yet one is not different in status from the other, so we must learn that different life-styles are perfectly viable. We need cultural heterogeneity in order to have an interesting life, and also in order to invent the new life-styles needed in a fast-changing culture. What we do not need is the "different is inferior" viewpoints that have so frequently characterized humankind's interpersonal relations.

CONCLUSION

Pluralism, then, is the development of interdependence, appreciation, and the skills for interacting intimately with persons from other cultures. It involves learning to enter social relationships where the rewards exceed the costs for both sides of the relationship. To achieve this state, we need more understanding of social-psychological principles and experimentation with new forms of social institutions, such as the catalysts.

My argument has been that our current attempts at integration, based on a legal framework, disregard individual differences and are attempts to eliminate cultural differences. This chapter advocates a shift from that perspective to one that provides for a marriage of the legal framework with our understanding of social-psychological principles. Rather than integration, as conceived of today, or assimilation, which involves the elimination of cultural differences, it advocates *additive multiculturalism,* where people learn to be effective and to appreciate others who are different in culture. Additive multiculturalism is, by its very nature, something that needs to be developed in the majority rather than in the minority of the population. As more members of the minority learn to integrate in jobs and are given a chance to do so, the majority must learn to relate to the minorities with a perspective of additive multiculturalism. Within that framework and over a period of many years, we should develop a pluralism that gives self-respect to all, appreciation of cultural differences, and social skills leading to interpersonal relationships with more rewards than costs.

REFERENCES

Abelson, R. P. (1959). Modes of resolution of belief dilemmas. *Journal of Conflict Resolution, 3,* 343–352.
Abelson, R. P., Aronson, E., McGuire, W. J., Newcomb, T. M., Rosenberg, M. J., & Tannenbaum, P. H. (1968). *Theories of cognitive consistency: A sourcebook.* Chicago: Rand McNally.

Albert, R. (1983) The intercultural sensitizer or culture assimilator: A cognitive approach. In D. Landis & R. Brislin (Eds.), *Handbook of intercultural training.* Beverly Hills, CA: Sage.

Amir, Y. (1969). Contact hypothesis in intergroup relations. *Psychological Bulletin, 71,* 319–342.

Amir, Y. (1976). The role of intergroup contact in change of prejudice and ethnic relations. In P. A. Katz (Ed.), *Toward the elimination of racism.* New York: Pergamon Press.

Berkowitz, L., & Walster, E. (1976). Equity theory: Toward a general theory of social interaction. In L. Berkowitz (Ed.), *Advances in experimental social psychology* (Vol. 9). New York: Academic Press.

Berry, J. W. (1984). Cultural relations in plural societies: Alternatives to segregation and their socio-psychological implications. In N. Miller & M. B. Brewer (Eds.), *Groups in contact: The psychology of desegregation.* Orlando, FL: Academic Press.

Berry, J. W., Kalin, R., & Taylor, D. M. (1976). *Multiculturalism and ethnic attitudes in Canada.* Ottawa: Minister of State for Multiculturalism.

Blau, F., & Ferber, M. (1986). *The economics of women, men, and work.* Englewood Cliffs, NJ: Prentice-Hall.

Brewer, M. B., & Kramer, R. M. (1985). The psychology of intergroup attitudes and behavior. *Annual Review of Psychology, 36,* 219–244.

Brislin, R. W., & Pedersen, P. (1976). *Cross-cultural orientation programs.* New York: Gardner Press.

Campbell, D. T. (1967). Stereotypes and perception of group differences. *American Psychologist, 22,* 812–829.

Campbell, D. T. (1969). Reforms as experiments. *American Psychologist, 24,* 409–429.

Castañada, A., James, R. L., & Robbins, W. (1974). *The educational needs of minority groups.* Lincoln, NE: Professional Educators Publishers.

Deutsch, M. (1969). Conflicts: Productive and destructive. *Journal of Social Issues, 25,* 7–41.

Dowdall, G. W. (1974). White gains from black subordination in 1960 and 1970. *Social Problems, 22,* 162–183.

Epps, E. G. (1974). *Cultural pluralism.* Berkeley, CA: McCatchan Press.

Feldman, J. (1974). Race, economic class and the intention to work: Some normative and attitudinal correlates. *Journal of Applied Psychology, 59,* 179–186.

Foa, U. G., & Donnenwerth, G. W. (1971). Love poverty in modern culture and sensitivity training. *Sociological Inquiry, 41,* 149–159.

Foa, U. G., & Foa, E. B. (1974). *Societal structures of the mind.* Springfield, IL: Charles C Thomas.

Goldstein, M., & Davis, E. E. (1973). Race and belief: A further analysis of the social determinants of behavioral intentions. *Journal of Personality and Social Psychology, 26,* 16–22.

Hennigh, L. (1975). Negative stereotyping: Structural contributions in a Bureau of Indian Affairs community. *Human Organization, 34,* 263–268.

Heradveit, D. (1979). *The Arab–Israeli conflict.* Oslo, Norway: Universitetforlaget.

Hofstede, G. (1980). *Culture's consequences.* Beverly Hills, CA: Sage.

Homans, G. C. (1974). *Social behavior: Its elementary forms.* New York: Harcourt Brace.

Jones, E. E., Kanouse, D. E., Kelley, H. H., Nisbett, R. E., Valins, S., & Weiner, B. (1972). *Attribution: Perceiving the causes of behavior.* Morristown, NJ: General Learning Press.

Kessler, R. C., Price, R. H., & Wortman, C. B. (1985). Social factors in psychopathology: Stress social support and coping processes. *Annual Review of Psychology, 36,* 531–572.

Lambert, W. E. (1973). *Culture and language as factors in learning and education.* Paper presented at the Symposium on Cultural Factors in Learning, Bellingham, WA.

Landis, D., & Brislin, R. (1983). *Handbook of intercultural training* (Vols. 1–3). New York: Pergamon Press.

Landis, D., Day, H. R., McGrew, P. L., Thomas, J. A., & Miller, A. B. (1976). Can a black "culture assimilator" increase racial understanding? *Journal of Social Issues, 32*(2), 169–183.

Lévy-Leboyer, C. (1984). *La crise des motivations.* Paris, France: Presses Universitaires de France.

Lewis, O. (1966). The culture of poverty. *Scientific American, 215,* 19–25.

Ley, D. (1974). *The black inner city as frontier outpost.* Washington, DC: Association of American Geographers.

Marx, G. T. (1967). *Protest and prejudice.* New York: Harper & Row.

Mosteller, F., & Moynihan, D. P. (1972). *On equality of educational opportunity.* New York: Random House.

Murphy, H. B. M. (1961). Social change and mental health. *Milbank Memorial Fund Quarterly, 39,* 385–445.

Murphy, H. B. M. (1965). Migration and the major mental disorders: A reappraisal. In M. B. Kantor (Ed.), *Mobility and mental health.* Springfield, IL: Charles C Thomas.

Myrdal, G. (1944). *An American dilemma.* New York: Harper.

Naroll, R. (1983). *The moral order.* Beverly Hills, CA: Sage.

Naroll, R., Benjamin, E. C., Fohl, F. K., Fried, M. J., Hildreth, R. E., & Schaefer, J. M. (1971). Creativity: A cross-historical pilot survey. *Journal of Cross-Cultural Psychology, 2,* 191–198.

Nisbett, R. E., Caputo, C., Legant, P., & Marecek, J. (1973). Behavior as seen by the actor and as seen by the observer. *Journal of Personality and Social Psychology, 27,* 154–164.

Novak, M. (1972). *The rise of unmeltable ethnics.* New York: Macmillan.

Pettigrew, T. F. (1969). Racially separate or together? *Journal of Social Issues, 25*(1), 43–69.

Progress against poverty: 1964–74. *Focus on Poverty Research, 1976, 1,* 8–12.

Rothbart, M. (1976). Achieving racial equality: An analysis of resistance to social reform. In P. A. Katz (Ed.), *Toward the elimination of racism.* New York: Pergamon.

Schuman, H., & Hatchett, S. (1974). *Black racial attitudes: Trends and complexities.* Ann Arbor, MI: Institute of Social Research.

Seelye, H. N. (1975). *Teaching culture.* Skokie, IL: National Textbook.

Seligman, M. E. P. (1975). *Helplessness: On depression, development and death.* San Francisco: Freeman.

Sherif, M. (1968). If the social scientist is to be more than a mere technician. *Journal of Social Issues, 24*(1), 41–61.

Simonton, D. K. (1975). Sociocultural context of individual creativity: A transhistorical time-series analysis. *Journal of Personality and Social Psychology, 32,* 1119–1133.

Skinner, B. F. (1953). *Science and human behavior.* New York: Macmillan.

Taylor, D. A. (1974). Should we integrate organizations? In H. Fromkin & J. Sherwood (Eds.), *Integrating the organization.* New York: Free Press.

Taylor, D. M., & Jaggi, V. (1974). Ethnocentrism and causal attribution in a south Indian context. *Journal of Cross-Cultural Psychology, 5,* 162–171.

Thibaut, J., & Kelley, H. H. (1959). *The social psychology of groups.* New York: Wiley.

Thurow, L. C. (1969). *Poverty and discrimination.* Washington, DC: Brookings Institution.

Triandis, H. C. (1975). Culture training, cognitive complexity and interpersonal attitudes. In R. Brislin, S. Bochner, & W. Lonner (Eds.), *Cross-cultural perspectives on learning.* New York: Halstead/Wiley.

Triandis, H. C. (Ed.). (1976). *Variations in black and white perceptions of the social environment.* Urbana: University of Illinois Press.

Triandis, H. C., & Davis, E. E. (1965). Race and belief as determinants of behavioral intentions. *Journal of Personality and Social Psychology, 2,* 715–725.

Triandis, H. C., & Vassiliou, V. (1967). Frequency of contact and stereotyping. *Journal of Personality and Social Psychology, 7,* 316–328.

Tucker, L. (1966). Some mathematical notes on three-mode factor analysis. *Psychometrika, 31,* 279–311.

Turner, C. B., & Wilson, W. J. (1976). Dimensions of racial ideology: A study of urban black attitudes. *Journal of Social Issues, 32*(2), 139–152.

Vassiliou, V. V., Triandis, H. C., Vassiliou, G., & McGuire, H. (1972). Interpersonal contact and stereotyping. In H. C. Triandis (Ed.), *The analysis of subjective culture.* New York: Wiley.

Ward, C., & Hewstone, M. (1985). Ethnicity, language, and intergroup relations in Malaysia and Singapore: A social psychological analysis. *Journal of Multilingual Multicultural Development, 6,* 271–296.

Weldon, D. E., Carlston, D. E., Rissman, A. K., Slobodin, L., & Triandis, H. C. (1975). A laboratory test of effects of culture assimilator training. *Journal of Personality and Social Psychology, 32,* 300–310.

X (Clark), C. (Ed.). (1973). The white researcher in black society. *Journal of Social Issues, 29*(1), 1–119.

B. Symbolic versus Realistic Group Conflict

4

Symbolic Racism

David O. Sears

Throughout our history, white Americans have singled out Afro-Americans for particularly racist treatment. Of all the many immigrant nationalities that have come to these shores since the seventeenth century, Afro-Americans have consistently attracted the greatest prejudice based on their group membership and have been treated in the most categorically unequal fashion.

In the early 1960s, optimism abounded about finally putting to rest the most glaring symptoms of this tragic flaw in American democracy. Explicit discrimination against blacks had seemingly become a thing of the past except in some vestigial practices of the old Confederacy. By the end of that decade, federal court decisions and civil rights legislation, and their active enforcement by the Kennedy and Johnson administrations, had put an end to formal segregation and discrimination in almost all areas of southern social and political life as well. Most of these actions had the support of northern whites, and even white southern public opinion moved dramatically to support general principles of racial equality (Greeley & Sheatsley, 1971). As the 1970s dawned, the main formal barriers to racial equality seemed to be crumbling, with the full approval of the white majority.

But with the end of most formal barriers came recognition of still further obstacles. And during the late 1960s and early 1970s, there was disquieting evidence of continued white resistance to full racial equality. Public support for the U.S. Supreme Court became sharply polarized around its liberal civil rights decisions, and calls for the impeachment of Chief Justice Warren were common (Murphy & Tanenhaus, 1968). In 1964, in California, two thirds of the electorate voted to overturn a state law forbidding overt racial discrimination in housing, though the state had relatively few blacks and no unusual history of racial discrimination or racial conflict (Wolfinger & Greenstein, 1968). Over the next few years, riots broke out in hundreds of black ghettos across the country, generating fear and condemnation among whites. In both 1964 and 1968, George Wallace's candidacy for the presidency, with its barely disguised appeal to antiblack sentiments, did surprisingly well in both North and South. "White backlash" became a topic of anxious conversation in the White House and elsewhere. "Backlash" local candidates, such as Louise Day Hicks in Boston or Sam Yorty in Los Angeles, ran well at the polls. For the first time, moderate blacks mounted serious and sometimes successful candidacies for higher office

---

DAVID O. SEARS • College of Letters and Sciences, University of California, Los Angeles, California 90024.

in such majority-white electorates as Massachusetts and Los Angeles. But even then, the vote was strongly polarized by race and, among whites, by level of racial prejudice (Becker & Heaton, 1967; McConahay & Hough, 1976; Sears & Kinder, 1971). School desegregation plodded along "at all deliberate speed," which was very slow indeed, and its main instrument, "busing," was strongly opposed by most whites.

This seemed sharply paradoxical. Egalitarian public policies were being implemented on a massive scale, backed by overwhelming white support for the formal principles of racial equality. But there were clear warning signs of widespread opposition to further implementation. This paradox raised serious questions about the level of individual racism among whites, that is, about whites' attitudes toward blacks and toward racial equality. Various views came forward. Perhaps racism was just in hiding, momentarily cloaked by whites' need to appear tolerant in a new era insisting on overt tolerance, but ready to spring "out from under the rocks" when the coast was clear. It did seem that the old forms of racial prejudice, supporting a segregationist social system, so common in the pre–World War II generation, were dying out. Younger generations of whites were plainly more racially liberal (Campbell, 1971). But perhaps the issues were changing, and with them, the public agenda. Racism might actually have been increased in the North by the personal impact of government racial policies that for the first time directly affected the lives of northern whites. Alternatively, these new issues may have activated values that had been peripheral to racial issues when the public agenda was dominated by segregation and thus may have stimulated new configurations of support and opposition.

In that context, we proposed that a new form of racism had emerged in white America, which we termed *symbolic racism* (Sears & Kinder, 1970). This was not racism composed of derogations of and antagonism toward blacks *per se*, or of support for formal inequality. Rather, it blended some antiblack feeling with the finest and proudest of traditional American values, particularly individualism. It has now been over a decade and a half since this concept was proposed, a time of great change in American politics and in American society. Much research has been done since then. It seems appropriate to take stock of what we have learned and how the notion of symbolic racism has fared.

This chapter, then, presents a kind of current status report on symbolic racism. I will first review the original thinking behind it, describe how it was tested empirically, and summarize the key findings relevant to it. Its main critiques will be considered. Finally, I will turn to ways in which the concept has been shaped and modified in the years since it was first proposed, and I will evaluate how it helps us understand the large issues in race relations of our day.

THE SYMBOLIC RACISM APPROACH

A POLITICAL FOCUS

The notion of symbolic racism was introduced to explain a rather specific phenomenon: the political role of whites' racial attitudes. There can be no doubt that white response to an increasingly politicized black population has had a major impact on postwar American politics (Kinder & Sanders, 1986). Public opinion on racial matters throughout this period has affected who holds power and makes policy (Converse, Clausen, & Miller, 1965; Converse, Miller, Rusk, & Wolfe, 1969; Fiorina, 1981; Kinder & Sears, 1981; Pettigrew, 1971). Dissatisfaction with the national administration's pushing of racial equality—too rapidly or not rapidly enough—has contributed to growing cynicism about government in general (Miller, 1981). And some feel that a major partisan realignment is occurring, spurred in part by the politics of race (Carmines & Stimson, 1980, 1984; Markus, 1979).

Much research had been done in the 1960s on black protest, inspired by the many ghetto riots of the era (e.g., Aberbach & Walker, 1973; Feagin & Hahn, 1973; Fogelson, 1971; National Advisory Commission on Civil Disorders, 1968; Sears & McConahay, 1973). As startling as this change in blacks' actions was, it soon became evident that the black population was not in a position of great political power, owing to its small fraction of the electorate, its poverty and ghettoized location, and the magnitude of the white backlash against the riots. Because whites' attitudes as much as blacks' actions would ultimately dictate the pace of racial progress, much research attention shifted at the point to the white population.

Our own research on whites began at that time with two main goals. One was to assess the power of racism in determining whites' political responses. Hence, we have looked, since the early 1970s, at the role of whites' racial attitudes in determining their responses to racial policies such as busing (e.g., Sears & Allen, 1984; Sears et al., 1979, 1980), to black candidates (e.g., Kinder & Sears, 1981; McConahay & Hough, 1976; Sears, Citrin, & Kosterman, 1985; Sears & Kinder, 1971), and to tax and spending reductions affecting programs benefiting blacks (Sears & Citrin, 1985). Most of these studies involved secondary analysis of data collected for other purposes and used whatever measures of racial attitudes were available, without attempting to specify very exactly the nature of the racism at work.

Our other goal was to develop the notion of a new kind of racism: symbolic racism. Here, too, our concern was with the role of racism in determining the mass white public's political responses—but here we were particularly interested in specifying the *kind* of racism that was involved, especially whether it was a familiar and old-fashioned form of racial prejudice, or a product of real racial threats, or a new, more symbolic, form of racism (Kinder & Sears, 1981; McConahay, 1982; McConahay & Hough, 1976).

THE CONTENT OF SYMBOLIC RACISM

From the beginning, a central contention was that symbolic racism was replacing "old-fashioned racism" as a determinant of whites' responses to political matters (Sears & Kinder, 1970, 1971). McConahay (1982) made this contrast most explicitly. He described old-fashioned racism as "open bigotry," particularly revolving around three specific contents: (a) pre–Civil War racial stereotypes; (b) restrictions on interracial social contacts, such as social distancing and segregation; and (c) opposition to equal access or equal opportunity for persons of all races, along with support for racial discrimination. We argued that old-fashioned racism was disappearing: relatively few whites still believed in the innate inferiority of blacks as a race or supported formal discrimination in schooling, jobs, public accommodations, and other areas of life. A vanishing set of ideas was likely to have much-reduced political power.[1]

Symbolic racism was proposed as a new form of racial attitude, composed of

---

[1]We used the term *generalized egalitarianism* in our earliest research, to label the same dimension later labeled *old-fashioned racism*, using the opposite pole to highlight the fact that almost everyone subscribed to general principles of racial equality (see Sears & Kinder, 1970, 1971). The point of the term *symbolic racism* was to emphasize the fact that it centers on symbols rather than on the concrete realities of life, especially of the individual's own personal life. However, as McConahay (1982) pointed out, the focus on symbolic content does not clearly distinguish symbolic racism from old-fashioned racism because the latter also focuses on symbols (e.g., "beliefs and stereotypes rooted in socialization and not in personal experience"—McConahay, 1982, p. 705). McConahay therefore prefers the term *modern racism*. A different term might have been better, in retrospect, but *symbolic racism* fit the contrast it was invented to serve—it was not old-fashioned, and not rooted in personal experience—and there is some advantage in continuing to use a label in fairly wide use.

> a blend of antiblack affect and the kind of traditional American moral values embodied
> in the Protestant Ethic . . . a form of resistance to change in the racial status quo based
> on moral feelings that blacks violate such traditional American values as individualism
> and self-reliance, the work ethic, obedience, and discipline. (Kinder & Sears, 1981, p.
> 416)

It is measured with items that are

> almost wholly abstract, ideological, and symbolic in nature . . . with no conceivable
> personal relevance to the individual, but have to do with his moral code or his sense of
> how society should be organized. (Sears & Kinder, 1971, p. 66)

Symbolic racism was therefore conceptualized as being a joint function of two separate
factors: antiblack affect and traditional values.

The notion of symbolic racism was originally developed by Sears and Kinder (1970,
1971) to explain the findings of a survey on the Los Angeles mayoralty elections of 1969
that pitted a black liberal challenger, Tom Bradley, against a white conservative incumbent, Sam Yorty. The respondents were white suburbanites in the city of Los Angeles.
The survey itself had been developed and conducted by Thomas Pettigrew and his
collaborators as part of their program of research on white electoral responses to black
mayoral candidates (e.g., Pettigrew, 1971). McConahay and Hough (1976) conducted a
second survey on the same election, using some of the same items, and Kinder and Sears
(1981) participated in the analyzed data from Pettigrew's follow-up survey on the 1973
Los Angeles mayoralty election matching the same two candidates. The concept of symbolic racism was, therefore, originally generated inductively to describe the results from
items that had been developed by other researchers for other purposes; the items were
not generated deductively to measure a preexisting concept.[2] In later studies, additional
items were generated to measure the symbolic racism concept more precisely. Thus,
measurement of symbolic racism has been evolving slowly over time.

At this point, there is a reasonably clear consensus on the content of symbolic racism.
It falls into two main categories: (a) antagonism toward blacks' "pushing too hard" and
moving too fast, especially (though not exclusively) through the use of violence, and (b)
resentment toward special favors for blacks, such as in "reverse discrimination," racial
quotas in jobs or education, excessive access to welfare, special treatment by government,
or unfair and excessive economic gains by blacks. A third possible category is (c) denial of
continuing discrimination: the belief that discrimination in areas such as jobs or housing
is a thing of the past because blacks now have the freedom to compete in the marketplace
and to enjoy things they can afford.[3]

TESTING FOR SYMBOLIC RACISM

Operationalizing symbolic racism has involved using items from each of these categories. Table 1 shows some typical items: (a) antagonism toward blacks' demands, that is,
blacks' being too demanding (McConahay, 1982; McConahay & Hough, 1976) or pushing
themselves where they're not wanted (Kinder & Sears, 1981) or civil rights leaders'
pushing too fast (Sears & Allen, 1984); (b) resentment about special favors for blacks, that
is, government's or public officials' making a special effort to help minorities (Kinder &
Sears, 1981; Sears & Allen, 1984; Sears & Citrin, 1985), or blacks' having got more than

---

[2]It should be noted that Pettigrew's analysis (1971) of such local elections as that of Louise Day
Hicks, in Boston, based on similar data, closely resembles our own.
[3]McConahay (1982) has used this third category in his work, but Kinder and Sears (1981) have not. I
incline toward Kinder's view (1985) that such perceptions are less manifestations of symbolic racism
than colored by it, but the distinction is perhaps a subtle one.

TABLE 1. Items Measuring Symbolic Racism

Antagonism toward blacks' demands

Blacks are getting too demanding in their push for equal rights. (Agree)[b,c]
Blacks shouldn't push themselves where they're not wanted. (Agree)[a]
Some say that the civil rights people have been trying to push too fast. Others feel they haven't pushed fast enough. (Trying to push too fast)[d]
It is easy to understand the anger of black people in America. (Disagree)[b,c]

Resentment about special favors for blacks

Over the past few years, the government and news media have shown more respect to blacks than they deserve. (Agree)[b]
Over the past few years, blacks have got more economically than they deserve. (Agree)[b]
The government should *not* make any special effort to help blacks and other racial minorities because they should help themselves. (Agree)[e]
Do you think blacks who receive money from welfare programs could get along without if they tried, or do they really need the help? (Could get along)[a]
Do you think Los Angeles city officials pay more, less, or the same attention to a request or complaint from a black person as from a white person? (More)[a]

Denial of continuing discrimination

How many black people in Louisville and Jefferson County do you think miss out on jobs or promotions because of racial discrimination? (None)[b]
Blacks have it better than they ever had it before. (Agree)[c]

[a] Kinder and Sears (1981).
[b] McConahay (1982).
[c] McConahay and Hough (1976).
[d] Sears and Allen (1984).
[e] Sears and Citrin (1985).

they deserve (Kinder & Sears, 1981; McConahay, 1982); and (c) a denial of continuing discrimination, that is perceptions of discrimination against blacks (Kinder & Sears, 1981; McConahay, 1982); and lack of sympathy with the anger of blacks (McConahay & Hough, 1976).

Although these items were not, for the most part, derived in any formal deductive sense from the concept of symbolic racism, they all share its two underlying elements: antiblack affect and traditional values. All three categories of items express antiblack affect in terms of antagonism, resentment, and anger toward blacks' wishes and a lack of sympathy with them. And all express underlying individualistic values in rejecting the assumption that the individual black's fate is or should be determined by that of the group as a whole, that is, the assumption that the individual black's fate is not determined by treatment of blacks as a group, and that demands for help and special favors should not be granted to blacks as a group.

Consequently, the symbolic racism model involves a two-step process, as shown in the solid lines in Figure 1: the conjunction of traditional values and antiblack affect produces symbolic racism, which in turn produces opposition to problack policies and black candidates. This full model has been tested by Sears *et al.* (1985), predicting opposition to Jesse Jackson; the second step was tested by McConahay and Hough (1976) and Kinder and Sears (1981), predicting opposition to Tom Bradley, and by Sears and Allen (1984), predicting antibusing attitudes.

Some tests of this symbolic racism model have also added political conservatism as an independent symbolic predisposition predicting these same dependent variables (Kinder & Sears, 1981; Sears & Citrin, 1985; Sears & Kinder 1971). In these cases, it is treated as independent of racism, which is carried by the symbolic racism term.

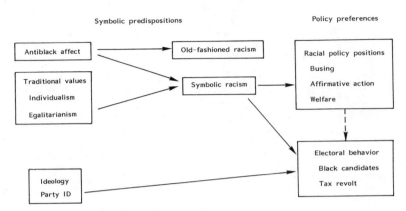

FIGURE 1. The symbolic racism approach.

A variant of the symbolic racism approach suggests that current racial policy issues can themselves become highly symbolic, thus adding their own influence over voting behavior. The most obvious case is "busing," which has been the instrument for the electoral defeat of various probusing school-board members, judges, and ballot measures. This second variant is depicted with a dotted line in Figure 1.

Symbolic Politics

The concept of symbolic racism was developed as part of a broader theory of symbolic politics. This theory holds that much adult political behavior results from symbolic predispositions acquired before full adulthood. These predispositions are viewed as being learned, and as reflecting the norms dominating the young individual's informational environment. In adulthood, they can be evoked by symbols in the current informational environment and are presumed to be the primary determinants of adulthood policy preferences and voting behavior. This particular version of a symbolic politics theory was first tested empirically in a study of the Watts riots, in which the residues of preadult socialization were invoked to explain blacks' and whites' conflicting responses to the symbols of black protest in general, and to the rioting in particular (Sears & McConahay, 1973).

The general symbolic politics approach is depicted in Figure 2. Most studies have relied on just three basic symbolic predispositions—racial attitudes, ideological self-labeling, and party identification—as predictors of political responses to the Vietnam war (Lau, Brown, & Sears, 1978), the energy crisis (Sears, Tyler, Citrin, & Kinder, 1978), the Watts riots (Sears & McConahay, 1973), national health insurance (Sears, Lau, Tyler, & Allen, 1980), the California tax revolt (Sears & Citrin, 1985), and antibusing attitudes (Sears, Hensler, & Speer, 1979).

It should be emphasized that the theory of symbolic politics is a more general account of political behavior than is the symbolic racism approach *per se*, which is primarily focused on the dynamics of racial conflict. Studies in the more general symbolic-politics vein have often assessed the impact of racial attitudes on political behavior, but usually by treating them in an omnibus fashion, considering neither distinctions among types of racism nor their antecedents. For examples, see studies of the origins of antibusing attitudes and their role in presidential voting (Sears *et al.*, 1979, 1980), and of the persistence of racial attitudes through the life span (Miller & Sears, 1986).

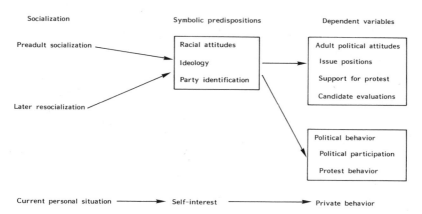

FIGURE 2. A theory of symbolic politics.

THE EFFECTS OF SYMBOLIC RACISM

THE POLITICAL EFFECTS

The first general proposition was that symbolic racism has a major effect on racial policy preferences and on voting behavior in racially relevant elections. It has therefore been tested as a predictor of whites' positions on policy issues such as busing, affirmative action, and welfare (Kluegel & Smith, 1983; Sears & Allen, 1984; Sears & Citrin, 1985), and of voting behavior in contests involving black candidates, such as Tom Bradley in Los Angeles (Kinder & Sears, 1981; McConahay & Hough, 1976; Sears & Kinder, 1970, 1971) or Jesse Jackson for the presidency (Sears et al., 1985), white candidates perceived as widely differing in racial policies (Sears et al., 1985), or referenda seemingly influenced by racial concerns, such as tax reduction (Sears & Citrin, 1985).

These empirical tests have typically combined symbolic racism items into scales and then correlated them with whites' policy preferences and voting behavior in multiple regression (OLS) equations. Representative data are shown in Table 2. For example, Kinder and Sears (1981) and McConahay and Hough (1976) found that, in two elections, symbolic racism related quite strongly to voting against Tom Bradley, the black candidate for mayor of Los Angeles, among white suburbanites. McConahay (1982) and Sears and Allen (1984) reported strong effects of symbolic racism on whites' opposition to busing. Kluegel and Smith (1983) reported similar effects of symbolic racism on opposition to affirmative action.

In large-sample survey studies, however, the importance of symbolic racism depends on the absolute level of prediction it affords—usually, how much variance it explains. The amount of variance explained depends, of course, to some extent on the reliabilities of the symbolic racism measure and the dependent variables. These, in turn, depend partly on the number of symbolic racism items available in any given study and on how well those items fit the conceptual definition of symbolic racism. Because the number of appropriate items varies widely across studies, no precise, simple, and uniform estimate of absolute impact can be made. But even in the absence of such an estimate, a ballpark estimate can be based on studies at the high end of measurement reliability, those that use substantial multi-item scales of symbolic racism. As Table 2 shows, these scales generated standardized regression coefficients (betas) of .47, .39, .36, and .34 with the use of quite reliable dependent variables, and with the inclusion of some

TABLE 2. Effects of Symbolic Racism on Whites' Political Attitudes

Study	Sample	Type of racism	Number of items	Dependent variable	Bivariate correlation	Regression analysis		
						Other variables in model	Standardized coefficient for racism scale	R^2
1. Kinder and Sears (1981)	Los Angeles suburbs (1969)	Symbolic racism	8	Vote for white vs. black mayoral candidate	—	Racial threat Opposition to busing	.36	.25
2. Kinder and Sears (1981)	Los Angeles suburbs (1973)	Symbolic racism	13	Vote for white vs. black mayoral candidate	—	Racial threat Opposition to busing	.34	.14
3. McConahay (1982)	Louisville (1976)	Symbolic racism	6	Opposition to busing	.51	Racial threat Old-fashioned racism Racial affect	.47	.28
4. McConahay (n.d.)	Louisville (1977)	Symbolic racism	5	Opposition to busing	—	Racial threat Old-fashioned racism	.39	.23
5. Sears and Citrin (1985)	California (1979)	Symbolic racism	2	Support for tax revolt	.30	Party ideology	.24	.13

other racial attitudes in the models (Kinder & Sears, 1981; McConahay, 1982, n.d.). At the low end of reliability are studies that have used only one- or two-item measures of symbolic racism. For example, Sears and Allen (1984) presented 12 analyses of opposition to busing, based on data from seven different surveys. In an effort to maintain comparability across surveys, only one symbolic racism item was used in each analysis. Even so, the betas averaged a healthy .26 (with several self-interest and demographic variables also included in each equation). Sears and Citrin (1985) used a two-item symbolic-racism scale to predict positions on an issue with no manifest racial content: support for the California tax revolt. Nevertheless, this scale generated a bivariate correlation of .30 with support for the tax revolt, as well as a beta of .24 when included in an equation with ideology and party identification. In short, multi-item scales incorporating the essence of the symbolic racism concept generated standardized regression coefficients approaching .40, with opposition to busing or relevant candidate evaluations used as the dependent variables. Even when minimal measures of symbolic racism were used, the betas still averaged around .25.

These effects of symbolic racism would seem to me quite strong, by the standards of research in this area, particularly considering the other variables used in most of these equations. In partisan elections, these effects are not as strong as those of party identification, of course. But in ostensibly nonpartisan elections, or in predicting issue positions, they are as strong as those of any other symbolic predispositions.[4]

OLD-FASHIONED RACISM

Our second general proposition was that symbolic racism now has a much stronger political impact than does old-fashioned racism. An initial question is whether the two are really independent. Symbolic racism presumably has a strong component of nonracial traditional values, whereas old-fashioned racism does not, so they should be statistically somewhat independent. Nevertheless, they share common roots in antiblack affects, so they are bound to be highly correlated. In fact, they can be distinguished empirically, especially with statistical techniques that do not demand orthogonality, such as oblique rotations of factor analyses. McConahay (1986) found two such factors in oblique rotations of racial items in two surveys in Louisville in 1976 and 1977. Bobo's oblique rotations (1983) of 1972 and 1976 National Election Studies (NES) data obtained at least two factors, very closely resembling symbolic and old-fashioned racism (though in each case the last factor was of borderline acceptability). Nevertheless, in all three studies, the old-fashioned and symbolic racism factors were highly correlated (in McConahay's data, $r = .68$ and .70, respectively, and in Bobo's, in the .50 to .60 range). Clearly a very strong common dimension of racism runs through all the items in both scales, but the two are different variants on this basic theme and can be distinguished statistically.[5]

---

[4]The R^2 on the most racially relevant dependent variables averages around 25% with symbolic racism, other symbolic predispositions, and demographic variables in the equation. Using more remote dependent variables or ignoring other relevant predictors reduces the R^2 to the 10%–15% range. The R^2 could be increased substantially by adding variables that are still more proximal to the equation, such as candidate evaluations, in the case of elections, or the perceived effects of a policy, in the case of issue positions (see Campbell et al., 1960; Kluegel & Smith, 1983; McClendon, 1985; Rabushka, 1982; Shanks & Miller, 1985). We have chosen not to include these variables because we doubt the necessary assumptions about one-way causality.

[5]This contrast of highly correlated but separate dimensions in whites' racial attitudes is a common finding in the literature on whites' racial attitudes (also see Bobo, 1983; Brigham, Woodmansee, & Cook, 1976; Weigel & Howes, 1985). The contrast between these two dimensions has been at the heart of our analysis from the beginning, contrary to the interpretations of Bobo (1983) and Sniderman and Tetlock (1986), who have viewed our research as ignoring this multidimensionality.

Symbolic racism does have a much stronger political impact than does old-fashioned racism. Kinder and Sears (1981) found so little old-fashioned racism among Los Angeles suburbanites that they did not even test its effects. McConahay (1982, n.d) found in two studies that symbolic racism had strong effects on opposition to busing, whereas old-fashioned racism had considerably weaker effects (betas of .40 and .31 for symbolic racism, and .10 and .20 for old-fashioned racism). Bobo (1983, p. 1206) also used two predictors closely resembling old-fashioned and symbolic racism (though he did not label them as such). The strongest effects were generated by items most closely resembling symbolic racism (such as evaluations of whether or not civil rights leaders were pushing too hard, or of black militants), but his "segregationism" measure (support for the general principle of segregation, for segregated neighborhoods, and belief in racial differences in intelligence) had only trivial effects on opposition to busing.

PERSONAL RACIAL THREAT

Our third general proposition was that symbolic racism has a far stronger influence than does personal racial threat over whites' political responses in racially relevant situations. Direct personal racial threat, which we defined as one instance of short-term material self-interest, is, of course, only one of several potential determinants of opposition to racial change other than symbolic or old-fashioned racism. But it is of special interest for several reasons. It has been one of the major manifest themes of whites' resistance to racial change: much of the rhetoric of the antibusing movement was phrased in directly self-interested terms, describing white parents who did not want their own children bused, and the *Bakke* case stemmed from a simple self-interested complaint. Moreover, widespread self-interested resistance to change would make an especially persuasive political case: helping a relatively small racial minority at the expense of serious harm to the large white majority would be hard for political leaders to justify. Finally, self-interest has a long and honored history in democratic, economic, and psychological theory: the utilitarian tradition has long taught Americans to believe in simple hedonic theories of human preference and action. In the roster of possible explanations, then, self-interest has a special claim on our attention.

Consequently, much of our research has contrasted the effects of symbolic racism with those of personal racial threat. Threat has been operationalized with a wide variety of both objective and subjective indicators of the direct impact of racial change on whites' own personal circumstances, such as having children in public schools that participate in racial busing programs, perceiving it as likely that one's own children might be bused, fearing integration of one's own neighborhood, or fearing personal victimization by blacks' crimes.

The several relevant studies have almost all shown that direct personal racial threat has little or no effect on whites' political attitudes. Kinder and Sears (1981) investigated such threats in the areas of crime, schools, neighborhood, and jobs and found that they affected neither voting for the black challenger in the Los Angeles mayoralty elections nor symbolic racism. Kluegel and Smith (1983) found similarly slender effects on opposition to affirmative action. Their numerous tests of the main effects of self-interest turned up weak and inconsistent findings (though mixed with a few potentially meaningful interactions with age, some expected and some contrary to expectation, whose *post hoc* explanation will require replication and further test). Jacobson (1985) also found weak effects of self-interest on support for affirmative action.

The most focused and extensive research, however, has been done on whites' opposition to busing. This literature has been reviewed most recently by Sears and Allen (1984). Here, the racial threats have included having children in the public schools in school districts that bus for integration, living in all-white neighborhoods, and feeling attached to the neighborhood and unwilling to move. Some of these studies have used national data (Bobo, 1983; Kinder & Rhodebeck, 1982; Sears et al., 1979, 1980), some statewide data (Gatlin, Giles, & Cataldo, 1978), and others local data (Kinder & Sears, 1981; McConahay, 1982; Miller, 1981).[6] Most of these studies show no impact at all of personal racial threat on whites' opposition to busing. However, there is some modest evidence that it has significantly increased opposition in one phase of such desegregation controversies, when busing has been court-ordered but not yet implemented (Sears & Allen, 1984).

CRITIQUES

A substantial amount of evidence has therefore accumulated in favor of the three original propositions of the symbolic racism approach: that symbolic racism is a major determinant of whites' political responses to racially relevant questions, and that old-fashioned racism and direct personal racial threat are not. This work has been no freer of criticism than any other concerned with race relations, however. Let me first discuss some critiques that seem to me off-target before turning to some more genuine problems.

MEASUREMENT AND LABELING

The exact items used to index symbolic racism have varied somewhat from one study to the next. These variations have led to some confusion about the operationalization and labeling of both symbolic racism and self-interest.

One confusion seems to be between studies that test a general symbolic-politics theory and those testing for symbolic racism (Bobo, 1983; Schuman, Steeh, & Bobo, 1985; Sniderman & Tetlock, 1986). We have done a series of studies in the general symbolic-politics vein, testing a series of hypotheses on the role of whites' racial attitudes in American political life, but not bearing on the symbolic racism versus old-fashioned racism distinction that is central to the symbolic racism approach. One such hypothesis has been that whites' racial attitudes are socialized early in life and persist through adulthood (Miller & Sears, 1986). A second, discussed earlier, has been that whites' racial attitudes explain whites' political responses to racial issues better than does self-interest (Sears et al., 1979, 1980). A third was that group-specific values were at the most politi- cally potent level of abstraction in the sense of having greater clout over racial policy preferences than do more abstract values (Sears, Huddy, & Schaffer, 1986). A fourth suggested that racial attitudes were central to whites' reactions to Jesse Jackson's can- didacy in the 1984 national elections and, in turn, to a possible realignment of southern whites toward the Republican Party (Sears et al., 1985).

All these studies have required robust and reliable measures of racial attitudes in general, but not measures of symbolic racism in particular. Moreover, they were all based on secondary analysis of the two standard general-purpose surveys, the National Elec- tion Studies and the General Social Surveys, which have not attempted to measure symbolic racism specifically. As a result, in each study, we used omnibus scales of racial attitudes, disregarding the distinction between symbolic and old-fashioned racism. This

---

[6]Some of these studies have used measures of symbolic racism, and some, omnibus measures of racial attitudes. That distinction is irrelevant here, because the purpose is simply to assess the effects of personal threat, which tends to be only weakly correlated with either (see Bobo, 1983; Kinder & Sears, 1981).

distinction was irrelevant to the hypotheses motivating these studies and could not be made precisely in most of these data bases in any case.

It is noteworthy that, even in this undifferentiated, omnibus form, whites' racial attitudes had major political effects. Omnibus scales of racial attitudes in the National Election Studies' 1972, 1976, and 1984 studies yielded betas of .39 and .31 on whites' opposition to busing (Sears et al., 1979, 1980) and .32 on their opposition to Jackson (Sears et al., 1985). But no claim was made in any of these cases about the role of symbolic racism because it had not been measured. Rather, the core of the evidence on symbolic racism comes from studies explicitly indexing symbolic racism with items such as those shown in Table 1 (or as its kin, "modern racism"), and contrasting it with old-fashioned racism (Kinder & Sears, 1981; McConahay, 1982; McConahay & Hough, 1976; Sears & Allen, 1984; Sears & Citrin, 1985). The separate purposes of these two sets of studies should be apparent, but perhaps it is worth reemphasizing the distinction here.

A second apparent confusion concerns the labels used for different measures of racial attitudes. At one extreme, when using these omnibus scales of racial attitudes, which probably encompass both old-fashioned and symbolic racism, we have consistently used general labels such as *racial intolerance* (Miller & Sears, 1986; Sears et al., 1979) or *racial prejudice* (Miller & Sears, 1986; Sears et al., 1980). At the other extreme, we have used narrow descriptive labels (such as *expressive racism* or *racial affect*) for collections of items too narrow to measure even symbolic racism fully (Kinder & Sears, 1981; Sears et al., 1985). In short, the term *symbolic racism* has been reserved for relatively pure cases of it, and other descriptive labels have been used for measures of racial attitudes that are either more general or more specific than the symbolic racism notion.[7]

A third and more understandable confusion has arisen concerning our treatment of policy attitudes on the two most controversial contemporary racial issues: busing and affirmative action. We have treated them as dependent variables in some studies, when we have tested the effects of symbolic racism and racial threat on such issue positions (Kinder & Sears, 1981; Sears & Allen, 1984; also see Kluegel & Smith, 1983). In other studies we have treated them as aspects of symbolic racism, and thus as subsets of that independent variable, when we have tested its effects on voting behavior or positions on other policy issues (Kinder & Sears, 1981; Sears & Citrin, 1985). It is understandably confusing when a given variable is treated as an independent variable in some analyses and as a dependent variable in others, all concerned with approximately the same model.

The reason for these disparate practices is that policy issues such as busing and affirmative action, which themselves contain the basic elements of symbolic racism, can perforce become highly symbolic issues in their own right, capable of energizing racially based responses to candidates and to other issues. This process by which new issues themselves become symbolic will be discussed later. Tests of these two separate steps in this process necessarily require treating such racial policy positions as dependent variables in the first instance, and as part of the independent variable in the second. When such policy positions have been included as part of a symbolic racism measure, the theory, the analytic strategy, and the empirical justification have been laid out quite explicitly (see Kinder & Sears, 1981; Sears & Citrin, 1985).

Finally, some criticism has focused on our treatment of self-interest. Some have argued that we define *self-interest* too narrowly and should consider benefits or threats to the group, not just to the self; that we should consider subjective as well as objective interests; that ideology should not be analyzed separately from self-interest, because they

[7]In no study has the label *symbolic racism* been applied to a scale containing old-fashioned racism items, contrary to Bobo's (1983) and Sniderman and Tetlock's (1986) statements about two papers (Sears et al., 1979, 1980) which neither dealt with symbolic racism nor used the term.

are inextricably entwined; and that our analyses of self-interest are insensitive to interacting conditions under which it would prove to be very powerful (Bobo, 1983; Sniderman &
Tetlock, 1986). We will consider the question of group interests below, but the other
points have been dealt with rather clearly elsewhere in detail. We have tested the effects
of subjectively defined racial threats extensively, and they prove also to have null effects
(e.g., Kinder & Sears, 1981); ideology and self-interest simply have proved so far not to be
closely correlated (e.g., Sears et al., 1980); and we have reported quite an extensive roster
of specific conditions under which self-interest does affect political preferences, even
though these conditions prove to be the exception rather than the rule (Sears & Allen,
1984; Sears & Citrin, 1985).[8]

Social Desirability and Respondent Duplicity

Another issue that has complicated discussions of symbolic racism concerns the
honesty of respondents' self-reported racial attitudes. One of the heartening changes in
American race relations since World War II is that overt expressions of old-fashioned
racism have become increasingly unfashionable. This change is heartening for the cause
of tolerance because it means that most of the white public believes overt racial bigotry is
not polite and, in that sense, accepts the norm of tolerance. It is not necessarily so
heartening for social scientists, who must then worry about whether their respondents
are telling the truth.

Fairly strong evidence has accumulated that whites do underreport their true levels
of old-fashioned racism under some circumstances. Simple verbal reports do elicit less
racial prejudice than do more unobtrusive measures (Crosby, Bromley, & Saxe, 1980).[9] It
is also more obvious to respondents that old-fashioned racism items are measuring racism than it is that symbolic racism items are (McConahay, 1986). And in several experiments, McConahay (1986) showed that measures of old-fashioned racism are more readily biased than are measures of symbolic racism because of such situational conditions as
the race of the interviewer. All this might suggest, to caricature the point, that symbolic
racism measures "true" racism, whereas measures of old-fashioned racism are invalid
because they simply elicit facework—the respondent's attempt to appear tolerant—and
thus mere lip service to the principles of equality.

But one must be somewhat cautious about inferring too much invalidity in measures
of racism. Most of the research on bias has been conducted on college students in plainly
experimental situations, not on adult white respondents confronted with white interviewers in the normal survey context. Nevertheless, old-fashioned racism items do probably lend themselves to some facework, with respondents attempting to appear more
racially tolerant than they really are, to gain social approval. It would be naive to assume
that whites in general now feel free to express their full measure of racism, however open
some individuals may be about it. There is too much available evidence on such biases.

[8]Sniderman and Tetlock (1986) were critical of virtually every aspect of the symbolic racism approach. Yet, they ultimately seemed to come to a very similar account of contemporary politics.
They, too, concluded that racism continues to be a potent political factor in white America today
(more in the terms of symbolic racism than in those of old-fashioned racism, though still discernible
in the latter), that the level of white racism as measured in surveys can generally be trusted, that
racial policy attitudes and voting behavior regarding black candidates are caused both by racism
and by nonracial traditional values, and that personal racial threat does not have a major, across-
the-board effect but may have an effect under special circumstances. See Kinder (1986) for a detailed
response.
[9]It is interesting that the legendary LaPiere (1934) study of attitude–behavior inconsistency found
widespread nondiscriminatory behavior paired with equally widespread expressed prejudice, quite
the opposite of the current concern.

Nevertheless, we have argued from the beginning that symbolic racism is not *simply* a socially acceptable means of expressing genuinely inegalitarian beliefs and policy preferences (Sears & Kinder, 1970, 1971). To be sure, symbolic racism is a fairly socially acceptable way to express such strong primordial antiblack affects as fear and anger. But I would suggest that the overwhelming rejection of old-fashioned racist positions is now mostly quite genuine; by wide majorities, whites now really do reject the old doctrines of racial inferiority, formal discrimination, and legalized segregation.[10]

GROUP INTEREST AND GROUP CONFLICT

Our research has focused mainly on symbolic racism and personal racial threat as predictors of whites' political responses. Bobo (1983, 1986) and others have quite rightly pointed to another category of potentially important predictors: group interest. Members of a particular group may support policies (or candidates) that they view as supporting the interests of their own group and may oppose those that they view as opposing these interests.

Conventional forms of group interest theory are quite similar to self-interest theories, in that political responses are hypothesized to be controlled by perceptions of the effects of policies or candidates on the material interests of the public. They differ in whose interests are at stake—the group's or the individual's. Group interest could well rest on self-interest, in that one could perceive one's own well-being as being intimately connected to the fate of one's group. Or group interest could be independent of self-interest, in that one might favor policies that help one's group even if they do not affect one's own well-being consequentially. But a group interest theory should have little in common with symbolic racism, which speaks to value conflicts rather than material interests.

Presumably, issues of race pit the interests of blacks and whites against each other, so the most relevant version of a group interest approach is realistic group-conflict theory (Levine & Campbell, 1972). Demands and protests by blacks may trigger a realistic sense of threat among whites regarding their own group's interests and privileges, which in turn may generate opposition to policies changing the racial status quo. Bobo's statement of this idea (1983) is perhaps the most explicit: "most notions of group conflict involve both objective conditions of competition and conflict between individual group members, shifts in relative group statuses, *and* the subjective assessment of a threat posed by outgroup members to individual and collective interests" (p. 1200).

A second version of the group interest idea is based on Marxist analysis:

> Groups that occupy a dominant position in the social structure routinely manufacture an interpretation of reality and a set of normative presumptions that serve their interests. Dominant groups . . . seek to impose a sense of order on the pattern of social relations and to persuade both themselves and their subordinates that the current organization of relationships is appropriate and equitable. (Jackman & Muha, 1984, p. 759).

This is the view that Bobo presents in the current volume. It assumes that the dominant group develops an ideology supporting and rationalizing its privileged position, to help it maintain its hegemony. Hence, the more a subordinate group rebels and threatens that superior position, the more strongly and creatively the dominant group adheres to its superiority-justifying ideology.

In this latter form, a group interest theory potentially comes very close to a symbolic racism approach. Whites' responses against blacks' violations of traditional values can be

---

[10]This seems to me to remain the position of Kinder and McConahay as well (see Kinder, 1986; McConahay, Hardee, & Batts, 1981).

interpreted as their defense of an ideology that justifies their hegemony. Whites' long-standing individualistic ideology asserts that all people of whatever color have equal opportunity, and that it is up to the individual to work hard enough to succeed. This ideology disadvantages blacks because they, by reason of their color, do, in fact, have less real opportunity and cannot be expected, as individuals, to succeed as well as whites. Moreover, individualism renders illegitimate government policies intended to benefit an entire group because they advantage the undeserving as well as the deserving. Hence, whites' political responses to demands on behalf of blacks as a group, and to government policies that especially advantage blacks as a group, should, according to this second version of group interest theory, be intimately related to their support for individualistic values. This prediction is very similar to that of the symbolic racism approach. The main difference lies in the role of threat to group hegemony, which is not part of the symbolic racism approach.

The group interest approach has been developed empirically in most detail in two papers by Bobo (1983, 1986; see also Rothbart, 1976). His analyses make two main points. One is that the group interest approach provides another explanation for the same basic data that the symbolic racism approach has generated. He has attributed the relationship between whites' antagonism toward black militants and demanding civil-rights leaders, on the one hand, and their opposition to busing, on the other, as reflecting the clash of blacks' demands with whites' defense of their group's privileged positions (Bobo, 1983). Similarly, he has attributed the effects of symbolic racism on opposition to racial policies to hegemony-justifying ideology. In terms of the symbolic racism items shown in Table 1, by rendering illegitimate blacks' collective demands and special government action to aid blacks as a group, white hegemony will be maintained; similarly, denying continuing discrimination against blacks makes illegitimate both blacks' demands and special favors granted to them (Bobo, 1986). His second point, mainly qualitative and historical, is that this analysis successfully accounts for postwar changes in white public opinion on racial issues (Bobo, 1986).

In principle, this notion that group interest contributes heavily to whites' resistance to change is highly plausible. Vanneman and Pettigrew (1972) and Pettigrew (1971) developed such ideas in their important early work on fraternal deprivation, especially with regard to whites' voting in the 1960s for George Wallace. The notion is also consistent with the results from various empirical inquiries into the political ramifications of a group-based calculus (e.g., Guimond & Dubé-Simard, 1983; Klein, 1984), as well as with much political theory. Development of the group interest approach is also useful because it crystallizes an important alternative to the self-interest and symbolic racism approaches. It emphasizes whites' sense that blacks pose a threat to their collective situation—to their economic position, status, or power—whether or not they are threatened personally themselves. The group interest approach is easily contrasted with the self-interest approach, which involves a direct threat to the self, and with symbolic racism, which involves a challenge to one's values and arousal of antiblack feelings, whether or not material interests of the self or group are threatened.

However, two distinctions seem to me central in contrasting the symbolic racism, group-interest, and self-interest approaches, and Bobo's research has not yet succeeded in making them (see Sears & Kinder, 1985, for a more detailed account of this point). One concerns attitudes toward the relevant groups. Symbolic group affects should be distinguished from perceived benefits for or threats to the in-group. A symbolic politics approach concerns itself centrally with symbolic affects toward groups (see Conover & Feldman, 1981). However, it views such evaluations as independent of any tangible costs or benefits to group well-being. A person might disparage groups such as punk rockers or the fifth-century B.C. Spartans or might cheer on the Boston Celtics and the African

National Congress, even though feeling that none of those groups are likely to tangibly aid or harm his own group's well-being.

The home turf for group interest theory, in contrast, is a group conflict in which tangible goods are at stake, such as a territorial dispute over oil-rich lands or two Mafia families' feuding over the control of drug trafficking in a particular area (though even apparently tangible stakes may often be trivial on inspection, and one may therefore be led to suspect that the conflict is mainly symbolic, as in the case of the British-Argentine war over the Falkland Islands). The key question is which is involved in whites' opposition to problack policies: symbolic group affects or some perception of tangible threats posed by blacks to the interests of whites as a group? The available research has not yet succeeded in making this contrast.[11]

A second consequential distinction is between self-interest and group interest. Bobo suggested that, for group interest to be really powerful, it must evoke self-interest, in the form of perceived interdependence of the self's outcomes with those of the group. A symbolic politics approach would assume that group symbols (such as *black militants* or *Zionists* or *niggers*) can be potent political forces even in the complete absence of any perceived self–group interdependence over tangible outcomes. Although the group interest alternative is well worth exploring, I am skeptical that its more self-oriented versions will be the most fruitful. So far, the best evidence is that white public opinion is not much influenced by direct, personal racial threats. What is more likely is that the major impacts of group conflict will involve more symbolic versions of group interest, in which affects toward the groups in question are no more than that and do not imply much real or felt material interdependence between the self and either the in-group or the out-group.

Bobo also failed to distinguish group interest from group conflict. Even if whites' sense of their own collective interest is powerful, they still may vary in the extent to which they perceive the two races' interests as necessarily in conflict. Whites vary considerably in whether or not they see blacks' and whites' real interests as necessarily in conflict. They disagree about whether or not school desegregation will produce educational gains for black children without corresponding losses for white children, or whether President Reagan's economic program will aid both blacks and whites, rather than providing gains for affluent whites at the expense of poor blacks. In both cases the non-zero-sum assumption may, in fact, be right or wrong, but that is irrelevant.

Additional research may or may not show that the central ingredients of a group conflict theory influence resistance to change in the racial status quo. The challenge will come in attempting to test *directly* for evidence of differential effects of (a) perceptions of threat to the hegemony of the dominant group, (b) perceived group conflict, and (c) antiblack affect and violations of traditional values without any particular sense of group threat. Jessor and Sears's analysis (1986) of the 1985 NES pilot study is directed to exactly that point: whites' opposition to racial policy is not related significantly to perceived interdependence with either the in-group as a whole (whites) or the out-group as a whole (blacks). It is dependent, however, on perceived conflict between the racial groups, and on various versions of antiblack affect, as the symbolic racism approach would expect.

---

[11]For example, I would argue that Bobo's two indicators of group interest, items evaluating black militants and civil rights leaders, reflect symbolic racism instead. Whites might have negative affects toward such symbols as *black, militant,* or *protest* for any number of reasons other than racial competition over scarce resources. Whites may dislike black militants because of their aggressive championing of blackness. The Anglo tradition has been to dislike blackness for its own sake, long before European explorers traveled to Africa (Jordan, 1968). And much research conducted in the 1960s concluded that part of whites' ambivalence about civil rights protest was based on a distaste for direct confrontation as a style of politics.

THE BROADER THEORY

The symbolic racism approach was intended first and foremost to account for whites' responses to racially relevant political attitude objects, especially racial policy and black candidates. As indicated above, the data seem to support rather strongly its three central propositions: (a) that symbolic racism has a powerful role in determining whites' responses to such attitude objects, whereas neither (b) old-fashioned racism nor (c) personal racial threats do. But the symbolic racism approach went well beyond such proximal predictors of whites' current political responses. As depicted in Figure 1, the theory, if it may be called that, also asserted that symbolic racism stems (d) from residues from preadult socialization, (e) and from antiblack affect and traditional American values, and (f) not from current racial threats. It also contended (g) that affects toward racially relevant attitude objects dominated cognitions toward them, and (h) that such attitude objects could themselves become so affectively charged as to themselves become symbolic, and to function similarly to symbolic racism. It is appropriate now to turn to these additional points.

Perhaps the most complete test of the full symbolic-racism model, including its presumed antecedents, uses the 1984 National Election Studies pre- and postelection surveys. This analysis is quite supportive, as shown in Table 3. Antiblack affect and traditional values both have a strong impact on whites' racial policy preferences. Together, they added over 20% to the variance explained by basic demographic variables, and their effects are reduced little by the addition of controls on ideology and party identification. Similarly, evaluations of Jesse Jackson were strongly influenced by anti-

TABLE 3. A Symbolic Racism Analysis of the 1984 Presidential Election[a]

Predictors	Racial policy		Evaluations of Jesse Jackson		Reagan–Mondale preference
Demographics R^2 (adjusted)	3.0%	3.0%	3.6%	3.6%	6.3%
Black thermometer	.20**	.20**	.24**	.20**	−.01
Individualism	.03	.00	.02	−.03	.08**
Equality	.30**	.22**	.22**	.09*	.06**
Cumulative R^2	17.9%	—	15.5%	—	—
Ideology	—	.17**	—	.07	.12**
Party ID	—	.06	—	.17**	.64**
Cumulative R^2	—	21.2%	—	—	—
Racial policy	—	—	—	.19**	.04*
Cumulative R^2	—	—	—	22.8%	—
Jackson evaluation	—	—	—	—	.11**
Cumulative R^2	—	—	—	—	69.5%
N	1,912		1,893		1,934

[a]From the 1984 National Election Studies pre-/postnational survey. The individualism and equality measures were six-item scales; ideology and party identification were three-item scales based on bipolar self-ratings and thermometer evaluations of each pole; racial policy was the mean of four items on aid to minorities, spending on blacks, perception of whether or not civil rights leaders were pushing too fast, and support for busing; and thermometer evaluations of Jackson, Reagan, and Mondale were used to construct the last two dependent variables. Each column is a separate regression equation with the dependent variables shown at the top. Entries are standardized regression coefficients (betas). Pairwise deletion was used. The demographic controls in each equation included region, education, income, subjective social class, sex, and dummy variables for being Jewish or Catholic.
*$p < .05$; **$p < .001$.

black affect, traditional values, and racial policy, the last mediating some of the effects of the first two. These data support the main thrust of the symbolic racism approach: antiblack affect and traditional values have stronger effects on racial policy than do such conventional political variables as ideology and party identification, and along with racial policy, they retain strong effects on evaluations of black candidates even when these conventional political variables are controlled for. Though this analysis is generally supportive of the overall model, it would be useful to look more carefully at each of its components.

ANTIBLACK AFFECT

The central justification for using the term *racism* was the presumption that antiblack affect played a role in the effects of symbolic racism. Presumably, antiblack affect is acquired fairly early in life, according to numerous studies of children's racial socialization (see Harding, Proshansky, Kutner, & Chein, 1969; Proshansky, 1966). It is probably acquired nonverbally in many cases, with or without direct interracial contact. It is a spontaneous and direct affect, perhaps without strong cognitive mediation, in the vein described by Zajonc (1980). It may be experienced subjectively as fear, avoidance and a desire for distance, anger, distaste, disgust, contempt, apprehension, unease, or simple dislike (see McConahay, 1986).

However, if predictors with no manifest racial content (e.g., traditional American values alone) could explain opposition to racial policies and black candidates just as well, or if symbolic racism could explain opposition to nonracial policies and white candidates just as well as it did more racially relevant attitudes, then invoking the term *racism* would be unnecessary and indeed inappropriate. So the involvement of antiblack affect is a key element.

It is clear to almost everyone, researchers and respondents alike, that old-fashioned racism items do, in fact, index antiblack attitudes, but such is not the case for symbolic racism. Some other researchers question whether it measures racism at all (e.g., Sniderman & Tetlock, 1986), and ordinary people often tend not to perceive it as reflecting racist content (McConahay, Hardee, & Batts, 1981). What evidence do we have that antiblack affect is really involved, rather than, say, antipathy toward excessively greedy demands that might have been made by any group?

Three general strategies have been used to isolate a distinctive effect of antiblack affect. It should be a factor if (a) direct measures of antiblack affect have significant effects; (b) the effects of symbolic racism (or racial attitudes in general) persist with controls on relevant other *nonracial* attitudes, such as general political ideology; and/or (c) symbolic racism influences evaluations of racially relevant attitude objects (e.g., liberal black candidates) more than those of comparable racially neutral objects (e.g., liberal white candidates). Let us evaluate the success of each strategy in turn.

Direct measures of antiblack affect have, to date, been rather crude. Osgood, Suci, and Tannenbaum (1957) and others argued that a single evaluative factor underlies most such attitudes. In that vein, the main measuring instrument has been the "feeling thermometer" used by the National Election Studies, which measures simple evaluations of "blacks," "whites," and other objects on a warm–cold scale. Little effort has been made to measure any more qualitatively differentiated types of affects toward blacks (though see the recent effort of Jackman & Muha, 1984, to separate warmth from closeness).

The effects of this most direct measure of antiblack affect on whites' racial policy preferences are illustrated in Table 3 with data from the National Election Studies. It has a raw correlation of .24 with racial policy and retains a strong effect (standardized regression coefficient of .20) in a fully specified symbolic-politics model. The effects of antiblack affect on racial policy are fairly typical. In the 1972, 1976, and 1980 NES surveys, it correlated .20, .25, and .28 with the same racial-policy scale. It had a significant effect on opposition to busing in McConahay's (1982) analysis of 1975 Louisville data, even though scales of both symbolic and old-fashioned racism were included in the equation.

The direct role of antiblack affect in determining policy and other preferences is an important, but not the only, basis for asserting that racism plays a role in these political evaluations. Another consists of evidence that measures of symbolic racism predict racial policy and evaluations of black candidates with key nonracial dimensions controlled. Table 3 shows that both racial policy and Jackson evaluations were strongly influenced by racial attitudes with ideology and party identification controlled. Sears and Kinder (1971) found that symbolic racism continued strongly to influence preferences for Mayor Yorty with general political conservatism controlled. Similarly, symbolic racism contributed to support for the California tax revolt even with controls on ideology and preferences about the magnitude of government spending (Sears & Citrin, 1985).

Third, there is evidence that such racial attitudes influenced evaluations of the black candidate, Jesse Jackson, more than those of such liberal whites as Walter Mondale or Gary Hart, and had no effect at all on evaluations of the conservative white, Ronald Reagan (Sears et al., 1985). Similarly, the standardized regression coefficients for the black thermometer on presidential choice in the 1968–1984 NES surveys ranged from +.05 to −.03, and for racial policy, from .04 (1976) to .14 (1972), with a mean of .08 (with demographics, party identification, and ideology also in the equations). All of these candidates were white, of course. The only national white candidate whose evaluations were strongly affected by racial attitudes in this period was George Wallace.[12] All this points to an essential role for specifically antiblack affect, but its influence focuses particularly on racial policy positions, evaluations of black candidates, and voter choice in black–white contests.

These data simply treat the thermometer ratings for "blacks" in general. But there is evidence that whites have more differentiated evaluations of blacks than that, when different subgroups of blacks are considered. Oblique rotations of factor analyses of an extended range of racially linked thermometer evaluations indicate that "blacks" fall on the same factor as "working-class blacks," "black politicians," and "black young people," but "black activists," "black militants," and "civil rights leaders" fall on a second factor in factor analyses of the evaluation of various black groups.[13] These two dimensions also yield very different levels of negative affect toward blacks. Just as few whites today endorse segregation, few dislike blacks categorically; the scale mean on the items in the first factor was 62.9. On the other hand, whites are typically much more negative toward black activists; the scale mean on the items in the second factor was 43.5 (Jessor & Sears, 1986).

These two dimensions suggest that mainstream blacks are both differentiated from and evaluated considerably more favorably than black radicals. Moreover, these mainstream blacks fall on the same factor as "whites" and "white politicians" when these latter items are included in the factor analysis. This does not mean that antiblack affect is unimportant; the black thermometer has a significant effect almost no matter how it is treated.[14] But it does suggest that one component of antiblack affect is tied to negative

[12]In 1968, the black thermometer and racial policy drew raw correlations of .22 and .32 and betas of .12 and .19 on his evaluations; in 1972, correlations of .11 and .40 and betas of .03 and .22. But by 1980, even he was not evaluated in racial terms: correlations of .07 and .18 and betas of .04 and .08.

[13]In this analysis, based on the 1985 NES pilot study, both factors are fairly strong, yielding eigenvalues of 3.58 and 1.27, though they are correlated ($r = .40$).

[14]For example, if the difference between evaluations of blacks and of whites is used instead of the black thermometer in Columns 2 and 4 of Table 3, the effects change very little; the betas are .21 and .20, respectively.

evaluations of black radicals (Jessor & Sears, 1986; also see Rusk & Weisberg, 1972). Research on these feeling thermometers has not yet sufficiently disentangled black radicalism from radicalism in general.

Finally, there is some evidence that this second factor of antiblack affect, focused on black activism, is linked more tightly to contemporary politics than is the first, focused on mainstream blacks. In the 1984 National Elections Study, an expanded measure of antiblack affect, comprised of thermometer evaluations of blacks, civil rights leaders, and black militants, correlated more strongly with racial policy and Jackson evaluations than did the simple black thermometer and had considerably stronger effects on them in full symbolic-politics models (Sears et al., 1985).

TRADITIONAL VALUES

The original conception of symbolic racism was that it represented a blend of antiblack affect with traditional Protestant values. The latter have been enumerated variously as including values of hard work, individualism, thrift, punctuality, sexual repression, and delay of gratification, as opposed to laziness, seeking of favoritism and handouts, impulsivity, and so on (see Kinder & Sears, 1981; McConahay & Hough, 1976; Sears & Kinder, 1971, Sears & McConahay, 1973).[15] An important point about these values is that they contain no manifest racial content. People also apply them to many situations in society that have no relevance to racial conflict at all, and on such occasions, they are presumably completely irrelevant to racial matters. It is only when they are mixed with antiblack affect that individual racism of a symbolic nature can be said to be present.[16]

Most of these values fall into the general category of *individualism*. Yet, it is by no means the only traditional value that applies to racial policy. Lipset and Schneider (1978), Feldman (1983), and others have suggested that whites' attitudes toward racial policy represent trade-offs between individualism and equal opportunity, which they argue is just as fundamental an American value. Both values are very commonly held by Americans because almost all believe that people's outcomes should depend to some degree on the work that they do, and that equal opportunity should be provided to all, to some extent. However, both could have independent effects because the two values are not logically opposed, people do vary in their levels of commitment to them, and, indeed, it is easy to imagine people who variously believe in both, one, or neither.

Several recent studies have tested the relative effects of these traditional values on racially relevant dependent variables and, somewhat to our consternation, have found that egalitarian values are uniformly the stronger of the two. In the 1984 NES study, equality values had a substantial impact on racial policy and evaluations of Jesse Jackson, but individualism had no impact on either one, as shown in Table 3. Feldman (1983) reported a similar result with somewhat different items from the 1972 NES survey. Sears, Huddy, and Schaffer (1984), using the 1983 NES pilot study, found that egalitarian values substantially influenced racial policy (with antiblack affect included in the equation), but

---

[15]In this book (Chapter 5), Bobo observes that many of these same values emerge in old-fashioned racism as well. In this, he is, of course, quite right; they were particularly prominent in early European, especially Anglo, stereotypes of Africans and, later, slaves: happy-go-lucky, lazy, sexual, dirty, musical, childish, and so on (see Jordan, 1968). But I would argue that they are more involved in the manifest content of symbolic racism because they are central to all three of its content areas. They seem to me peripheral to two main areas of old-fashioned racism—social distance and formal discrimination—though clearly involved in old-fashioned stereotyping.

[16]Such values can have antiblack effects in the absence of such individual racism because they can produce institutional racism (Carmichael & Hamilton, 1967; Jones, 1971;1971; Knowles & Prewitt, 1969).

that individualism failed to have a significant effect. In their own national survey, Kluegel and Smith (1983) found that equal opportunity values strongly predicted support for affirmative action, whereas individualism failed to have even statistically significant effects. In a national survey done in 1983, Huddy, Sears, and Cardoza (1986) found that egalitarian values had twice as strong an effect as individualism on a standard racial-policy item on special aid to minorities. Egalitarian values also had significantly enhanced support for various versions of bilingual education, whereas individualism had no effect in any case.

Why does egalitarianism have this consistent, and rather strong, advantage over individualism? It is not because of any confounds with antiblack affect. Table 3 is representative of most of these analyses in showing that egalitarian values are stronger both in simple bivariate correlations and in more fully specified symbolic racism models that include antiblack affect. The advantage it could conceivably stem from superior measurement of egalitarian values. This seems unlikely because, in the 1984 NES study, the reliability (Cronbach alpha) of egalitarianism was actually lower than that of individualism, (.59 to .65, for six-item scales). In several of these cases, there was actually more variance in individualism than in egalitarianism. Moreover, Table 3 shows that individualism had somewhat stronger effects than egalitarianism did in predicting Reagan–Mondale preference, so it is not generally inconsequential. So the advantage of egalitarianism does not seem to be trivially methodological.

It seems most appropriate, then, to conclude, at least provisionally, that egalitarianism does have stronger effects than individualism. If this conclusion proves to be correct, it would alter our view of symbolic racism. It would imply that resistance to racial change is more rooted in genuine resistance to equality than is implied by our original emphasis on perceptions that blacks violate nonracial individualistic values such as ambition, hard work, and delayed gratification. It would be a more pessimistic view of race relations.

THE ROLE OF CONSERVATIVE IDEOLOGY

General political conservatism played no central role in the original symbolic racism model, as depicted in Figure 1. But there are reasons to believe that it might be centrally involved in such political matters. There is substantial evidence that Americans' ideological self-labels, like their party identifications, are highly stable over time (Converse & Markus, 1979), and that they are fairly strong determinants of policy and candidate preference (Conover & Feldman, 1981; Levitin & Miller, 1979; also see Sears et al., 1979, 1980, 1985; Sears & Citrin, 1985). This evidence suggests that ideological self-descriptions are important symbolic predispositions. Other interpretations of ideology are common, of course, particularly those beginning with normative definitions of ideology (Converse, 1964; Kinder & Sears, 1985). However, many persons who do not meet that normative definition still have and use such a self-label quite meaningfully, as just indicated.

These ideological self-labels tend not to be closely related to simple antiblack affect. For example, over the 1968–1984 NES studies, their mean correlation with the black thermometer item was +.04. On the other hand, they correlated +.29, on the average, with the racial policy scale shown in Table 3. These correlations are consistent with various causal hypotheses.

Many political activists on the left view general conservatism as simply a rationalization for white racism. However, a number of studies have showed that self-labeling as a political liberal or conservative contributes to racially relevant dependent variables above and beyond the effects of symbolic racism or racial attitudes more generally, and adding it to the predictive equation does not markedly diminish the role of racism (Sears & Citrin,

1985; Sears & Kinder, 1971; Sears et al., 1979, 1980). For example, comparisons of columns 1 and 2 in Table 3 show that adding ideology to the predictive equation for racial policy diminishes the role of antiblack affect scarcely at all, though ideology is itself a significant predictor. Similarly, ideology does not markedly diminish the role of antiblack affect in predicting evaluations of Jesse Jackson (compare columns 3 and 4 in Table 3). So, plainly, political ideology is not just a rationalization for racism.

A second possible role for ideology is as a summary indicator of traditional values. Liberals have traditionally supported values of equality, and conservatives, values of individualism, so it is plausible that these values are adequately summarized by self-identification as a liberal or a conservative. Ideological self-identification was, in 1984, fairly substantially correlated with traditional values ($r = .26$ with individualism, and .40 with equal opportunity). But values and ideology have independent effects; ideology is not simply a surrogate for traditional values. For example, in the 1984 data, ideology and equality values both have independent effects on each of the dependent variables shown in Table 3.

In short, the available evidence suggests that general political ideology is indeed fairly closely linked to most of the political responses we have been concerned with, those with manifest racial content as well as those without. But it accounts for the influences of neither racism nor traditional values on racially relevant dependent variables. And it frequently does have fairly strong effects independent of symbolic racism or other racial attitudes. So conservative ideology is not merely a surrogate for racism, nor is symbolic racism just one aspect of conservative ideology. They generally make independent contributions to whites' political responses.[17]

Affect and Cognition

The original notion of symbolic racism portrayed a relatively simple relationship between cognition and affect: symbolic racism resulted when antiblack affect was joined with affects toward the symbols of traditional values. Racial policy preferences clearly have much complex cognitive rationale behind them, such as that busing would subject white children to repeated violence or to markedly worse education. However, the symbolic politics theory with which we were working assumed that much of this complex cognitive apparatus was rationalization of the negative feeling about blacks lying behind such policy preferences. This assumption was given support by the seeming indifference of this cognitive apparatus to many of the facts; for example, passionately opposed busing plans often actually involved busing very few white children into ghetto schools, relatively few children were victimized by even petty violence in the schools, and data on desegregation often indicated, at most, minor negative effects on white children's academic performance.

However the symbolic racism approach did not regard traditional values as mere rationalizations for antiblack affect. There is no reason to assume that racism fuels whites' commitments to the symbols of traditionalism. Such symbols surely are as affective, and perhaps as strong. Rather, they were hypothesized to contribute additively to racially relevant political attitudes above and beyond the effects of antiblack affect, as shown in Figure 1.[18]

---

[17]There is some evidence of interaction: Sears and Kinder (1971) and Sears et al. (1979) found that conservatives of whatever racial attitude and liberals high in symbolic racism (or racial intolerance) responded rather similarly to the Yorty–Bradley race and busing; liberals with tolerant racial attitudes were the deviants.

[18]Sniderman and Tetlock (1986) mistakenly interpreted symbolic racism as nothing more than a convenient rationalization for antiblack sentiment phrased in terms of traditional values. They also

In the intervening years, sociopsychological theory on such matters has expanded considerably. One could now identify at least three general points of view, ranging from the dominance of affect to the dominance of cognition (though there are, in addition, those who despair of ever being able to isolate the effects of affect from those of cognition). The affect-dominant view is that affect is experienced immediately, quickly, and spontaneously, without any necessary cognitive content (Zajonc, 1980), and that affects are strong and enduring, whereas cognitions are epiphenomenal and are readily manipulated to rationalize those feelings (Festinger, 1957; Rosenberg, 1960). This view has much in common with Allport's original analysis of racial prejudice (1954), that one's personal values influence the cognitive categorization process, producing "partisan" or "autistic" thinking that serves simply to rationalize one's values (see pp. 24, 164).

This affect-dominant view might be contrasted with the wide variety of models that assume decision making to be centrally influenced by such cognitive variables as expectations, attributions, and intentions. Among these models are value-expectancy theories (Edwards, 1954; Feather, 1982), rational choice theories (Page, 1978), theories of reasoned action (Ajzen & Fishbein, 1980), and some attribution theories (Kelley, 1967). In some of these theories, affect has a substantial independent role as an unexplained prior, such as the subjective utility of a particular choice alternative. But in others, affect is a mere by-product of cognition; for example, the attributions made about a particular event dictate the affects toward it (Weiner, 1982).

The original notion of symbolic racism had its psychological roots mainly in the first of these three viewpoints: affects are classically conditioned responses to specific stimuli, and supportive cognitions are, in large part, rationalizations of those primitive affective responses. As in Zajonc's theorizing (1980), affect is more closely associated with a particular stimulus and does not depend on cognition; it is primary and basic.

Two contrary theories hold that racial policy preferences are determined more cognitively. One is that they are generated by moderately rational assessments of the societal costs and benefits of the policy in question; for example, attitudes toward busing are determined by assessments of its probable educational benefits, juvenile crime, prejudice reduction, and so on (Armor, 1980; Rothbart, 1976; Stinchcombe & Taylor, 1980). A second treats cognitive attributions of blacks' outcomes as determinants of policy preferences. Whites tend to believe that blacks' various disadvantages are partly due to their not trying hard enough to get ahead (Rothbart, 1976; Schuman, 1969), even though they are less likely to believe in blacks' native inferiority. And Feldman (1983) showed that both external attributions of the causes of poverty that emphasize unequal opportunity and internal attributions that focus on lack of adherence to the work ethic are related to explanations for racial inequality and to policy preferences (also see Kluegel & Smith, 1983).

A complete theory should take such cognitive variables as cost–benefit expectations and attributions into consideration. The major analytical problem is to determine their causal role: Are they causes, or effects, or both? Although it would be nice to believe that new statistical technologies, such as two-stage least-squares regression, can unravel these tangled causal flows, I am skeptical that they will take us very far in this direction. Finding appropriate instruments, highly correlated with one but not both of the variables whose causal relation is in question, seems to me likely to prove the exception rather than the rule in this literature.

---

described low correlations between antiblack affect and conservatism as strong disconfirmations of the symbolic racism model, as if conservatism were thought also to be a mere rationalization for antiblack affect. Both interpretations are incorrect; the notion of symbolic racism suggests that both traditional values and conservatism produce variance in racially relevant political responses independent of that produced by antiblack affect (e.g., Sears & Citrin, 1985; Sears et al. 1979, 1980, 1985).

Two sets of recent findings suggest the value of a more cognitively driven view. Simple thermometer evaluations of "blacks" have relatively weaker effects than do more specific subgroups of blacks (Bobo, 1983; Jessor & Sears, 1986). One interpretation is that affect toward "blacks" most influences policy preferences when embedded in a more cognitive context. The greater impact of the thermometer evaluations dealing with more specific and connotatively consensual labels of subcategories of blacks, such as black militants or working-class blacks, might be explained this way.

Second, a simple symbolic-politics theory would predict that affects toward racial equality would be a simple function of affects toward its two constituent elements: race and equality in general. But one recent study (Sears et al., 1986) showed that racial equality values had considerably more impact on racial policy than did their two constituent elements: antiblack affect and general equality values. This finding suggests that embedding antiblack affect in the equality context gave it a force that it did not have as an isolated and thus cognitively more spare symbol. Perhaps such symbols, when presented completely in the abstract, are too cognitively impoverished to evoke a strong response.

The critical political factor, then, may be whether a given symbol evokes cognitive schemata in many members of the general public. Fiske (1982) contended that affects influence our attitudes and behavior primarily when we have a cognitive schema about the domain in question, because affect is stored with the knowledge structure; when the schema is not evoked, neither is the affect. A newspaper story about an unemployed, unmarried black woman on welfare, with three illegitimate children, receiving no spousal or child support, might trigger the affects associated with blacks on welfare, primarily because the story evokes a familiar schema about them. Hence, embedding symbols of equality explicitly in a racial context may evoke schemata in many Americans that the more abstract consideration of either alone does not.

One important implication would be that, without such consensual schematic thinking, public opinion may be too splintered to be mobilized readily by any given symbol. A second implication is that any individual may have multiple schemata about one attitude object. Different schemata may be evoked (or "primed") by different cues in the informational environment. Media attention to one issue area as opposed to another may dictate the basis on which a president's performance is evaluated (Iyengar & Kinder, 1985), perhaps because media attention evokes a particular schema. Public support for tax reduction may vary as a function of which schema is most widely evoked: one focused on welfare-state programmatic goals or one dominated by cynical evaluations of government inefficiency, waste, fraud, and so on (Sears & Citrin, 1985). Similarly, McConahay (1986) suggested that whites high in modern racism may be quite ambivalent about blacks, capable of swinging strongly between support and opposition depending on the most salient cues (or, in the present terms, on which schema is evoked). And Kinder and Sanders (1986) have recently shown that whites' attitudes toward affirmative action are more powerfully determined by racial attitudes when affirmative action is presented as providing unfair advantages to blacks than when it is presented as reverse discrimination against whites. Changing the meaning of the attitude object changes the predispositions it elicits.

WHEN ATTITUDE OBJECTS BECOME SYMBOLIC

This discussion of symbolic racism embeds it in the general framework of a more general theory of symbolic politics. Although this theory has not been fully elaborated in any one place, some of its elements have been (e.g., in Huddy et al., 1986; Sears, 1983, 1984; Sears & Whitney, 1973; Sears et al., 1986). It begins with the notion that mass politics is centrally influenced by symbolic predispositions. These are affective responses to particular symbols that are (a) stable over time—indeed, often quite long-standing within the individual's life span; (b) consistent over presentations of manifestly similar represen- tations of the symbol or the attitude object; and (c) powerful, in that they dictate affects toward new attitude objects paired to the original symbol (see Sears & Whitney, 1973).

Some of these symbolic predispositions fit the classic model of early-socialized at- titudes. In the United States, antiblack affect seems typically to be acquired early in the school years (Katz, 1976), and most have acquired a political party identification before late adolescence (at least, until recently; see Campbell, Converse, Miller, & Stokes, 1960; Converse, 1975; Shanks & Miller, 1985). But some symbolic predispositions may be acquired in adulthood, often in response to attitude objects that are associated with other powerful symbols or experiences. These new symbolic predispositions can presumably be detected by the same tests as are used with earlier-socialized ones: stability, consisten- cy, and power.

Several previous studies have dealt with attitude objects that become newly symbolic in adulthood. There is evidence that "the Watts riot" became newly symbolic for many adults in the mid-1960s, especially for blacks in the Watts area and environs, who in- creasingly came to believe, in the weeks and months following that riot, that it had been a symbolic political protest (rather than a meaningless outburst or set of instrumental criminal actions), and that it would have positive effects for blacks. These two beliefs became more consistent with each other over time, giving rise to "protest ideology," in which the violence was disapproved but was viewed as an effective means of protest. Young blacks in particular seemed to become resocialized to this new view of protest (Sears & McConahay, 1973, Chapter 11).

"Vietnam" became a symbol through the late 1960s and the early 1970s, initially generating quite inconsistent attitudes (Verba, Brody, Parker, Nie, Polsby, Ekman, & Black, 1967), weakly linked with preexisting predispositions (Lau et al., 1978). But by 1980, it had itself become a powerful symbolic predisposition, dictating attitudes toward newly arising symbols of international intervention (Sears, Steck, Lau, & Gahart, 1983). "Proposition 13" took on some considerable symbolic value for Californians in the late 1970s, and it remains a potent symbol whenever they consider taxes (Sears & Citrin, 1985). "Bilingual education" has considerable symbolic value, especially when formu- lated in terms of maintaining a child's fluency in a native non-English language (Huddy et al., 1986). Similarly, "Jesse Jackson" became a potent symbol in the 1984 campaign because he became a personalized symbol of blacks' demands. By the end of that cam- paign, the Jackson symbol itself appeared to become a significant contributor to pre- Reagan votes and Republican party identification, especially among southern whites (Sears et al., 1985).

In this same vein, I would argue that "busing" and "affirmative action" have become symbolic in recent years. It is easy to demonstrate this for "busing"; it generates highly stable attitudes (Converse & Markus, 1979), which are highly consistent with other racial attitudes (Kinder & Sears, 1981; Sears et al., 1979), and has considerable force over voting decisions (Kinder & Sears, 1981; Sears & Citrin, 1985). Less work has been done on attitudes toward affirmative action, but it yields similar patterns (Kluegel & Smith, 1983).

The process by which such an object becomes symbolic is one that requires further research. Some preliminary ideas have been laid out earlier (Sears, 1983, 1984), having to do with the information flow on the object, its association with other symbolic predisposi- tions, the consensus on its meaning, social polarization, and the like. But a fuller descrip- tion is beyond the scope of this chapter.

LONG-TERM SOCIAL CHANGE

If the political role of old-fashioned racism has been usurped by symbolic racism, one might legitimately ask how and why this has happened. Both old-fashioned racism and symbolic racism are assumed to be socialized fairly early in life and stable within individuals over long periods of time. If that assumption is correct, however, two implications would follow: early socialization on race should have changed, from a focus on old-fashioned racism to one on symbolic racism; and persistent cohort differences should be detectable, with the older generation retaining its old-fashioned racism, and the younger, its symbolic racism. None of these assumptions has yet been tested adequately (see Miller & Sears, 1986).

Why might the nature of early socialization on racial issues have changed? As political events have transpired, the attitude objects presented to the mass public plainly have changed. Many changes have occurred in American race relations since World War II (Farley, 1984; Wilson, 1978). Southern resistance and legal segregation have largely been overcome, and "reverse discrimination" and "busing" have come forward as issues. The old objects focused principally on race, blacks, and racial issues; the new objects pit individualistic values against egalitarian ones, perhaps, along with the ever-present symbols of race. Similarly, the change in the political climate has changed the nature of the white political candidates involved in racial issues, and thus, the symbolism surrounding them. The notorious southern racists of an earlier era, such as Senator Bilbo, Governor Faubus, Governor Ross Barnett of Mississippi, "Bull" Connor, and the early George Wallace standing in the schoolhouse door, were symbols of massive southern resistance to change. In the late 1960s, they were replaced by northerners like Sam Yorty, Frank Rizzo, and Louise Day Hicks, who fought racial change directly but without being so explicitly antiblack. In the late 1970s and 1980s, they, in turn, have been replaced by conservatives such as Ronald Reagan, Ed Meese, David Stockman, and Ed Koch, for whom racial issues are quite secondary, although their nonracial values have major implications for the well-being of blacks. Such changes in attitude objects, along with the continued high salience of racial issues, ought to change the content of early political socialization on race, within the family, in the media, in the schools, on the playground, and everywhere else.

Such change in early political socialization is suggested by Ward's findings (1985). The generation he interviewed, born after World War II, tended to be split on issues of symbolic racism, whereas their parents were split on issues of old-fashioned racism (specifically, miscegenation). Ward assumed that the old-fashioned racism in some of the parents resulted in the socialization of a "reservoir of racism" in their offspring, which manifested itself in the latter's symbolic racism some 20 years later. So the parent–child correlations on racism were very high, but the issues that split the two generations were quite different, reflecting the change in the racial attitude objects on the public agenda.

A second possibility is that there has merely been a change in cultural expression while the same underlying attitudes remain. This is the more ominous implication of the finding that racial policy preferences are better predicted by egalitarian values than by individualism. Symbolic racism may really be composed of resistance to racial equality; only the battlefield has changed, not the war. To be sure, the old-fashioned rednecks were at least up-front about their prejudice, so a white person's assurance of tolerance may be a mixed blessing for blacks. But in the long run, a reduction in overtly demeaning communication is sure to have a positive effect in many aspects of our society.

CONCLUSIONS

The line of research centering on symbolic racism holds that racism continues to pervade white America, that it continues to have a powerful effect on racial policy preferences and voting behavior, and that such effects are largely symbolic and surprisingly independent of any direct impact that racial issues have on whites' private lives. The form that white racism takes today is quite different than that of 30 years ago; overt bigotry is much reduced. This is part of what has plainly been a major change in the cultural climate about race. These changes most probably reflect genuine changes in the white public's attitudes, though, to some extent as well, a change in patterns of overt expression. Either way, major changes have occurred in the policies and practices of our public and private institutions.

Although these liberalizing changes are important and should be applauded, it remains important to assess the extent to which whites' political positions continue to depend on race. Our efforts have addressed this question. Clearly any one research program can take only one cut at such a complex matter. And we have focused particularly on the contrast of symbolic racism with self-interest because, frankly, much of the political debate has centered on that contrast.

Some find offensive the underlying dynamics postulated by the symbolic politics approach, especially the notion that racism lurks behind attitudes seemingly innocent of manifest racial content. Bobo (1983), for example, suggested using the term *sophisticated prejudice* instead of *symbolic racism* because *racism* is too pejorative. There is no doubt that *racism* is pejorative, but so is *prejudice;* none of us likes to think we are either racist or prejudiced. Many people do not believe that holding the views reflected in the symbolic racism items shown in Table 1 means that one is really racist; they feel that one can agree to such items without being racist.

It is a cliché to note that the measurement of any underlying dimension is, with present technology, only probabilistic; the score of any one individual is determined by numerous factors other than the theoretical dimension of primary interest, including error of measurement. Nevertheless, if there is a single individual in the United States, black, white, red, yellow, or brown, who is not somewhat racist and prejudiced against blacks, this condition strikes me as a remarkable feat of resistance to a quite overwhelming saturation of centuries of cultural socialization. It is difficult to read Shakespeare's *Othello* without being impressed by how ingrained racist assumptions about blacks have been in the Western world since the beginning of extensive contact between Europe and Africa. Cultural norms on such matters are so ubiquitous that it seems to me doubtful that variation in their acceptance is anchored by their complete absence. I see little to be gained by pretending that what we are dealing with is somehow nicer than racism. Perhaps it is a consequence of our adherence to individualistic values that we tend to take such matters personally; certainly, many do. It is hard for me to see why individuals should hold themselves morally responsible for reflecting some rudiments of a nearly universal cultural socialization, even though it does seem proper to feel some obligation to resist its most destructive elements.

A second offensive aspect of the symbolic racism approach stems from its assumption that racism is often an irrational response to long-standing predispositions rather than a reasonable response to the realities of life. This is sometimes taken as a charge that the individual is often irrational. That charge, too, seems to me to have some truth in it. It should be noted that a fundamental and seemingly rather straightforward assumption of the symbolic politics approach is that the process is politically symmetrical. I would presume that the political left, right, and center are all quite even-handedly subject to the same psychological dynamics. Hence, support for radical or problack causes, such as support for a protest interpretation of ghetto riots, is determined just as fulsomely by symbolic predispositions as is support for conservative or antiblack positions (e.g., see Sears & McConahay, 1973).[19]

---

[19]For a contrary interpretation of the symbolic politics approach, see Sniderman and Tetlock (1986).

Plainly, the cultural climate in America has changed since World War II. Almost all institutions have been at least formally desegregated, and many in much more than a token sense (Farley, 1984). Government can no longer indulge in flagrantly discriminatory actions. Few whites any longer prefer strict segregation or believe in major, inherent, intractable racial inferiorities. All these changes are real. Moreover, they are changes of great societal importance because consensual social norms govern a great deal of public behavior, both official and informal (however much private attitudes may depart from the norm). Openly discriminatory legislation is no longer a serious possibility, and it is rarely possible to be openly insulting to blacks on racial grounds. Both barriers are firmly grounded in white opinion.

Nevertheless, our findings suggest that underlying racism continues to have an important political force. The old forms do not; politicians can no longer make political hay by preaching segregation and racial inferiority. But the new forms do; politicians can complain about demands and special favors and can insist that blacks need no special government action to achieve parity. Indeed, the Reagan administration has gone to court to dismantle affirmative action agreements painstakingly negotiated by local governments.

Any observer of American life would be guilty of wishful thinking if he or she imagined that racism would suddenly disappear, after nearly five centuries as a major complex of national and cultural belief. It is deeply ingrained throughout Western culture. It appears not to be as responsive to reality experiences as one might wish, whether they consist of benign interracial contacts or simply the absence of personal racial threats. Discovering whether symbolic racism is mostly antiblack affect and traditional values or a selfish defense of group privilege will require more pointed research. Either way, the needs that black leadership now press have come into conflict, we argue, with traditional American values that have had nothing themselves to do with race, adding strength to whites' resistance to change. This threatens, perhaps, to freeze blacks in their current status, surely not a pleasant prospect.

The symbolic racism view is not, then, a particularly optimistic one. It may seem old-fashioned to suggest it, but if it is correct that socialization and education are partly responsible for racism, they can also be partly responsible for its reduction. Differences of color have produced stereotypes and prejudice throughout history and in a vast variety of cultures. But any whose memory still spans the lynchings of Negroes in the 1930s and the exclusion of blacks from the professional baseball and basketball leagues of the immediate postwar period must feel optimistic about what has been accomplished in this land, and about what further must be within our reach.

ACKNOWLEDGMENTS

I would like to express thanks to Jack Citrin, Leonie Huddy, Tom Jessor, Donald R. Kinder, and John B. McConahay for their helpful comments on this manuscript, and Rick Kosterman for help with the data analyses.

REFERENCES

Aberbach, J. D., & Walker, J. L. (1973). *Race in the city: Political trust and public policy in the new urban system*. Boston, MA: Little, Brown.
Ajzen, I., & Fishbein, M. (1980). *Understanding attitudes and predicting social behavior*. Englewood Cliffs, NJ: Prentice-Hall.
Allport, G. W. (1954). *The nature of prejudice*. Garden City, NY: Doubleday Anchor.

Armor, D. J. (1980) White flight and the future of school desegregation. In W. G. Stephan & J. R. Feagin (Eds.), *School desegregation: Past, present, and future.* New York: Plenum Press.

Becker, J. F., & Heaton, E. E., Jr. (1967). The election of Senator Edward W. Brooke. *Public Opinion Quarterly, 31,* 346–358.

Bobo, L. (1983) Whites' opposition to busing: Symbolic racism or realistic group conflict? *Journal of Personality and Social Psychology, 45,* 1196–1210.

Brigham, J. C., Woodmansee, J. J., & Cook, S. W. (1976). Dimensions of verbal racial attitudes: Interracial marriage and approaches to racial equality. *Journal of Social Issues, 32,* 9–21.

Campbell, A. (1971). *White attitudes toward black people.* Ann Arbor, MI: Institute for Social Research.

Campbell, A., Converse, P. E., Miller, W. E., & Stokes, D. E. (1960). *The American voter.* New York: Wiley.

Carmichael, S., & Hamilton, C. V. (1967). *Black power.* New York: Vintage.

Carmines, E. G., & Stimson, J. A. (1980). The racial reorientation of American politics. In J. C. Pierce & J. L. Sullivan (Eds.), *The electorate reconsidered.* Beverly Hills, CA: Sage.

Carmines, E. G., & Stimson, J. A. (1984). The dynamics of issue evolution: The United States. In R. J. Dalton, S. C. Flanagan, & P. A. Beck (Eds.), *Electoral change in advanced industrial democracies.* Princeton, NJ: Princeton University Press.

Conover, P. J., & Feldman, S. (1981). The origins and meaning of liberal/conservative self-identifications. *American Journal of Political Science, 25,* 617–645.

Converse, P. E. (1964). The nature of belief systems in mass publics. In D. E. Apter (Ed.), *Ideology and discontent.* Glencoe, IL: Free Press.

Converse, P. E. (1975). Public opinion and voting behavior. In F. I. Greenstein & N. W. Polsby (Eds.), *Handbook of political science* (Vol. 4). Reading, MA: Addison-Wesley.

Converse, P. E., & Markus, G. B. (1979). Plus ça change . . . : The new CPS election study panel. *American Political Science Review, 73,* 32–49.

Converse, P. E., Clausen, A. R., & Miller, W. E. (1965). Electoral myth and reality: The 1964 election. *American Political Science Review, 59,* 321–336.

Converse, P. E., Miller, W. E., Rusk, J. G., & Wolfe, A. C. (1969). Continuity and change in American politics: Parties and issues in the 1968 election. *American Political Science Review, 63,* 1083–1105.

Crosby, F., Bromley, S., & Saxe, L. (1980). Recent unobtrusive studies of black and white discrimination and prejudice: A literature review. *Psychological Bulletin, 87,* 546–563.

Edwards, W. (1954). The theory of decision-making. *Psychological Bulletin, 51,* 380–417.

Farley, R. (1984). *Blacks and whites: Narrowing the gap?* Cambridge, MA: Harvard University Press.

Feagin, J. R., & Hahn, H. (1973). *Ghetto revolts: The politics of violence in American cities.* New York: Macmillan.

Feather, N. T. (Ed.). (1982). *Expectations and actions: Expectancy-value models in psychology.* Hillsdale, NJ: Erlbaum.

Feldman, S. (1983). Economic individualism and American public opinion. *American Politics Quarterly, 11,* 3–30.

Festinger, L. (1957). *A theory of cognitive dissonance.* Evanston, IL: Row, Peterson.

Fiorina, M. P. (1981). *Retrospective voting in American national elections.* New Haven, CT: Yale University Press.

Fiske, S. T. (1982). Schema-triggered affect: Applications to social perception. In M. S. Clark & S. T. Fiske (Eds.), *Affect and cognition: The 17th Annual Carnegie Symposium on Cognition.* Hillsdale, NJ: Erlbaum.

Fogelson, R. M. (1971). *Violence as protest: A study of riots and ghettos.* Garden City, NY: Doubleday.

Gatlin, D. S., Giles, M. W., & Cataldo, E. F. (1978). Policy support within a target group: The case of school desegregation. *American Political Science Review, 72,* 985–995.

Greeley, A. M., & Sheatsley, P. B. (1971). Attitudes toward racial integration. *Scientific American, 223,* 13–19.

Guimond, S., & Dubé-Simard, L. (1983). Relative deprivation theory and the Quebec nationalist movement: The cognition–emotion distinction and the personal-group deprivation issue. *Journal of Personality and Social Psychology, 44,* 526–535.

Harding, J., Proshansky, H., Kutner, B., & Chein, I. (1969). Prejudice and ethnic relations. In G. Lindzey & E. Aronson (Eds.), *The handbook of social psychology* (Vol. 5). Reading, MA: Addison-Wesley.

Huddy, L., Sears, D. O., & Cardoza, D. (1986). *Dynamics of support for bilingual education in the non-Hispanic mass public: A symbolic politics analysis.* Unpublished manuscript, University of California, Los Angeles.

Iyengar, S., & Kinder, D. R. (1985). Psychological accounts of agenda-setting. In S. A. Kraus & R. M.

Perloff (Eds.), *Mass media and political thought: An information-processing approach*. Beverly Hills, CA: Sage.

Jackman, M. R., & Muha, M. J. (1984). Education and intergroup attitudes: Moral enlightenment, superficial democratic commitment, or ideological refinement. *American Sociological Review, 49,* 751–769.

Jacobson, C. K. (1985). Resistance to affirmative action: Self-interest or racism? *Journal of Conflict Resolution, 29,* 306–329.

Jessor, T., & Sears, D. O. (1986). *Realistic and symbolic explanations for racial conflict*. Paper presented at the annual meeting of the Midwest Political Science Association, Chicago.

Jones, J. M. (1971). *Prejudice and racism*. Reading, MA: Addison-Wesley.

Jordan, W. D. (1968). *White over black: American attitudes toward the Negro, 1550–1812*. Chapel Hill: University of North Carolina Press.

Katz, P. A. (1976). The acquisition of racial attitudes in children. In P. A. Katz (Ed.), *Towards the elimination of racism*. Elmsford, NY: Pergamon Press.

Kelley, H. H. (1967). Attribution theory in social psychology. In D. Levine (Ed.), *Nebraska symposium on motivation*. Lincoln: University of Nebraska Press.

Kinder, D. R. (1985). *The continuing American dilemma: White resistance to racial change forty years after Myrdal*. Unpublished manuscript, University of Michigan.

Kinder, D. R. (1986). The continuing American dilemma: White resistance to racial change forty years after Myrdal. *Journal of Social Issues, 42,* 151–171.

Kinder, D. R., & Rhodebeck, L. A. (1982). Continuities in support for racial equality, 1972 to 1976. *Public Opinion Quarterly, 46,* 195–215.

Kinder, D. R., & Sanders, L. M. (1986). *Survey questions and political culture: The case of whites' response to affirmative action for blacks*. Paper presented at the annual meeting of the American Political Science Association, Washington, DC.

Kinder, D. R., & Sears, D. O. (1981). Prejudice and politics: Symbolic racism versus racial threats to the good life. *Journal of Personality and Social Psychology, 40,* 414–431.

Kinder, D. R., & Sears, D. O. (1985). Public opinion and political action. In G. Lindzey & E. Aronson (Eds.), *Handbook of social psychology* (3rd ed.). New York: Random House.

Klein, E. D. (1984). *Consciousness and group politics: The rise of the contemporary feminist movement*. Cambridge: Harvard University Press.

Kluegel, J. R., & Smith, E. R. (1983). Affirmative action attitudes. Effects of self-interest, racial affect, and stratification beliefs on whites' views. *Social Forces, 61,* 797–824.

Knowles, L. L., & Prewitt, K. (Eds.). (1969). *Institutional racism in American*. Englewood Cliffs, NJ: Prentice-Hall.

LaPiere, R. T. (1934). Attitudes vs. actions. *Social Forces, 13,* 230–237.

Lau, R. R., Brown, T. A., & Sears, D. O. (1978). Self-interest and civilians' attitudes toward the war in Vietnam. *Public Opinion Quarterly, 42,* 464–483.

Levine, R. A., & Campbell, D. T. (1972). *Ethnocentrism: Theories of conflict, ethnic attitudes, and group behavior*. New York: Wiley.

Levitin, T. E., & Miller, W. E. (1979). Ideological interpretations of presidential elections. *American Political Science Review, 73,* 751–771.

Lipset, S. M., & Schneider, W. (1978). The Bakke case: How would it be decided at the bar of public opinion? *Public Opinion, 1,* 38–44.

Markus, G. E. (1979). The political environment and the dynamics of public attitudes: A panel study. *American Journal of Political Science, 23,* 338–359.

McClendon, M. J. (1985). Racism, rational choice, and white opposition to racial change: A case study of busing. *Public Opinion Quarterly, 49,* 214–233.

McConahay, J. B. (n.d.). *Is it still the blacks and not the buses: Self-interest vs. racial attitudes as correlates of opposition to busing in Louisville, a replication*. Unpublished manuscript, Duke University.

McConahay, J. B. (1982). Self-interest versus racial attitudes as correlates of anti-busing attitudes in Louisville: Is it the buses or the blacks? *Journal of Politics, 44,* 692–720.

McConahay, J. B. (1986). Modern racism, ambivalence, and the modern racism scale. In S. L. Gaertner & J. Dovidio (Eds.), *Prejudice, discrimination, and racism: Theory and research*. New York: Academic Press.

McConahay, J. B., & Hough, J. C., Jr. (1976). Symbolic racism. *Journal of Social Issues, 32,* 23–45.

McConahay, J. B., Hardee, B. B., & Batts, V. (1981). Has racism declined in America? *Journal of Conflict Resolution, 25,* 563–579.

Miller, S. (1981). *Contemporary racial conflict: The nature of white opposition to mandatory busing*. Unpublished doctoral dissertation, University of California, Los Angeles.

Miller, S., & Sears, D. O. (1986). Stability and change in social tolerance: A test of the persistence hypothesis. *American Journal of Political Science, 30,* 214–236.

Murphy, W. F., & Tanenhaus, J. (1968). Public opinion and the United States Supreme Court. *Law and Society Review, 2,* 357–384.

Osgood, C. E., Suci, G. J., & Tannenbaum, P. H. (1957). *The measurement of meaning.* Urbana: University of Illinois.

Pettigrew, T. F. (1971). *Racially separate or together?* New York: McGraw-Hill.

Proshansky, H. M. (1966). The development of intergroup attitudes. In Lois W. Hoffman & M. L. Hoffman (Eds.), *Review of child development research* (Vol. 2). New York: Russell Sage Foundation.

Rabushka, A., & Ryan, P. (1982). *The tax revolt.* Stanford, CA: Hoover Institution.

Report of the National Advisory Commission on Civil Disorders. (1968). New York: Bantam.

Rosenberg, M. J. (1960). An analysis of affective-cognitive consistency. In C. I. Hovland & M. J. Rosenberg (Eds.), *Attitude organization and change.* New Haven: Yale University Press.

Rothbart, M. (1976). Achieving racial equality: An analysis of resistance to social reform. In P. A. Katz (Ed.), *Towards the elimination of racism.* New York: Pergamon Press.

Rusk, J. G., & Weisberg, H. F. (1972). Perceptions of presidential candidates: Implications for electoral change. *Midwest Journal of Political Science, 16,* 388–410.

Schuman, H. (1969). Sociological racism. *Transaction, 7,* 44–48.

Schuman, H., Steeh, C., & Bobo, L. (1985). *Racial attitudes in America: Trends and interpretation.* Cambridge: Harvard University Press.

Sears, D. O. (1983). The persistence of early political predispositions: The roles of attitude object and life stage. In L. Wheeler & P. Shaver (Eds.), *Review of personality and social psychology* (Vol. 4). Beverly Hills, CA: Sage Publications.

Sears, D. O. (1984). *Attitude objects and political socialization through the life cycle.* Paper presented at the annual convention of the American Political Science Association, Washington, DC.

Sears, D. O., & Allen, H. M., Jr. (1984). The trajectory of local desegregation controversies and whites' opposition to busing. In N. Miller & M. B. Brewer (Eds.), *Groups in contact: The psychology of desegregation.* New York: Academic Press.

Sears, D. O., & Citrin, J. (1985). *Tax revolt: Something for nothing in California* (enlarged ed.). Cambridge: Harvard University Press.

Sears, D. O., & Kinder, D. R. (1970). *The good life, "white racism," and the Los Angeles voter.* Paper delivered at the annual meeting of the Western Psychological Association, Los Angeles.

Sears, D. O., & Kinder, D. R. (1971). Racial tensions and voting in Los Angeles. In W. Z. Hirsch (Ed.), *Los Angeles: Viability and prospects for metropolitan leadership.* New York: Praeger.

Sears, D. O., & Kinder, D. R. (1985). Whites' opposition to busing: On conceptualizing and operationalizing group conflict. *Journal of Personality and Social Psychology, 48,* 1141–1147.

Sears, D. O., & McConahay, J. B. (1973). *The politics of violence: The new urban blacks and the Watts riot.* Boston: Houghton-Mifflin. (Reprinted by University Press of America, 1981.)

Sears, D. O., & Whitney, R. E. (1973). Political persuasion. In I. deS. Pool, W. Schramm, F. W. Frey, N. Maccoby, & E. B. Parker (Eds.), *Handbook of communication.* Chicago: Rand-McNally.

Sears, D. O., Tyler, T. R., Citrin, J., & Kinder, D. R. (1978). Political system support and public response to the 1974 energy crisis. *American Journal of Political Science, 22,* 56–82.

Sears, D. O., Hensler, C. P., & Speer, L. K. (1979). Whites' opposition to "busing": Self-interest or symbolic politics? *American Political Science Review, 73,* 369–384.

Sears, D. O., Lau, R. R., Tyler, T. R., & Allen, H. M., Jr. (1980). Self-interest vs. symbolic politics in policy attitudes and presidential voting. *American Political Science Review, 74,* 670–684.

Sears, D. O., Steck, L., Lau, R. R., & Gahart, M. T. (1983). *Attitudes of the post-Vietnam generation toward the draft and American military policy.* Paper presented at the annual meeting of the International Society of Political Psychology, Oxford, England.

Sears, D. O., Huddy, L., & Schaffer, L. G. (1984). *Schemas and symbolic politics: The cases of racial and gender equality.* Paper presented at the 19th Annual Carnegie Symposium on Cognition, Carnegie-Mellon University, Pittsburgh.

Sears, D. O., Citrin, J., & Kosterman, R. (1985). *The white response to Jesse Jackson in 1984.* Paper presented at the annual meetings of the American Psychological Association, Los Angeles, and the American Political Science Association, New Orleans.

Sears, D. O., Huddy, L., & Schaffer, L. G. (1986). A schematic variant of symbolic politics theory, as applied to racial and gender equality. In R. R. Lau & D. O. Sears (Eds.). *Political cognition: The 19th Annual Carnegie Symposium on Cognition.* Hillsdale, NJ: Erlbaum.

Shanks, J. M., & Miller, W. E. (1985). *Policy direction and performance evaluation: Complementary explanations of the Reagan elections.* Paper delivered at the annual meeting of the American Political Science Association, New Orleans.

Sniderman, P. M., & Tetlock, P. E. (1986). Symbolic racism: Problems of motive attribution in political analysis. *Journal of Social Issues, 42,* 129–150.

Stinchcombe, A. L., & Taylor, D. G. (1980). On democracy and school integration. In W. G. Stephan and J. R. Feagin (Eds.), *School desegregation: Past, present, and future.* New York: Plenum Press.

Vanneman, R. D., & Pettigrew, T. F. (1972). Race and relative deprivation in the urban United States. *Race, 13,* 461–486.

Verba, S., Brody, R. A., Parker, E. B., Nie, N. H., Polsby, N. W., Ekman, P., & Black, G. S. (1967). Public opinion and the war in Vietnam. *American Political Science Review, 61,* 317–333.

Ward, D. (1985). Generations and the expression of symbolic racism. *Political Psychology, 6,* 1–18.

Weigel, R. H., & Howes, P. W. (1985). Conceptions of racial prejudice: Symbolic racism reconsidered. *Journal of Social Issues, 41,* 117–138.

Weiner, B. (1982). The emotional consequences of causal attributions. In M. S. Clark & S. T. Fiske (Eds.), *Affect and cognition: The 17th Annual Carnegie Symposium on Cognition.* Hillsdale NJ: Erlbaum.

Wilson, W. J. (1978). *The declining significance of race.* Chicago: University of Chicago Press.

Wolfinger, R. E., & Greenstein, F. I. (1968). The repeal of fair housing in California: An analysis of referendum voting. *American Political Science Review, 62,* 753–769.

Zajonc, R. B. (1980). Feeling and thinking: Preferences need no inferences. *American Psychologist, 35,* 151–175.

5

Group Conflict, Prejudice, and the Paradox of Contemporary Racial Attitudes

Lawrence Bobo

INTRODUCTION

The status of black Americans is the longest standing and most glaring exception to the American promise of freedom and equality. For this, as well as other reasons, social psychologists have long sought to shed light on the ways in which racial attitudes, beliefs, and values affect and are affected by patterns of black–white relations. Black–white relations now seem more complex and contradictory than ever before. From basic economic and demographic indicators to indicators of racial attitudes and beliefs, simultaneous patterns of progress, deterioration, and lack of change can be discerned.

I am concerned with the underlying meaning of race to white and black Americans (although, as in most of the literature in this area, disproportionate attention is given to white attitudes). This attempt to impose theoretical coherence on the complexities of racial attitudes and beliefs must begin, however, by recognizing a crucial shift in the character of black–white relations. The basic issues that define significant points of conflict and controversy in black–white relations have changed in many ways. Foremost among these changes has been a shift in focus from eliminating discrimination in access to public schools, facilities, employment, and the like, to a concern with mandatory school desegregation and the use of hiring goals or quotas; a shift from removing formal exclusionary barriers to implementing the measures needed to ensure full inclusion and participation; a shift, that is, *from stuggles over acquiring basic civil rights to struggles over actually redistributing educational, economic, political, and social resources.*

For many social psychologists, these changes have signaled a need to modify their traditional conceptions of prejudice in order to understand the changes in attitudes associated with these more global shifts in black–white relations. Others have stressed the increasing importance of group conflict processes because these broader changes have pushed to the forefront of black–white relations explicit and increasing concern about the allocation of scarce resources and values, such as educational and job opportunities. Thus, this chapter is concerned with efforts to apply social-psychological theo-

LAWRENCE BOBO • Department of Sociology, University of Wisconsin, Madison, Wisconsin 53706.

ries of group conflict and of prejudice to an understanding of the nature and consequences of contemporary racial attitudes.

Many years ago, Gordon Allport (1954) noted that distinguishing the effects of prejudice from those of group conflict on intergroup relations would be a very difficult task. He
suggested that "Realistic conflict is like a note on an organ. It sets all prejudices that are
attuned to it into simultaneous vibration. The listener can scarcely distinguish the pure
note from the surrounding jangle" (p. 233). Thus, it is with some trepidation that this
chapter takes up the task of trying to clarify the distinctive social-psychological significance of group conflict and prejudice in the racial attitudes of white and, to a lesser
degree, black Americans. Recent theoretical and empirical work has, however, raised this
question anew and in the process has improved our conceptual leverage on these issues.
As a result, an attempt to distinguish the "pure note" of group conflict from that of
prejudice seems warranted.

The approach taken in this chapter is more that of a speculative essay than a traditional literature review. This approach is chosen, precarious though it may be, because
there is a need for a discussion of broad theoretical issues raised by the controversy about
the relative importance of group conflict and prejudice for contemporary racial attitudes.
The departure from traditional literature reviews takes two forms. First, I propose and
elaborate on a theoretical framework for understanding the place of group conflict in
intergroup belief systems, and I attempt to specify ways of conceptualizing and measuring group conflict motives. Second, I take a quite catholic approach to the material as the
research draws not only on the work of social psychologists, but also on that of historians, demographers, political scientists, and sociologists. The final outcome, I hope, is a
better sense of the distinctive roles of prejudice and group conflict in racial attitudes as
well as a sense of fruitful directions for future research.

Theoretical controversy of the kind examined here has occurred before within social
psychology as well as in other disciplines. For example, Clark (1965), although not exclusively concerned with racial attitudes and relations, asserted that social psychology
devoted too little attention to questions of power and political conflict. Rose (1956) argued
that we shouldn't assume that prejudice underlies discrimination because "patterns of
intergroup relations (including mainly discrimination and segregation) are quite distinct
from attitudes of prejudice in that each has a separate and distinct history, cause, and
process of change" (p. 173). Like Rose, Blumer (1958b) called for greater attention to the
organization of society: to competing interests, differences in power, and situational
contexts, which he saw as the underlying forces in intergroup relations. Allport (1962)
took issue with these and similar assertions that social structure was more important than
individual prejudice. He argued that societal factors are "distal causal factors" in intergroup behavior, whereas individual personality is always the "proximal causal factor."
Allport suggested an important link between the two, however: conformity to group
norms. In a similar vein, Williams (1965), too, noted that social structure and personality
are linked but added that we should be careful to distinguish "prejudice" as driven by
feelings of competitive threat or the protection of vested interests from "prejudice" as
driven by psychological affective or expressive needs.[1]

---

[1]In some instances, this controversy took on a polemical character. For example, Rose (1956) asserted
that "no study of prejudice, using any definition or any theory, helps us much in understanding
what is going on in the desegregation process today. The explanation is apparently to be looked for
in terms of legal, economic, political and social structural forces" (p. 176). Similarly, Blumer (1958b)
argued that "the preoccupation of students [of race relations] with the study of prejudice has
turned their attention away from the actual association of races and led them into a detached and
artificial world. It is not surprising, therefore, that the vast body of research findings on studies of
racial prejudice has not led or contributed to theoretical knowledge of the behavior of racial groups
in their relations with each other" (p. 434).

A similar dialogue over societal versus personality factors in intergroup relations arose among historians with respect to attempts to explain the rise of slavery and racist ideology. In a controversial paper, the Handlins (1950) argued that black indentured servants were regarded and treated much the same as white servants when they first arrived in the American colonies in 1619. Over a period of roughly 40 years, they argued, the status of black servants deteriorated, whereas that of white servants improved. Thus, by around 1660, blacks had been reduced to a cheap, available, and easily exploited pool of servants whose bondage was viewed as lifelong. Importantly, this analysis suggested a gradual, not a rapid, degradation of blacks and transformation of the attitudes toward them. Such a pattern of events was more consistent with the view that antiblack prejudice *resulted* from the establishment of slavery, than with the claim that a deep psychological antipathy toward blacks preceded slavery. Instead, the rise of a new mode of organizing social life, a slave economy, led to the development of attitudes and beliefs justifying and reinforcing that new social form.

Degler (1959) challenged these claims, pointing to evidence that, from the earliest moment of their arrival, blacks had been treated differently—more harshly—than white servants (see also the exchange of letters of Degler, 1960, and Handlin & Handlin, 1960). In contradistinction to both positions, Jordan (1962) noted that the available information for the years in question, especially 1619–1640, was very sparse and at best inconclusive. He argued for a compromise position, which held that economic, political, and cultural factors conducive to the rise of slavery as an institution worked simultaneously with antiblack prejudice to foster the ultimate subjugation of blacks. The enslavement of blacks and the existence of individual-level prejudice, Jordan (1968) wrote, "may have been equally cause and effect, continuously reacting upon each other, dynamically joining hands to hustle the Negro down the road to complete degradation" (p. 80).

More recently, Fredrickson (1971b) questioned this conclusion and, indeed, the very terms of the debate that assumed that black slavery was a unique departure requiring special explanation. Although accepting Jordan's basic claim that prejudice played a role in the rise of slavery, Fredrickson argued that the real question was why not *all* black indentured servants were regarded as bound for a lifetime of servitude. Many were freed, just as their white counterparts were, when their term of service was completed. In Fredrickson's account, the forces that paved the way for black enslavement were the absence of any deep-seated cultural bias, at that time, against the institution of slavery and several societal factors (e.g., the political vulnerability of African blacks as compared to white European indentured servants, as well as the growing demand for a stable labor supply) that had, by the 1660s, led to the *de facto* (and later *de jure*) enslavement of a large number of blacks (see also Harris, 1964). From this point of view, it is as incorrect to claim that prejudice played no role in the rise of slavery as it is to assign prejudice the same causal weight as other societal factors. In particular, Fredrickson (1971b) argued

> that "virulent prejudice," as compared to milder forms of ethnocentrism and stereotyping, followed in the wake of enslavement and probably did not take full possession of the white mind until slavery had become fully established as the basis of the economic and social order. (p. 246)

This argument is lent further support by the fact that a full articulation of theories of the permanent, innate inferiority of blacks followed the rise of the abolitionists' moral challenge to slavery and the Northern industrialists' challenge to economic policies conducive to plantation-based commodities and slave labor (Fredrickson, 1971a).

Several lessons are to be drawn from these earlier examinations of the role of societal versus personality—more loosely, group-conflict versus prejudice—approaches to intergroup relations. First, societal and personality approaches are not mutually exclusive frameworks of analysis. It sometimes seems that these approaches are irreconcilable because the former tends to assume that intergroup attitudes and behavior are guided by an interest-based, rational calculus, with interests being a function of position in the social structure. Personality or prejudice approaches, in contrast, tend to emphasize individual-level, psychological, and often irrational bases of intergroup relations. The present discussion seeks to avoid this constraining, and misleading, opposition by suggesting that certain types of attitudes and beliefs reflect group-based interests imposed by the social structure; that is, there are aspects of personality that reflect societal level processes and do so in a manner that should not be construed as "prejudice." Second, if this observation is to inform empirical research, then the relevant concepts need to be well defined, and appropriate measurement strategies must be outlined. Third, theory must be informed by an analysis of the sociohistorical context of group relations, as well as by the rules of cognitive functioning. The historically specific and socially relevant content of racial attitudes and beliefs cannot be derived from the psychological attributes of individuals alone. In particular, periods of substantial shift in the character of attitudes, such as the rise of sophisticated proslavery doctrines and, later, the scientific racism that accompanied the rise of Jim Crow, were inextricably linked to, and perhaps primarily driven by, larger economic, political, and cultural forces. Contemporary research on the growing complexity and subtlety of racial attitudes would benefit from a balanced concern with societal and personality factors (Pettigrew, 1985). Furthermore, research on racial attitudes and beliefs must be based on an analysis of the changes and continuities in the sociohistorical context of black–white relations. The relative economic and political status of blacks and whites, patterns of residential and school segregation, and enduring cultural beliefs are all important inputs to prevailing patterns of racial attitudes and beliefs.

The main question, then, is what role, if any, does group conflict play in racial attitudes in the contemporary United States? A full answer to this question requires a conception of group conflict and of group conflict motives, as well as a specification of the ways in which the latter differ from prejudice and other racial attitudes. Before addressing each of these matters, however, it would be instructive to consider why the question arises in the first place.

THE PROBLEM: PROGRESS AND RESISTANCE

The attitudes of white Americans toward black people have undergone sweeping and dramatic change over the past several decades. In 1942, approximately 60% of whites believed that blacks were less intelligent than whites (Hyman & Sheatsley, 1956, p. 35). By 1964, that figure had declined to less than 25% (Hyman & Sheatsley, 1964; see also Schuman, 1971, p. 383). A substantial majority of white Americans in 1942 approved of the blatantly discriminatory proposition that "white people should have the first chance at any kind of job," whereas in 1972 nearly 100% of whites in a national survey rejected that statement. But just as survey research has chronicled such changes for the better, opposition to policies such as school busing (80%–90%; see Schuman, Steeh, & Bobo, 1985) and affirmative action (roughly 80%; see Lipset & Schneider, 1978) remain impediments to certain forms of racial change.

Research on racial attitudes thus increasingly presents a paradox: Although there is continuing improvement in whites' beliefs about blacks and support for the general principles of racial equality and integration (Taylor, Sheatsley, & Greeley, 1978), there is pronounced opposition to specific policies aimed at improving the social and economic position of blacks, as well as to participation in social settings where blacks are a substantial majority (Farley, Schuman, Bianchi, Colasanto, & Hatchett, 1978; Smith, 1981). Pettigrew (1979) described this paradox as follows: "White Americans increasingly reject racial injustice in principle, but are reluctant to accept the measures necessary to eliminate the injustice" (p. 119).[2]

Students of democratic theory have also examined the extent to which abstract democratic principles are applied in more concrete situations (Prothro & Grigg, 1960). Jackman (1978), in particular, stressed this type of approach to the conceptualization of racial attitudes. Others have drawn on the distinction she made between racial principles and applied measures of racial policy preferences. Thus, recent research by Schuman, Steeh, and Bobo (1985) indicates that, across a number of important issues (access to public accommodations, discrimination in jobs, residential integration, and school integration), whites were more positive in attitude toward the principle of racial egalitarianism than toward policies to implement such principles. This disparity applied in terms of both lower absolute levels of support for implementation and less positive trends over time. In sum, this research demonstrated that one major characteristic of American racial attitudes is a gap between "principles and implementation."

The sustained positive movement on questions concerning the abstract goals of equal treatment and integration suggest that a fundamental change in racial norms has taken place (Schuman et al., 1985). This transformation in normative climate, however, has not eliminated race as a concern in American social and political life, nor has it resulted in support for strong efforts to equalize the opportunities afforded to blacks and whites. Research concerned with accounting for these patterns of "progress and resistance" has resulted in five broad approaches and answers.

First, a number of theories point to an underlying residue of prejudice and racism that is currently manifested in less overt ways (Crosby, Bromely, & Saxe, 1980; Donnerstein & Donnerstein, 1976; Gaertner & Dovidio, 1981; Kinder & Sears, 1981; Rogers & Prentice-Dunn, 1981). For example, Gaertner and Dovidio (1981) identified "aversive racists," people who have some degree of negative feelings toward blacks and yet are committed to a nonprejudiced self-image. A series of experiments suggests that the outcome, at least in situations involving ambiguous racial norms, is discriminatory treatment of blacks. Second, others have suggested that many contemporary proposals for racial change involve important value-violations. For instance, Lipset and Schneider (1978) noted that affirmative action programs, especially those involving quotas, are perceived as violating the values of individualism and meritocratic advancement. Others have argued that court orders for school desegregation and busing are viewed as violating the value of majority rule (Stinchcombe & Taylor, 1980) and the general cultural motif of noncoercive, voluntary compliance (Taylor, 1986). Third, some research (McClendon, 1985; McClendon & Pestello, 1982) points to pragmatic objections to racially neutral features of certain policies such as the cost, time, or safety considerations raised by school busing. Fourth, some researchers stress the importance of group-interested ideologies (Jackman & Muha 1984; Jackman & Senter, 1983) and realistic group-conflict motives (Bobo, 1983; Smith, 1981; Wellman, 1977). Finally, a number of researchers have alerted us to different cognitive processes that affect racial attitudes and perceptions. These processes include a tendency toward more extreme reactions, both positive and negative, to out-group members (Linville & Jones, 1980); the observation that ambivalent feelings can lead to "amplified" reactions of positive and negative valence (Katz, 1981); the differential consequences of distinct "modes" (e.g., genetic versus environmental) of

[2]A similar description of white racial attitudes had been offered by Dr. Martin Luther King, Jr., as early as 1967. He argued that the attitudes of most whites fell in between the polar extremes of segregationism and a deep commitment to racial justice. King said that many whites were "uneasy with injustice, yet unwilling to pay a significant price to eradicate it" (p. 13).

explaining racial inequality (Apostle, Glock, Piazza, & Suelzle, 1983); and an examination of the impact of general and racially specific beliefs about social stratification on racial attitudes (Kluegel & Smith, 1982).

Despite critical differences in interpretation and analysis, these five strands of research share, to varying degrees, three assumptions about contemporary race relations. The first of these assumptions pertains to the far-reaching normative change in standards for interracial relations and conduct. In particular, it is assumed that this important transformation in racial norms does not easily extend to support for large-scale racial change or to fully color-blind behavior. Next, although this point is often treated more implicitly than explicitly, it is assumed that the character of the issues themselves has changed. Some have explicitly characterized the shift as being from equal rights or procedural issues to equal opportunity or redistributive issues (Kluegel & Smith, 1982). More generally, it is clear that, after 1965, there were key changes in law and politics pertaining to race, in the form and the articulated ideology of black political activism, in the status of many blacks, and in the questions that social researchers pursued (see Schuman *et al.*, 1985, Chapters 1 and 6). Finally, these two assumptions have resulted in a general concern about understanding the gap between "principles and implementation" or, more broadly, about explaining the apparent limitations on racial progress (Blackwell, 1982; Rothbart, 1976).

For the present purposes, this problem is framed as the need to explain the emergence and character of an ideology of "bounded" racial change. It is argued that there is a nascent view that, although blacks are entitled to full citizenship rights, moving beyond equal rights to ensuring equal opportunities, or to implementing policies that may impose substantial burdens on whites, is an illegitimate goal. In particular, the tendencies to attribute racial inequality to the shortcomings of blacks themselves (Kluegel, 1985; Schuman, 1971) and to view the opportunity structure as fair and open (Kluegel, 1985) are key elements of the ideology of bounded racial change. This emergent understanding of race relations is not adopted in a consistent and uniform fashion by all whites. But to the extent that many accept this view and to the extent that it is perceived as the current trend in opinion, it influences and constrains public dialogue and mass opinion (Noelle-Neumann, 1974, 1984). This view, then, becomes a cultural force that needs to be understood in its own right (Prager, 1982). Indeed, such a nascent ideology has the potential to crystallize into a politically potent set of attitudes and beliefs.

Although this problem can be addressed by means of different research methods and the ideas advanced by any (or all) of the five approaches outlined above, this chapter focuses on two theories that have grown primarily out of the recent survey research literature and that have a fairly direct concern with the gap between principles and implementation: realistic group conflict and symbolic racism. (This focus restricts concern to the dynamics of public opinion on race, leaving interpersonal attitudes and behavior largely untouched.) The latter theory, based in a prejudice tradition, contends that whites' attitudes have perhaps become more sophisticated but still reflect a basic nonrational antipathy toward blacks. Thus, whites may respond positively to survey questions about general racial principles, but they allow the depth of their antiblack prejudice to emerge when asked about issues such as school busing. The group conflict theory, as developed here, contends that white support for the principle of racial justice is a real but limited commitment. The commitment is limited in that it often fails to be translated into support for concrete policy change insofar as blacks are perceived as significantly competing for the resources that whites possess and value. These types of theories are not mutually exclusive (Allport, 1954; Williams, 1965), nor do they exhaust the possible factors shaping contemporary racial attitudes. For these reasons, this chapter concludes with a brief discussion of integrating the group-conflict-versus-prejudice debate into a more complex framework that recognizes the several approaches outlined above. I now turn to a discussion of group conflict and ideological processes in racial attitudes.

GROUP CONFLICT AND RACIAL IDEOLOGY

DEFINITIONS

Social or group conflict involves—in a paraphrase and modification of Coser (1956)—a struggle over values or claims to status, power, and other scarce resources in which the aims of the conflict groups are not only to gain the desired values, but also to affect, change, or injure rivals. The specific tactics employed can range from efforts at influence or persuasion, to the use of positive inducements, to forms of constraint or coercive action (Gamson, 1968). Recent racial conflict in the United States has involved litigation and the pursuit of legal redress, conventional political action (voting and lobbying), and unconventional political action, such as nonviolent protest and mass demonstrations, as well as urban rioting (Himes, 1966, p. 3). All of these tactics have been used, to varying degrees, in the pursuit of (or to prevent) social change; all involve efforts to alter the distribution of power, wealth, and status between social groups (McAdam, 1982, p. 26) or to prevent such change from occurring (Taylor, 1986).

Realistic conflicts derive from incompatible—though not necessarily irreconcilable—group interests. According to Fireman and Gamson (1979), a "group can be assumed to have an objective interest in a collective good to the extent that the good promotes the long-run wealth and power of the group and the viability of its design for living (whether or not these consequences are known to group members)" (p. 24). Or more broadly, a group's objective interests involve the "shared advantages or disadvantages likely to accrue to" a group and its members as a result of interaction with other groups (Tilly, 1978, p. 54). Group interests are based in social structural conditions—in particular, long-standing patterns of inequality of power, wealth, and status that establish opposing interests (Jackman & Jackman, 1983, p. 6).

Three clarifications need to be made. First, objective group interests do not invariably become subjectively perceived interests, but they do, in the long-run, "exert an important influence on subjective ones" (Fireman & Gamson, 1979, p. 24). This point is especially pertinent to a discussion of intergroup ideologies where a more powerful or dominant group may promote ideas and interpretations that obscure a subordinate group's realization of its interests. Second, it is important to distinguish between personal interests and group interests. Outcomes that benefit (or injure) an individual may not benefit (or injure) a group and its position. But more important, part of what separates theories of social conflict from simple utilitarian logic is a concern with the solidary ties that exist among people with a shared group identity (Fireman & Gamson, 1979). Third, group interests have consequences for individuals. Insofar as individuals are socialized to identify with particular groups and their values, the group and its social position become part of the individual's social identity. More specifically, group members may develop a sense of investment in, or a felt need to challenge, some pattern of structural inequality on the basis of their group membership (Blumer, 1958a; Bobo, 1983; Tajfel & Turner, 1979; Wellman, 1977; Wilson, 1973).

In addition, realistic group conflict is distinguished from "nonrealistic" conflict in that it is directed toward achieving some group-interested outcome (Coser, 1956, pp. 48–55). It is goal-oriented, whereas nonrealistic conflict involves a nonspecific release of hostility or aggressive psychological impulses. Where dispute is focused on a delimited issue or set of issues concerned with the distribution of power, wealth, or status between social groups, and involves clearly defined groups with differing objectives, there is realistic conflict. Disputes lacking these features, especially those lacking a concern with the rival objectives of the conflict groups, are nonrealistic. Although cognitive processes and intergroup affective orientations enter into both types of conflict, nonrealistic conflict is largely reducible to nonrational psychological impulses.

THE CURRENT SOCIAL CONTEXT

Other than the fact of observable differences in skin color and the historically important identities of black and white Americans, the pivotal features of race relations in the United States are extensive residential segregation of the races, economic inequality, and inequality in political power. Although there has been real progress in each domain, most blacks still confront different chances in life than those that await most whites.

With respect to residential segregation, in 1965 the Taeubers documented extensive separation of blacks and whites. They concluded that, regardless of region, city size, economic base, local laws, and the extent of other forms of discrimination, there was "a very high degree of segregation of the residences of whites and Negroes" (Taeuber & Taeuber, 1965, p. 35). Van Valey, Roof, and Wilcox (1977) concluded that, between 1960 and 1970, the level of residential segregation by race had changed very little. Farley (1977) demonstrated that racial segregation was not only more extensive in absolute terms than the segregation of social classes, but that it occurred regardless of social class. For example, his analysis of 1970 Census data indicated that "whites who have more than a college education are more residentially segregated from similarly well educated blacks than they are from whites who have never completed a year of school" (p. 514). Although there is some evidence of increasing black suburbanization (Frey, 1985), a recent analysis of 1980 Census data indicated some, but far from striking, progress in reducing the overall residential segregation of blacks and whites in the nation's larger cities (Taueber, 1983a,b).

It should be noted that such segregation is inconsistent with the expressed desires of many blacks. As Farley et al. (1978) reported in their study of Detroit area residents that most blacks prefer to live in neighborhoods integrated 50-50.[3] What is more, most whites have no absolute objection to residential integration (Farley et al., 1978; Schuman et al., 1985). Many whites do, however, express little enthusiasm for neighborhoods with substantial numbers of blacks. Farley and colleagues (1978, p. 335) found that, as the number of blacks mentioned in an integrated neighborhood setting neared one-third, 57% of the whites interviewed said they would feel uncomfortable, 41% said they would probably try to move out of such a neighborhood, and fully 73% said they would not consider moving into such a neighborhood. In addition, Schuman et al. (1985) reported that, when questions about possible degrees of neighborhood integration mentioned large numbers of blacks, education ceased to have a positive effect on such attitudes (see also Jackman & Muha, 1984; Smith, 1981). In sum, not only are blacks and whites separated as a matter of fact, but many whites prefer to live in neighborhoods that are clearly white in character.

One major consequence of residential segregation is the segregation of schools. Despite years of litigation, increasingly forceful court mandates, and heated debates, the public schools are still largely segregated. In 1974, more than 40% of black students attended schools with 90% or more minority enrollment (Orfield, 1978, p. 57). Segregation is especially clear-cut in large northern metropolitan areas. In the city of Los Angeles, for example, figures for 1974–1975 revealed that more than 60% of black students attended schools with 99–100% minority enrollment (Orfield, 1978, p. 182). Although the

[3]Blacks did, however, express reluctance to become the first or lone black family in a white neighborhood (Farley, Bianchi, & Colasanto, 1979).

mandate of the *Brown* decision has been considerably fulfilled in rural southern areas (Farley, 1984; Rodgers, 1975), the decision has had much less impact on the nation's larger cities. The level of school segregation may, in fact, be worsening because of white enrollment losses, court rulings disallowing "metropolitan plans" that consolidate city and suburban school districts, and the apparent effective end of pressure under the Reagan administration to use busing as a remedy for school segregation. Indeed, one recent investigation concluded that, after noteworthy progress in reducing isolation in the schools between 1968 and 1976, "Overall, segregation slightly increased between 1976 and 1980" (Hochschild, 1984, p. 31).[4]

Blacks also lag behind whites economically. Even though substantial progress has been made, blacks still have lower levels of earnings, yearly income, and occupational attainment than whites (Farley, 1984). The level of unemployment among black adult males is roughly twice that among comparable whites and has been so for more than 30 years (Bonacich, 1976; Farley, 1984). Moreover, the percentage of blacks who have dropped out of the labor force entirely has risen to 13%, more than two and one-half times the rate (5%) among whites (Farley, 1984). Blacks are three times more likely than whites to have incomes below the poverty level (Farley, 1984), and roughly half of all black children can expect to spend some time below the poverty level (U.S. Bureau of the Census, 1983). There are indicators of vulnerable progress in other areas as well. Some reports suggest that the percentage of blacks entering college (*Wall Street Journal*, May 29, 1985, pp. 1, 24) and going on to graduate and professional schools (Berry, 1983) has begun to decline.

Even in the absence of direct personal experience with these problems, there is evidence suggesting that many whites have some awareness of black disadvantage. Survey data indicate that many whites acknowledge at least some degree of racial inequality and acknowledge the effects of past discrimination on blacks (Apostle *et al.*, 1983; Kluegel & Smith, 1982; Lipset & Schneider, 1978). Because inequality may be explained in many different ways (Apostle *et al.*, 1983), because the extent of the inequality may be misjudged (Robinson, 1983), and because the extent of ameliorative efforts may be exaggerated (Kluegel & Smith, 1982), white awareness of inequality and discrimination does not directly result in support for efforts to achieve equality.

Segregation and economic inequality notwithstanding, the basic rights of blacks as citizens have been given greater strength and efficacy by court rulings, by the actions of several presidents and the administrative agencies under their control, and by congressional enactment. As Wilson (1980) has pointed out, "Instead of reinforcing racial barriers created during the pre-industrial and industrial periods, the political system in recent years has tended to promote racial equality" (p. 17). In addition, organizations like the National Association for the Advancement of Colored People, the National Urban League, and the Leadership Conference on Civil Rights act as vigorous watchdogs. Such groups regularly press for the full implementation of civil rights policies and actively respond to efforts to weaken or reverse such policies. Two indicators of the continuing influence of these and similar organizations can be found in the recent strengthening and

[4]As in the case of residential integration, black preference for integrated schools is very high (near 100%) and quite stable over time (Schuman *et al.*, 1985). Blacks, however, are split nearly evenly on the question of school busing and, like whites, have shown decreasing support for federal intervention to bring about school integration. It is not clear whether the change among blacks is mainly a capitulation to white resistance or some more genuine rejection of the forceful implementation of school desegregation. Schuman *et al.* (1985) did present evidence that blacks and whites frequently—though not uniformly—offer different explanations for opposing busing, and Bobo (1984) presented evidence suggesting that whites may have become negative toward implementing school integration before the change among blacks.

25-year extension of the Voting Rights Act and, at a more symbolic level, in the establishment of a national holiday honoring the birthday of Martin Luther King, Jr.

Blacks remain, however, a numerical minority in a democratic political system. According to figures compiled by the Joint Center for Political Studies, blacks still hold less than 2% of all elective offices (*Washington Post*, June 9, 1985, p. A5). Thus, the ballot box and conventional politics generally have not always been the most effective means for blacks to achieve their political ends. Political gains have frequently required protest or "insurgent politics" (Eisinger, 1974; Lipsky, 1968; McAdam, 1983; Morris, 1984). Indeed, civil rights came to be viewed as the nation's most important problem during the height of nonviolent black protest and mass demonstration, roughly 1963–1965 (Smith, 1980), and for the entire decade from 1960 to 1970 concern about race issues ranked second in public concern and media coverage, following concern about the war in Vietnam (Funkhouser, 1973). Moreover, the passage of key legislation (the Civil Rights Act of 1964 and the Voting Rights Act of 1965) was closely linked to major protest efforts and the sense of crisis and urgency they created (Brauer, 1977; Burstein, 1979; Garrow, 1978; Lawson, 1976; McAdam, 1983; Zashin, 1978). In sum, many of the crucial gains that blacks have made came through the establishment of effective political networks and organizations of their own (Morris, 1984) and through protest politics. The historical record of black recourse to insurgent politics is underscored by blacks' tendency to feel alienated from white society (Schuman & Hatchett, 1974; Turner & Wilson, 1976), to express fairly high levels of power discontent and group consciousness (Gurin, Miller, & Gurin, 1980; Pitts, 1974; Shingles, 1980), and to endorse protest and demonstration as legitimate political tools (Bobo, 1985; Eisinger, 1974; Isaac, Mutran, & Stryker, 1980; Robinson, 1970).

One of the important changes that laid the cultural groundwork for the civil rights struggle of the 1950s and 1960s was the discrediting of theories of biological racism. A general shift away from notions of distinct "races" and theories of "social Darwinism" began in the 1920s (Gossett, 1963, Chapter 16; Sitkoff, 1978, Chapter 8). This trend accelerated in the 1930s and 1940s in response to Nazi Germany's racism. These changes in ideas were readily applied to the "Negro problem" in the United States (Sitkoff, 1978, p. 190). One of the clearest examples of the ultimate impact of this changing cultural attitude toward "prejudice" is the often hotly debated Footnote 11 to the *Brown* decision which cites the Clarks' doll selection studies (1947) and Myrdal's *An American Dilemma* (1944) as substantiation of the fact that discrimination and prejudice had damaged black children (Wilkinson, 1979).

Not only did academe turn against notions of biological racism, but much of the propaganda in the United States during World War II portrayed racism as inherently antidemocratic. As Woodward (1974) noted, "American war propaganda stressed above all else the abhorrence of the West for Hitler's brand of racism and its utter incompatibility with the democratic faith for which we fought" (p. 131). This ideological struggle bore clear relevance to the place of blacks at that time and became an important basis for appeals to end segregation (Woodward, 1974, pp. 130–134).

Any complete explanation of racial attitudes must attend to this backdrop of real social inequalities between the races, the presence of black political organization and activism, the existence of protective legislation, the disrepute accorded notions of biological racism, and the rhetoric of American democracy. The first of these considerations means that whites, on average, have a real stake in maintaining race relations as they are and no benefits to gain by implementing equal opportunity policies. Therefore, they remain ahead by resisting further change. The four latter considerations set limitations on the ways in which inequality can be culturally justified or defended. A belief system that tends to espouse only constrained or "bounded" racial change has resulted. In addition to racial prejudice, it is argued here that this set of beliefs reflects the operation of several specific group-conflict motives as well as a larger ideological process. In general, it is the expectation of group conflict theory that whites, as members of a dominant group, will tend to develop and adopt attitudes and beliefs that defend their privileged, hegemonic social position. Such an ideology, however, emerges and functions within the limitations set by the current social structure and cultural milieu.

GROUP CONFLICT MOTIVES AND RACIAL ATTITUDES

Group conflict is not an inevitable outcome of structural inequality. For this reason, study of the social-psychological processes through which conflict emerges is needed. In particular, empirical study of the role of group conflict in racial attitudes and ideology requires a specification of the attitudinal forms that group conflict motives assume.

Previous research has taken a variety of approaches. Sherif (1966) examined the effects of a competitive situation on perceptual processes and in-group cohesion and explored the effects of superordinate goals on the reduction of intergroup tensions. More recently, Tajfel and Turner (1979) provided an empirically grounded theoretical statement on the role of group identity and social comparison processes in group conflict. Yet, Blumer's observation (1958a) that racial attitudes involve a sense of group position provides the most direct starting point for the present argument. Blumer suggested that racial attitudes consist of a feeling of in-group superiority, a sense of a proprietary claim to certain resources, and a sense that the out-group poses a threat to the position of the in-group. Each of these attitudes is a social product, and taken together, they constitute a sense of group position.

A handful of empirical work has sought to document the effects of the sense of group position on racial attitudes. Drawing on in-depth interviews with several prototypical respondents from a survey of San Francisco Bay area residents, Wellman (1977) found that whites frequently objected to large-scale racial change. These objections, he concluded, were not grounded in a form of prejudice but appeared to serve as a defense of group privilege. Smith's analysis (1981) of national survey data for the period 1954–1978 showed that whites' willingness to send their children to integrated schools varied substantially with the number of blacks involved. He found that "whites of all regional, cohort, and educational attainment groups share a common self-interest in their unwillingness to accept minority dominance" (p. 569). Bobo's reanalysis (1983) of data used in two papers on symbolic racism showed that attitudes toward the black political movement were important determinants of whites' position on school busing. These effects were interpreted as evidence of group conflict because attitudes toward black activists involved a sense of political threat. Relatedly, Giles and Evans (1984) also treated attitudes toward the black political movement as a form of perceived racial threat. They cautioned, however, that such questions do not bear a simple relation to objective status characteristics. Other research points to an increasing element of status threat in white racial attitudes, especially among otherwise liberal whites (Caditz, 1976). There is also research indicating that economically vulnerable whites respond more negatively to black protest (Ransford, 1972), as well as to other racial attitude questions (Cummings, 1980), than do whites of higher economic status.

These investigations have not, however, aimed to provide a general definition of group conflict attitudes or to elaborate on the various forms that such attitudes may take. Toward this end, it is suggested that group conflict motives are attitudes directly concerned with the competitive aspects of group relations and attempts to alter those relations. They concern the distribution of scarce values and resources between social groups, as well as attempts to affect the process and pattern of their distribution. More specifically, three types of attitudes reflect group conflict motives: perceptions of incompatible group interests, perceptions and evaluations of relative group standing (fraternal deprivation), and perceived threats or challenges to group interests. Each type of attitude invokes a sense of in-group position vis-à-vis an out-group, and yet, these attitudes are not primarily expressions of intergroup affective orientations or trait beliefs about an out-group (stereotypes).

To elaborate, perceptions of incompatible group interests concern the extent to which groups are perceived as having conflicting interests and objectives. In addition, they concern beliefs about the group benefits (and consequences) of proposals for change. Very general questions of this type might take the following form: "As blacks move ahead economically, more and more whites fall behind." Kluegel and Smith (1983) provided evidence that a question concerning the zero-sum structure of economic opportunities is related to white attitudes toward affirmative action. More specific questions could concern the differing political objectives of blacks and whites, or beliefs about who is helped or hurt by policies like school busing or affirmative action.[5]

Fraternal deprivation involves a sense that one's membership group is at a disadvantage with respect to a particular out-group (Runciman, 1966; Vanneman & Pettigrew, 1972; Williams, 1975). As treated here and elsewhere (Sears & Kinder 1985), this type of attitude involves a direct expression of satisfaction or dissatisfaction with the position of the in-group along some dimension (power, wealth, or status) relative to an out-group. This sort of attitudinal expression has also been termed a *group grievance* (Isaac *et al.*, 1980; Useem, 1980, 1981) and a *form of power discontent* (Aberbach, 1977; Gurin *et al*, 1980). Considerable evidence suggests that such group-level discontents played an important role in the black urban unrest of the late 1960s (Abeles, 1976; Caplan & Paige, 1972), as well as in reactions to other social movements (Guimond & Dube-Simard, 1983), and in white voting for black candidates for political office (Vanneman & Pettigrew, 1972).

Perceptions of incompatible group interests and fraternal deprivation are attitudes focused on the structure of group relations; that is, they concern the conditions and characteristic features of group relations. Perceived threat, in contrast, concerns reactions to the primary sources or agents of pressure for social change. Attempts to alter the structural relations between groups may come from the actions of specific individuals or groups, or from broad and diverse social movements. To the degree that a social movement commands widespread, sustained media coverage, elite attention, and public salience, the response of the mass public becomes an indicator of perceived threat.

For example, blacks or Jews could be asked about their reactions to groups like the Ku Klux Klan or neo-Nazi organizations. Or to take a less extreme case, respondents could be asked to evaluate groups like ROAR or BUSTOP (antibusing groups that formed in Boston and Los Angeles, respectively). Importantly, there should be a group basis to such evaluations. As some have suggested, "The experience of threat is not entirely an individual matter. The self-conception is made up of group memberships, and the individual is threatened whenever an important membership group seems to be the object of threat" (Turner, 1969, p. 821). Groups or social movements seeking social change can be

---

[5]In the context of U.S. race relations, both whites and blacks have reason to minimize concern about conflicting group interests. As Jackman and Muha (1984) argued, it is to a dominant group's advantage to avoid the introduction of explicitly hostile or competitive perceptions, as doing so would damage the potential for amicable, paternalistic relations. Similarly, a subordinate group, especially one that is a numerical minority, can more readily base an appeal for change in the language of common values and fairness, than in the language of redistributing resources like wealth and power. Insofar as both dominant and subordinate group members have reason to minimize their conflicting interests, questions concerning incompatible group interests may not result in strong racial polarization in response, and such questions may have weaker relations than the other group conflict motives to racial policy attitudes.

attitude objects. Indeed, social protest has been conceptualized as a communicative process that aims, among other things, not only to affect specific targets but to address and influence the larger bystander public (Lipsky, 1968; Turner, 1969). Insofar as the groups are real and seek concrete objectives, for some they may represent a voice for desired ends, whereas for others they constitute a threat to important values and interests. The extent to which reactions to such movements are realistic then becomes an empirical question.

Research on political tolerance has addressed this point. Sullivan, Piereson, and Marcus (1982) found that blacks and Jews (and other liberal whites) tended to feel threatened by right-wing extremist groups such as the KKK, whereas more conservative whites tended to feel threatened by left-wing groups. Interestingly, Sullivan *et al.* found little differences between the correlates of perceived threat among blacks and Jews as compared to other whites, even though the two former groups presumably confronted more real-world external threats. The data do not rule out a purely psychological basis for feelings of threat; indeed, some of the open-ended comments reflect simple prejudice (Sullivan *et al.*, 1982, pp. 165–175), but it appears that, on the whole, people are capable of realistically assessing threats to what they take as their values and interests. Shamir and Sullivan (1983) provided cross-national data (for the United States and Israel) that also indicate that expressions of perceived threat are based more in real-world politics than in psychological insecurity or projection.

Research by Bobo (1985) is more directly concerned with threat in the racial context. Using national survey data, he examined changes between 1964 and 1980 in the attitudes of blacks and whites toward the black political movement and the correlates of such attitudes. The trend analysis indicated significant differences between blacks and whites in patterns of change over time. Although both groups appeared to respond to the ebb and flow of actual black-protest activity, the trajectory of change suggested important group-interested differences. White attitudes moved from a clear rejection of black activism during the tumultuous 1960s to a more moderate stance by the late 1970s. For example, 51% of whites in 1980 said that blacks were pushing for change at "about the right speed," an increase of 26% from 1968. Fully 63% of blacks interviewed in 1964 felt civil rights leaders were pushing "at about the right speed." That figure had dropped to 49% by 1980, as more and more blacks expressed the feeling that things were moving "too slowly." In addition, the degree of racial polarization on this item was quite striking. For example, in 1964, 74% of whites said blacks were moving "too fast," compared to only 9% of blacks, a difference of 65 percentage points. The trend analysis was supplemented with data on the correlates of a measure of perceived threat. Bobo found that general (nonracial) beliefs about social protest, along with indicators of the perceived incompatibility of group interests and fraternal deprivation, were strong predictors of the level of perceived threat. Indeed, these effects were substantially independent of intergroup affective orientations, political conservatism, and other background-control variables. The full set of results suggests that, to a considerable degree, attitudes toward the black political movement index concern with a real-world social-protest movement that attempted to affect the distribution of rights and resources between blacks and whites.

There is an implicit structure to the group conflict motives described above. This structure is depicted in Figure 1. As the model indicates, perceptions of the general structure of group relations (perceptions of incompatible group interests) precede a sense of fraternal deprivation. The latter, in turn, is related to the level of perceived threat. Perceived threat, among the group conflict motives, should be the most direct determinant of racial policy attitudes (attitudes toward policies like affirmative action or school busing). Indeed, Bobo (1985) found that, among the three types of group conflict motives, only perceived threat had a direct effect on attitudes toward government intervention on

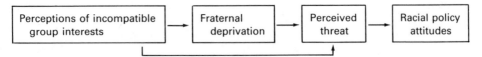

FIGURE 1. Heuristic model of the structure of group conflict attitudes and their relation to racial policy attitudes.

behalf of black interests. There should, however, be important feedback dynamics. Insofar as increased external threat serves to increase perceived threat, the latter should enhance feelings of fraternal deprivation, which, in turn, should exacerbate the perception that groups have incompatible group interests. This is not to argue that conflict invariably breeds greater conflict. Open dispute can activate a number of processes that facilitate negotiation and compromise (Williams, 1965, 1977).

CONFLICT AND POSITIVE CHANGE

Open conflict and dispute can effectively dramatize a groups' grievances (see Morris, 1984, pp. 268–269, for a striking example.) Himes (1966) argued that racial conflict can lead to greater recognition and more meaningful consideration of racial problems. Indeed, as Turner (1969) argued, without some form of protest or threat to the status quo, the grievances of a minority group might go unnoticed. Challenge and conflict can also create a bargaining atmosphere and can foster greater mutual respect among antagonists (Killian & Grigg, 1971).

With respect to attitudes and attitude change, Riley and Pettigrew (1976) found that dramatic political events led to a positive change in racial attitudes. They reported data on the attitudes of white Texans before and after Eisenhower's decision to send troops into Little Rock, Arkansas, in 1957. They also had data collected shortly before and after the assasination of Martin Luther King, Jr. Despite some countervailing movement among those with initially negative attitudes, both occurrences produced overall positive shifts on pertinent racial attitudes. In the case of the attitudinal impact of the assasination of Dr. King, Riley and Pettigrew were able to rule out the possibility of simply having captured a preexisting trend by comparing two preoccurrence surveys, separated by several months, that showed no changed. Crain and Mahard (1982) found that open dispute and conflict preceding the implementation of school desegregation not only fostered more positive attitudes among black students, but generally improved the school racial climate. In terms of national survey data, Schuman et al. (1985) reported that change in the attitudes of individuals (as opposed to change resulting from cohort replacement) toward greater support of racial principles was more characteristic of the turbulent 1960s than of the quiescent 1970s.[6]

[6]It is instructive to consider the possible positive effects of open conflict through an analogy to interpersonal relations. Within any ongoing dyadic relationship, there may be unacknowledged matters of strain or tension. Sometimes, these unacknowledged problems (e.g., an inequitable division of household chores or child-care duties between husband and wife) lead to serious feelings of grievance and exploitation on the part of the person shouldering the greater burden. The point at which the problem is directly confronted (e.g., the wife tells her husband that she is performing an unfair share of the household chores) may be highly emotional and unpleasant. One person's claim to being a good and fair person is being challenged. As a result, both individuals may dislike and avoid the "unmasking" encounter itself (Scanzoni, 1972, pp. 61–102; Speigel 1968). However, the problem situation will continue if it is not openly addressed. In short, an unwanted and potentially unpleasant encounter may be needed to compel recognition of a problem. With respect to racial issues and conflict, many whites may disapprove of the system-challenging actions and demands of black activists, but dialogue and progress are less likely without them.

IDEOLOGICAL HEGEMONY AND RACIAL ATTITUDES

The ideas and research summarized above not only suggest ways in which group conflict enters into racial attitudes but also suggest that racial attitudes may serve ideological purposes. Recent sociological theories of ideology have made use of Gramsci's concept of ideological hegemony (Gitlin, 1980; Gramsci, 1971; Williams, 1973). Ideological hegemony is said to exist when the ideas of one group dominate or exert a predominant influence on the major cultural and social institutions (Fermia, 1975, p. 29; Williams, 1960, p. 587). These ideas explain social reality—in particular, inequalities between social groups—in a manner that defends and justifies such inequalities. A dominant group is truly hegemonic when people of all stations in life, dominant and subordinate, accept the vision of society as espoused by the dominant group. In this respect, Gramsci's notion of hegemony corresponds to Marx's dictum (1964) that "the ideas of the ruling class are, in every age, the ruling ideas" (p. 78). Gramsci, however, added an element of exchange and indeterminancy that elevates the role played by human subjectivity. For Gramsci, the economic base of society creates rough boundaries on ideas but does not predetermine or directly create ideological belief systems (the "superstructure").

In fact, Gramsci held that there may exist contradictory elements within an ideological belief system and that such contradictions often reflect the differing interests of social groups (Fermia, 1975, p. 37). Similarly, Jackman and Senter's work (1983) on group images in the race, gender, and class contexts emphasized that social groups are engaged in a process of exchanging ideas and interpretations. They are involved in efforts, within the existing social and cultural institutions, to influence and control one another.

On the basis of these observations, the present argument maintains that dominant group attitudes and beliefs involve a strain toward, or a pursuit of, hegemony. A dominant group seeks to articulate a set of beliefs that persuades themselves, as well as others, that their privileged status is for the general good. Within the context of racial relations, this tendency is aptly characterized as the pursuit of racial hegemony.

This ideological process is the product of the confluence of social structural conditions (inequality and segregation) and the effects of long-standing group identities; that is, the ideological element in racial attitudes is a product of the interaction of inequality and ethnocentrism. As used here, the term *ethnocentrism* refers to a sense of positive in-group distinctiveness and commitment (Van den Berghe, 1967; Williams, Dean, & Schuman, 1964) not emotional hostility toward an out-group. Together, these factors establish a set of group interests and motivate a particular direction for attitudes, beliefs, and interpretations.

Although dominant groups do attempt to propagate ideas that secure and advance their interests, such ideas seldom reign without some challenge from subordinates, difficulties introduced by unanticipated political or economic exigencies, or the influence of other internalized attitudes and values that might weaken or contradict the ideological commitment of dominant group members. As concerns an analysis of changing racial belief systems in the United States, blacks mounted a strong political challenge to their subordination in the 1950s and 1960s based on a direct appeal to the general values— what Myrdal (1944) termed the "democratic creed"—of the dominant group. They were facilitated in this effort by a number of changing conditions. A massive migration of blacks from the rural South to the North (Farley, 1968) enhanced their political influence (Lawson, 1976; Myrdal, 1944; Sitkoff, 1971, 1978) and increased their economic and social freedom. Also, by this time, many of the ideas used to justify black subordination were clearly on the defensive in academe and in the rhetoric of many prominent political figures. A unanimous U.S. Supreme Court authoritatively repudiated racial segregation. For a period of time, especially during the middle through the late 1960s, an era that some have characterized as a Second Reconstruction, the courts, Congress, and the executive branch appeared to be engaged in a coordinated effort to secure and protect the rights of blacks (Brauer, 1977). The high degree of unanimity at the level of national leadership provided legitimation for many of the changes blacks were demanding. As a practical political matter, moreover, many of the changes initially demanded by blacks had their focus on *de jure* segregation and discrimination in the South (Woodward, 1974; Zashin, 1978). The combination of these occurrences resulted in considerable external pressure, both political and cultural, and internal value-based pressure to support the ideals of racial equality and integration (see Katz, 1967, for a similar point).

At the same time, there was initially little reason for northern whites to believe that adherence to these principles would require any changes in their own position in society or that of their children. But as the issues shifted fom largely southern problems of state-imposed segregation and voting hindrances, to economic and other redistributive issues of national scope (e.g., school busing, affirmative action, and the economic decline of urban areas), many whites no doubt came to sense a greater threat to their position in life. This sense of threat was probably amplified by the use of political slogans like Black Power (Aberbach & Walker, 1970) and the urban unrest of the late 1960s (Ashmore & Del Boca, 1976). Group conflict and ideological processes have thus contributed to the gap between support for racial principles and support for full implementation of such principles, that is, to the development of an ideology of bounded racial change.[7]

The general process is summarized in Figure 2. To recapitulate, conditions of inequality and ethnocentrism establish conflicting group interests, which, in turn, translate into interpretive tendencies on the part of dominant and subordinate group members. These interpretive tendencies favor group interests. But as Figure 2 makes clear, the final outcome, the prevailing state of intergroup attitudes and beliefs, is influenced by exchanges between dominant and subordinate groups, by relevant cultural values and beliefs (e.g., equality and fairness), and by other aspects of the patterning of group relations (e.g., the extent and type of the contact between the group members, the past history of competition and conflict, and the clarity of group boundaries).

PROGRESS AND RESISTANCE REVISITED

At many points in U.S. racial history, those advocating more progressive racial attitudes did not necessarily express an overarching commitment to full racial equality (Turner & Singleton, 1978). For instance, many early opponents of slavery opposed it as a moral evil. All the same, they shared with their slave-owning contemporaries a belief that blacks and whites could not exist as equals in the same society. These people tended to become active participants in colonization movements (i.e., efforts to find a new homeland for blacks; see Fredrickson, 1971a). Similarly, there were liberal as well as conservative politicians in the South after the fall of Reconstruction who were not rabid "Negrophobes," but who nonetheless were committed to preserving white hegemony (Woodward, 1974). Only the radical populists proposed anything near coequal part-

---

[7]The process described here can be understood in terms of Katz's functional theory of attitudes (1960). In particular, the substantial and growing support for the racial principles of integration and equality may occur because these attitudes increasingly serve a value-expressive function for the respondents. Such questions speak in more abstract terms to important cultural values, such as individualism and equality. Questions on implementation, however, speak to more concrete social and policy change. As a result, the low levels of support for implementation imply a larger utilitarian element in such attitudes. Questions regarding principles and implementation evidently address different motivational needs of respondents. The former tap into general values, whereas the latter tap a concern about group position.

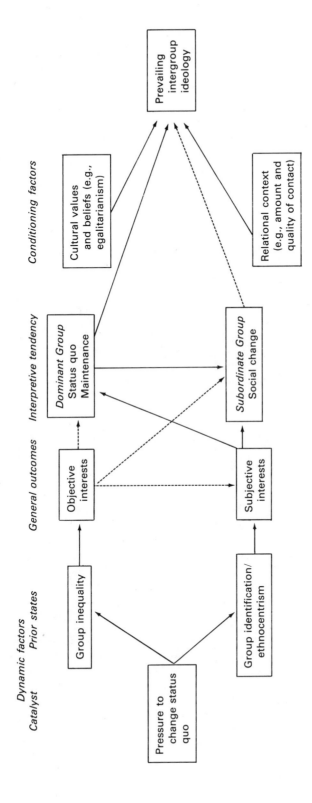

FIGURE 2. Schematic representation of the ideological hegemony process. ------ = Influences; --------- = strong influences.

nership with blacks as part of their efforts to coalese the poor masses. Indeed, as Woodward (1974) suggested, the threat posed to economically and politically powerful whites by this potential coalition was a critical factor in the rise of Jim Crow laws and practices.

Two historically important examples of the admixture of positive and negative racial beliefs are to be found in the beliefs of Thomas Jefferson and Abraham Lincoln. Jefferson's writings indicate that he believed black enslavement to be at odds with the U.S. Constitution; yet, he personally owned many slaves. In a letter to a friend, Jefferson spoke about his own attitudes toward slavery: "You know that nobody wishes more ardently to see an abolition not only of the [African slave] trade but of the condition of slavery; and certainly nobody will be more willing to encounter every sacrifice for that object" (Takaki, 1979, p. 43). Although recognizing the contradiction and agonizing over it, Jefferson kept most of his slaves. In addition, there is evidence suggesting that he treated his slaves brutally (Takaki, 1979, p. 44), and Jefferson was perhaps the first American to venture the speculation that blacks were inherently less intelligent than whites (Jefferson, 1972; see also Takaki, 1979, pp. 47–50). As Fredrickson (1975) noted, Lincoln also held complex, contradictory views on race. He had been one of the strong advocates of colonization as a way to solve the race problem; in general, he felt that whites and blacks could not exist as civil equals in the same country. The motives of both men appear to have come from a combination of prejudice—in particular, a distaste for the mixing of black and white races—and an ideological commitment to the white control of major social and political institutions (Fredrickson, 1975; Takaki, 1979).

The acceptance of some progressive racial ideals—in the above examples, an objection to black slavery—did not guarantee a deep commitment to a racially equal and fully integrated society. In the past, such disjunctures or contradictions in belief have involved both prejudice and group-interested ideology. It seems likely that the inchoate ideology of bounded racial change evident in contemporary racial attitudes also involves such a combination of motives.

PREJUDICE AND RACIAL ATTITUDES

DEFINITIONS

Prejudice is a term that is often used synonymously with simple "bias" (see the discussion in Ehrlich, 1973). But it is also invoked as a motive force in explaining such occurrences as the rise of black slavery in the United States (Degler, 1959; Jordan, 1968). In its more formal social-psychological use, prejudice has generally been "thought of as irrationally based, negative attitudes against certain ethnic groups and their members" (Pettigrew, 1982, p. 28). Or as others have put it, prejudice is "an emotional, rigid attitude . . . toward a group of people" (Simpson & Yinger, 1972, p. 24). Prejudice, then, is an emotional antipathy based on an inaccurate and rigidly held stereotype (see Allport, 1954, pp. 6–10).

Recent research has treated stereotyping as a cognitive process separable from affective orientations toward an out-group (see Ashmore & Del Boca, 1981; Brewer & Kramer, 1985; Miller, 1982). There is considerable evidence suggesting not only that stereotypes, or some simplified cognitive structure that aids information processing, are necessary, but that stereotypes can be fruitfully studied without a concern with prejudice (see essays in Hamilton, 1981). Yet, an affective orientation toward a group is to be regarded as a prejudice only to the degree that it is based on an underlying inaccurate stereotype that resists modification (Allport, 1954; Seeman, 1981). There may, in fact, be real differences between groups that inform the images people hold of one another and the evaluations they make (Campbell, 1967). For that reason, affective hostility alone, in the absence of an exaggerated or *faulty* stereotype, may not be a form of prejudice.

Symbolic Racism

A theory of prejudice labeled *symbolic racism* has been applied to the gap between principles and implementation. The theory and concept have been defined and elaborated upon on several occasions, and some important differences have emerged among its various advocates (compare Kinder & Sears, 1981, to McConahay, Hardee, & Batts, 1981). One central definition was provided by Kinder and Sears (1981), who argued that symbolic racism involves

> a blend of antiblack affect and the kind of traditional American moral values embodied in the Protestant Ethic. Symbolic racism represents a form of resistance to change in the racial status quo based on moral feelings that blacks violate such traditional American values as individualism and self-reliance, the work ethic, obedience, and discipline. (p. 416)

It is argued that socialization to negative feelings toward blacks merges with other basic values to form psychological resistance to contemporary proposals beneficial to blacks as a group. Thus, the gap between principles and implementation is evidence of, or an aspect of, the emergence of a new form of prejudice. Older forms of antiblack sentiment (segregationist attitudes and beliefs) are being replaced by a new symbolic racism (opposition to school busing). The symbolic racism researchers assert that the amalgam of antiblack affect and traditional values is a new form of prejudice best understood from the perspective of a new "sociocultural theory" of prejudice. There are several reasons to question this account of the gap between principles and implementation and, more specifically, to note that, in a number of critical featues, symbolic racism does not depart from more traditional conceptions of prejudice.

First, symbolic racism is a theory of prejudice (see also Brewer & Kramer, 1985). The proponents of the concept do not venture to explicitly differentiate the concept and/or theory of symbolic racism from the notion of prejudice as traditionally defined. Instead, it is argued that symbolic racism cannot be indexed by "old-fashioned" or passé racial beliefs (Kinder & Sears 1981; McConahay *et al.*, 1981). The main point of differentiation from prejudice, then, is at the level of measurement, not at the level of theoretical development. In addition, the symbolic racism researchers also make frequent use of the terms *prejudice* and *intolerance.* Kinder and Sears (1981, p. 416) explicitly argued that symbolic racism is a variant of prejudice. McConahay *et al.* (1981, p. 577) contended that their "modern" or symbolic racism scale definitely measured an aspect of prejudice.

The main interpretive frame of the symbolic racism researchers also emphasizes the nonrational origins of opposition to implementing racial change. This is a distinctive feature of theories of prejudice (see Wellman, 1977, pp. 14–15). The main tests of symbolic racism have the aim of demonstrating two things: (a) that rational self-interest and group conflict do not influence attitudes toward school busing (McConahay, 1982; Sears, Hensler, & Speer, 1979; Sears, Lau, Tyler, & Allen, 1980) or voting against a black candidate for political office (Kinder & Sears, 1981); and (b) that some measure of racial attitudes and political conservatism does predict such attitudes.

As a result, it might be expected that the concept of symbolic racism would be operationalized with questions concerning clearly emotional and stereotyped orientations toward blacks. The general strategy, however, has been to rely on questions concerning a number of contemporary racial problems and disputes, especially attitudes toward black political activism and influence. From the present perspective, when attitude questions concerned with black protest and political influence are used to index symbolic racism, a theory of prejudice has incorporated elements of group conflict and group conflict motives (Bobo, 1983). Questions that explicitly invoke concern about real-world political actors and events, and that arguably tap a dominant groups' sense of political threat from a contentious subordinate group, are being treated as indicators of prejudice.

Second, and more broadly, a strong case can be made that white racial attitudes have long involved some degree of less positive affect toward blacks than toward whites and a belief that blacks lack certain positively valued traits to be found in whites (e.g., industriousness, a capacity for hard work, and most of the qualities associated with the Protestant Ethic). Johnson (1949) pointed out that, after the Civil War, an ideology of laissez-faire individualism developed in the South as a way of justifying black subordination without the institution of slavery. These beliefs had clear origins in earlier proslavey doctrines. In particular, southern whites emphasized that blacks "would not work without compulsion" (Johnson, 1949, p. 130). This central claim had three subsidiary points:

> (1) The Negro needs the direction of the white man in order to be industrious and actually prefers it to supervision of another Negro; (2) without this supervision and compulsion the Negro degenerates; and (3) the Negro is inherently *lazy, shiftless, and licentious.* (Johnson, 1949, p. 131; italics added)

Takaki (1970) noted that, during the nineteenth century, whites in the North and the South regarded blacks as lacking the Protestant qualities of hard work, obedience, and restraint that they (the whites) possessed. Whites in the nineteenth century viewed blacks, he argued, as a peculiar mixture of children, who needed paternal protection and guidance, and savages, who required constant monitoring because they might engage in violence, crime, or sexual debauchery. All in all, Takaki (1970) concluded:

> The image of the Negro served a need shared by whites, North and South; it performed an identity function for white Americans during a period when they were groping for self-definition. It is significant to note the way whites imagined the Negro in relation to themselves: the Negro was mentally inferior, naturally lazy, childlike, unwholesome, and given to vice. He was the antithesis of themselves and of what they valued: industriousness, intelligence, and moral restraint. (p. 42)

Takaki (1979) broadened and refined this point is his later work. There, he began with Gramsci's notion of hegemony and argued that whites have, since the American Revolution, striven to differentiate themselves from others. This differentiation has served to provide a source of identity and, crucially, played a part in the pursuit of various self- and group-interested ends (i.e., the taking of Indian lands, the enslavement of blacks, discrimination against Oriental laborers, and so on).

More concretely, the attitudes and beliefs of Thomas Jefferson provide a vivid example of how certain values became linked to a justification of white privilege. Jefferson argued that the United States should be a fundamentally new nation based on republican values. This ideology of republicanism held that the character and fate of a nation rest not so much on wealth and power, as was the case in Europe, as on the degree of value consensus and the public virtue of its citizenry. Virtue was a product of reason, self-reliance, industriousness, and moral restraint. These qualities, of course, were viewed as more characteristic of whites than of blacks (Takaki, 1979, p. 64). Although slavery, with the enormous power it gave one person over the life of another, introduced temptations that might weaken adherence to these values, the gravest threat to republicanism came from the same forces that threatened the institution of slavery. For Jefferson, the increasing industrialization and commercialization of the North, along with the attendant pressures for a stronger federal government that would further facilitate these developments, would only undermine the southern way of life and republican values. The pastoral character of the farm and the plantation were, in his view, most conducive to the maintenance of virtue. Thus, despite Jefferson's moral discomfort with slavery, many of his letters, speeches, and other writings would become a basis for certain secessionist, states' rights, and proslavery positions. Indeed, like many other southern whites, according to historian Robert Shalhope (1976), "Jefferson clung to an ideology—to a way of life with identity and meaning in a changing world—which rested on slavery. The exploitation of the black was legitimized in terms of preserving higher values—a republican society" (p. 556).

Historians are not the only researchers to have pointed to whites' sense of themselves as a group endowed with valued traits that were absent or underdeveloped in blacks. A classic work in the empirical prejudice-stereotyping tradition (Katz & Braly, 1933) found laziness to be one of the primary traits attributed to blacks.[8] Campbell (1967) noted that salient differences between groups, especially in highly valued traits (i.e., industriousness and moral restraint), are likely to be a central focus of group stereotypes. Additionally, concern with such perceived trait differences between groups continues to inform more contemporary research on group images (Jackman & Senter, 1983).

It is possible, however, that the distinguishing feature of contemporary prejudice, and hence of symbolic racism, is the concern with black "pushiness" expressed in white attitudes. This concern about the illegitimacy of blacks' demands may be what sets current prejudice apart from older manifestations of prejudice. Although the expressions of concern about black demands and their legitimacy are more widespread—perhaps for concrete historical reasons, namely, a nationally oriented civil rights movement covered by national news media—this type of racial attitude is by no means an entirely new occurrence (see Rudwick, 1967; Wilson, 1980). For example, Rudwick (1964) explained that, in the Chicago riot of 1919, the Detroit riot of 1943, and especially the East St. Louis riot of 1917,

> unskilled whites manifested tension after they considered their jobs threatened by Negroes. There was also concern because [recent black] migrants had overburdened the housing and transportation facilities. Everywhere, efforts of Negroes to improve their status were defined as arrogant assaults, and whites insisted on retaining competitive advantages enjoyed before the Negro migration. (p. 218)

The connection between the white public sentiment in these riot-torn cities of the early twentieth century and today's prevailing racial attitudes is the presence of some pressure or demand for change presented by blacks. The concern with black "pushiness," then, could plausibly be viewed as part of a dominant group's attempt to interpret subordinate group challenges as illegitimate, and yet to do so in a manner that offers an ostensibly principled defense of a privileged group position (Jackman & Muha, 1984).

The upshot of this is twofold. First, racial attitudes in the United States, at least for the past 150 years, have involved a blend of antiblack affect and traditional moral values. Indeed, theories of prejudice have been routinely concerned with intergroup affect and stereotyping, that is, with feelings and beliefs about the traits of group members. Second, the perception of some trait difference between blacks and whites can and has been used

---

[8]In addition, symbolic racism is in some respects similar to the authoritarian personality (Adorno, Frenkel-Brunswik, Levinson, & Sanford, 1950). Both Sears and colleagues and Adorno *et al.* have suggested that intergroup attitudes must be measured in subtle ways because blunt or coarse outgroup derogation is culturally unacceptable. Both have also argued that intergroup attitudes involve a considerable element of reverence for traditional values and political conservatism. In particular, Adorno *et al.*'s ethnocentrism scale and political economic conservatism scale and symbolic racism are motivated by quite similar ideas.

to rationalize a group advantage. As Jackman and Senter (1983) argued, perceived trait differences can serve the ideological needs of dominant groups.

Still, there remains the possibility that a substantial shift in the character of prejudice has taken place, thus creating a need for new measures of prejudice. The above comments suggest a different approach to explaining the changing content of racial attitudes. The major change between present-day attitudes and those characteristic of whites in the nineteenth century is that trait differences between blacks and whites are less likely to be viewed as inherent or of biological origin. As Schuman (1971) noted, "a considerable portion of the white urban population believes that the source of Negro hardships lie within Negroes themselves, but denies that this source is inborn and unchangeable" (p. 386; see also Apostle et al., 1983). That is, the predominant interpretation holds that the problem is blacks' level of motivation and effort, not their genetic endowment.

Jackman and Senter (1983) added, on the basis of an analysis of national survey data on group images concerning the traits of intelligence, dependability, and laziness, that most whites do not posit the existence of large, categorical differences between themselves and blacks. Instead, they tend to express only small, qualified distinctions in those traits that favor whites. These small and qualified differences, however, are given a strong negative evaluation. This evaluative overlay is sufficient to justify a dominant group advantage. Jackman and Senter explained that "the perception of small but derogatory differences represents a hardening line of defense against challenge" (p. 332).

These sorts of changes—though certainly, in part, the result of prejudice, as the symbolic racism researchers have effectively argued—are also driven by alterations in the economic, political, and social context. The image of blacks as permanently and categorically inferior to whites has been shorn of its economic, political, and social underpinnings. Blacks are no longer enslaved. Slave labor is not crucial to any aspect of the economy, and slavery is reviled throughout the world. Blacks are no longer segregated and discriminated against under the majesty of law as was the case during the reign of Jim Crow; nor do they engage in the symbolically humbling behaviors (e.g., passivity and accommodation) required under Jim Crow. On the contray, their legal right to full citizenship has been codified through legislation, legal interpretation, and the actions of administrative agencies. Moreover, blacks have more effective political power than they had in earlier periods. In view of these facts and the discrediting of notions of biological racism, it is understandably less common to find that the predominant mode of accounting for racial inequality involves genetic thinking and blatantly segregationist sentiments.

Insofar as important inequalities remain, it should be expected that new attitudes and beliefs, amenable to the current context, will begin to arise to explain and defend those inequalities. These new attitudes and beliefs emerge naturally from one group's "side" of social experience as they attempt to provide meaning and order in their lives. The bent of these emerging views will be such as to support a privileged group's hegemonic position. A key psychological basis for this tendency is the sense of group position. It has been suggested that the most persuasive argument for resistance to large-scale racial change in the present social context is an appeal to the value of individualism (Jackman & Muha, 1984). Policies that are premised on the recognition of group characteristics are resisted, ostensibly, because they violate the ideal of individualism.

At minimum, it seems unlikely that theories of prejudice alone can provide a full explanation of the contemporary paradox of racial attitudes. Indeed, the gap between principles and implementation suggests that racial attitudes have both positive and negative currents, a set of characteristics that on its face poses difficulties for a prejudice interpretation. The symbolic racism researchers have taken two slightly different positions on this problem. Kinder and Sears (1981) noted that "since the explicitly segregationist, white supremacist view has all but disappeared, it can no longer be a major political force" (p. 416). They asserted, however, that prejudice must still be operating, although in some new fashion. The task, then, is to conceptualize and measure the new manifestations of prejudice—hence, the notion of symbolic racism. As Kinder and Sears (1981) argued, "What has replaced [segregationist, white supremacist views], we suggest, is a new variant that might be called symbolic racism" (p. 416). From this point of view, support for racial principles is of little contemporary political consequence. McConahay et al. (1981) pressed this point further. They argued that whites can perceive the racist content of survey questions on racial principles and thus give the socially desirable response. New, modern racism items do not suffer from this contamination, McConahay et al. claimed, because people do not perceive the racist content of believing, for example, that blacks have too much political influence. In either treatment, the point is that prejudice has grown more sophisticated.

Although accurately describing an important change in the character of racial attitudes, both accounts are problematic. No sustained analysis of why this shift in attitudes has occurred is provided. If the root of the problem is a form of prejudice, then it is difficult to understand why there would be any pressure to change from segregationist attitudes to some newer, more relevant form of voicing an irrational hostility toward blacks. Furthermore, it is not entirely accurate to view segregationist beliefs and attitudes as merely a simpler, older form of prejudice (though many analysts have done so). The rise of white supremacist practices and ideology, especially the rise of segregation, although partially the result of prejudice, can also be traced to a combination of political exigencies (e.g., increased black voting and the Populist movement), cultural trends (e.g., social Darwinism), and the active protection of group interests (Cell, 1982; Fredrickson, 1971b; Woodward, 1974). According to Cell (1982), "Segregation is at the same time an interlocking system of economic institutions, social practices and customs, political power, law, and ideology, all of which function both as means and ends in one group's efforts to keep another (or others) in their place within a society that is actually becoming unified" (p. 14). Any new set of attitudes said to be derivative of segregationist attitudes may also reflect a group-interested ideology tailored to new circumstances. I suggest that a major contributor to the greater complexity of racial attitudes is the natural process of a dominant group's interpreting social events and proposals for change in a manner that allows the maintenance of its hegemony under very different structural (economic and political) and cultural conditions.

American historical experience and culture do make available, however, an unflattering image of blacks as lazy and dependent slaves, carefree minstrels, and potentially dangerous vagabonds. This image may even involve a deeply ingrained color complex that permeates Western society (Jordan, 1968). It must also be noted that this cultural baggage, though not as prominent or ubiquitous as it once was, is still dimly implicated in the racial attitudes of black and white Americans (Prager, 1982). In this more limited sense, the theory of symbolic racism rightly cautions us that prejudice has not vanished. Yet, the theory may exaggerate the importance of prejudice as such, especially insofar as attitudes toward black political activism are viewed as indicators of this concept.

If there had been no civil rights movement or urban riots, or if these events had gone without media coverage and sustained elite attention, then attitudes toward black activists and activism might well amount to an abtracted racial resentment. None of these conditions obtain. On the contrary, the mass media provided intensive coverage of black protest (Funkhouser, 1973; Garrow, 1978), the mass public developed fairly clear assessments of the aims of civil rights leaders (Sheatsley, 1966), and political leaders and institutions helped focus public attention on black grievances. Indeed, some have argued—and have provided data from national surveys that suggest—that the presidential elections of 1964 and 1968 served to make race one of the key features of conventional partisan political alignments and political thinking among the mass public (Carmines & Stimson, 1982). The recent designation of Martin Luther King's birthday as a national holiday has also served to embed more deeply in American culture an awareness of black protest as a vehicle for social change.

EMPIRICAL ASSESSMENTS

The empirical research on symbolic racism has resulted in several consistent findings and contributions to our understanding of racial attitudes. First, indicators of objective, tangible personal threats from blacks (e.g., living in an area where a busing plan is being implemented) do not predict related racial-policy attitudes (Bobo, 1983; Sears, Hensler, & Speer, 1979, 1980) or a willingness to vote for black candidates for political office. Second, other types of racial attitudes, in particular those concerning contemporary race problems (e.g., welfare dependency and crime) and black political activism, are the strongest predictors of opposition to policies and candidates likely to improve the status of blacks relative to that of whites. In addition, neither the contemporary race problem nor the black political activism attitudes appear to be related to measures of tangible personal threat. Third, measures of political ideology (self-identification as a liberal or a conservative) are also important predictors of racial policy attitudes and a willingness to support black political candidates. Fourth, and more broadly, this line of speech has helped to focus attention on some real changes in the character of white racial attitudes.

These clear-cut findings and contributions do not, however, firmly substantiate the main theory. Early research on symbolic racism treated prejudice as a single unitary dimension (Sears, Hensler, & Speer, 1979, 1980). Subsequent research has shown that racial attitudes have several reasonably distinct but correlated dimensions (Bobo, 1983). The most important of these dimensions for predicting school busing opposition is attitude toward black political activism.

This latter finding is congenial to a group conflict interpretation of racial attitudes once the conception of "interests" is broadened to include a sense of collective or group interest, with the latter indexed by measures of perceived threat. The symbolic racism researchers have typically conceptualized self-interest as a tangible personal risk. Yet, as others have noted (Bobo, 1983; Kluegel & Smith, 1983; Pettigrew, 1985), there are other viable conceptualizations of "interests" in an issue or outcome. The narrow definition preferred by the symbolic racism researchers is depoliticized and tends to overlook the potential for subjectively meaningful links between perceived collective and personal interests. Thus, the relationship between attitudes toward black political activism (perceived threat) and specific racial policy attitudes is plausibly interpreted as a manifestation of a group conflict. Indeed, research reviewed earlier—which showed substantial black–white polarization in attitudes toward the black political movement, racial differences in trends over time on such attitudes, and a clear relationship to other group-conflict and social-protest attitudes—argues in favor of group conflict approach (Bobo, 1985).

Still, prejudice plays a role. In particular, there is evidence suggesting that "old-fashioned" prejudice retains contemporary political relevance. McClendon (1985) reported a connection between support for school busing and traditional segregationist attitudes net of the effect of modern racism. Jacobson (1985) found similar results for affirmative action attitudes. It is not the case, in sum, that prejudice needs new avenues of expression.

CONCLUSIONS

Recent research has rekindled a focused controversy over the relative importance of group conflict and prejudice in racial attitudes and relations. The case for either interpretation should not be pressed too far. Racial attitudes are complex, involving affective orientations, stereotypes, modes of explanation, group conflict motives, and several other types of attitudes, values, and concerns. This chapter has had the goal of clarifying the distinctive contribution of group conflict and group conflict motives while stressing that prejudice and group conflict approaches are not mutually exclusive. As others have noted, one process can readily feed into the other (Allport, 1954; Williams, 1965). For the present, if there is a general conclusion to be reached, it is that, alongside our traditional concern with individual prejudice, we should recognize the importance of group conflict. In short, racial attitudes can simultaneously involve group-interested ideology and irrational hostilities.

At the beginning of this chapter I suggested that a core problem touched on in a broad range of social-psychologically oriented research on race is the problem of resistance to more profound forms of racial change. A loosely coherent set of attitudes and beliefs that, among other things, attributes continuing patterns of black–white inequality to the dispositional shortcomings of blacks themselves and the otherwise fair operation of the economic and political system has developed and now characterizes much of the white population. I labeled this nascent set of beliefs an ideology of bounded racial change because although it involves support for the extension of basic citizenship rights to blacks the ideology also involves vigorous opposition to change that might impose substantial burdens on whites.

The growing complexity and subtlety of racial attitudes and beliefs, which the ideology of bounded racial change clearly reflects, derives from a social context still characterized by considerable black–white economic inequality, limited black political empowerment, extensive residential segregation by race, other historical trends and the influence of enduring cultural values and beliefs. At the individual level, a number of social-psychological factors contribute to adherence to this ideology, especially a concern with group position that enters public opinion as perceptions of incompatible group interests, feelings of fraternal deprivation, and perceived threats posed by the black political actors who have pressured for social and political change.

REFERENCES

Abeles, R. P. (1976). Relative deprivation, rising expectations, and black militancy. *Journal of Social Issues, 32,* 119–137.
Aberbach, J. D. (1977). Power consciousness: A comparative analysis. *American Political Science Review, 71,* 1544–1560.
Aberbach, J. D., & Walker, J. L. (1970). The meanings of black power: A comparison of white and black interpretations of a political slogan. *American Political Science Review, 64,* 367–388.
Adorno, T. W., Frenkel-Brunswik, E., Levinson, D. J., & Sanford, R. N. (1950). *The authoritarian personality.* New York: W. W. Norton.
Allport, G. W. (1954). *The nature of prejudice.* Reading, MA: Addison-Wesley.
Allport, G. W. (1962). Prejudice: Is it societal or personal? *Journal of Social Issues, 18,* 120–134.
Apostle, R. A., Glock, C. Y., Piazza, T., & Suelzle, M. (1983). *The anatomy of racial attitudes.* Berkeley: University of California Press.
Ashmore, R. D., & Del Boca, F. K. (1976). Psychological approaches to understanding intergroup conflicts. In P. A. Katz (Ed.), *Towards the elimination of racism.* New York: Pergamon Press.
Ashmore, R. D., & Del Boca, F. K. (1981). Conceptual approaches to stereotypes and stereotyping.

In D. L. Hamilton (Ed.), *Cognitive processes in stereotyping and intergroup behavior.* Hillsdale, NJ: Erlbaum.

Berry, M. F. (1983). Blacks in predominantly white institutions of higher learning. In J. D. Williams (Ed.), *The state of black America.* New York: National Urban League.

Blackwell, J. E. (1982). Persistence and change in intergroup relations: The crisis upon us. *Social Problems, 29,* 325–346.

Blumer, H. (1958a). Race prejudice as a sense of group position. *Pacific Sociological Review, 1,* 3–7.

Blumer, H. (1958b). Recent research on race relations: United States of America. *International Social Science Bulletin, 10,* 403–477.

Bobo, L. (1983). Whites' opposition to busing: Symbolic racism or realistic group conflict? *Journal of Personality and Social Psychology, 45,* 1196–1210.

Bobo, L. (1984). *Racial hegemony: Group conflict, prejudice, and the paradox of American racial attitudes.* Doctoral dissertation, University of Michigan, Ann Arbor.

Bobo, L. (1985, August). *Racial differences in response to the black political movement.* Paper presented at the 1985 Annual Meeting of the American Sociological Association, Washington, D.C.

Bonacich, E. (1976). Advanced capitalism and black/white relations in the United States. *American Sociological Review, 41,* 34–51.

Brauer, C. (1977). *John F. Kennedy and the Second Reconstruction.* New York: Columbia University Press.

Brewer, M. B., & Kramer, R. M. (1985). The psychology of intergroup attitudes and behavior. *Annual Review of Psychology, 36,* 219–243.

Burstein, P. (1979). Public opinion, demonstrations and the passage of antidiscrimination legislation. *Public Opinion Quarterly, 43,* 157–172.

Caditz, J. (1976). *White liberals in transition: Current dilemmas of ethnic integration.* New York: Spectrum Books.

Campbell, D. T. (1967). Stereotypes and the perception of group differences. *American Psychologist, 22,* 817–829.

Caplan, N., & Paige, J. M. (1971). A study of ghetto rioters. *Scientific American, 219,* 15–21.

Carmines, E. G., & Stimson, J. A. (1982). Racial issues and the structure of mass belief systems. *Journal of Politics, 44,* 2–20.

Cell, J. W. (1982). *The highest stage of white supremacy: The origins of segregation in South Africa and the American South.* London: Cambridge University Press.

Clark, K. B. (1965). Problems of power and social change: Toward a relevant social psychology. *Journal of Social Issues, 21,* 4–20.

Clark, K. B., & Clark, M. (1947). Racial identification and preferences in Negro children. In T. M. Newcomb & E. L. Hartley (Eds.), *Readings in social psychology.* New York: Holt.

Coser, L. A. (1956). *The functions of social conflict.* New York: Free Press.

Crain, R. L., & Mahard, R. E. (1982). The consequences of controversy accompanying institutional change: The case of school desegregation. *American Sociological Review, 47,* 697–708.

Crosby, F., Bromely, S., & Saxe, L. (1980). Recent unobtrusive studies of black and white discrimination and prejudice: A literature review. *Psychological Bulletin, 87,* 546–563.

Cummings, S. (1980). White ethnics, racial prejudice, and labor market segmentation. *American Journal of Sociology, 85,* 938–958.

Degler, C. N. (1959). Slavery and the genesis of American race prejudice. *Comparative Studies in Society and History, 2,* 49–66.

Degler, C. N. (1960). Letters to the editor. *Comparative Studies in Society and History, 2,* 491–495.

Donnerstein, E., & Donnerstein, M. (1976). Research in the control of interracial aggression. In R. Green & E. O'Neal (Eds.), *Perspectives on aggression.* New York: Academic Press.

Ehrlich, H. J. (1973). *The social psychology of prejudice.* New York: Wiley.

Eisinger, P. K. (1974). Racial differences in protest participation. *American Political Science Review, 68,* 592–606.

Farley, R. (1968). The urbanization of Negroes in the United States. *Journal of Social History, 1,* 241–258.

Farley, R. (1977). Residential segregation in urbanized areas of the United States in 1970: An analysis of social class and racial differences. *Demography, 14,* 497–518.

Farley, R. (1984). *Blacks and whites: Narrowing the gap?* Cambridge: Harvard University Press.

Farley, R., Schuman, H., Bianchi, S., Colasanto, D., & Hatchett, S. (1978). Chocolate city, vanilla suburbs: Will the trend toward racially separate communities continue? *Social Science Quarterly, 7,* 319–344.

Farley, R., Bianchi, S., & Colasanto, D. (1979). Barriers to racial integration of neighborhoods: The Detroit case. *Annals of the American Academy of Political and Social Science, 441,* 97–113.

Fermia, J. (1975). Hegemony and consciousness in the thought of Antonio Gramsci. *Political Studies,* *23,* 29–48.

Fireman, B., & Gamson, W. A. (1979). Utilitarian logic in the resource mobilization perspective. In M. N. Zald & J. D. McCarthy (Eds.), *The dynamics of social movements.* Cambridge, MA: Winthrop.

Fredrickson, G. M. (1971a). *The black image in the white mind: The debate on Afro-American character and destiny, 1817–1914.* New York: Harper & Row.

Fredrickson, G. M. (1971b). Toward a social interpretation of the development of American racism. In N. I. Huggins, M. Kilson, & D. M. Fox (Eds.), *Key issues in the Afro-American experience* (Vol. 1). San Francisco: Harcourt Brace Jovanovich.

Fredrickson, G. M. (1975). A man but not a brother: Abraham Lincoln and racial equality. *Journal of Southern History, 16,* 39–58.

Frey, W. H. (1985). Mover destination selectivity and the changing suburbanization of metropolitan whites and blacks. *Demography, 22,* 223–243.

Funkhouser, G. R. (1973). The issues of the sixties: An exploratory study in the dynamics of public opinion. *Public Opinion Quarterly, 37,* 62–75.

Gaertner, S. L., & Dovidio, J. F. (1981). Racism among the well-intentioned. In E. G. Clausen & J. Bermingham (Eds.), *Pluralism, racism, and public policy: The search for equality.* Boston: G. K. Hall.

Gamson, W. A. (1968). *Power and discontent.* Homewood, IL: Dorsey Press.

Garrow, D. J. (1978). *Protest at Selma: Martin Luther King, Jr., and the Voting Rights Act of 1965.* New Haven, CT: Yale University Press.

Giles, M. W., & Evans, A. S. (1984). External threat, perceived threat, and group identity. *Social Science Quarterly, 65,* 50–66.

Gitlin, T. (1980). *The whole world is watching: Mass media in the making and unmaking of the new left.* Berkeley: University of California Press.

Gossett, T. (1963). *Race: The history of an idea in America.* New York: Schocken.

Gramsci, A. (1971). *Selections from the prison notebooks* (ed. and trans. by Q. Hoare & G. N. Smith). New York: International Publishers.

Guimond, S., & Dube-Simard, L. (1983). Relative deprivation theory and the Quebec nationalist movement: The cognition–emotion distinction and the personal-group deprivation issue. *Journal of Personality and Social Psychology, 44,* 526–535.

Gurin, P., Miller, A. H., & Gurin, G. (1980). Stratum identification and consciousness. *Social Psychology Quarterly, 43,* 30–47.

Hamilton, D. L. (Ed.). (1981). *Cognitive process in stereotyping and intergroup behavior.* Hillsdale, NJ: Lawrence Erlbaum.

Handlin, O., & Handlin, M. F. (1950). Origins of the southern labor system. *William and Mary Quarterly, 7,* 199–222.

Handlin, O., & Handlin, M. F. (1960). Letters to the editor. *Comparative Studies in Society and History, 2,* 488–490.

Harris, M. (1964). *Patterns of race in the Americas.* New York: W. W. Norton.

Himes, J. S. (1966). The functions of racial conflict. *Social Forces, 45,* 1–10.

Hochschild, J. L. (1984). *The new American dilemma: Liberal democracy and school desegregation.* New Haven, CT: Yale University Press.

Hyman, H. H., & Sheatsley, P. B. (1956). Attitudes toward desegregation. *Scientific American, 195,* 35–39.

Hyman, H. H., & Sheatsley, P. B. (1964). Attitudes toward desegregation. *Scientific American, 211,* 16–23.

Isaac, L., Mutran, E., & Stryker, S. (1980). Political protest orientations among black and white adults. *American Sociological Review, 45,* 191–213.

Jackman, M. R. (1978). General and applied tolerance: Does education increase commitment to racial integration? *American Journal of Political Science, 22,* 302–324.

Jackman, M. R., & Jackman, R. W. (1983). *Class awareness in the United States.* Berkeley: University of California Press.

Jackman, M. R., & Muha, M. J. (1984). Education and intergroup attitudes: Moral enlightenment, superficial democratic commitment, or ideological refinement? *American Sociological Review, 49,* 751–769.

Jackman, M. R., & Senter, M. S. (1983). Different, therefore unequal: Beliefs about trait differences between groups of unequal status. In D. J. Treiman & R. V. Robinson (Eds.), *Research in social stratification.* Greenwich, CT: JAI Press.

Jacobson, C. K. (1985). Resistance to affirmative action: Self-interest or racism? *Journal of Conflict Resolution, 29,* 306–329.

Jefferson, T. (1972). *Notes on the State of Virginia* (ed. by W. Peden). New York: W. W. Norton.

Johnson, G. (1949). The ideology of white supremacy, 1876–1910. In F. M. Green (Ed.), *The James Sprunt Studies in History and Political Science: Essays in southern history* (Vol. 31). Chapel Hill: University of North Carolina Press.

Jordan, W. D. (1962). Modern tensions and the origins of American slavery. *Journal of Southern History, 28,* 18–30.

Jordan, W. D. (1968). *White over black: American attitudes toward the Negro, 1550–1812.* New York: W. W. Norton.

Katz, D. (1960). The functional approach to the study of attitudes. *Public Opinion Quarterly, 24,* 163–204.

Katz, D. (1967). Group process and social integration: A system analysis of two movements of social protest. *Journal of Social Issues, 23,* 3–22.

Katz, D., & Braly, K. (1933). Racial stereotypes of one hundred college students. *Jouranl of Abnormal and Social Psychology, 28,* 280–290.

Katz, I. (1981). *Stigma: A social psychological analysis.* Hillsdale, NJ: Lawrence Erlbaum.

Killian, L., & Grigg, C. (1971). *Racial crisis in America: Leadership in conflict.* Englewood Cliffs, NJ: Prentice-Hall.

Kinder, D. R., & Sears, D. O. (1981). Prejudice and politics: Symbolic racism versus racial threats to the good life. *Journal of Personality and Social Psychology, 40,* 414–431.

King, M. L., Jr. (1967). *Where do we go from here? Chaos or community?* New York: Bantam.

Kluegel, J. R. (1985). If there isn't a problem, you don't need a solution: The bases of contemporary affirmative action attitudes. *American Behavioral Scientist, 28,* 761–787.

Kluegel, J. R., & Smith, E. R. (1982). Whites' beliefs about blacks' opportunity. *American Sociological Review, 47,* 518–532.

Kluegel, J. R., & Smith, E. R. (1983). Affirmative action attitudes: Effects of self-interest, racial affect, and stratification beliefs on whites' views. *Social Forces, 61,* 797–824.

Lawson, S. (1976). *Black ballots: Voting rights in the South, 1944–1969.* New York: Columbia University Press.

Linville, P., & Jones, E. E. (1980). Polarized appraisals of out-group members. *Journal of Personality and Social Psychology, 38,* 689–703.

Lipset, S. M., & Schneider, W. (1978). The *Bakke* case: How would it be decided at the bar of public opinion? *Public Opinion, 1,* 38–44.

Lipsky, M. (1968). Protest as a political resource. *American Political Science Review, 62,* 1144–1158.

Marx, K. (1964). Existence and consciousness. In T. Bottomore (Ed.), *Karl Marx: Readings in sociology and social philosophy.* New York: McGraw-Hill.

McAdam, D. (1982). *Political process and the development of black insurgency, 1930–1970.* Chicago: University of Chicago Press.

McAdam, D. (1983). Tactical innovation and the pace of insurgency. *American Sociological Review, 48,* 735–754.

McClendon, M. J. (1985). Racism, rational choice, and white opposition to racial change: A case study of busing. *Public Opinion Quarterly, 49,* 214–233.

McClendon, M. J., & Pestello, F. P. (1982). White opposition: To busing or to desegregation? *Social Science Quarterly, 63,* 70–82.

McConahay, J. B. (1982). Self-interest versus racial attitudes as correlates of anti-busing attitudes in Louisville: Is it the buses or the blacks? *Journal of Politics, 44,* 692–720.

McConahay, J. B., Hardee, B. B., & Batts, V. (1981). Has racism declined in America? *Journal of Conflict Resolution, 25,* 563–580.

Miller, A. G. (1982). Historical and contemporary perspectives on stereotyping. In A. G. Miller (Ed.)., *In the eye of the beholder: Contemporary issues in stereotyping.* New York: Praeger.

Morris, A. D. (1984). *The origins of the civil rights movement: Black communities organizing for change.* New York: Free Press.

Myrdal, G. (1944). *An American dilemma: The Negro problem and modern democracy.* New York: Random House.

Noelle-Neumann, E. (1974). The spiral of silence: A theory of public opinion. *Journal of Communication, 24,* 43–51.

Noelle-Neumann, E. (1984). *The spiral of silence: Public opinion-our social skin.* Chicago: University of Chicago Press.

Orfield, G. (1978). *Must we bus? Segregated schools and national policy.* Washington, DC: Brookings Institution.

Pettigrew, T. F. (1979). Racial change and social policy. *Annals of the American Academy of Political and Social Science, 441,* 114–131.

Pettigrew, T. F. (1982). Prejudice. In S. Thernstrom, A. Orlov, & O. Handlin (Eds.), *Dimensions of ethnicity: Prejudice.* Cambridge: Belknap Press (Harvard University Press).

Pettigrew, T. F. (1985). New black-white patterns: How best to conceptualize them? *Annual Review of Sociology, 11,* 329–346.

Pitts, J. P. (1974). The study of race consciousness: Comments on new directions. *American Journal of Sociology, 80,* 665–687.

Prager, J. (1982). American racial ideology as collective representation. *Ethnic and Racial Studies, 5,* 99–119.

Prothro, J. W., & Grigg, C. M. (1960). Fundamental principles of democracy: Bases of agreement and disagreement. *Journal of Politics, 22,* 276–294.

Ransford, H. E. (1972). Blue collar anger: Reactions to student and black protest. *American Sociological Review, 37,* 333–346.

Riley, R. T., & Pettigrew, T. F. (1976). Dramatic events and attitude change. *Journal of Personality and Social Psychology, 34,* 1004–1015.

Robinson, J. P. (1970). Public reaction to political protest: Chicago, 1968. *Public Opinion Quarterly, 34,* 1–9.

Robinson, R. V. (1983). Explaining perceptions of class and racial inequality in England and the United States of America. *British Journal of Sociology, 34,* 344–366.

Rodgers, H. (1975). On integrating the public schools: An empirical and legal assessment. In H. Rodgers (Ed.), *Racism and inequality: The policy alternatives.* San Francisco: Freeman.

Rogers, R. W., & Prentice-Dunn, S. (1981). Deindividuation and anger-mediated interracial aggression: Unmasking regressive racism. *Journal of Personality and Social Psychology, 41,* 63–73.

Rose, A. M. (1956). Intergroup relations vs. prejudice. Pertinent theory for the study of social change. *Social Problems, 4,* 173–176.

Rothbart, Myron. (1976). Achieving radical equality: An analysis of resistance to social reform. In P. A. Katz (Ed.), *Towards the elimination of racism.* New York: Pergamon Press.

Rudwick, E. (1967). *Race riot at East St. Louis, July 2, 1917.* New York: World Publishing.

Runciman, W. G. (1966). *Relative deprivation and social justice.* Berkeley: University of California Press.

Scanzoni, J. (1972). *Sexual bargaining: Power politics in the American marriage.* Chicago: University of Chicago Press.

Schuman, H. (1971). Free will and determinism in beliefs about race. In N. C. Yetman & C. H. Steele (Eds.), *Majority and minority: The dynamics of racial and ethnic relations.* Boston: Allyn & Bacon.

Schuman, H., & Hatchett, S. (1974). *Black racial attitudes: Trends and complexities.* Ann Arbor, MI: Institute for Social Research.

Schuman, H., Steeh, C., & Bobo, L. (1985). *Racial attitudes in America: Trends and interpretations.* Cambridge: Harvard University Press.

Sears, D. O., & Kinder, D. O. (1985). Whites' opposition to busing: On conceptualizing and operationalizing group conflict. *Journal of Personality and Social Psychology, 48,* 1141–1147.

Sears, D. O., Hensler, C. P. & Speer, L. K. (1979). Whites' opposition to busing: Self-interest or symbolic politics? *American Political Science Review, 73,* 369–384.

Sears, D. O., Lau, R. R., Tyler, T. R., & Allen, H. M. (1980). Self-interest or symbolic politics in policy attitudes and presidential voting. *American Political Science Review, 74,* 670–684.

Seeman, M. (1981). Intergroup relations. In M. Rosenberg & R. H. Turner (Eds.), *Social psychology: Sociological perspectives.* New York: Basic Books.

Shalhope, R. E. (1976). Thomas Jefferson's republicanism and antebellum southern thought. *Journal of Southern History, 42,* 529–556.

Shamir, M. & Sullivan, J. L. (1983). The political context of tolerance: The United States and Israel. *American Political Science Review, 77,* 911–928.

Sheatsley, P. B. (1966). White attitudes toward the Negro. *Daedalus, 95,* 217–238.

Sherif, M. (1966). *Group conflict and cooperation.* London: Routledge & Kegan Paul.

Shingles, R. D. (1980). Black consciousness and political participation: The missing link. *American Political Science Review, 75,* 76–91.

Simpson, G. E., & Yinger, J. M. (1972). *Racial and cultural minorities: An analysis of prejudice and discrimination.* (4th ed.). New York: Harper and Row.

Sitkoff, H. (1971). Harry Truman and the election of 1948: The coming of age of civil rights in American politics. *Journal of Southern History, 37,* 597–616.

Sitkoff, H. (1978). *A new deal for blacks: The emergence of civil rights as a national issue: Vol. 1. Depression decade.* New York: Oxford University Press.

Smith, A. W. (1981). Racial tolerance as a function of group position. *American Sociological Review, 46,* 558–573.

Smith, T. W. (1980). America's most important problem-A trend analysis. *Public Opinion Quarterly, 44,* 164–180.

Speigel, J. P. (1968). The resolution of the role conflict within the family. In N. W. Bell & E. F. Vogel (Eds.), *A modern introduction to the family.* New York: Free Press.

Stinchcombe, A., & Taylor, D. G. (1980). On democracy and school integration. In W. G. Stephan & J. R. Feagin (Eds.), *School desegregation: Past, present, and future*. New York: Plenum Press.

Sullivan, J.L., Piereson, J. E., & Marcus, G. E. (1982). *Political tolerance and American democracy*. Chicago: University of Chicago Press.

Taeuber, K. E. (1983a). *Racial residential segregation, 28 cities, 1970–1980* (Working Paper No. 83-12). Madison: University of Wisconsin, Center for Demography and Ecology.

Taeuber, K. E. (1983b). *Research issues concerning trends in residential segregation* (Working Paper No. 83-12). Madison: University of Wisconsin, Center for Demography and Ecology.

Taeuber, K. E., & Taeuber, A. F. (1965). *Negroes in cities: Residential segregation and neighborhood change*. Chicago: Aldine.

Tajfel, H., & Turner, J. C. (1979). An integrative theory of intergroup conflict. In W. S. Austin & S. Worchel (Eds.), *The social psychology of intergroup relations*. Monterey, CA: Wadsworth.

Takaki, R. T. (1970). The black child-savage in ante-bellum America. In G. B. Nash & R. Weiss (Eds.), *Race in the mind of America*. San Francisco: Holt, Rinehart, & Winston.

Takaki, R. T. (1979). *Iron cages: Race and culture in 19th century America*. Seattle: University of Washington Press.

Taylor, D. G. (1986). *Public opinion and collective action: The Boston school desegregation controversy*. Chicago: University of Chicago Press.

Taylor, D. G., Sheatsley, P. B., & Greeley, A. M. (1978). Attitudes toward racial integration. *Scientific American, 238*, 42–49.

Tilly, C. (1978). *From mobilization to revolution*. Reading, MA: Addison-Wesley.

Turner, C. B., & Wilson, W. J. (1976). Dimensions of racial ideology: A study of urban black attitudes. *Journal of Social Issues, 32*, 139–152.

Turner, J., & Singleton, R. (1978). A theory of ethnic oppression: Toward a reintegration of cultural and structural concepts in ethnic relations theory. *Social Forces, 56*, 1001–1018.

Turner, R. H. (1969). The public perception of protest. *American Sociological Review, 34*, 814–831.

U.S. Bureau of the Census. (1983). *Current population reports, Series P-60, No. 138, Characteristics of the population below the poverty Level: 1981*. Washington, DC: U.S. Government Printing Office.

Useem, B. (1981). Solidarity model, breakdown model, and the Boston anti-busing movement. *American Sociological Review, 45*, 357–369.

Van den Berghe, P. L. (1967). *Race and racism: A comparative perspective*. New York: Wiley.

Van Valey, T. L., Roof, W. C., & Wilcox, J. E. (1977). Trends in residential segregation: 1960–1970. *American Journal of Sociology, 87*, 826–844.

Vanneman, R. D., & Pettigrew, T. F. (1972). Race and relative deprivation in the urban United States. *Race, 13*, 461–486.

Wellman, D. T. (1977). *Portraits of white racism*. New York: Oxford University Press.

Wilkinson, J. H. (1979). *From Brown to Bakke, the Supreme Court and school integration: 1954–1978*. New York: Oxford University Press.

Williams, G. (1960, Oct.–Dec.). Egemonia in the thought of Antonio Gramsci: Some notes on interpretation. *Journal of the History of Ideas*, pp. 585–597.

Williams, R. (1973). Base and suprestructure in Marxist cultural theory. *New Left Review* (82), pp. 3–16.

Williams, R. M., Jr. (1965). Social change and social conflict: Race relations in the United States, 1944–1964. *Sociological Inquiry, 35*, 8–25.

Williams, R. M., Jr. (1975). Relative deprivation. In L. A. Coser (Ed.), *The idea of social structure*. New York: Harcourt Brace Jovanovich.

Williams, R. M., Jr. (1977). *Mutual accommodation: Ethnic conflict and cooperation*. Minneapolis: University of Minnesota Press.

Williams, R. M., Jr., Dean, J. P., & Suchman, E. A. (1964). *Strangers next door: Ethnic relations in American communities*. Englewood Cliffs, NJ: Prentice-Hall.

Wilson, W. J. (1973). *Power, racism, and privilege: Race relations in theoretical and sociohistorical perspective*. New York: Free Press.

Wilson, W. J. (1980). *The declining significance of race* (2nd ed.). Chicago: University of Chicago Press.

Woodward, C. V. (1974). *The strange career of Jim Crow* (3rd rev. ed.). New York: Oxford University Press.

Zashin, E. (1978). The progress of black Americans in civil rights: The past two decades assessed. *Daedalus, 107*, 239–262.

II

RACISM TOWARD BLACKS: HOW GENERALIZABLE?

6

Racism in Black and White

A Bicultural Model of Reaction and Evolution

James M. Jones

INTRODUCTION

Racism is an elusive, emotional, and historically pervasive fact of American society. In contemporary society, the problems heretofore viewed in the context of a historical legacy that includes involuntary slavery, constitutional denial of equal rights, legal support of second-class citizenship, and ubiquitous and various forms of physical, emotional, social, economic, and psychological exploitation and oppression of black Americans of African descent are now normalized as problems of equal opportunity for *minorities*. The use of the term *minority* denotes an expansive confluence of disadvantage associated with being different in any of numerous ways, including physical or mental disability, nonnormative sexual preference, the status of being an immigrant or refugee, aged, chronic poverty, and ethnicity characterized by color. In addition, being female, although not a condition of minority status, does often qualify for being included among the less advantaged.

Why are so many people disadvantaged? When we add up the numbers of people connected with the groups described above, surely they no longer represent a *minority* of Americans; yet, they still seem to share the characteristics of disadvantage. How is it that a *majority* of Americans are disadvantaged? The view taken here is that the racism developed and refined with regard to black Americans served as a spawning ground for the evolution of a society in which normative values ensure that *difference*, defined in a variety of ways, will be associated with disadvantage. It is further suggested that the most blatant difference that defined the initial problem of racism, black skin and its biological roots, further masked the more fundamental problem of a cultural ethos of invidious comparison and in-group preference.

The problems of racism in America are critically affected by the intersection of biological and cultural opposites (Jones, 1972, 1986b). Black against white defines in absolute terms the cultural differences between Africa and Europe around 1500. Those cultural differences continue, as do the values placed on their expression. Over the years, we have come to define *equality* in terms of biology, for example, skin color or sex. Thus, when it appears that the legal and constitutional aspects of biologically based disadvan-

JAMES M. JONES • Department of Psychology, University of Delaware, Newark, Delaware 19716.

tage have been eliminated or dramatically curtailed, many feel as though the problem has been solved (cf. Kleugel & Smith, 1986).

However, if the problem is based on cultural differences (i.e., ethnicity) *as well as* biological differences (skin color, features, etc.), then to eliminate color as a basis of discrimination solves only part of the problem. The remaining biases attributed to cultural features of group identification and in-group preference continue to exert powerful effects on the judgment of merit and on the allocation of resources.

In this multiethnic society, ethnicity and skin color are highly correlated, unlike in Europe and Africa, where ethnicity in general is independent of skin color. Thus, it is not always clear to what extent skin color and/or cultural characteristics form the basis of in-group identification or out-group discrimination. Thus, the reduction of color-based discrimination has an unknown impact on the practices of culture-based discrimination.

This chapter addresses the issue of the cultural dynamic in racism. It takes the model of blacks as generic to the understanding of the form, practice, and consequences of racism in America.

THE ROLE OF CULTURE IN RACISM

I have suggested that there are three forms of racism: *individual, institutional,* and *cultural* (Jones, 1972, 1986b). Of the three, cultural racism is the more subtle, insidious, and pervasive. Several different approaches to the concept of culture emphasize the human response to environmental circumstances. Kroeber and Kluckhohn (1952) suggested that

> culture consists in patterned ways of thinking, feeling and reacting, acquired and transmitted mainly by symbols, constituting the distinctive achievements of human groups, including their embodiments in artifacts; the essential core of culture consists of traditional (i.e., historically derived and selected) ideas and especially their attached values. (p. 86)

Hofstede (1980) considered culture "the interactive aggregate of common characteristics that influence a human group's response to its environment" (p. 25). Finally, Triandis (1976b) advanced the notion of *subjective* culture as a "group's characteristic ways of viewing the man-made part of its environment" (p. 3). Although the strict biological concept of race no longer enjoys support, a more practical definition was offered by van den Berghe (1967): "A group that is socially defined on the basis of physical (ie, biologically based) criteria" (p. 9). The concepts of *culture* and *race* are joined by van den Berghe in his definition of *ethnicity* as "A group that is socially defined on the basis of cultural criteria" (p. 9).

Black Americans represent a distinctive human group socially defined on the basis of *both* physical and cultural criteria. Historically, the physical criterion of skin color formed the basis of oppression and stigmatization. For many Americans, cultural characteristics were presumed to have biological roots. However, the reality of black culture includes collective and cumulative adaptation to social stigma, oppression, and racism. To the extent that blacks are perceived as a race, the criteria for culture tend to be ignored. To the extent that blacks are perceived as an ethnic group, the primary cultural criteria are those deriving from the common characteristics associated with their adaptation to an oppressive and stigmatizing environment.

In contemporary society, the focus has been on ameliorating those sources of discrimination and bias against blacks as a race. Therefore, the antidiscrimination clauses refer to race, color, or creed. To the extent that such "physical criteria" are no longer used as a basis for discrimination, the problem of racism *appears* to be gone. However, concern with cultural racism goes well beyond skin color in seeking to understand those adaptations to and characteristic ways of perceiving the environment that distinguish blacks and form the basis of continued disadvantage.

A recent summary of national statistics showing black–white gaps on nearly every indicator of social, economic, or physical well-being highlights the problem of black disadvantage (Jones, 1986b). In August, 1985, then Secretary of Health and Human Services Margaret Heckler introduced the final report of a governmental Task Force on Black and Minority Health (cf. Malone, 1985), noting that, whereas there had been a steady improvement in the overall health of U.S. citizens, *"there [is] a continuing disparity in the burden of death and illness experienced by Blacks and other minority Americans as compared with our nation's population as a whole"* (Heckler, 1985, p. ix).

For example, in 1900, life expectancy for the U.S. population was 47.3 years; by 1983, it had risen to 75.3 years. However, the life expectancy for blacks, although improving from 33 to 69.6 during this same period, continued to be 5.6 years shorter than that of the population as a whole. Similarly, infant mortality for blacks has declined by over half since 1960, falling from 44.3 deaths per 1,000 live births to 19.2 deaths in 1983. During this same period, however, the rate for whites fell from 22.9 to 9.7. Thus, over a 20-year period, the black–white infant-mortality ratio went from 1.93 to 1.98. The problem has become relatively worse.

Table 1 documents the relative mortality consequences of being black in America. Black men and women are at greater risk of death than whites by each of eight different causes.

These health disparities themselves suggest a problem in need of attention. However, the basic problem of ill health and mortality risk is exacerbated by the social perceptions that seek to account for them. Black inequality is largely seen by white Americans as a result of black individual inadequacy. Recent evidence shows that whites perceive that black–white economic discrepancies emanate *not* from structural barriers (discrimination, racism, etc.), but from black individual inadequacies (lack of motivation and ability; cf. Kluegel & Smith, 1986). The severity of racism and its cumulative contribution to the disadvantages represented by economic, social, educational, and health disparities is often understated or ignored. Thus, understanding black people and their culture is made more difficult by a failure to recognize the cumulative role that systematic oppression has played in their evolution.

It is customary in analyses of racism to focus on the problem of the racists: white

TABLE 1. Age-Adjusted Death Rates by Selected Cause, Race, and Sex, United States, 1980 (Rate per 100,000 Population)[a]

	Black male	White male	Relative risk	Black female	White female	Relative risk
Total deaths (all causes)	1,112.8	745.3	1.5	631.1	411.1	1.5
Heart disease	327.3	277.5	1.2	201.1	134.6	1.5
Stroke	77.5	41.9	1.9	61.7	35.2	1.8
Cancer	229.9	160.5	1.4	129.7	107.7	1.2
Infant mortality	2,586.7	1,230.3	2.1	2,123.7	962.5	2.2
Homicide	71.9	10.9	6.6	13.7	3.2	4.3
Accidents	82.0	62.3	1.3	25.1	21.4	1.2
Cirrhosis	30.6	15.7	2.0	14.4	7.0	2.1
Diabetes	17.7	9.5	1.9	22.1	8.7	2.5

[a] From M. M. Heckler (1985), *Report of the Secretary's Task Force on Black and Minority Health. Vol. 1. Executive Summary* (Table 5, p. 67) by M. M. Heckler, 1985, Washington, DC: Department of Health and Human Services.

people, institutions, or society. In the following pages, I will consider the problem of racism from the perspective of black Americans. Racism is a fact of great impact on the development of black people individually and collectively. To understand that evolution is, in part, to understand the dynamics of racism.

RACISM AND BLACK CULTURE

The first distinction to be made is that black culture can be viewed in both *reactionary* and *evolutionary* terms. That is, as Kroeber and Kluckhohn (1952) noted, culture is "considered as a product of action [and] as a conditioning element of future actions" (p. 181). Thus, the African legacy surely provided cultural conditioning for the actions required to survive slavery and subsequent oppression. In addition, the emergence of black culture was also a product of the experiences peculiar to slavery, oppression, and the related edifice of racism. The African legacy provides the *evolutionary* underpinnings of black culture, and the adaptations to the "peculiar institution" and subsequent centuries of oppression and systematic disadvantage account for its *reactionary* components.

REACTIONARY VIEW

This approach suggests that black Americans lost whatever culture they may have had in Africa, and that, if there is any black culture at all, it consists in the collective adaptations that blacks have made to a racist and oppressive society. Because many of these so-called adaptations are considered maladaptive in the larger society, a "culture-of-poverty" or "cultural-disadvantage" perspective describes this conception (Lewis, 1961).

EVOLUTIONARY VIEW

This view suggests that black culture represents the unfolding of a cultural core laid in an African past and characterized in function, if not form, across the cultures of the African diaspora.

Both of these elements of black culture place black Americans of African descent at risk in this society (Jones, 1979, 1985, 1986b). The added ingredient of *power*, a central element of racism that distinguishes it from other forms of bias such as prejudice and ethnocentrism, transforms the cultural legacy of British colonial racism and imperialism into an intricate pattern of racist control by

- Oppressing and dehumanizing blacks in ways that created a hostile, pernicious, and largely untenable environment to which they as a group had to adapt. That adaptation now is characterized by the "reactionary" perspective of black culture.
- Establishing a cultural context in which certain attributes and values (among them, white skin) were laid up as the standard of conduct and competence against which all alternatives were judged. Beginning with skin color, the black presence and cultural style were viewed as a persistent and deficient alternative.

If one believes that black culture has a significant evolutionary component deriving from an African legacy, just as black color clearly derives from that same legacy, then black Americans are disadvantaged not only by the color of their skin, but by the character of their culture.

There is one other perspective that needs to be considered. Cole (1970) suggested that black culture consists of three parts:

1. *Mainstream experience.* Blacks, like all citizens of this country, participate in the "American Way." Differences exist, to be sure, but we all "die and pay taxes," although some die sooner and some pay proportionately more in taxes!

2. *Minority experience.* The sense of being a numerical political or power minority is shared with other groups, such as, at varying times, other ethnic groups, poor people, women, and older people. When one is in such a situation, the concerns with powerlessness, discrimination, and disadvantage lead to feelings of distrust, vigilance, development of "political" personalities, and, often, common perspectives and experiences.

3. *Black experience.* Those experiences peculiar to being black in this society, comprised of both reactionary and evolutionary components, describe aspects of black culture that do not include features common to others. Cole (1970) included among these features *soul* (defined as "long-suffering") and *style* (described as individual patterns of expression). Thus, black culture consists of three dimensions of experience that provide points of contact with, as well as points of departure from, other groups. Trying to integrate these experiences in one person or culture presents what Boykin (1983) called the "triple quandary." At the least, black people must be bicultural to function effectively in this society. The challenge for a black person is to integrate the instrumentalities and expressiveness of two worlds when they are often in conflict with each other.

Cultural racism, then, represents black disadvantage on two counts. First, most ethnic groups (including the founding Anglos) have evolved in a cultural context predicated on exploiting opportunity for advancement and accomplishment in a basically meritocratic environment. This kind of evolution is contrasted with that of black Americans, whose cultural evolution occurred in a context of denial, limitation, and oppression. Survival in such a context required reactions to a hostile and unforgiving circumstance. If "How shall I survive this day?" is the measure of both possibility and accomplishment, needless to say, black Americans have been adapting to a very different environment from the one that now proclaims equality of opportunity for all.

Second, the characteristics of African culture appear, on most salient dimensions, to be not only *different* from those handed down through the western European colonization of America, but often *opposed.* Over the years, several writers have pointed to basic racial and cultural differences between blacks and whites. Usually, the differences noted reflect the view of black inferiority either by virtue of nature (e.g., intelligence) or nurture (e.g., "inability" to delay gratification or improvidence; cf. McDougall, 1921). I have identified five dimensions of human experience and predilection that seem most commonly associated with black–white differences; time perspective, rhythm, improvisation, oral expression, and spirituality. These dimensions of human experience provided the foundation of black survival because they were not only characteristic of Africans at the time, but precisely the kind of skills and predilections that enabled them to survive slavery and the ensuing centuries of oppression.

TRIOS

TRIOS is an acronym standing for these five dimensions of human experience: *T*ime, *R*hythm, *I*mprovisation, *O*ral expression, and *S*pirituality. The concepts emerged from an analysis of racial differences in sports performance (Jones & Hochner, 1973); African religion and philosophy (Jones, 1972; Mbiti, 1970); Trinidadian culture (Jones & Liverpool, 1976); and psychotherapy with black clients (Jones & Block, 1984).

These five dimensions reflect basic ways in which individuals and cultures orient themselves to living (see Figure 1). They refer to how we experience and organize life,

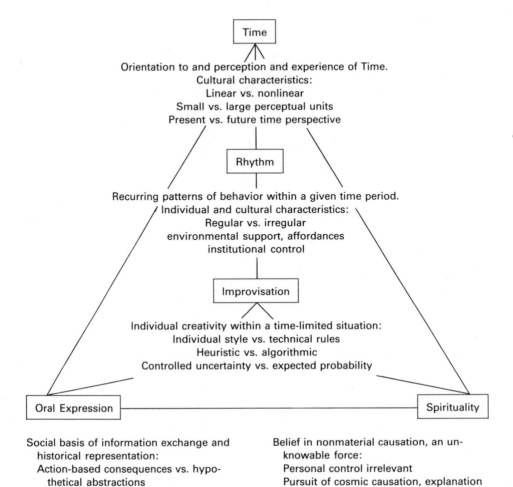

FIGURE 1. TRIOS: A quintet of cultural concepts.

make decisions, arrive at beliefs, and derive meaning. TRIOS is important because, on these dimensions of human experience, we will find divergences between the Euro-American and Afro-American perspective. The culture in which we live has evolved from the Euro-American perspective, but both have interacted and necessarily share in the fabric of contemporary culture. The matter is in part one of emphasis and preference.

TRIOS stands as a set of conceptualized dimensions of human perception and experience organized as a clustered "culture–personality" orientation. In considering the question of cultural differences, the dimensions of TRIOS are represented as two poles of possiblity. On one extreme is the materialistic, future-oriented, iconographic, individualistic profile of the hardworking, narrowly driven high-achiever. On the other extreme is the spiritual, present-oriented, orally expressive, socially responsive profile of the gregarious, flexible, easy-going, affectively driven person. These idealized polarities form the dialectical basis of cultural and personality synthesis. One model of this synthesis is biculturalism.[1]

[1]A detailed account of the essential features of each of the TRIOS elements is given in Jones (1986a).

BICULTURALISM IN BLACK AMERICANS: STRATEGIES FOR COPING WITH RACISM[2]

W. E. B. DuBois observed the facts of biculturalism among black Americans in his *Souls of Black Folk* (1903):

> After the Egyptian and Indian, the Greek and Roman, the Teuton and Mongolian, the Negro is a sort of seventh son, born with a veil, and gifted with second-sight in this American world,—a world which yields him no true self-consciousness, but only lets him see himself through the revelation of the other world. It is a peculiar sensation, this double-consciousness, this sense of always looking at one's self through the eyes of others, of measuring one's soul by the tape of a world that looks on in amused contempt and pity. One ever feels his twoness,—an American, a Negro; two warring ideals in one dark body, whose dogged strength alone keeps it from being torn asunder. (p. 214)

Racism is the veil, and biculturality is the struggle, the continuing adaptation to this ever-present reality.

As Blauner (1970) pointed out, one enduring and inescapable feature of black life and culture is the persistence of a political, moral, and psychological struggle against a system of oppression, denigration, denial, and disadvantage. Black heroes, not surprisingly, are always persons who have achieved some measure of success in that struggle, particularly when that success carries with it opportunities for other black people. In this light, the creation of a national holiday in honor of Dr. Martin Luther King, Jr., is a most significant accomplishment not only for black Americans, but for all American people. It stands as a symbol of the legitimate existence of black people in this country and, even more, of the recognition of the importance of a positive resolution of that struggle for human rights for the entire society.

It is significant also to note that Dr. King embodies a biculturalism of both style and accomplishment. His education was both within (Morehouse College) and outside (Boston University) the veil. His eloquence and oratory, from the preacher's pulpit to printed pages, capture another bicultural dimension.

Biculturalism, then, defines both a strategy for penetrating the veil and the cumulative behavioral and psychological consequences of those strategic enactments. However, there are clearly many different strategies and correspondingly different consequences. Two broadly conceived differences are discussed below.

BICULTURALISM AS A CENTRAL TENDENCY—THE MELTING POT

The central-tendency approach to biculturalism assumes that blacks adapt or acculturate to prevailing norms of performance, accomplishment, attitude, and behavior by incorporating aspects of the *Afro* and *American* features outlined above into a single constellation of ethnic and personality traits. The melting-pot view (Glazer & Moynihan, 1963) suggests that prevailing norms guide the incorporation of traits and behaviors toward a common instrumental purpose. Thus, if American-ness is viewed as including individualistic, future-oriented, goal-directed behavior, nuclear family constellations, cognitive and intellective expressions of intelligence, and so on, then this view suggests

---

The elaboration of the Time concept and its organizing role in black culture and personality is developed further in Jones (1986a).

[2]The biculturalism idea is quite similar to the concept of androgyny (Bem, 1974). In both cases, it is assumed that functional types of behavior can be characterized by gender or racial types but are also *independent* of those types. With biculturality, also, we find a tendency to draw distinctions between the *instrumental* and the *expressive* characteristics, the former being associated with whites and males, the latter with blacks and females.

that any and all ethnic groups should assimilate to these beliefs, values, and practices as a condition for advancement. The American overshadows the Afro in this case, and assimilationist strategies seem to be the inevitable outcome.

Writing a decade later, Glazer and Moynihan (1976) acknowledged that the ethnic foundation seemed to have become more important in recent years. Thus, ethnicity represented a strong statement of identity that was expressed by a

> sudden increase in tendencies by people in many countries and in many circumstances to insist on the significance of their group distinctiveness and identity and on new rights that derive from this group character. (p. 3)

These authors went on to note that

> doing without ethnicity in a society as its subgroups assimilate to the majority group may be as utopian and as questionable an enterprise as the hope of doing without social class in a society. (p. 5)

The strong insistence of ethnicity for black Americans came in the late 1960s as the "Black Power" or "Black Is Beautiful" movement. The important point to note is that the melting-pot or central-tendency approach presented a central option, apparently adopted by both sides. As Cleaver (1968) noted then, you were either part of the problem or part of the solution. Thus, ethnicity was opposed to the melting pot. Black pride was opposed to assimilation. Integration was equated with assimilation and the loss of ethnic identity.

What is here referred to as the central-tendency approach is equivalent to the "nomothetic" approach to measurement. Its basic principle is that experience or capacity can be ordered across all people so that a single underlying dimension can be extracted. Thus, people may be compared one to the other on the degree to which they possess a given attribute. Trait psychology—indeed, scientific psychology—rests on the nomothetic properties of measurement and comparison.

The central tendency or nomothetic approach operates on three basic premises:

1. One can and does assign value to dimensions of human character and ability, based on the norms or values of society.
2. One can assess the standing of *every* citizen along these dimensions.
3. One can evaluate the *merit* of citizens on the basis of the value assigned to the behavior and the standing one attains in its expression. This merit then becomes the basis for the allocation of rewards.

The central-tendency approach represents a majority-rule strategy by which normative expectancies often define acceptability. The most constantly enjoined expression and operation of such a central tendency is the testing movement, particularly the IQ test. It is assumed that intellective ability (IQ) is a major dimension of value, that IQ tests are valid measures of that ability, and that one can assign opportunity and allocate rewards on the basis of one's standing on that measure. The ongoing battles over testing point out, often in dramatic form, the operation of this approach and its negative as well as positive consequences.

BICULTURALISM AS VARIANCE: ETHNICITY

In contrast to the central-tendency approach, the variance model does not limit a person or group to a single expression of its standing on a dimension of value. Rather, one may be located at different places at different times, depending on situational, dispositional, and related factors. This approach to biculturalism assumes that the normative values and attributes are instrumental in the society and necessarily must be incorporated into any plan of advancement. It does not, however, assume that those culturally valued attributes must be expressed at all times, are enduring and permanent features of one's makeup, and govern the behavior of people over situations.

The variance approach is equivalent to the *idiographic* route to knowledge. It is predicated on the idea that a detailed analysis of individual experience can reveal important information about a person that cannot be obtained through some normative comparison. If the nomothetic analysis is deductive, the idiographic approach is basically inductive. Whereas the former suggests the kind of person one ought to be to be successful in society, the latter suggests the kind of society that would evolve from the kind of people who make it up.

The problem of being a minority person in this society follows from the nomothetic or central-tendency bias, which defines positive values by comparison with the normative features of the society's majority people. Whereas the idiographic approach builds a view of society as the aggregation of the diversity of its members, the nomothetic approach dictates uniformity by its comparison of all to a common standard.

The idiographic approach identifies the aspects of traditional culture or ethnicity as those that are *expressive* of one's identity. It also takes into account those features of the broader society that consistently get rewarded and hence define the *meritocracy* (Herrnstein, 1971). The strategy, then, for an Afro-American bicultural person, is to identify and develop those instrumentalities, and to select the situations and contexts in which their expression may serve instrumental goals.

The Chinese in Hong Kong similarly draw a distinction between modernity and westernization. *Modernity* refers to the need to develop technologies that are instrumental for collective development and advancement in a modern technological world. Acknowledging the need for modernization is distinctly different from accepting the cultural values of individualism and competitiveness that are associated with modernity in the Western world. Therefore, the Hong Kong Chinese reject westernization while embracing modernity (Bond & King, 1985).

The variance approach, then, does not argue, for example, that blacks are present-oriented, and whites are future-oriented. Rather, this approach looks for the range of contexts and situations in which different styles or tendencies may be expressed. As a strategy for penetrating the veil, it is quite clear that one may adopt those behaviors that appear to be instrumental in a given situation, and that that identified situation then becomes an eliciting condition for the behavior in question. This variance approach is similar to how Snyder (1974) described high self-monitors. According to Snyder, high self-monitors are characterized by their desire to behave in ways that are situationally appropriate. Thus, their behavior would be expected to vary across situations in accordance with their perception of normatively appropriate behavior. This predicted increase in behavioral variability has been demonstrated in several studies (Snyder, 1981, 1983). Similarly, the notion of improvisation also implies a degree of situational variability driven primarily by an individual's feelings and immediate objectives.

The point to make regarding the central-tendency versus the variance approach is that the latter requires a contextual or situational analysis. When we discuss group differences, we must be clear that the two approaches being discussed here offer different accounts of observed group differences. If we consider a concept like temporal orientation, then, to the extent that future orientation is valued positively, and one's capacity or tendency is measurable, rewards will be allocated in response to behaviors that reflect that tendency. Thus, by a central-tendency analysis, members of a group that did not score high on the measure of that attribute would either fare poorly in competition for rewards or be obliged to make a *fundamental* change in their character over a period of time. Cultural assimilation seems to be a necessary consequence of the central-tendency approach.

By contrast, although there might be a measurable difference in future orientation between two groups, in the variance model the distributions are largely overlapping. That is, members of both groups behave in both future and present orientation ways. It may be that, over time, more members of one group behave in present-oriented ways than do members of another group. However, for any given situation, the large majority of persons in both groups have the capacity to make future-oriented decisions and to benefit from the consequences. Thus, individuals within these distributions have a bidirectional possibility that is situationally determined. Attempts to measure or assess one's standing on the dimension may fail to capture this behavioral flexibility if the measurement is done in a context that is judged inappropriate for the expression of this flexibility.

The cultural meaning attached to the decisions associated with the behavioral enactments defines the identify and personality of members of the group (Errington, 1984). Understanding the bicultural person necessarily requires understanding the strategies under which bidirectional movement occurs, including the eliciting conditions and the goals to which choices are made are tied.

The broad questions of acculturation often take on political urgency, as they seem to pit giving up one's heritage against making it in the system. In many respects, the central-tendency approach does tend to require this choice (I do not, however, regard this necessarily as a conscious choice). Thus, in this view, as one moves toward the opposite polarity, one necessarily moves away from the prevailing cultural orientation. This movement is not required in the variance or idiographic model. One might further assume that, other things being equal, natural expression occurs within one's "primary" culture, whereas the majority culture may hold the key to instrumental behaviors. It may be, further, that aspects of one's own expressive culture take on instrumentality in the majority culture (e.g., Richard Pryor and Eddie Murphy have successfully exploited their indigenous cultural experiences for great public gain). The variance model allows one to move back and forth across cultures to develop and maintain a duality in terms of both values and behavioral styles. Thus, the prevailing tendency in social and behavioral science to take a nomothetic approach to racial and ethnic differences fails to capture the more subtle complexity of the situationally based variance model of biculturalism.

REMEDIES FOR RACISM

For black Americans, racism has been a fact of life for over three centuries. The systematic exploitation, oppression, and discrimination has been not only a constant companion of daily living but a statutory barrier to normality. What Myrdal (1944) called the *American Dilemma* is the ambivalence and hypocrisy that black coping strategies must address.

There is a peculiar double jeopardy that characterizes the black situation in America. The American dilemma is a dilemma for blacks as well, being, perhaps, of even greater magnitude than for whites. This country was built with the substantial assistance, commitment, and sacrifice of black people. It has emerged as a leader in human rights around the world, in part because of the human rights struggles that have taken place on this soil. Black Americans feel that their rights in this society, cannot be legislated, granted, or bestowed: they are *birth rights*.

The legacy of racism, slavery, and oppression is one that is not easily calculated. Surviving such a brutal and pernicious system required adaptations of myriad and subtle consequences. Distrust and suspicion were reinforced at every turn. The limitation of such distrust on development and motivation can only be conjectured at this point, but it surely must include both the realy explanation for failure and the preemption of effort.

Nevertheless, blacks have struggled, advanced, and contributed consistently to the greatness that is America—in spite of the ambivalence of knowing that one could die for the freedoms the country represents without having them for oneself. So perhaps it is the biculturalism idea that bridges this ambivalence gap. Perhaps it is continued distrust that maintains substantially segregated social relations even among those blacks who participate widely in the economic, political, and educational life of this country. Perhaps some variant of "separate and I'll take what I can get" is the solution adopted by black Americans, as well as by other disadvantaged groups. Racial integration is, to some extent, an inevitable consequence of widening opportunities, but it is not necessarily a goal of social engineering or racial advancement.

Black Americans continue now to combat racism, and its remedies follow several different courses. It is convenient to organize considerations of remedial approaches around the forms of racism I have discussed earlier: individual, institutional, and cultural.

INDIVIDUAL RACISM

There continue to be large numbers of whites who believe that black people as a group are inferior. Some believe this is a biological condition and cite IQ test scores as evidence. Others believe that it is a condition of cultural evolution and cite reactions to oppression and slavery as the culprits. Still others do not necessarily assert black inferiority verbally but *behave* as if they believed it. We might label these types of racist feelings as *dominative, aversive,* and *symbolic,* respectively (cf. Gaertner & Dovidio, 1986a; Kovel, 1970; McConahay, 1986; McConahay & Hough, 1976).

In general, each of these characterizations of individual racists is based on negative racial attitudes. The remedies, in general, involve changing these attitudes. The basic ways in which attitude change has been attempted by social psychologists have been through interracial contact under conditions that promote positive association (cf. Stephan & Brigham, 1985, and Miller & Brewer, 1984, for recent reviews and empirical analyses of the status of the concept). The evidence suggests that, when positive interracial contact is promoted in cooperative group contexts and is sanctioned by relevant authority in situations where a meaningful exchange of relatively personal or individualistic information is possible, there is likely to be positive attitude change (e.g., Braddock, 1985; Miller, Brewer, & Edwards, 1985). It has also been demonstrated that, when contact is promoted and the conditions are not right, negative consequences can occur (cf. Epstein, 1985).

One of the assumptions of the contact hypothesis is that ignorance and negative inaccurate stereotyping preempt the ability to perceive people as individuals instead of as members of a group that is different. Thus, contact, when properly arranged, can reduce the inaccuracies and, it is apparently implied, can demonstrate that the different group is less different than might have been assumed from a distance.

To the extent that blacks and whites are similar (want the same things and agree on the best ways to get them), contact might well prove to be a major procedure for reducing individual racism. Indeed, Cook (1985) reported several years of research on interracial contact that support not only the notion that interracial attitudes (liking, for example) become more positive but, perhaps more important, majority group members are more likely "to extend the implications of the equality principle to members of outgroups not previously included" (p. 6). The implication of this finding is that interracial contact may extend the boundaries of the in-group to include people who are members of what previously had been considered the out-group. Because the application of justice principles is characteristically reserved for (or at least is disproportionately applied to) in-group members, this result is probably more significant than the simple racial attitude or stereotype changes (cf. Gaertner & Dovidio, 1986b).

However, interracial contact does not always reveal racial similarity. To the extent that groups have differing agendas, styles of behaving, and so on, the contact may promote a sense of difference rather than similarity. The net effect of the increased salience of group difference has not been systematically explored.

The neoconservative reaction to the Johnson agenda for civil rights continues, and conflict between earlier supporters of the black civil rights struggle and black leaders is a major impediment to contemporary black progress. This reaction is widespread as a rejection of the methods by which racial inequities are reduced (affirmation action, business set-asides, busing, and so on). Whereas the policy of the Reagan administration has been to dismantle these remedies for inequality, the white citizens of this country perceive that the remedies are sufficiently effective to warrant their view that there is no residual discrimination that is not more than compensated for by these remedies (Kleugel & Smith, 1986).

It is therefore not surprising that interracial contact *per se*, even under the favorable conditions proposed by the contact hypothesis, may not necessarily reduce racist attitudes. It may, in some cases, exacerbate them.[3] The fact that continued institutional discrimination, predicated in part on historical disadvantage and an operational philosophy that is inherently disadvantageous to groups that were not involved from the beginning, complicates the matter.

In general, individual racists are portrayed as the dominative type (Kovel, 1970), virulent, emotional, and antiblack. However, recent work in intergroup relations and social cognition suggests that antiblack attitudes may be less a function of out-group discrimination than of in-group favoritism (Brewer, 1979), and that the racial stereotypes on which these attitudes rest may result from biases inherent in the cognitive processing of social information (Hamilton, 1986; Linville, Salvoey, & Fisher, 1986). This in-group preference is based in part on the tendency to want to preserve privilege, and also on the notion that similar others share positive attributes and values and thereby enhance our own sense of self-esteem (Tajfel & Turner, 1974).

The cognitive perspective emphasizes both frequency and familiarity. Thus, if a group to which one belongs is also a numerical majority, specific attributes observed among its members are not strongly associated with the fact of group membership. However, for numerically smaller groups, the observation of specific attributes in individual group members increases the likelihood that the attribute will be associated with group membership itself (Hamilton, 1986; Hamilton & Gifford, 1976).

The familiarity aspect of stereotyping is based on intergroup contact. The more contact one has with the members of a group, the more variation in behaviors is observed, and the more complex is the resultant schema of group characteristics (Linville *et al.*, 1986). This complexity of perception leads to more conservative attributions of *group-based* characteristics. In both the numerousness and familarity models, the out-group members tend to be perceived in more extreme ways, *either* more or less positively relative to in-group members. The critical determinant of which way the out-group mem-

---

[3]For example, the attempts to integrate the police and fire departments around the country with blacks, Hispanics, and women have created dramatic conflict in many cities. The simple fact is that the best interests of whites as a group, or individually, are not served by policies that serve the best interests of blacks as a group. At least, that is the short-term perception of many whites. The effect of contact in these situations is not positive.

ber will be perceived depends on the quality of the attribute or performance being judged. If it is positive, it becomes more positive. If it is negative, it also becomes more negative. The prevailing tendency to view black behaviors that reflect cultural difference as negative reinforces the tendency to evaluate black behavior in general in more negative ways.

Perhaps the key remedy to the biases conceived in this social cognition perspective revolves around a specific component of the intergroup contact idea. That is, as long as the groups continue to be perceived as different even though racial desegregation or even racial integration takes place, and as long as the central normative values of a color-blind but culturally biased judgment system is in place, group contact may not reduce bias as much as it could. However, when strategies are designed to make intergroup contact meet the conditions of reducing the salience of prior group boundaries, and correspondingly to make the in-group feeling of we-ness salient, then the powerful forces of the cognitive processing of social information, in-group favoritism, and self-enhancement can promote rather than undermine intergroup relations. Recent work along these lines (Miller & Brewer, 1986; Gaertner, 1985; Ashmore, 1985) has shown promising results.

The simple view of individual racism is of people who are ignorant, misinformed, and subject to stereotypical thinking and perception. The work of social psychology has been highly sophisticated in teasing apart these conditions and in developing theories to address them and applications that ameliorate this form of the problem. I would certainly applaud the continued research, development, and application of this scientific work as a tool for reducing individual racism.

INSTITUTIONAL RACISM

Institutional racism is not only more complicated but more pernicious than individual racism. Major institutions of the United States were conceived in a societal context that systematically exploited, oppressed, and generally remained unopen to black people. The result of such systematic practices is still not fully understood. To assume that two decades of still-grudging opportunity are sufficient to justify equal treatment regardless of race and historical injustices is patently unfair. This is not to argue that taking race into account will not prove unfair to certain people now, but from the perspective of institutional racism, the problem continues and even grows.

The problem of institutional racism was hailed by the Kerner Commission (1968) as the root cause of the riots of the 1960s and the growing schism between white and black society. The remedy put into place then was a systematic plan to force institutions (at least, those over whom the federal government had some control) not only to stop discrimination (which the legislation of the mid-1960s addressed) but to affirmatively reduce the gap caused by the government-supported conspiracies of previous centuries.

The critical aspect of institutional racism that distinguished it from prejudice and from individual racism was the notion that institutions can produce racist consequences whether they do so intentionally or not. The present administration has not only proposed to dismantle affirmative action but has already gone on record as supporting the idea that intentionality must be proved before institutional discrimination can be found!

Another critical point about institutional racism involves a historical consideration. Many immigrant ethnic groups (Cubans, Jamaicans, East Indians, Asians, etc) have come to this country and are in many cases doing better economically and even educationally than blacks. What these groups face when they arrive in this country is a range of opportunities that have been systematically denied black people over the years. Black society, at least many aspects of it, has been developed in a context of limitation, exploitation, and denial. That cumulative experience surely must take a toll on the motivation, expectation, and interpretation of opportunities. Again, we do not know what this cumulative legacy is, but it is surely implicated in the growing schism *within* black society. The fear that a permanent underclass of black urban dwellers is emerging is a legacy of institutional racism that the modest successes of blacks who have emerged in the middle class does not obviate. Moreover, the belief that the problems of the black underclass are economic and not racial again understates the cumulative effects of racism and their continuing role in this human tragedy.

Clearly, affirmative action is a critical remedy to institutional racism. It was so perceived by Lyndon Johnson and was so practiced, with significant positive results, for nearly two decades. Retrenchment of affirmative action can only be seen as throwing in with those who intentionally, or out of ignorance, fail to understand the depths of institutional racism and the cumulative effects that such discrimination has on the development and possibility of a people.

It is significant that American business has not been so quick as we might intuitively expect to join the anti-affirmative-action bandwagon. It acknowledges that the demographic trends in this society suggest that the ethnic minority groups will be a major portion of the work force from which to draw in the decades to come. If affirmative-action and equal-employment-opportunity programs can be made to work, they may well be foreseen as a strategy of preparing for the future. Like nearly every other systematic action designed to help minorities, these problems have positive implications for the entire society (Bell, 1973).

A related point concerns the utilization of human resources. The remedy to institutional racism, it seems to me, is the adoption of a strategy that assumes that basic capacities are normally distributed across known human groups. The failure to learn how to provide these groups with opportunities—and the failure to prevent them from succumbing to pernicious and unhealthy circumstances—is a failure of the entire society. We need all of our people, and to the extent that we do not provide for full participation, we fail as a nation. The nation failed when it operated in an open racist fashion. It continues to fail when it permits children to die, boys and men to go without work, youth to go uneducated, and women to be victimized by drugs and maintained by welfare. If we were as resolute in eliminating the despair and hopelessness that is a continuing legacy of institutional racism as we were in reaching farther and farther into space, or in maintaining our elegant *pas de deux* with the Soviet Union, we surely would have eliminated or at least controlled these problems. It does little good to blame the victims for their fate. It is also not useful to assume they have no role to play in the circumstances of their life.

But unfortunately, the problem of institutional racism is itself embedded in a larger problem: cultural racism. On January 14, 1986, Secretary of Education William Bennett conducted a class at a black elementary school in Atlanta, Georgia. His visit was part of the preparation for the first celebration of the national holiday honoring Dr. Martin Luther King, Jr. Bennett stated that he saw no conflict between his endorsement of the teachings of Dr. King and his administration's efforts to dismantle affirmative action. He put it this way:

> People of good will disagree about the means, [but] I don't think anybody disagrees about the ends . . . I think the best means to achieve the ends of a colorblind society is to proceed as if we were a colorblind society. . . . I think the best way to treat people is as if their race did not make any difference. (Sawyer, 1986, p. A8)

The idea of a color-blind society assumes that the problem is somehow biological. It asserts that there are no meaningful biological differences and that, therefore, race doesn't matter: we are all the same. Although race may not matter, culture does. We are not all the same, as we have evolved from and continue to evolve different cultural legacies. Schofield's analysis (1986) of a desegregated school argues persuasively that the maintenance of a color-blind society inhibits the acknowledgment of group differences, an inhibition that, in turn, precludes the successful adaptation of students to the desegregation context. Moreover, the school itself fails to benefit from the diversity of its constituent populations. Secretary Bennett considers the cultural tradition of Western civilization the common denominator for all U.S. citizens (Bennett, 1985). Although Bennett argued that *race* doesn't make a difference, he argued quite clearly that *culture* does make a difference.

It seems likely that Secretary Bennett would not support the idea that culture does not make a difference or that a culture-blind society was ideal. That cultural legacy is itself a guide to centuries of racial exploitation and oppression. For all of its positive and important features, that legacy is also the legacy of cultural racism.

CULTURAL RACISM

The concept of *cultural racism* represents a widespread confusion between biology and culture or ethnicity. Whether one is considering race or ethnicity, the salient factor is that the groups, however defined, occupy significant social positions in society. The social position occupied is consistently lower for minority than for majority groups. The reason for the lower position in society is *either* biological *or* cultural.

Historically, the problem of racism has been seen in biological terms. Black people of African descent were judged to be less capable than those of western European descent in nearly every sphere of performance, intelligence, judgment, and accomplishment. This belief served to justify continued oppression of blacks by whites individually, as well as systemically.

The change in racism over the years is perhaps best understood as a change in the degree to which this belief in biological inferiority has continued to provide the rationale for the discriminatory treatment of black Americans. To the extent that it is not normatively acceptable to believe in biological inferiority, it is believed that evidence of inferior social standing is based on maladaptive responses to this historical treatment. A belief in the development of a pathological *culture* (of poverty, oppression, or simple disadvantage) now provides the explanation for continued group disparities between blacks and majority whites.

The concept of *cultural racism* (Jones, 1972) has as its character the overlay of power onto ethncocentrism. That power has two components, equally significant but not equally understood. As Jordan (1969) noted concerning the early ethnocentrism of the English:

> [The consequence of] the Englishman's ethnocentrism tended to distort his perception of African culture in two opposite directions. While it led him to emphasize differences and to condemn deviations from the English norm, it led him also to seek out similarities (where perhaps none existed) and to applaud every instance of *conformity to the appropriate standard*. (p. 25; italics added)

Thus, the dual power to define difference as deficient and to reinforce conformity to prevailing standards is the essential character of cultural racism.

These two forms of cultural racism (disregarding difference and seducing similarity) both serve to homogenize the possibilities for black Americans. This is true not only for black but for all groups.

So who is the perpetrator of cultural racism? It is elusive because it is endemic to the culture. We believe, until something or someone comes forward to demonstrate otherwise, that there are certain relationships that increase the probability of goal attainment. We are an achieving society, so in some sense, the ultimate human values are those that are productive of (instrumental toward) the attainment of the goals we share. By and large, these goals have been defined in material terms.

The questions that an analysis of cultural racism must address are: What cultural differences are being denied or repressed, and if we can identify them, can we show that they could make a positive contribution to society? Arguments have been advanced against the concept of black culture on the grounds that a culture must form a basis for positive organization and advancement. It must contain elements of pride that are worthy of support. Critiques of the concept of black culture claim that there is nothing unique to black society that is worthy of support. When given opportunities, this analysis continues, blacks are not distinguishable in any important way from whites. From this perspective, perhaps institutional racism is the Maginot Line. Once it has been brought under control, racism as a problem will no longer exist. The present analysis of cultural racism suggests that this may not be the case.

One line of reasoning that I take as support for the cultural arguments is work in social influence (Latane & Wolf, 1981; Nemeth, 1986). The aspect of this work that is particularly important is the analysis of *both* majority and minority influence in social interaction. Nemeth (1986) drew the distinction clearly:

> In most studies comparing majority and minority influence, there is an emphasis on influence in the sense of "prevailing." Within this context, evidence exists that majorities exert more public influence and that minority influence when it occurs, tends to operate primarily at the latent level. [The present formulation argues that] differences between majority and minority influence are in fact more extensive once influence is considered in a broader context. In particular, it is proposed that exposure to persistent minority views fosters greater thought about the issue [which] tends to be divergent rather than convergent . . . and people tend to be better decision makers because they attend to more aspects of the situation and reexamine premises. By contrast, . . . exposure to persistent majority views fosters convergent thinking and leads to an unreflective acceptance of the majority position. (p. 23)

Although this portrayal of the influence of different perspectives on group decision-making describes a positive contribution of difference based on numerical and power asymmetries, it remains to be demonstrated that a similar positive consequence may accrue to interactions in other composite group situations.

CONCLUSION

The primary assumption of cultural racism is that our way is the best way; the majority rules, and tradition prevails. The antidote to this approach is the implementation of the principles of diversity, which recognize the biological idea that diversity promotes adaptability and increases genetic fitness and evolutionary success. The requirements for making positive strides in this area include:

1. Identifying the characteristics and capabilities of ethnic groups that derive from their evolution in and adaptation to the cultural context of discrimination and disadvantage. It is clear that the resourcefulness, inventiveness, and improvisation attendant on achieving in this society contribute to a resiliency that may be instructive of a wider range of human capabilities.

2. Learning how these characteristics may make a positive contribution to the attainment of the goals we generally share.

3. Providing interactional settings in which these majority and minority viewpoints and approaches can co-occur, so as to learn more about possibilities than a one-dimensional approach permits.

4. Conceiving participation patterns and valuations of them that do not stigmatize the minority relative to the majority contribution.

Enforced similarity may be as disadvantageous as the rejection of difference. The concept of pluralism is perhaps the best approach to understanding a society in which cultural racism is reduced. More particularly, the idea of *additive* multiculturalism (Triandis, 1976a; Chapter 3, this volume) is congruent with the idea advanced here that bicultural adaptation is a critical dimension of the black reaction to racism.

It is an important task to develop ways of incorporating diversity not only in the development of intergroup attitudes, but in the determination of a system for the allocation of resources. It is easy to reject color as a basis for the allocation of resources. However, being committed to a "color-blind" society does not solve the problem, as Schofield's analysis (1986) suggests. In reality, it is far more difficult to reject cultural differences in personality and behavioral style as bases of reward. The critical question of racism must go beyond the biological roots to confront the cultural question. The multidimensional model of human character and conduct is demanded in a multicultural society. Those who are and have been culturally different know this fact very well. Those who have enjoyed the advantage of defining the norm still have this lesson to learn.

Two basic beliefs are necessary to convert the problem of racism to our collective advantage:

- There is strength in diversity, and efforts to integrate the major institutions of this society will ultimately strengthen both the institutions and this society.
- We are no stronger as a nation than the weakest among us. We must therefore extend opportunity to all and, more than that, have the resolve to strengthen weakness and to eliminate human suffering and injustice wherever they are found.

REFERENCES

Ashmore, R. (1985). Sex stereotypes and implicit personality theory. In D. L. Hamilton (Ed.), *Cognitive processes in stereotyping and intergroup behavior.* Hillsdale, NJ: Lawrence Erlbaum.

Bell, D. (1973). *Race, racism and American law.* Boston: Little Brown.

Bem, S. L. (1974). The measurement of psychological androgyny. *Journal of Consulting and Clinical Psychology, 42,* 155–162.

Bennett, W. (1984). *To reclaim a legacy.* Washington, DC: Department of Education.

Blauner, R. (1970). Black culture: Myth or reality? In R. Whitten & J. Szwed (Eds.), *Afro-American anthropology.* New York: Free Press.

Bond, M. H., & King, A. Y. C. (1985). Coping with the threat of westernization in Hong Kong. *International Journal of Intercultural Relations, 9,* 351–363.

Boykin, A. W. (1983). The academic performance of Afro-American children. In J. Spence (Ed.), *Achievement and achievement motives.* San Francisco: W. H. Freeman.

Boykin, A. W. (1986). The triple quandary and the schooling of Afro-American children. In U. Neisser (Ed.), *The school achievement of minority children: New perspectives.* Hillsdale, NJ: Lawrence Erlbaum.

Braddock, J. H. (1985). School desegregation and black assimilation. *Journal of Social Issues, 41*(3), 9–22.

Brewer, M. B. (1979). In-group bias in the minimal intergroup situation: A cognitive-motivational analysis. *Psychological Bulletin, 86,* 307–324.

Cleaver, E. (1968). *Soul on ice.* New York: McGraw-Hill.

Cole, J. B. (1970). Culture: Negro, black and nigger. *Black Scholar, 1,* 40–44.

Cook, S. W. (1985, Oct. 18–19). *Research on changing dominant group attitudes that legitimate social injustice.* Paper presented at the 20th Annual meeting of the Society of Experimental Social Psychology. Evanston, IL.

DuBois, W. E. B. (1903). *Souls of black folk.* Chicago: A. C. McClurg.

Epstein, J. L. (1985). After the bus arrives: Resegregation in desegregated schools. *Journal of Social Issues, 41*(3), 23–44.

Gaertner, S. L. (1985). *When groups merge: Reducing the salience of group boundaries*. Paper read at the Meetings of the American Educational Research Association, Chicago.

Gaertner, S. L., & Dovidio, J. F. (1986a). The aversive form of racism. In J. F. Dovidio & S. L. Gaertner (Eds.), *Prejudice, discrimination and racism*. Orlando, FL: Academic Press.

Gaertner, S. L., & Dovidio, J. F. (1986b). Prejudice, discrimination and racism: Problems, progress and promise. In J. Dovidio & S. Gaertner (Eds.), *Prejudice, discrimination and racism*. Orlando, FL: Academic Press.

Glazer, N., & Moynihan, D. P. (1963). *Beyond the melting pot*. Cambridge: Harvard University Press.

Glazer, N., & Moynihan, D. P. (1976). *Ethnicity: Theory and experience*. Cambridge: Harvard University Press.

Hamilton, D. L. (1986). Cognitive bases of stereotyping. In J. F. Dovidio & S. L. Gaertner (Eds.), *Prejudice, discrimination and racism*. Orlando, FL: Academic Press.

Hamilton, D. L., & Gifford, R. (1976). Illusory correlation in interpersonal perception: A cognitive basis of stereotypic judgments. *Journal of Experimental Social Psychology, 12*, 392–407.

Heckler, M. M. (1985). *Report of the Secretary's Task Force on Black and Minority Health: Vol. 1. Executive summary*. Washington, DC: Department of Health and Human Services.

Herrnstein, R. (1971). I.Q. *Atlantic Monthly, 228*(3), 43–64.

Hofstede, G. (1980). *Culture's consequences: International differences in work-related values*. Beverly Hills, CA: Sage.

Jones, J. M. (1972). *Prejudice and racism*. Reading, MA: Addison Wesley.

Jones, J. M. (1979). Conceptual and strategic issues in the relationship of black psychology to American social science. In A. W. Boykin, A. J. Franklin, J. F. Yates (Eds.), *Research directions of black psychologists*. New York: Russell Sage.

Jones, J. M. (1985, June 22–26). *TRIOS: A model of biculturality in black Americans*. Paper presented at the First International Conference on Cultural Values and Collective Action. Nags Head, NC.

Jones, J. M. (1986a). Cultural differences in temporal perspectives: Instrumental and expressive behaviors in time. In J. McGrath (Ed.), *Research on time: Studies toward a social psychology of time*. Beverly Hills, CA: Sage.

Jones, J. M. (1986b). Racism: A cultural analysis of the problem. In J. F. Dovidio & S. L. Gaertner (Eds.), *Prejudice, discrimination and racism*. Orlando, FL: Academic Press.

Jones, J. M., & Block, C. B. (1984). Black cultural perspectives. *Clinical Psychologist, 37*, 58–62.

Jones, J. M., & Hochner, A. R. (1973). Racial differences in sports activities: A look at the self-paced versus reactive hypothesis. *Journal of Personality and Social Psychology, 27*, 86–95.

Jones, J. M., & Liverpool, H. (1976). Calypso humour in Trinidad. In A. Chapman & H. Foot (Eds.) *Humour: Theory and research*. London: Wiley.

Jordan, W. D. (1969). *White over black: American attitudes toward the Negro, 1550–1812*. Baltimore: Penguin Books.

Kerner, O. (1968). *Report of the National Advisory Commission on Civil Disorders*. New York: Bantam Books.

Kleugel, J. R., & Smith, E. R. (1986). *Beliefs about inequality: Americans' views of what is and what ought to be*. Chicago: Aldine.

Kovel, J. (1970). *White racism: A psychological history*. New York: Pantheon.

Kroeber, A. L., & Kluckhohn, C. (1952). *Culture: A critical review of concepts and definitions*. New York: Random House.

Latane, B., & Wolf, S. (1981). The social impact of majorities and minorities. *Psychological Review, 88*, 438–453.

Lewis, O. (1961). *The children of Sanchez: Autobiography of a Mexican family*. New York: Random House.

Linville, P. W., Salvoey, T., & Fisher, G. W. (1986). Stereotyping and perceived distributions of social characteristics: An application to ingroup–outgroup perception. In J. Dovidio & S. L. Gaertner (Eds.), *Prejudice, discrimination and racism*. Orlando: FL: Academic Press.

Mbiti, J. (1970). *African philosophy and religions*. New York: Doubleday.

McConahay, J. B. (1986). Modern symbolic racism. In J. F. Dovidio & S. L. Gaertner (Eds.), *Prejudice, discrimination and racism*. Orlando, FL: Academic Press.

McConahay, J. B., & Hough, J. C. (1976). Symbolic racism. *Journal of Social Issues, 32*, 23–45.

McDougall, W. (1921). *Is America safe for democracy?* New York: Scribner.

Miller, N., & Brewer, M. B. (Eds.). (1984). *Groups in contact: The psychology of desegregation*. Orlando, FL: Academic Press.

Miller, N. & Brewer, M. B. (1986). Categorization effects on ingroup and outgroup perception. In J. Dovidio & S. Gaertner (Eds.), *Prejudice, discrimination and racism*. Orlando, FL: Academic Press.

Miller, N., Brewer, M. B., & Edwards, K. (1985). Cooperative interaction in desegregated settings: A laboratory analogue. *Journal of Social Issues, 41*(3), 63–80.

Myrdal, G. (1944). *An American dilemma: The Negro problem and modern democracy*. New York: Harper.

Nemeth, C. (1986). Differential contributions of majority and minority influence. *Psychological Review, 93,* 23–32.

Sawyer, K. (1986, January 15). King scholars steal Bennett's lines. *Washington Post,* p. A8.

Schofield, J. W. (1986). Causes and consequences of the colorblind perspective. In J. F. Dovidio & S. L. Gaertner (Eds.), *Prejudice, discrimination and racism.* New York: Academic Press.

Snyder, M. (1974). Self-monitoring of expressive behavior. *Journal of Personality and Social Psychology, 30,* 526–537.

Snyder, M. (1981). On the influence of individuals on situations. In N. Cantor & J. F. Kihlstrom (Eds.), *Personality, cognition and social interaction.* Hillsdale, NJ: Erlbaum.

Snyder, M. (1983). The influence of individuals on situations: Implications for understanding links between personality and behavior. *Journal of Personality, 51,* 497–516.

Stephan, W. G., & Brigham, J. C. (1985). Intergroup contact. *Journal of Social Issues, 41*(3), 1–8.

Triandis, H. C. (1976a). The future of pluralism. *Journal of Social Issues, 32,* 179–208.

Triandis, H. C. (1976b). *Variations in black and white perceptions of the social environment.* Urbana, IL: University of Illinois Press.

van den Berghe, P. (1967). *Race and racism: A comparative perspective.* New York: Wiley.

7

Racism toward Hispanics
The Culturally Monolithic Society

Albert Ramirez

The topic of prejudice and racism is one that has occupied social psychology for many years. Almost every contemporary social psychology textbook has a chapter devoted to prejudice, discrimination, or interracial group relations, with numerous references to the studies conducted in these areas. How many of the studies discussed in these chapters, however, are based on research conducted with or about Hispanics? In order to answer this question, the present writer surveyed the relevant chapters of 17 contemporary and widely used social psychology textbooks. In the hundreds of studies referred to in these 17 textbooks in their discussion of prejudice and discrimination, only 4 studies dealt specifically with Hispanics. Does this mean that no research relevant to or indicative of prejudice against Hispanics has been conducted? Hardly. What this exclusion of Hispanics in social psychology textbooks demonstrates is an almost total lack of awareness concerning Hispanics as victims of prejudice and discrimination, and of the psychological literature that exists that is relevant to the Hispanic experience in this country.

The objective of this chapter is to present and review the psychological research on Hispanics relevant to the issues of prejudice, discrimination, and racism. The review is by no means an exhaustive one; it is selective in two major ways. First of all, though the term *Hispanic* is in the title and has been used thus far in this chapter, almost all of the research to be discussed focuses on the Chicano, or Mexican-American—which is the largest of the Hispanic groups in this country—and does not deal to any significant degree with the other two major Hispanic groups: Puerto Ricans and Cuban-Americans. Although at times the more general term *Hispanic* may be used, it should be kept in mind that the inferences and conclusions drawn by the present writer are based on research focusing on the Mexican-American. Second, even with respect to the Chicano research, the studies presented here are selective in that they represent the way which the present writer has decided to analyze and interpret the psychological research pertaining to prejudice and racism toward Mexican-Americans. The two major types of perspectives on the Hispanic experience to be used by this writer are those that reflect a culturally monolithic system and those that reflect a culturally pluralistic system.

ALBERT RAMIREZ • Department of Psychology, University of Colorado, Boulder, Colorado 80309-0345.

THE CULTURALLY MONOLITHIC SYSTEM VERSUS THE CULTURALLY PLURALISTIC SYSTEM

A culturally monolithic system is one in which human behavior is viewed from the normative perspective of one cultural group; individuals or groups who vary from this norm are thus labeled as deviant, disadvantaged, or just plan inferior (Romano, 1970; Vaca, 1970). In a culturally monolithic system, the individuals and groups who are labeled are usually ethnically, racially, and/or culturally different from the dominant cultural group. In a culturally monolithic system, therefore, the dominant group's values, beliefs, and lifestyles serve as the standard of comparison and the point of reference. In short, a culturally monolithic system is one in which the dominant cultural group has the power, resources, and authority to define itself in positive, normative ways and to define the out-group in negative, dysfunctional ways—thus rationalizing the continuation of vesting power in itself and away from other groups.

The alternative to a culturally monolithic system is a pluralistic one. A pluralistic system is one in which the differences that exist among diverse groups—whether these be religious or ethnic, racial groups—are cherished and are respected for their worth; the differences are, in fact, cultivated for the benefits they bring to all people in that society. In a pluralistic system, power is independent of racial or cultural group; that is, one's perceived social power is not related to his or her racial or ethnic group affiliation.

There are other elements that distinguish a monolithic from a pluralistic system. In the former, the type of contact between dominant-group members and minority-group members tends to be based on nonequal-status (i.e., a dominant–subordinate) relationships. The dominant-group member is usually the employer, supervisor, or person in authority, whereas the minority-group member is typically the supervised and subordinate individual. In a pluralistic system, such contact is based on the presumption of equal social status between individuals from both the dominant and the ethnic-minority groups. In a monolithic system, the contact between the two groups tends to be a formal, structured one, rather than an informal, intimate one, as might be the case in a pluralistic system. Finally, in both a monolithic system and a pluralistic system, we find an inevitable interdependence between the dominant cultural group and the minority cultural groups. In the monolithic system, however, it is a negative interdependence based on competing and mutually exclusive superordinate goals; the only way the dominant group can maintain its resources and power is by not allowing other groups to reach their goal of increased resources and power. A culturally pluralistic system is characterized by those interracial group contacts that have been found to lead to positive intergroup relations (Amir, 1976).

The conceptualization of the Hispanic experience—including explanations for the prejudice, discrimination, and racism that confront Hispanics in this country—is completely different, depending on whether these intergroup relations and dynamics are interpreted from a culturally monolithic perspective or from a culturally pluralistic perspective. Not surprisingly, the model of interpretation is itself a function and a reflection of the system—the society—in which it is imbedded. What this means is that the definition, conceptualization, and interpretation of the Hispanic experience in this society have been predominantly from a culturally monolithic perspective.

CULTURALLY MONOLITHIC ASSUMPTIONS ABOUT THE MEXICAN-AMERICAN

The culturally monolithic approach to the study of the Mexican-American is based on the *a priori* assumption that Chicanos' problems—including the fact that they may be victims of prejudice and discrimination—can be attributed to their individual, internal dynamics and to the group's cultural characteristics. The labels used to describe Chicanos are pejorative, extremely negative, and in complete opposition to the labels used to describe the members of the dominant cultural group. For example, some of the value orientations ascribed to Mexican-Americans and to Anglo-Americans (Saunders, 1954; Vaca, 1970; Zintz, 1969) follow:

Mexican-American values	Anglo-American values
Present-oriented	Future-oriented
Immediate gratification	Deferred gratification
Passive	Active
Low level of aspiration	High level of aspiration
Non-goal-oriented	Goal-oriented
Non-success-oriented	Success-oriented
External locus of control	Internal locus of control

As can be noted, those "positive" values ascribed by the Anglo are primarily based on western European, Judeo-Christian ethics and are focused primarily on the ideology of individualism. Individualism centers on the belief system that (a) individuals should work hard and compete successfully with others; (b) those individuals who do work hard should be and will be rewarded with success (wealth, power, and status); and (c) those who do not succeed fail because of lack of effort and motivation (Feagin, 1975). The values ascribed to Mexican-Americans are viewed as negative and, by virtue of the terms that are used to label these values, as completely opposite to those of the dominant cultural group. If one believes in a just world (Lerner & Miller, 1978), which fits nicely with the ideology of individualism, it easily follows that Chicanos get what they deserve. Because they are not future-oriented, success-oriented, internal, or goal-oriented, it is no wonder that members of the dominant group are prejudiced against them. The underlying assumption, in addition to the one that Chicanos are to blame for any prejudice and discrimination directed at them, is that these patterns of prejudice and discrimination would cease to exist if only Mexican-Americans would become more like Anglo-Americans. The ascribed values and stereotypes associated with Chicanos serve as the rationalization for the continued oppression, racism, and discrimination that is directed toward them. As long as the dominant society can "explain" the Chicano experience in this country in terms of these negative cultural characteristics, it need not blame itself for Chicanos' lower educational attainment, higher unemployment, and lower socioeconomic status.

Aspirations and Expectations of Chicanos

The aspirations and expectations of minority-group members have received considerable attention from social scientists. The general conclusions of these investigators have been that, among certain ethnic groups (Jewish-Americans and Japanese-Americans), there exist high levels of aspiration, whereas low levels of aspiration are characteristic of other ethnic minority groups (black Americans and Mexican-Americans). Unfortunately, the interpretations of the results of these studies have frequently been quite ethnocentric and culturally deterministic. Thus, certain characteristics of the Jewish culture have been viewed as leading to a high level of achievement (Etzioni-Halevy & Halevy, 1977). Similarly, the achievement of Japanese-Americans has been attributed to the similarities between the Japanese and American cultural systems (Caudill & DeVos, 1956), the assumption being that only cultures that have characteristics similar to the American culture can attain high levels of achievement. In this regard, the concept of assimilation has also been used to explain the success of these groups (Montero & Tsukashima, 1977). In contrast, Hispanics and blacks have been characterized as having low levels of aspiration, although a growing number of studies have shown that such conclusions are unwarranted. With respect to blacks, for example, Picou (1973) found that the occupational aspirations of rural black and white students were similar, and that father's occupation and education, as well as academic performance, were much better predictors of aspirations than race. Similar results were obtained by Nichols (1977).

With respect to the aspirational level of Mexican-Americans, much of the early research reflected a strong bias both in preempirical assumptions and in methodological approaches (Heller, 1966; Madsen, 1964; Tuck, 1946; Wendling & Elliott, 1968). Not surprisingly, therefore, these studies described Mexican-Americans as having low educational aspirations and expectations. Other studies, however, have indicated that Mexican-Americans do not differ from Anglos in level of aspiration (Anderson & Johnson, 1968; Juarez & Kuvlesky, 1968; Kuvlesky, Wright, & Juarez, 1971). Chavez & Ramirez (1983) found that both employed and unemployed Chicanos have equally positive work aspirations, although the discrepancy between occupational aspirations and expectations was greater among the unemployed group, as might be anticipated.

With respect to the concept of expectancy, Rotter's theory (Rotter, Chance, & Phares, 1972), focusing on the construct of locus of control, has generated much research and controversy. Most studies have found internal control to be associated with greater mastery tendencies and achievement striving (Phares & Lamiell, 1976), characteristics that one would expect to be related to positive educational and occupational outcomes. Rotter (1975) suggested that individuals from cultures with a high fatalistic and passive orientation are more likely to demonstrate an external locus of control. Because, from the culturally monolithic perspective, fatalism and passivity are stereotypes of Chicanos, the expectation would be that Mexican-Americans would manifest a high level of externality in their locus-of-control orientation. With respect to locus of control in Hispanics, the results are inconsistent. Some studies report greater externality among Chicanos (Scott & Phelon, 1969), whereas Garza and Ames (1974) found Chicanos to be more internal than Anglos. In addition, Garza (1977) found that, in assessing the appropriateness of the five subscales of the I-E scale for comparing Anglos and Chicanos, only two subscales showed cultural equivalence.

The concept of expectancy has also been used to explain the effect of the self-fulfilling prophecy on minority children (Rosenthal & Jacobson, 1968), the process by which a teacher's expectations are communicated to and internalized by the student. The U.S. Commission on Civil Rights (1973), observing classes in three states, found that Anglo-American students were praised more often by their teachers than were Chicano students, and that Chicano students received less attention; not surprisingly, the class participation of these students was lower. Whitehead and King (1973) examined differences in managers' expectations and evaluations of Mexican-American workers. The lower expectations held by the managers were communicated implicitly and explicitly. Nevertheless, Chicanos continued to have positive work attitudes and behaviors (Davidson & Gaitz, 1974), as well as positive occupational aspirations and expectations (Chavez & Ramirez, 1983).

Ramirez and Chavez (1982) analyzed a subset of the data obtained from the 1979 National Longitudinal Survey of youth ranging from 14 to 22 years of age; 6,143 of these were white, non-Hispanic, and 1,652 were Hispanic. The results indicated that, for the most part, both groups had the same level of work commitment and willingness to work. In addition, the educational and occupational aspirations and expectations were quite similar and in a fairly high direction. Regardless of research to the contrary, however, the stereotype of the Mexican-American as having lower educational occupational aspirations and expectations, as being passive, and as having an external locus of control continues to remain firmly entrenched and relatively unchanged.

INTELLECTUAL AND EDUCATIONAL ABILITIES OF CHICANOS

Another rationalization for the different treatment of Mexican-Americans—particularly Chicano youth in the school setting—has been their supposed lower intelligence and abilities and the problems created by these assumed deficiencies and disadvantages (Mercer, 1975). The assessment devices used to make these judgments, of course, reflect the culturally monolithic character of the American educational system and serve to legitimize the continued existence of this monolithic approach to education. The result of such an educational system is that Chicano children have often been assigned to classes for the mentally retarded and have rarely been assigned to classes for gifted students (Mercer, 1977). Mercer (1973), however, found that, when Chicanos and Anglos were equated on such sociocultural variables as family size, parents' job, urban family background, and parental generation level, they showed no significant differences in IQ scores. In spite of the extensive research indicating the cultural bias of these tests (Garcia, 1977; Mercer, 1977; Olmedo, 1977; Padilla & Ruiz, 1973), the predominant interpretation of ethnic group differences in scores is still based on the culturally monolithic paradigm.

In order to demonstrate the effect of culture-specific tests, some ethnic-minority social scientists have developed tests standardized on their own ethnic group. Not surprisingly, the specific ethnic group that serves as the normative group and from whose culture the test items were developed scores significantly higher on these tests. For example, Williams (1975) developed the BITCH-100 (Black Intelligence Test of Cultural Homogeneity) and found that black students scored significantly higher on this test than did white students. The present writer has developed a test called CISCO (Chicano Intelligence Scale of Cultural Orientation), consisting of the 28 multiple-choice items shown in Figure 1. Figure 2 presents the results from studies conducted at the University of Colorado with 81 Chicano students and 133 Anglo-American students. Out of a possible score of 140 (28 items × 5 points per correct item), the average score for Anglo students was 36.4 (SD = 14.42) and the mean for Chicanos was 93.3 (SD = 24.03). An appropriate label has been designated for each particular I-CO level. If the results from this test were interpreted in the same manner as the traditional IQ test results, the conclusion would be that 16% of Anglo-American university students are severely defective and 52% are moderately defective.

In spite of the research indicating the methodological problems and the preempirical biases of many intelligence and achievement tests in some of this research going back to the 1930s (Sanchez, 1932, 1934), the lower scores of Mexican-American children on these tests are still attributed to dysfunctional characteristics within themselves (low self-esteem, poor motivation, and negative attitudes) and/or within their ethnic minority culture. Chicano family values have been described as counter to high achievement in school (Carter, 1970; Demos, 1962). This culturally monolithic interpretation has led to the rationalization of different treatment of Mexican-American children and to their placement in compensatory-education types of programs (Arciniega, 1973), in spite of the findings of a number of studies that indicate a positive relationship between achievement and Spanish cultural influence in the home (Garcia, 1981; Henderson, 1972; Henderson & Merritt, 1968).

LANGUAGE ATTITUDES

Language and culture are intertwined; the language used by the culture serves as the official vehicle for transmitting the culture's values, beliefs, and ideologies. Another

Circle the letter of the correct answer.
 1. Which one of the following is not associated with el movimiento?
     a. Miguel Aleman   b. Rodolfo Gonzales   c. César Chávez   d. Reis Tijerina
 2. Cuál de las siguientes organizaciones no es una organizacion chicana?
     a. LULAC   b. PASO   c. American G.I. Forum   d. RUCA
 3. One important ingredient of tortillas de harina:
     a. corn flour   b. vegetable oil   c. white flour   d. corn starch
 4. Mis padres y los Silvas son compadres, porque yo soy el _____ de los Silvas.
     a. ahijado   b. primo hermano   c. huerfano   d. nieto
 5. The treaty signed by the United States and Mexico in 1848 is known as the Treaty of:
     a. Guadalupe Hidalgo   b. Chapultepec   c. San Joaquin   d. Chamizal
 6. Cuál de los siguientes se encuentra con menos probabilidad en el barrio?
     a. una iglesia   b. una panaderia   c. un salon de baile   d. una camara de comercio
 7. A light-complected Mexican-American boy is likely to be nicknamed _____ by his friends.
     a. blanco   b. gringo   c. prieto   d. güero
 8. Rosita Alvirez: a. murió de tres tiros   b. se casó con Hipolito   c. tubo dos hijos y una
     hija   d. no le gustaba ir a bailes
 9. That part of the southwestern United States from which it is believed the Aztecs migrated
     before they settled in Mexico City is:
     a. San Diego   b. Aztlan   c. Colorado   d. Santa Barbara
10. El pollo es al mole como la tripa es al:
     a. chorizo   b. arroz   c. menudo   d. gaspacho
11. The Chicano writer who was killed by a policeman in East Los Angeles in 1970 was:
     a. Francisco Madero, Jr.   b. Ruben Salazar   c. José Espinosa   d. Juan Gallo
12. Canciones rancheras tienen una calidad especial cuando cantadas por:
     a. Trini Lopez   b. Libertad Gomez   c. Roberto Medina   d. Jorge Negrete
13. The poem "I Am Joaquin" was written by:
     a. Joaquin Castillo   b. César Chavez   c. Miguel Aleman   d. Rodolfo Gonzales
14. La bandera del soldado:
     a. azul, blanca, colorada   b. verde, blanca, colorada   c. amarilla, blanca, colorada d. ver-
     de, blanca, amarilla
15. Chante and canton:
     a. champion   b. home   c. shirt   d. song
16. Como un acto de fe y de sacrificio muchos chicanos dejan de tomar ó comer sus antojitos
     favoritos durante:
     a. la cuaresma   b. la chota   c. las posadas   d. una cruda
17. A person who is my madrina is my:
     a. step-mother   b. legal guardian   c. mother-in-law   d. god-mother
18. Estas son las mañanitas que cantaba:
     a. la vieja Inez   b. el rey David   c. el Chicanito   d. la reina Maria
19. Carnalismo is:
     a. a purely physical attraction   b. a relationship through kinship   c. sins of the flesh   d. a
     feeling of brotherhood
20. El compositor mexicano famoso por todo el mundo:
     a. Lee Treviño   b. Augustin Lara   c. Jose Torres   d. Pedro Armindariz
21. El grito de Dolores is most associated with:
     a. Benito Juarez   b. Emiliano Zapata   c. Pancho Villa   d. Padre Hidalgo
22. Cuál de estos terminos no aparece en el movimiento chicano?
     a. huelga   b. venceremos   c. asimilado   d. teatro campesino
23. Elected in El Paso, 1972, as Chairman of La Raza Unida Party was:
     a. Alberto Casso   b. Corky Gonzales   c. José Angel Gutierrez   d. César Chávez
24. Arroz con _____:
     a. lengua   b. pollo   c. tamales   d. naranjas

FIGURE 1. Chicano Intelligence Scale of Cultural Orientation (CISCO).

25. Chicano term for the police:
   a. la migra   b. la chota   c. el gabacho   d. el pachuco
26. El barrio es el hogar de:
   a. la migra   b. la chota   c. el gabacho   d. el pachuco
27. Pocho was written by:
   a. Angel Gutiérrez   b. Rodolfo Gonzales   c. Jose Villareal   d. Pedro Infante
28. La Virgin de Guadalupe se aparecio ante de:
   a. Cristol Colón   b. Juan Diego   c. Jesus Villa   d. Pedro Pistolas

FIGURE 1. (*Continued.*)

important basis for prejudice and discrimination within a culturally monolithic system, therefore, is reflected in its reaction to individuals who are perceived as speaking the language of the dominant cultural group differently. The Mexican-American's speaking of English with a Mexican accent has served as another rationalization for different treatment and for prejudice (Ortego, 1969). Barker (1947) observed 30 years ago that Mexican-American bilinguals in Tucson, Arizona, manifested a feeling of inferiority with respect to their Mexican accent in speaking English. Krear (1971) also demonstrated the common occurrence of parents with limited English ability speaking only English with their children so that they would not grow up with an accent that would reduce their social and economic opportunities.

The diversity of attitudes toward accented speech is illustrated in a study by Thompson (1973). The English pronunciation of 50 Mexican-American male adults from Austin,

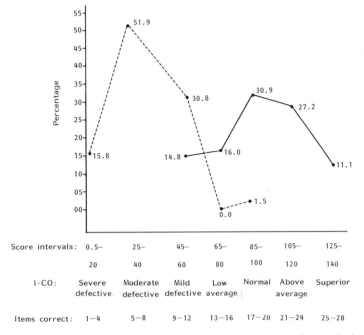

FIGURE 2. Performance of Chicano and Anglo students on the Chicano Intelligence Scale of Cultural Orientation. Key: Chicanos = ———; Anglos = — — — —.

Texas, was analyzed and classified as Spanish-influenced, northern, or regional Texan. Although adopted pronunciation was not significantly related to the usual categories of frequency of Spanish use, age, social class, social mobility, or education, it was related to attitude toward accent. Those who had adopted the regional Texan pronunciation believed that accent was of primary important in obtaining employment, and most reported having consciously developed their Texan pronunciation. On the other hand, respondents with northern or Spanish-influenced English indicated that, other than fluency, the only criterion was the ability to do the job.

Several studies contrasting standard English and accented English have been conducted. In addition to investigating reactions to English and Spanish, Politzer and Ramirez (1973a,b) asked the same listeners to rate four speakers who spoke English with a marked Spanish accent. The Mexican-American and Anglo-American children in both studies (third-, sixth-, ninth-, and twelfth-graders in monolingual schools and third-graders in a bilingual school) downgraded the accented speech relative to both standard English and Spanish. In another California investigation with elementary and high school students, Brekke (1973) elicited attitudes toward standard American-accented and Mexican-American-accented English from 262 Anglo and Chicano students, half of whom were preadolescents (mean age of 16 years). For each of four speakers, the listeners were asked to judge ethnic background, to judge educational and occupational level, to evaluate speech characteristics on 3 scales, and to evaluate speaker characteristics on 10 scales. Ethnic background was consistently distinguished accurately, and the judged educational and occupational levels of the standard speakers were higher. On the three speech scales, a greater distinction between the two speech styles was made by the older group, and the preadolescent Mexican-Americans rated the accented-English speakers as being significantly more correct, more acceptable, and more valuable than did the other groups. On the 10 speaker characteristics, the older group again evidenced more of a gap between the two speech styles than did the younger students. Furthermore, whereas the ethnicity of the rater did not effect the evaluation of the standard speakers, the Mexican-American students rated accented-English speakers significantly more favorably than did Anglo students on six of the scales.

Studies with college students have also revealed a negative stereotype of speakers of accented English. In a Los Angeles study by Arthur, Farrar, and Bradford (1974), 48 Anglo college students rated four pairs of matched guise voices on 15 adjective scales. Although all the speakers were identified as Mexican-American, they were consistently rated more positively on scales related to success, ability, and social awareness when speaking the local standard of English than when speaking Chicano English, the local ethnic dialect. Similar results were obtained by the present writer in an informal study conducted with students in his class. Mexican-American students were more likely to evaluate the standard-English speaker as more progressive, successful, and educated than the person who spoke English with a Chicano accent. This was the outcome even though most of the Mexican-American students in this class were intimately involved in the Chicano movement on campus and perceived themselves as activists and, in some cases, as militants.

Noting the frequent association of inferior status with accented speech, as well as the increased acceptance of ethnic speech as a badge of in-group loyalty, Ryan and Carranza (1975) sought evidence of the functional separation of speech styles. Sixty-three Mexican-American, black, and Anglo female high-school students in Chicago were asked to rate the personalities of male speakers of standard English and of Mexican-American-accented English in two contexts (home and school) and with two sets of rating scales (status-stressing and solidarity-stressing). Although the standard-English speakers received more positive ratings in every case, the differences were significantly greater in the school context than in the home context, and on status-stressing scales than on solidarity-stressing scales. Anglo students rated accented speakers significantly lower on status scales than did either black or Mexican-American students.

Language attitude research in general has shown that individuals are sensitive to language variation, language style, and the accent characteristics of speech; that individuals report not being completely satisfied with their own speech styles; and that speech tends to be modeled according to the speech of those with whom one identifies. Further, the research strongly suggests that attitudes toward speech are related to the expectations and/or evaluations of the personality characteristics of the speaker and/or other behavior characteristics of the speaker. The research on a phenomenon particularly germane to Chicanos—accent—indicates a negative attitude in this country toward Chicano-accented speech, evidenced by the consistent devaluation of Chicano-accented speech as compared to so-called standard, unaccentuated speech. Furthermore, this negative evaluation of speech-accentedness appears to generalize into negative evaluations of the behavioral characteristics of the speaker.

CHICANO ETHNIC IDENTITY AND ACCULTURATION

From the culturally monolithic perspective, strong ethnic identity among members of minority groups is perceived as negative and as detrimental to the development of an integrated American society. At the same time that ethnic minority groups are stigmatized and discriminated against by the dominant culture, and structural and institutional barriers are maintained to prevent the economic growth of these groups, they are criticized for not assimilating and becoming part of the "melting pot" that supposedly characterizes American culture. At the same time that they are prevented from becoming "true Americans," Mexican-Americans are criticized for sticking together and for developing group cohesiveness and a strong sense of ethnic identity.

Salazar (1972) interviewed 150 Mexican-Americans in the El Paso, Texas, area about their preferred identity terms. Of those interviewed 36% preferred to call themselves Mexican-American, 23% preferred Mexican/Mexicano, and 17% preferred Chicano. Younger respondents, 44% of those in the age category of 15–20, preferred Chicano, whereas the 31-to-41 and 41-to-50 age groups showed a greater preference for Mexican-American. Native Mexican-born respondents identified with Mexican/Mexicano most often, as did respondents with both parents born in Mexico. In terms of language used at home, those who reported speaking more English at home related more to Mexican-American, those speaking some Spanish and some English most often preferred Mexican-American and Chicano, and those who spoke more Spanish than English preferred Mexican/Mexicano.

Stoddard (1970) asked Mexican-Americans their perceptions concerning their and Anglos' criteria in identifying Chicanos. Mexican-American respondents ranked family name as the most commonly used criterion used by themselves to identify each other, with language second. Language was the most common criterion attributed to Anglo use to identify Chicanos, with skin color as the second factor.

The age at which ethnic and racial differences are perceived was investigated by Werner and Evans (1968). These investigators conducted doll-play interviews with 40 Chicano 4- and 5-year-old boys and girls, with and without exposure to school experience. Two sets of dolls were used in each interview, one set had yellow hair and "flesh-toned skin" (authors' words), and the other set had black hair and brown skin. The doll identified as "most like me" by the children who had had some school experience was predominantly white, whereas the darker doll was identified as "most like me" by children who had not been exposed to the school experience. One major problem with this study was the fact that the investigators gave the children a very limited choice between "dark"- and "light"-skinned dolls, even after stating in the beginning that "Mexican Americans are characterized by a wide range of skin color."

Rohrer (1973) used a somewhat more realistic method to test 4-year-olds' perceptions of ethnic and racial differences by showing color photographs of white, Mexican-American, and black individuals to student members of the same three groups as those depicted in the photographs. The white children surpassed the minority children in correct group identification. Both sexes in the black and white groups tended to identify with their own group. Mexican-American males showed a tendency to identify with the white over their own group, whereas the opposite was true for Mexican-American females. Preference patterns revealed that the introduction of a Mexican-American group and choice altered the previous pattern of overall white preference because both Mexican-Americans and blacks tended to prefer the Mexican-American over the white choice.

Rice, Ruiz, and Padilla (1974) used the color photograph method to investigate person perception, self-identity, and ethnic group preference in Anglo, black, and Chicano preschool and third-grade children in Kansas City, Missouri. All of the children in this study were able to discriminate between the photographs of the white and black males, but the preschool subjects were unable to make the discrimination between the Anglo and Chicano photographs. All subjects indicated the appropriate photograph when asked which looked most like them. Among the preschool subjects, neither the blacks nor the Chicanos expressed a significant preference for their own ethnic group, whereas a significant number of the Anglo subjects selected the Anglo photograph as the one they liked the best. At the third-grade level, only the Chicano subjects displayed a strong preference for their own ethnic group. Two major problems with this study were that the photographs used were only of males and that the experimenters used were Anglo females.

A study by Leyva (1975) explored the relationship between "Chicanismo" and educational aspirations and expectations among Mexican-American high-school students. Those students who identified with the concept of *Chicanismo* were more likely to have higher educational aspirations and expectations than those Mexican-American students who did not identify with Chicanismo. Lampe (1975) found that those individuals who labeled themselves Chicanos held more positive attitudes toward blacks and less positive attitudes toward Anglos than those person who used *Mexican-American* or *Spanish-American* as self-labels. Penalosa and McDonagh (1966) found that the most upwardly mobile Chicanos were more likely to use labels specific to their Mexican-ness.

These studies of Chicano ethnic identity indicate that the most common approach to determining ethnic self-identity among Chicanos is to inquire about terms or labels used to identify themselves, and that there is much diversity among terms in different populations. The concept of ethnic identity, however, is not a choice between identification with "Mexican" and identification with "American" cultural values, which would involve loss in either choice: The choice of one would involve a loss of the benefits and experiences of the other. Chicano ethnic identity is grounded in diversity—evolving from a multicultural ethnic background and the contemporary experience of living in a society that allows exposure to, and often involves functioning in, at least two cultures.

The conception of Chicano ethnic identity as pluralistic is in opposition to the dominant culture's conception of ethnic identity, which seeks to minimize differences and to promote "sameness" and "ethnic homogeneity." This line of thought is often justified by an argument that proposes cultural uniformity as necessary in order to reduce intergroup hostilities and prejudices. As interest in the concept of ethnic identity has increased, so has interest in the concept of acculturation. Within recent years, therefore, the questions of acculturation, multiculturalism, and ethnic identity among Mexican-Americans have received more attention by both Anglo and Hispanic social scientists. A number of studies have focused on the characteristics of the acculturated Mexican-American, the nonacculturated Mexican-American (Cordova, 1970), and the bicultural Mexican-American (Ramirez & Castaneda, 1974). Other studies have focused on the measurement of these concepts (Olmedo, Martinez, & Martinez, 1978; Padilla, 1980). In addition, there is a growing amount of research that indicates a significant relationship between biculturalism and a number of measures that serve as indicators of positive mental health and adjustment. M. Ramirez (1977) and Ramirez, Garza, and Cox (1980) have found that multicultural Mexican-Americans demonstrate greater flexibility of personality functioning as well as greater development of certain cognitive skills. The work by Szapocznik, Scopetta, Kurtines, and Arnalde (1978) also indicates that bicultural Cuban-American adolescents tend to demonstrate greater psychological adjustment than those Cuban-Americans who participate solely in either the Cuban or the Anglo culture.

Unfortunately, the dominant causal analysis of acculturation processes has all too often reflected the culturally monolithic perspective, which has tended to analyze acculturation dynamics from a social-problem–cure approach. Thus, the assumption that certain types of negative psychological attributes may characterize Mexican-Americans who are not acculturated has sometimes led to a deficit model of interpretation (Child, 1943; Stonequist, 1964), and a belief on the part of social scientists that there are inherent deficiencies within the Mexican-American viewpoint and that progress will occur only through acculturation to the Anglo-American value system and viewpoint (Montiel, 1970). Such conclusions have been reached even though a number of studies have found a significant relationship between identification with traditional Mexican-American culture and a variety of positive attitudes and behaviors (Derbyshire, 1968; Ramirez, 1969; Vigil, 1979).

As is the case with the other research areas discussed thus far, the study of ethnic identity and acculturation has been and even now continues to be a function of existing interracial group relations in this country, particularly those intergroup relations based on domination and subordination (i.e., asymmetrical power relations). As suggested by Proshansky and Newton (1973), problems of group identification do not occur for those groups that have status and power; it is only those groups that do not have status and power that often have problems with ethnic identity. Similarly, the so-called problem of acculturation and assimilation is never one that is ascribed to the cultural groups in power and with status; invariably, only those groups without power or status are defined as having problems with acculturation and assimilation. The "problems" of acculturation and ethnic group identification, therefore, demonstrate and are indicants of asymmetrical power relations in American society.

A USPI–ESPI ANALYSIS OF INTERRACIAL GROUP RELATIONS

As indicated in the preceding section, the social science approach to the study of the Mexican-American has historically been one that conceptualizes Chicanos and/or their culture as the causal agent, what Ryan (1971) referred to as blaming the victim, and the present writer, as the culturally monolithic approach. Thus, such problem behaviors as poor school performance (Carter, 1970) or juvenile delinquency (Heller, 1966) have been attributed to such factors as low self-esteem, lack of proper role models, or cultural values that do not foster proper nonproblem behavior. The framework, on either an internal or an external level of explanation, has been identical, because the problem behavior is seen as starting from the Mexican-Americans as individuals or from the values of their Chicano culture. It is possible, of course, to view the so-called problem behaviors and the determinants as being the consequences of living in a culturally monolithic—or racist—society. From this point of view, the assumed determinants that explain Chicanos' experiences are themselves problem behaviors stemming from exposure to racist systems. As discussed in the previous section, some of the assumed determinants have been low self-esteem, a low level of aspiration, and negative attitudes toward education. If racism and exposure to a culturally monolithic system are indeed the central explanatory concept, one may derive the following model:

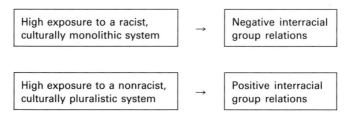

The following conceptualization is based on the premise that one element of a racist and culturally monolithic system is that the social power and influence structure is systematically related to race, thereby contributing to an attitude on the part of both minorities and nonminorities that people of color are to be perceived as being less legitimate sources of authority and therefore as having less social influence. Such a system is referred to by the present writer as a USPI system: "unequal social power and social influence." It is expected that, in a USPI system, the attribution occurs rather naturally, because in such a system the power structure is predominantly white, with positions of less authority being more likely to be occupied by people of color. In a USPI system, therefore, the relationship between social power and race or ethnicity is not random but highly systematic; consequently, those individuals being socialized in such a system (for example, children in a USPI school setting) learn the association between legitimacy of authority and race or ethnicity. In such a system, aspects of the dominant group (language, cultural values, and beliefs) serve as the principal vehicles for communication and social interaction and are viewed as prescriptive and normative. Such a system reinforces and validates the belief that minorities are "less than" or "inferior to," and these beliefs are unfortunately sometimes internalized by the minorities themselves (Knowles & Prewitt, 1969). Such internalization of prejudice by the minority person is associated with other problem behaviors and attitudes such as low self-esteem and low motivation. For example, Dworkin (1964) found significant differences between Mexican-Americans born in Mexico and those born in the United States with respect to their stereotypes of Anglos and in their own self-images, with the U.S.-born Chicanos holding more negative stereotypes about both themselves and Anglos. Buriel and Vasquez (1982) also found that the own-group stereotypes held by Chicanos become more negative with each successive generation.

In short, a USPI system has all the features that are associated with the culturally monolithic system as described in the first part of this paper. The USPI system is one in which asymmetric and unequal power relations exist between groups, and one, therefore, in which the intergroup relations are based on domination and subordination (Apfelbaum, 1979). An ESPI system ("equal social power and social influence"), on the other hand, would be one in which the association between ethnicity and legitimacy of authority is random, so that the individuals being socialized in such system have no empirical basis for linking authority with the race or ethnicity of individuals (Ramirez, 1977a). An ESPI system has the characteristics discussed earlier with respect to the culturally pluralistic system.

For some time now, the present writer has been interested in the relationship between the social influence and the ethnicity of the communicator or influencing agent; it is the results of these studies that led to the development of the USPI–ESPI model. In these studies, social power has been conceptualized as potential social influence, and social influence has been defined as a change in a person's cognition, attitude, or behavior that has its origins in another person or group (French & Raven, 1959). One of the studies occurred in a school setting in which both the power structure and the students were predominantly black (Dembroski, Lasater, & Ramirez, 1978). This study compared the influence of a black communicator with that of a white communicator. Although the context in which this study was conducted was not in the strict sense an ESPI system as defined above, it may be construed as being more in this direction than in the direction of a USPI system, in which the power structure is predominantly white and those students being socialized in the system are predominantly black. Another study (Ramirez & Lasater, 1977), conducted in a school setting in which the authority structure was white and Chicano students comprised one fourth of the student body (a USPI system), compared the influence of a Chicano communicator with that of an Anglo communicator. One of the major differences between the two studies, therefore, was the authority structure of the schools in which the study was conducted; the black students were in a school in which the authority structure was entirely black, and the Chicano students were in a school where the authority structure was entirely Anglo. Both groups, therefore, had been exposed to two different systems regarding the legitimization of social power and authority, and one's race and ethnicity. The results of these studies indicated that black students were more likely to be influenced by the black communicator than by a white communicator. The Chicano students, on the other hand, were more likely to be influenced by the Anglo communicator, a finding suggesting that perhaps these students had internalized the system practices and attitudes concerning the association between legitimacy of authority and being Anglo.

Another study with Chicano adults (Ramirez, 1977b) yielded similar results; the Chicanos were more likely to comply to the request of an Anglo communicator than to the request of a Chicano communicator. Little and Ramirez (1976) found that Chicano children attempted to represent themselves better when tested by an Anglo than when tested by a Chicano.

Such results indicate the effects of being socialized in a culturally monolithic system, where the most powerful positions are occupied by Anglos and the least powerful positions are held by Chicanos. The types of experiences that Chicanos have in a culturally pluralistic, or ESPI, system are quite different from the types of experiences that they have in a cultural monolithic, or USPI, system. The effects of these two types of systems were further investigated in a later study (Ramirez & Soriano, 1982). USPI–ESPI was measured by having the students check the appropriate response category to the following questions: "At your high school, what percentage of the (a) students, (b) teachers, and (c) school administrators are Chicano?" The response categories were 0%, 1–3%, 4–9%, 10–24%, 25–49%, 50–74%, and 75–100%. A high-USPI school was one in which there were a large number of Chicano students and a small percentage of Chicano faculty and administrators. The results indicated that Mexican-American university students who had attended high-USPI senior high schools had had negative high-school experiences, whereas those who had attended low-USPI schools had had more positive high-school experiences. For example, those who had attended high-USPI schools were more likely to agree with such statements as "Throughout my education, I have seen much prejudice and discrimination; at home I have felt more confident about myself than at school; I have always felt dumb at school." High-USPI students were less likely to agree with such statements as "Most of my best friends in high school are going to college; throughout my education, I have been encouraged to do well by my teachers and other school officials; I feel that my past schooling has adequately prepared me to attend college." How attitudes and beliefs are communicated in such systems is further evidenced by the fact that 84% of the students who had attended high-USPI schools stated that their high school counselors had either never mentioned college to them or, if they did, advised them against going to college. Of those students who had attended low-USPI schools, 92% stated that their school counselors had advised them to attend college.

It is expected that the results would be similar if conducted in other social systems within American society. Like the educational system, these other systems are also USPI, because they reflect the overall society, which is culturally monolithic. For example, the media system has been interpreted within a USPI framework (Ramirez, 1985a) because it (a) attributes positive aspects of Hispanic consumer behavior to the acculturated Hispanic; (b) attributes negative aspects of Hispanic consumer behavior to the nonacculturated Hispanic; (c) uses a culturally monolithic model to interpret Hispanic consumer behavior; (d) stereotypes Hispanics in its advertising, presenting them as a Frito Bandito, the macho male, or the temperamental and emotional Latino; and (e) uses few Hispanics in positions of power and as sources of influence. In a variety of settings in which the present writer has discussed intergroup relations with groups of individuals from diverse backgrounds, the results of an intergroup relations and contact questionnaire developed by the writer (see Figure 3) clearly indicate that both Anglos and Chicanos are unlikely to have interacted to any significant degree with Chicanos in positions of power or authority. The reason is readily apparent, as the existing USPI system allows ethnic minority persons low accessibility to such positions.

PSYCHOLOGY AND THE CULTURALLY PLURALISTIC SYSTEM

The preceding discussion of the USPI–ESPI model represents one approach to the study of ethnic-minority and dominant-group relations, focusing primarily on the concepts of social power and social influence. Because power and influence are central aspects of group relations, these two types of systems can also be used to categorize the models, theories, and perspectives that have been used to study Chicanos. Some examples of these are presented in Table 1. As will be noted, there are a significantly greater number of USPI approaches to the study of the Mexican-American. There is, however, a growing literature on the importance of adopting theoretical orientations to the study of the Chicano that are more pluralistic and multicultural (Buriel, 1984; Garza & Lipton, 1984; Johnson, 1978; Ramirez, 1983; Ramirez & Ossorio, 1983), and that move away from the traditional approaches that conceptualize behavior from the normative perspective of the dominant sociocultural group (Baldwin, 1979; Rappaport, Davidson, Wilson, & Mitchell, 1975). American social psychology has to begin to take seriously the criticism that it has demonstrated little appreciation of the sociostructural and sociocultural determinants of human behavior (Stryker, Sarabia, Lopez, Castillo, Burillo, Tajfel, Torregrosa, Kelman, Ridruejo, & Harre, 1983). This criticism is especially valid regarding the dominant approach that has been used to study American ethnic minority groups, particularly blacks, Hispanics, native Americans, and Asian Americans. Of these groups, most of the research has been on blacks. Because blacks have been studied primarily from the culturally monolithic perspective, there is a strong relationship between the dominant approach used to define the Hispanic experience, as discussed in the first section of this chapter, and the traditional approaches that have been used to define the black experience in this country. Thus, the deficit–deficiency models that have been used to characterize the black family (Frazier, 1939; Moynihan, 1965; Rainwater, 1970) are, for all intents

Please check one space only that most nearly reflects your situation.

	All of my own group	Mostly of my own group	Equally of my group and other group(s)	Mostly of other group(s)	All of other group(s)
My Work					
1. My co-workers	———	———	———	———	———
2. My supervisors	———	———	———	———	———
3. Persons I supervise	———	———	———	———	———
4. My close friends at work	———	———	———	———	———
My Neighborhood					
5. My neighbors	———	———	———	———	———
6. My close friends in my neighborhood	———	———	———	———	———
7. My neighbors whose home I often visit	———	———	———	———	———
8. My neighbors who often visit me	———	———	———	———	———
My Personal Life					
9. My closest friends	———	———	———	———	———
10. Persons I have close & meaningful relationships with	———	———	———	———	———
11. Social functions that I attend with friends	———	———	———	———	———
12. Persons I discuss personal problems with	———	———	———	———	———
My Society					
13. My teachers	———	———	———	———	———
14. My employers	———	———	———	———	———
15. My spiritual counselors, priests, clergy	———	———	———	———	———
16. My physicians, dentists	———	———	———	———	———

Please answer the following questions after completing the above.
(1) Go back and think about what your answers mean in terms of intergroup relationships and pluralism.
(2) What effect have your intergroup experiences had on your attitude and behavior?
(3) Put yourself in the place of someone you know who is of another group.
   (a) How might that person answer the same questions?
   (b) What effect might his or her intercultural experiences have had on his or her life?

FIGURE 3. An intergroup relations and contact questionnaire. (Developed by the author.)

and purposes, identical to the ones used to conceptualize the Chicano family and its purported value systems. The research attributing Chicano chihdrens' failure in school to their low self-esteem and negative self-image parallels the early research on the supposed negative self-concept and self-hatred of black children.

There is, however, a large amount of research that clearly demonstrates that black children have the same level of self-esteem as do white children (Banks, 1976; Bridgeman & Shipman, 1975; Taylor, 1976). The more recent approaches to the study of multiculturalism, acculturation, and ethnic identity among Hispanics are similar to recent

TABLE 1. Models Used to Study Chicanos

USPI Models	ESPI Models
1. Blaming the victim (critiqued by Ryan, 1971).	1. Flexibility, unity, and expansion (Ramirez, 1983).
2. Marginal man (Stonequist, 1964).	2. Integration with Mexican-American culture (Buriel, 1984).
3. Conflict-replacement (Child, 1943; Heller, 1966; Madsen, 1964; Sommers, 1964; critiqued by Ramirez, 1984).	3. Interactional (Garza & Lipton, 1984; Johnson, 1978).
4. Damaging culture (Clark, 1959; Humphrey, 1944; Kluckhohn & Strodtbeck, 1961; Rubel, 1966; Saunders, 1954; critiqued by Ramirez & Castañeda, 1974, and by Buriel, 1984).	4. Multiculturalism, cultural pluralism (same as above, plus Ortego, 1970; Ramirez, 1983, 1985b; Ramirez, Garza, & Cox, 1980; Ramirez & Ossorio, 1983; Romano, 1969).
5. Cultural deprivation, determinism; pathology (same as above, plus Johnson, 1970; Ulibarri, 1960; Zintz, 1969; critiqued by Brischetto & Arciniega, 1973; Montiel, 1970; Rocco, 1970; Romano, 1970, 1973; Vaca, 1970).	
6. Culture of poverty (Banfield, 1970; Burma, 1970; Lewis, 1966, 1968).	

research focusing on black identity and transformation stages (Cross, 1971; Thomas, 1971). The research on black intelligence and achievement relates directly to the research discussed earlier with respect to Chicano intelligence and achievement; most of the research on black intelligence and achievement has been based on either a genetic inferiority model or a cultural deficiency model (Deutsch, 1967; Herrnstein, 1973; Jensen, 1969; Shockley, 1971). The assumptions and interpretations regarding the speech dialect of blacks are similar to those regarding the Chicano dialect. As is the case for children's use of a Chicano dialect, black children's use of black English has been labelled as substandard and deficient, in spite of the growing evidence that black speech represents a legitimate alternative dialect with its own descriptive rules for syntax and pronunciation (Smitherman, 1977; White, 1984). Finally, the more recent and pluralistic approaches in the study of the Hispanic experience are closely related to those approaches describing the richness and diversity of the black experience (Jones, 1980; White, 1984).

The above discussion is not meant to suggest that identical theoretical paradigms will necessarily serve to describe the reality and the experience of all ethnic minority groups in contemporary American society. The sociostructural and sociocultural reality and experience of each of these groups, though in many ways similar and comparable, are at the same time unique and diverse. The appreciation and recognition of this uniqueness and diversity need to be reflected in our methodological approaches and conceptual models, what Ramirez and Ossorio (1983) referred to as an *ethnic* or *multicultural psychology*, the main features of which are:

1. A conceptual framework that makes individual, group, and cultural differences an essential and systematic aspect of the general phenomenon of human behavior and development.
2. A neutral, symmetric notation and vocabulary for thinking and talking across the boundaries generated by commitments to particular social groups, substantive theories, methodological ideologies, or value orientations.
3. A systematic elucidation of major cultural perspectives, accomplished within those perspectives, in regard to their paradigmatic assumptions, presuppositions, outlooks, and choice principles.

4. The derivation of methodological and theoretical commitments as exemplifying the corresponding cultural perspectives.
5. A systematic elucidation of the correspondences among the formulations of a given cultural perspective and its derivatives, when those formulations are accomplished within a set of other cultural perspectives and their methodological and conceptual derivatives.
6. The analysis and investigation of sociocultural phenomena that are distinctively associated with societies that are ethnically pluralistic or multicultural to a significant degree. Two important special cases may be noted here. The first case involves phenomena associated with cultural displacement (i.e., cases where individuals must function wholly or in important ways in a culture other than that into which they are socialized; these cases include immigrant, refugees, and indigenous ethnic minorities). The second case involves phenomena associated with differential eligibilities, including power differentials between privileged (usually majority) groups and underprivileged (usually minority) groups. (pp. 284–285)

The adoption of such approaches to the study of ethnic minority groups is especially necessary in the study of prejudice and discrimination because, unfortunately, some of the earlier models that purportedly studied prejudice and discrimination were themselves racist and ethnocentric, reflecting the biases and prejudices of the investigators and theorists. As psychology continues to move from culturally monolithic to culturally pluralistic approaches to investigating prejudice, racism, and discrimination, it may serve as a model and as an influencing force in converting our society from a culturally monolithic system to a culturally pluralistic one—a society in which prejudice, racism, and discrimination will no longer serve as the dominant factors governing interracial group relations in this country.

REFERENCES

Amir, Y. (1976). The role of intergroup contact in change of prejudice and ethnic relations. In P. A. Katz (Ed.), *Towards the elimination of racism.* New York: Pergamon Press.

Anderson, J. G., & Johnson, W. H. (1968). *Sociological determinants of achievement among Mexican-American students.* ERIC Clearinghouse on Rural Education and Small Schools, New Mexico State University.

Apfelbaum, E. (1979). Relations of domination and movements for liberation: An analysis of power between groups. In W. G. Austin & S. Worchel (Eds.), *The social psychology of intergroup relations.* Monterey, CA: Brooks/Cole.

Arciniega, T. A. (1973). The myth of the compensatory education model in education of Chicanos. In R. O. de la Garza, Z. A. Kruszewski, & T. A. Arciniega (Eds.), *Chicanos and Native Americans: The territorial minorities.* Englewood Cliffs, NJ: Prentice-Hall.

Arthur, B., Farrar, D., & Bradford, B. (1974). Evaluation reactions of college students to dialect differences in the English of Mexican Americans. *Language and Speech, 17,* 255–270.

Baldwin, J. A. (1979). Theory and research concerning the notion of Black self-hatred: A review and reinterpretation. Journal of Black Psychology, 5, 51–77.

Banfield, E. C. (1970). *The unheavenly city: The nature and future of our urban crisis.* Boston: Little, Brown.

Banks, W. C. (1976). White preference in blacks: A paradigm in search of a phenomenon. *Psychological Bulletin, 83,* 1179–1186.

Barker, G. C. (1947). *Social functions of language in a Mexican American community.* Unpublished doctoral dissertation, University of Texas, Austin.

Brekke, A. M. (1973). *Evaluational reactions of adolescent and pre-adolescent Mexican American and Anglo American students to selected samples of spoken English.* Unpublished doctoral dissertation, University of Minnesota, Minneapolis.

Bridgeman, B., & Shipman, V. C. (1975). *Disadvantaged children and their first school experience.* Report prepared for Project Head Start, Washington, DC: Office of Child Development.

Brischetto, R., & Arciniega, T. (1973). *Chicanos and native Americans: The territorial minorities.* Englewood Cliffs, NJ: Prentice-Hall.

Buriel, R. (1984). Integration with traditional Mexican-American culture and socio-cultural adjustment. In J. L. Martinez, Jr. & R. H. Mendoza (Eds.), *Chicano psychology*. New York: Academic Press.

Buriel, R., & Vasquez, R. (1982). Stereotypes of Mexican descent persons. *Journal of Cross-Cultural Psychology, 13,* 59–70.

Burma, J. (1970). *Mexican Americans in the U.S.: A reader.* New York: Pitman.

Carter, T. P. (1970). *Mexican Americans in school: A history of educational neglect.* Englewood Cliffs, NJ: College Entrance Examination Board.

Caudill, W., & DeVos, G. A. (1956). Achievement culture and personality: The case of the Japanese-Americans. *American Anthropologist, 58,* 1102–1126.

Chavez, R., & Ramirez, A. (1983). Employment aspirations, expectations, and attitudes among employed and unemployed Chicanos. *Journal of Social Psychology, 119,* 143–144.

Child, I. L. (1943). *Italian or American? The second generation in conflict.* New Haven, CT: Yale University Press.

Clark, M. (1959). *Health in the Mexican American culture: A community study.* Berkeley, CA: University of California Press.

Cordova, I. R. (1970). The relationship of acculturation, achievement, and alienation among Spanish-American sixth grade students. In H. S. Johnson & W. G. Hernandez (Eds.), *Educating the Mexican American.* Valley Forge, PA: Judson Press.

Cross, W. (1971). The Negro-to-Black conversion experience: Toward a psychology of black liberation. *Black World, 20,* 13–27.

Davidson, C., & Gaitz, C. (1974). Are the poor different? A comparison of work behavior and attitudes among the poor and non-poor. *Social Problems, 22,* 229–245.

Dembroski, T. M., Lasater, T. M., & Ramirez, A. (1978). Communicator similarity, fear-arousing communications and compliance with health care recommendations. *Journal of Applied Social Psychology, 8,* 254–269.

Demos, G. A. (1962). Attitudes of Mexican-American and Anglo-American groups toward education. *Journal of Social Psychology, 57,* 249–256.

Derbyshire, R. L. (1968). Adolescent identity crisis in urban Mexican Americans in East Los Angeles. In E. B. Brody (Ed.), *Minority group adolescents in the United States.* Baltimore: Williams & Wilkins.

Deutsch, M. (1967). *The disadvantaged child.* New York: Basic Books.

Dworkin, A. G. (1964). Stereotypes and self-images held by native-born and foreign-born Mexican-Americans. *Sociology and Social Research, 49,* 214–224.

Etzioni-Halevy, E., & Halevy, Z. (1977). The Jewish ethic and the spirit of achievement. *The Jewish Journal of Sociology, 19,* 50–55.

Feagin, J. R. (1975). *Subordinating the poor: Welfare and American beliefs.* Englewood Cliffs, NJ: Prentice-Hall.

Frazier, E. F. (1939). *The Negro family in the United States.* Chicago: University of Chicago Press.

French, J. R., & Raven, B. H. (1959). The bases of social power. In D. Cartwright (Ed.), *Studies in social power.* Ann Arbor: University of Michigan Press.

Garcia, H. D. C. (1981). *Bilingualism, confidence, and college achievement* (Report No. 318). Baltimore: Center for Social Organization of Schools, Johns Hopkins University.

Garcia, J. (1977). Intelligence testing: Quotients, quotas, and quackery. In J. L. Martinez, Jr. (Ed.), *Chicano psychology.* New York: Academic Press.

Garza, R. T. (1977). Personal control and fatalism in Chicanos and Anglos: Conceptual and methodological issues. In J. L. Martinez, Jr. (Ed.), *Chicano psychology.* New York: Academic Press.

Garza, R. T. & Ames, R. E., Jr. (1974). A comparison of Anglo- and Mexican-American college students on locus of control. *Journal of Consulting and Clinical Psychology, 42,* 919.

Garza, R. T., & Lipton, J. P. (1984). Foundations for a Chicano social psychology. In J. L. Martinez, Jr., & R. H. Mendoza (Eds.), *Chicano psychology.* New York: Academic Press.

Heller, C. S. (1966). *Mexican-American youth: Forgotten youth at the crossroads.* New York: Random House.

Henderson, R. W. (1972). Environment predictors of academic performance of disadvantaged Mexican-American children. *Journal of Consulting and Clinical Psychology, 38,* 297.

Henderson, R. W., & Merritt, C. G. (1968). Environmental backgrounds of Mexican American children with different potentials for school success. *Journal of Social Psychology, 75,* 101–106.

Herrnstein, R. (1973). *IQ in the meritocracy.* Boston: Little, Brown.

Humphrey, N. D. (1944). The changing structure of the Detroit Mexican family. *American Sociological Review, 9,* 622–626.

Jensen, A. (1969). How much can we boost IQ and scholastic achievement? *Harvard Educational Review, 39,* 1–123.

Johnson, D. (1978). A metatheory for Chicano psychology: The case for a minority based metatheory. *Atisbos: Journal of Chicano Research, Summer–Fall,* 36–60.

Johnson, K. R. (1970). *Teaching the culturally disadvantaged: A rational approach.* Palo Alto, CA: Science Research Associates.

Jones, R. L. (1980). *Black psychology.* New York: Harper & Row.

Juarez, R. Y., Kuvlesky, W. P. (1968). *Ethnic group identity and orientation toward educational attainment: A comparison of Mexican-American and Anglo boys* (ERIC: Ed 028.467).

Kluckhohn, F., & Strodbeck, F. L. (1961). *Variations in value orientations.* New York: Harper.

Knowles, L. L., and Prewitt, K. (1969). *Institutional racism in America.* Englewood Cliffs, NJ: Prentice-Hall.

Krear, S. W. (1971). The role of the mother tongue at home and at school in the development of bilingualism. In N. N. Wagner & M. J. Maug (Eds.), *Chicanos: Social and psychological perspectives.* St. Louis: C. V. Mosby.

Kuvlesky, W., Wright, D., & Juarez, R. (1971). A comparison of Mexican-American, Negro and Anglo youth. *Journal of Vocational Behavior, 1,* 231–244.

Lampe, P. (1975). Mexican-American self-identity and ethnic prejudice. *Cornell Journal of Social Relations, 10,* 223–237.

Lerner, M. J., & Miller, D. T. (1978). Just world research and the attribution process: Looking back and ahead. *Psychological Bulletin, 85,* 1030–1057.

Lewis, O. (1966). The culture of poverty. *Scientific American, 215,* 19–25.

Lewis, O. (1968). *A study of slum culture: Backgrounds for La Vida.* New York: Random House.

Leyva, R. (1975). Educational aspirations and expectations of Chicanos, non-Chicanos, and Anglo-Americans. *California Journal of Educational Research, 26,* 27–39.

Little, J. & Ramirez, A. (1976). Ethnicity of subject and test administrator: Their effects on self-esteem. *Journal of Social Psychology, 99,* 149–150.

Madsen, W. (1964). *Mexican Americans of south Texas.* New York: Holt.

Mercer, J. R. (1973). *Labeling the mentally retarded.* Berkeley: University of California Press.

Mercer, J. R. (1975). Sociocultural factors in educational labeling. In M. J. Begab & S. A. Richardson (Eds.), *The mentally retarded and society: A social science perspective.* Baltimore: University Park Press.

Mercer, J. R. (1977). Identifying the gifted Chicano child. In J. L. Martinez, Jr. (Ed.), *Chicano psychology.* New York: Academic Press.

Montero, D., & Tsukashima, R. (1977). Assimilation and educational achievement: The case of the second generation Japanese-American. *The Sociological Quarterly, 18,* 490–503.

Montiel, M. (1970). Social science myth of the Mexican American family. *El Grito, 3,* 56–63.

Moynihan, D. P. (1965). *The Negro family: The case for national action.* Washington, DC: U.S. Government Printing Office.

Nichols, N. J. (1977). Black or white socioeconomically disadvantaged pupils—They aren't necessarily inferior. *The Journal of Negro Education, 43,* 443–449.

Olmedo, E. L. (1977). Psychological testing and the Chicano: A reassessment. In J. L. Martinez, Jr. (Ed.), *Chicano psychology.* New York: Academic Press.

Olmedo, E. L., Martinez, J. L., & Martinez, S. R. (1978). Measure of acculturation for Chicano adolescents. *Psychological Reports, 42,* 159–170.

Ortego, P. (1969). Some cultural implications of a Mexican American border dialect of American English. In R. I. Duran & H. R. Bernard (Eds.), *Introduction to Chicano studies.* New York: Macmillan.

Ortego, P. D. (1970). Montezuma's children. *El Grito, 3,* 39–50.

Padilla, A. M. (1980). The role of clinical awareness and ethnic loyalty in acculturation. In A. M. Padilla (Ed.), *Acculturation: Theory, models, and some new findings.* Boulder, CO: Westview Press.

Padilla, A. M., & Ruiz, R. A. (1973). *Latino mental health: A review of literature.* Washington, DC: U.S. Government Printing Office.

Penalosa, F., McDonagh, E. C. (1966). Social mobility in a Mexican-American community. *Social Forces, 44,* 498–505.

Phares, E. J., & Lamiell, J. (1976). To internal–external control, interpersonal judgements of others in need, and attribution of responsibility. *Journal of Personality, 43,* 23–38.

Picou, S. (1973). Black–white variations in a model of the occupational aspiration process. *Journal of Negro Education, 42,* 117–122.

Politzer, R. L., & Ramirez, A. G. (1973a). *Judging personality from speech: A pilot study of the attitudes toward ethnic groups of students in monolingual schools* (R & D Memo No. 107). Stanford, CA: Stanford University Center for Research and Development in Teaching.

Politzer, R. L., & Ramirez, A. G. (1973b). *Judging personality from speech: A pilot study of effects of bilingual education on attitudes towards ethnic groups* (R & D Memo No. 106). Stanford, CA: Stanford University Center for Research and Development in Teaching.

Proshansky, H., & Newton, P. (1973). Colour: The nature and meaning of Negro self-identity. In P. Watson (Ed.), *Psychology and race*. Chicago: Aldine.

Rainwater, L. (1970). *Behind ghetto walls: Black family life in a federal slum*. Chicago: Aldine.

Ramirez, A. (1977a). Chicano power and interracial group relations. In J. L. Martinez, Jr. (Ed.), *Chicano psychology*. New York: Academic Press.

Ramirez, A. (1977b). Social influence and ethnicity of the communicator. *Journal of Social Psychology, 102,* 79–91.

Ramirez, A. (1985a). *Hispanic consumer behavior: Social psychological perspectives*. Paper presented at the American Psychological Association Convention, Los Angeles.

Ramirez, A. (1985b). *El multiculturalismo y la aculturacion: Un analisis socio-psicologico*. Paper presented at the Bi-National Conference on Psychology, Cuture, and National Identity, National Autonomous University of Mexico, Mexico City.

Ramirez, A., & Chavez, R. (1982). Family- and work-related attitudes and aspirations of Hispanic and non-Hispanic youth. Paper presented as part of symposium, *Hispanic youth employment: Research and policy issues,* National Council of La Raza, Washington, DC.

Ramirez, A., & Lasater, T. M. (1977). Ethnicity of communicator, self-esteem, and reactions to fear-arousing communications. *Journal of Social Psychology, 102,* 79–91.

Ramirez, A., & Ossorio, P. (1983). Ethnic psychology: An approach to the study of race, ethnicity, and culture. In W. C. McCready (Ed.), *Culture, ethnicity, and identity: Current issues in research*. New York: Academic Press.

Ramirez, A., & Soriano, F. (1982). Social power in educational systems: Its effects on Chicanos' attitudes toward the school experience. *Journal of Social Psychology, 118,* 113–119.

Ramirez, M. (1969). Identification with Mexican-American values and psychological adjustment in Mexican American adolescents. *International Journal of Social Psychiatry, 15,* 151–156.

Ramirez, M. (1977). Recognizing and understanding diversity: Multiculturalism and the Chicano movement in psychology. In J. L. Martinez, Jr. (Ed.), *Chicano psychology*. New York: Academic Press.

Ramirez, M. (1983). *Psychology of the Americas*. New York: Pergamon Press.

Ramirez, M. (1984). Assessing and understanding biculturalism-multiculturalism in Mexican-American adults. In J. L. Martinez, Jr., & R. H. Mendoza (Eds.), *Chicano psychology*. New York: Academic Press.

Ramirez, M., & Castaneda, A. (1974). *Cultural democracy, bicognitive development, and education*. New York: Academic Press.

Ramirez, M., Garza, R. T., & Cox, B. G. (1980). *Multicultural leader behaviors in ethnically mixed task groups* (Technical Report). Washington, DC: Office of Naval Research, Organizational Effectiveness Research Program.

Rappaport, J., Davidson, W. S., Wilson, M. N., & Mitchell, A. (1975). Alternatives to blaming the victim or the environment: Our places to stand have not moved the earth. *American Psychologist, 30,* 525–528.

Rice, A. S., Ruiz, R. A., & Padilla, A. M. (1974). Person perception, self-identity, and ethnic group preference in Anglo, black, and Chicano preschool and third-grade children. *Journal of Cross-Cultural Psychology, 5,* 100–108.

Rocco, R. R. (1970). The Chicano in the social sciences: Traditional concepts, myths, and images. *Aztlan, 1,* 75–98.

Rohrer, G. K. (1973). Racial and ethnic identification and preference in young children. *Dissertation Abstracts International, 33,* 3404–3405.

Romano, O. (1969). The historical and intellectual presence of Mexican Americans. *El Grito, 2,* 41.

Romano, O. (1970). Social science, objectivity, and the Chicanos. *El Grito, 4,* 4–16.

Romano, O. (1973). The anthropology and sociology of the Mexican-Americans. In O. Romano (Ed.), *Voices*. Berkeley, CA: Quinto Sol Publications.

Rosenthal, R., & Jacobson, L. (1968). Pygmalion in the classroom: Teacher expectations and pupils' intellectual development. New York: Holt, Rinehart & Winston.

Rotter, J. B. (1975). Some problems and misconceptions related to the construct of internal versus external control of reinforcement. *Journal of Consulting and Clinical Psychology, 43,* 56–67.

Rotter, J. B., Chance, J., & Phares, E. J. (1972). *Applications of social learning theory of personality*. New York: Holt, Rinehart & Winston.

Rubel, A. J. (1966). *Across the tracks: Mexican Americans in a Texas city*. Austin, TX: Hogg Foundation for Mental Health.

Ryan, E. B., & Carranza, M. A. (1975). Evaluative reactions toward speakers of standard English and Mexican American accented English. *Journal of Personality and Social Psychology, 31,* 855–863.

Ryan, W. (1971). *Blaming the victim.* New York: Random House.

Salazar, J. H. (1972). *Self-designation patterns of a traditional ethnic minority in a modern society: Conflict, consensus and confusion in the identity crisis* (ERIC Document File, No. EDO66256).

Sanchez, G. I. (1932). Group differences and Spanish-speaking children—A critical review. *Journal of Applied Psychology, 16,* 549–558.

Sanchez, G. I. (1934). The implications of a basal vocabulary to the measurement of the abilities of bilingual children. *Journal of Social Psychology, 5,* 395–402.

Saunders, L. (1954). *Cultural differences and medical care: The case of the Spanish-speaking people of the southwest.* New York: Russell Sage Foundation.

Scott, J. D., & Phelon, J. G. (1969). Expectancies of unemployable males regarding source of reinforcement. *Psychological Reports, 25,* 911–913.

Shockley, W. (1971). Negro IQ deficit: Failure of a "malicious coincidence" model warrants new research proposals. *Review of Educational Research, 41,* 227–248.

Smitherman, G. (1977). *Talkin and testifyin: The language of black America.* Boston: Houghton Mifflin.

Sommers, V. S. (1964). The impact of dual cultural membership on identity. *Psychiatry, 27,* 332–344.

Stoddard, E. (1970). Ethnic identity of urban Mexican American youth. *Proceedings of the Southwest Sociological Association,* Dallas, TX.

Stonequist, E. V. (1964). The marginal man: A study in personality and culture conflict. !n E. Burgess & D. J. Bogue (Eds.), *Contributions to urban sociology.* Chicago: University of Chicago Press.

Stryker, S., Sarabia, B., Lopez, E. M., Castillo, J. C., Burillo, F. J., Tajfel, H., Torregrosa, J. R., Kelman, H. C., Ridruejo, P., & Harre, R. (1983). *Perspectivas y contextos de la psicologia social.* Barcelona, Spain: Editorial Hispano Europea, SA.

Szapocznik, J., Scopetta, M. H., Kurtines, W., & Arnalde, M. A. (1978). Theory and measurement of acculturation. *Inter-American Journal of Psychology, 12,* 113–130.

Taylor, R. L. (1976). Psychosocial development among black children and youth: A re-examination. *American Journal of Orthopsychiatry, 46,* 4–19.

Thomas, C. (1971). *Boys no more.* Beverly Hills, CA: Glencoe Press.

Thompson, R. M. (1973). *Social correlates of regional pronunciation in Mexican American English.* Paper presented at the Linguistics Society of America, Ann Arbor, MI.

Tuck, R. D. (1946). *Not with the first: Mexican-Americans in a southwest city.* New York: Harcourt, Brace.

Ulibarri, H. (1960). Teacher awareness of socio-cultural differences in multicultural classrooms. *Sociology and Social Research, 45,* 49–55.

U.S. Commission on Civil Rights. (1973). *Teachers and students* (Report V: Mexican American education study: Differences in teacher interaction with Mexican American and Anglo American students). Washington, DC: U.S. Government Printing Office.

Vaca, N. A. (1970). The Mexican American in the social sciences: II. 1936–1970. *El Grito, 4,* 17–51.

Vigil, D. (1979). Adaptation strategies and cultural life styles of Mexican American adolescents. *Hispanic Journal of Behavioral Sciences, 1,* 375–392.

Wendling, A., & Elliott, D. S. (1968). Class and race differentials in parental aspirations and expectations. *Pacific Sociological Review, 11,* 123–133.

Werner, N. W., & Evans, I. M. (1968). Perception of prejudice in Mexican-American preschool children. *Perceptual and Motor Skills, 27,* 1039–1046.

White, J. L. (1984). *The psychology of blacks: An Afro-American perspective.* Englewood Cliffs, NJ: Prentice-Hall.

Whitehead, C. J., & King, A. S. (1973). Differences in managers' attitudes toward Mexican and non-Mexican-Americans in organizational authority relations. *Social Science Quarterly, 53,* 760–761.

Williams, R. L. (1975). The BITCH-100: A culture-specific test. *Journal of Afro-American Issues, 3,* 103–116.

Zintz, M. V. (1969). *Education across cultures.* Dubuque, IA: Kendall/Hunt.

8

Seeking Convergence in Race Relations Research

Japanese-Americans and the Resurrection of the Internment

Don T. Nakanishi

Like many other scholars, I had parceled out white attitudes toward different racial groups almost as if there were no important similarities and differences in the ways whites imaged or treated them. Yet I knew that the reality of white America's experience was dynamically multiracial. What whites did to one racial group had direct consequences for others. And whites did not artificially view each group in a vacuum; rather, in their minds, they lumped the different groups together or counterpointed them against each other.

Ronald Takaki, *Iron Cages* (1979)

We are experiencing on a massively universal scale a convulsive ingathering of people in their numberless groupings of kinds— tribal, racial, linguistic, religious, national. It is a great clustering into separateness that will, it is thought, improve, assure, or extend each group's power or place, or keep it safe or safer from the power, threat, or hostility of others. This is obviously no new condition, only the latest and by far the most inclusive chapter of the old story in which after failing again to find how they can co-exist in sight of each other without tearing each other limb from limb, Isaac and Ishmael clash and part in panic and retreat once more into their caves.

Harold Isaacs, *Idols of the Tribe* (1975)

DON T. NAKANISHI • Graduate School of Education, University of California, Los Angeles, California 90024.

INTRODUCTION

Research on American race relations is at a critical divide. After a decade or more of collectively debunking demeaning myths and stereotypes about minority life, as well as challenging an array of earlier, order-based theories such as assimilation, the field has come to reflect a rich mosaic of new paradigmatic tendencies and goals. Race, which has always been a fuzzy concept, can no longer be analyzed on its own slippery terms. Instead, it now must be conjugated with often equally muddy notions of class and gender. Psychology and sociology, which previously could claim almost exclusive title to the domain of intergroup relations research, have had to give substantive ground to other methodological and analytical approaches. Recent contributions from disciplines as old as economics, history, literature, and political science, or seemingly new like ethnic studies or policy studies, have clearly led to a more provocatively pluralistic field of inquiry. And finally, among other major changes, research on American race relations has begun to reflect, slowly but nonetheless to a greater extent than it did before, the multiracial reality of America's past, present, and future. New research on Chicanos, American Indians, and Asian Pacific Americans have not supplanted, nor have they sought to supplant, the long tradition of scholarship on blacks. But they have provided added credence to viewing persistent societal conditions of poverty, discrimination, prejudice, and powerlessness from multiple vantage points of group experiences. These contributions on other nonwhite populations have augmented the research agenda on American race relations by demonstrating the continued importance of issues dealing with language, immigration, and land ownership. They have also underscored the need for new visions, interpretations, and conceptualizations of America's multiracial experience.

This chapter was intended to probe the generalizability of scholarship on American black–white relations for the Asian Pacific American experience. On simple reflection, though, it became obvious that this would be an awesome intellectual task. If properly and rigorously undertaken in a scientific manner, it would entail the testing and verification of a large body of theoretical propositions, hypotheses, and observations, which has been generated over the years. Indeed, as sociologist Hubert Blalock, Jr., illustrated in his influential treatise *Toward a Theory of Minority-Group Relations* (1967), the seemingly simple exercise of stockpiling testable theoretical propositions from past research can be a significant scholarly achievement in its own right. Blalock's work, which proposed close to 100 different testable hypotheses solely on the topics of prejudice and discrimination, could conceivably occupy entire departments of sociology and psychology for many years in seeking verification solely for the American experience, without ever gaining additional confirmation through cross-national investigations (Berreman, 1972). Therefore, in a strict methodological sense, this chapter will not attempt to test the generalizability to Asian Pacific Americans of existing research findings on black–white relations.

There is no doubt, though, that scholarship on Asian Pacific Americans, like that on other American racial and ethnic groups, has been and continues to be enriched by the sustained and multifaceted attention that the black experience has received. Scholars, journalists, policy analysts, activists, and creative writers have contributed to a large and impressive body of literature, which has had a major, ongoing impact on how all minority groups, as well as all issues related to racial inequality and minority status, have been approached. For example, major analytic and normative perspectives, be they variants of social Darwinism, cultural pluralism, internal colonialism, or assorted Marxist frameworks, which have guided analyses of the condition of American blacks, have been used at various junctures to explore the Asian Pacific American experience (Hirata, 1978). Similarly, recent contributions like Wilson's controversial book, *The Declining Significance of Race* (1978), which has yet to be applied fully to Asian Pacific Americans, will undoubtedly influence future inquiries on the group. The work, despite its potentially harmful policy implications, provides added credence for several recent analytic innovations in Asian American scholarship. It underscores, for instance, the importance of pioneering works by Takaki (1979), Ong (1981), and Cheng and Bonacich (1984) to an understanding of the longitudinal development of Asian Pacific Americans, like blacks, in the broader context of evolving societal structures, institutions, and belief systems. It also is consistent with current efforts by scholars to challenge the largely monolithic portrayals of Asian Pacific Americans and other minority groups in past research by highlighting their internal, within-group differentiation. Like blacks, Asian Pacific Americans are rarely viewed as a highly heterogeneous population with a myriad of real and symbolic levels of internal differentiation of social classes, generations, religions, gender, countries of origin, languages, and cultural norms. They are also rarely analyzed in terms of their varying degrees of access to and interaction with external groups, institutions, or processes, be they of American society or of their ancestral homelands. Among others, the recent studies by Nee and Nee (1974), Kim (1981), and Takahashi (1982) illustrate both the necessity and the promise of analyzing major within-group differences among Asian Pacific Americans.

The Asian Pacific American experience, though, cannot be fully understood through perspectives developed on black–white relations. One crucial difference lies in the limitations of the largely domestic focus of most research on blacks. In contrast, many crucial dimensions of the historical and contemporary experiences of Asian Pacific Americans must be analyzed in a broader international framework. For example, the extraordinary growth and diversification of the Asian Pacific American population since the mid-1960s, in which the group was transformed from predominantly American-born to largely foreign-born, cannot be captured without considering the political and economic conditions in Asian countries or the varied forms of involvement of the United States in Asia (Cheng & Bonacich, 1984). Likewise, the political participation of Asian Pacific Americans must be approached from both domestic and international perspectives (Nakanishi, 1986). Like blacks, Asian Pacific Americans were politically disenfranchised because of laws that prevented earlier immigrants from becoming naturalized. However, with the exception of the Garvey movement and current activities against apartheid in South Africa, the importance of so-called homeland politics has been less apparent and sustained for blacks than it has been for Asian Pacific Americans. And finally, as many writers have shown (TenBroek, Barnhart, & Mason, 1968; Isaacs, 1958; McClellan, 1971; Takaki, 1979), racial stereotypes and acts of racial prejudice and hatred against Asian Pacific Americans have their origins not only in evolving domestic racist ideologies and practices, but also in shifting American foreign attitudes toward and relations with Asian nations.

Generalizability, however, is a significant issue for the present and future development of scholarship and public policies dealing with American race relations. Although all racial groups, analyzed in terms of their internal features or relations with others, may have an assortment of unique differentiating characteristics, it is clear that our analytic insights, and the remedies we propose, could benefit from the continuous integration of group-specific and comparative insights, and more generally, from nomethetic and idiographic contributions to the topic (Przeworski & Teune, 1970). Unfortunately, for a variety of methodological and philosophical reasons, race relations research does not reflect or seek an adequate convergence of these intellectual approaches. It is highly likely that the plethora of specialized inquiries on specific group experiences from multiple levels of analysis will make it more difficult rather than simpler to seek interrelationships in the future. Indeed, we may be headed toward a crisis similar to that faced by international relations research since the mid-1960s, in which scholars of different theoretical persuasions began to lock themselves in "conceptual jails" (Rosenau, 1971), which prevented a meaningful synthesis of their approaches.

In race relations research, ethnic studies humanists, be they historians or literary analysts, have clearly revolutionized the field by unearthing a massive, rich, and largely "buried past" (Ichioka, 1974), using previously untapped primary documents written in non-English languages, oral historical techniques, and more generally, insights from the perspectives of minority people. Recent historiographic contributions, for example, have challenged the accuracy of earlier interpretations, especially the long-standing view that minority groups were simply passive spectators of the parade of major events and injustices in their past experiences (Wollenberg, 1976). As Daniels (1976) wrote about Asian American historiography:

> Most of the scholarship about Chinese in America, and in fact about Asian Americans generally, has focused on the opposition which they aroused, on the excluders rather than the excluded. There are many reasons for this: the lack of manuscript materials, the inability of most scholars interested in United States history to utilize Asian languages, and perhaps most important of all, a first overt and then covert kind of racism which tended to ignore the victims even while dissecting the oppressors. (p. 10)

Among many others, recent works by Nee and Nee (1974), Hansen and Mitson (1974), Lai (1976), Ichioka (1977), Yu, (1977), Vallangca (1977), Choy (1979), Kim (1981), Kwong (1981), Kikumura (1981), and Low (1982) have attempted to rectify this imbalance in previous historical treatments of the Asian Pacific American experience.

These rich and detailed studies challenge the nomothetically inclined social sciences and their approaches to American race relations. Specific spatiotemporal features, which are vividly highlighted in idiographic inquiries, are often overlooked, deemphasized, or displaced through methodological and analytical manipulations. It is not surprising, then, that a good deal of earlier and current social science research on minority groups, especially those that resort to the past to explain current conditions or are comparative in focus, have met the classic criticism of being ahistorical, historically inaccurate, or insensitive to significant group differences. This dilemma is shared by nearly all fields of inquiry. However, there are few issue areas like American race relations, where the findings, interpretations, and perspectives of the social sciences have been so easily transferred, usually without sufficient verification, to public policies, legal deliberations, and more generally, public debates, which have been both beneficial and detrimental to minority groups. This common intellectual dilemma, therefore, cannot be fully addressed by the field of race relations solely on its intellectual merits. It also must be considered in terms of its potential implications for public policies and group actions (Enloe, 1973; Ladner, 1973).

Generalizability ought to be one of the guiding ideals for research on American race relations, as well as in other scholarly domains. However, it would be fallacious to criticize the current state of the field, which may appear to be too eclectic, too specialized, and perhaps too ethnocentric for some—and provocatively pluralistic for others. With respect to most criteria of rigorous scholarship and informed policy thinking, the field has clearly benefited from the infusion of new disciplinary approaches, the increased representation of minority scholars, and the substantial growth of literature on all racial minorities. For Asian Pacific Americans, critiques of this new scholarship are available in many revealing and insightful assessments of psychological, literary, sociological, and historical approaches to the Asian Pacific American experience (Endo, 1980; Hirata, 1978; Hundley, 1976; Hune, 1977; Hurh & Kim, 1982; Kim, 1982; J. Liu, 1978; W. T. Liu, 1980; Lyman, 1977; Okamura, 1978; Sue, 1980). These reviews of the literature highlight the limitations and biases of long-standing perspectives such as assimilation and the so-called model minority thesis. They also recognize the paucity of research on groups other than Chinese- and Japanese-Americans, as well as the need for fresh theoretical and empirical inquiries into important but largely neglected issue-areas like political participation and the growing number of Asian Pacific Americans in poverty. Although all call for even more concerted research on Asian Pacific Americans, in which Asian Pacific Americans are the explicit focus of scholarly attention, they also recognize the necessity of drawing from and forging linkages with other established and emerging areas of study. Recent research on Asian Pacific Americans, for example, has benefited from analytic and methodological innovations not only in the study of blacks, but also in scholarship on other American racial and immigrant groups, women, Asian studies, and more generally, all forms of intergroup relations.

Indeed, if the field of race relations is to achieve its long-range goals of being truly interdisciplinary and multiracial, it should deliberately search for areas of convergence, as well as fully justify its potential domains of divergence. It must, in a figurative sense, occasionally attempt to put together the puzzle of American race relations with the pile of pieces of empirical and analytic insights that it has and must consider what additional pieces remain to be found.

SEEKING CONVERGENCE

The following discussion seeks to contribute to this search for convergence by analyzing in an interdisciplinary and multiracial fashion what is perhaps the most well-known and dramatic episode of racial prejudice and discrimination against an Asian Pacific American group: the World War II internment of Japanese-Americans. Rather than treating the event as past history, as a voluminous body of literature has done,[1] I will attempt to explore a somewhat puzzling, and yet profound, dimension of this tragedy: its recent resurrection by Japanese-Americans as the dominant issue area and focus of attention for the group. It will attempt to analyze the interaction of structural and psychological factors that led Japanese-Americans not only to depart from a prolonged and collectively shared period of silence and avoidance of the event, but more important, to identify with it in a highly visible, sustained, and multifaceted manner.

My reasons for exploring this phenomenon are twofold. First, the internment experience is one of the few major events in Asian Pacific American history that is familiar to most scholars and many members of the general public, and that receives at least some attention in current American textbooks, as well as studies on American race relations. Although some controversy remains about its wartime necessity (Commission on Wartime Relocation and Internment of Citizens, 1982; Irons, 1983; Weglyn, 1976), there are few who would dispute the interpretation that racism was at least one of its major underlying causes, or that the removal and imprisonment of 120,000 individuals for more than 4 years is an extraordinary action. However, like other significant events in the group histories of American racial minorities, the internment is usually viewed as a distant and past tragedy, which will probably never happen again, and which, more importantly, has had no enduring impact on or significance for the group or its members. It is largely considered a topic for historiographic investigation or for a classroom discussion on American history. It serves as another benchmark for illustrating the severity of

---

[1]For a general overview of the Japanese-American internment experience, see Weglyn (1976), Bosworth (1976), Daniels (1976), Girdner and Loftis (1969), and Grodzins (1949). *Americans Betrayed*. For a legal analysis of major internment-related cases, see TenBroek, Barnhart, and Matson (1968), Rostow (1962), Irons (1983), and Takasugi (1974). For reviews of the literature, see Okamura (1978).

America's past racial oppression, or in a more optimistic vein, as a frame of reference for assessing the progress that the society has made in improving its racial conditions.

The recent resurrection of this event by Japanese-Americans, though, suggests that these common notions of past racial victimization may be limited. They may be based more on simplistic value judgments about the resiliency of individuals and groups in coping with and coming to grips with such events rather than on in-depth empirical investigations. The following analysis provides an alternative and more rigorous treatment of the longitudinal significance of such events by drawing on data collected from multiple methodological approaches.[2] It gains its analytic insights from studies of survivors of major historical disasters like the Holocaust and the atomic bombing of Hiroshima, a body of literature that, in its infancy, was earlier applied to and then largely dismissed in relation to understanding the behavior of blacks *during* slavery (Degler, 1976). However, the empirical findings and theoretical generalizations from these works on the behavior of individuals *after* these disastrous episodes suggests that the latent collective response of Japanese-Americans to their internment experience should not be puzzling nor viewed as unique. By analyzing the Japanese-American case, perhaps we will not prematurely turn the page on past instances of racial victimization and, instead, will seek to empirically ascertain their possible enduring impact and significance for both the group and the larger society.

Another reason for analyzing the recent resurrection of the internment is that it reveals the shortcomings and ramifications of the popular view that Japanese-Americans are a successful or model minority, an interpretation that is often generalized to all other Asian Pacific American groups. This perspective was promulgated first by journalists and then by numerous scholars during and after the mid-1960s, a period of profound societal racial strife (Bell, 1985; Makaroff, 1967; Peterson, 1966; Varon, 1967). As Chun (1980) wrote, this view "created a glowing image of a population that, despite past discrimination, had succeeded in becoming a hard-working, uncomplaining minority deserving to serve as a model for other minorities" (p. 1). Its critics, however, have argued that this interpretation has been used invidiously to pit Asian Pacific Americans against other groups by placing them on a symbolic pedestal for others to emulate. More substantively, these critics argue that the perspective rests on an inadequate and normative analysis of selective aggregate-level census indicators and glosses over persistent and new forms of prejudice and discrimination faced by Asian Pacific Americans (Cabezas & Yee, 1977; Chun, 1980; Suzuki, 1977). And like some critics of Wilson's assessment of the emerging black middle class (Willie, 1978), these critics argue that the attainment of specific achievement levels by sectors of the Asian Pacific American population cannot be interpreted as meaning that equality of opportunity and societal acceptance have been gained, and that problems of institutional access, psychological well-being, or racial prejudice have been fully resolved.

In many respects, the model minority interpretation has served as one of the most important conceptual barriers to a meaningful convergence of analytical and empirical insights between Asian Pacific Americans and other racial groups. The perspective has often led researchers to conclude that Japanese-Americans—and more generally, all Asian Pacific Americans—have fully and irreversibly overcome their minority racial status. They are no longer affected by the similar structural and individual-level variables and forces that continue to restrict and prevent other racial groups from realizing their full potential as individuals and groups in this society. Many comparative analyses of

---

[2]The following analysis is based on in-depth interviews, archival materials analysis, and participant-observation of Japanese-American community organizations, which are more fully described in Nakanishi (1978).

racial minorities, as a result, begin with the simple and dichotomous premise that Asian Pacific Americans have succeeded and others have not. They then propose explanations, which are not always simple but are clearly dichotomous, to account for this seemingly monolithic difference among the groups (Lieberson, 1980; Ogbu, 1983). Moreover, the analytic generalizations that are usually drawn from this perspective are akin to those that have been extracted from the so-called European immigrant group analogy, which has been frequently used in examining the plight of blacks in northern urban centers. The crucial difference, however, is that Asian Pacific Americans provide an example of a racial minority that has seemingly lifted itself from its previous racial subordination in American society. The generalizations are that racial inequality is not a permanent and fixed condition for any group in this society, and that, over time, both the social structure and the group can attain a mutually beneficial accommodation. At the same time, this perspective of extraordinary group achievement has had a wide-range impact on Asian Pacific Americans in the realm of public policy. It has served to delegitimize and undermine attempts by Asian Pacific Americans seeking recognition and assistance for a variety of social needs of the group (U.S. Commission on Civil Rights, 1979). It also has excluded them from a wide array of governmental and private initiatives designed to enhance the quality of life and equality of opportunity for minority groups (Kuramoto, 1976).

However, if the popular and widely held view of Japanese-Americans as a successful or model minority represents a laudatory—and indeed, long-sought—affirmation of societal acceptance, why would the group resurrect, visibly identify with, and seek redress or recognition for an event that remains controversial and emotion-laden even after more than 40 years? Why would they engage in highly public activities, which would appear to jeopardize a uniquely positive stereotype of a racial group in American society? And more substantively, why would a group that has been portrayed as docile, eschewing public attention in politics for private economic achievement, suddenly take center stage on a seemingly no-win issue dealing with past racial victimization and keep it firmly atop the group's agenda for over a decade?

This is the second puzzling aspect of the recent activities of Japanese-Americans in relation to their internment experience. As we will see, this seemingly unprecedented action cannot be explained by the model minority thesis or by conventional perspectives on race relations, especially those that do not bridge idiographic and nomothetic approaches. It also provides another example of how research in race relations—in this case, the studies in support of the model minority perspective—can have significant, although perhaps largely unanticipated, consequences for both public policy deliberations and group actions. The rise and continued promulgation of this perspective in both journalistic and academic circles coincided with the resurrection of the internment. It served, on the one hand, as a major constraint on Japanese-American organizations for seeking governmental and public recognition for their past victimization. It also served, on the other hand, as one of the crucial elements of a dialectic process, which influenced the direction, momentum, and scope of the process of reawakening. And finally, this discussion will illustrate the necessity and analytic benefits of exploring such seemingly group-specific topics within an explicitly multiracial framework. By probing the resurrection of the internment in this manner, it will provide glimpses of a variety of largely overlooked areas of the convergence and divergence of the contemporary experiences of Japanese-Americans and other American racial minorities.

RESURRECTING THE INTERNMENT

I had nearly outgrown the shame and guilt and the sense of unworthiness. This trip, this pilgrimage, made comprehensible, finally, the traces that remained and would always remain, like a needle. That hollow ache I carried during the early months of internment had shrunk, over the years, to a tiny sliver of suspicion about the very person I was. It had grown so small sometimes I'd forget it was there. When I first read, in the summer of 1972, about the pressure Japan's economy was putting on American business and how a union in New York City had printed up posters of an American flag with MADE IN JAPAN written across it, then that needle began to jab. I heard Mama's soft, weary voice from 1945 say, "It's all starting over." I knew it wouldn't. Yet neither would I have been surprised to find the FBI at my door again. I would resist it much more than my parents did, but deep within me something had been prepared for that. Manzanar [concentration camp] would always live in my nervous system, a needle with Mama's voice. (Houston & Houston, 1973, p. 170)

Since the mid-1960s, after a seemingly prolonged and collectively shared period of silence, Japanese-Americans began to confront their World War II internment experience. Although this latent response to a past tragedy may not be unprecedented, it hardly follows a predictable or prescribed itinerary or set of rules. Survivors of other major disasters, for instance, have commonly exhibited a complex tug-of-war between remembering and forgetting their previous experiences. Yet, it has not been possible to forecast when and how the struggle of underlying psychological forces such as guilt, shame, repression, and vulnerability will be contested and resolved.[3]

The unpredictability of this reawakening stems, to a large extent, from the fact that surviving *through* and *after* a tragic event is a different and uniquely defined experience for each group of survivors. Each survival experience not only carries a distinct imprint from its disastrous episode but also evolves and is influenced by a different constellation of external factors and events, be they real or symbolic, historical or current, which serve to differentiate one group of survivors from another. For example, the viewing of a poster "of an American flag with MADE IN JAPAN written across it" may have triggered memories of the internment for Nisei (second-generation Japanese-American) writer Jeanne Wakatsuki Houston, but it probably would not have the same impact or symbolic meaning for other survivors, such as the Hiroshima *hibakusha*. On the other hand, as Lifton (1969) observed, "mass-media reports of people dying from A-bomb disease, and reports of nuclear weapons testing; as well as the annual August 6th ceremony, the sight of the A-Bomb Dome, [and] war or war-like behavior anywhere in the world" (p. 485) do serve to generate recollections of the Hiroshima explosion for its survivors. Although the underlying process, which Lifton called "symbolic reactiviation," may be comparable for survivors of both the Internment and Hiroshima, the specific signals or stimuli that bring memories and related symbolisms to the surface are not the same and probably vary in terms of their frequency of appearance. Indeed, different groups of survivors may exhibit similar forms of postdisaster behavior, but each approaches the dilemma of survival from unique and group-specific contexts and perspectives.

The resurrection of the internment by Japanese-Americans in recent years probably could not have been foreseen. For over two decades after the successful passage of the Evacuation Claims Act in 1948, which allowed Japanese-Americans to file claims "for damages to or loss of real or personal property . . . that is a reasonable or natural consequence of the evacuation" (Chuman, 1976; Hosokawa, 1969), the Japanese-American community rarely, if ever, engaged in formal organized activities dealing specifically with their internment experience. There were no pilgrimages to the former concentration camps; no legislative campaigns to rescind Executive Order 9066, which President Franklin Delano Roosevent issued to remove Japanese-Americans from the western states; and no organizations that sought to educate the general public about the injustices and losses

[3]See, for example, Niederland (1962, 1972), Lifton (1969), Erikson (1976), Wolfenstein (1957), and Janis (1971).

suffered by Japanese-Americans during the war. When references were made to the internment, especially by the Japanese American Citizens League (JACL) during the late 1940s and early 1950s in successsfully overturning a number of long-standing anti-alien and anti-Japanese laws (Chuman, 1976), they functioned almost exclusively as tools of advocacy and public relations. These references were used, in large measure, to show other Americans that Japanese-Americans were loyal and patriotic (Hosokawa, 1969). Two frequently used themes—that no acts of sabotage were committed by Japanese-Americans during the war, as well as stories of Japanese-American soldiers who provided "proof in blood" of their loyalty to America—served to buttress the view that the Internment was wrong, and yet, it provided Japanese-Americans with unexpected opportunities to demonstrate their worth as American citizens.

The internment, in many respects, came to symbolize a test of character for the Nisei. Although the test may have been unnecessary and unconstitutional, Nisei passed it with flying colors. They deserved recognition as full-fledged and equal American citizens, much as did World War II veterans of other racial and ethnic minorities at the time. However, in promoting this specific interpretation of the internment, very little was revealed about how the event adversely affected Japanese-Americans, especially the first-generation, alien Issei. Japanese-Americans, to be sure, were portrayed as victims, but little was said about their victimization. Although one might fault Nisei leaders, as well as a number of scholars who wrote about the Internment, for promulgating this narrow assimilationist view of the event, there is good reason to believe that both the American public and Japanese-Americans were not ready for a fuller discourse on the internment.

Indeed, the avoidance of a number of unresolved issues stemming from the internment for nearly two decades following the war at the collective level mirrored an analogous process of repression and denial at the individual level for most Japanese-Americans. As I will discuss more fully later, it was not uncommon for third-generation (Sansei) children to have acquired only the most basic and straightforward facts about their elders' internment experience, such as the names and locations of the concentration camps. They gained little understanding of the personal and group impact of being abruptly removed from homes and incarcerated in desolate locales; of the decisions by many to volunteer for military service or for others to seek repatriation to Japan; or of the extent of racial hatred and wartime hysteria that prevailed. The late Amy Ishii, a founder of the Manzanar Committee, a group that began, in the late 1960s, to plan annual pilgrimages to the Manzanar concentration camp in Central California and to offer public educational forums on the internment, commented on the difficulties of sharing the internment experience with Sansei (Hansen & Mitson, 1974):

> Women, if they've ever been raped, don't go around talking about it, you know, "I was a victim of rape," or anything like that. This is exactly the kind of feeling that we as evacuees, victims of circumstance, had at the time of the evacuation. A lot of Nisei and Issei are actually ashamed of the fact that they were in a concentration camp. You just don't talk about having been a victim of rape, and I think this is where our mental block is; therefore, it is very hard for the young people to go to their parents and ask them "Have you had this experience?" (p. 14)

Shame and guilt are often associated with the repression of a stressful or traumatic experience (Himmelfarb, 1971; Lifton, 1969; Niederland, 1972; Wolfenstein, 1957). But the following observation by Herbert Muhlen (1962) of a Nazi death camp survivor who remained in Germany after the war suggests a more commonsensical, alternative reason that the Sansei might have been offered such a limited description of the Internment:

> A Jewish woman in Hamburg was asked by her eight-year-old daughter, "What is a concentration camp?"

"Something like a vacation resort," she replied, "but not so much fun."

Both she and her husband had been in a concentration camp. After liberation, they had settled in their old home town, where they operated a successful, middle-sized factory. They belong to the Jewish congregation, attend services on holidays, and have an equal number of Jewish and Gentile friends.

"I do not want my daughter to be shocked and hurt by knowledge of the horrors," this woman explains. "I want her to grow up in a normal world as a normal child." (pp. 189–190)

And finally, it might be noted that, although the bulk of the literature on the internment appeared during the 20-year period following the war, very little found its way into American textbooks or the mass media (Okamura, 1976). Most works treated the event as past history. Many discussed the broader legal significance of evacuating and incarcerating Japanese-Americans, but none applied those historical lessons to an analysis of the McCarthy era's Internal Security Act of 1950, with its Title II provisions for the establishment of detention camps at locations such as Tule Lake, which was used during the internment. Indeed, the first work to draw parallels between the internment and Title II was *Concentration Camp USA* by Charles Allen, Jr., which appeared in 1966. At the same time, unlike the body of literary works and personal accounts written by survivors of the Nazi death camps, only a handful of books about the internment were written by Japanese-Americans during the two-decade period after the war.[4]

After this prolonged and collectively shared period of silence, Japanese-Americans resurrected the internment. Far from being a cataclysmic event, this resurrection represented a gradual process of reawakening, which was influenced initially by events and individuals outside the Japanese-American community. The first, and perhaps the broadest, impetus for this resurrection during the mid-1960s came from the general impact that the Black Power movement had on Japanese-Americans and other identifiable groups in American society, especially in terms of their group identities and their perceived status in the society. Harold Isaacs (1975) provided the most eloquent interpretation of the rippling effect of this dynamic societal reexamination:

> This crisis of "black" and "American" identity would by itself be crisis enough. But its effects in these years was to shake up all the other groups in the society located in various stations along the road from being "out" to being "in." It brought on change in the perception and self-perception of the "group" that had always been seen by all the others as "in"—the white Protestants of northern European origins who had been seen as the dominant majority "group" of the society and, who now began to be loosely and commonly lumped together under the pejorative label "Wasp." In other mostly non-white groups—the Mexican-Americans and other Spanish-speaking groups, the American Indians, the Chinese-Americans and Japanese-Americans—something of the black pattern began to be reproduced, with radical fringe groups appearing and reflecting—and momentarily speaking for—the much more widely felt and deeply laid feelings of whole populations that their status in the society and their image of themselves had to change. (pp. 20–21)

It was within this context of multiple group redefinition that the term *Asian American* and later *Asian Pacific American* was born and eventually gained popular usage to reflect the

---

[4]See Okamura (1978) for a review of the voluminous literature on the internment experience. Indeed, one of the very few works on the internment written by a Japanese-American before the mid-1960s was John Okada's novel, *No-No Boy* (1957). It was long considered taboo by the Japanese-American establishment and was not widely read by Japanese-Americans until the late 1960s. It sympathetically portrays the plight of a Japanese-American who answered "no" to two controversial questions regarding political loyalty and volunteering for military service, which were asked all Japanese-Americans while they were incarcerated. If they answered in the negative to these two questions, individuals were sent to the special Tule Lake concentration camp. See Weglyn (1976) for a fuller discussion.

commonality of experiences and the need to seek unity among the diverse Asian ethnic populations in the society (Uyematsu, 1971). The first group to carry this name was the Asian American Political Alliance, which was founded in the mid-1960s by Chinese, Japanese, and Filipino Americans in the Berkeley area as an alternative voice to the largely accommodationist orientations of long-standing organizations in Asian American communities (Nakanishi, 1986).

This climate of redefinition also stimulated discussions of ethnic identity and spurred interest, especially among Asian American college students, in the past history of Asian Americans. One of the most frequently and intensely examined events was the internment because it powerfully illustrated the common history of racial oppression that Asian Americans shared with other racial minorities. It was also a highly significant, and yet psychologically repressed, shared experience in the life histories of the parents and grandparents of Sansei students. Most Sansei, as in Muhlen's example, had been sheltered from knowing about most, and especially the traumatic, aspects of the internment by their elders, and had not been taught about the event in their previous schooling. Indeed, the Sansei, who are the "heirs" of the internment (Bergman & Jucovy, 1982; Epstein, 1977), played a crucial role not only in resurrecting the event from its buried past, but also in demonstrating its relevancy to the contemporary Japanese-American community. In ways that were highly private and highly public, the Sansei would not allow the older generations to forget the internment.

The second major influencing factor for this reawakening was the specific concern that black leaders such as Martin Luther King, Jr., Stokeley Carmichael, and H. Rap Brown voiced in relation to the existence and potential use of concentration camps in the United States during 1967 and 1968 (Brown, 1969; Okamura, 1974). Their concerns were expressed in the aftermath of ghetto riots and antiwar demonstrations and focused on the provisions of Title II of the 1950 Internal Security Act. These provisions were "statutorily legislated in 1950 by reference to the World War II concentration camp experience of resident Japanese," and created the legal appartus for "establishing concentration camps into which people might be put without benefit of trial, but merely by executive fiat . . . simply by an assumption . . . that an individual might be thinking about engaging in espionage or sabotage" (Okamura, 1974, p. 73).

The emerging nationwide uproar over Title II by black activists and civil libertarians, as well as the various calls for its repeal, initially had an impact on a small, and essentially Sansei and leftist-oriented, sector of the Japanese-American community. Indeed, the top leadership of the JACL, which was and remains the only national civil-rights group for Japanese-Americans, was initially opposed to using its resources and reputation for what was perceived to be a controversial, no-win legislative pursuit. Concern about the issue, though, broadened as individuals like Raymond Okamura and groups like the Asian American Political Alliance organized substantial grass-roots support within the Japanese-American community to propel a diverse cross section of Japanese-American groups, especially the JACL, into a major, 4-year campaign for the repeal of Title II (Okamura, 1974). Title II eventually "became a viable issue which large segments of the Japanese American could identify" (Kanno, 1974, p. 107). And as the late Edison Uno (1974) wrote:

> It sparked the imagination of Japanese Americans throughout the United States who utilized the Title II issue to enlighten and sensitize politicans, public media, educators, and the general public about the gross injustices of mass incarceration—in the past or future. What other group in our country could legitimately seek to repeal such a reprehensible law as Title II? Once we realized that we should no longer suffer the pain and agony of false guilt, we accepted our experience as part of our Japanese American heritage, that part of our history which involved a struggle for survival against tremendous odds which would test the character and spirit of each of us. (p. 110)

The Title II repeal campaign was the first major organized activity that Japanese-Americans undertook in relation to the internment after close to two decades of silence, and it unexpectedly demonstrated the potential for politically mobilizing the group. It had its origins in the black movement and was, in many respects, dedicated to showing solidarity with that movement. As Okamura (1974) wrote:

> [We] felt it was imperative for Japanese Americans to assume the leadership in order to promote Third World unity. Japanese Americans had been the passive beneficiaries of the Black civil rights movement, and this campaign was the perfect issue by which Japanese Americans could make a contribution to the overall struggle for justice in the United States. (p. 76)

The Title II campaign, though, was the first of many contributions that Japanese-Americans subsequently sought to make to prevent another internment from happening again to them or to other Americans. Coupled with both the initiation of annual pilgrimages to Manzanar concentration camp in December 1969 and the general atmosphere of group redefinition, the movement "sparked the imagination" of Japanese-Americans into considering other unfinished business of their internment experience and also sustaining and broadening the process of reawakening. Indeed, the successful repeal of Title II provided Japanese-Americans not only with a sense of the efficacy of pursuing other internment-related activities, but also with a new and powerful symbolic message that the internment was beginning to be recognized as wrong and deplorable by a growing number of American citizens, politicians, organizations, and media. Although Japanese-Americans had received some prior recognition, especially in academic works, that the internment should not have happened, they were still plagued by the historical legacy of the event and its close affiliation with the horrors of Pearl Harbor and World War II in the minds of many Americans. For example, a 1967 public opinion poll commissioned by the JACL's Japanese American Research Project provided a glimpse of this legacy when it was revealed that "80 percent of Californians approved evacuation in 1942, and a quarter century later, 48 percent still did" (Hosokawa, 1969, p. 497). The JACL's initial reluctance to join the Title II repeal movement probably stemmed from this and other more intuitive assessments of the American public's sentiments about the internment. This assessment reinforced the JACL's long-standing policy of avoiding activities, especially those dealing with the internment, that might undermine the acceptance of Japanese-Americans and unexpectedly foment another round of anti-Japanese backlash and prejudice.

To be sure, the Title II movement did not convince all Americans that the internment was wrong. But it did serve to acquaint more Americans with the event than ever before, and to allow Japanese-Americans to begin to confront the myths surrounding their internment experience, which continued to affect them during their postwar survival period. Indeed, by accentuating the linkage between Title II and the internment, Japanese-Americans made Title II the first of a series of challenges to the wisdom and necessity of the internment rather than solely a contemporary public policy issue (Nakanishi, 1978). Moreover, the repeal of Title II served to broaden the support and appeal of subsequent internment-related activities within the Japanese-American community. After the issue was embraced by the JACL, as well as a number of religious, civil rights, and media organizations, the act of resurrecting the internment was no longer perceived as an exclusively Sansei or leftist cause. It could be and was embraced both politically and psychologically by diverse sectors of the Japanese-American community.

THE PAST AS PRESENT

The resurrection of the internment during the late 1960s signaled the beginning of a new collective response to the internment. By identifying with it in both a highly publicized manner such as the Title II campaign and a more intensely private and commemorative fashion like the Manzanar pilgrimage, Japanese-Americans made a concrete and symbolic statement that the internment should no longer be treated as past history or a forgotten past by either other Americans or Japanese-Americans. Indeed, the slogan of the Title II campaign, "It happened once, can it happen again?" was directed as much toward Japanese-Americans as toward the general public. Far from being a momentary or faddish phenomenon, the resurrection of the event during the late 1960s served for the Japanese-Americans as the starting point for an intense, prolonged, and often controversial period of political actions and creative activities, as well as collective and personal reexamination of the internment.

Since the late 1960s, the internment has been the preeminent issue area for Japanese-American communities and organizations across the nation. Numerous public forums and "Days of Remembrance" activities have been held annually from Seattle to New York. Pilgrimages have been organized to nearly all the former concentration camps. And an extraordinary array of literary works, textbooks, theatrical productions, and motion pictures, in which Japanese-Americans occupy center stage, have been developed.[5] Moreover, Japanese-American organizations have vigorously pressed for even greater public and governmental recognition that the internment was not only wrong and unjust but also had a damaging impact on Japanese-Americans both individually and as a group. Since the early 1980s, for example, former Japanese-American civil service employees, who were summarily fired from their jobs as a result of Executive Order 9066, have gained back pay and civil service credit from cities such as Los Angeles, Seattle, and San Francisco, as well as from the state governments of California and Washington.[6] More significantly, Japanese-Americans and other Asian American organizations launched major legislative and legal campaigns to gain redress and monetary reparations for losses and damages from the internment experience and filed successful *coram nobis* lawsuits in relation to the three major Supreme Court decisions that tested the constitutionality of the evacuation and internment orders; *Korematsu v. U.S.*, *Hirabayashi v. U.S.*, and *Yasui v. U.S.* (Irons, 1983). And finally, during the past decade more and more Japanese-Americans from all walks of life—be they celebrated World War II veterans or so-called no-no boys,[7] professionals or working men and women, or English-speaking or Japanese-speaking individuals—have begun the arduous psychological task of "working through" (Janis, 1971; Lane, 1964) their personal internment experiences, and have openly discussed both the immediate and enduring consequences of their wartime victimization (Nakanishi, 1978).

The resurfacing of these memories has continued, but it was most dramatically and powerfully exhibited during the public hearings held by the presidential Commission on Wartime Relocation and Internment of Civilians in 1981. This nine-member body, which was established by Congress and President Jimmy Carter as a result of concerted lobbying by the JACL and Japanese-American congressional representatives, was charged with the following mandates:

1. Review the facts and circumstances surrounding Executive Order Number 9066, issued February 19, 1942, and the impact of such Executive Order on American citizens and permanent resident aliens.
2. Review directives of United States military forces requiring the relocation and, in

---

[5]In 1982, for example, the East-West Players Theatre Company, the oldest Asian American theatrical organization, dedicated its entire season to dramatic works on the internment. Also see *Amerasia Journal*, Vol. 8, 1981, which devotes over 50 pages to testimonies that were given in 1981 at the hearings of the Commission on Wartime Relocation and Internment of Civilians.
[6]*Pacific Citizen*, April 15, 1983, p. 1.
[7]See Okada, (1957) and Weglyn (1976).

some cases, detention in internment camps of American citizens, including Aleut
civilians, and permanent resident aliens of the Aleutian and Pribilof Islands; and
3. Recommend appropriate remedies. (Commission on Wartime Relocation and Internment of Civilians, 1982, p. 1)

Some Japanese-American groups, like the Chicago-based National Coalition for Japanese
American Reparations, bitterly opposed this so-called commission strategy as being an
unnecessarily cautious legislative compromise, and they subsequently filed a separate
and successful class-action lawsuit against the federal government to gain monetary
reparations.[8] However, there was no question that the public hearings eventually captured the attention of more Japanese-Americans and received greater media attention
than any previous Internment-related activity. In total, "more than 750 witnesses: evac-
uees, former government officials, public figures, interested citizens, and historians and
other professionals who have studied the subjects of commission inquiry" testified before
packed audiences throughout the nation (Commission on Wartime Relocation and Internment of Civilians, 1982, p. 3).

Although some of the testimonies dealt with previously well-researched topics like
the Internment's legal significance (Irons, 1983; Rostow, 1962; Takasugi, 1974; TenBroek,
Barnhart, & Matson, 1968), a number of heretofore buried aspects of the internment
finally surfaced during the hearings. For example, earlier works had shown that the
wartime incarceration had an all-encompassing economic impact on Japanese-Americans,
involving not only personal losses of property, income, and savings, but also the structural destruction of a viable ethnically based economy (Fugita & O'Brien, 1980). The
commission hearings extended scholarly understanding of these economic consequences
through personal accounts of being permanently displaced from previous means of live-
lihood in professions, farming, or fishing, and through analyses of the short- and long-
term losses of being forced to abruptly sell businesses and property. Various scholars also
challenged the Federal Reserve Bank's often-cited figure of $400 million in property losses
at the time of the internment as being a misleading underestimate, and they argued that
total economic losses were at least three or four times greater. One researcher, Larry
Boss, presented evidence that economic damages, excluding personal income, would
now be in excess of $6 billion if an annual inflation rate of 6% were applied to the original
losses (Commission on Wartime Relocation and Internment of Civilians, 1982). Similarly,
the hearings not only reaffirmed the findings of earlier works on the social disorganiza-
tion of the Japanese-American family unit in adapting to the abnormal situation of life in
concentration camps (Broom & Kitsuse, 1973; Kitano, 1976), but also revealed the largely
hidden, long-range changes in family relations in readjusting to life after the camps. And
finally, testimonies were given on rarely examined medical problems directly related to
detention, the possible collusion between JACL leaders and government officials on the
decision to remove the Japanese-Americans from the western states, and the enduring
psychological impact of the internment on both those who survived and subsequent
generations.

After considering these testimonies, as well as an unprecedented collection of government documents obtained through the Freedom of Information Act, the commission
issued its final report, *Personal Justice Denied* (1982). Its major conclusion was that

Executive Order 9066 was not justified by military necessity and the decisions that

[8]By a 2–1 decision, the U.S. Court of Appeals for the District of Columbia Circuit overturned an
earlier U.S. District Court dismissal of a class action lawsuit, *Hohri v. United States*, which was filed
by the National Coalition for Japanese American Redress on behalf of the 120,000 Japanese-Americans who had been interned. The decision allows these former internees to sue the federal
government.

> followed from it—exclusion, detention, the ending of detention, and the ending of exclusion—were not founded upon military considerations. The broad historical causes that shaped the decisions were race prejudice, war hysteria, and a failure of political leadership. (p. 35)

The report also urged Congress and the President to implement the following five recommendations to redress injustices to Japanese-Americans during the war: (a) issue a resolution recognizing "that a grave injustice was done" (p. 40) and offer a formal apology; (b) pardon individuals like Korematsu, Hirabayashi, and Matsui who were wrongly convicted of violating curfew and detention measures; (c) "direct the Executive agencies to which Japanese Americans may apply for the restitution of positions, status, or entitlements lost in whole or in part because of acts or events between December 1941 and 1945" (p. 40); (d) establish a special educational and research fund to encourage studies and public-oriented educational projects on the internment; and finally (e) appropriate $1.5 billion in order to provide "a one-time per capita compensatory payment of $20,000 to each of the approximately 60,000 surviving" Japanese-Americans who had been incarcerated during World War II (p. 40). Several bills, which are based on these recommendations, have been introduced in the House and Senate since the issuance of the report, but no formal actions have been taken.

The recent resurrection of the internment has spawned an extraordinary level of organized activity by Japanese-Americans. However, it would be simplistic to assume that this prolonged reencounter with the tragedy has operated in a social vacuum, or that it can be viewed as an unimpeded and noncontroversial act of group self-determination. As in other postsurvival experiences, a unique set of events and circumstances both within and outside the Japanese-American community has dialectically influenced the direction, momentum, and scope of this process. To begin with, the resurrection of the internment in the late 1960s coincided with the promulgation of the model minority interpretation of the Japanese-American experience. This laudatory designation, as mentioned above, portrayed Japanese-Americans as having faced seemingly insurmountable racial and economic barriers in the past, like other American racial minorities, but as now exhibiting high aggregate-level indicators of group socioeconomic and educational attainment. William Peterson (1966), a demographer, was one of the first of many journalists and scholars to offer this bold and heroic pronouncement. As the following passage illustrates, the internment served as a major cornerstone of his argument:

> Barely more than twenty years after the end of the war-time camps, this is a minority that has risen above even prejudiced criticism. By any criterion that we choose, the Japanese Americans are better than any other group in our society, including native-born whites. They have established this remarkable record moreover, by their own almost totally unaided effort.
> Every attempt to hamper their progress resulted only in enhancing their determination to succeed. Even in a country whose patron saint is the Horatio Alger hero there is no parallel to this success story. (p. 1)

This view, which was an updated version of the notion that the internment tested the character and determination of Japanese-Americans, continuously worked at loggerheads with efforts by Japanese-Americans not only to work on the unfinished business of the internment individually and collectively, but also to redefine their group status and experiences in American society.

Like earlier interpretations, the success-story thesis treated the internment as past history. Although Japanese-Americans were recognized as victims, their victimization was seen as temporary and as having no lasting adverse consequences for the group or its individual members. Instead, they were now viewed as a model minority, "better than any other group in our society," which others, especially other racial minorities, should emulate in overcoming their racial subordination. If Japanese-Americans could succeed "by their own almost totally unaided effort" despite their long history of racial segregation and persecution, then it logically followed that other groups could do the same without special governmental, legal, or private intervention. The thesis indeed provided an ironic twist to the classic "blaming-the-victim" perspective in race relations research.

More important, this thesis had a direct impact on the process of resurrecting the internment at the individual and collective levels. In many respects, this glowing image of postwar Japanese-American progress and societal acceptance, which originated during the height of the civil rights movement, provided many Japanese-Americans with a self-fulfilling justification for not psychologically departing from their long-standing repression and avoidance of their internment experience. As a result, many opposed early and even current Internment-related activities, which might subvert this positive group image and work against a renewed sense of self-esteem. It provided many Japanese-Americans with a defensive rationale for letting bygones be bygones and led many to settle psychologically on the view, which S. I. Hayakawa consistently argued as a syndicated columnist and then as a U.S. Senator, that the internment was a "blessing in disguise" (Tachiki, 1971).

The model minority perspective also served to undermine the significance and legitimacy of many group-level internment activities. They came to be interpreted as nothing more than reflections of contemporary American fads rather than latent collective responses to a disastrous shared experience, as the renewed interest in the Holocaust, for example, is often portrayed (Himmelfarb, 1971). If the internment was not viewed as having an enduring impact on Japanese-Americans, then the pilgrimages to former concentration camps and the dramatic and literary works on the internment, as well as the varied ways in which young Japanese-Americans sought to learn more about their elders' wartime victimization, could be summarily categorized as further examples of ethnic revival, a search for roots, or other forms of behavior that merely mimicked broader current popular moods (Daniels, 1971). Finally, the success-story thesis, as mentioned above, served to negate many legitimate policy concerns of Japanese-Americans and other Asian Pacific American groups. More specifically, it served as one of the major counterarguments against monetary reparations for Japanese-Americans in legislative deliberations. If Japanese-Americans are so well off today, as some have argued from the model minority perspective, then why pay them for something that happened so long ago? Or in another ironic twist on the view that other racial minorities should follow the Japanese-American example, some have argued that if Japanese-Americans are given reparations for the internment, then what would prevent blacks, Chicanos, native Americans, and other groups from making similar claims for past and present victimization and suffering?

Despite the many real and symbolic ramifications of the success-story thesis for Japanese-Americans, there were other events and developments that served to propel and provide added credence to sustaining the process of resurrecting the internment. Throughout the 1970s, and the 1980s as well, the increased impact of Japan's trade policies and practices on numerous sectors of the weakening American economy generated a new round of anti-Japanese sentiments and hostilities. There were, for example, persistent references to the tragedy of Pearl Harbor, the continued use of the derogatory term *Japs*, and campaigns calling for the boycott of Japanese consumer products by the auto industry and the whale preservation movement. Although these sentiments and activities may not have been aimed directly at Japanese-Americans, these and other signals have been imbued with unique, group-specific symbolic meanings for Japanese-Americans. These meanings have their origins in the internment and other historical periods of anti-Japanese hatred, when distinctions were not drawn between Japanese-Americans and the government and people of Japan (Nakanishi, 1978).

The continuing reappearance of these signals, beginning in the mid-1970s, has not necessarily been perceived as a prelude to another internment, in the way that such symbolic elements have been observed among survivors of other major traumatic episodes (Erikson, 1976; Lifton, 1969). Nonetheless, these signals have underscored the necessity for Japanese-Americans to go beyond the Title II campaign. They have provided added incentive to further confront the myths about the internment, and to be psychologically sensitive to and politically vigilant about even seemingly minor or remote episodes that resemble these wartime experiences. For example, Japanese-American organizations lodged formal protests against President Carter and his presidential transition team when it was learned that a prominent Japanese-American wartime veteran, who was being considered for the ambassadorship to Japan, had been questioned about his political loyalties. Carter's staff wondered whether he could unequivocally represent American interests in tough bargaining situations with his ancestral homeland. Concern was also raised during the height of the Iranian hostage episode when vengeful and hysterical calls, akin to those heard after Pearl Harbor, were made for the mass round-up and deportation of all Iranian students in the United States because of their presumed ties to the despised Ayatollah.

In recent years, Japanese-American and other Asian American groups have organized to combat a series of racially motivated acts of violence against Asians in different parts of the nation. For example, they launched a major grass-roots campaign to successfully appeal and overturn the light sentences that had been given to two unemployed Detroit auto workers who, in 1982, used a baseball bat to kill a Chinese-American named Vincent Chin. (The two men mistook Chin for a Japanese and, therefore, for someone who was viewed as having taken away their jobs.) And finally, Japanese-American organizations gained renewed justification for pursuing the goal of further educating the American public about the internment after the presidential commission released its final report. Although many newspaper editorials called for some form of redress, there were a large number of commentaries and letters to the editor that vehemently opposed the commission's recommendations, especially monetary reparations, by drawing a groundless and yet highly emotional connection between the internment and Japan's wartime atrocities in Asia, especially its treatment of American prisoners of war.[9]

The continued resurrection of the internment has evolved in relation to this unique dialectic between real and symbolic external forces of group acceptance and group threat. These external forces have prolonged the complex and common tug-of-war between remembering and forgetting at the individual level. They have also shaped a collective response, which has been both defensive and assertive. Like other postsurvival experiences, these external forces, on the one hand, have prevented Japanese-Americans from resurrecting the internment in a totally constraint-free sociopolitical context. On the other hand, though, they have provided Japanese-Americans with new and unanticipated opportunities, situations, and rationales for further charting their latent collective response to their earlier victimization. However, aside from these external factors, there have been several major internal developmental changes in the political behavior of Japanese-Americans, which have coincided with and molded this sustained process of reawakening.

Since the mid-1970s, there has been a dramatic increase in the overall political involvement of Japanese-Americans, especially in electoral politics, but also in other forms

[9]*Pacific Citizen*, February 3, 1983.

of political behavior, such as protest activities. Although Japanese-Americans have a rich, but largely unexamined, political history (Nakanishi, 1986), no previous era has approached current levels of political participation. In contrast to earlier periods, the 1970s and 1980s have witnessed the election and appointment of more mainland Japanese-Americans to public office than in all previous years combined. At the same time, a greater diversity of political and social-service organizations have been founded, and a substantial number of Japanese-Americans have been mobilized for a variety of political issues and causes, some of which, like the legal defense of Iva Ikuko Toguri D'Aquino (nee "Tokyo Rose"), had long been viewed by the group's leadership as socially taboo and too controversial (Duus, 1979; Uyeda, 1978).

To be sure, this major developmental change in the political involvement of Japanese-Americans has coincided with and been affected by the overall increase in political participation and assertiveness of all racial minorities, especially blacks, since the mid-1960s. With respect to internment-related issues, this heightened political involvement has provided Japanese-American organizations with more political resources, both internal and external, than were available during the Title II repeal campaign. For example, Japanese-American organizations, like the JACL, which had previously channeled their legislative concerns such as Title II through the long-standing Hawaiian-Japanese-American congressional delegation of U.S. Senators Daniel Inouye and Sparky Matsunaga, have benefited from the election of mainland Japanese-American politicians. They have come to view two California members of Congress, Norman Mineta and Robert Matsui—and to a much smaller extent former Senator S. I. Hayakawa of California—as their principal legislative liaisons in lobbying for mainland Japanese-American issues like the creation of the presidential fact-finding commission. In contrast to the Hawaiian legislators, however, none of the three mainland officials has represented sizable Japanese-American constituencies. At the same time, other Japanese-American organizations, especially those that have opposed the JACL's strategies and goals, have found their own legislative allies among non-Japanese-American politicians who have benefited from the electoral support of local Japanese-American voters. Michael Lowry of Seattle, for example, introduced the first Japanese American reparations bill in the House in 1979 shortly after his election. And finally, it is clear that recent internment-related efforts have benefited from the growth of a new sector within the Japanese-American community composed of young public-interest attorneys and their community-based organizations, like the Asian Law Caucus of Oakland, which were chiefly responsible for filing the successful *coram nobis* lawsuits.

However, it also is apparent that the continued resurrection of the internment has had its own independent effect on the increased political involvement of the Japanese-American community. Internment-related issues have dominated the organizational agendas of Japanese-American groups since the mid-1970s. These issues have not only provided long-standing groups like the JACL with a renewed purpose for existing but have also spurred the creation of new organizations and the elevation of new community leaders whose principal *raison d'être* has been pursuing the unfinished business of the internment. Similarly, efforts to mobilize communitywide support for an array of political issues, such as opposing redevelopment projects in many local Japanese-American communities by Japan-based corporations, have often been couched in political symbolism relating to the internment (Gee, 1976). And perhaps most important, a growing number of Japanese-American leaders of diverse ideological persuasions have come to believe that, aside from broader external causes, such as racism and war hysteria, the internment occurred because Japanese-Americans were politically naive, lacked sufficient political representation, and were politically passive (Nakanishi, 1978). As a result, many Japanese-Americans have placed a unique, group-specific symbolic meaning on the dramatic increase in their political participation, be it electoral involvement or protest activities, as being crucial not only in advancing their present group interests, but also in preventing a recurrence of a disastrous historical condition.

CONCLUSION

George Santayana may have been right when he argued that those who do not learn from history are condemned to repeat it. However, what should be learned from the past, as well as how the past should be applied to the present, is not always obvious. By resurrecting the internment in the late-1960s Japanese-Americans have made both a concrete and a symbolic statement that their World War II experiences should not be forgotten, and that they should develop a new collective response to their past victimization. And yet, in making this declaration, it was far from apparent what actions, if any, Japanese-Americans would undertake in relation to the event, or what insights, interpretations, or lessons they would derive from it. The internment, like other historical events and disasters, does not automatically yield its share of profound lessons for its survivors, nor does it provide specific guidance on what to do with them. In some instances, such as the Title II repeal movement, present circumstances may provide a specific sociopolitical context for approaching the past. However, in most instances, the link between the past and the present are probably not as direct, intuitive, or compelling (Jervis, 1976). And as the Japanese-American case illustrates, numerous structural and psychological boundaries may prevent or delay survivors from seeing such a link and, more important, from sustaining it once it is finally recognized.

The latent collective response of Japanese-Americans to the internment suggests that we should modify our outlook on the past. As in most works on the internment, we tend to treat major events in the experiences of American minority groups as past history. They are largely relegated to historiographic inquiries or to classroom history lessons and are rarely viewed as having contemporary relevancy. Emphasis is placed on revealing the immediate causes and effects of such events rather than on probing their enduring consequences or significance in the development of the group over time (Lifton, 1969). By treating these events in this limited fashion, we also place on overly optimistic interpretation on the resiliency of individuals in reassembling their lives and mental outlooks after such episodes. We tend to compartmentalize their victimization, to place it within the rigid spatiotemporal boundaries of personal life histories, and generally to overlook the prolonged nature of their survival experiences.

The resurrection of the internment also underscores the necessity for seeking greater convergence in race relations research. The Japanese-American case, for example, cannot be rigorously analyzed without an attempt to bridge the paradigmatic gaps between the idiosyncratic and nomothetic approaches, as well as the seemingly mutually exclusive levels of analysis of psychological and structural inquiries. The perspective offered here of treating survival experiences dialectically considering the longitudinal interplay and group-level processes is intended to be a contribution to this search for convergence. It seeks to extend our understanding of survival experiences beyond the individual-level, clinical-psychiatric observations that have largely dominated the literature on this topic (Bergman & Jucovy, 1982; Epstein, 1977; Lifton, 1969; Niederland, 1962, 1972; Wolfenstein, 1957). Instead, this perspective gains its analytic insights from Kai Erikson's pioneering study *Everything in Its Path* (1976), which explored both the immediate individual and the collective consequences of a disastrous flood that struck a Pennsylvania mining town. However, by examining the resurrection of the internment by Japanese-Americans, we gain glimpses of the longitudinal dimensions of survival experiences, as well as the potentially prolonged latency of individual and collective responses to such episodes. We also gain insights into the multiple forms of latent collective responses that are not purely psychological, and that can be cultural as well as political.

The discussion also reaffirms the use of a multiracial framework and the probing of the interrelationships and commonalities in the shared experiences of all American minority groups, while being critically cognizant of their distinctiveness. The latent collective response of Japanese-Americans to the internment did not evolve in a social vacuum, and it was far from being an unimpeded and noncontroversial act of group self-determination. It developed, on the one hand, in relation to a highly specific set of real and symbolic external forces of group acceptance and group threat. In this regard, the countervailing influences of Japanese-Americans' unique, laudatory image as a model minority, the continued influence of United States–Japan relations on their group status, and the specific popular myths that have continued to persist about their wartime incarceration cannot be minimized. On the other hand, though, the event's emergence in the mid-1960s cannot be separated from the extraordinary nature of race relations at that time, as well as the impact that the heightened assertiveness and search for redefinition by all minority groups, especially blacks, had on resurrecting the internment. Both directly and indirectly, blacks and other minority groups provided Japanese-Americans with a new social context from which to establish a different collective response to the internment, to stimulate the working through of individual traumas, and to reveal the broader legal and social relevancy of the internment for current race relations. However, in sustaining this reencounter with their past racial victimization, and in seeking redress and reparations so that extraordinary government actions like the internment will never happen again, perhaps Japanese-Americans have done more than heed Santayana's famous aphorism. Perhaps they have also revealed aspects of the experiences of all minority groups, which should no longer be buried.

REFERENCES

Allen, C., Jr. (1966). *Concentration camps, USA*. New York: Marzani & Munzelli.

Bell, D. A. (1985). The triumph of Asian Americans. *The New Republic* (July 15–22), pp. 24–31.

Bergman, M. S., & Jucovy, M. E. (Eds.). (1982). *Generations of the Holocaust*. New York: Basic Books.

Berreman, G. D. (1972). Race, caste, and other invidious distinctions in social stratification. *Race, 13*, 10–23.

Blalock, H., Jr. (1967). *Toward a theory of minority-majority relations*. New York: Capricorn Books.

Bosworth, A. P. (1976). *America's concentration camps*. New York: W. W. Norton.

Broom, L. & Kitsuse, J. (1973). *The managed casualty: The Japanese American family in World War II*. Berkeley: University of California Press.

Brown, H. R. (1969). *Die nigger die!* New York: Dial Press.

Cabezas, A. & Yee, H. (1977). *Discriminatory employment of Asian Americans: Private industry in the San Francisco–Oakland SMSA*. San Francisco: Asian.

Cheng, L. & Bonacich, E. (Eds.). (1984). *Labor immigration under capitalism: Asian workers in the United States before World War II*. Berkeley: University of California Press.

Choy, B.-Y. (1979). *Koreans in America*. Chicago: Nelson-Hall.

Chuman, F. (1976). *The bamboo people: Japanese Americans and the law*. Del Mar, CA: Publisher's, Inc.

Chun, K.-T. (1980). The myth of Asian American success and its educational ramifications. *IRCD Bulletin, 15*, 1–12.

Commission on Wartime Relocation and Internment of Citizens. (1982). *Personal justice denied*. Washington, DC: Commission on Wartime Relocation and Internment of Citizens.

Daniels, R. (1971). *Concentration camps USA: Japanese Americans and World War II*. Hinsdale, IL: Dryden Press.

Daniels, R. (1976). Asian historians and East Asian immigrants. In N. Hundley, Jr. (Ed.) *The Asian American: The historical experience*. Santa Barbara: ABC-Clio Press.

Degler, C. (1976). Why historians change their minds. *Pacific Historical Review, 45*, 167–184.

Duus, M. (1979). *Tokyo Rose: Orphan of the Pacific*. Tokyo: Kodansha International.

Elder, G. (1974). *Children of the Great Depression*. Chicago: University of Chicago Press.

Endo, R. (1980). Social science and historical materials on the Asian American experience. In R. Endo, S. Sue, & N. Wagner (Eds.), *Asian Americans: Social and psychological perspectives* (Vol. 2). Palo Alto, CA: Science and Behavior.

Enloe, C. (1973). *Ethnic conflict and political development*. Boston: Little, Brown.

Epstein, H. (1977). Heirs of the Holocaust. *New York Times Magazine* (June 19), pp. 12–15.

Erikson, K. (1976). *Everything in its path*. New York: Simon & Schuster.

Fugita, S. & O'Brien, D. (1980). Economics, ideology, and ethnicity. In R. Endo *et al.* (Eds.), *Asian Americans* (Vol. 2). Palo Alto, CA: Science and Behavior.

Gee, E. (Ed.). (1976). *Counterpoint: Perspectives on Asian America*. Los Angeles: Asian American Studies Center, University of California, Los Angeles.

Girdner, A., & Loftis, A. (1969). *The great betrayal*. New York: Macmillan.

Grodzins, M. (1949). *Americans betrayed*. Chicago: University of Chicago Press.

Hansen, A., & Mitson, B. (Eds.). (1974). *Voices long silent*. Fullerton: California State University, Fullerton, Japanese American Oral History Project.

Himmelfarb, M. (1971). Never Again! *Commentary, 52,* 73–76.

Hirata, L. C. (1978). The Chinese American in sociology. In E. Gee (Ed.), *Counterpoint*. Los Angeles: Asian American Studies Center, University of California, Los Angeles.

Hosokawa, B. (1969). *Nisei: The quiet American*. New York: William Morrow.

Houston, J. W., & Houston, J. D. (1973). *Farewell to Manzanar*. San Francisco: Houghton Mifflin.

Hundley, N., Jr. (Ed.) (1976). *The Asian American: The historical experience*. Santa Barbara: ABC-Clio Press.

Hune, S. (1977). *Pacific migration to the United States: Trends and themes in historical and sociological literature*. Washington, DC: Research Institute on Immigration and Ethnic Studies, Smithsonian Institution.

Hurh, W. M., & Kim, K. C. (1982). Race relations paradigms and Korean American research: A sociology of knowledge perspective. In E.-Y. Yu, E. Phillips, & E. S. Yang (Eds.), *Koreans in Los Angeles*. Los Angeles: Center for Korean-American and Korean Studies, California State University, Los Angeles.

Ichioka, Y. (1974). *A buried past*. Berkeley: University of California Press.

Ichioka, Y. (1977). The early Japanese quest for citizenship: The background of the 1922 Ozawa case. *Amerasia Journal, 4,* 1–22.

Irons, P. (1983). *Justice at war*. New York: Oxford University Press.

Isaacs, H. (1958). *Images of Asia*. New York: Capricorn.

Isaacs, H. (1975). *Idols of the tribe*. New York: Harper & Row.

Janis, I. (1971). *Stress and frustration*. New York: Harcourt Brace Jovanovich.

Jervis, R. (1976). *Perception and misperception in international politics*. Princeton: Princeton University Press.

Kanno, H. (1974). Broader implications of the campaign to Title II. *Amerasia Journal, 2,* 105–108.

Kikumura, A. (1981). *Through harsh winters: The life of a Japanese immigrant woman*. Novata, CA.: Chandler & Sharp.

Kim, E. (1982). *Asian American literature*. Philadelphia: Temple University Press.

Kim, I. (1981). *New urban immigrants: The Korean community in New York*. Princeton: Princeton University Press.

Kitano, H. (1976). *Japanese Americans*. Englewood Cliffs, NJ: Prentice-Hall.

Kuramoto, F. (1976). Lessons learned in the federal funding game. *Social Casework, 57,* 208–218.

Kwong, P. (1981). *Chinatown, New York: Labor and politics, 1930–1950*. New York: Monthly Review Press.

Ladner, J. (Ed.). (1973). *The death of white sociology*. New York: Vintage Books.

Lai, H. M. (1976). A historical survey of the Chinese left in America. In E. Gee (Ed.), *Counterpoint*. Los Angeles: Asian American Studies Center, University of California, Los Angeles.

Lane, R. (1964). *Political ideology*. New York: Free Press.

Lieberson, S. (1980). *A piece of the pie*. Berkeley: University of California Press.

Lifton, R. (1969). *Death in life: Survivors of Hiroshima*. New York: Vintage Books.

Liu, J. (1978). Toward an understanding of the internal colonial model. In E. Gee (Ed.), *Counterpoint*. Los Angeles: Asian American Studies Center, University of California, Los Angeles.

Liu, W. T. (1980). Asian American research: Views of a sociologist. In R. Endo, S. Sue, & N. Wagner (Eds.), *Asian Americans: Social and psychological perspectives* (Vol. 2). Palo Alto, CA: Science and Behavior.

Low, V. (1982). *The unimpressible race: A century of educational struggle by Chinese in San Francisco*. San Francisco: East-West Publishers.

Lyman, S. (1977). *The Asian in North America*. Santa Barbara: ABC-Clio Press.

Makaroff, J. (1967). America's other racial minority: Japanese Americans. *Contemporary Review, 210*, 310–314.

McClellan, R. (1971). *Heathen Chinese: A study of American attitudes towards China, 1890–1905*. Columbus: Ohio State University Press.

Muhlen, N. (1962). *The survivors: A report on the Jews in Germany today*. New York: Thomas Crowell.

Nakanishi, D. T. (1978). *Can it happen again? The enduring impact of the Holocaust and evacuation on the political thinking of American Jewish and Japanese American leaders*. Ph.D. dissertation, Harvard University.

Nakanishi, D. T. (1986). "Asian American politics: An agenda for research." *Amerasia Journal*.

Nee, B., & Nee, V. (1974). *Longtime Californ': A documentary study of an American Chinatown*. Boston: Houghton Mifflin.

Niederland, W. G. (1962). Psychiatric consequences of persecution. *American Journal of Psychotherapy, 26*, 191–203.

Niederland, W. G. (1972). Clinical observations on the survivor syndrome. In R. S. Parker (Ed.), *The emotional stress of war, violence, and peace*. Pittsburgh: Stanwix House.

Ogbu, J. (1983). Minority status and schooling in plural societies. *Comparative Education Review, 27*, 168–190.

Okada, J. (1957). *No-no boy*. Rutland, VT: Charles E. Tuttle.

Okamura, R. (1974). "Campaign to repeal the Emergency Detention Act," *Amerasia Journal, 2*, 71–111.

Okamura, R. (1976). The concentration camp experience from a Japanese American perspective and review of Michi Weglyn's *Years of Infamy*. In E. Gee (Ed.), *Counterpoint*. Los Angeles: Asian American Studies Center, University of California, Los Angeles.

Ong, P. (1981). Chinese labor in early San Francisco: Racial segmentation and industrial expansion. *Amerasia Journal, 8*, 69–92.

Peterson, W. (1966). Success story: Japanese American style. *New York Times Magazine*. (January 9), pp. vi–20.

Przeworski, A., & Teune, H. (1970). *The logic of comparative social inquiry*. New York: Wiley-Interscience.

Rosenau, J. N. (1971). *The scientific study of foreign policy*. New York: Free Press.

Rostow, E. (1962). *The sovereign prerogative*. New Haven: Yale University Press.

Sue, S. (1980). Psychological theory and implications for Asian Americans. In R. Endo, S. Sue, & N. Wagner (Eds.). *Asian Americans: Social and psychological perspectives (Vol. 2)*. Palo Alto, CA: Science and Behavior.

Suzuki, B. (1977). Education and the socialization of Asian Americans: A revisionist analysis of the "model minority" thesis. *Amerasia Journal, 4*, 23–51.

Tachiki, A., *et al.* (Eds.). (1971). *Roots*. Los Angeles: Asian American Studies Center, University of California, Los Angeles.

Takahashi, J. (1982). Japanese American responses to race relations: The formation of Nisei perspectives. *Amerasia Journal, 9*, 29–58.

Takaki, R. (1979). *Iron cages: Race and culture in 19th century America*. New York: Alfred A. Knopf.

Takasugi, R. (1974). Legal analysis of Title II. *Amerasia Journal, 2*, 95–104.

TenBroek, J., Barnhart, E. N., & Matson, F. (1968). *Prejudice, war, and the Constitution*. Berkeley, CA: University of California Press.

U.S. Commission on Civil Rights (Ed.). (1979). *Civil rights issues of Asian and Pacific Americans: Myths and realities*. Washington, DC: U.S. Commission on Civil Rights.

Uno, E. (1974, Fall). Therapeutic and educational benefits. *Amerasia Journal, 2*, 109–111.

Uyeda, C. (1978). The pardoning of "Tokyo Rose": A report on the restoration of American citizenship for Iva Ikuko Toguri. *Amerasia Journal, 5*, 69–94.

Uyematsu, A. (1971). The emergence of Yellow Power in America. In T. Amy (Ed.), *Roots*. Los Angeles: Asian American Studies Center, University of California, Los Angeles.

Vallangca, R. V. (Ed.). (1977). *Pinoy: The first wave, 1898–1941*. San Francisco: Strawberry Press.

Varon, B. (1967). The Japanese Americans: Comparative occupational status, 1960 and 1950. *Demography, 4*, 809–819.

Weglyn, M. (1976). *Years of infamy*. New York: William Morrow.

Willie, Charles V. (1978). The inclining significance of race. *Society, 15*, 1–15.

Wilson, W. (1978). *The declining significance of race*. Chicago: University of Chicago Press.

Wolfenstein, M. (1957). *Disaster: A psychological essay*. Glencoe, IL: Free Press.

Wollenberg, C. (1976). *All deliberate speed*. Berkeley, CA: University of California Press.

Yu, C. Y. (1977). Rediscovering voices: Chinese immigrants and Angel Island. *Amerasia Journal, 4*, 123–140.

9

Stereotypical Images, American Indians, and Prejudice

Joseph E. Trimble

> When you walk down a street in Rapid City, South Dakota, behind a Lakota man or a young Lakota girl, and you look into the eyes of whites who walk toward you, what do you see? You see fear. You see hatred. You see it in their eyes, even when they try to hide it with a smile. On the street, in the middle of town, in midday, why are they afraid? Why do whites look at Indians that way?
>
> The whites still don't see the Indians as human beings. They see animals.

Anonymous, in Steiner (1976)

Fear and hatred and the feeling of being less than human—don't these feelings occur for any group that has been subjected to rejection, isolation, persecution, incarceration, and extermination? And wouldn't these feelings continue when every effort to subdue a group was met with active or passive resistance? Don't these feelings reinforce and justify any effort to exclude a group from full participation in the pursuit of their inalienable rights? Answers to these questions demand more than mere academic inquiry; they demand answers that reflect the history of intergroup relations, especially ones in which one group forms to subdue another. In this chapter, we explore certain social-psychological elements that have fostered negative intergroup relations between Euro-Americans and American Indians. As we do so, some light may be shed on the feelings of fear, hatred, and inferiority cited above.

Fear, hatred, and feelings of inferiority are attitudes; they are also instrumental in promoting and maintaining racist beliefs and discriminatory practices. They are inventions "propagated among the public by an exploiting class for the purposes of stigmatizing some group as inferior so that the exploitation of either the group itself or its resources or both may be justified" (Cox, 1948, p. 49). Fear, hatred, and inferiority can also become highly institutionalized "norms for dealing with another group [as they

JOSEPH E. TRIMBLE • Department of Psychology, Western Washington University, Bellingham, Washington 98225.

reinforce] images of actual or perceived relationships between the groups" (Sherif, 1969, p. 269). Once the attitudes become normalized, the dominant group searches for differences among out-group members to *justify* racism and discrimination—to the point where the differences actually become factual and immutable (Marx, 1970).

HISTORICAL BEGINNINGS

Almost from the moment that Euro-Americans made contact with America's indigenous population, attitudes and impressions were formed. Noting in his journal, Columbus observed that the Arawak (the Caribbean tribe he first contacted) "are so guileless and so generous with all that they possess . . . they invite anyone to share it and display as much love as if they would give their hearts" (Vigneras, 1960, p. 194). Other explorers and settlers also noted the gentleness and peacefulness of the Indians they contacted (cf. Berkhofer, 1978).

However, as most students of American history will remember, whatever positive characterizations were recorded about American Indians, most were overwhelmingly overshadowed by negative attributions. Typical of the many negatively slanted descriptions are the words of an early Virginia traveler, Samuel Purchas, who noted that Indians were "more brutish than the beasts they hunt, more wild and unmanly than that unmanned wild country . . . captivated also to Satan's tyranny in foolish pieties, mad impieties, wicked idleness, busie and bloudy wickednesse" (quoted in Berkhofer, 1978, p. 21).

Early character descriptions of the American Indian basically fell into two general categories. On the one hand, there was the image of the "good Indian" who appeared to be

> friendly, courteous and hospitable. Modest in attitude, if not always in dress, the noble Indian exhibited great calm and dignity in bearing conversation. . . . Brave in combat, he was tender in love for family and children. The Indian, in short, lived a life of liberty, simplicity and innocense. (Berkhofer, 1978, p. 28).

Then there was the image of the "bad Indian," whose habits and customs, when

> not brutal . . . appeared loathsome to Whites. Filthy surroundings, inadequate cooking, and certain items of diet repulsive to white taste tended to confirm a low opinion of Indian life. Indolence rather than industry, improvidence in the face of scarcity, thievery and treachery added to the list of traits on [the negative] side. (Berkhofer, 1978, p. 28).

The negatively slanted images aided in developing a federal policy and fueled the fires of rampant racism and discrimination that persist to this very day.

Gunnar Myrdal (1944), in writing about America's attitudes toward blacks, suggested that whites were basically ambivalent about the status and character of blacks. Although some historians, social psychologists, and others may contest Myrdal's contention, colonial Euro-Americans were *never* ambivalent toward American Indians. Francis Parker (quoted in Berkohofer, 1978) stated over a century ago that "Spanish civilization crushed the Indian; English civilization scorned and neglected him; French civilization embraced and cherished him" (p. 115). The Euro-American attitudes were, for the most part, justified by the images that best suited their cause: the crushing took the form of genocide, the scorn and neglect took the form of isolation and relocation, and the embrace and passion took the form of overt paternalism. As one traces the historical developments concerning Indian affairs for the past 200 years, genocide, isolationism, and paternalism highlight the policies dealt out by the federal government.

The Indian was judged by most to be incompetent, backward, and incapable of managing their own affairs, and our early forefathers set up a colonial structure in which the Indian was forced into a hostile form of dependence (Hagen, 1962). In about 1830, the control of Indian affairs was assigned to the war department; about 20 years later the responsibility was shifted to the Office of Indian Affairs, which eventually became the present-day Bureau of Indian Affairs (BIA).

COLONIALISM AND ITS IMPACT

Colonialism is a policy that emphasizes "the domination of a people by a culturally different and more powerful group over which they have little influence" (Anders, 1980, p. 690). Typically, under colonial rule, a dominant group controls and directs the life-style of a perceived subordinate group. The U.S. government, through the Bureau of Indian Affairs, has done just that: the everyday life of the American Indian has been under colonial control for the better part of 150 years. The American Indians are the only American ethnic-minority group that has a special agency assigned exclusively to the governance of its affairs.

The colonial posture of any government has all of the elements of racist and discriminatory practices. In the case of American Indians, several policies have been enacted over the years that basically led to the denial of civil and human rights. Essentially, our federal government's early policy toward American Indians was shaped by an attitude similar to that of the Supreme Court of the State of Washington, which concluded that

> The Indian was a child, and a dangerous child, of nature, to be both protected and restrained. . . . True, arrangements took the form of treaty and of terms like "cede," "relinquish," "reserve." But never were these agreements between equals [but rather] between a superior and an inferior. (quoted in *Indian Tribes*, 1981, p. 35)

Yes, early Indian–white contacts were fairly amicable. Settlers needed—depended on, in many instances—the Indian to assist them in surviving the harsh New England winters, to understand the complex unexplored environments and to handle and manage relationships between tribes. But because of the constant flow of immigrants, more land was soon needed for settlement, and accommodation was rapidly replaced with competition. And under the "doctrine of discovery," land not immediately occupied was staked out and claimed, even though that very land might well have been part of a territorial domain claimed by a tribe.

Our Continental Congress recognized that the "doctrine of discovery" was hardly ample justification for squatting. They also recognized that Indian–white skirmishes (some referred to them as massacres) could no longer be tolerated. In an effort to regulate conflict and land settlement issues, the first Congress embarked on the policy of negotiating treaties with the aboriginal tribes.

One treaty in 1787 concerning lands in the Northwest Territory proclaimed that "the utmost good faith shall always be observed towards the Indians; their lands and property shall never be taken from them without their consent; and, in their property, rights, and liberty, they shall never be invaded or disturbed" (*Indian Tribes*, 1981, p. 18).

The first Congress wanted to both accommodate the first Americans and to protect them from the encroachment of immigrants. Despite the honorable intent of our early elected representatives, a vast number of settlers and colonialists were convinced that the best policy was one of extermination: genocide. Maintaining "the utmost good faith" required patience, tolerance, and the recognition of the Indian as an equal. Not so, said the characterizations and stilted, biased imagery. Our history books are filled with numerous accounts of the battles, wars, slaughter, pillage, rape, and murder carried out between Indians and whites. The extermination policy, although not formal and legislated, was quietly endorsed by many eighteenth- and nineteenth-century leaders. Andrew Jackson, for example, revered by some as a progressive President, was a noted Indian figher who, in 1817, claimed, "I have long viewed treaties with the Indians as an absurdity" (quoted in Svensson, 1973, p. 19).

EXTERMINATION, RELOCATION, AND ISOLATION

The informal and insidious policy of extermination was replaced with a more formalized policy of relocation and isolation. And beginning about 1830, large numbers of Indians were *forced* to leave their ancestral homes for reserved land set aside for settlement west of the Mississippi. Never mind the treaties. Relocation and isolation meant that the Indian problem would be out of the way for a while. And as colonialism prevailed, the minority Indian had no rights, no power, no status, and little support.

Relocation and isolation were hardly sufficient policies to stop the flow of immigrants and the pressing need for more land. The reservation policy did protect some tribes; an invisible boundary could be policed by the U.S. Army, but it could not guarantee that unoccupied lands would not be taken by settlers. And toward the end of the nineteenth century, it was clear to Congress that colonialism had to shift to a position of promoting a pluralist, assimilationist policy. Under a diluted and paternalistic policy of "separate but equal," Indians were given the opportunity to own and manage property in the hopes that they would eventually blend in and adopt the "American" way of life.

Pluralism and assimilation didn't work either, for beneath the fabric of the Indian ethos was an enduring sense of dignity and reverence for traditional custom, legend, and spiritualism. This ethos somehow transcended all efforts to control and regulate it, and it managed to bring the Indian into the twentieth century amidst paternalism, poverty, fear, hatred, and frustration. And in recognition of the Indians' persistence in surviving despite the policies of extermination, isolation, and assimilation, the U.S. Congress in 1924 conferred citizenship rights to all Indians born within the territorial boundaries of the United States.

THEN CAME CITIZENSHIP

Along with citizenship, one ordinarily receives voting privileges. Yet, some 14 years after Indians were granted full citizenship, some seven states continued to deny Indians the right to vote; New Mexico and Arizona continued to deny their sizable Indian population voting privileges right through to 1948, when they were court-ordered to stop the practice (*Indian Tribes*, 1981). Despite the court precedent, the tribes in Utah in the 1950s had to bring suit to gain a right to vote in state elections. And in South Dakota, when it was clear that the Sioux had gained a majority in certain local school-board elections, whites were able to successfully appeal to the state to change the structure so that they would (once again) hold the majority vote. In Arizona and New Mexico, in 1973, whites challenged the Indian right to occupy elected positions on local government boards on the basis that Indians reside on untaxed lands (Kemnitzer, 1978). Indians may be citizens, but their struggle to realize their rights, particularly through voting, continues to be challenged, in large part because of their unique relationship with the federal government, a relationship established by the government to regulate and control Indian affairs.

AND NOW THEY CALL FOR TERMINATION

Beginning in the mid-1940s, there has been a growing sentiment on the part of a number of politicians, citizens, and corporate officials to absolve the government of all its responsibilities toward Indians. This policy is typically referred to as *termination* and implies that treaty responsibilities with federally recognized tribes should be eliminated. Many sympathetic to a termination policy point to the 1985 Indian Affairs federal budget of close to $90 million as a futile and inflated venture—futile because the 1.6 million American Indians who desire benefits from the staggering budget remain close to the bottom of just about every socioeconomic category: unemployment rates, median family income, median years of education, incidences of certain diseases and alcoholism are all either disproportionately higher or lower (depending on the category) than in any other ethnic-minority population in the United States. Other critics argue that as long as Indians are dependent on the federal government, no substantial progress and growth can occur in Indian communities. And still others argue that far more important national needs can be addressed with $90 million than meeting treaty responsibilities.

Although the termination policy is quite a way from becoming formal government policy, many Indian leaders rightly fear that it may be the final gesture that would end two centuries of colonial domination and, in turn, amplify the existing problems to an uncertain magnitude.

CONTEMPORARY EXAMPLES OF DISCRIMINATION

The historical course of Indian affairs in the United States demonstrates the rampant efforts of government policy to mold and shape the destiny of an indigenous people. Viewed as incapable of self-governance, as well as with fear, hatred, and distrust, the Indian, under colonial control, was forced into a paternalistic, wardlike state. Tribes, willing or not, relied on the government for direction and support for just about every phase of daily life. Within the past few decades, efforts have been taken to give the tribes more autonomy in governing their destiny, and that policy is paying off in some areas of the country. Nonetheless, Indian–white relationships are still largely controlled and strained by an antiquated image, and that image, seemingly cherished by many non-Indians, continues to fan the flames of racism and discrimination. Some illustrations of present-day discriminatory practices can be found in the following arenas.

LAW ENFORCEMENT

Bahr, Chadwick, and Strauss (1972) found, in a study of legal practices among Indians in Seattle, that levels of legal action for Indians were significantly greater than for the non-Indian population. Further, their research showed that about 20% of the Indians sampled in Seattle believed that they had been arrested because they were Indian.

Numerous legal complications persist concerning law enforcement practices on Indian reservations. Plagued by legal entanglements and questions of jurisdiction, reservation tribes continue to struggle with maintaining law and order. Many tribal officials complain that county law-enforcement agencies will not respond to complaints arising on reservations. County sheriffs argue that they have no jurisdiction on reservation lands because of their unique trust status with the government. Consequently, many felons go unconvicted and many crimes go unsolved. All the while, the federal government maintains the responsibility for law enforcement, mainly for serious offenses, and, according to many, has not yet fully lived up to that task (*Indian Tribes*, 1981).

EDUCATION

In the early 1970s, the Bureau of Indian Affairs (BIA) investigated parent complaints concerning the practices occurring in a federally controlled Indian school. Among other things, the BIA found evidence of criminal malpractice and evidence of physical and psychological cruelty: some of the Indian youth were allegedly handcuffed and locked in their rooms for as long as two days. In another investigation, a white school principal was dismissed from his post when it was learned that he had ducked the heads of Indian youth into toilets as a form of punishment for truancy and for being suspected of drinking alcohol. Another white principal of a BIA school was reported as making statements such as "All Indians are brain-drains," "Indian culture belongs in museums," and "They are even worse than our coloreds, and the best you can do is just leave them alone."

In 1968, the U.S. Congress authorized a thorough investigation of the status of Indians in the educational system (U.S. Senate, 1968–1969). The findings point out that: (a) the government has failed in living up to responsibilities for providing educational opportunities for Indians; (b) the failure has created a severe and self-perpetuating cycle of poverty and unemployment; (c) the schools fail to understand the cultural differences among Indian students; as a consequence, the schools blame their own failure on the Indian student and, in so doing, reinforce a defensive attitude, and Indians, in turn, retaliate by viewing the school as an alien institution; and (d) the relationship between the schools and the Indian community is demeaning. Low self-esteem and self-confidence, encouragement of apathy, and a sense of alienation result, leaving many Indian youth with the feeling that they have been "pushed out" of the educational system. Simply stating that many Indians drop out of school is hardly sufficient.

In the 1970s, American Indians achieved a median of eight years of education, the lowest of any ethnic-minority group in the United States. And in the late 1960s, a survey of the educational status of Indians in Oklahoma found that 6% of the 60,000 Indians in the state had no formal schooling whatsoever, and that close to 60% had not gone beyond the eighth grade. In one particular school in western Oklahoma, with an Indian enrollment of 129, there were 635 reports of absenteeism in 1 year alone among Indian students (Trimble, 1972).

Many researchers have attributed the high rates of absenteeism and dropping out to the racist attitudes of white administrators and teachers, which, in turn, cause in the Indians a distinct lack of interest in schoolwork, academic difficulty, and general behavioral problems.

There is some hope, as many Indian educators and sensitive school administrators are reporting encouraging results. The 1980 U.S. Census shows that the median years of education had increased to 10. And many more Indian youth are attending institutions of higher learning than ever before. In spite of the gains, though, many Indian communities continue to complain that racist practices occur in many of the schools.

EMPLOYMENT

The employment position of the Indian youth is much less favorable than that of any other ethnic-minority group in the country. In parts of some states, it is not uncommon to find better than 75% of the Indian labor force either unemployed or underemployed. Yearly trends are variable. In 1940, nearly one-third of all Indian males were unemployed. By 1960, the rate had climbed to 39%; in 1970, the rate dropped to 12%. Rates for Indian women, as one might suspect, tend to run much higher than those for men (Feagin, 1978).

Most employed Indians can be found in the blue-collar and service-worker categories, although there is some evidence that more are moving into the professional technical categories—from 2.6% in 1940 to 9.8% in 1970 (Hraba, 1979). It should come as no surprise, then, that the median family income of Indians in 1970 was $5,800; where 1 in 10

U.S. families in 1970 fell below the poverty line, nearly 33% of Indians were declared as officially poor (Feagin, 1978). In 1965, the Indians in one county in northwestern Oklahoma reportedly had a median family income of $347 a year, and only 23 of 55 Indians in that county reported earnings of $2,500 or more during that year (Trimble, 1972). Svensson (1973) noted that "urban Indians shared the disadvantages under which virtually all Indians have operated . . . an average per capita cash income of only $900 and a median family income of $3,600" (p. 35).

Many attribute the unemployment problems to discrimination, lack of training opportunities, and the inability to develop and sustain viable employment opportunities on and near reservation communities. Yes, the government and the BIA are keenly aware of the problems, and steps have been taken to provide remedies. In the early 1950s, the BIA launched what has become known as the *employment relocation program.*

In 1952, about 5,000 reservation Indians were directly relocated to urban areas with the promise of finding gainful employment. In the years that followed, one in every three relocated families eventually returned to their reservation homes (Trimble, 1972). It turned out that, as the number who were relocated increased, the number of projected jobs decreased. More than that, relocated families found they were "part of a machine and not part of nature," and that the urban environment was distressing, rampant with discrimination, and lacking in social support. In commenting on the urban experience, Ablon (1971) stated "that the chief problems Indians struggle with in the city are employment, marital discord and difficulties with the law" (p. 204). More to the point, where relocated, Indians were given a promise of a new and better life, but what they found "was no job, no decent place to live and a culture that was difficult if not impossible to assimilate" ("An Indian", 1971, p. 99).

The American Indian has also experienced numerous problems in the areas of religious practices, fishing rights, health care delivery, and land claims. In a heavily documented report in 1981, the U.S. Commission on Civil Rights best summarized the status of Indian rights in the United States. In the main report, the commission concluded that

> (1) recent conflicts over Indian rights have exacerbated the continuing equal protection problems Indians face; and (2) non-Indians have erroneously attacked and characterized Indian rights as unlawful discrimination against non-Indians; [and] that civil rights violations are promoted by public ignorance of Indian rights and by the failure of appropriate parties to respond promptly to any infringement of Indian rights. (*Indian Tribes*, 1981, p. 188)

The general public is largely unaware of the problems Indians are facing in the last quarter of the twentieth century. Much of what the public knows is fed largely by a host of antiquated stereotypes that serve to promote ignorance and the practice of discrimination and racial prejudice. The pervasiveness of Indian-oriented stereotypes in textbooks, films, research literature, and the news media is discussed in the next section. Following this, some research findings are presented that suggest that stereotypes about Indians can change over time.

PREVALENCE OF STEREOTYPICAL IMAGES

Few non-Indians have had any direct contact with American Indians, yet nearly all non-Indians seem to have some kind of opinion about the first Americans. Most of their information has been derived from historical writings, television, motion pictures, or hearsay. Tourists who visit Indian areas, especially reservations, often do so to confirm what they already "know," rather than to learn something new. Indeed, many think that the Indians' culture is standing still—that Indians are oddities or curios. The writings of historians and social scientists do little to dispute these notions because they are framed in an "ethnographic present" that leads the reader to believe that what is being described still exists. D'Arcy McNickle (1973), an American Indian historian, argued that many portrayals of American Indians are "seen as components of 'culture areas' frozen in ecological domains and social systems" (p. 6). The static stance taken by many writers envelops much of the information available about the first Americans. Certainly, this view dovetails with that of many present-day Americans.

Over the years, an assortment of stereotypes has been developed to describe American Indians. Many of these stereotypes are holdovers from early Indian–white relationships; they range from the benign observation that Indians are untamed, innocent, and pure lovers of nature to the more caustic description of Indians as savages, animals, and murderers. During more recent times, the tone of the stereotype has calmed down somewhat, but although Indians are viewed in more passive terms, the stereotype remains. For example, it is not uncommon today to hear Indians described as quiet, taciturn, or passive; yet, this image still conveys the stereotype of "the silent Indian." The wooden cigar-store Indian, as he stands alone, staring off into space, saying nothing, is the notion of an Indian of many Americans.

In social situations, Indians "usually sit or stand quietly, saying nothing [until they seem to] disappear into the background, merging with the wall fixtures" (Wax & Thomas, 1961, p. 306). Cultural anthropologists Wax and Thomas (1961) noted that, in similar situations, "the white man will become undiscourageably loquacious. A silent neighbor will be peppered with small shoptalk in the hope that one of his rounds will trigger an exchange and a conversational engagement" (p. 306). The tendency toward silence is a product of the socialization experiences of many Indian youth. Wax and Thomas argued that the Indian is "brought up to remain motionless and watch. Outwardly he appears to freeze. Inwardly, he is using all of his senses to discover" (p. 306). From the non-Indian's perspective, silence appears to be an unacceptable personality trait; for many Indians, it is a strength and a value that guides their actions.

Social scientists have noted other stereotypical images of American Indians. Braroe (1965) found that Jasper Cree Indians were stereotyped as being childish, irresponsible, "worthless parasites," and generally intolerable. Although the Cree did not accept this imposed imagery, Braroe argued that they tended to act in ways that supported the stereotype. James (1961) noted the negative terms used by the local dominant community to describe the Ojibwa who lived nearby as "dirty," "drunken," "lazy," and "immoral." Yet, these negative perceptions were accompanied by a sense of "romaticism" that James attributed to "oldtimers"—older Indians who had been victims of the onslaught of colonialism. James stated that "this negative stereotype is not simply a product of white imagination or bigotry. It is a white judgment, motivated by white values, concerning white experiences with reservation Indians" (p. 732). Similar perceptions were found by Gordon MacGregor (1946) among whites living on or near the Pine Ridge Sioux Reservation in South Dakota. White attitudes varied according to white and Indian socioeconomic levels. Although many whites feared the Indians, most perceived them to be inferior and wished them to remain so.

For anyone familiar with Indian–white relationships, the existence of negative Indian stereotypes is not surprising. Other, more benign images do exist, but they seem to be overshadowed by the more offensive ones. Whether it is justified or not, the existence of negative imagery is unhealthy and does little to promote harmony between groups. Rather, such imagery keeps groups apart and prevents them from learning about and appreciating the value of diversity in a pluralistic society.

TEXTBOOK STEREOTYPES

Textbooks aid and abet the development of stereotypical images of the American Indian. The writers of these texts often take poetic license in their descriptions of Indians and Indian life, both past and present. In reviewing literature written for adolescents to determine the accuracy of the portrayal of American Indians, Anne Troy (1975) found far more inaccurate than accurate accounts of customs, tribes, dates of historical importance, and current living patterns. The novels she reviewed were built on the traditional and historical images of "the dirty, drunken, cruel and warring savage" and "the glorified, noble but naive native" (p. 34). Keith Beaman (1969), a free-lance writer, reported similar findings. Indians were described as "noble savages" when they provided aid to colonists and settlers, but as "treacherous savages" and, more recently, "filthy savages," when they fought the militia and settlers in defense of their land.

The most comprehensive review of the portrayal of American Indians in textbooks was undertaken by the American Indian Historical Society (AIHS) in San Francisco (cf. Costo, 1970). The AIHS, through the efforts of 32 Indian scholars, examined more than 300 books dealing with American Indian history and culture. The reviewers concluded that "not one [book] could be approved as a dependable source of knowledge about the history and culture of the Indian people in America. Most of the books were . . . derogatory to the Native American. Most contained misinformation, distortions, or omissions of important history" (Costo, 1970, p. 11). Alarming and shocking as this may sound, it is more discouraging to note the AIHS finding that "all of these books are currently being used in the schools of this country" (p. 11).

The AIHS reviewers found frequent references to "primitive, degraded, filthy, war-like, savage" Indians. Some authors were a little more imaginative. In one text, the reviewers found Indians grouped with "riffraff, fugitives from justice, runaway slaves . . . whose forays over into Georgia made life hideous" (p. 41). In the same text, a chapter is given the rather dubious title of "Bold, Flamboyant Savages of the Western Plains" (p. 41). In other texts, the reviewers often found the phrase "Indians and animals," suggesting a relationship between the two. Similarly, Indians were often referred to as "savage and hostile to settlers," with no balancing statements that might have indicated any blame or shame on the part of the settlers for the historical course of events or for Indian–white relationships.

In another book, a rather pointed reference documented:

> Unnatural affection, child-murder, father-murder, incest, a great deal of heriditary cursing, a double fratricide, and a violation of the sanctity of dead bodies—when one reads such a list or charges against any tribe or nation, either ancient or in modern times, one can hardly help concluding that somebody wanted to annex their land (p. 41).

FILM AND STEREOTYPES

The motion picture and television industries have produced a large number of films that convey still another version of the culture and history of the American Indian. For the most part, films are biased and present unflattering or distorted and fallacious images of American Indian history and culture. Like their counterparts in print—novels and textbooks—films have both created and perpetuated many negative images of Indians. Most films depict the constant struggle between settlers, ranchers, and local tribal groups, although some have dealt with historic events such as the Battle of Little Big Horn or the "Sand Creek Massacre." More recently, Hollywood producers' attempts to portray Indian life and culture in realistic terms have given birth to such films as *Standing Tall, A Man Called Horse, Little Big Man,* and *When the Legends Die.*

Indian culture and history have been portrayed in some rather unususal, and often crude, ways, but invariably negatively. Anthropologist Murray Wax (1971) argued that

> a distorted image of the warrior aspect of native cultures has permeated American society via the movies. . . . This has been accompanied by a thematic counterpointing of Indian–white relationships in which Indians are placed in a small handful of stock roles (e.g., villainous raiders of peaceable settlers; noble red man defending his land; beautiful barbarian maiden trying to establish peace between the irrascible males of two different cultures). (p. 180)

Thus the Indian becomes the infamous "bad guy"—enemy and scourge of the cavalry and white settlers. An Indian portrayed as a "good guy" is usually a "scout" for the military, the "handmaiden" of a white trapper or settler, or the white hero's sidekick. In such examples, the role is always *subordinate* to that of the hero; and the character is inevitably inferior to whites, but slightly more sophisticated than other Indians. Rarely are Indians portrayed as heroes. In short, the image of the "primitive savage" has prevailed in Hollywood's portrayal of the Indian.

An even more insidious characterization of the first American occurs as the film is edited. Films show "Indians," not Sioux or Arapahos or Kiowas. Moviegoers are given a stereotypical picture of an incredibly diverse population group and thus see nothing of the diversity. In this way, the Indian culture becomes standardized as well as stereotyped. When tribal names are mentioned, it is usually only to enhance the little historical truth that the film actually does contain. The overall image, however, has been one of Indians lurking in the bushes, hiding behind rocks, or stalking white heroes. Film directors and wardrobe and makeup designers have developed a highly stylized and consistent "Indian." Extras wear feathers of one sort or another or cloth headbands carelessly tied about their heads. "Chiefs," or Indian leaders, are invariably clad in warbonnets. Indeed, the number of feathers worn is often a good indicator of status or "power." Most Indian historians, as well as Indians themselves, note that the warbonnet was indigenous only to Northern Plains tribes such as the Sioux, the Cheyenne, the Crow, or the Arapaho. Yet, every "Hollywood tribe" is led by someone wearning a warbonnet, just as all Indians, regardless of tribe or band, ride horses, fight constantly, and use nonverbal signals (e.g., smoke signals, bird calls, and the beat of drums) to communicate with one another.

Most Hollywood Indians speak either no English or, at best, a broken English interspersed with grunts, groans, and "ughs." In some films, Indian extras speak in foreign dialects—usually gibberish or nonsense syllables—in an effort to "authenticate" their Indian roles. One producer actually recorded the Indian dialogue in English, reversed the tape, and dubbed it in to represent a tribal dialect. To their credit, some producers actually had their extras learn their parts in a tribal dialect, such as Lakota (Sioux) or Navajo. Even here, however, what Hollywood produced was usually a disastrous mutilation of the true language, and actors and actresses said things that made no sense in context. In one film, for example, a "Sioux," costumed as a Hollywood Indian (i.e., wearing nothing that resembled the traditional dress of the Tetons), speaks in Lakota to an interpreter. The Indian's words, "White man, you are nothing!" are translated as "I have been traveling a long time to talk with you!" The audience never knows the difference.

In many cases, the extras who play Indians in these films were hired because they "looked Indian," yet were often not Indians at all. Mexican-Americans, Greeks, Italians, or other "appropriately dark-skinned" peoples played most Indian roles. When Indians do play themselves on the screen, their complexions are sometimes darkened with makeup.

With little respect, sensitivity, or appreciation for tribal customs or reality, Hollywood producers have created their own image of the American Indian. That it is a false image has never penetrated the minds of most moviegoers. How could it, when it reinforces so well what they have already learned in classrooms and from textbooks and novels?

RESEARCH THEMES AND STEREOTYPES

Social and behavioral science research efforts appear to confirm many of the stereotypes held by a less knowledgeable public, simply because of the attention certain topics have received. Although researchers are attempting to provide understanding of and solutions to specific areas of concern, they are unintentionally feeding stereotypes.

The most apparent of these stereotypical foci are alcoholism and self-destructive behavior among Indians. The research community has paid a great deal of attention to these two substantive areas, which reflect the stereotypical view of the "drunken, suicidal Indian."

An abundance of articles dealing with alcoholism and mental health among American Indians and Alaskan natives exists in the literature. Kelso and Attneave (1981) compiled some 1,360 articles on Indian mental-health topics. The reviewers broke down the citations into 10-year increments to illustrate publication trends. In the area of studies on discrimination, the authors noted that only 7 references appear from 1930 to 1959; from 1960 to 1969, the number of citations increased to 17, and from 1970 to 1979, the number jumped to 58. The increase in studies on discrimination certainly coincided with the heightened interest in civil rights issues that occurred in the 1970s.

It is of interest that close to 30% of the discrimination citations are related to problems of acculturation and cultural adaptation. Following that category, the authors cited some 18 articles concerning discrimination in school settings. Other discrimination-related citations deal with such topics as crime, health, politics, legal matters, and human relations issues. Kelso and Attneave also cited some 50 publications dealing with suicide and 152 on the subject of alcoholism.

In another biography, Mail and McDonald (1980) listed 969 citations dealing exclusively with alcoholism among American Indians; 24 of these citations deal directly with alcoholism and discrimination. A review of the discrimination citations reveals that about 50% are concerned with criminal arrest patterns and that another 29% focus on the role that attitudes play in the relationship between alcohol consumption and discriminatory practices toward Indians.

Both bibliographies clearly show a strong connection between discrimination and mental health problems. More to the point, it could be assumed that a large contributing factor to the incidence of Indian alcoholism and mental health problems is racism and discrimination.

Suicide or self-destructive behavior seems to be inordinately high among American Indian youth. In their review of the literature related to suicide among Indians, May and Dizmang (1974) reported that Indian suicide rates were higher than those of the general population and that such rates varied from one tribe to another. Miller and Schoenfeld (1971) investigated suicide rates among a sample of Navajo men and women. They found more attempted than actual suicides and suggested that research—and treatment— should focus on such attempted suicides. Moreover, they found no significant difference between the overall suicide rates or suicide-attempt rates of Navajos and those of the general population. Psychiatrist James Shore (1975) argued that, although suicide rates were unusually high in some areas, the stereotype of the "suicidal Indian" had actually been drawn from the publicity given to a small number of tribes that do have unusually high suicide rates. Shore also maintained that such publicity had convinced members of other tribes that had relatively low rates that self-destructive behavior was one of their major mental-health problems. In fact, if suicide is identified as a major mental-health problem by a tribe, community, or village, it must be recognized as such, whether or not the actual suicide rates support this view. Nonetheless, suicide rates and the publicity given to them have certainly contributed to the stereotype of the "suicidal Indian."

Alcoholism among American Indians and Alaskan natives has received even more research and public attention than suicide. The scope of the articles ranges from an analysis of drinking patterns among certain tribes specifically and among Indians generally to descriptions of treatment programs and services. Nancy Lurie (1971) argued that drinking among American Indians was perhaps the world's oldest ongoing protest demonstration. Yet, alcoholism levels among Indians and Alaskan natives does contribute to the maintenance of the "drunken Indian" stereotype. The stereotype has become both a curse and a legacy; it can be found in historical accounts, in Hollywood "images," and in the actual incidence levels and alcoholism rates of Indian people around the country.

Writing on the subject of Indian alcoholism, Westermeyer (1972) maintained that two distinctive patterns of drinking occurred among the Chippewa: "white drinking" and "Indian drinking." He argued that most drinkers shifted back and forth between the two patterns, depending on the situation. "White drinking" (drinking in a style peculiar to non-Indians) served as an entry into the dominant American culture, whereas "Indian drinking" (often binge drinking in group settings) occurred only among other Indians. In each case, the pattern and apparent reasons for drinking differed (cf. Ferguson, 1968; Lemert, 1958; Waddell, 1975).

In another article, Westermeyer (1974) exposed myths about Indian drinking that he found in the research literature. He identified three major themes: (a) Indians are unable to hold their liquor; (b) alcoholism rates are unusually high among Indians; and (c) alcoholism is a major problem among Indian people. Westermeyer argued that these mythical themes were typically framed in broad, sweeping generalizations. He added that many misconceptions evolved from findings in single-community or reservation-based groups. Westermeyer noted, for example, that many of the physiological studies intended to assess metabolic rates of alcohol absorption had been poorly designed. Finally, Westermeyer strongly argued that many of the alcohol-related research findings simply reinforced long-standing myths about Indian drinking and were not really based on solid research findings.

The emphasis given to suicide and alcoholism among Indians is somewhat unflattering. Moreover, those who prefer to cling to their notion of the Indians as "drunken and suicidal" are not likely to be influenced by contradictory evidence. But a deemphasis on suicide and alcoholism themselves and a corresponding emphasis on the role of treatment and prevention sensitive to the Indian life-style can help erode the pejorative implications of those stereotypes.

On the one hand, the number of research citations on Indian suicide rates and alcoholism acts much as does a lightning rod. Indians and some non-Indians alike are deeply concerned about the problems, and because of the enormity of the topics, researchers and practitioners are drawn to them to seek explanations and solutions. In fact, many Indian professionals consider alcoholism to be the number one mental-health problem among Indians. Yet, the attention given to the topics serves to confirm the self-serving stereotypical images of many racist-minded non-Indians, in whom no amount of factual evidence will alter deep-seated prejudicial convictions. Most Indian professionals recognize the dilemma. So, in spite of the pitfalls, research on alcoholism and suicide will continue until the problems are significantly reduced or are eradicated altogether.

THE NEWS MEDIA AND STEREOTYPES

News photographers and cartoonists continue to portray American Indians as they were a century or more ago. The Indians most often seen in photographs are clad in stereotypical features, beaded headbands, and decorative clothing. Certainly, the Indian of the cartoonist's pen is a caricature of one or more of the commonly held stereotypes of Indians. The emphasis is on artifacts, rather than on contemporary human beings. It is as if the images of the photojournalist are frozen in the past.

The news coverage by eight national and regional newspapers of the 1973 occupation of the small southwestern South Dakota village of Wounded Knee was reviwed. The Wounded Knee incident lasted 71 days. During that period, and later as well, the news media devoted a great deal of space to the various skirmishes and day-to-day circumstances related to the confrontations. During the 71-day period of the occupation, the eight papers published 244 stories (3,530 column inches), with 94 photos and 22 political cartoons alongside the written text. A content analysis of the photos and cartoons sheds some interesting light on the characterization of American Indians in the news media.

The Wounded Knee incident was an American Indian concern; thus, Indians should have been the central theme of photos and cartoons; in fact, that was the case. In 15% of the photos, government and state agents and attorneys were also shown with various Indians who were involved in the incident. How were the Indians portrayed by the media? Of the photos that showed only American Indians, 54% depicted the Indians in "traditional" garb (braids, feathers, and headbands), and only 26% portrayed the "militant" Indian (in long hair, beaded or decorated vests, and "Billy Jack" hats). Only 5% of the photos showed the American Indians in typical everyday reservation clothing: jeans, boots, western hats, and so on. In virtually all of the political cartoons, the Indians wore feathers of one sort or another, "warpoint," moccasins, and stereotypically traditional garb.

Biased characterization of the Indian by the press serves no real purpose. The light in which the Indian is portrayed reflects neither the nature nor the characteristics of contemporary Indian life. Modern Indians simply do not fit the non-Indians' stereotype of their ancestors. Journalists, news photographers, and cartoonists seem to experience difficulty in portraying modern American Indians, especially when they want to be certain that the reader will recognize the subject as an American Indian. As long as contemporary Indians are portrayed as though they still live and dress as some of them did years ago, stereotypical and unrealistic images will be perpetuated. Far too many people, and especially young people, believe that Indians still wear feathers, live in wigwams or teepees, and "roam" the prairies as they did years ago. The journalistic responsibility for portraying the Indian in more positive and realistic terms must be met. Until that occurs, the public needs to be reminded that caricatures and fictitious images are just that.

Journalistic portrayals of Indians also affect Indians. Many are offended by the continued misrepresentation and the inaccurate characterization of their people. Others, unfortunately, try to live up to such images. Vine Deloria (1969) eloquently stated: "Experts paint us as they would like us to be. Often we paint ourselves as we wish we were or as we might have been." He continued, "To be an Indian is in a very real sense to be unreal and ahistorical" (p. 9). The image rendered through the news media continues to perpetuate a mythical lifestyle and character. It helps the public to identify the characters in the story. Some Indians know what the public expects and comply with that expectation by sporting contrived regalia. But sooner or later, the charade must come to an end.

When that happens, the Indian can then be cast in the role of a twentieth-century human being instead of some historical, romantic character.

Some Data on Changing Stereotypes

About 1970, during the social upheaval and protest surrounding ethnic-minority and civil-rights issues, the subject of stereotypes of American Indians achieved some attention. At that time, an effort was made to identify the stereotypes held of American Indians by both Indians and non-Indians following the procedures of the classic work on stereotypes by Katz and Braly (1933).

In our initial study, we asked 131 Indian and non-Indian graduate and undergraduate students from colleges in Oklahoma to list as many words as they could that accurately and succinctly described the American Indian. The combined lists produced 38 separate and distinct single-word traits. About 2 months later, the 38-word list was administered to 136 Indian and non-Indian American students. The subjects were instructed to select 15 words from the list of 38 single-word traits, choosing those that seemed most typical of American Indians. Following this task, another group of Indian and non-Indian subjects were asked to select from the list one word that seemed to be the most typical trait of the group. After completing their task, the subjects were asked to rank their 15 chosen words from "most typical" to "least typical," using "most typical" as a benchmark. Results from this 1970 study appear in Table 1.

A statistical analysis of the results suggested a lack of agreement between the non-Indian and Indian samples for the ranked traits, with little or no relationships between the rankings of the two samples. Despite the absence of an overall relationship, some interesting findings did emerge. There was some agreement between the groups on the ranking of particular traits. For example, both groups converged on the traits "proud" and "drunkards" and tended to rank them as "moderately descriptive" of American Indians. The traits "stoic" and "savage" were regarded by both groups as "less descriptive." However, there was strong disagreement between the two groups in ranking the

TABLE 1. Average Rankings of Descriptive
Traits of American Indians in 1970

| | Average ranking[a] | |
Trait	Non-Indian	Indian
Artistic	14.3	7.2
Backward	8.5	11.5
Brave	13.8	10.9
Defeated	12.5	2.1
Distrustful	7.1	13.2
Drunkards	5.5	4.4
Ignorant	3.8	14.1
Lazy	3.1	6.6
Mistreated	14.1	2.8
Proud	2.9	3.4
Quiet	9.7	4.9
Savage	10.9	12.5
Shy	6.7	9.2
Stoic	11.7	13.8
Suspicious	4.4	7.9

[a] Kendall's tau = −.09; z = 0.47, nonsignificant.

traits "defeated," "ignorant," and "mistreated." The Indian sample regarded the traits "distrustful" and "ignorant" as "less descriptive" of Indians than the non-Indian sample. On the other hand, the non-Indian sample considered the trait "mistreated" "much less descriptive" than did the Indian sample.

In 1973, the same 15 single-word traits were used with another sample of 122 non-Indian and Indian graduate and undergraduate students from academic institutions in Oklahoma. The subjects were instructed to review the lists of traits and to add any traits that they felt should be included. Following their review, a second group were asked at a later time to rank the traits according to the criteria followed by the 1970 sample. Results from the 1973 ranking appear in Table 2.

The 1970 and 1973 rankings differed somewhat because new traits were added to the original 15-word list. The 1970 traits "stoic," "savage," "distrustful," "quiet," and "brave" were excluded from the 1973 list; among those traits added in 1973 were "unreliable," "stubborn," "poor," "ignored," and "faithful." Apparently, conventional stereotypes had been replaced with those that more accurately reflected the current circumstances of the American Indian. "Poor" and "ignored," for example, seem to reflect a greater concern about the social welfare and status of Indians.

The 1973 results introduced some other interesting data. Basically, even with the addition of new traits, there was some overall agreement between the two samples in ranking the traits. Specifically, both groups showed strong agreement on the ranking of the traits "artistic," "backward," "ignorant," "ignored," "mistreated," "poor," and "suspicious," with "artistic," "backward," and "ignorant" receiving low rankings and "ignored" and "mistreated" receiving high rankings.

In an attempt to further our understanding of change and stereotypes, two more samples of 100 non-Indian and Indian graduate and undergraduate students were again selected in 1976 from academic institutions in Oklahoma. This sample was given exactly the same instructions that had been given to the 1973 sample. The results from the 1976 study are presented in Table 3.

The results of the 1976 study were similar to the findings in 1973. First, the listing of

TABLE 2. Average Rankings of Descriptive
Traits of American Indians in 1973

Trait	Average ranking[a]	
	Non-Indian	Indian
Artistic	10.4	12.6
Backward	13.3	14.3
Defeated	4.1	13.4
Drunkards	3.9	7.8
Faithful	13.6	3.7
Ignorant	14.2	13.8
Ignored	2.1	2.6
Lazy	11.7	9.5
Mistreated	2.7	2.1
Poor	5.5	6.3
Proud	6.6	4.8
Shy	9.1	10.9
Stubborn	11.9	5.9
Suspicious	8.8	8.1
Unreliable	7.3	10.8

[a] Kendall's tau = .48; $z = 2.53$, $p < .01$.

TABLE 3. Average Rankings of Descriptive
Traits of American Indians in 1976

Trait	Average ranking[a]	
	Non-Indian	Indian
Artistic	8.9	10.1
Defeated	14.1	14.3
Drunkards	6.8	9.1
Easy-going	14.2	14.0
Faithful	12.8	4.2
Ignored	6.7	4.9
Lazy	10.0	13.2
Militant	2.3	2.1
Mistreated	1.9	5.8
Native	3.7	2.7
Patient	11.3	12.8
Proud	8.6	7.4
Shy	12.2	11.3
Strong	6.1	3.7
Stubborn	5.5	8.2

[a] Kendall's tau $= .65$; $z = 3.26$, $p < .0007$.

traits in the 15-word limit was again altered: the 1973 traits "unreliable," "suspicious," "poor," "ignorant," and "backward" were replaced in 1976 with "easy-going," "militant," "native," "patient," and "strong." The emergence of the new traits indicated a move away from the use of negatively oriented characteristics toward the use of traits that reflected the then-current social state of affairs and more psychologically oriented attributes. The inclusion of some new traits again supported the notion that certain social conditions may influence the ways in which groups are perceived and characterized.

Perhaps the most outstanding finding that emerged from the 1976 study was the level of overall agreement between the two groups in their selection of the 15-trait list. In fact, the high correlation of the overall ranking suggests a strong level of agreement between the two sample groups in their ranking of traits. For example, both groups converged at the low end on the ranking of the traits "defeated," "easy-going," "patient," and "shy," and at the high end on the ranking of "native" and "militant." The Indian sample ranked "faithful" much higher than did the non-Indian sample, but the ranking of this trait represented the only major point of departure between the two groups.

Table 4 lends some additional insight into the overall pattern of these studies, with its summary of the results fround over the six years. Only six descriptive traits were included in all six of the 15-word lists compiled by the six different sample groups, but none of these traits were ranked consistently across the samples. For some traits, such as "shy" and "lazy," the ranking went down from "moderately descriptive" in 1970 to "least descriptive" in 1976. The ranking of the trait "defeated" also went through some interesting changes: in 1970, the Indian sample ranked "defeated" high ("more" to "most descriptive"); in 1976, the Indian sample ranked this trait low ("least descriptive"). The trait "drunkards" went through a similar, although not quite so striking, change in its ranking by the Indian samples. When treated with appropriate statistical procedures, the rankings of these six traits showed a tendency toward intergroup agreement. In 1970, there was almost no agreement ($-.06$); by 1973, a marginal level of agreement had emerged ($.33$); in 1976, both groups strongly agreed on the ranking of the six traits ($.87$).

TABLE 4. Ranking Changes in Descriptive Traits of American Indians[a,b]

| | Study years[c] | | | | | |
| | 1970 | | 1973 | | 1976 | |
Traits	NI	I	NI	I	NI	I
Artistic	14.3	7.2	10.4	12.6	8.9	10.1
Defeated	12.5	2.1	4.1	13.4	14.1	14.3
Drunkards	5.5	4.4	3.9	7.8	6.8	9.1
Lazy	3.1	6.6	11.7	9.5	10.0	13.2
Mistreated	14.1	2.8	2.7	2.1	1.9	5.8
Shy	6.7	9.2	9.1	10.9	12.1	11.3

[a] List includes only those traits that were consistently listed in each sample year.
[b] The reader is reminded that the numbers ranking the traits varied, as did the individuals in each successive sample.
[c] Numerous correlation coefficients were calculated, with the following results: 1970, NI × I $= -.06$; 1970 × 1973, NI × NI $= -.20$; 1970 × 1976, NI × NI $= -.06$; 1973 × 1976, NI × NI $= -.33$; 1973, NI × I $= .33$; 1970 × 1973, NI × I $= .33$; 1970 × 1976, NI × I $= -.20$; 1973 × 1976, NI × I $= .47$; 1976, NI × I $= .87$, $pp = .0083$; 1970 × 1973, I × I $= .20$; 1970 × 1976, I × I $= .06$; 1973 × 1976, I × I $= -.47$. Only the 1976 NI × I yielded statistically significant results.

Agreement patterns were also obtained by comparing the rankings of the respective groups. The 1970 and 1973 Indian samples showed a little agreement (.20), although the 1970 and 1976 samples had shown almost no agreement; however, the 1973 and 1976 Indian samples showed slightly more agreement than had been found in the 1970–1973 comparison (.47). The 1970–1973, 1970–1976, and 1973–1976 non-Indian comparisons produced similar results ($-.20$, $-.06$, and .33). The 1970–1973 and 1973–1976 comparisons between the non-Indian (NI) and the Indian (I) samples also produced comparable results, along with the emergence of some interesting patterns. The 1970–1973 non-Indian and Indian samples showed moderate agreement (.33). The pattern shifted to a small negative relationship when the 1970 non-Indian sample was contrasted with the 1976 Indian sample ($-.20$) but increased to a moderately positive level of agreement when the 1973 non-Indian sample was contrasted with the 1976 Indian sample (.47). The fluctuations in the between-group comparisons are not statistically significant and could be chance occurrences. The directional trends of the agreement patterns, however, suggest variations in the ways in which American Indians were described by the same traits over the course of the 6-year period.

What do the results obtained from the small study mean? What implications do they have for our understanding of the ways in which American Indians are characterized by themselves and by non-Indians? What conclusions can be drawn from the results? How do these conclusions contribute to our understanding of stereotyping in general?

The results of these three sets of examples do point out that groups can change their stereotypes. More specifically, the words that individuals and groups use and prioritize to describe others—and the value that they place on these word descriptions—can change over even a short span of time. Two groups can also agree to some extent on the use of certain words to describe one of the groups. Our results showed a greater level of agreement between the two 1976 samples than between the two 1970 and 1973 samples. In addition, the 1976 samples selected less negatively slanted words than had the previous samples. The strong agreement between the 1976 samples, compared with the earlier studies, is puzzling. Certainly, the results could have been due to chance; on the other hand, it seems more likely that the commonality of agreement was due to a multitude of factors operating at the time of study. In Oklahoma in 1976, the needs and issues of American Indians were very evident in the press; American Indians themselves were more expressive. Such attention and orientation may therefore have swayed the perceptions of the sample.

The 1970s were a time of rapid social change in the United States. Indeed, the civil rights movement played a major role in drawing attention to the oppressed status of America's ethnic-minority populations. For the American Indian, the 1970s were seen as a time to draw attention to past civil injustices, unfulfilled treaty responsibilities, and errant discrepancies in the federal government's mismanagement of Indian affairs. Indians also seized the occasion to remind America that they, too, were living in the twentieth century and that seemingly ageless stereotypical images would no longer be tolerated and ignored.

Yes, Indian activist groups like the American Indian Movement and the National Indian Youth Council borrowed tactics used by blacks and Chicanos. They were effective. And part of those tactics required effective and skillful use of the media. Indian activists, through the media, reminded America that the Indian was not a vanishing species, that their land and culture were not for sale, and that there was a good deal of "unfinished business" to be tended to.

Most likely, the attention that the media gave to the Indian during the 1970s contributed to the changes in stereotypes found in Oklahoma. At the time of the study, Oklahoma had the largest Indian population and the most number of different tribes of any state. And the activists recognized all too well that Indians were likely to receive a good deal of press in the state. To an extent, they were right.

Were the images found among that small sample of 1976 similar to what we would find in the 1980s? Probably. Indians now, more than ever, are pushing strongly for self-governance of tribally controlled lands and the federal government's obligations under treaty arrangements. The problems of unemployment, health, alcoholism, and educational progress still remain, despite gradual progress in all areas.

INDIANS, BLACKS, AND RACISM

Are the racist and discriminatory experiences of Indians similar to those of America's other ethnic-minority populations? How do they compare with those of blacks, the group to which much of the research literature is devoted? On the surface, the needs and problems of ethnic minorities are similar in many respects; hence, the answer to the first question above is a resounding "yes." But at another, more complex level of analysis, the problems and experiences with racism among American Indians are unique, and so, the answer must be "no." Because of the complex makeup of the Indian population in the United States, it is an oversimplification to claim that Indians and blacks share very similar problems and that racist practices are comparable simply because the alleged common enemy is the white. It may prove instructive at this point to highlight the basic differences of the two groups in terms of their relationships with the dominant American culture.

As every student of American history knows, the Indian is indigenous to the Americas. Almost from the beginning of the colonial effort, Indians and their culture were seen as threats, either to be eliminated or to be assimilated. Blacks are immigrants, not of their own choosing. They were brought to America to assist the Anglo-American to "tame the wilderness and cultivate the land"; and in certain instances, they were recruited to fight against the Indian. The settlers coveted Indian land even after it was set aside by treaty agreement with the federal government. After much of the Indian land was confiscated, stolen, or wrenched away, especially in the mid-southern states, blacks were brought in to work it for their white overseers.

In the course of colonization and throughout the entire settlement of the West, the Anglo-Americans pushed the Indians to abandon their aboriginal ways and to become "like everyone else." Blacks, on the other hand, were invariably excluded from just about every Anglo institution and were left, in many ways, to devise their own culture. Indians, unlike blacks, historically, were always reminded that their vast cultural differences presented problems for them and the dominant culture. As a consequence, the ethnocidal practice of removing Indian youth from reservations to attend Anglo-controlled boarding schools was viewed as a convenient strategy for creating the "white-acculturated Indian." Black schools were created, yes, but not for the purpose of destroying culture; rather, they were created as a token gesture to provide blacks with the skills to manage affairs in their own communities. Strange as it may seem, Indians were historically welcomed in the educational institutions of the dominant culture—even actively recruited. On their graduation, many white school and university officials would point with pride to the effect that education had had on "taming the savage mind."

In the late 1950s, blacks consolidated their efforts to seek their rights to be free from discrimination in voting, housing, use of public facilities, employment, and the right to attend schools and colleges of their own choosing. Civil rights became the rallying point around which protests, demonstrations, and riots revolved. The civil rights legislation of that tumultuous era benefited not only blacks but every other ethnic-minority population in the United States. In a sense, blacks wanted the same rights as whites. Indians, on the other hand, were not so wanting—for the bulk of the tribal governments really wanted to retain a sovereign status within a pluralistic society and the right to exist as separate political entities. Hence, civil rights legislation posed a problem for Indians. They wanted the rights provided by legislation, and they also wanted to retain entitlements provided by treaties. In a word, Indians wanted equality, but they also wanted to remain separate tribal entities.

The basic civil rights issue for Indians centers on a maintenance of cultural independence attainable only through preservation of the reservation land use. Provided by treaties with the United States, the more than 200 reservation and land-settlement areas make an ideal setting for promoting tradition and customs and maintaining tribal identity. Today, more than ever in the history of the United States, the reservation is home, a retreat and haven away from the world of the dominant culture. With some exceptions, the tribes govern in a manner consistent with tradition. Tribal members abide by tribal law first. Residents are free to practice ceremonials, to speak distinct languages, and to follow a life-style free of the strictures of a paternalistic government. So distinct is the status of the Indian that, in 1973, a separate Division of Civil Rights was established by the U.S. Department of Justice to handle Indian civil rights.

So as Indians demand their civil rights, "there is the danger that their separate tribal rights may be overlooked in the process" (*Indian Tribes*, 1981, p. 39). The rights of sovereignty and independent self-government are viewed as far more sacred and meaningful than having a full slate of rights as outlined in the civil rights legislation. Indians see the legislation as assimilationist propaganda and are quite reluctant to accept the standards and conditions that come with full acceptance. Thus, in the main, Indians are more in favor of a separate-but-equal status than they are of total desegregation: Indians essentially want the same rights as all citizens of the United States, but at the same time, they do not aspire to adopt and internalize the ways of the dominant society. The land base and their unique status afford them that right and that choice.

Indians have suffered discriminatory and racist practices similar to those suffered by blacks. However, blacks never signed treaties with the United States and, as a consequence, must deal with the government and the dominant culture in a different way. Furthermore, blacks were never allocated separate land bases, nor were they subjected to the multitude of unique hardships and oppressive acts carried out against the indigenous peoples of the Americas. Anthropologist Luis Kemnitzer remarked:

> No other group of people have the heritage of conquest and theft of homeland, of treatments as savages and sub-humans, of decimination of kin by disease, military action, of dissolution of sacred institutions, of demoralization and dehumanization as Native Americans have. . . . No other group of people are so imbued with a need for individual autonomy and privacy and all this means as Indians are. (1978, pp. 15–16)

The federal government is ambivalent toward the Indian in a way that it is not toward blacks. The ambivalence stems from the failure of past efforts to meet the needs of Indians; inherited guilt from past failures, including illegal land claims, genocide, ethnocide, and the prolonged impoverished of Indian communities; and the increasing pressure from congressional and industrial representatives to terminate federal responsibilities and abrogate treaty obligations.

In spite of all the failures, the American Indians, this country's indigenous population of 1.5 million, perseveres. Perhaps the strength to survive is embedded in an identification with one's tribal heritage. The strength of that identification is most likely a source of psychological survival that transcends all other forms of intervention (Trimble, 1986).

SUMMARY AND CONCLUSIONS

In this chapter, we have examined a number of factors that have fed racist and prejudicial practices toward American Indians. We opened our discussion by pointing out how early historical images shaped federal government policy. Early settlers and colonialists viewed the Indians as primitive children but nonetheless wise in their knowledge of the ecology and subtlety of the "new world." Thus, early on, most settlers promoted a policy of accommodation. That policy changed to one of extermination and subsequently isolation as the presence of the Indian was seen as a threat to colonial settlement and westward migration. In time, the policy of isolation was intensified, eventually resulting in the present-day policies of assimilation and termination. All the while, the prevailing image of the Indian as a dependent, helpless child has prevailed.

Over the course of time, numerous words have been coined to characterize and describe the American Indian. Most appear to have negative implications; many are false and inaccurate. Many textbook writers, particularly, have contributed to the perpetuation of false images by portraying the history of American Indians inaccurately. Often, these writers have used words that are offensive and degrading to Indians and non-Indians alike. Some journalists, news photographers, and political cartoonists continue to bias their material with portrayals of Indians reminiscent of a century or so ago. The film industry has done the same. These portrayals not only lack historical authenticity but neglect the positive cultural aspects of contemporary American Indians. The themes are far from flattering and serve to feed a seemingly unyielding public, a public that thrives on seeing the American Indian only in the context of the past.

In more subtle ways, research on the American Indian lends credence to a few negative beliefs about Indians. Researchers and practitioners are eager to find explanations and solutions for deviant behaviors such as alcoholism and suicide, but the continued discussion of alarming rates of abuse subtly feeds the public image of the Indian as a "drunkard" and "suicidal." Very little attention is given to those Indians who abstain from drinking, or to those who have maintained sobriety after a bout with alcohol.

Similarly, little attention has been paid to Indians who have earned professional degrees or who have made significant contributions in their respective fields. The negative and deviant themes of much social science research on the American Indian should be balanced with efforts that recognize and identify the inherent strengths of Indians.

With some degree of assurance, we can say that the prevalent image is not truly representative of the way many, if not most, Indians think of themselves. Indians tend to recognize that the stereotypical image is not complimentary. Yet, despite the inaccurate nature of most of the unflattering imagery, it still persists. Once, these stereotypes might have had a functional value. Enough evidence exists today to suggest that many of these stereotypical images are mythical and archaic and are thus no longer functional.

We can continue to moralize and attempt to understand why archaic and inaccurate images persist. Such moralizing may lead to change, but in the interim, it does little to foster an appreciation of cultural diversity or to promote positive intergroup relations. A more practical approach is to pursue an understanding of the functional nature of stereotypes and to emphasize the use of those stereotypes that enhance group solidarity and foster an appreciation of cultural diversity. This seems to be a modest request.

REFERENCES

Ablon, J. (1971). Cultural conflict in urban Indians. *Mental Hygiene, 55,* 199–205.

Anders, G. C. (1980). Theories of underdevelopment and the American Indian. *Journal of Economic Issues, 14*(3), 681–701.

An Indian lives in the city. (1971, June 14). *Newsweek,* pp. 94–102.

Bahr, H. M., Chadwick, B. A., & Struass, J. H. (1972). Discrimination against urban Indians in Seattle. *The Indian Historian, 5,* 4–11.

Beaman, K. (1969, September 12). American Indians are still called "filthy savages." *New York Times Educational Supplement, 2834,* 20.

Berkhofer, R. F. (1978). *The white man's Indian: Images of the American Indian from Columbus to the present.* New York: Vintage Books.

Braroe, N. W. (1965). Reciprocal exploitation in an Indian–White community. *Southwestern Journal of Anthropology, 21,* 166–178.

Costo, R. (Eds.). (1970). *Textbooks and the American Indian.* San Francisco, California: Indian Historian Press.

Cox, O. (1948). *Caste, class, and race.* New York: Monthly Review Press.

Deloria, V. (1969). *Custer died for your sins.* New York: Avon.

Feagin, J. R. (1978). *Racial and ethnic minorities.* Englewood Cliffs, NJ: Prentice-Hall.

Ferguson, F. N. (1968). Navajo drinking: Some tentative hypotheses. *Human Organization, 27,* 159–167.

Hagen, E. E. (1962). *On the theory of social change.* Homewood, IL: Dorsey Press.

Hraba, J. (1979). *American ethnicity.* Itasca, IL: Peacock.

Indian tribes: A continuing quest for survival. (1981). A report of the United States Commission on Civil Rights. Washington, DC: U.S. Government Printing Office.

James, B. J. (1961). Sociological-psychological dimensions of Ojibwa acculturation. *American Anthropologist, 63*(4), 721–746.

Katz, D., & Braly, K. W. (1933). Racial stereotypes of 100 college students. *Journal of Abnormal and Social Psychology, 28,* 280–290.

Kelso, D. R., & Attneave, C. L. (Eds.). (1981). *Bibliography of North American Indian mental health.* Westport, CN: Greenwood Press.

Kemnitzer, L. S. (1978). Native Americans. In K. V. Chandras (Ed.), *Racial discrimination against neither white-nor-black American minorities.* San Francisco: R & E Associates.

Lemert, E. M. (1958). The use of alcohol in three Salish Indian tribes. *Quarterly Review of Studies on Alcohol, 19,* 90–107.

Lurie, N. O. (1971). The world's oldest on-going protest demonstration: North American Indian drinking patterns. *Pacific Historical Review, 40,* 311–332.

MacGregor, G. (1946). *Warriors without weapons.* Chicago: University of Chicago Press.

Mail, P. D., & McDonald, D. R. (Eds.). (1980). *Tulapai to Tokay.* New Haven, CN: HRAF Press.

Marx, G. T. (1970). Civil disorders and agents of social control. *Journal of Social Issues, 26*(1), 19–57.

May, P. A., & Dizmang, L. H. (1974). Suicide and the American Indian. *Psychiatric Annals, 4*(9), 22–28.

McNickle, D. (1973). *Native American tribalism: Indian survivals and renewals.* New York: Oxford University Press.

Miller, S. I., & Schoenfeld, L. S. (1971). Suicide attempt patterns among the Navajo Indians. *International Journal of Social Psychiatry, 17*(3), 189–193.

Myrdal, G. (1944). *An American dilemma: The Negro problem and modern democracy.* New York: Harper & Row.

Sherif, M. (1969). *Social psychology.* New York: Harper & Row.

Shore, J. H. (1975). American Indian suicide—fact and fantasy. *Psychiatry, 38,* 86–91.

Steiner, S. (1976). *The vanishing white man.* New York: Harper & Row.

Svensson, F. (1973). *The ethnics in American politics: American Indians.* Minneapolis, Burgess.

Trimble, J. E. (1972). *An index of the social indicators of the American Indian in Oklahoma.* Oklahoma City: Oklahoma Indian Affairs Commission, Oklahoma Office of Community Affairs and Planning.

Trimble, J. E. (1986). American Indians and interethnic conflict: A theoretical and historical overview. In J. Boucher, D. Landis, & K. Arnold (Eds.), *Interethnic conflict: Myth and reality.* Beverly Hills, CA: Sage.

Troy, A. (1975). The Indian in adolescent novels. *The Indian Historian, 8*(4), 32–35.

U.S. Senate. (1968–1969). Hearings before the Subcommittee on Indian Education of the Committee on Labor and Public Welfare, Parts 1–5, 90th Congress. Washington, DC: U.S. Government Printing Office.

Vigneras, L. A. (1960). *The journal of Christopher Columbus* (C. Jane, trans. rev.). London: Hakluyt Society.

Waddell, J. O. (1975). For individual power and social credit: The use of alcohol among Tucson Papagos. *Human Organization, 34,* 9–15.

Wax, M. (1971). *Indian Americans: Unity and diversity.* Englewood Cliffs, NJ: Prentice-Hall.

Wax, R. H., & Thomas, R. K. (1961). American Indians and white people. *Phylon, 22*(4), 305–317.

Westermeyer, J. J. (1972). Chippewa and majority alcoholism in the Twin Cities: A comparison. *Journal of Nervous and Mental Diseases, 155,* 327–322.

Westermeyer, J. J. (1974). The drunken Indian—myths and realities. *Psychiatric Annual, 4,* 29–36.

10

Racism and Sexism
Comparisons and Conflicts

Pamela Trotman Reid

Are racism and sexism parallel or separate processes? Can we apply findings from one area of research to the other? Obviously, any response to such questions must be conditional, subject to definitions of the terms themselves as well as to the specific circumstances under which the questions are answered. These questions are necessarily asked, however, in light of this society's long-standing interest in racial prejudice and its increased awareness of discrimination based on gender. For this reason, there is a need to understand the extent to which the biased treatment of women may be legitimately compared to that of blacks. In other words, can it be determined whether racism and sexism are parts of a generalized response set, or if they are two different behaviors? In this chapter, the analysis has two components. In the first part, an examination of racism and sexism is presented with respect to a variety of dimensions relative to the assessment of the existence of parallelism: the definitions, the causes, and the scope of the problems. This review emphasizes social-psychological perspectives, although it is recognized that many other disciplines, such as economics, history, and political science, have contributed to the literature on racism and sexism. The second part of the chapter deals with the impact of both processes on black women, who have dual identities and are oppressed under each. In addition, the possibility that these processes may have an additive effect is explored. Specifically, in the second part of the chapter, the conflicts arising from the racism and sexism that are presented to black women are examined. It is suggested that black women may need special consideration because of their unique position relative to the movements both for women's equity and for black civil rights.

COMPARISONS OF SEXISM AND RACISM

DEFINITIONS OF RACISM AND SEXISM

The terms *racism* and *sexism* are frequently used in research literature and in discussion without definition. Indeed, the terms may have such widespread usage that most

PAMELA TROTMAN REID • Department of Psychology, University of Tennessee at Chattanooga, Chattanooga, Tennessee 37403.

people believe they are aware of what is meant. However, it seems necessary to examine carefully the various ways in which the terms are described so that we may determine whether the concepts described in various situations are actually similar.

Consideration of the terms *racism* and *sexism* may begin with the definitions in the 1975 edition of *Webster's New Collegiate Dictionary*. *Racism* was defined first as "a belief that race is a primary determinant of human traits and capacities and that racial differences produce an inherent superiority of a particular race." In the second definition, provided by the synonym *racialism*, there is reference to prejudice or discrimination. The same dictionary defined *sexism* as "prejudice or discrimination against women." There is obviously some imbalance in the development of the two concepts based on this common source. In defining racism, there is the assumption of a belief system that can support or, at least, explain any discriminatory attitudes or behavior. For sexism, no such system is explicitly presented in the definition. The lack of any explanation for sexism may result either from an assumption of a common experience that does not need explication, or from the fact that the concept of sexism does not yet have the history of examination and research that racism has.

Another definition of *racism* is the classic in social psychology from the preface to the 1954 edition of *The Nature of Prejudice* (Allport, 1979): "an antipathy based upon a faulty and inflexible generalization. It may be felt or expressed. It may be directed toward a group as a whole, or toward an individual because he is a member of that group" (p. 9). This description of racism—or more accurately, of "negative ethnic prejudice"—appears to be as easily applicable to the concept of sexism as it is to racism. The definition includes the mode of racist expression, covert or overt; sexist attitudes and behavior may also take these forms. The definition indicates the process involved in racism (faulty generalization), a process identical to the stereotyping that occurs in sexism. Finally, the affective dimension described by Allport (antipathy) and the object of the negative expression (an individual or a group) are both common to racism and sexism. In fact, Allport recognized that sex was the basis of certain discriminatory behavior. He pointed out examples of antifeminism, which he stated clearly demonstrated the basic characteristics of prejudice (pp. 33–34).

Parallelism between racism and sexism may also be inferred from an examination of the definition developed more recently by Chesler (1976). In his review of contemporary theories of racism, Chesler focused on "institutional white racism," describing it in this way: "acts or institutional procedures which help create or perpetuate sets of advantages or privileges for whites and exclusions or deprivations for minority groups" (p. 22). Important to this definition is Chesler's assumption of "an ideology of explicit or implicit superiority or advantage of one racial group over another, plus the institutional power to implement that ideology in social operations" (p. 22). The picture of blacks as powerless with respect to social institutions is also reflected in the discrimination experienced by women. Both groups have had to deal with the expectation and assumption that white men were better suited to certain positions, such as supervisory and managerial positions (Kanter, 1977). Both groups have a history of exclusion from prestigious community organizations and clubs (e.g., the Jay Cees for the first time accepted women as members in 1986). In addition, both groups have faced limitations on their acceptance to schools and universities. As defined in this research, then, institutional racism appears to have strong parallels with institutional sexism. Although the similarities of sexism to racism are evident for the mode of expression and the process in both the Allport and the Chesler definitions, neither addresses the root or the cause of the negative feelings that exist. The causes of racism and sexism have, however, been offered as an explanation in a number of other theories.

CAUSES OF RACISM AND SEXISM

Ashmore and Del Boca (1976) distinguished between explanations of prejudice that focus on intrapersonal factors and those that emphasize interpersonal relations. The intrapersonal theories have frequently been applied to racist behavior, especially by black researchers. When racism is attributed to intrapersonal factors, personality or cognitive processes are proposed. For example, Biassey (1972) stated that "much of prejudice and racism in America is paranoid in origin and developed by the self-serving, defensive maneuvers of the majority" (p. 353). Comer (1980) similarly defined *racism* as "a low-level defense and adjustment mechanism utilized by groups to deal with psychological and social insecurities" (p. 363). Delany (1980) also described racism as being the result of a disturbed personality. He called it a "classic pathology with the usual destructive behavior" and as a sickness that "runs deep in the history of this nation" (p. 368). Research on cognitive causes of racism has typically examined the role of perception, cognitive consistency, and belief system congruency. For example, Mezei (1971) found that race was more important than belief congruency in determining social intimacy. Katz (1976) also demonstrated the existence of cognitive components in the development of racism. She found that, in children, the perception of racial differences in physical appearance was accompanied by an awareness of racial status.

The intrapersonal factors are not typically used to describe the roots of sexism. Instead of being labeled as pathological, individuals with sexist attitudes are considered either misinformed, uninformed, or obtuse. Although some writers have suggested that sexists experience anxiety about changing roles or that liberated women are perceived as a threat to the male ego, sexists are more frequently viewed as lacking sensitivity to women's perspectives than as having a deep-seated personality problem. In fact, although most researchers support explanations of racism that focus on the individual level (Ashmore & Del Boca, 1976), feminist theorists emphasize societal-level and political causes of sexism (Hyde, 1985).

Among the interpersonal factors in racial prejudice acquisition that have been investigated are socialization processes, conformity to societal norms, and attribution theory. Researchers have shown how parents, peers, schools, and mass media have instructed the individual directly and indirectly in the dominant cultural belief patterns (Ashmore & Del Boca, 1976). Studies of attitudes toward women have also demonstrated the importance of socialization and the agents of that process (Shaffer, 1985). In addition to the pressures of family and society, racist belief systems are supported by the type of information available through the media concerning blacks and other underrepresented groups. The image of these groups is distorted; thus, the media actually encourage faulty attributions about the roots of social problems relevant to the specific group (Ashmore & Del Boca, 1976). This distortion of image, as well as the other interpersonal factors, appears to be equally applicable to women and to blacks.

The problems of racism and sexism are most accurately described as having multiple causes. Intrapersonal, interpersonal, and societal factors must be recognized as contributors having summative, as well as interactive, effects. Early childhood experiences, familial attitudes, media influences, and peer and social group standards—all play a role in the final pattern of attitudes and behaviors that are adopted by white individuals toward blacks and by males toward females. In a comprehensive review of the early developmental precursors of racial and gender attitudes, Katz (1983) underscored the complexity of the issues involved. She noted that explanations rooted in biological, cognitive, and learning theories have been proposed to explain children's responses to gender and racial differences. Although Katz suggested the existence of several similarities in the developmental processes underlying race and sex discrimination, she also indicated that there are differences. One important difference is that gender-role expectations change with age, whereas racial attitudes seem to be more fixed. It appears, then, that racism and sexism must be understood in terms of a number of dimensions. Therefore, an evaluation of the scope of the problems of racism and sexism may be a starting point in pursuing an understanding of these concepts and the extent to which each affects American social behavior.

SCOPE OF RACISM AND SEXISM

"Racism is as American as apple pie" was a favorite saying of H. Rap Brown, a civil rights activist of the late 1960s. Although racist attitudes and practices certainly exist in many societies, there appears to be a uniqueness in the present form and function of racism as practiced toward blacks in the United States in comparison with the racism practiced in some other countries. Indeed, several researchers have noted that the type of racism directed at blacks in the United States has resulted from a combination of economic, historic, political, religious, and social conditions that are peculiar to this society (Comer, 1980; Delaney, 1980). Blackwell (1985) suggested that the resulting U.S. brand of racism may be seen in the adaptations that the black community has made by forming an amalgamation of African and American cultures. The adaptations made by the black people, he suggested, emanated from the segregation and exclusion from mainstream social institutions that both forced and allowed the establishment of parallel black institutions. Black people, rejected by the white community, developed their own sets of community standards and goals. In addition to the lack of social status, the minority position of blacks in a society controlled by majority rights contributes to keeping black people on the fringes of power.

The dimensions of sexism seem to have little parallelism with those of racism. First of all, the sexism practiced in the United States is not considered uniquely American. In fact, the universality of sexist practices, assumptions, and policy have been proclaimed by feminist writers from diverse disciplines (Rogers, 1981). Although a few feminist anthropologists argue that, through the domestic sphere, women have the ability to wield great social power, most research has focused on demonstrating that all women are oppressed whether they realize it or not. With respect to social standing in public areas, it can be argued that women have long been on the fringes. They have been excluded and discriminated against in many segments of the labor force and in the political arena. However, although women, like blacks, have been grossly underrepresented in positions of power and authority, *women are not a minority group*, despite an attempt to claim that underdog status for them (e.g., Hacker, 1981).

Hacker and Weisstein (cited in Cox, 1981) have both used the term *minority group* to demonstrate the similarity of the status of women and blacks in the United States. They have identified similarities in the stereotyped behaviors ascribed to each, in the rationalizations of status for each, and in discrimination against and the adaptive behaviors of each. However, by minimizing the issue of numbers, Hacker and Weisstein have failed to recognize the differences in the scope of each problem and the prognosis for improvement. The problem of racism toward blacks as a uniquely American issue, is very much related to the minority (meaning few in numbers) position of blacks. One reason is that the elimination of racism may be viewed as benefiting a group of "outsiders" (nonwhites), who constitute only a small proportion of the population. For the most part, white people do not believe that the elimination of racism will actually provide any personal gain for them (Pence, 1982). Contributing to the notion that racism impacts only negatively on the victims is the isolation that may often be found to exist between the racial groups. It is completely within the realm of possibility for a white person to live all of his or her life without ever engaging in a personal relationship with a black person. The fact that many white people are unacquainted with any black person makes racism almost a theoretical issue for them. It also contributes to the belief that the elimination of racism would help only blacks. On the other hand, sexism is, at the same time, both a personal issue and a universal problem. Even a white man (the traditional embodiment of sexual oppression) may become concerned about discrimination directed at his mother, his wife, his daughter, or a female friend. The socialization of men and women is intertwined intimately at a level that different ethnic groups will probably never attain. Although whites and blacks may be socialized without being aware of each other, this is not likely for girls and boys.

The issue of numbers also makes it clear that, even at their most effective, the most blacks may hope to achieve is some level of proportional representation. It is, at least theoretically, possible for white women to become the dominant force in the society. The possibilities may be illustrated by the dramatic gains of women in a variety of areas since only the mid-1970s. For example, the percentage of women in managerial and admin-istrator positions increased from 17.6% in 1972 to 27.5% in 1982; women employed as lawyers and judges increased from 3.8% to 14.1% during the same period; those in personnel and labor relations, from 31% to 49.95% (Blackwell, 1985, pp. 39–40). It should be noted that these data do not distinguish between the gains of white women and black women. Although black men and women have also made gains since the mid-1970s, it often appears that the ceiling may have been reached and that some advantages are slipping away. Support for the claims that blacks are in a worse economic position now than they were in the mid-1970s is found in the *Current Population Reports* (cited in Blackwell, 1985, p. 55). The downward shifting of economic conditions for blacks, who are historically bound to the lower classes, has also been found to have had a deleterious effect on their educational advances. Poverty levels among women are also more common. Examining the data on the feminization of poverty, it should be noted that blacks and other minority women contribute disproportionately to this problem. As we will discuss in the second section of this chapter, black women experience double discrimination.

METHODOLOGICAL ISSUES

Researchers frequently suggest that the solution to many social problems lies in a better understanding of the issues involved. To facilitate understanding, then, they propose to do more research, ignoring the fact that the research methods themselves may interfere with progress toward the goal of understanding. The assumption is that the more research available, the clearer the problem and its solution will become. However, analyses of research on racism and sexism indicate that, in many instances, methodological bias may obfuscate rather than clarify the issues under investigation. In fact, it may be demonstrated that bias in research not only exacerbates some aspects of the racism and sexism problems but actually represents a subtle manifestation of the researchers' biases. Examination of some of the assumptions, biases, foci, and goals of research on women has identified some of the areas that are a problem. Many of these areas seem similarly relevant to studies of blacks (and to studies of other ethnic minority groups).

In her review of feminist criticism of methodology, Grady (1981) demonstrated that bias exists at every stage of the research process. She found that the traditional (i.e., white male as norm) perspective dominates the selection of topics for research, the subject selection, the operationalization of variables, the conceptualization preceding tests of sex differences, and the interpretation of the results. Additionally, it appeared that there was a male bias in the determination of whether an investigation would be published. The bias evidenced in the research on women may also be seen in research on ethnic minorities. In the selection of topics, scientists have obviously been influenced by gender-role stereotypes. Some research questions frequently studied in women have not, until recently, been investigated among men, for example, the relationship of moods to hormonal cycles and the effect of parental age on offspring. Williams (1980) assessed the work of white researchers in the black community with respect to topic selection. He concluded that, in many studies, researchers "looked for and found pathology," while ignoring strengths and adaptive capacities. According to Williams, the majority of problems researched in black communities are system-induced (e.g., health, education, and penal), yet, the researchers continue to investigate the black victims as the root of the problems. In research, women, too, have been cast as problems, not victims. Hare-Mustin (1983) examined sex bias in psychotherapy and concluded that psychological problems of women reflect societal conditions and attitudes. She noted, however, that the solutions offered deal with the individual and actually combine with other sexist forces affecting women's lives. Unger (1979) also noted that psychological research is designed to focus on internal causes as the source of problems. In studies on both women and black men, the issues are typically "how these people are different" (from white men) and "how that difference can be minimized."

Feminists have also claimed bias in research studies on the grounds that there is often no conceptual justification for the many instances of all-male samples. It has been shown that, even in comparative behavioral investigations, animal samples are typically limited to males (Hyde & Rosenberg, 1976). On the other hand, until recently, the selection of female-only samples has been rare (Hyde, 1985). Research on females was considered valid only if a comparison male group existed.

The problem of sample selection in race research has two aspects. First, as in research on women, there is a tendency to accept only studies that compare blacks with whites. Korchin (1980) revealed his experience of a rejection comment from a journal reviewer who assessed his research as "fatally flawed" because there was no comparison of his black sample with a white group. His anecdote is not at all unique. The value of studying diverse groups as an end in itself has not yet been fully appreciated. Additionally, in race research, there appears to be an assumption that greater homogeneity exists among blacks (and other ethnic minorities) than among whites. For this reason, very little attention has been paid to socioeconomic differences, to cultural background differences, or even to sex and age differences (Jackson, 1980). In fact, Gary (1980) noted that there is a tendency for white researchers "to focus on the lowest income groups of black subjects, and to concentrate on captive subjects (prisoners, mental patients, school children)" (pp. 448–449).

The selection of subjects, then, clearly shapes the outcome of findings and represents scientists' implicit assumptions. There are obvious parallels for racism and sexism in how scientists approach investigations in each area because blacks and white women continue to be seen as deviants or as deficient in comparison to a white male norm. Sue (1983) stressed the importance of bicultural research that would "emphasize understanding of ethnic minority groups in their own terms" (p. 588). Sue believes that psychologists err in allowing the "etic" approach (an acceptance of core similarities in all humans) to dominate their thinking and research. Although he recognized that the assumption of "universals" has some validity, he suggested that the recognition of cultural variance is also a valid and necessary objective.

Wallston (1981) observed that the socialization of researchers is another important part of the bias problem. She argued that professors have "the tendency to train people in our own image" (p. 607). As most professors are white men, traditional training often amounts to educating people to evaluate problems using the standards and norms of white men. Sue (1983) pointed out that, although the past notion of Anglo-Saxon cultural superiority is not accepted by most, training, testing, and other practices in education proceed as if it were. Many professional women and black men will admit that it is difficult for them to analyze their black and/or female experiences without the traditional perspectives they have adopted from their professors. They cannot easily develop theoretical frameworks that do not use terms and assumptions previously defined by white men. It may be even more difficult, however, for experienced white male researchers to accept new concepts, refutations of theoretical principles, or reinterpretations of long-standing data. Parlee (1981) believes that new theoretical perspectives will need powerful proponents. She suggested that women will have to become reviewers and editors if they wish to "determine what research is 'methodologically sound' enough and 'interesting' enough to publish" (p. 641). The same suggestion has been made with respect to black scientists. In the field of psychology, however, whereas white women have made some strides toward increasing their numbers among publishing decision-makers, the success of blacks in gaining access to the publication network has been relatively slight.

The analysis and interpretation of research data from a biased perspective has been demonstrated in studies of race differences as well as of sex differences. The most insidious aspect of this problem is that the bias may not be apparent, even to careful observers, because the researchers appear to follow sound methodological practice. For example, Jones (1983) was able to reveal the bias in published research comparing black and white children only by a complete reanalysis of the data. In his analysis, contrary to the published findings, black children were not more aggressive than white children. The actual difference was in his assumption that same-race, not cross-race, interactions should be used as the basis for the statistical comparisons. An example of research interpretation suggesting deviance in the black community is the labeling of black female assertiveness as "black matriarchy" and dominance. Similarly, interpretation bias has been found in the analysis of female behavior when expectations of inferiority are built into the variable labels. Unger (1979) cited the example of the terminology used in perception research, that is, "field-dependent versus field-independent." She pointed out that the value-laden term *dependent*, given to behavior that is more often female, promotes the conclusion that one perceptual type is better than the other. She suggested that an alternative term—for example, *field-sensitive*—would have very different connotations. Another example of sex bias has been noted in researchers' interpretation of parental behavior. When a child does not have the benefit of regular paternal influence, the circumstance is termed *father absence*; if it is the mother's influence that is missing, the term is *maternal deprivation*. The implication is that maternal deprivation is a worse condition, and the unproven assumption is that mothers are more necessary to a child's well-being. A more extensive analysis of methodological concerns from a feminist perspective is provided by Wallston and Grady (1985).

CURRENT PERCEPTIONS OF RACISM AND SEXISM

White racism has been a topic of continuing concern to blacks in recent years. The concern is due to the reemergence of white hostility in subtle, as well as blatant, ways after an apparent decline during the heyday of the civil rights movement. The reappearance of overt racist behavior has been attributed to the belief on the part of many whites, and even some blacks, that racism is no longer an issue to which our society need attend. The fact that blacks have entered many areas of public and private employment, that political awareness among blacks has increased, and that admission to educational institutions and to public accommodations seems assured by law appears to many as *prima facie* evidence that racial discrimination is a thing of the past. There is actually little research support for the claim that racism has disappeared (Sue, 1983).

Articles about the "new racism" have appeared with some regularity over the past few years in periodicals and newspapers, such as the *Washington Post* and *The New Republic*. Despite many counterclaims that racism in the United States is now different, there is a growing recognition that behaviors that were unacceptable and defined as *racist* a decade ago are now increasingly apparent. Barker (1981) explained that past emphasis on explanations of racism in terms of inferiority and superiority simply concealed some of the other reasons for racial prejudice. He hypothesized a link between race and national unity, suggesting that racism exists because certain groups are perceived as "outsiders." McConahay and Hough (1976) theorized that racism is now more complex than in the past. They suggested that symbolic issues associated with blacks (e.g., busing and welfare) offer the opportunity for hostile expression while direct antiblack sentiments are suppressed. This *symbolic racism* has been defined as the feeling by whites that blacks are making illegitimate demands for changes (Sears & McConahay, 1973). Although the concept of out-groups and the use of symbolic codes are not really new, the fact that research still attempts to define *racism* indicates that important questions still have not been satisfactorily resolved.

Concurrent with the surges and declines of attentiveness to racism have been changes in the amount of significance attached to instances of sexism in our society. Today, sexual harassment, violence toward women, pornography, and rape are among the topics subjected to public scrutiny. A number of programs have been instituted to encourage equity in the education of women in nontraditional areas. Women are slowly gaining acceptance in formerly all-male occupations. Attention to training male personnel in the avoidance of overt discrimination is an important component in the management of many large companies. Widely adopted editorial policies exist that recommend non-sexist language in books and articles. Yet, only a few decades ago, sexism was little more than a joke. An example of the disregard of sexist attitudes 50 years ago is found in a 1945 research study on prejudice (Dyer, cited in Allport, 1979). In the experiment, the researcher disregarded boys' negative statements about girls while recording expressions of prejudice against other groups. Not only were the hostile comments about girls rejected as examples of prejudice, they were, in fact, believed to be normal responses of adolescent boys. Researchers today are consistently reminded to guard against obviously sexist hypotheses and to investigate their previously conceived assumptions regarding sex-role behavior. In fact, concern about sex roles appears to have overtaken attention to race relations, as indicated easily by the number of articles, books, journals, and magazines devoted to each subject.

In examining the parallels between racism and sexism, one must wonder whether one set of data may be sufficient to explain most dimensions of discrimination. Although many commonalities exist, the number of differences suggests that problem solving in one area may not be facilitated by the practice of too quickly generalizing to the other. On the surface, it appears that types of discriminatory behavior, psychological effects, and even social responses to discrimination are similar for blacks and white women. However, the tendency of social scientists to discuss racism and sexism on an abstract level limits the applicability of research to real-world conditions. In fact, although scientists appear to consider racism and sexism discrete problems, under several conditions the processes may be interacting. What impact might result from this interaction? What conflicts occur for the victims? To investigate some of the issues, we must go beyond abstractions and consider some specifics. Black women provide an example of those who are influenced by both racism and sexism. Although there are other ethnic-minority women who are also influenced by both processes, there is more research available on black women than on other minority-group women.

RACE AND SEX CONFLICTS: THE CASE OF BLACK WOMEN

The possibility that race and sex prejudice may have interactive, or even additive, results has seldom been considered by social scientists. Psychological research and theory have typically ignored the possibility that gender differences may mediate reactions to racial characteristics. Similarly, studies of discrimination based on sex often fail to recognize the existence of race as a factor. In this section of the chapter, therefore, consideration is given to the problems of dual identity for ethnic minority women, that is, an examination is made of their identification as members of an ethnic minority group and as women. Specifically, the case of black women is considered because of their greater numbers among ethnic minorities and because of the long history of discrimination against blacks in the United States. This section also explores the conflicts that black women experience as the result of their dual allegiance to the civil rights movement and the women's movement. Race and gender stereotypes, as well as the available research data, are examined for their impact on present behavior and attitudes.

GENDER DIFFERENCES IN THE TREATMENT OF BLACKS

Historically, the sexual attractiveness of black women was vigorously denied by white women and even by white men, despite evidence of many sexual liaisons between black female slaves and their white male masters. The denials and distortions of the relationship of white men and black women during slavery have helped to erase the image of black women as victims; instead, a stereotype of black women as licentious and promiscuous has developed. Hooks (1981) suggested that white men were able to act out their misogynistic attitudes through their treatment of black women. She cited documentary evidence that colonial white men terrorized black women through rape and sexual torture. White women, Hooks hypothesized, either were convinced that black women deserved such treatment or accepted them as scapegoats. Other researchers (Ashmore & Del Boca, 1976; Simpson & Yinger, 1953) have used the defense mechanism concepts, repression and guilt, and projection theory to make a similar point about the sexual exploitation of black women during slavery. These researchers have described a theory of antiblack prejudice in which whites projected their tabooed sexual drives onto blacks.

This apparent early recognition of sexual differences among blacks, however, was considered only when it served the purposes of the oppressors. The idea that black women or men were eligible for any privileges or power because of gender was certainly a notion treated as absurd and impractical. Both black women and black men were treated in the past as children with no rights to respect, power, or authority because of their adulthood. In social status and in discrimination, therefore, it has been assumed that black men and black women are social equals. Although many of the attitudes and prejudices of the past have been disgarded, this assumption of "equality under oppression" appears to remain. The volumes of books devoted to the study of racism attest to this assumption by their failure to discuss the relationship of gender or sexual status to the facets and forms of racial discrimination that existed in the past or have developed over the years (e.g., Barker, 1981; Dorn, 1979; Katz, 1978; Willie, 1983). In fact, the consequences of racism have not been gender-blind. The reality of the masculinity or femininity of black persons has often been integrally related to the reactions of white men and white women. Furthermore, the domains of maleness and femaleness have also been defined as important by black men and women for themselves as they have struggled to be accepted into the mainstream of American society. There has even developed an idealization of the mainstream model of gender roles in the black community, even when the likelihood of maintaining the ideal was considered low (Hannerz, 1969).

SEXISM: CONFLICT WITH BLACK MEN

White behavioral and social scientists note with much interest the efforts of past and present-day European immigrants to become acculturated and accepted into the American mainstream. Similar efforts by black families have, on the other hand, often been derided and misinterpreted. One aspect of black family life that has received this treatment in research and popular media is black family relationships. The well-accepted myth is that the black woman is the head of a matriarchal structure. The stereotype of the controlling black woman has gained such strength, despite refuting empirical evidence and denials by black researchers (Jackson, 1973; Willie, 1983), that the actual relationship between black women and black men has not been fully recognized. For this reason, it has been a surprise to some that the patriarchal philosophy is alive and strong in the black community and that some black men have fully adopted a sexist perspective.

It is increasingly obvious that many black men strongly desire the recognition and control that they believe is due to all *men*. In fact, some black men, in the effort to enhance male power, suggest that black women should restrict their thrust for opportunities and self-determination. Hare (1978), for example, in discussing the inequities of full-time earnings based on race and sex, complained that black women's gains have severely limited "the black male's ability to prevail and compete in a perpetually patriarchal society" (p. 4). His unquestioning acceptance of men's rights and power is also evident in his statement that "the black man will be able to *bring the woman along* in our common struggle, so we will not need a black women's liberation movement" (Hare, 1971, p. 34; italics added). Hare has not been alone in his desire for black women to stand aside while black men take leadership positions or in his predictions of disaffection between black men and black women if they do not. Staples (1981), in fact, blamed the economic independence of black women, past and present, for dissolved marriages and suggested that educational and economic success "detracts" from a woman's desirability as a mate.

There are also black men who, rather than proclaim their sexism, appear to ignore the importance of gender differences in determining the black experience. Jenkins (1982) and Pugh (1972), for example, both discussed the black experience from a psychological perspective and yet almost completely excluded any mention of issues related to sex. The denial of the gender factor by black men, in effect, suggests the strategy advocated by Staples (1981), that is, attack racism first and, afterward, consider what to do about the problem of sexism. This approach, however, requires women to relinquish their needs as women and to postpone their liberation.

Black women have recognized for many years that "sexism could serve black men as well as it has whites if they too could manage to get ahead at the expense of their women" (Torrey, 1979; p. 47). Even during the abolitionist era, Sojourner Truth, a black suffragist, warned "if colored men get their rights, and not colored women theirs, you see the colored men will be masters over the women, and it will be just as bad as before" (cited in Hood, 1978; p. 48). Although some black men believe that the civil rights movement's main goal has been to establish a black male power structure, many others agree with black women who view the freedom of black men as inextricably tied to that of black women (e.g., Casenave, 1981). Research has shown that these beliefs are backed by actions—for example, egalitarian decision-making characterizes black husband–wife relationships (Mack, 1974)—and that black men participate in child care more often than white men (Daneal, 1975). Black men are not alone, however, in their divisions with respect to race and sex allegience. Black women have also made claims and counterclaims regarding the side that they should take. Often, an adversarial position is drawn that has black men on one side and white women on the other; black women are left to decide where they should stand.

Dual Identity: Conflict for Black Women

The double bind in which black women find themselves consists of the conflicting demands of racial identity and gender identity. For most black women, there is a clear solution to this dilemma: end racism *and* sexism. The consensus is strong. Black women who castigate white women for their role in the oppression of blacks (e.g., LaRue, 1970), together with those who view black men as "absorbing the dominant white male disease" (Lorde, 1979), recognize the need to respect all human potential. However, black women seriously question the notion that they have the power to effect such social changes, and they wonder who does and who will. Taking sides with white women is critically assessed by some. For example, LaRue (1970) asked, "if white women remained silent while white men kept the better positions and opportunities, can we really expect them to be more open-minded when placed in direct competition for jobs?" (p. 19). Additionally, few black women expect that white women will rectify the injustices of the society. In fact, black women who work in white organizations have often learned to be wary of whites who wish to act as interpreters of their experience (Gilkes, 1983). With respect to their positive or negative influence on black men, both Sojourner (1979) and ya Salaam (1979) contended that black women do not have the power to affect black men outside the sphere of home and family.

Although black women may view their power as limited, many are socialized to accept the responsibility of working toward the "betterment of their race." The women who seem to have a commitment to serving their community through active involvement cope with their frustrations, in part, by giving high value to their own experiences. One woman described the situation this way:

> If I could change anything in my life, I don't think I would. . . . You really do grow; you learn a lot from life; it makes you very strong; you have to be strong; you don't have much choice; you learn responsibility at a very early age, because you have to. (quoted in Gilkes, 1983, p. 135)

The goals toward which black women apply themselves are varied and often conflicting. Yet, the poignancy of the effort must be recognized in the articles, books, and speeches given day after day. Perhaps, the spirit of many is captured in the words of a black woman, a mother, a community organizer, and a women's rights activist: "In black women's liberation . . . we're fighting for the right to be different and not be punished for it. . . . I want the right to be black and me" (Wright, 1972, p. 608). However, frequently, black women are judged against standards constructed for white women.

Race Differences in the Treatment of Women

The race difference most often cited in demographic and research literature is the employment participation rate of black and of white women. Black women are the second highest in the percentage employed of any female labor group (Asian American women are highest). Black women contribute more income and share more family power with their spouses than do women in comparable white families (Richmond-Abbott, 1983).

Additionally, McAdoo (1980) found no differences in the types of jobs held by black middle-class mothers who were married and by those who were single parents. Obviously, however, the single-parent families were more vulnerable to economic stress because of differences in overall income (Walker & Wallston, 1985).

Along with the expectation of their economic contributions, black women are also called on by their families to fulfill traditional duties and to give emotional support (McAdoo, 1978). In response to the demands for energy, resources, and time, black women have developed a life-style of involvement in an extended kin network that appears to characterize them more than it does white women. Regardless of social class status, the majority of black women remain connected to relatives and "fictive kin" through their adult lives, participating in an exchange of child care and emotional and financial help (McAdoo, 1980). Although the network of relatives and friends is regarded as a valuable cultural pattern that supports black women, it is a double-edged sword. Those who get assistance must also give. Belle (1982) noted that, for women struggling in poverty, the assistance received does not always compensate for the additional stress placed on them by the responsibility to reciprocate the aid.

The importance of family and work notwithstanding, we must also consider, as part of the treatment of women, the public and private standards that society establishes to judge feminine value. All children, boys and girls, develop feelings of self-respect and self-esteem based in large part on society's reactions to them. Society sets standards not only for appropriate behavior but also for physical attractiveness. The standard set for the ideal American woman is unambiguously white. In fact, the black woman is the antithesis of the American standard. This point is repeated in the print, film, and television images of black women. In their rare appearances in children's books, black female characters were found to be presented in stereotypical female roles (e.g., mother or maid) and to be depicted as unattractive (Dickerson, 1980). Black female characters on television programs were high in dominance, high in nurturance, and low in achievement behavior; they were portrayed as significantly different from white women (Reid, 1979). Based on her analysis of media images, Rawles (1978) emphatically stated that "identifying with the image of white femininity is an exercise in self-hate for black women" (p. 245). Although white women also decry the stereotyping and the limited images of white women's roles, they are not, as black women are, subjected to the consistent and virtually unrelenting representation of themselves on television as castrating, immoral, and ugly.

RACISM: CONFLICT WITH WHITE WOMEN

The notion that black women hold values that differ from those of white women has been successfully dispelled by the results of a large-scale survey conducted in 1974 and 1979 under the sponsorship of Virginia Slims cigarettes. Heiss (1981) analyzed these survey data on motivation for marrying, acceptance of nontraditional family forms, and acceptance of reasons for divorce. Race commonalities were more evident than differences. Yet, although many values of black and white women are the same, the social and economic conditions under which they live their lives are, in the main, widely disparate. Bernard (1981) described the world of white women as "primarily a middle-class, if not a wholly egalitarian, world" (p. 254). This middle-class classification has also been given to the women's movement by others (Bardwick, 1979; Frieze, Parsons, Johnson, Ruble, & Zellman, 1978). The world of black women, however, is best typified as lower-class and poor, although it is the middle-class and professional black women who are more likely to have the education and opportunity to give voice to black concerns.

Despite differences in economic levels, black women are at least as likely as white women to advocate female liberation (Hemmons, 1980) and are even twice as likely to approve the women's movement goals (Harris poll, cited in Torrey, 1979). Therefore, a question often arises about the lack of the noticeable participation of black and other minority women in national and local women's organizations. Although black and white women share a common oppressor, white men, there are many differences in life experiences that suggest to some black women the need for separate paths (Hood, 1978). Among the differences between white women and black women are the conflicting allegiance to race versus sex that black women often experience, but that white women do not; the greater level of social acceptability that white women receive compared with black women; and finally, the fact that white women are necessary to the existence of white men, whereas black women are not necessary. Although the differences in lifestyles and expectations may explain, to some extent, the absence of black women from women's movement activities, the presence of racism is also part of the answer.

From the earliest days of the suffragist movement, there has been a recognition by white women that black women and black men were both their allies and their competitors in the struggle for political power. There were, of course, among the women's movement, staunch abolitionists. Hooks (1981) claimed, however, that there is "little historical evidence to document the assertion that white women as a collective group or white women's rights advocates are part of an anti-racist tradition. . . . They attacked slavery, not racism" (p. 125). The fact that some white women are clearly racist has not escaped the notice of black women who have attempted to align themselves with feminist organizations. Although Alice Walker (1982) declared it "inherently an impossibility" to be both truly feminist and racist, the late civil rights activist Fannie Lou Hamer described the conflict with white women this way: "The white woman felt like she was more than us . . . you know the white male, didn't go and brainwash the black man and the black woman, he brainwashed his wife too. He made her think that she was an angel" (quoted in Hood, 1978, p. 50).

Just as some black men have ignored the needs of black women as women and have rejected the notion that sexism is an important problem for them, white women have frequently ignored the unique needs of black women as blacks. This omission has been interpreted as rejection and racism. It is evident in many of the growing number of scholarly books in fields such as psychology, sociology, and history that *women* means white women, and that other women are treated as afterthoughts, if included at all. Just as white men have overlooked the attitudes, contributions, and perspectives of white women, black women have been similarly treated. For example in Strasser's history (1982) of American housework, only one paragraph was devoted to black women's plight; their importance was seen as being the new servant class, as Irish and other immigrant workers moved up in social status. Greenspan (1983) did not give any consideration to racial factors in her book on women's therapy; neither did Scarf (1980) in hers on depression, nor did Notman and Nadelson (1978) in theirs on health care. One explanation for these omissions is that the authors did not believe that any racial differences existed among white and ethnic minority women. This seems highly unlikely. A more plausible explanation is probably that consideration of ethnic differences remains unimportant to many white researchers, whether they are male or female. Gaertner's explication (1976) of liberal racist behavior includes the definition of the aversive racist as one who "tries to avoid contact with blacks." This concept supports the notion that the exclusion of ethnic concerns may be interpreted as racism, whether conscious or not.

Even when the concerns of black women are incorporated into the feminist discussion, the problem of racism is not often considered in much depth. A review of psychology-of-women textbooks showed that most offered token or no references to Afro-American women (Brown, Goodwin, Hall, & Jackson-Lowman, 1985). Admittedly, some white women are uncomfortable about dealing with this problem (Pence, 1982). One example of this discomfort is the discourse on black women and racism found in Bernard (1981). She began her exploration of racism toward blacks by focusing on the hatred it engendered among black women for whites and ended by claiming that black women hate white women for taking black men. No discussion of the detrimental effect of racism on black women was included. A brief reference to white women's racism during the suffragist era was explained by the fact that it "made more sense to have [Southern Congressmen] as allies than as enemies of the women's [sic] cause" (p. 340). Increasingly, however, the realization of the impact of racism as a daily event in the lives of black women has become evident, as many recent women's studies textbooks and courses have attempted to include ethnic minority issues and to present relevant research on these issues (e.g., Hyde, 1985; Richmond-Abbott, 1983).

CONFLICTS IN RESEARCH

The paradox of the black woman's situation is, to paraphrase de Beauvoir (cited in Bernard, 1981), "that they belong at one and the same time to the white world, to the male world and to the other spheres in which those worlds are challenged; shut up in their world, surrounded by the others, they can settle down nowhere in peace" (p. 20). Compounding the double conflict of racism and sexism for black women is the fact that few others understand the pressures endured. The extent of the divisions with black men because of sexism and with white women because of racism are infrequently assessed; the comparisons most often made treat sex and race as separate phenomena. Gurin and Pruitt (1978) pointed out the effect of assessing race and sex discrimination separately. For example, economic comparisons that examine the relative position of black men to white men and black women to white women result in the conclusion that black men experience greater discrimination, despite evidence indicating that black women have the lowest salaries of any race–sex group. The comparison that would indicate the results of black women's experiencing both sex and race discrimination is typically neglected. This was the case in a study of the relationship of racism and sexism in the job market (Szymanski, 1976). The indicator of sexual discrimination was the ratio of white female to white male median earnings. The indicator of racial discrimination was the ratio of black male to white male median earnings. Black females were alternately considered "Third World people" and "women," as the need of the study dictated.

Similarly distorted assessments have been made of comparisons that purport to demonstrate both race and sex effects for educational attainment (Gump & Rivers, 1975) and occupational aspirations (Gurin & Epps, 1975). One negative example was found in a recent book on the psychology of sex roles. Richmond-Abbott (1983) reviewed the research on early-school sex-role socialization and found agreement on the fact that teachers give less attention to girls, and that school materials are not relevant to blacks. However, she then concluded that black girls were considered less deviant in the class than black boys, and that the likelihood of some black female teachers meant that the school experience "probably doesn't hurt their [black girls'] self-image as much as it might hurt their female white classmates" (p. 136). This conclusion, drawn from research that did not compare the sex–race groups, is not unusual. In effect, it underscores the observation that there exists a dearth of research and documentation on the effects of discrimination specifically directed at the black girl or the black woman.

In assessments of research in the area of sexism and racism, it has become apparent that the analysis of these processes as independent functions is inadequate. Instead, racism and sexism should be examined in relationship to each other (Smith & Stewart, 1983). It has been suggested, therefore, that researchers adopt a model of research that incorporates a contextual and an interactive framework, that is, a model in which the experiences of black women are compared with those of the other three gender–race groups within specific social situations, rather than the continued use of sex and race as independent status characteristics.

The need for an understanding of the interactive process of racism and sexism has been demonstrated in only a few studies. For example, an investigation of high-school students' career development suggested that, for black female adolescents, the effects of racism and sexism are combined as well as independent (Chester, 1983). Adams's analysis (1983) of sex and race status characteristics on dominance behavior in college students indicated the need to consider context in social situations. Adams found that black women did not respond as predicted by their sex or race group. In fact, she concluded that the statuses associated with sex and race were not constant across situations and did not combine by any simple averaging process. Lykes (1983) concurred in the assessment of context as an important factor in determining behavior in situations of discrimination. An exploration of the effects of institutional oppression and individual prejudice on black women indicated that highly successful black women depend on contextual cues and use them to respond differently to the sexism and the racism that they encounter. Specifically, Lykes found that situational factors, such as the racial composition of the workplace, affected both the degree of directness and the flexibility of coping in black women.

The investigators who recommended the interactive and contextual approach presumed this methodological strategy capable of affecting the integration of the disparate views of black women that have emanated from society and the social sciences. The question that must also be considered, however, is whether an accurate description of black women's behavior will in any way resolve or ameliorate the conflicts of gender and race identity that will be encountered. Although investigations into the forms and purposes of discrimination could be developed further, at some point the focus of research should be shifted to illuminate the means by which discrimination and its effects can be minimized.

DIVERSITY VERSUS DIVISIONS

The Hunter College Women's Studies Collective (1983) admitted that "women are divided not only by race and class but also by age and sexual orientation" (p. 12). They argued, however, that any resistance to one type of discrimination is resistance to all. Although in theory this seems to be sound reasoning, the argument is unconvincing in light of the evidence that many workers committed to one cause exhibit much less concern about other inequities. Bardwick (1979) appeared to concur in this assessment. She stated that "divisiveness within the women's movement came about in the first place because of the diversity of women. . . . Divisiveness between women is increased when a commitment to women seems to require less commitment to men and to children" (p. 151). It would appear, therefore, almost unnatural to expect that black women (or white women) could or would totally divorce themselves from the policies and practices of their fathers, brothers, sons, and husbands.

Nevertheless, the increased effort by many feminist groups to integrate the concerns, problems, and positions of black and other ethnic-minority women with those of white women is a positive step toward eliminating some of the racial divisions and conflicts now existing. We can continue to seek our commonalities in addition to recognizing our differences. Yet, the difficulty in avoiding racist traps in interpreting data and making assumptions is greater than many realize. We have all been socialized into the same society, although with different perspectives on it. Both sexism and racism are ingrained in our society's expectations, and they operate together in ways we are trained to accept. The admission of this condition may allow us to examine more realistically the possibilities for positive social change.

SUMMARY AND CONCLUSIONS

A review of the social-psychological literature reveals many similarities between the processes of racism and sexism. The definitions of each indicate the operation of a basic belief system that describes the objects of the discrimination, either women or minorities, as inferior to white men. Multiple causes—interpersonal, intrapersonal, and societal— appear to be necessary to explain the development and manifestation of each process. Analyses of methodological strategies demonstrated that bias exists in research on race and sex discrimination based on assumptions, samples, procedures, and interpretations. The commonalities found between the two processes, however, are not sufficient cause to ignore the many differences. The differences, in fact, lead to the conclusion that racism and sexism must be studied and understood as they operate separately in society.

Among the differences between racism and sexism, the difference of scope appears to have the most far-reaching implications for social power. The manifestation of racism in the United States is described as resulting from some uniquely American situations, whereas sexism is viewed as more universal in form and practice. The significance of the numerical minority status of ethnic group members contrasts with the proportions of women in society. The notion is that women have, at least theoretically, the potential for equal status through numbers. In current perspectives on the progress of women versus ethnic minorities in the drive toward equity with white men, although the retreat from affirmative action goals is viewed as having affected both civil rights and women's movements, the concerns of race relations are believed to be overshadowed by interest in women's issues.

Although racism and sexism are distinct processes, these forms of discrimination may combine or interact for some women, specifically in the case of black women, whose dual identification impacts on their experiences. Conflicts for black women arising from their interactions with white women, white men, and black men present unique sets of issues and problems. Although the race and sex equity movements both claim that black women should join their ranks, each group has exhibited some extent of discrimination against them. The results indicate that black women have been most disadvantaged, economically and socially, when compared to the other race–sex groups.

Although some efforts have been made to incorporate the concerns of ethnic minority women into predominantly white women's organizations, the dilemmas that arise from their diversity are not expected to be resolved quickly or easily. Ultimately, the problem of discrimination has societal, as well as individual, solutions. Research is needed to address the concerns of race and sex bias by increasing the information base available on women of all backgrounds. Richardson (1982) underscored this point when she asked:

> What body of knowledge is one left with when any generalization or abstraction about women as a group is subject to what seems to be an unending series of qualifications. As opposed to the *reductio ad absurdum* argument . . . this sensitivity to the interacting forces of other social statuses and roles with that of gender demands new conceptual tools and a constant critical revision of what is known? (p. 48)

The use of diversity in research and theory development must be used, as Richardson suggested, not only to prevent divisiveness, but to promote social equity for various race and gender groups.

ACKNOWLEDGMENTS

In preparing this chapter, I have benefited greatly from the comments of Dr. Irvin D. Reid. Dr. Barbara S. Wallston also provided helpful assistance and comments.

REFERENCES

Adams, K. A. (1983). Aspects of social context as determinants of black women's resistance to challenges. *Journal of Social Issues, 39*(3), 69–78.

Allport, G. W. (1979). *The nature of prejudice. 25th Anniversary Edition.* Reading, MA: Addison-Wesley.

Ashmore, R. D., & Del Boca, F. K. (1976). Psychological approaches to understanding intergroup conflicts. In P. A. Katz (Ed.), *Towards the elimination of racism.* New York: Pergamon Press.

Bardwick, J. (1979). *In transition.* New York: Holt, Rinehart & Winston.

Barker, M. (1981). *The new racism.* Frederick, MD: Aletheia.

Belle, D. (1982). Social ties and social supports. In D. Belle (Ed.), *Lives in stress: Women and depression.* Beverly Hills, CA: Sage.

Bernard, J. (1981). *The female world.* New York: Free Press.

Biassey, E. L. (1972). Paranoia and racism in the United States. *Journal of National Medical Association, 64,* 353–358.

Blackwell, J. E. (1985). *The black community: diversity and unity* (2nd ed.). New York: Harper & Row.

Brown, A., Goodwin, B. J., Hall, B. A., & Jackson-Lowman, H. (1985). A review of psychology of women textbooks: Focus on the Afro-American woman. *Psychology of Women Quarterly, 9*(1), 29–38.

Casenave, N. (1981). Black men in America: The quest for manhood. In H. P. McAdoo (Ed.), *Black families.* Beverly Hills, CA: Sage.

Chesler, M. A. (1976). Contemporary sociological theories of racism. In P. A. Katz (Ed.), *Towards the elimination of racism.* New York: Pergamon Press.

Chester, N. L. (1983). Sex differentiation in two high school environments: Implications for career development among black adolescent females. *Journal of Social Issues, 39*(3), 29–40.

Comer, J. P. (1980). White racism: Its root, form, and function. In R. L. Jones (Ed.), *Black psychology* (2nd ed.). New York: Harper & Row.

Cox, S. (1981). *Female psychology: The emerging self* (2nd ed.). New York: St. Martin's Press.

Daneal, J. (1975). *A definition of fatherhood as expressed by black fathers.* Unpublished doctoral dissertation, University of Pittsburgh.

Delany, L. T. (1980). The other bodies in the river. In R. L. Jones (Ed.), *Black psychology,* (2nd ed.). New York: Harper & Row.

Dickerson, D. P. (1980). *The role of black females in selected children's fiction.* Unpublished manuscript, Howard University.

Dorn, E. (1979). *Rules and racial equality.* New Haven, CT: Yale University Press.

Frieze, I. H., Parsons, J. E., Johnson, P. B., Ruble, D. N., & Zellman, G. L. (1978). *Women and sex roles.* New York: Norton.

Gaertner, S. L. (1976). Nonreactive measures in racial attitude research: A focus on "liberal." In P. A. Katz (Ed.), *Towards the elimination of racism.* New York: Pergamon Press.

Gary, L. E. (1980). A mental health research agenda for the black community. In R. L. Jones (Ed.), *Black psychology* (2nd ed.). New York: Harper & Row.

Gilkes, C. T. (1983). Going up for the oppressed: the career mobility of black women community workers. *Journal of Social Issues, 39*(3), 115–139.

Grady, K. (1981). Sex bias in research design. *Psychology of Women Quarterly, 5*(4), 628–636.

Greenspan, M. (1983). *A new approach to women and therapy.* New York: McGraw-Hill.

Gump, J. P., & Rivers, L. W. (1975). A consideration of race in efforts to end sex bias. In E. E. Diamond (Ed.), *Issues of sex bias and sex fairness in career interest measurement.* Washington, DC: Department of Health, Education and Welfare, National Institute of Education.

Gurin, P., & Epps, E. (1975). *Black consciousness, identity, and achievement.* New York: Wiley.

Gurin, P., & Pruitt, A. (1978). Counseling implications of black women's market position, aspirations and expectancies. In *Conference on the Educational and occupational needs of black women* (Vol. 2). Washington, DC: National Institute of Education.

Hacker, H. M. (1981). Women as a minority group. In S. Cox (Ed.), *Female psychology: The emerging self* (2nd ed.). New York: St. Martin's Press.

Hannerz, U. (1969). *Soulside: Inquiries into ghetto culture and community.* New York: Columbia University Press.

Hare, N. (1971, June). Will the real black man please stand up? *The Black Scholar, 2,* 32–35.

Hare, N. (1978, April). Revolution without a revolution: the psychology of sex and race. *The Black Scholar, 9,* 2–7.

Hare-Mustin, R. T. (1983). An appraisal of the relationship between women and psychotherapy: 80 years after the case of Dora. *American Psychologist, 38,* 593–601.

Heiss, J. (1981). Women's values regarding marriage and the family. In H. P. McAdoo (Ed.), *Black families*. Beverly Hills, CA: Sage.

Hemmons, W. M. (1980). The women's liberation movement. In L. Rodgers-Rose. *The black woman*. Beverly Hills, CA: Sage.

Hood, E. F. (1978, April). Black women, white women: Separate paths to liberation. *The Black Scholar, 9* 45–56.

Hooks, B. (1981). *Ain't I a woman: Black women and feminism*. Boston: South End Press.

Hunter College Women's Studies Collective. (1983). *Women's realities, women's choices*. New York: Oxford University Press.

Hyde, J. S. (1985). *Half the human experience: the psychology of women* (3rd ed.). Lexington, MA: Heath.

Hyde, J. S., & Rosenberg, B. G. (1976). *Half the human experience: the psychology of women*. Lexington, MA: Heath.

Jackson, J. J. (1973). Black women in a racist society. In C. Willie, B. Kramer, & B. Brown (Eds.), *Racism and mental health*. Pittsburgh: University of Pittsburgh Press.

Jackson, J. J. (1980). *Minorities and aging*. Belmont, CA: Wadsworth.

Jenkins, A. H. (1982). *The psychology of the Afro-American*. New York: Pergamon Press.

Jones, J. M. (1983). The concept of race in social psychology: from color to culture. In L. Wheeler & P. Shaver (Eds.), *Review of personality and social psychology*. (Vol. 4). Beverly Hills, CA: Sage.

Kanter, R. M. (1977). Women in organizations: Sex roles, group dynamics, and change strategies. In A. Sargent (Ed.), *Beyond sex roles*. St. Paul: West.

Katz, J. H. (1978). *White awareness: Handbook for anti-racism training*. Norman: University of Oklahoma Press.

Katz, P. A. (1976). The acquisition of racial attitudes in children. In P. A. Katz (Ed.), *Towards the elimination of racism*. New York: Pergamon.

Katz, P. A. (1983). Developmental foundations of gender and racial attitudes. In R. Leahy (Ed.), *The child's construction of social inequality*. New York: Academic Press.

Korchin, S. J. (1980). Clinical psychology and minority problems. *American Psychologist, 35,* 262–269.

LaRue, L. (1970). The black movement and women's liberation. *Black Scholar, 1*(7), 36–42.

Lorde, A. (1979). Feminism and black liberation: the great American disease. *Black Scholar, 10*(8), 17–20.

Lykes, M. B. (1983). Discrimination and coping in the lives of black women: Analyses of oral history data. *Journal of Social Issues, 39*(3), 79–100.

Mack, D. (1974). The power relationship in black and white families. *Journal of Personality and Social Psychology, 30,* 409–413.

McAdoo, H. P. (1978, November). Factors related to stability in upwardly mobile black families. *Journal of Marriage and the Family*, pp. 761–776.

McAdoo, H. P. (1980). Black mothers and the extended family support network. In H. P. McAdoo (Ed.), *The black woman*. Beverly Hills, CA: Sage.

McConahay, J. B., & Hough, J. C. (1976). Symbolic racism. *Journal of Social Issues, 32*(2), 23–45.

Mezei, L. (1971). Perceived social pressure as an explanation of shifts in the relative influence of race and belief on prejudice across social interactions. *Journal of Personality and Social Psychology, 19,* 69–81.

Notman, M. T., & Nadelson, C. C. (1978). *The woman patient*. New York: Plenum Press.

Parlee, M. B. (1981). Appropriate control groups in feminist research. *Psychology of Women Quarterly, 5*(4), 637–644.

Pence, E. (1982). Racism—A white issue. In G. T. Hull, P. B. Scott, & B. Smith (Eds.), *All the women are white, all the blacks are men, but some of us are brave*. Westbury, NY: Feminist Press.

Pugh, R. W. (1972). *Psychology and the black experience*. Monterey, CA: Brooks/Cole.

Rawles, B. (1978). The media and their effect on black images. In Lipman-Blumen (Ed.), *Conference on the educational and occupational needs of black women* (Vol. 2). National Institute of Education.

Reid, P. T. (1979). Racial stereotyping on television: A comparison of the behavior of both black and white television characters. *Journal of Applied Psychology, 64,* 465–471.

Richardson, M. S. (1982). Sources of tension in teaching the psychology of women. *Psychology of Women Quarterly, 7*(1), 45–54.

Richmond-Abbott, M. (1983). *Masculine and feminine: Sex roles over the life cycle*. Reading, MA: Addison-Wesley.

Rogers, S. C. (1981). Woman's place: a critical review of anthropological theory. In S. Cox (Ed.), *Female psychology: The emerging self* (2nd ed.). New York: St. Martin's Press.

Scarf, M. (1980). *Unfinished business: Pressure points in the lives of women*. New York: Ballantine.

Sears, D. O., & McConahay, J. B. (1973). *The politics of violence: The new urban blacks and the Watts riot*. Boston: Houghton Mifflin.

Shaffer, D. R. (1985). *Developmental psychology: Theory, research and applications.* Belmont, CA: Brooks/Cole.
Simpson, G. E., & Yinger, J. M. (1953). *Racial and cultural minorities: An analysis of prejudice and discrimination.* New York: Harper & Row.
Smith, A., & Stewart, A. (1983). Approaches to studying racism and sexism in black women's lives. *Journal of Social Issues, 39*(3), 1–15.
Sojourner, S. (1979). The perpetuation of myths. *Black Scholar, 10*(8), 31–32.
Staples, R. (1981). Race and marital status: An overview. In H. P. McAdoo (Ed.), *Black families.* Beverly Hills, CA: Sage.
Strasser, S. (1982). *Never done: The history of American housework.* New York: Pantheon Books.
Sue, S. (1983). Ethnic minority issues in psychology: A reexamination. *American Psychologist, 38*(5), 583–592.
Szymanski, A. (1976). Racism and sexism as functional substitutes in the labor market. *The Sociological Quarterly, 17*, 65–73.
Torrey, J. W. (1979). Racism and feminism: Is women's liberation for whites only? *Psychology of Women Quarterly, 4*(2), 281–293.
Unger, R. K. (1979). *Female and male.* New York: Harper & Row.
Walker, A. (1982). One child of one's own. In G. T. Hull, P. B. Scott, & B. Smith (Eds.), *All the women are white, all the men are black, but some of us are brave.* Westbury, NY: Feminist Press.
Walker, L. S., & Wallston, B. S. (1985). Social adaptation: A review of dual earner family literature. In L. LaAbate (Ed.), *Handbook of family psychology.* Homewood, IL: Dow Jones Ervin.
Wallston, B. S. (1981). What are the questions in psychology of women? A feminist approach to research. *Psychology of Women Quarterly, 5*(4), 597–617.
Wallston, B. S., & Grady, K. E. (1985). Feminist methodology and the crisis in social psychology. In V. E. O'Leary & R. K. Unger (Eds.), *Women, gender and social psychology.* Hillsdale, NJ: Erlbaum.
Williams, R. L. (1980). The death of white research in the black community. In R. L. Jones (Ed.), *Black psychology* (2nd ed.). New York: Harper & Row.
Willie, C. V. (1983). *Race, ethnicity, and socioeconomic status.* Bayside, NY: General Hall.
Wright, M. (1972). I want the right to be black and me. In G. Lerner (Ed.), *Black women in white America.* New York: Pantheon Books.
ya Salaam, K. (1979). Women's rights are human rights! *Black Scholar, 10*(6), 9–16.

III

SOCIAL POLICY

A. Desegregation

11

School Desegregation
The Social Science Role

Harold B. Gerard

My main credential for writing this article is that I spent some of the best years of my life studying what happened to children from the year before to five years after desegregation (Gerard & Miller, 1975). We have the dubious distinction of having collected more desegregation data than anyone since Coleman (Coleman, Campbell, Hobson, McPartland, Mood, Weinfield, & York, 1966). Coleman studied 600,000 children in all 50 states, whereas we studied 1,800 children in a single school district over a period of 6 years, collecting detailed data on each child from a number of perspectives. We had hoped that our data would still the critics by demonstrating that minority achievement, achievement-related attitudes, and self-esteem would improve from pre- to postdesegregation, as would school performance, with no adverse effects on white pupils. We had also hoped that interethnic attitudes would improve. This was the heart of the expectations in the historic 1954 *Brown v. Board of Education* U.S. Supreme Court Decision (see Stephan, 1978), and I fully expected to find confirming evidence.

In this chapter, I hope to point out what can charitably be called slippage in the psychology underlying the *Brown* decision, especially as regards the Social Science Statement submitted to the Court by social psychologists Isidor Chein, Kenneth Clark, and Stuart Cook. This statement, which was submitted to the court in support of the plaintiffs, was vague about how desegregation would correct the harms of segregation. All that it said, in effect, was that, because the minority child was now in a classroom with whites, he or she would no longer have the status of an outcast or a pariah. This knowledge would somehow impart to the child the self-image necessary to do well in school and later to enter the mainstream of American society. The "lateral-transmission-of-values hypothesis," which was implicit in the Coleman Report, and in the minds of other workers in the early 1960s, was somewhat more sophisticated than the pariah hypothesis. In discussing the hypothesis, I will attempt to show how our data bear on its various assumptions. I would like to close the article with some general observations about the relationship between social science research and social policy and also to show how social scientists should avoid getting black eyes.

This article is based on an address presented at the meeting of the Western Psychological Association, Los Angeles, April, 1981.

HAROLD B. GERARD • Department of Psychology, University of California, Los Angeles, California 90024.

THE SOCIAL SCIENCE STATEMENT

In an issue of the *Personality and Social Psychology Bulletin* (PSPB), Stuart Cook (1979) underscored a judgment he had made earlier (Wiegel, Wiser, & Cook, 1975) that those of us who have deigned to study the consequences of school desegregation have been misguided, unhelpful, and merely reactive. We have chosen to waste our time revealing disappointing result after disappointing result in our evaluation studies rather than applying what we know to make desegregation work. The big questions of course are: What do we really know and how can we apply what we may know to the desegregated classroom?

I can understand Cook's frustration over the general lack of positive effects, especially as he was one of three framers of the Social Science Statement. In his article, Cook (1979) answered the question: Did we mislead the Court? His answer was No—principally, he went on to say, because the conditions for real integration, which were outlined in the statement, are rarely met in the typical mixed classroom, although the framers argued that these conditions "can generally be satisfied in the public schools." Thirty-two prominent social scientists signed the statement. If I had been asked to do so, I probably would have signed it, too.

In retrospect, however, it was extraordinarily quixotic to assume that the following conditions, as specified in the statement, would or could be met in the typical school system: (a) firm and consistent endorsement by those in authority; (b) the absence of competition among the representatives of the different racial groups; (c) the equivalence of positions and functions among all participants in the desegregated setting; and (d) interracial contacts of the type that permit learning about one another as individuals. What could the framers have been thinking about while believing that the conjunction of these four conditions could be met in the typical American school? As a former teacher in a New York City junior high school that was predominantly black but was supposedly integrated, I can personally attest to the extraordinary difficulty of meeting any one of the four conditions, much less all four. My teaching stint occurred not long before *Brown*.

By 1954, two of the framers, Clark and Cook, had devoted most of their careers to the study of prejudice. Cook had been the director of the Commission on Community Interrelationships of the American Jewish Congress, which later became the Research Center for Human Relations at New York University. The commission had as its primary focus the understanding and amelioration of anti-Semitism and antiblack prejudice. Cook, more than any other psychologist, has devoted his entire career to the understanding and reduction of prejudice, a goal he still pursues quite vigorously. Kenneth Clark and his wife, Mamie, pioneered some of the early, better-controlled research on prejudice, and he has continued to be an active worker in the field. The resounding conclusion from Cook's and Clark's own research and the many other studies that had appeared by 1954 is that prejudice is extraordinarily refractory to any attempts to change it. It is a virulent cancer that infects our entire culture from the lowest to the highest rung of the socioeconomic ladder. It is deeply embedded in the fabric of the American character. How, then, can we easily meet these four conditions outlined in the statement?

The first condition, firm and consistent endorsement by those in authority, requires commitment to a posture that, for most white Americans, is antithetical to their acknowledged or unacknowledged prejudice. By *those in authority*, I assume the framers meant the entire chain of command from the classroom teacher, school principal, and superintendent to the school board and town council. That chain is literally as strong as its weakest link. Recalcitrance or equivocation at any level will spell doom for the levels below. The effects of a strife-torn school board that is unwilling or unable to give its full support to desegregation will permeate the entire system. As soon as the community at large senses recalcitrance by the board in the face of a court order, antidesegregation forces within the community will be mobilized. A crack in a community's resolve provides the room necessary for prejudice to widen it into a chasm.

I would add here that the logistics of communitywide, two-way mandatory busing, especially in sprawling urban areas, is an additional source of community resistance. Much of the so-called white flight that occurred in the 2 years following the implementation of court-ordered mandatory busing was attributable to the unwillingness of white parents to have their children bused across town. There has been some evidence of possible "black flight" in Boston as well, presumably for the same reason (Armor, 1980). Los Angeles experienced a 62% white pupil loss in the junior-high-school grades that were involved in the busing program. On the other hand, in San Diego, where Judge Welsh approved a voluntary busing program, white flight attributable to busing has been negligible in spite of rather substantial participation in the plan by minority pupils. It thus appears that, in spite of their prejudice, most white parents are willing to accept desegregation achieved through one-way busing as long as their own children can continue to go to their neighborhood school. As in the nation at large, the vast majority of whites are staunchly opposed to two-way busing. There are limits, therefore, on how willing they are to accept the law of the land as interpreted by the courts.

The authority support condition, as stipulated in the Social Science Statement, did not anticipate the situation as represented by the demography and geography in our large northern urban centers; it was rather myopically focused on small dual school systems in the South that were maintained by *de jure* segregation. In Cook's own words (1979), "The fact that busing would pit the values associated with neighborhood schools against those of racial integration—with two presidents, the Congress, and a majority of citizens endorsing the former—could not at that time have been anticipated" (p. 430).

Perhaps we should forgive them for their short-sightedness in this respect. The only problem is that the legal doctrine that has been built on *Brown* is now cast in concrete, and its application to large urban *de facto* segregated districts is resulting in the resegregation of many of those districts as a result of white flight. I am still willing to give the framers and signers the benefit of the doubt in not having anticipated the logistics of northern urban busing, but I do have trouble understanding their lack of acknowledgment of strong widespread community opposition to two-way busing. When it comes to schools, which are typically supported out of local property taxes, community support is often the effective, if not the ultimate, authority, the law of the land notwithstanding.

The second condition is that there be an absence of competition among the representatives of the different racial groups. Were the framers here suggesting that it would be relatively easy to change the structure and norms of the typical American classroom? Aggressive competitiveness runs deep in our culture, pervading every corner of society, including, most certainly, the classroom (Pepitone, 1972; Schofield & Sagar, 1977; Suls & Sanders, 1979; Veroff, 1978). By the time a child starts school, he or she has been imbued with the competitive spirit that fits right in with the teaching methods and grading system found in the typical school. The teacher has been trained to mete out rewards to the successful competitor. Our child-rearing methods prime the child for school and later life.

Is the teacher as change agent equipped to foster cooperation among his or her pupils? Hechinger and Hechinger (1974) presented evidence that competitiveness tends to occur even in classrooms where competition is actively discouraged. In light of this fact, what hope does the teacher have of prevailing against the countervailing norm? Furthermore, is the teacher able to deal with the effects of subcultural diversity represented in the typical mixed classroom? We know, both from life and the laboratory, that strong in-group versus out-group feelings tend to develop in such a context (Gerard &

Hoyt, 1974; Tajfel, 1979). These feelings are probably part of the roots of prejudice itself. What in the background and training of the average teacher would enable him or her to cope with these naturally occurring intergroup schisms? Given the competitive bent of most pupils and a general tendency for the teacher to endorse and foster such competition, the potentially hostile intergroup feelings between subgroups of pupils from different backgrounds, and his or her own prejudice, the teacher is necessarily confronted with a herculean task in trying to significantly change the situation.

There is also the important consideration of the probable cultural gap between the teacher, the vast majority of whom are white and middle-class, and the lower socioeconomic-status minority child. Kay Bikson, who worked with us, collected data indicating that teachers—and this goes for both white and minority group teachers—tend to underrate the intelligence and ability of a minority child who displays ghetto speech mannerisms. In the study, the teachers heard short speech excerpts of children whom they did not know and rated each child on a number of semantic-differential-type scales. The data show that the typical teacher is likely to prejudge a child on the basis of speech mannerisms (and probably on other kinds of earmarks as well) by downgrading the minority child relative to his or her performance on objective measures.

I assume that the next condition, that there be an equivalence of positions and functions among all participants in the desegregated setting, refers principally to the children themselves and not to teachers and administrators. To believe that this requirement, which embodies one of Gordon Allport's conditions (1954) for the reduction of intergroup prejudice, could easily be met in the typical mixed classroom ignores what life is really like in such a classroom. Our own longitudinal data and cross-sectional data from the Coleman Report show a widening achievement gap between white and minority children as they move through the grades. By the sixth grade, the gap is more than two grade-equivalents wide. Given that the minority children are already one-down by virtue of their minority status, the fact that their academic performance is, on the average, far below that of their white peers places them in double status jeopardy, both in relation to their white peers and in the eyes of the typical teacher. So how can we hope to meet the condition of equal status in the traditional classroom when, desegregation or not, the average classroom has not changed all that much since we were in school?

Our data show that teachers tend to normalize their grades no matter what the absolute level of achievement is in their classroom. By that I mean they will distribute the same proportion of A's, or whatever the grade for excellent work is called, B's, C's, and so forth, irrespective of their pupils' average absolute performance. It is as though their adaptation level shifts to meet the average level of performance in their class. Thus, a class of very bright pupils will tend to be undergraded relative to their actual achievement level, and a class of slow pupils will tend to be overgraded.

What we find in our own data is that, in the year just prior to the start of the desegregation program, whites were being undergraded if their normalized grades are compared with their normalized scores on state-mandated achievement tests, whereas both black and Mexican-American children were overgraded. One year after desegregation, there was still a tendency for teachers to undergrade whites and to overgrade minority pupils, which is evidence of a double standard, but over time, we have seen a progressive diminution of the difference in scores. By the end of the third year after segregation, the teachers' grading practices appeared to be completely normalized, as indicated by the negligible discrepancies between grades and achievement for all three groups.

All would be well if academic performance as well as the grade-achievement discrepancy had converged in the years following desegregation, but it did not. The relative achievement standing of minority pupils progressively worsened as they moved through the grades. The effect of gradual grade normalization had the effect of lowering minority grades and increasing white grades, the latter increasing because the poorer performance of the minority pupils provided the teacher with a lower performance anchor. This state of affairs could only have had an adverse effect on the minority pupil's status in the classroom and on his or her self-esteem. Also, because grades, as used in the traditional classroom, signal success or failure, they may spur or reduce motivation. Whites would tend to be encouraged and minority pupils discouraged, and in turn, their performance might be affected and the achievement gap, therefore, exacerbated. Such a situation contains all the necessary ingredients for creating Myrdal's vicious circle (1944) right in the classroom. In fact, we have some suggestive evidence that, as compared with pre-desegregation achievement, white performance increased somewhat and black performance decreased somewhat in the years following desegregation. The only clearly salutary effects we found were for the white children who were initially very poor performers. They showed an increase in both self-esteem and achievement.

Given these facts, it would be nearly, if not totally, impossible to provide the children with the experience of equal status contact. The teacher would literally have to be a genius social engineer with enormous sensitivity to create such a contact situation. How, then, could the framers have been deluded into believing that such contact could be generally satisfied in the public schools, where the coin of status in the classroom is good grades?

The fourth and final condition listed in the statement, that interracial contacts among the children should be of the type that permit learning about each other as individuals, is somewhat more vague than the other three. What is meant here, I assume, is that contact should somehow cut through the mutual stereotypes that each group has of the other. What little evidence we do have about this requirement indicates that stereotypes tend to persist rather than dissolve in the mixed classroom. Furthermore, we found only a minuscule number of cross-ethnic work-partner or friendship sociometric choices, especially by whites, with virtually no change over the postdesegregation years we studied. Thus the evidence is strong that self-segregation occurred within the classroom. There was little meaningful contact, let alone contact that would permit learning about each other as individuals. It is likely that the vicious circle was in full bloom.

To sum up at this point, for the four conditions to be met in the typical school, the teacher would have to be a social engineering whiz. How many of those of us with our supposed sophistication in group dynamics would undertake the task? The truly embarrassing question is: What do we actually know about intergroup contact that could really make a difference in how a desegregation program is implemented? In 1954, the framers extrapolated from Myrdal (1944), from the Clark and Clark (1939) doll studies, and from the Kardiner and Ovesey (1951) study of black self-esteem to argue that segregation inflicts damage on black self-esteem. They also maintained, on the basis of Klineberg's earlier studies (1935), that the higher IQs of blacks living in the North compared with those of blacks who remained south of the Mason–Dixon line represent evidence supporting the success of a desegregated experience. (They failed to take fully into account the fact that most blacks in the North lived under conditions that were often no less segregated than in the South.) They also argued that, because President Eisenhower, as one of his first executive orders on entering the White House in 1953, had desegregated the armed services, desegregation of the schools could also be successfully accomplished by government decree. This argument ignored marked differences between the military situation, where men and women, black and white, were facing a common enemy in Korea and the complex nexus of circumstances represented by school desegregation, especially in the North. It also ignored the fact that, in school desegregation, the participants are children, and thus, a good deal of emotion is engendered in their parents.

In his PSPB article, Cook (1979) attempted to evade the bad predictions by blaming the system, but it was that self-same system about which the predictions had been made, a system with which the framers were intimately acquainted. Excuse not accepted.

THE BASIS FOR THE LATERAL-TRANSMISSION-OF-VALUES HYPOTHESIS

I would next like to run through what I consider the more sophisticated set of assumptions that social scientists held either explicitly or implicitly in the early to mid-1960s, when desegregation was getting under way. (Virtually nothing had happened in the way of implementing desegregation during the 10 years following *Brown*.) These assumptions embody the lateral-transmission-of-values hypothesis and provide it with an underlying dynamic. The hypothesis predicts that, through classroom contact with their white peers, who should outnumber them, minority pupils will experience what is tantamount to a personality change by absorbing the achievement-related values of the higher-achieving whites and will thus start achieving themselves. The way this supposed transformation via elbow rubbing happens is contained in the assumptions that I now enumerate:

1. First, we assume that the achievement gap is not due to a difference in native ability. This has been an abiding faith held by the majority of social scientists, but definitive evidence remains as elusive as ever. The genotypes underlying intelligence are undoubtedly extremely complex, involving numerous genes and their interactions, which probably manifest as many different phenotypes. Therefore, even if it were possible to identify the genotypes, any conclusions about innate racial differences would, at best, be tenuous. At this point, the only reasonable working assumption is that there are no differences.

2. Given that there are no innate differences, the achievement gap exists because of a difference in orientation toward educational attainment within the white and minority communities, which is internalized by the children growing up in those communities. The evidence here from our own study and from the work of others is confusing, to say the least. I was struck, when first reading the Coleman Report, that blacks evidenced higher achievement motivation than whites on the measures used. The black children in the sample also reported that their parents spent more time helping them with schoolwork than did the whites. Others have reported similar evidence (Debord, Griffin, & Clark, 1977; Epps, 1975; Proshansky & Newton, 1968; Weinberg, 1975). In spite of the lack of confirming evidence and evidence to the contrary, most social scientists, I suspect, still believe that there is an achievement-value deficit among black and certain other minority-group children. What does come through in some of the studies is that aspirations among blacks are not functionally related to the path required to reach lofty goals. Part of the stigma of lower social status is a lack of personal efficacy in realizing academic and vocational goals, which induces a sense of helplessness in not being able to exercise control over circumstances.

3. Achievement orientation deficits are reversible and are easier to reverse in the younger child. Our findings here are disappointing and are in agreement with most of the data collected around the country (Bradley & Bradley, 1977; St. John, 1975). A troubling sidelight is the very low correlation we found between actual achievement, as measured by standardized tests, and achievement orientation, as measured by the stock-in-trade instruments that psychologists use. Are these values (or traits, if you will) so ephemeral and easily overwhelmed by situational forces, or are we misguided in the kinds of trait and value measures we typically use?

4. Social influence will occur in any group, so that the norms of conduct, beliefs,

values, and attitudes of the majority will influence the minority. The work supporting this assumption represented my own limited area of expertise when I began the study (Deutsch & Gerard, 1955; Gerard, 1953, 1954). The work that has been done has been almost exclusively in the laboratory, where particular attitudes are concocted on the spot and are therefore usually not intense. There is no systematic evidence supporting the idea that the majority can change deep-seated values held by the minority. Some work coming mainly out of European laboratories suggests that, on the contrary, a staunch minority may influence the majority in profound ways (Moscovici, 1976).

In any event, the majority influence assumption has been a key one in the desegregation literature. The prescription usually offered, which is based strictly on intuition, is that the number of minority children in a classroom should be no more than 40% and no less than 20%, which supposedly represents a minimum critical mass. To this day, there is no evidence supporting the efficacy of these boundary figures. Incidentally, in the tug of war between the schools and the courts, a consensus has never been reached on what percentage figures define a desegregated school.

A social psychologist, in supporting this majority influence assumption, might argue that minority values would change because of both informational influence and normative pressures (Deutsch & Gerard, 1955). The white majority in the classroom, through their achievement-related behavior both in word and by deed, would provide minority children with information representing a new benchmark toward which to strive. Normative pressures derive from the desire of the minority children to be accepted by their white peers. Because grades are the coin of status, the minority child will presumably strive to do well in the new, high-achieving classroom. Using a structural-equations model, Murayama and Miller (1979) found evidence in our data supporting this normative-pressures model. That is, good grades do tend to enhance the child's sociometric status. As not many minority children improved their performance, we can assume that the normative pressures that did exist did not turn the trick. For normative pressures to be felt by the minority child, he or she would have to perceive that acceptance was a reasonable likelihood. Given the lack of any true integration over the course of 5 years, the perceived likelihood was undoubtedly low. Others, like Irwin Katz (1964), have argued for a model emphasizing the reverse process: Acceptance leads to reduced threat and increased self-esteem, which, in turn, result in improved performance. There was no evidence in our data that would support such a causal sequence.

5. A crucial condition for effective social influence to occur is an implicit assumption underlying the lateral transmission hypothesis, namely, that there are no strong barriers to communication in the classroom. To the extent that the racial subgroups are truly integrated socially, there will be fluid communication between the groups. As I have pointed out, there was little evidence that real integration had occurred even after 5 years of the mixed-classroom experience. A subassumption here is that, the earlier in his or her school career the child is placed in a mixed classroom, the more likely it is that he or she will experience true integration. Again, we found no supporting evidence. Self-segregation was as true for the younger children—those who started with desegregation in the first and second grades—as it was for the older ones.

6. Salutary effects for the minority children will be mediated by the higher level of instruction in the desegregated as compared with the segregated classroom. This assumption argues that the teacher will pitch the material at the level of the white majority, and to stay in the running, the minority children will exert themselves and use more of their capacities. That this normalization does not occur is clear from our achievement data. The anecdotal evidence we have indicates that teachers, to cope with the new range of abilities, invariably used some variant or other of ability groupings, especially for reading and math.

7. Assumption 6 is based on a more fundamental notion that competition is good and will lead to improved performance. Research data here, as for most of the assumptions, are sparse. There is some evidence that, when performance discrepancies are small, some form of bootstrapping will occur through social comparison (Thorton & Arrowood, 1966; Toda, Shinotsuka, McClintock, & Stech, 1978). There is reason to believe, however, that, when the discrepancy is large, as is the case between minority and white pupils, each group will tend to render the other noncomparable as a performance referent, and the desired bootstrapping will not occur in the lower group.

8. An assumption related to and supporting Assumptions 6 and 7 is that, if the performance standard for a person is raised, he or she will improve in order to meet the new standard. For this to occur, however, the person must be motivated to reach the higher standard, and it must also not exceed his or her potential grasp; the performance situation must somehow be tractable for the person. The laboratory research on achievement motivation has explored some of its psychological parameters, but our knowledge is still rudimentary. We would find considerable disagreement among educators and psychologists on how best to program a curriculum to optimize learning, a curriculum that would take account of the nexus of individual and social-psychological factors that operate in the classroom. Our data indicate that, whatever curricula and methods were used, they did not achieve the desired end.

9. Teachers will treat children similarly regardless of ethnic background. This assumption, which is a keystone of the lateral transmission hypothesis, was clearly not met in our data, and I would venture to guess that it is still not being met in schoolrooms across the country. There are fairly consistent findings that teachers pay more attention to white than to minority pupils. As pointed out earlier, there is also evidence that teachers underrate minority children. In our own data, we found that teachers who tended to undervalue the achievement of minority pupils as compared with whites—and most teachers did—tended to have an adverse affect on the performance of the minority children in their classes (Rosenthal & Jacobson, 1968). Not only that, minority children in such classes tended to be more isolated from their white peers than were minority children in the classrooms of less bigoted teachers. The teachers' behavior seemed to set an example for the white students.

In the mid-1960s, a number of psychologists argued that teachers in segregated minority schools tended to be punitive and rejecting of their pupils, whereas teachers in white schools were more likely to use various forms of positive reinforcement. It would therefore follow that, in the mixed but predominantly white classroom, minority children would experience positive rather than negative forms of reinforcement that would then enable them to flower. According to Katz (1964), one of the proponents of this argument, self-reinforcement as well as self-discouragement is a consequence of social learning mediated by social reinforcement and modeling. In terms of what actually happens in the classroom, with all of its bigotry and invidious comparison, this nice-sounding theory was just another pie in the sky.

10. That desegregation will increase the minority child's self-esteem was the real heart of the *Brown* decision. In the decision itself and in the Social Science Statement, as well as in the writings of many social scientists at the time, two separate, but not mutually exclusive, hypotheses appear to underlie the assumption. The one stressed the most was the pariah hypothesis: On being thrust into the previously all-white classroom, the child would see herself or himself in a new light and would conclude that he or she was just like and as good as everybody else—like all those whites out there and here in the classroom. This simple-minded notion, which ignores the realities of the classroom, deserves to be caricatured.

The original contention in *Brown*, that segregation itself generates low self-esteem, has been called into question (Epps, 1975, 1979; Porter & Washington, 1979; Wylie, 1979). The original Clark and Clark (1939) doll studies, which figured so prominently in 1954, have been shown to have serious methodological flaws and interpretive problems (Brand, Ruiz, & Padilla, 1974; Stephan & Rosenfeld, 1978). Also, work by Taylor and Walsh (1979) indicates that, when occupational level is controlled for, black self-esteem is, if anything, higher than white self-esteem. The black child growing up in a black family with black friends and relatives probably develops as strong feelings of self-worth as does the white child growing up in a white world. Thrusting the black child into a predominantly white, status-oriented classroom does nothing to enhance the black child's self-esteem. Instead, we find that self-esteem diminishes after desegregation, a consequence that is understandable in the light of recent research on the effect of ability comparison information on self-attributions (Ames, 1978; Ames, Ames, & Felker, 1977; Harvey, Cacioppo, & Yasuna, 1977; Levine, 1983; Nicholls, 1975; Sanders, Gastorf, & Mullen, 1979; Stephan & Rosenfeld, 1978; Wortman, Costanza, & Witt, 1973).

The second, less prominent, hypothesis predicting that desegregation will increase the black child's self-esteem argues that this self-esteem increase will be mediated by the experience of successful competition with white peers. By comparing his or her performance with that of whites in the class, the minority child will realize that he or she is just as good as they are. Would that that would have happened, but it did not.

11. The final assumption, to which I have alluded a number of times, is that increased self-esteem will lead to improved performance. Because goal-setting depends on expectation of success and failure, and because self-esteem can be translated into such expectations, higher self-esteem ought to lead to the setting of higher goals and subsequent improved performance. Also, if we build on the discussion of the previous assumption, the process is assumed to be circular, as higher performance will, in turn, lead to increased self-esteem. Again, there is little evidence of that outcome from data around the country.

In summary, we have found no real evidence to support the lateral transmission hypothesis, either directly in the measurement of values and self-esteem or indirectly in the form of improved performance. The lid that was on minority performance in the segregated classroom is still there.

SOCIAL SCIENCE AND PUBLIC POLICY

At this point, after the heartache and disappointment, I consider myself a realist rather than a pessimist. Social scientists were wrong in the belief that change would come easily. There are so many resistances to overcome, many of which should have been anticipated, but many of us were blinded by our ideology into thinking that we could have our utopia in one fell swoop of mandated busing. Simply mixing children in the classroom and trusting to a benign human nature could never have done the trick. If this nation is to survive, it must eventually achieve equal, desegregated opportunity for all in housing, education, and employment. What I am questioning here are the assumptions underlying the belief that school desegregation, as implemented in the typical school district, will be an instrument to achieve that end.

Social scientists have only lost credibility in the process of essentially entering the political arena prematurely. I can imagine what the David Stockmans of the world are saying about social scientists. Cook (1979) argued that social scientists should be out there helping to make desegregation work. The trouble is that a good deal of damage has been done by recommendations that were based, not on hard data, but mostly on well-meaning rhetoric. Urban districts are not resegregating and becoming less effective in teaching our children. Social scientists and educators have to start learning how to engineer effective integration. Some tentative baby steps have finally been made along these lines (Aronson, Stephan, Sikes, Blaney, & Snapp, 1978; Johnson & Johnson, 1975; Slavin, 1980). Funds for more of it will come from God knows where.

The hard sciences invest a great deal of money and effort in what is called research and development (R&D), in which ideas generated from basic research are developed for application to real-world physical problems. In physics, for example, basic research findings in crystallography are applied to developing solid-state devices for the communications industry. Typically, the investment in development far exceeds that of the original basic research, probably by a factor of 10 or more. Often, years of effort by many scientists and engineers are spent developing a device before it is ready for use in some ongoing communication system. Much time may then be spent actually implementing the device's real-world use with months or even years of field trials. Then, and only then, when the device has proved itself useful and reliable, will those responsible for large-scale operating systems approve its widespread use.

We in the social sciences have missed the essential R&D link in the chain of applying ideas to practical problems. Communication between the ivory tower and the real world of family, school, and workplace has never been good; mostly, it has been nonexistent. In the tower, basic researchers play their interesting little games with 2×2 designs while therapists, educators, and managers attempt to cope with real people. If we are ever going to gain credibility with the lay public and with those in charge of the collective purse strings, we are going to have to follow something of the implementation model used by the hard sciences, so that when we make recommendations about how to deal with an issue like school segregation, we have the facts and experience to back us up. This can only be done with careful research on such things as the effect of performance on self-esteem and vice versa, on the effects of social categorization on prejudice and vice versa, on the effects of competition and cooperation on intergroup attitudes and vice versa, and so on. We already have some rudimentary knowledge of these problems. But then, we have to take what we know and try to apply it, on a small scale at first, to the school setting, with a laboratorylike approach in which we use the best scientific minds available. In the process, we will be forced to go back to the drawing board many times until we develop a program that will really work. This will not happen overnight. The investment required will be enormous both in person years and dollars.

One of the most serious deterrents to successful R&D and systems engineering in the social sciences is the academic reward structure we ourselves perpetuate, especially in psychology. Promotion to tenure and beyond is best achieved by publishing as many short, neat, and methodologically simple papers as possible. By far, the best way to climb the academic ladder is to hit on a simple experimental paradigm, like a paired-associate learning task, a conformity situation, or a fear arousal procedure, and then crank out studies that vary one or another experimental variable that might possibly affect the criterion response. The faculty member who commits himself or herself to a long-term, messy evaluation study is definitely at risk.

Given the keen competition for a limited number of academic jobs these days, a young person who sets out to do a longitudinal study in some real-world context would be foolish, given the standards used by promotion committees. Better to make your studies short, numerous, and focused on a narrow problem that will be of interest to your own limited group of fellow workers around the country, who then can be counted on to write glowing letters of praise to support your promotion. Typically, these mutual admiration societies of co-workers number no more than a couple of dozen people worldwide. Members of these groups can also be relied on to help each other get research grants.

This climate fosters comfortable little cliques that continue to grind out esoterica that, typically, have little or no bearing on the fire fighting going on in clinics, schools, hospitals, prisons, and factories.

Earlier, I pointed out aspects of the culture in the typical classroom that impede true integration, and I have ended by railing at the culture in the typical psychology department that offers no reward for risk taking in the study of real-world problems. Changing the classroom is an enormous task that we psychologists could, in our own way, facilitate indirectly by changing our own norms. That is something over which we do have some control.

It seems that whatever rhetoric is in the ascendance at the time determines how we, as a nation, attempt to solve our social problems. Somehow, we will muddle through; families, children, and workplaces will survive still another Washington administration. We will keep muddling until we are prepared to make a real commitment to research on, development of, and systems engineering for social problems.

REFERENCES

Allport, G. W. (1954). *Prejudice*. Cambridge, MA.: Addison-Wesley.
Ames, C. (1978). Children's achievement attributions and self-reinforcement: Effects of self-concept and competitive reward structure. *Journal of Educational Psychology, 70,* 345–355.
Ames, C., Ames, R., & Felker, D. W. (1977). Effects of competitive reward structure and valence of outcome on children's achievement attributions. *Journal of Educational Psychology, 69,* 1–8.
Armor, D. (1980). White flight and the future of desegregation. In W. G. Stephan & J. R. Feagin (Eds.), *School desegregation: Past, present and future*. New York: Plenum Press.
Aronson, E., Stephen, C., Sikes, J., Blaney, N., & Snapp, M. (1978). *The jigsaw classroom*. Beverly Hills, CA.: Sage.
Bradley, L. A., & Bradley, G. W. (1977). The academic achievement of black students in desegregated schools: A critical review. *Review of Educational Research, 47,* 399–449.
Brand, E. S., Ruiz, R. A., & Padilla, A. M. (1974). Ethnic identification and preference: A review. *Psychological Bulletin, 81,* 860–890.
Clark, K. B., & Clark, M. (1939). Development of consciousness of self and the emergence of racial identification in Negro children. *Journal of Social Psychology, 10,* 591–599.
Coleman, J. S., Campbell, E. Q., Hobson, C. J., McPartland, J., Mood, A. M., Weinfield, F. D., & York, R. L. (1966). *Equality of educational opportunity*. Washington, DC: Office of Education, U.S. Government Printing Offic.
Cook, S. W. (1979). Social science and school desegregation: "Did we mislead the Supreme Court?" *Personality and Social Psychology Bulletin, 5,* 420–437.
Debord, L. W., Griffin, L. J., & Clark, M. (1977). Race and sex influence in the schooling processes of rural and small town youth. *Sociology of Education, 50,* 85–102.
Deutsch, M., & Gerard, H. B. (1955). A study of normative and informational influence upon individual judgement. *Journal of Abnormal and Social Psychology, 51,* 629–636.
Epps, E. G. (1975). Impact of school desegregation on aspirations, self-concepts and other aspects of personality. *Law and Contemporary Problems, 39,* 300–313.
Epps, E. G. (1979). Impact of school desegregation on the self-evaluation and achievement orientation of minority children. *Law and Contemporary Problems, 78,* 57–76.
Gerard, H. B. (1953). The effect of different dimensions of disagreement on the communication process in small groups. *Human Relations, 6,* 249–271.
Gerard, H. B. (1954). The anchorage of opinions in face-to-face groups. *Human Relations, 7,* 313–326.
Gerard, H. B., & Hoyt, M. F. (1974). Distinctiveness of social categorization and attitudes toward ingroup members. *Journal of Personality and Social Psychology, 29,* 836–842.
Gerard, H. B., & Miller, N. (1975). *School desegregation*. New York: Plenum Press.
Harvey, J. H., Cacioppo, J. T., & Yasuna, A. (1977). Temporal pattern of social information and self-attribution of ability. *Journal of Personality, 45,* 281–296.
Hechinger, G., & Hechinger, F. M. (1974). Remember when they gave A's and D's? *New York Times Magazine* (May 5), pp. 84, 86, 92.
Johnson, D. W., & Johnson, R. (1975). *Learning together and alone: Cooperation, competition and individuation*. Englewood Cliffs, NJ: Prentice-Hall.
Kardiner, A., & Ovesey, L. (1951). *The mark of oppression*. New York: Norton.

236 HAROLD B. GERARD

Katz, I. (1964). Review of the evidence relating to the effects of desegregation on the intellectual performance of Negroes. *American Psychologist, 19,* 381–399.

Klineberg, O. (1935). *Negro intelligence and selective migration.* New York: Columbia University Press.

Levine, J. M. (1983). Social comparison and education. In J. M. Levine & M. C. Wang (Eds.), *Teacher and student perceptions: Implications for learning.* Hillsdale, NJ: Erlbaum.

Moscovici, S. (1976). *Social influence and social change.* London: Academic Press.

Murayama, G., & Miller, N. (1979). Re-examination of normative influence processes in desegregated classrooms. *American Educational Research Journal, 16,* 273–284.

Myrdal, G. (1944). *An American dilemma: The Negro problem and modern democracy.* New York: Harper.

Nicholls, J. (1975). Causal attributions and other achievement-related cognitions: Effects of task outcome, attainment value, and sex. *Journal of Personality and Social Psychology, 31,* 379–389.

Pepitone, E. A. (1972). Comparison behavior in elementary school children. *American Education Research Journal, 9,* 45–63.

Porter, J. R., & Washington, R. W. (1979). Black identity and self-esteem: A review of studies of black self-concept. *Annual Review of Sociology, 5,* 53–74.

Proshansky, H., & Newton, P. (1968). The nature and meaning of Negro self-identity. In M. Deutsch, I. Katz, & A. R. Jensen (Eds.), *Social class, race and psychological development.* New York: Holt, Rinehart & Winston.

Rosenthal, R., & Jacobson, L. (1968). *Pygmalion in the classroom. Teacher expectations and pupil's intellectual development.* New York: Holt, Rinehart & Winston.

St. John, N. (1975). *School desegregation.* New York: Wiley.

Sanders, G. S., Gastorf, J. W., & Mullen, B. (1979). Selectivity in the use of social comparison information. *Personality and Social Psychology Bulletin, 5,* 377–380.

Schofield, J. W., & Sagar, H. A. (1977). Peer interaction patterns in an integrated middle school. *Sociometry, 40,* 130–138.

Slavin, R. E. (1980). Cooperative learning. *Review of Educational Research, 50,* 315–342.

Stephan, W. G. (1978). School desegregation: An evaluation of predictions made in *Brown vs. Board of Education. Psychological Bulletin, 85,* 217–238.

Stephan, W. G., & Rosenfeld, D. (1978). Effects of desegregation on race relations and self-esteem. *Journal of Educational Psychology, 70,* 670–679.

Suls, J., & Sanders, G. S. (1979). Social comparison processes on the young child. *Journal of Research and Development in Education, 13,* 79–89.

Tajfel, H. (Ed.). (1979). *Differentiation between social groups: Studies in the social psychology of intergroup relations.* London: Academic Press.

Taylor, N. C., & Walsh, E. J. (1979). Explanations of black self-esteem: Some empirical tests. *Social Psychology Quarterly, 42,* 242–252.

Thorton, D. A., & Arrowood, A. J. (1966). Self-evaluation, self-enhancement and the locus of social comparison. *Journal of Experimental Social Psychology, Supplement I,* 40–48.

Toda, M., Shinotsuka, H., McClintock, C. G., & Stech, F. J. (1978). Development of competitive behavior as a function of culture, age, and social comparison. *Journal of Personality and Social Psychology, 36,* 825–829.

Veroff, J. (1978). Social motivation. *American Behavioral Scientist, 21,* 709–730.

Weigel, R. H., Wiser, P. L., & Cook, S. W. (1975). The impact of cooperative learning experiences on cross-ethnic relations and attitudes. *Journal of Social Issues, 31,* 219–244.

Weinberg, M. (1975). The relationship between school desegregation and academic achievement: A review of research. *Law and Contemporary Problems, 39,* 240–270.

Wortman, C. B., Costanza, P. R., & Witt, T. R. (1973). Effect of anticipated performance on the attributions of causality to self and others. *Journal of Personality and Social Psychology, 27,* 372–381.

Wylie, R. C. (1979). *The self-concept: Theory and research on selected topics* (rev. ed.). Lincoln: University of Nebraska Press.

12

The 1954 Social Science Statement and School Desegregation
A Reply to Gerard

Stuart W. Cook

In his article "School Desegregation: The Social Science Role" (see Chapter 11), Harold Gerard deplores the quality of the Social Science Statement submitted to the U.S. Supreme Court at the time of its historic 1954 decision to desegregate the schools. He characterizes the statement as quixotic, myopically focused, short-sighted, unsophisticated, and based on well-meaning rhetoric rather than research. In view of the fact that the statement was presented to the Court as a review of the available research evidence and cited more than 40 publications of social scientists and educators, this characterization appears to question either the professional qualifications or the ethical standards of those who prepared and signed it. Gerard describes his own "realism" about school desegregation, developed in part, he indicates, as a consequence of the disappointing results of his case study of desegregation in the Riverside, California, elementary schools (Gerard & Miller, 1975). By overgeneralizing his own results and failing to take account of the results of many similar studies, he presents a misleading picture of the research outcomes on school desegregation and the complexities of interpreting them. He concludes his chapter by urging that social science not repeat the mistake of "entering the political arena prematurely," as he feels it did in the case of school desegregation.

To some extent, Gerard's derogation of the Social Science Statement follows from his misunderstanding of the historical context of the statement and of the potential contributions of social science at different stages in the development and implementation of social policy. However, whatever the origins of his misrepresentations, they must be corrected in the interest of preserving an accurate account of a significant event in the history of psychology. Such a correction is the primary purpose of this article.

This chapter is reprinted from *American Psychologist*, 1984, 39(8), 819–832.

STUART W. COOK • Department of Psychology and Institute for Behavioral Science, University of Colorado, Boulder, Colorado 80309.

THE HISTORICAL CONTEXT

To appreciate the nature of the Social Science Statement, it is necessary to know the historical context in which it was prepared. In 1953, the Supreme Court agreed to reconsider a long-standing aspect of judicial policy relevant to constitutional guarantees against racial discrimination. Earlier, under a "separate but equal" interpretation of these guarantees, the Court had refused to disapprove state laws that required or permitted segregation. Such laws existed in 17 states and the District of Columbia. They affected the conditions of schooling for 8 million white and 2.5 million black children.

Under the joint title *Brown v. Board of Education of Topeka* (1954), the Court consolidated four cases[1] in which black parents argued that government-enforced segregation of public schools deprived black children of equal educational opportunity, even if tangible school facilities were equal. In constitutional terms, these parents were arguing that "separate but equal" education was a discriminatory deprivation of their rights to equal protection of the laws under the Fourteenth Amendment.

Before the Court hearing, social scientists prepared a review of evidence and theory relevant to the effects of segregation on black children.[2] Thirty-two anthropologists, psychiatrists, psychologists, and sociologists signed the review and presented it to the Supreme Court as an appendix to the plaintiff's legal briefs. The issue facing the Court, it must be emphasized, was not *de facto* racial segregation due to residential patterns but *de jure* government-enforced separation of blacks and whites into separate schools even if the children lived in the same neighborhoods. The reason for highlighting the circumstances under which the Social Science Statement was written is to call attention to its focus on the effects of government-enforced segregation and what differences might be expected if children were not forced to attend segregated schools under a public policy of this kind. In contrast, little or no attention was being given at the time to the question of steps that might be taken to *correct* the effects of school segregation on children who had grown up under its influence. Because the constitutional issue revolved around the consequences of legalized segregation, the prevention of such consequences in the future was at issue, rather than remediation of the effects already created. Failure to recognize this could lead one to infer from the statement predictions about the consequences of desegregation that were never made.

THE SOCIAL SCIENCE STATEMENT

The statement was titled "The Effect of Segregation and the Consequences of Desegregation: A Social Science Statement" (1953). It began with an examination of the effects of segregation, prejudice, and discrimination and their social concomitants (as reflected in such factors as poor housing, disrupted family life, and other substandard living conditions) on black children. It was asserted that, in the course of their development, such children learn from their environment that they belong to a group that has inferior status in American society. They react to this knowledge with a sense of humiliation and feelings of inferiority and come to entertain the possibility that they are, in fact, worthy of second-class treatment. This reaction, in turn leads to self-hatred and rejection of being black.

The effects of this experience were said to differ by social class. Aggressive, anti-

---

[1]The Supreme Court reviewed five related cases at the same time. A separate opinion was rendered in one of the five, *Bolling v. Sharpe* (1954).
[2]The Social Science Statement was drafted by Isidor Chein, Kenneth B. Clark, and Stuart W. Cook.

social, and delinquent actions were said to be more likely to appear in children of lower socioeconomic classes. Children from middle and upper socioeconomic classes were more likely to show withdrawal and submissive behavior and/or exaggerated conformity to middle-class standards.

Another consequence of the awareness of inferior social status was said to be the lowering of personal ambition. This is reflected, for example, in a depression of educational aspirations. Such effects "impair the ability of the child to profit from the educational opportunities provided him" ("The Effect of Segregation," 1953, p. 430).

The effect on children from the white majority group was said to be that they learned to derive unjustified personal status from the superiority attached by society to being white. This provided such children an unrealistic basis for self-evaluation.

With respect to the effect of government enforcement of discrimination *per se*, it was pointed out that living in an underprivileged environment tends to cause feelings of inferiority only insofar as this experience is perceived as an indicator of low social status and as a symbol of inferiority. Studies were cited as showing that, from the earliest school years, children are aware of status differences between whites and blacks. Government-enforced segregation was said to be a major contributor to this awareness for two reasons: (a) enforced segregation results from the decision of the majority group without the consent of the segregated group and is commonly so perceived; and (b) historically, segregation patterns have involved an assumption of inferiority of blacks dating back to slavery days.

A third of the text of the Social Science Statement dealt with potential difficulties that might be encountered in making the change from segregation to desegregation. Before examining these, we should first recall that such problems were not a part of the question the Court had to decide. If the justices were to conclude that government-enforced segregation of schools had led to less than equal educational opportunity for black children, the Fourteenth Amendment, with its requirement for equal protection under the laws, implied abandoning such government policy. Such a change would be called for regardless of the consequences of desegregation.

In its discussion of the potential difficulties of desegregating, the Social Science Statement dealt with two prevalent fears. The first concerned school achievement; the second, potential interracial conflict. The school achievement question had two aspects. One was apprehension about the potentially negative effects of desegregated education on the school achievement of whites. Such apprehensions were said to be unfounded.[3] The other concerned the possibility of damaging minority students by putting them at a competitive disadvantage in schools with white students. The discussion of this possibility recognized the initial educational disadvantage of formerly segregated black students. The case was made that this did not depend on innate racial differences in intelligence and, by implication, that the black–white achievement gap would eventually be eliminated. Nothing was said about how long this would take, but because the argument was by analogy to Klineberg's data (1935) on the increment in average black IQ with number of years lived in the North following migration from the South, the implied expectation was that achievement gain in desegregated schools would be a gradual process.

When it turned to the fear of potential interracial conflict, the statement called attention to what had been learned from desegregation in the armed services, public housing, and industry. Because, with rare exceptions, such desegregation had been carried out without incidents of violence, it was assumed that this would also be the case in the

---

[3]With rare exceptions, subsequent studies have consistently found that desegregation does not affect the school achievement of white students.

public schools. As to whether desegregation might be accompanied by the development of more favorable racial attitudes and friendlier race relations, the statement noted that this result had been found in interracial housing, employment, the armed services, the merchant marine, and recreational settings. However, care was taken to call the justices' attention to the *conditions* under which this outcome could be anticipated. It was asserted that these conditions "can generally be satisfied" in public schools.

THE IMPACT OF THE STATEMENT

Whether or not the Court was influenced in its decision by the Social Science Statement is uncertain. Some observers have seen a relation between it and an oft-quoted passage from the Court's opinion: "To separate them from others of similar age and qualifications solely because of their race generates a feeling of inferiority as to their status in the community that may affect their hearts and minds in a way unlikely ever to be undone" (*Brown v. Board of Education*, 1954, p. 494). Another passage in the opinion bears a strong resemblance to wording in the statement:

> Segregation of white and colored children in public schools has a detrimental effect upon the colored children. The impact is greater when it has the sanction of the law; for the policy of separating the races is usually interpreted as denoting the inferiority of the Negro group. A sense of inferiority affects the motivation of a child to learn. Segregation with the sanction of law, therefore, has a tendency to retard the development of Negro children and to deprive them of some of the benefits they would receive in a racially integrated school system. Whatever may have been the extent of psychological knowledge at the time of *Plessy v. Ferguson,* this finding is amply supported by modern authority. (p. 494)

As a footnote to this passage, the opinion listed seven social science references that the Social Science Statement had also cited. (For a detailed exposition of the grounds for believing that the Court used social science to document its key finding that segregated education for black children was not equal education—and hence, was discriminatory—see Rosen, 1972.)

On the other hand, historical analysis of the events surrounding the Court's decision has persuaded others that the Social Science Statement served a quite different function. According to this analysis, the justices knew that segregated schools were favored by a large majority of the population. They were worried about the possibility that a decision to desegregate would not be accepted. For this reason, they felt they must appeal to the conscience of the nation for support. They used the evidence presented in the Social Science Statement to this end (Kluger, 1976, p. 705 ff.; Taylor, 1981).[4] (Kluger, 1976, reached this conclusion on the basis of interviews with former staff associates of the justices.)

Was the Social Science Statement Myopically Focused and Short-Sighted?

Gerard's most general accusation is that the Social Science Statement "did not anticipate the situation as represented by the demography and geography in our large urban centers, but it was rather myopically focused on small dual systems in the South that

---

[4]A third position is that the Social Science Statement had no effect on the Court (Cahn, 1955; van den Haag, 1957). The argument is that the statement merely reiterated ideas about the consequences of desegregation that were common knowledge and provided no basis for deciding the constitutional issue. To some extent, this position overlaps the interpretation that the Court used the statement only to arouse support for its decision.

were maintained by *de jure* segregation." And later, "Perhaps we should forgive them for their short-sightedness in this respect." Still later, "I am still willing to give the framers and signers the benefit of the doubt in not having anticipated the logistics of northern urban busing, but I do have trouble understanding their lack of acknowledgement of strong widespread community opposition to two-way busing."

These statements simply overlook the history of the judicial actions that were in process in 1954 and reflect Gerard's first major area of ignorance about the Social Science Statement. As noted above, the statement focused on segregation mandated by or permitted by laws then current in 17 states. Under these laws, black children were being bused out of their neighborhoods to all-black schools. Material presented to the Court had to be relevant to the effects of such practices or to the consequences of discontinuing them. It was not until 1971, 17 years after the *Brown v. Board of Education* (1954) decision, that the Court dealt with the question of desegregating schools as a corrective for segregation brought about by government-supported actions in the past. In a case originating in Charlotte, North Carolina (*Swann v. Charlotte-Mecklenberg Board of Education*, 1971), the Court for the first time declared that desegregation plans assigning both black and white students to their neighborhood schools might not be sufficient to correct for past governmental discrimination. The reason was the "Such plans may fail to counteract the continuing effects of past school segregation resulting from discriminatory location of school sites or distortion of school size in order to achieve or maintain an artificial racial separation" (p. 28). Where such discrimination had led to all-black or all-white neighborhoods and neighborhood schools, the Court said that other ways of achieving desegregated schools would be required. Where necessary, these would include busing.

However, in 1954, 17 years earlier, the Court was concerned only with the constitutionality of its separate-but-equal policy. For social scientists to have addressed the justices on any topic other than the human consequences of their current policy would have been highly inappropriate. It would have been presumptuous in the extreme to have raised the problem of *de facto* segregation in northern and western metropolitan areas. In other words, the absence from the Social Science Statement of an anticipation of opposition to two-way busing in large urban centers, which led Gerard to characterize it as myopic and short-sighted, reflected the specific historical context in which the statement was prepared.

Was the Social Science Statement Vague about How Desegregation Would Correct the Harm of Segregation?

Gerard criticizes the Social Science Statement as follows:

> This statement, which was submitted to the court in support of the plaintiffs, was vague about how desegregation would correct the harms of segregation. All that it said, in effect, was that because the minority child was now in a classroom with whites, he or she would no longer have the status of an outcast or pariah. This knowledge would somehow impart to the child the self-image necessary to do well in school and later enter the mainstream of American society.

This quote reflects Gerard's second major area of ignorance about the Social Science Statement. For the reasons noted above,—that is, the nature of the constitutional issue facing the Court,—the statement focused on the consequences of *segregation*. In describing its contents in the introductory paragraph, the statement said: "It is with these issues only that this paper is concerned. Some of the issues have to do with the consequences of *segregation*, some with the *problems of changing* from segregation to unsegregated practices" ("The Effect of Segregation," 1953, p. 427; italics added). Nowhere in the statement was there mention of any potential effect of *desegregation* in imparting a new self-image to black children. The only mention of school performance occurred in the context of reassuring the justices that putting white and black children in the same schools need not jeopardize the education of the white children nor damage the black children. Gerard's account of what the statement said on these matters is entirely imaginary. As we shall see, this confusion between what the statement said and what he represents it as having said pervades Gerard's entire chapter.

WAS THE SOCIAL SCIENCE STATEMENT INCORRECT REGARDING THE GENERATION OF LOW SELF-ESTEEM UNDER SEGREGATION?

Gerard asserts that "the original contention in *Brown*, that segregation itself generates low self-esteem, has been called into question." As authority for this statement, he cites Epps (1975, 1978), Porter and Washington (1979), and Wylie (1979). Before examining what these reviewers did, in fact, say, we should first examine the relevant aspect of the Social Science Statement itself:

> As minority group children learn the inferior status to which they are assigned—as they observe the fact that they are almost always segregated and kept apart from others who are treated with more respect by the society as a whole—they often react with feelings of inferiority and a sense of personal humiliation. Many of them become confused about their own personal worth. On the one hand, like all human beings, they require a sense of personal dignity; on the other hand, almost nowhere in the larger society do they find their own dignity as human beings respected by others. Under these conditions, the minority group child is thrown into a conflict with regard to his feelings about himself and his group. He wonders whether his group and he himself are worthy of no more respect than they receive. This conflict and confusion leads to self-hatred and rejection of his own group. ("The Effect of Segregation," 1953, p. 429)

Later on, the statement indicates that "studies have shown that from the earliest school years children are not only aware of the status differences among different groups in the society, but begin to react with the patterns described above" (p. 431). In support, the statement cites 11 published works. What the cited articles and books indicate is that society-level analyses by sociologists and anthropologists had called attention to lowered self-esteem among black children and had traced it to the inferior status of blacks officially endorsed by laws that required segregation (e.g., Davis, 1939; Frazier, 1949; Myrdal, 1944). Psychiatrists had drawn similar conclusions from case studies (Dai, 1948; Kardiner & Ovesey, 1951). Psychologists had interpreted their projective studies with dolls, photographs, and drawings as confirming those from other disciplines. The collective judgments of social scientists had been published in an article by Deutscher and Chein (1948). These investigators had questioned the social scientists thought most likely to be informed on the effects of segregation, namely, 849 members of the American Ethnological Society, the Division of Personality and Social Psychology of the American Psychological Association, and the members of the American Sociological Society who concentrated in social psychology or race relations. Of the 517 who replied, 90% expressed the opinion that enforced segregation had detrimental psychological effects on segregated groups, even if equal facilities were provided. As summarized in one of Gerard's references (Porter & Washington, 1979), "Studies done prior to the mid-1960s were virtually unanimous in finding a high degree of identification with and preference for white among preschool black children" (p. 55).

Each of the four articles that Gerard cites as "calling into question" the position of the Social Science Statement on self-esteem is a review of the literature on self-esteem or self-concept. These reviewers, like others, pointed out that, beginning in the mid-1960s, the picture regarding black self-esteem changed radically. At that time, research results began to show that black self-esteem in segregated situations is as high or higher than that of whites. The studies producing these results mostly measured self-esteem with self-report questionnaires. However, some were straightforward replications of the pre-1954 studies using projective techniques (e.g., Datcher, Savage, & Checkosky, 1974; Hraba & Grant, 1970; Winnick & Taylor, 1977).

Rather than interpreting the new results as casting doubt on the pre-1954 results, as Gerard implies they did, the reviewers noted that there have been many confirmations of *both* the earlier and the more recent findings, and they explored possible reasons for the change in findings from the earlier to the later studies. One suggestion they offered is that there has been a significant change in the self-esteem of black children over time. This was postulated by Hraba and Grant (1970) in their "Black Is Beautiful" article. Datcher *et al.* (1974) offered the same interpretation of similar findings. Powell and Fuller (1970) raised the same possibility in relation to findings based on questionnaires. Underlying the interpretation in these articles was the observation that the increase in black self-esteem paralleled such historical developments as the emergence of Martin Luther King, Jr., as a national hero, the growth of black pride and the black power ideologies, the accession of blacks to big city political leadership, and the media exposure of prominent black leaders, artists, and athletes.

A second suggestion emphasized methodological and conceptual differences between studies conducted in the two time periods. The early research emphasis had been on indirect measures (e.g., dolls, drawings, puppets, and toys) for assessment of self-esteem, whereas the more recent studies emphasized self-report questionnaires and rating scales. The possible relevance of such a shift is that much of the earlier evidence indicating low self-esteem among legally segregated black children was based on indirect measures, whereas most of the later evidence showing high self-esteem had been based on self-report measures. Moreover, as research on self-esteem progressed in the 1960s, a distinction emerged between two subconcepts, one dealing with racial self-esteem and the other with personal self-esteem. The former refers to feelings about one's ethnic group and the latter to feelings about oneself, that is, personal worth, competence, and self-approval. Indirect measures like those evaluating the characteristics of white or brown dolls have tended to focus on racial self-esteem, but the self-report questionnaires and ratings have usually examined personal self-esteem.

Although the view that black self-esteem has changed since the pre-1954 period is entirely plausible, some writers have suggested that what the self-report questionnaires actually reflect is a new norm of racial pride rather than internalized self-esteem. Indicative is the fact that clinicians have expressed skepticism about whether verbal statements indicating high levels of self-esteem among black children dependably reflect the reality of their true feelings. For example, the psychiatrist Spurlock (1973) wrote about her study of black children (ages 4 to 9) as follows:

> The findings of the study were highly suggestive that the mouthing of the beauty of Blackness by many Black children is a reaction formation. A striking finding is that this characteristic appears most frequently among those children from lower socioeconomic groups; that is, they react by saying that Black is Beautiful but they do not really feel it as being so. (p. 156)

Similarly, the clinical psychologist Mamie Clark, in commenting on whether real change has taken place in the black child's self-esteem, indicated, "From my general observations, the children's perceptions of themselves as black, and all the negatives that connotes, have not changed significantly since my first studies in the 1930s and 1940s" (Poussaint, 1974, p. 140). There are clear warnings implied in such statements that social desirability considerations may influence self-evaluative responses to questionnaires or interviews about aspirations and self-concept.

Reviewers have criticized many features of both racial self-esteem and personal self-esteem studies. Paralleling the concern noted above about social desirability influences operating on self-report questionnaires has been a questioning of the projective assumption that favorable attributes assigned to opposite-color stimulus objects (photographs, dolls, etc.) can be interpreted as implying low regard for one's own racial group or self. These criticisms are just as severe for recent studies as they are for those on which the Social Science Statement was based (Wylie, 1979). On the other hand, the fact that identical projective procedures consistently produced a black preference for white stimulus objects in an earlier time period and generally, although not always, a black preference for black stimulus objects in a later time period leads one to take more seriously the inference that a real change in racial self-esteem has occurred.

None of the above discussion is meant to imply that the role of segregation in determining minority self-esteem is yet fully understood. Two things should be clear, however. One is that what social scientists said to the Supreme Court about the relationship between legally enforced segregation and the self-esteem of black children reflected an interdisciplinary consensus based on the best evidence available at the time. The other is that later research provides no defensible grounds for questioning the historical accuracy of that evidence.

What Did the Social Science Statement Say about the Effect of Desegregation on the Self-Esteem of Black Children?

Gerard attributes the following prediction to the Social Science Statement:

> That desegregation will increase the minority child's self-esteem was the real heart of the *Brown* decision. In the decision itself, and in the Social Science Statement, as well as in the writings of many social scientists at the time, two separate, but not mutually exclusive, hypotheses appear to underly the assumption. The one stressed the most was the pariah hypothesis: On being thrust into the previously all white classroom, the child would see herself or himself in a new light and would conclude that he or she was just like and as good as everybody else—like all those whites out there and here in the classroom. This simple-minded notion, which ignores the realities of the classroom, deserves to be caricatured.

Perhaps a caricature is in order, but not the one suggested. Nothing remotely resembling "this simple-minded notion"—nor any other prediction about the effect of desegregation on self-esteem—appeared in either the Supreme Court's opinion or the Social Science Statement.

Given that the Social Science Statement said nothing explicitly about the effects of desegregation on the self-esteem of black children, what might one reasonably infer about what it implied? Recall that the statement addressed a type of segregation in which black children were, by law, bused away from their neighborhood schools to more distant blacks-only schools, and that this busing characterized their entire elementary and secondary education. If one overlooks this, one might inappropriately infer, as Gerard does, that the statement implied that any type of desegregation for any period of time under any conditions would enhance black self-esteem. A more legitimate inference, however, would be that black children who attend desegregated schools throughout their educational careers under a constitutional assurance of their equality would show higher self-esteem than did earlier children who attended segregated schools under the stigma of official segregation. The fact that such an inference can no longer be tested (because changes have taken place simultaneously with school desegregation) provides no justification for misattributing some other prediction to the Social Science Statement.

However, testing other predictions (e.g., that black children bused from segregated schools in black neighborhoods to desegregated ones outside their neighborhoods will, after 1 or more years, show enhanced self-esteem) is clearly of practical interest and, if related to the conditions of desegregation, of theoretical interest as well. Regarding his own case study of the Riverside schools, Gerard notes:

> Thrusting the black child into a predominantly white, status-oriented classroom does nothing to enhance the black child's self-esteem. Instead, we find that self-esteem diminishes after desegregation, a consequence that is understandable in the light of recent research on the effect of ability-comparison information on self-attributions.

Reviewers of the research literature in this area have concluded their reviews as follows: Two of them found a trend for desegregated blacks to have lower self-esteem than segregated blacks (St. John, 1975, based on 25 studies; Stephan, 1978, based on 20 studies). Three found the existing studies too inconsistent to reveal a trend (Christmas, 1973; Epps, 1978; Zirkel, 1971). One found none of the nine studies examined to fulfill the necessary criteria to enable one to draw a conclusion (Wylie, 1979). One (Weinberg, 1977) examined 60 studies and found that, in 29 of the 60, the desegregated blacks had the higher self-esteem.

A number of considerations must be kept in mind in interpreting self-esteem outcomes of desegregation studies. One of these concerns the duration of the desegregated educational experience. Various observers have suggested that black children may suffer a blow to self-esteem in the first years of desegregation but may experience a gradual rise in self-esteem thereafter. Research limited to a brief time span is unable to test this possibility. The best test of a hypothesis inferred from the 1954 Social Science Statement would be a comparison of self-esteem in young black adults who had been educated entirely in segregated schools with self-esteem in others who had received all of their education in desegregated schools. Although such a comparison is not likely to be made, St. John (1975) described four studies that approximate it. These studies made cross-sectional comparisons of adult blacks who attended desegregated schools with those who did not. Although calling attention to possible alternative interpretations of the results of these studies, St. John concluded, "Thus, in the long run, desegregation is usually found associated with higher self-esteem" (p. 55).

Another difficulty with the expectation that short-range desegregation should enhance self-esteem is created by a ceiling effect in self-esteem measurement. As noted in the preceding section, since the mid-1960s the measured level of self-esteem in black children in segregated schools is as high as or higher than that of white children. Regardless of the interpretation placed on this finding (i.e., whether it is internalized or, alternatively, is a socially desirable response reflecting a strong black-pride norm), one would hardly anticipate a further enhancement of self-esteem under desegregation.

In summary, the research results on black self-esteem following desegregation are inconclusive and difficult to interpret. If any inference can be made from the Social Science Statement, it is that being educated entirely in desegregated schools would result in higher self-esteem. A few studies have found this result; however, the results are subject to alternative explanations. A possible methodological difficulty—that is, high predesegregation scores on self-esteem questionnaires—may make it difficult to measure change in self-esteem even when it occurs.

WHAT DID THE SOCIAL SCIENCE STATEMENT SAY ABOUT THE EFFECT OF DESEGREGATION ON THE SCHOOL ACHIEVEMENT OF BLACK CHILDREN?

Although the Social Science Statement nowhere predicted improvement in the school achievement of black children as a consequence of desegregation, it did attribute

impaired ability to profit from education to the depressing impact of legalized segregation. Moreover, it reassured the Court that there was no reason to be apprehensive about
the eventual adjustment of black children to classroom competition with white students.
Hence, despite the absence of an explicit prediction, it seems reasonable to *infer* that the
justices were led to believe that the achievement of black children would improve under
desegregation.

On the other hand, in discussing the temporary nature of the initial achievement
handicap of segregated black students, the statement drew on the IQ analogy in which
improvement had been found to be related to *number of years* of northern residence. It was
clear that the anticipated favorable effects were to occur over the long run, and nothing
was said to suggest that the achievement differential could be eliminated in a brief span of
time.

Gerard summarizes his view of whether desegregation has improved black school
achievement as follows: "All would be well if academic performance as well as the grade–
achievement discrepancy had converged in the years following desegregation, but it did
not. The relative achievement standing of minority pupils progressively worsened as
they moved through the grades." The results of his own study were consistent with this
appraisal: "We, in fact, have suggestive evidence that, as compared with predesegregation achievement, white performance increased somewhat and black performance decreased somewhat in the years following desegregation."

The picture emerging from reviews of the many studies of achievement under school
desegregation is more congruent with the inference from the Social Science Statement
than with Gerard's findings. Major reviews have been made by Bradley and Bradley
(1977), Crain and Mahard (1978, 1982), St. John (1975), Stephan (1978), and Weinberg
(1977). St. John (1975) summarized 64 studies with the conclusion that school desegregation has not been shown to be successful, nor has it been shown to be unsuccessful, in
raising the achievement levels of black students. Based on a review of 20 studies, Bradley
and Bradley (1977) reached the same conclusion. Stephan (1978) stated that, of the 34
published and unpublished studies he examined, 10 showed an increase in achievement
under desegregation, 23 showed a mixture of increases and no effects, and 1 showed a
decrease. Concentrating on 49 studies of *planned* desegregation (omitting studies of other
mixed-race schools), Weinberg (1977) judged that 60% of them showed achievement
gains for blacks. Based on 73 studies, Crain and Mahard (1978) reported positive effects in
40 and negative effects in 12. Of these studies, 39 involved mandatory desegregation
plans; of these, 24 reported achievement gains and 5 showed losses.

In addition to these reviews by traditional methods, three meta-analyses were carried out between 1975 and 1982 (Crain & Mahard, 1982; Krol, 1978; Wortman & Bryant,
1985). Each concluded that desegregation had had a beneficial effect on black student
achievement. Subsequently, a panel of social scientists conducted a coordinated series of
meta-analyses; following the procedures described by Glass, McGaw, and Smith (1981),
each meta-analyzed all or part of a common pool of 19 methodologically superior studies.
Thomas Cook (1983) undertook a critique and synthesis of the various analyses, comparing them to the three meta-analyses conducted earlier. He drew three key conclusions: (a)
Desegregation had not caused decreases in black achievement; (b) desegregation had not
caused an increase in achievement in mathematics; and (c) desegregation had increased
reading levels as measured by the mean effect size but not by the median or modal effect
size. The gain was between 2 and 6 weeks, or approximately 1 month in grade-level
terms.

Of special relevance to the position taken in the 1954 Social Science Statement is an
observation reported in four of the above reviews. Crain and Mahard (1978), St. John
(1975), and Weinberg (1977) all noted that achievement in desegregated schools exceeded

that in segregated schools more frequently for children in the earliest school grades (kindergarten, first, and second). In a subsequent review, Crain and Mahard (1982; see also Crain & Mahard, 1981, 1983) provided further support for this finding: from a total set of 93 studies, they isolated 23 that (a) studied students desegregated at either the kindergarten or first-grade level and (b) were methodologically the strongest, that is, either used black students in a segregated school as a control group or compared scores with those of earlier cohorts. These 23 studies analyzed 45 samples of students in 18 different cities. Of the 45 samples, 40 showed positive effects on black student achievement ($p < .001$). Of those for which Crain and Mahard could estimate an effect size, desegregation raised achievement by a quarter of a standard deviation. Conversion from standard deviation units to grade equivalents on norms for the Comprehensive Test of Basic Skills led to an estimate of achievement gain in grade-equivalent terms of 0.3 year.[5] Such children may reflect the greater potential of school desegregation when this desegregation does not have to overcome the effects of prior experience in segregated schools.[6]

Equally relevant to the position of the Social Science Statement is that several analysts of school desegregation (Crain & Mahard, 1978; Orfield, 1973, 1978) have stressed the difference in perspective represented by short-term versus cumulative achievement gains. Short-term effects measured over 1 or 2 years, when found at all, are typically small. If the effects of desegregation on achievement are evaluated in these terms, they will be underestimated, in part because they fall far short of closing the black–white achievement gap. The wisdom of a cumulative perspective was convincingly illustrated by Jones (1984). In a paper titled "White–Black Achievement Differences: The Narrowing Gap," he traced the school achievement performance of white and black children through successive testings between 1971 and 1982 by the National Assessment of Educational Progress (1981). He found both steady and impressive improvement by black children and a progressive narrowing of the black–white achievement gap. Noting several possible explanations (e.g., equal opportunity programs, higher black incomes, and broader societal participation by blacks), Jones wrote as follows about the possibility that his findings may reflect cummulative effects of school desegregation:

> It is possible that the trend reflects long-term effects of school desegregation, even though such effects have proven elusive to investigation in shorter time spans (e.g., Gerard, Chapter 11; Gerard & Miller, 1975). Perhaps school desegregation failed during its early years, often marked by tension and strife, but more recently has had beneficial educational effects for minority students. Or perhaps, as concluded by Crain and

[5]Any study comparing desegregated and segregated students must be concerned with the possibility that more able or more academically motivated children have somehow been selected into the desegregated schools—or vice versa. Thomas Cook (1983) noted the possibility that studies beginning with desegregation at kindergarten or first grade may encounter a problem of underadjustment for initial differences between desegregated experimental groups and segregated controls, at least by comparison with studies of older children. The problem can be traced to the fact that pretests given in kindergarten or first grade necessarily measure academic readiness, whereas those given in later grades measure academic achievement. A pretest–posttest correlation (needed to correct for initial differences between experimental and control groups) between academic readiness and academic achievement might be expected to be lower than one between two measures of academic achievement. Such a reduced pretest–posttest correlation might have the consequence of artifactually increasing the estimate of the desegregation effect in studies beginning at kindergarten and first grade by comparison with those beginning later. Of course, if the selection bias placed less able or less academically motivated students in the desegregated schools, then the effect of the reduced correlation would be to decrease the estimate of the desegregation effect.

[6]One meta-analytic review (Wortman & Bryant, 1985) found that the largest achievement advantage for desegregation occurred at Grades 7 and 8, with the next largest occurring at Grades 1–6. This review was based on 31 methodologically "acceptable" studies screened from a pool of 155 that initially seemed relevant.

Mahard (Crain & Mahard, 1978; Crain, Mahard, & Narot, 1982), achievement gains are seen for black students attending desegregated schools from kindergarten or first grade, but not for black students whose desegregated education began in later school years.

Among its other features, the wording of this statement calls attention to the fact that the effects of desegregation on achievement may be evaluated against either or both of two reference points. One is achievement level under segregation, that is, relative achievement gain in segregated and desegregated schools. The other is the size of the black–white achievement gap, that is, whether under desegregation the gap narrows, widens, or remains the same by comparison to its size under segregation. Obviously, the latter criterion is affected by the impact of desegregation on the achievement of white students as well as of blacks.

The weight of the evidence, contrary to Gerard's interpretation, is that desegregation, particularly when begun early and viewed cumulatively, accelerates black achievement gain. Procedures that further enhance this effect are described later in this chapter.

THE SOCIAL SCIENCE STATEMENT AND THE EFFECT OF DESEGREGATION ON RACE RELATIONS AND ATTITUDES

Parts I and II of the Social Science Statement dealt with the effects of legalized, separate-but-equal segregation on the self-esteem and school achievement of black children. Part III, in contrast, dealt with possible problems in making the change from segregation to desegregation. Two potential difficulties were examined. One of the two concerned school achievement, already discussed above. The other dealt with an entirely different matter, namely, whether desegregation provoked or prevented interracial tension and conflict. Behind this question was concern about whether a Court order to desegregate would be accepted or, alternatively, might be met with massive resistance. As relevant evidence, the Social Science Statement cited studies of successful desegregation in the wartime army, in wartime industry, and in postwar public housing. It called attention to instances of tension, such as protest strikes, but reported that these had been temporary and had been quieted by forceful leadership. It pointed out that previously segregated whites and blacks had often been found to associate under desegregation without serious friction and often in considerable harmony.

By 1974, school desegregation had taken place more-or-less unnoticed in an estimated 5,000–6,000 small and medium-sized communities of the southern United States (Cohen, 1974). This was precisely the geographic locale to which the Social Science Statement had been addressed. On this point, the statement appears prophetic indeed.

The statement supplemented the above comments with others that raised the possibility of positive attitudinal outcomes and enumerated the conditions under which these might be anticipated. Gerard characterizes the applicability of these conditions to public schools as "extraordinarily quixotic." In view of his emphasis on the misleading nature of this material, the relevant section of the Social Science Statement is quoted here:

> Under certain circumstances, desegregation not only proceeds without major difficulties, but has been observed to lead to the emergence of more favorable attitudes and friendlier relations between races. Relevant studies may be cited with respect to housing, employment, the armed services and merchant marine, recreation agencies, and general community life.
>
> Much depends, however, on the circumstances under which members of previously segregated groups first come in contact with others in unsegregated situations. Available evidence suggests, first, that there is less likelihood of unfriendly relations when the change is simultaneously introduced into all units of a social institution to

which it is applicable—e.g., all of the schools in a school system or all of the shops in a given factory.

The available evidence also suggests the importance of consistent and firm enforcement of the new policy by those in authority. It indicates also the importance of such factors as: the absence of competition for a limited number of facilities or benefits; the possibility of contacts which permit individuals to learn about one another as individuals; and the possibility of equivalence of positions and functions among all of the participants within the unsegregated situation. These conditions can generally be satisfied in a number of situations, as in the armed services, public housing developments, and public schools. ("The Effect of Segregation," 1953, p. 437)

Gerard presents reasons for believing that educational authorities (e.g., school boards, principals, and teachers) will not support desegregation, notes the traditional competitive atmosphere of classrooms, describes the black–white achievement gap as an indicator of unequal status, and pictures self-segregation within classrooms that prevents learning about members of other ethnic groups as individuals. There is certainly no reason to doubt the accuracy of Gerard's description of the conditions of his own study and of many other instances of desegregation. These conditions, of course, reflect the absence of just those circumstances that the Social Science Statement informed the justices were necessary for the emergence of more favorable attitudes and friendlier relations. On the other hand, it is equally accurate to say that desegregated schools are sometimes characterized by conditions quite different from those Gerard describes. For example, an estimate based only on contacts made by the Center for the Social Organization of Schools at Johns Hopkins University indicated that a minimum of 14,000 teachers had gone so far as to build interracial cooperation into their classrooms through the use of interracial learning teams (Hollifield & Slavin, 1983). Although many of these teachers were individual volunteers, others had been involved through programs initiated by their school districts. The latter changed their instructional methods as part of an institutional change rather than on the basis of personal convictions. The significance of this is that, once school district leaders decide to support desegregation, more effective classroom procedures and extracurricular programs can be quickly put into practice.

To the extent that the Social Science Statement's sentence "These conditions can generally be satisfied in . . . public schools" is taken as a prediction that they *would* characterize school desegregation, it should be pointed out again that the social scientists in 1954 had in mind desegregation that would integrate black students into their neighborhood schools. To look backward, as Gerard does, at conditions of desegregation that have prevailed during a decade of metropolitan resistance to two-way busing of students away from their neighborhood schools brings in considerations that could not possibly have affected the 1954 statement. It may be this misunderstanding regarding the nature of the desegregation being talked about that accounts for some of Gerard's misrepresentations of that document.

Given that the conditions under which school desegregation has occurred have varied widely, what have been the effects on racial attitudes and relationships? Of the reviews of this literature published between 1970 and 1978, one reported primarily positive results (Weinberg, 1977). Weinberg reviewed two groups of studies. The first dealt with schools that became interracial by means other than planned desegregation. On the basis of 46 studies of such schools carried out in the period 1940–1975, the review concluded "with high confidence that interracial interaction usually leads to the development of positive racial attitudes" (p. 211). A second group of 39 studies were conducted in schools that had undergone planned desegregation. The reviews of these findings showed "positive racial attitudes among blacks and/or whites in most of the cases" (p. 212).

However, six other reviewers judged the research outcome to be unclear. One of these, Carithers (1970), characterized 15 studies of interracial contact, cleavage, and attitude change as having "seemingly inconsistent results" (p. 38). Another, St. John (1975), described the attitudinal outcomes of 23 studies of mixed-race schools as being inconsistent but with negative outcomes being somewhat more frequent than positive ones. In 17 studies in which the criterion variable was sociometric choice rather than attitude, she concluded that the results showed predominantly no effect or a mixture of positive and negative effects. The third reviewer (Cohen, 1975) examined 24 studies involving interracial schools in the period 1968–1974; only two of these dealt solely with nonvoluntary desegregation. She reported the same mixed results for racial attitude and acceptance as had been found by St. John.

A fourth reviewer (Schofield, 1978) cited 14 studies of the attitudinal outcomes of attending mixed-race schools as yielding few firm conclusions. She reached the same conclusion when the outcome variable was intergroup behavior rather than attitude. The fifth reviewer, McConahay (1978), examined studies conducted since 1960 on the effect of planned school desegregation on attitudes and concluded that methodological problems render them all uninterpretable. When he examined studies in which the outcome variables included interracial behavior and/or friendship choice, he found only four studies in which the methodology was sufficiently sound to warrant serious attention. He judged the combined outcome of these four studies to be positive. The sixth reviewer, Stephan (1978), also decided that no firm conclusions could be drawn from the 18 studies that he had examined on the effects of multiracial schools on attitudes. In these studies, he observed that an increase in white prejudice toward blacks was found somewhat more frequently than a decrease.

However, as described in the next section, when desegregated classrooms are characterized by the conditions of contact described in the Social Science Statement, the race relations outcomes are quite different from those summarized in these reviews.

THE SOCIAL SCIENCE STATEMENT AS A CONTRIBUTION TO PUBLIC POLICY

In addition to describing the content of the Social Science Statement as "well-meaning rhetoric," Gerard believes that it may have been damaging both to society and to social science. With respect to the former, he writes, "Perhaps we should forgive them for their short-sightedness. The only problem is that the legal doctrine that has been built into *Brown* is now cast in concrete, and its application to large urban *de facto* segregated districts is resulting in resegregation of many of those districts as a result of white flight."[7] With respect to the damage to social science, he says, "Social scientists have only lost credibility in the process of essentially entering the political arena prematurely. I can imagine what the David Stockmans of the world are saying about social scientists."

As a protection against future premature contributions to public policy, Gerard recommends that social scientists incorporate in their work the research-and-development (R&D) stage often encountered in the hard sciences. He illustrates this by noting that ideas generated from basic research (as, e.g., in crystallography) are developed for application to real-world physical problems (as, e.g., in solid-state devices for the communications industry). As this process applies to school desegregation, Gerard elaborates as follows:

> This can only be done with careful research on such things as the effect of performance

[7]The extent to which school desegregation is a cause of white flight has been extensively studied. Conclusions very different from those stated by Gerard are found in Farley (1975), Orfield (1976), Pettigrew and Green (1976), and Rossell (1975–1976).

on self-esteem and vice versa, on the effects of social categorization on prejudice and vice versa, on the effects of competition and cooperation on intergroup attitudes and vice versa, and so on. We already have some rudimentary knowledge of these problems. But then, we have to take what we know and try to apply it, on a small scale at first, to the school setting with a laboratorylike approach in which we use the best scientific minds available. In the process, we will be forced to go back to the drawing board many times until we develop a program that will really work.

There can be little disagreement about the value of the R&D model when more effective methods of implementing programs are needed and when circumstances allow time and provide resources for their development. However, it is somewhat ironic to note that one of the best examples of application of the model has been the research on the facilitation of effective school desegregation. Building on laboratory research in such areas as cooperation and competition, the motivating effects of group membership and commitment, and the contact hypothesis, three research groups and a number of individuals have field-tested innovative methods of restructuring classroom learning assignments and rewards for academic performance.[8] All use small learning teams, heterogeneous in ethnic group and ability level. All also use classroom tasks that make the team members interdependent and thus induce intrateam helping. Most reward the teams as a whole for their members' cumulative performance. Some distribute rewards on the basis of competition between teams, whereas others do so on the basis of each team's success in reaching a teacher-set performance standard.

Classroom experiments in desegregated schools have compared these methods with traditional methods used in control classrooms that are similar in race and ability. The results have been impressive. The self-esteem of minority students has been measured in seven studies, positive results being found in five of the seven (e.g., Blaney, Stephan, Rosenfield, Aronson, & Sikes, 1977; Geffner, 1978). Gains in school achievement have been measured in 15 studies; in 11 of these, the classrooms with learning teams showed significantly higher achievement than control classes (e.g., Edwards, DeVries, & Snyder, 1972; Slavin & Oickle, 1981). Race relations have been measured in 13 studies. The race relations measure most frequently used in these studies has been the proportion of cross-racial friendship choices. In 11 of the 13 studies, race relations have been significantly more favorable among children taught in cooperating student teams (e.g., Johnson & Johnson, 1981; Slavin, 1979).

Two recent reviews have summarized the results of classroom research on interracial learning teams (Johnson, Johnson, & Maruyama, 1984; Slavin, 1983). Gerard refers to this work but downgrades its potential significance by referring to it as "tentative baby steps." When compared to the small amount learned from the scores of redundant studies of desegregation in schools using traditional teaching methods, a more appropriate metaphor might be that of a giant step forward. To say this, however, is not to underestimate the immense task of incorporating cooperative learning into the schools.

The constructive potential of work such as that described above has led to an alternative definition of the R&D model as applied to school desegregation:

> It is regrettably the case that social scientists have generally responded to the challenge of school desegregation in a reactive rather than an innovative fashion. Their role has been to evaluate the outcome of desegregation experiences just as these have occurred. They have not, by contrast, proposed and studied alternative methods by which school desegregation might be carried out.

[8]One subset of such studies was conducted at the Center for the Social Organization of Schools, Johns Hopkins University, by Slavin, DeVries, and their associates. Another subset was carried out by Aronson and his co-workers at the University of Texas and the University of California, Santa Cruz. A third subset is the work of David and Roger Johnson and associates at the University of Minnesota.

> An innovative orientation to school desegregation, as opposed to a purely reactive one, would ask whether a given teaching method, or a particular social arrangement in the classroom, or some other factor, might yield positive outcomes. In other words, an innovative approach would initiate and study the effects of alternative strategies for implementing integration in the schools. (Weigel, Wiser, & Cook, 1975, p. 220)

It should be noted, however, that the value of the R&D model for the development of public policy is limited. It is most useful at the implementation stage of new policy. If society has decided, for example, to care for the mentally ill in community rather than institutional settings, or to educate the handicapped in regular rather than special classes, or to educate minority and majority group children in the same schools, it needs the assistance of social science in developing the most effective methods for the new way of doing things. Even under such circumstances, other factors may determine the nature of policy implementation methods before R&D has a chance to play a role. For example, a political leader, wishing to receive credit for a new human-service policy, may insist on initiating a program before anything can be learned about the relative effectiveness of alternative procedures for carrying it out.

However, at other stages of policy formation or change, other roles for social scientists will be more appropriate. For example, policy decisions must often be made under conditions in which both relevant facts and relevant values are multifaceted and uncertain. Here, the social scientist's contribution is to guide policymakers to the most satisfactory decision-making process (Hammond, McClelland, & Mumpower, 1980).

Sometimes policy formation or policy change can be guided by answers to critical questions. When concerned decision-makers are willing both to wait for answers and to provide resources for getting them, social scientists can often be helpful. Such was the case in the early 1970s when concern about the effect of TV violence on children led Congress and the Surgeon General to commission new research on the question. The results of the new research played a part in obtaining a commitment from TV networks to reduce the amount of violence in programs, particularly during children's viewing hours. Under circumstances like these, the social science role is again to provide research results—but not in the R&D framework.

In still other cases, either policy consideration may be moving too fast to wait for new research, or new research is not possible because of practical considerations. In such circumstances, a body of relevant knowledge may be available from which clear inferences can be drawn about a proposed policy decision. For example, a recent U.S. Supreme Court decision on the minimum size of juries contained a 10-page discussion of relevant legal and social science literature on group size and jury size (Tanke & Tanke, 1979). Such events remind us that we must neither underestimate the potential value of social science knowledge to significant societal decisions nor overlook our obligation to make that knowledge available when and where it is needed.[9] Is it "entering the political arena prematurely" to add such knowledge to the other factors that policymakers are considering? The social scientists who framed and signed the 1954 Social Science Statement to the Supreme Court thought not.

---

[9]How to accomplish this in the area of judicial decision-making presents social scientists with ethical dilemmas as well as with problems of how to communicate scientific knowledge in such a way that it will be accepted, understood, and applied. The adversary system of introducing evidence in litigation encourages the selection of favorable facts and the omission of unfavorable ones. The presentation of conflicting evidence by opposing experts weakens confidence in the objectivity of their testimony and may cause it to be disregarded. Alternative procedures for providing policy-relevant information to the courts—as well as to legislatures and executive agencies—are badly needed. Three such procedures—"blue ribbon" scientific committees, science courts, and standing expert panels—were discussed by Hennigan, Flay, and Cook (1980).

Gerard's fear that social scientists have lost credibility seems out of touch with recent developments. Although he was certainly correct in implying that "the David Stockmans of the world" disparage the social sciences, the last decade has seen the application of social science research to an extraordinary range of policy questions. The eight volumes of the *Evaluation Studies Review Annual* detail the application of research methods to policy and program in such diverse areas as juvenile delinquency, education, mental health services, criminal justice, physical health, labor, income maintenance, housing, safety, energy conservation, substance abuse, environmental protection, and financial policy. Almost all of this research has been supported by public funds. Moreover, surveys of a wide spectrum of government policymakers have shown that they believe that social science serves to enlighten their understanding of the problems with which they deal (Caplan, Morrison, & Stambaugh, 1975; Knorr, 1977; Patton, 1978; Rich, 1977). These developments indicate that the role of social science in the development and implementation of public policy is steadily growing and that, rather than losing credibility, social scientists are gaining greater acceptance from the elected officials and civil servants responsible for a wide variety of policy actions. Nevertheless, the social science potential in policy formulation and implementation remain largely unused. (For a thorough exploration of the causes and possible remedies, see Weiss, 1977.)

SUMMARY

In 1954, when the U.S. Supreme Court was considering whether state laws enforcing school segregation were unconstitutional, it had before it a Social Science Statement summarizing the evidence regarding the psychological effects on children of government-mandated segregation. There are grounds for believing that the Court made use of the statement in formulating its decision to ban state laws requiring or permitting school segregation (*Brown v. Board of Education*, 1954). Because this decision has been widely regarded as the critical final step in abandoning legal and judicial support for racial discrimination in the United States, the statement has occupied a prominent spot in the history of psychology.

In Chapter 11, Gerard asserts that the Social Science Statement's central conclusions have been "questioned," alleges that it "myopically" omitted critical information about the difficulties of desegregation, and attributes to it discredited predictions about the consequences of school desegregation. In this chapter, the basis for questioning the statement's conclusions is shown to be untenable, the "myopic" omissions are shown to be irrelevant to the constitutional issue before the Supreme Court in 1954, and the discredited predictions are shown to be missing from the statement altogether.

Most relevant to a defensible inference from the Social Science Statement regarding the consequences of desegregation are studies in which desegregation begins in kindergarten or first grade or studies that cover the entire duration of students' schooling. The results of such studies have provided the most consistent evidence of the advantages of desegregated as compared to segregated schools.

In contrast, most studies of school desegregation have been of quite limited duration and have, of necessity, studied the self-esteem, achievement, and race relations of children who began their education in *de facto* segregated schools and later entered desegregated schools. Although such studies are of interest, little can be predicted about their outcomes from the content of the Social Science Statement. The results of such studies have been reviewed many times, both by traditional methods and by meta-analyses. These reviews are summarized in this article. The conclusions and interpretations reached are different from those stated by Gerard. It appears that he has overgeneralized the disappointing results of his own study (Gerard & Miller, 1975).

In contrast to Gerard's view, this article calls attention to an evident increase in the credibility of the social sciences as reflected by the extraordinary range of policy questions to which social science research is now being applied. This development suggests that the social science role in public policy has been steadily growing and will continue to grow in the future. Classroom experiments have demonstrated that self-esteem, school achievement, and race relations can be improved by desegregation procedures that are based on established psychological theory. A meaningful role for social scientists in the future would be to conduct research in desegregated schools that might help to maximize the effectiveness of such procedures. In contrast, a meaningful role for social scientists in 1954 was to relate already available knowledge of the consequences of segregation to the policy decision being made at the time.

REFERENCES

Blaney, N. T., Stephan, S., Rosenfield, D., Aronson, E., & Sikes, J. (1977). Interdependence in the classroom: A field study. *Journal of Educational Psychology, 69*(2), 121–128.

Bolling v. Sharpe, 347 U.S. 497 (1954).

Bradley, L. A., & Bradley, G. W. (1977). The academic achievement of black students in desegregated schools: A critical review. *Review of Educational Research, 47*, 399–449.

Brown v. Board of Education of Topeka, 347 U.S. 483 (1954).

Cahn, E. (1955). Jurisprudence. *New York University Law Review, 30*, 150–159.

Caplan, N., Morrison, A., & Stambaugh, R. (1975). *The use of social science knowledge in policy decisions at the national level.* Ann Arbor, MI: Institute for Social Research.

Carithers, M. W. (1970). School desegregation and racial cleavage, 1954–1970: A review of the literature, *Journal of Social Issues, 26*(4), 25–47.

Christmas, J. J. (1973). Self-concept and attitudes. In K. S. Miller & R. M. Dreger (Eds.), *Comparative studies of blacks and whites in the United States.* New York: Seminar Press.

Cohen, D. K. (1974). The equity package: Cities, families and schools, *Society, 12*(1), 39–40.

Cohen, E. G. (1975). The effects of desegregation on race relations. *Law and Contemporary Problems, 39*(1), 271–299.

Cook, T. D. (1983). *What have black children gained academically from school desegregation: Examination of the meta-analytic evidence* (Report to National Institute of Education). Evanston, IL: Northwestern University.

Crain, R. L., & Mahard, R. E. (1978). Desegregation and black achievement: A review of the research. *Law and Contemporary Problems, 42*(3), 17–56.

Crain, R. L., & Mahard, R. E. (1981). Minority achievement: Policy implications of research. In W. D. Hawley (Ed.), *Effective school desegregation: Equity, quality and feasibility.* Beverly Hills, CA: Sage.

Crain, R. L., & Mahard, R. E. (1982). *Desegregation plans that raise black achievement: A review of the research.* Santa Monica, CA: Rand Corporation.

Crain, R. L., & Mahard, R. E. (1983). The effect of research methodology on desegregation achievement studies: A meta-analysis. *American Journal of Sociology, 88*, 839–854.

Crain, R. L., Mahard, R. E., & Narot, R. (1982). *Making desegregation work.* Cambridge, MA: Ballinger.

Dai, B. (1948). Problems of personality development among Negro children. In C. Kluckhohn, H. Murray, & D. Schneider (Eds.), *Personality in nature, society and culture.* New York: Knopf.

Datcher, E., Savage, J. E., Jr., & Checkosky, S. F. (1974). School type, grade, sex and race of experimenter as determinants of racial preference and awareness in black and white children. *Journal of the Social and Behavioral Sciences, 20*, 41–49.

Davis, A. (1939). The socialization of the American Negro child and adolescent. *Journal of Negro Education, 8*, 264–274.

Deutscher, M., & Chein, I. (1948). The psychological effects of enforced segregation: A survey of social science opinion. *Journal of Psychology, 26*, 259–287.

Edwards, K. J., DeVries, D. L., & Snyder, J. P. (1972). Games and teams: A winning combination. *Simulation and Games, 3*, 247–269.

The effect of segregation and the consequences of desegregation: A social science statement. Appendix to appellants' briefs: *Brown v. Board of Education of Topeka, Kansas* (1953). *Minnesota Law Review, 37*, 427–439.

Epps, E. G. (1975). Impact of school desegregation on aspirations, self-concepts and other aspects of personality. *Law and Contemporary Problems, 39*(2), 300–313.

Epps, E. G. (1978). Impact of school desegregation on the self-evaluation and achievement orientation of minority group children. *Law and Contemporary Problems, 42*(3), 57–76.

Farley, R. (1975). School integration and white flight. In G. Orfield (Ed.), *Symposium on school desegregation and white flight*. Washington, DC: Center for National Policy Review, Catholic University Law School.

Frazier, E. (1949). *The Negro in the United States*. New York: Macmillan.

Geffner, R. (1978). *The effects of interdependent learning on self-esteem, inter-ethnic relations, and intra-ethnic attitudes of elementary school children: A field experiment*. Unpublished doctoral dissertation, University of California, Santa Cruz.

Gerard, H. B., & Miller, N. (1975). *School desegregation*. New York: Plenum Press.

Glass, E. V., McGaw, B., & Smith, M. L. (1981). *Meta-analysis in social research*. Beverly Hills, CA: Sage.

Hammond, K. R., McClelland, G. H., & Mumpower, J. L. (1980). *Human judgment and decision-making: Theories, methods and procedures*. New York: Praeger.

Hennigan, K. M., Flay, B. R., & Cook, T. D. (1980). "Give me the facts": Some suggestions for using social science knowledge in deciding on national policy. In R. F. Kidd & M. J. Saks (Eds.), *Advances in applied social psychology* (Vol. 1). Hillsdale, NJ: Erlbaum.

Hollifield, J., & Slavin, R. E. (1983). Disseminating student team learning through federally funded programs: Appropriate technology, appropriate channels. *Knowledge, 4*, 576–589.

Hraba, J., & Grant, G. B. (1970). Black is beautiful: A reexamination of racial preference and identification. *Journal of Personality and Social Psychology, 16*, 398–402.

Johnson, D. W., & Johnson, R. T. (1981). Effects of cooperative and individualistic learning experiences on inter-ethnic interaction. *Journal of Educational Psychology, 73*, 444–449.

Johnson, D. W., Johnson, R. T., & Maruyama, G. (1984). Goal interdependence and interpersonal attraction in heterogeneous classrooms: A meta-analysis. In N. Miller & M. B. Brewer (Eds.), *Groups in contact: The psychology of desegregation*. New York: Academic Press.

Jones, L. V. (1984). White-black achievement differences: The narrowing gap. *American Psychologist, 39*, 1207–1213.

Kardiner, A., & Ovesey, L. (1951). *The mark of oppression*. New York: Norton.

Klineberg, O. (1935). *Negro intelligence and selective migration*. New York: Columbia University Press.

Kluger, R. (1976). *Simple justice*. New York: Knopf.

Knorr, K. (1977). Policymakers' use of social science knowledge: Symbolic or instrumental? In C. H. Weiss (Ed.), *Using social research in public policymaking*. Lexington, MA: D. C. Heath.

Krol, R. A. (1978). A meta-analysis of comparative research on the effects of desegregation on academic achievement. *Dissertation Abstracts International, 39*, 6011. (University Microfilms No. 69-07, 962)

McConahay, J. B. (1978). The effects of school desegregation upon student racial attitudes and behavior: A critical review of the literature and a prolegomenon to future research. *Law and Contemporary Problems, 42*(3), 77–107.

Myrdal, G. (1944). *An American dilemma*. New York: Harper & Row.

National Assessment of Educational Progress. (1981). *Three national assessments of reading: Changes in performance, 1970–80*. Denver, CO: Education Commission of the States.

Orfield, G. (1973). School integration and its academic critics. *Civil Rights Digest, 5*(5), 3–10.

Orfield, G. (1976). White flight research. *Social Policy, 6*(4), 24–31.

Patton, M. Q. (1978). *Utilization-focused evaluation*. Beverly Hills, CA: Sage.

Pettigrew, T. F., & Green, R. L. (1976). School desegregation in large cities: A critique of the Coleman "white flight" thesis. *Harvard Educational Review, 46*(1), 1–53.

Porter, J. R., & Washington, R. E. (1979). Black identity and self-esteem: A review of studies of black self-concept, 1968–1978. *Annual Review of Sociology, 5*, 53–74.

Poussaint, A. F. (1974, August). Building a strong self-image in the black child. *Ebony, 29*, 138–143.

Powell, G. J., & Fuller, M. (1970). Self-concept and school desegregation. *American Journal of Orthopsychiatry, 40*, 303–304.

Rich, R. F. (1977). Uses of social science information by federal bureaucrats: Knowledge for action versus knowledge for understanding. In C. H. Weiss (Ed.), *Using social research in public policymaking*. Lexington, MA: D. C. Heath.

Rosen, P. L. (1972). *The Supreme Court and social science*. Urbana: University of Illinois Press.

Rossell, C. H. (1975–1976). School desegregation and white flight. *Political Science Quarterly, 90*, 675–695.

St. John, N. (1975). *School desegregation: Outcomes for children*. New York: Wiley.

Schofield, J. W. (1978). School desegregation and intergroup relations. In D. Bar-Tal & L. Saxe (Eds.), *The social psychology of education*. Washington, DC: Hemisphere Press.

Slavin, R. E. (1979). Effects of biracial learning teams on crossracial friendships. *Journal of Educational Psychology, 71*, 381–387.

Slavin, R. E. (1983). *Cooperative learning*. New York: Longman.

Slavin, R. E., & Oickle, E. (1981). Effects of cooperative learning teams on student achievement and race relations: Treatment by race interactions. *Sociology of Education, 54*, 174–180.

Spurlock, J. (1973). Some consequences of racism for children. In C. V. Willie, D. M. Cramer, & B. S. Brown (Eds.), *Racism and mental health*. Pittsburgh: University of Pittsburgh Press.

Stephan, W. G. (1978). School desegregation: An evaluation of predictions made in *Brown v. Board of Education*. *Psychological Bulletin, 85*, 217–238.

Swann v. Charlotte-Mecklenberg Board of Education, 402 U.S. 1 (1971).

Tanke, E. D., & Tanke, T. J. (1979). Getting off a slippery slope: Social science in the judicial process. *American Psychologist, 34*, 1130–1138.

Taylor, W. L. (1981). *Brown* in perspective. In W. D. Hawley (Ed.), *Effective school desegregation: Equity, quality and feasibility*. Beverly Hills, CA: Sage.

van den Haag, E. (1957). Prejudice about prejudice. In R. Ross & E. van den Haag (Eds.), *The fabric of society*. New York: Harcourt, Brace & World.

Weigel, R. A., Wiser, P. L., & Cook, S. W. (1975). The impact of cooperative learning experiences on cross-ethnic relations and attitudes. *Journal of Social Issues, 31*(1), 219–244.

Weinberg, M. (1977). *Minority students: A research appraisal*. Washington, DC: National Institute of Education, Department of Health, Education, and Welfare.

Weiss, C. H. (1977). *Using social research in public policy making*. Lexington, MA: D. C. Heath.

Winnick, R. H., & Taylor, J. A. (1977). Racial preference—36 years later. *Journal of Social Psychology, 102*, 157–158.

Wortman, P. M., & Bryant, F. B. (1985). School desegregation and black achievement: An integrative review. *Sociological Methods and Research, 13*, 289–324.

Wylie, R. C. (1979). *The self concept: Theory and research on selected topics* (Vol. 2, rev. ed.). Lincoln: University of Nebraska Press.

Zirkel, P. A. (1971). Self-concept and the "disadvantage" of ethnic group membership and mixture. *Review of Educational Research, 41*(3), 211–225.

B. Busing

13

School Busing
A Time for Change

David J. Armor

It is conventional to mark 1954, the year of the U.S. Supreme Court's famous *Brown* decision, as the beginning of the great school busing controversy. Indeed, that landmark case spelled the doom of the dual school system, as well as the end of many other discriminatory policies and practices against blacks and other minority groups. But at the time of *Brown*, the battle was in the South, which challenged the Court's basic goal of ending separate schools for blacks and whites. Could anyone have foreseen that the greatest controversy would not be over the goal of *Brown*, but over the remedies imposed to attain that goal, especially school busing? This controversy over busing has lasted for almost two decades, touching every part of the nation, and is still smoldering in many cities today.

The school busing controversy proper began with the Supreme Court's *Swann* decision in 1970, which for the first time permitted a lower court to order mandatory busing away from neighborhood schools. A less-noticed but equally important policy approved by *Swann* was the use of racial balance formulas in the design of a desegregation plan. Although upheld only as a "starting point" for a plan, soon racial balance was being embraced by desegregation experts and other courts as the fundamental definition of desegregation and its ultimate criterion of success.

The combination of racial balance goals and mandatory busing has had an enormous impact on creating, sustaining, and shaping the controversy over school desegregation. In fact, I will go further and argue that this particular combination of means and ends has led to school desegregation policies that have been counterproductive, if not self-destructive, in many school districts. Unless more reasonable alternatives are fashioned and promoted, the original aims of the desegregation movement could well be lost.

This chapter attempts to support the argument by reviewing recent developments in the school desegregation arena, particularly those affecting remedial policies such as busing. Drawing on recent court actions as well as new research findings, the chapter evaluates three interconnected issues whose outcomes will most likely determine the long-term viability of school desegregation goals and remedies.

The first issue, already mentioned, is the emergence of racial balance formulas in the definition of desegregation and in the monitoring of its success. The second concerns the

DAVID J. ARMOR • National Policy Analysts, 5006 Klingle Street, N.W., Washington, DC 20016.

efficacy of mandatory busing, a remedy imposed, in large part, to fulfill the racial balance goal. The critical question here has been the extent to which opposition to busing and "white flight" have undermined the attainment of desegregation as originally envisioned.

The third issue, likewise, has been influenced by the second: the expansion of segregation litigation and remedies to include both city and suburban areas. These metropolitan cases, as they are called, are a response to the dwindling white populations in central-city school districts. Ironically, this condition has been greatly exacerbated by mandatory busing, the very remedy advocated by most courts and many experts as the only way to attain desegregation.

It appears now, more clearly than before, that the future course of school desegregation—if, indeed, it has such a course—will be played out on the metropolitan stage. The demographic realities in our larger cities, where most minorities live, leave no other alternative. The concluding question is whether past and present court decisions offer opportunities for realistic and feasible metropolitan desegregation plans, or whether they have poisoned the well, so to speak, by creating legal obstacles that will hamper or prevent the development of such remedies for many years to come.

REMEDY AND DEFINITIONS OF DESEGREGATION

Charting the changes in desegregation definitions and remedies is a fascinating study of the interplay between judicial policy and social science research. If we consider one case at a time, the changes are incremental and carefully crafted to be consistent with prior cases. Further, lower courts always state allegiance to the principals enunciated in existing higher-court opinions. When one compares the desegregation remedies imposed during the 1970s with the explicit conclusions of *Brown*, however, a comprehensible nexus is absent. A link is provided only by the gradual evolution of novel remedial theories from a series of cases and policy studies during the 1960s.

INITIAL APPROACHES

The clear constitutional violation found in *Brown* was the officially sanctioned assignment of black and white students to separate schools; that is, segregation was defined as the "dual" school system. From some legal perspectives, a proper remedy for this violation, or "de-"segregation, would be nullification of the official action and the assignment of students to school on a nonracial basis. Indeed, similar language was used in the decision.

In the concept of nonracial student assignment, at least two methods would appear to qualify as desegregation: allowing students to attend any school of their choice or assigning students on a geographic basis, or a combination of both. Unfortunately, the Supreme Court has never explicitly defined the term *nonracial assignment*, and in fact, such straightforward remedies have rarely been approved by that body.

The Supreme Court did not discuss specific remedial issues in the first *Brown* opinion, other than in a footnote reference to nonracial student assignment. After special hearings, remedy was taken up in a subsequent decision about 1 year later, commonly known as *Brown II* (1955). Interestingly, again, no specific remedies or guidelines were offered in this second opinion, in spite of its stated purpose. Only the broadest of principles were put forth, including a mandate "to achieve a system of determining admission to the public schools on a nonracial basis." This is merely a restatement of language in the first opinion, and as such, it hardly presaged the types of mandatory busing remedies that became commonplace 15 years later. On the contrary, it can be fairly argued that mandatory busing to achieve racial ratios is a violation of the nonracial prescription.

The Supreme Court held that school districts should design their own desegregation plans, taking into account a number of practical consideration, including facilities and "revision of . . . attendance areas into compact units." The lower courts, being in the best position to evaluate local conditions, were granted broad authority to review these plans and to judge their adequacy "to effectuate a transition to a racially nondiscriminatory school system."

It did not help matters, of course, when many southern school districts defied court orders by refusing black children entrance into white schools, or by devising any number of tactics to maintain separate schools, such as creating new black and white school districts. On the other hand, many southern districts did adopt open enrollment policies (known as *freedom-of-choice plans*) or redrew school attendance zones on a geographic basis.

It was readily apparent, however, that residential patterns, together with white reluctance to attend black schools, meant that these types of remedies would have a limited impact. Policies that were racially neutral in the literal sense would not guarantee that most black and white children would go to school together. Put another way, ending official segregation was not desegregation in the sense of eliminating predominantly black and predominantly white schools.

REMEDY IN THE 1960s

The major thrust of desegregation plans throughout most of the 1960s was to open white schools to black students, mainly through freedom-of-choice plans. Toward the end of that decade, two significant events occurred that were to have far-reaching consequences. The first was the Supreme Court's *Green* decision in 1968 and its famous "root and branch" holding; the second was the U.S. Commission on Civil Rights report on "Racial Isolation in the Public Schools" (1967), which gave high visibility and important status to a social science definition of segregation.

Green was a significant portent of mandatory busing. First, it clarified remedy to the extent of ruling out freedom of choice, stating that such a plan is "not an end in itself." Although the Court did not declare freedom-of-choice plans unconstitutional, it did declare them unacceptable when other techniques were available, such as zoning, "promising speedier and more effective conversion to a unitary, nonracial school system."

Further, a school board had an "affirmative duty" to eliminate racial discrimination "root and branch," and "to come forward with a plan that promises realistically to work, and promises realistically to work *now*." In judging effectiveness, the school board was ordered to design a plan that would "convert promptly to a system without a 'white' school and a 'Negro' school, but just schools."

Although general terms like *nonracial system* were also used in this opinion, for the first time the Supreme Court made it clear that remedy was concerned not only with ending official acts of separation, but also with an affirmative duty to eliminate predominantly black and white schools. In other words, for *de jure* dual school systems it is presumed that the official policy was the predominant cause of segregation, and therefore, a remedy must also be judged by its impact on racial composition. This new "results" test begged the question of whether or not factors other than official policies could contribute to segregation. Although this question was less important in the South, it would become a major dilemma for the courts when desegregation cases moved North.

The coming northern dilemma was foreseen by many civil rights groups, including the U.S. Commission on Civil Rights. Its comprehensive study on *Racial Isolation in the Public Schools* (1967), published shortly before the *Green* decision, made a strong case for extending desegregation to northern cities with *de facto* segregation. Just as *Green* had impact on judicial remedies, the *Racial Isolation* report set the agenda for school desegregation policy at all levels of government.

The key finding in the report was that segregation has harmful effects on black students regardless of whether its causes are *de jure* or *de facto*:

> The facts in this report confirm that racial isolation, whether or not sanctioned by law, damages Negro students by adversely affecting both their attitudes and achievement. . . . These [damages] cannot be erased without school integration. (pp. 190–191)

The report advocated a uniform standard for defining racially isolated schools. Noting that black attitudes and performance were poorer in majority-black schools than in majority-white schools, and that majority-black schools tended to have unstable enrollments, the report recommended that schools exceeding 50% black enrollment be considered racially imbalanced or isolated.

Believing that the courts were likely to deal with racial isolation only when it arose from official policy, and therefore that racial segregation in northern cities might not come under court jurisdiction, the report recommended further that Congress eliminate racial isolation by approving this standard for the entire nation and by giving the states the power and funding to enforce it.

Congress never implemented this policy, but within a few years the issue became largely academic. The federal courts were about to expand both liability and remedy to a scale never anticipated, finding segregation and ordering massive busing plans throughout the nation, including many northern cities.

Both *Green* and the commission report gave new meaning to desegregation remedies by putting the major focus on racial composition outcomes. But even these important and influential actions stopped short of racial balance formulas or mandatory busing away from neighborhood schools. Indeed, the commission report explicitly defined a desegregated school in absolute terms, without regard to the racial composition of an entire school district.

BUSING IN THE 1970s

Following the *Green* decision, numerous southern school districts that had adopted freedom of choice or geographic zoning plans—and whose schools were still racially imbalanced—were taken back to court for further remedy hearings. A case in point was the Charlotte-Mecklenburg school district, a large countywide district in North Carolina that had desegregated using geographic zoning and a freedom-of-choice transfer plan. On order from the district court, the local school board designed a new plan, enlarging the geographic zoning to increase desegregation and adopting a minority-to-majority (M-to-M) voluntary transfer plan. Unlike freedom of choice, M-to-M plans enhance desegregation by allowing only transfers that improve racial composition.

Citing the mandate of *Green*, the North Carolina district court rejected major portions of the local board plan, which left numerous predominantly black and white schools at the elementary level, and adopted instead a plan prepared by a court-appointed expert. The court plan called for substantial pairing and clustering of elementary schools, together with expanded cross-county busing, to attain an approximate 70% white and 30% black enrollment in each school—the districtwide percentage.

In justifying this large-scale busing plan, the district court invoked findings of intentional segregation in housing, making it necessary to reassign children to schools far outside their neighborhoods:

> The present location of white schools in white areas and of black schools in black areas is the result of a varied group of elements of public and private action. . . . There is so much state action embedded in and shaping these events that the resulting segregation is not innocent or 'de facto.' (Swann, 1970)

The Charlotte case was not the first to raise these issues nor the first to invoke racial balance criteria, but it was the first to be fully reviewed by the U.S. Supreme Court. In its ground-breaking Swann decision of 1971, the High Court upheld the basic findings and orders of the district court, thus sending desegregation remedies into new, uncharted, and eventually turbulent waters.

Interestingly, the Swann decision acknowledged the finding of the lower court that residential segregation resulted in part from state actions, which were translated into school segregation by neighborhood school policies. But the Supreme Court did not amplify or explore this causal theory to any substantial extent, other than saying that such a showing could be taken into account in fashioning a remedy. Thus, the new law established by Swann did not clearly depend on a finding of de jure housing segregation. The role of residential segregation was not addressed explicitly until a series of metropolitan decisions later in the decade.

Instead, the Court noted the difficulty that district and appellate courts were having in devising remedies under feasibility standards and stated that it was time to "amplify guidelines" for desegregation. Four major guidelines on remedy were formulated by the Court:

1. Racial balance goals, based on the districtwide percentage of blacks, were found acceptable as "starting points" for a plan, with the caveat that constitutionally required desegregation "does not mean that every school in every community must always reflect the racial composition of the school system as a whole."

2. Predominantly one-race schools were not in themselves unconstitutional, but school authorities should be concerned with their elimination and would be required to "satisfy the court that their racial composition is not the result of present or past discriminatory actions."

3. Plans to remedy past discrimination did not have to be racially neutral, and therefore noncontiguous school attendance zones, such as pairing, clustering, and satelliting, were within "the broad remedial powers of a court."

4. Assignment of children did not have to be to the school nearest their home, and mandatory busing could be used to implement a cross-town student reassignment plan.

The most striking feature of these guidelines is the final abandonment of a fundamental principle of Brown, namely, that schools must be organized on the basis of nonracial student assignment. For many years, the Court had struggled with the dilemma posed by the conflict between nonracial assignment and desegregation. Because of residential segregation and the operation of personal preferences, not all of which can be ascribed to the dual school system, the Court came to the ultimate realization that truly nonracial assignment methods would not eliminate predominantly black and white schools.

In Swann, the Court finally made a choice and came down on the side of desegregation outcomes. By declaring that student assignment remedies did not have to be racially neutral, a new remedial theory was born based on racial distinctions and, ultimately, racial preferences. The Court had come full circle, replacing a system of mandatory racial separation with a system of mandatory racial integration.

It would take us too far afield to analyze the legal issues raised by this new remedial theory. Suffice it to say that the abandonment of the racial neutrality principle for remedy plunged the Supreme Court into an intense legal controversy over the proper interpretation of the Equal Protection Clause of the Fourteenth Amendment. If the Fourteenth Amendment forbids laws that make racial distinctions, should it not also forbid Court-imposed remedies that make racial distinctions? The debate over this fundamental issue remains intense today, affecting not only school desegregation remedies but remedies in employment, housing, and many other areas where discrimination cases arise.

Although *Swann* took care of remedy in the South, where the dual school system was part of state law, it was still unclear how these cases and the evolving desegregation law would affect northern cities, where state-imposed dual school systems had never existed. A number of northern desegregation cases had been filed by the time of *Swann*, and a few had resulted in large-scale busing orders (such as in Pasadena and Pontiac). But the conditions in each of these cases were fairly unusual (e.g., in Pasadena, the final busing order was not appealed to the Supreme Court), and it was not clear whether they could be generalized to most northern cities.

The matter was settled in another landmark ruling by the Supreme Court in 1973. In its *Keyes* decision affecting the Denver school district, the Court concluded that a finding of intentional segregation in one part of a school district created a *prima facie* case of intentional segregation in all other parts of a district. Unless a school board could then prove that the portion where discrimination occurred was isolated from and unrelated to the rest of the district, a lower court could find the entire district a dual school system and could impose a systemwide remedy. By 1974, Denver had been ordered to adopt a mandatory busing plan to achieve racial balance in all of its schools.

With *Swann* and *Keyes* in place, extensive desegregation remedies were brought to many large cities in all parts of the nation. Mandatory busing plans to achieve approximate racial balance in all or most schools have been ordered or adopted in such diverse cities as Boston, Denver, Norfolk, Little Rock, Dallas, Memphis, Dallas, Fort Worth, Omaha, Seattle, San Francisco, Los Angeles, Dayton, Detroit, and most Florida cities. The list of large cities with court-approved voluntary plans is much shorter (e.g., Atlanta, Cincinnati, Chicago, Milwaukee, and San Diego), and even fewer large cities have escaped major desegregation lawsuits altogether.

In spite of *Swann*'s prescription that "year-by-year adjustments of the racial composition of student bodies" are not required by the U.S. Constitution, once these racial balance plans are in place they are rarely abandoned. In some cases, a lower court has found that the district is still not unitary, and in other cases, the racial balance plan has been incorporated into local school-board policy. As a consequence, most of these school districts have been making boundary adjustments to maintain racial balance for periods ranging up to 10–15 years.

For example, after the Denver racial balance plan had been in effect for about 10 years, the school board went back to court in 1984 requesting a declaration of unitary status and removal of an injunction on student assignment. The motion was denied by the district court in 1985 (*Keyes*, 1985). In contrast, the Norfolk school system was declared unitary in 1975, but the school board maintained the mandatory racial balance plan as a matter of policy. In 1983, the board adopted a new policy to end mandatory busing, but a new lawsuit was brought to prevent a return to neighborhood schools. A district court approved the new plan in 1984, and it was upheld on appeal (*Riddick*, 1984, 1986). Norfolk returned to neighborhood schools in 1986.

Los Angeles is one of the rare cases where mandatory busing was started (1978) and then stopped (1980) because of a change in state laws. The original state court order was based on *de facto* segregation, and it was ultimately overturned by a state constitutional amendment passed in 1978 requiring compatibility with the *de jure* rule of federal law. However, a new lawsuit was filed in federal court in 1981, and in 1985, following appeals on various legal issues, the suit was allowed to proceed. If *de jure* violations are found, mandatory busing could resume in Los Angeles.

Finally, the most significant new legal development during this period was brought about by a series of metropolitan desegregation cases. That topic will be taken up following a discussion of the white flight issue.

RACIAL BALANCE AND WHITE FLIGHT

Throughout the first 20 years of desegregation, the white flight phenomonen was given little recognition by the courts. This outcome is explained largely by language in *Brown II* cautioning that "the vitality of these constitutional principles cannot be allowed to yield simply because of disagreement with them." Generally, the courts have considered white flight simply another form of public opposition to busing. In recent years, however, some courts have paid more attention to the problem, partly because of better documentation of the massive white losses following the start of busing plans.

Quite aside from court deliberations, the problem of white flight has been a major focus of debate among desegregation experts. The argument has been intense over its magnitude, its causes, and its long-term implications for the success of desegregation. This last issue, sometimes called the *resegregation problem*, may be the key to the greater attention that the courts are paying to the white flight problem. It is one thing to ignore public protest and quite another to worry about whether the remedy may be aggravating, rather than alleviating, school segregation.

The purpose of this section is to give a status report on the white flight issue, highlighting areas of agreement as well as issues still in contention. In addition, this section presents some previously unpublished data that illustrate the degree to which white flight can reduce the effectiveness of massive busing remedies.

DISTRICTWIDE STUDIES

The greatest agreement among desegregation experts has emerged for studies of districtwide enrollment changes. The earliest group of studies, published during the mid-1970s, were necessarily based on relatively short durations of large-scale busing plans. This period was marked by considerable disagreement, with Coleman, Kelly, and Moore (1975) being the first to find a serious white-flight problem, whereas Rossell (1975) and Farley (1975) argued to the contrary.

By the late 1970s, following the expansion of data bases and the improvement of analytic techniques, most of the major national studies of white flight agreed with Coleman on the key point that mandatory busing significantly increased white flight during the year of implementation (Armor, 1978; Farley, 1976; Rossell, 1978). There was still disagreement, however, on the duration of the effect: Armor (1978) and Coleman and associates (1975) claimed that it was large and long-term in central-city districts with significant minority populations; Farley (1976) claimed that it was primarily a 1-year effect; and Rossell (1978) emphasized its small magnitude.

Further improvement in analytic techniques as well as expanded white flight data from new desegregation cases led Rossell to modify her earlier views about the size of the white flight effect. In a 1983 review, Rossell stated that "every time white pupils are reassigned to minority schools, 35 to 50 percent of them leave the school system" (p. 88). She also concluded that "a negative [white flight] effect last into the fifth year of desegregation in large, high-proportion-black, central-city school districts" (p. 93).

One national study analyzed white flight in over 1,200 school districts between 1968 and 1976 (Wilson, 1985). This study also showed that desegregation has a significant first-year effect on white flight but failed to confirm a long-term effect. The study also concluded that the effect appears to depend primarily on the degree of racial contact rather than on the type of desegregation plan (e.g., mandatory busing).

Wilson (1985) acknowledged that his data do not fully assess plan characteristics, and in particular, there is no estimate of the degree of mandatory busing, such as the number of students reassigned. This is a significant weakness of the study, in light of Rossell's finding that estimated white students' reassignment has a stronger impact on white flight than any other plan or school district characteristic. The inadequate measurement of student reassignment, together with the inclusion of hundreds of small school districts, makes it difficult to generalize Wilson's results to larger cities that have experienced mandatory busing plans.

The majority of national white-flight studies now concur that larger, central-city school districts with sizable minority enrollments experience significant long-term white flight following mandatory busing plans, providing those plans involve a substantial reassignment of white students. The major question remaining is whether these white losses are sufficient to cause resegregation.

SCHOOL-LEVEL STUDIES

A major reason for disagreement among white flight studies has been the difficulty in quantifying key desegregation plan characteristics. Desegregation plans differ greatly along several dimensions that impact on student transfers, including the number of schools in the plan, the grade levels covered, and the specific transfer techniques used. When a mandatory plan is involved, these variations determine the number of white and black students reassigned or "bused." If mandatory white reassignment is a primary determinant of white flight, then plan variations can lead to widely divergent districtwide white loss rates, even when other district and demographic characteristics are controlled.

The difficulty in interpreting districtwide white loss rates has led some investigators to assess white flight on a school-by-school basis within a district (Pride & Woodard, 1985; Rossell, 1986; Rossell & Ross, 1979). These studies, although few in number, have the advantage that losses for reassigned students can be compared directly with losses for students who remain in neighborhood schools. Moreover, school-level studies can investigate various factors that might affect the degree of white flight, such as the distance that students are bused or the racial composition of the receiving schools. Such relationships help to specify the processes and causes of white flight.

The paucity of school-level studies is due mainly to the limited availability of good student reassignment data. For some desegregation plans, such as geographic rezoning, it may be impossible to count reassignments accurately, whereas for other plans, the necessary school data may not be maintained by the school district. Accordingly, it might be useful here to present and discuss some hitherto unpublished school-level analyses of white flight. The data were originally assembled by the author for purposes of court testimony in three mandatory busing cases: Norfolk, Virginia; Seattle, Washington; and Los Angeles, California.

The basic approach of a school-level study is first to identify those schools and grade levels involved in a mandatory desegregation plan, and to count the number of students, by race, who will be reasssigned to "receiving" schools as part of the plan. The second step is to count the number of students who actually show up in those receiving schools the following year. The resultant white cohort loss rate is more properly called a *no-show rate*, rather than a white flight rate, because some students may find their way into other district schools rather than fleeing the district altogether.

A summary of the white no-show rates for the three cities is shown in Figure 1. Although these cities and desegregation plans had highly diverse characteristics, the massive losses due to mandatory busing were quite consistent for all three. Basically, the no-show rates of bused white students were 5–10 times greater than the loss rate for their nonbused counterparts and reached a remarkable average of 50% or higher in the two larger cities. (Nonbused rates are cohort losses the year before busing.)

The Norfolk data are especially interesting because they illustrate an elementary desegregation plan phased in over a two-year period. In the first year of the plan, implemented in the fall of 1970, 13 elementary schools in relatively close proximity were combined into five pairs and clusters. In spite of the shorter distances, the no-show rate for white students assigned to black schools was 34%, compared to 4% for all nonbused students. In 1971, the busing program was expanded by a pairing and clustering of the remaining 23 elementary schools, many of which were on opposite sides of the city. The no-show rate for these white students climbed to 42%, a figure suggesting that the distance of the busing might well have been related to the degree of white flight.

The Seattle data are also revealing. Seattle is one of the few large cities to implement mandatory busing without a court order or other governmental pressure. This circumstance led some commentators to speculate that Seattle had more community support for mandatory busing and therefore would not experience a serious white-flight problem. The data fail to support this speculation. Seattle's no-show rates were quite comparable to no-show rates in the other two cities, both of which were acting in response to court orders or pressures.

The 1978 Los Angeles plan was adopted during court litigation, when a court order was anticipated but before formal hearings had concluded. At that time, the school board believed that white flight would be minimized if the plan was limited to Grades 4–8, keeping primary grades and high schools intact. Again, the data offer no support for this belief. The average Los Angeles no-show rate was the highest documented anywhere in the white-flight literature. The only way partial plans limit white flight is by reducing it at those schools or grade levels excluded from the plan, which, of course, reduces the white-loss rate for the district as a whole. For the students actually bused, there appears to be no amelioration whatsoever.

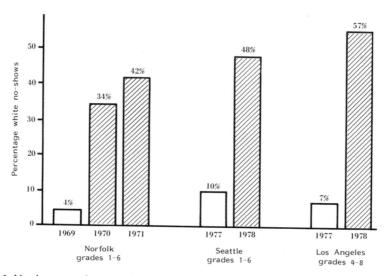

FIGURE 1. No-show rates for newly bused white students. Key: striped bar = bused; open bar = not bused.

Needless to say, no-show rates at these levels can defeat the two primary advantages claimed for mandatory plans over voluntary plans: integrating minority schools and equalizing the burden of busing. Projected school enrollments in Los Angeles—assuming no flight—anticipated that, of the 65 predominately minority schools in the plan, 42 would become over 40% white and only 1 would have fewer than 30% white students. In fact, the no-show rate was so high that only 12 of these schools became over 40% white, whereas 30 ended up being less than 30% white. Further, although roughly equal numbers of minority and white students were assigned to ride buses, the no-show rates meant that many buses from white schools were nearly empty. Overall, minorities outnumbered whites on buses by a factor of 2 to 1.

The very high no-show rate in Los Angeles, which necessarily involved some very long bus rides (60–80 minutes one way for some of the pairs and clusters), again raises the question of distance and other factors that might cause variation in white-flight rates. The Los Angeles data can be used to investigate these questions. Although the Los Angeles plan can be classified as partial, the size of the district means that over 150 schools were involved in the mandatory busing component—a number larger than most school districts in the nation. Moreover, detailed measurements are available for a number of school and plan characteristics, including the distance and the ethnicity of the receiving schools. This rich data set offers a unique opportunity to test assumptions about factors that may affect white flight.

The most surprising result from numerous regression analyses is the relatively small number of factors that had a significant impact on no-show rates (Armor, 1979). No important effects were found for such school characteristics as the ethnicity of the receiver (black or hispanic), socioeconomic status, the experience of the faculty or the principal, or desegregation-planning intensity. The same can be said for numerous plan characteristics, such as pairing versus clustering or whether pairs were selected by the local school community or were assigned by central staff. Among over 20 factors, the only statistically significant predictors of no-show rates were travel time, the achievement level of the receiving school, and grade level (junior highs having higher no-show rates than elementary schools).

The estimated no-show rates for varying travel times and receiver achievement levels are presented in Table 1. Basically, the no-show rates increased by about 10% for each 15-minute increase in travel time or for each 20-point increase in the percentage of students in the receiving school who achieved below the national median. The very high no-show rate for Los Angeles, compared to that for other cities, can therefore be explained in part

TABLE 1. Los Angeles No-Show Rates for
Bused White Students, by Travel Time and
Achievement Level of Receiving School[a]

Travel time	Percentage of receiver students achieving below the national median		
	30[b]	50	70[c]
20 minutes	16	27	38
35 minutes	26	36	47
50 minutes	36	46	57

[a] Based on a regression analysis using 65 minority receiving schools; white receivers excluded.
[b] White average.
[c] Minority average.

by long bus rides. The average bus ride in the Los Angeles plan took a little over 50 minutes one way. Of course, one cannot be sanguine about white flight for shorter routes; a 20-minute ride to the average minority receiver still produced no-show rates of nearly 40%.

The Los Angeles study also yielded the remarkable finding that the racial composition of the receiving school had no effect on white loss. When actual no-show rates are adjusted for distance and achievement level (based on minority receiver characteristics), there were no meaningful differences in the no-show rates at black, Hispanic, or white receiving schools. The results are summarized in Figure 2. Adjusted no-show rates at white receivers are 54%, compared to 50% at Hispanic receivers and 52% at black receivers.

This finding is not an artifact of the analysis, because only minority receivers were used to estimate regression coefficients. Moreover, low no-show rates were actually observed at higher achieving black receiving schools located near white senders. For example, the no-show rate for Windsor Hills, a middle-class black receiver located about 2 miles from two white senders in the Westchester area, was only 20%.

This result contradicts two popular notions in the desegregation literature. First, it fails to support the belief that white flight is more severe for black receivers than for Hispanic receivers. Second, it challenges the conventional wisdom that white flight is motivated primarily by avoidance of racial or ethnic contact. If the motivation were primarily racial, we would expect to see less white flight from white receivers than from minority receivers, after adjustments are made for distance and achievement level. On the contrary, the Los Angeles analysis suggests that the lower unadjusted no-show rates for white receivers are explained by their higher achievement levels and by their closer proximity to white sending schools.

The no-show analyses for these three cities contribute to our understanding of the causes of white flight. In particular, the findings here are consistent with the emerging conception that opposition to mandatory busing and its resultant white flight cannot be reduced to a simple model of racism (Armor, 1980; McClendon, 1985; Rossell, 1983). The traditional racism model holds that white flight is motivated primarily by a desire to avoid contact with minorities.

The existing evidence against this model is substantial: (a) attitude studies show

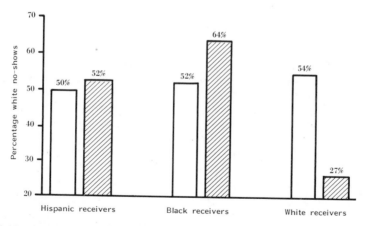

FIGURE 2. No-show rates for white students bused to Hispanic, black, and white receiving schools in Los Angeles, adjusted for distance and achievement level. Key: open bar = adjusted; striped bar = unadjusted.

substantially declining levels of racist attitudes, whereas opposition to mandatory busing remains persistently high (McClendon, 1985); (b) attitudinal and behavioral evidence shows little white resistance to voluntary busing, where large numbers of minority students are brought into white schools (Armor, 1980); and (c) national districtwide studies have shown that white reassignment, but not black reassignment, is significantly related to the rate of white flight (Rossell, 1978).

The school-level data support a more complex cost–benefit model of white flight (Armor, 1980; Rossell, 1983). This model holds that flight depends on the evaluation of the perceived benefits of reassignment versus its cost (and the cost of flight as well). The distance of a receiving school is an obvious cost, not only in lost time for the child but also in the reduced accessibility of the child or the school to the parent. The achievement level of the receiving school represents a perceived cost if it is lower than the sending school or a benefit if it is higher. Thus, white families tend to leave a district when assigned to a distant minority school with achievement levels lower than their current school. Minority families, on the other hand, may actually favor reassignment to a distant white school, providing it has higher achievement levels than their current school. Given the greater financial constraints on minorities, minority flight is seldom significant.

WHITE FLIGHT AND RESEGREGATION

Perhaps, the ultimate issue in the white flight debate is whether white losses caused by mandatory busing can be sufficient to render the plan ineffective, or at least less effective than alternatives. Although white flight itself is no longer in dispute, there is still considerable debate about the long-term effectiveness of mandatory versus voluntary plans. Even though a mandatory plan may cause more white flight than a voluntary plan, there may be enough whites remaining in a mandatory plan to produce more desegregation than would a voluntary plan.

Unfortunately, current research on this question is plagued by a number of technical shortcomings, and no definitive answer is available at this time. Nevertheless, it might be useful to summarize some of this current research and to explain the problems in the hope that future studies will discover solutions.

The most serious problem has been one of definition. The shift to racial balance definitions of desegregation has tended to discount the importance of white flight and to obscure its long-term impact on the resegregation of an entire district. *Resegregation of a district* means that the entire district becomes predominantly minority, and thus, no amount of racial balance can meaningfully desegregate most of its minority schools.

For example, assume that a district begins at 60% white and 40% minority, and that a mandatory desegregation plans aims to balance each school racially at about this level, plus or minus some tolerance of 5%–10%. Assume further that the mandatory plan coupled with demographic factors causes the district to become about 70% minority over a period of 5 years or so. According to the racial balance approach, the district would still be well desegregated if all schools were approximately 70% minority. But this district would clearly not be desegregated in the sense of its original racial composition, and indeed, the entire district might be considered segregated in comparison to some broader reference group (e.g., a metropolitan area).

This problem has affected two of the major studies on the effectiveness of alternative desegregation plans (Rossell, 1983; Smylie, 1983). Both of these studies used the index of dissimilarity as the main criterion of effectiveness. Because this index measures the departure from strict racial balance relative to the percentage of a minority in a district, it ignores both the level of white flight and the degree of contact between white and minority students. It must be conceded that mandatory plans do the best job of producing racial balance, but usually only at the cost of converting all schools to predominantly minority status.

Clearly, there is a need for studies that use some type of absolute index of white and minority contact that takes into account the loss of white students caused by a plan. Although a voluntary plan may not produce racial balance, it may preserve enrollment stability to the point where the absolute number of students in meaningfully desegregated schools (e.g., 50% minority plus or minus some deviation) is higher than for a mandatory plan. To date, this hypothesis has been thoroughly tested in only a few case studies—concerning the districts of San Diego, Chicago, Los Angeles, and Hattiesburg, Mississippi (Armor, 1980; Armor & Ross, 1981; Ross, 1983; Rossell, 1985). These case studies suggest the possibility that a voluntary plan can produce more long-term, stable desegregation than a mandatory plan, but they do not provide a sufficient basis for generalization.

Although there is no final answer on resegregation as yet, it is still the case that mandatory busing has caused significant white flight in most of the larger cities where it has been used. Given the reality of urban demographic trends, at the very least mandatory busing has aggravated the growing racial isolation of these cities. Whatever the balance of causes, the fact is that the public school systems in most larger cities are now predominantly minority and can no longer be desegregated by intradistrict methods. This fact brings up the issue of metropolitan desegregation, which has become a major focus of litigation during recent years.

METROPOLITAN DESEGREGATION

Given the dwindling white population in most large cities, metropolitan proposals seek to enhance the desegregation process by encompassing white student populations in both city and suburban regions. Although metropolitan remedies are not new, the legal and policy issues they raise have resisted rapid resolution, at least in comparison to intradistrict remedies. In spite of the seemingly definitive *Milliken* decision in 1974, the potential for broad application of "metro" remedies remained uncertain throughout the 1970s.

By 1985, however, a number of key court decisions had greatly clarified the metro situation. Although generalization is always hazardous in this field, the case law developed in the recent decisions has significantly lessened the prospects for metropolitan school desegregation, at least through court action. Ironically, the courts appear to have removed themselves from the thorniest problem of all—interdistrict segregation—even though they undoubtedly contributed to it by their insistence on intradistrict mandatory busing. Without court intervention, the growing segregation in large metropolitan areas presents an enormous challenge for those who want to increase opportunities for interracial contact.

Early Efforts and the Detroit Case

Some of the earliest attempts to develop metropolitan desegregation plans have been the most successful, in the sense of generating sustained community support within both city and suburban areas. Among these plans must be counted the METCO program in Boston and Project Concern in Hartford and New Haven, Connecticut. Begun in the mid-1960s and sustained with a combination of public and private financing, these programs bus minority children from the city to predominantly white suburban districts. One reason for the long-term popular success of these programs is that they are completely voluntary: not only for the city students who transfer to the suburbs, but for the participating suburban school districts that enroll them. Unfortunately, one of the most recent court developments in Milwaukee may put these sorts of programs in jeopardy, as we shall discuss presently.

On the legal side, metropolitan issues did not become a major court matter until the Richmond, Virginia, case, which finally reached the Supreme Court in 1972, following an appellate court decision denying metropolitan relief. The Supreme Court divided on a 4–4 vote, thereby delaying more definitive guidelines. The delay was brief; substantial clarification of the legal issues emerged in the 1974 *Milliken* decision, which affected the city of Detroit and its surrounding suburbs.

On liability, the Detroit case was similar in many respects to other northern desegregation cases. The plaintiffs alleged numerous constitutional violations involving school construction, boundary changes, optional attendance zones, and discriminatory transportation practices for the relief of overcrowding. In comparison with other cases, more expert testimony was offered in the area of housing segregation and discrimination, mostly on behalf of the plaintiffs; little testimony was offered by the defendants to rebut the contention that housing segregation was caused largely by official state action (Wolf, 1981). The district court agreed with most of the plaintiffs' assertions, including those about housing segregation, and held the Detroit school board liable for the intentional segregation of black and white students.

On the remedy, however, the district court parted company with other northern decisions. It concluded that Detroit could not be desegregated by the students within its own boundaries because the city system was nearly two-thirds black. Without finding the suburbs guilty of any specific unconstitutional actions—and, in fact, without making them regular parties to the action—the local court nevertheless ordered the largely white suburban districts to merge with the city district, and to attain racial balance by mandatory busing between the city and the suburbs. What was accomplished within the single district of Charlotte-Mecklenburg County would be accomplished in Detroit and its suburbs by dissolving school district boundaries. The new district would have encompassed at least 54 school districts and nearly 800,000 students, becoming the nation's second largest school district after the New York City district.

Following affirmation by an appellate court, the Supreme Court reversed the decision. Its *Milliken* decision established basic guidelines that have governed metropolitan cases since that time. Actually, the guiding principal was a variant of the *Swann* (1971) holding that the scope of the remedy must be determined by the scope of the violation:

> Specifically, it must be shown that racially discriminatory acts of the state or local school districts . . . have been a substantial cause of inter-district segregation.

The Court went on to describe two grounds on which an interdistrict remedy might be based: (a) where a discriminatory act of one district has a racial impact on an adjacent district or (b) where district boundaries were deliberately manipulated to have a racial impact. In a concurring opinion, Justice Stewart added a third ground: "purposeful, racially discriminatory use of state housing or zoning laws." Interestingly, although the Detroit district court found housing discrimination, the finding was not cast specifically within this interdistrict framework.

Most of the metropolitan lawsuits brought since *Milliken* have sought to establish one or more of these grounds, and often all three. Moreover, because housing segregation is far more pervasive than actions under the first two categories, plaintiffs have put special efforts into establishing housing violations. If housing discrimination can be proved to have interdistrict effects in one city, it may be possible to extend the proof to other cities, thereby providing the basis for metro remedies nationwide.

THE INDIANAPOLIS AND WILMINGTON CASES

The first two important metro cases to be resolved following *Milliken* involved Indianapolis, Indiana, and Wilmington, Delaware. (A third case, involving Louisville, is frequently cited as metro, but the city–suburban consolidation was adopted by state law and not by court order.) Both of these cases resulted in metropolitan remedies, which were decided locally in the mid-1970s but were not implemented until appeals were exhausted several years later.

These first major actions gave the impression that metro remedies were about to become commonplace. In retrospect, however, it is clear that the liability and remedy decisions for these two cities were based on fairly narrow grounds, and applications to other large cities never materialized.

In the Indianapolis case, the major constitutional violation involved a 1969 state law called *Unigov.* This act repealed a then-existing law requiring city and school district boundaries to expand together, thereby allowing the city of Indianapolis—but not the school district—to expand into the predominantly white Marion County suburbs. The district court also found official housing discrimination with interdistrict effects in the placement of public housing projects, all of which were located within the school district and none in other portions of the county (*United States,* 1976).

Because the Court found what amounted to a state-mandated boundary violation, it is not clear whether the housing violations alone would have justified a metropolitan remedy. No court had to decide this issue. It is noteworthy, however, that a consolidation of districts was not ordered, and the remedy was limited to the one-way busing of black children into white suburban school districts. This is perhaps the least controversial type of metropolitan remedy, as individual school districts maintain their autonomy and no white suburban students are required to be bused into the city.

In the case of Wilmington, the remedy was far more drastic. As in the Indianapolis case, the major constitutional violation found during the liability phase was the passage of a special state law preventing the predominantly black Wilmington district from annexing predominantly white suburban districts. Unlike in the Indianapolis case, the district court ordered the consolidation of Wilmington and the 10 suburban districts in New Castle County into one large district, with mandatory busing of whites into the city and blacks into the suburbs to achieve racial balance in all schools (Evans, 1975).

Although the key court decision was in 1975, the plan was not implemented until 1978. Interestingly, the plan was modified in 1981 by breaking the single large district into four smaller districts, each district taking a portion of the Wilmington district. In effect, the former Wilmington district ceased to exist. In addition, major changes were made in attendance zones to adjust for the racial imbalance developing since 1978, part of which may have been caused by white flight.

Some desegregation experts have claimed that metropolitan plans prevent or diminish white flight by cutting off suburban avenues of escape. This opinion was bolstered to some extent by the observation that large county districts in the South experienced less white flight than central-city districts following the start of mandatory busing. In the Wilmington case, however, which involved metropolitan consolidation as well as mandatory busing, the white flight was substantial.

Between 1974 and 1983, New Castle County white public-school enrollment in Grades 1–12 dropped from 65,000 to 33,000, and white nonpublic enrollment grew from 13,000 to 17,000. The share of white students in nonpublic schools, therefore, more than doubled, from 16% to 34%. Because white public enrollment elsewhere in Delaware dropped only from 36,000 to 30,000, demographic factors alone cannot account for the white losses in the New Castle County public schools. Similar levels of white flight have been documented for the Louisville–Jefferson County metropolitan plan, which also involved mandatory two-way busing (Armor, 1978).

ATLANTA AND THE HOUSING CASES

Wilmington was the last large-scale metropolitan consolidation and busing plan to be ordered by a federal court. Since 1979, the courts have issued major decisions in six more metropolitan cases, and none have ordered either consolidation or mandatory busing.

Five of the six cases relied heavily on showing housing discrimination, and four of these—involving Atlanta, Goldsboro, Cincinnati, and Kansas City, Missouri—found no liability whatsoever against defendant school districts, and no remedy has been ordered (some of these cases are still on appeal). In the fifth case—involving St. Louis—no explicit liability has been found against the suburbs, but they are cooperating in a voluntary city–suburban busing plan. The sixth case involves Little Rock, Arkansas, where both boundary and housing violations were affirmed by an appellate court in 1985, but the remedy was restricted to boundary adjustments and a metropolitanwide voluntary transfer plan.

Atlanta's is the only one of these cases in which a full housing case has been heard, including expert testimony on behalf of both the plaintiffs' and the suburban defendants' positions. In the other cases, either the defendants were dismissed before their side was presented, or they did not present a full housing defense. The Atlanta case has also been affirmed on appeal to the U.S. Supreme Court. Therefore, this case may be instructive about the ultimate fate of a strategy relying primarily on housing discrimination.

The housing violations raised in the Atlanta case are typical of those in all recent metro cases. The allegations about official discrimination in housing included the placement of public housing within black communities and a refusal to locate public housing in white suburban areas; racial covenants prohibiting the sale of property to minorities; discriminatory zoning laws establishing black or white housing areas or providing for minimum lot sizes; real-estate-agency practices of racial "steering"; and federal loan programs that demanded or encouraged racially homogeneous neighborhoods. It was further alleged that school districts shared in these violations, first by maintaining a dual school system, which worked to reinforce housing segregation, and second, as agencies of the state, which had created the housing segregation in the first place.

Most of the testimony on behalf of the Atlanta plaintiffs was anecdotal, establishing that various laws or practices had, in fact, existed, but without establishing the magnitude of their effects or—more important—their interdistrict nature. The key expert witness for the plaintiffs was Karl Taeuber, who presented U.S. Census data showing that the cost of housing in white suburban areas was within the reach of many black families living in Atlanta. He concluded that economic factors were not a substantial explanation of housing segregation, and that, instead, the alleged discriminatory actions were the primary causes of housing segregation in the Atlanta area. Taeuber did not attempt to substantiate his conclusions by quantifying the effects of economic or discriminatory factors on the degree of housing segregation.

The defendants (including the Atlanta school district) presented three expert witnesses—David Armor, William Clark, and Anthony Pascal—who carried out extensive analyses and simulations using both U.S. Census and survey data to quantify the effects of numerous factors on housing segregation. They testified that housing segregation was caused largely by a host of nondiscriminatory factors, with special emphasis on the cost and type of housing, job location, and personal preferences. For example, one simulation showed that, if all public housing units were distributed throughout the metropolitan area in the same proportion as housing stock, suburban black households would be increased by only 2% or 3% at most. Another simulation showed that black preferences for 50–50 neighborhoods, combined with white preferences for predominantly white neighborhoods—and rejection of 50–50 neighborhoods—could explain up to 90% of the existing housing segregation as measured by desegregation indices.

The district court ruled that official government actions had contributed to housing segregation in the past. But the court also found, based primarily on the defendants' expert testimony, that "present-day housing patterns are not caused by government discrimination." The court stated further that the causes of housing segregation were complex and varied, but that economic restraints and personal preferences appeared to be the strongest factors in housing decisions (*Armour*, 1984).

The status of the other five major metropolitan cases also shed some light on the prospects for housing and other interdistrict violation arguments. The highlights of these cases are summarized as follows:

Goldsboro, North Carolina. In 1981, the city school district of Goldsboro (78% black) sued the Wayne County school district (31% black), which entirely surrounds the city district, and demanded interdistrict relief. The alleged constitutional violations included a racially motivated failure to merge with the city, the maintenance of "white haven" schools in the county district, and the location of public housing entirely within the city district. Following the plaintiff's presentation of evidence, the district court found for the defendant, ruling that neither discriminatory intent nor effect had been established for any of these allegations. The district court also noted that Goldsboro black students had higher achievement-test scores than Wayne County black students. The lower court's opinion was upheld by an appellate court in 1984 (*Goldsboro*, 1984).

Cincinnati. The NAACP sued Cincinnati and all suburban school districts within Hamilton County for a series of alleged constitutional infractions, including an array of housing violations similar to those in Atlanta. This case did not even reach a hearing stage; the local court dismissed the charges in 1984 for failure to present a sufficient basis for litigation (*Bronson*, 1984).

St. Louis. The St. Louis case is a very complex one with an unusual outcome. Suit was originally brought against the St. Louis school district and the state of Missouri; suburban districts were not parties to the case. Following a finding of unconstitutional segregation on the part of the defendants, which included some housing violations but no boundary-change violations, the district court ordered a metropolitan plan involving many suburban districts. On appeal, an appellate court reversed the decision of the district court, holding that a metropolitan remedy could not be imposed without a liability trial involving the suburban districts. Subsequently, the suburbs settled by agreeing to a voluntary interdistrict transfer program. The district court approved the settlement and ordered the state to fund the transfer plan.

Kansas City, Missouri. This suit was brought against the city school district, numerous suburban districts, and the state of Missouri by a local civil-rights group. The alleged discriminatory actions included noncoterminous city and school district boundaries, a failure to merge city and suburban districts for racial reasons, a former dual school system, low numbers of black faculty and staff in the suburbs, and the same array of housing violations as in Atlanta. As in Goldsboro, the suburbs were dismissed in 1984 following the presentation of the plaintiffs' case, on the grounds that discriminatory intent and significant segregative effects had not been proved against the suburban defendants. The city district and the state were not dismissed, however, and they were eventually ordered to fashion an intradistrict remedy to be financed by the state (Jenkins, 1984).

Little Rock, Arkansas. The city school district of Little Rock sued the surrounding district of Pulaski County and the neighboring district of North Little Rock, an independent city. Unlike in the other five metro cases, this suit alleged a major boundary violation: in 1969, the county district halted its long-standing policy of allowing the city district to annex portions of the county district as the city's municipal boundaries expanded. Other allegations included a failure of the county to carry out its own desegregation plan, the construction of predominantly white "haven" schools, and the usual list of housing violations, including the location of public housing. The district court found against the defendants on all counts and ordered a metropolitan remedy that would consolidate all three districts and achieve racial balance by mandatory two-way busing. In 1985, an appellate court upheld the liability findings but reversed on the remedy, holding that a full metropolitan plan exceeded the scope of the violation. Instead, it ordered that the city district be expanded to be coterminous with the municipal boundaries, and that some sort of metropolitan voluntary plan be fashioned. The districts will keep their separate identity (*Little Rock,* 1984, 1985).

In the years since the 1974 decision, the lesson of *Milliken* has become clear, and it is a far different message than that delivered by *Swann* and *Keyes.* Although the courts have been accused of ignoring the relationship between violation and remedy in intradistrict cases, that relationship has become paramount in metropolitan cases. No major boundary-change remedies have been ordered (and upheld on appeal) without clear boundary-change violations. Even when sizable boundary violations are found, as in Little Rock, most remedies have focused on undoing the violation rather than on imposing massive metropolitan busing plans.

Perhaps most important, the attempt to make housing discrimination the major basis for metro remedies has apparently failed. There may well be additional cities where boundary violations will eventually be proved and metro remedies will be imposed. The failure of the housing strategy, however, makes it highly unlikely that court-ordered mandatory metropolitan remedies will become a nationwide phenomenon. Because mandatory metropolitan plans are not going to be adopted by any legislative body, the question becomes whether there is any feasible solution for the growing segregation in metropolitan areas.

NEW APPROACHES TO OLD PROBLEMS

If the assertion here is correct, and the courts have largely removed themselves from the growing problem of metropolitan school segregation, then solutions will not be easy. Worse than that, there will be no progress at all without a willingness on the part of the courts and other governmental agencies to admit the failures of past remedies and to experiment with new approaches. Above all, the willingness to test new approaches must not be extinguished by court actions to punish those who adopt innovative programs.

More specifically, at least three important initiatives are needed to reduce segregation in large metropolitan areas. First, the courts should allow voluntary programs in place of counterproductive mandatory busing plans. Second, state and federal agencies should experiment with new types of desegregation plans, such as that adopted by Wisconsin for the Milwaukee area. Finally, the courts must cooperate by adopting new standards and definitions of desegregation that will permit legislative initiatives to flourish.

Voluntary versus Mandatory

Racial balance is not required by the U.S. Constitution, as the U.S. Supreme Court constantly reminds us, and it makes little sense in most large cities that are predominantly minority. In a city that is 80% minority, racially balancing all schools according to the districtwide figure would make every school segregated. Yet, the lower courts have repeatedly imposed racial balance criteria as "starting points" and then have demanded enforcement via mandatory busing for years, as in the cases of Pasadena, Denver, Boston, and many other cities. In many of these cases, nearly all schools have become predominantly minority over time because of white flight. In light of this experience, the Supreme Court would perform an immense service for public education by modifying the *Swann* guidelines to prevent this common abuse of remedial powers.

Instead of racial balance, the Court should return to an absolute definition of desegregation, similar to that used by the U.S. Commission on Civil Rights in the late 1960s. Such definitions have both lower and upper limits for the percentage of minorities, such as 20%–50%, plus or minus some deviation of 5%–10% at either end. Aside from the increased flexibility offered by this formulation, it would solve the dilemma of defining desegregation in predominantly minority school-districts.

Without the burden of mandatory busing to achieve racial balance goals, voluntary programs can be very effective in generating meaningful desegregation for those students and parents who want it most—which would probably create the best climate for the purposes of both education and race relations. Obviously, in heavily minority districts, not all minority schools can be desegregated (regardless of method), and segregated minority schools should be candidates for enhanced educational programs. But at least some schools would be meaningfully desegregated, rather than having all schools' balanced but segregated.

In this regard, the 1986 appellate decision in the Norfolk case is especially noteworthy. For the first time, a southern school district is being permitted to dismantle a mandatory busing program and to return to a neighborhood school system with voluntary desegregation options. The appellate court acknowledged the white flight problem and stated that a school district should be permitted to adopt a voluntary plan when a mandatory plan has failed. The U.S. Supreme Court refused review, so the appelate decision stands as final law.

Legislative Initiatives: The Wisconsin Plan

The second requirement for progress is new legislative initiatives by state and federal agencies. Although it would be unrealistic to expect legislative action for either metropolitan consolidation or mandatory busing, there may well be legislative support for interdistrict voluntary desegregation programs, especially if such programs are linked with modified programs of the voucher type.

A case in point is a Wisconsin state program affecting Milwaukee and its surrounding suburbs. The Wisconsin "220" program permits minority students in the Milwaukee city district to transfer to participating suburban districts; likewise, suburban white students can transfer to the city district. The sending district keeps its per capita cost allotment for that student, and the receiving district also receives a per capita allotment. Thus, there are financial incentives for both the city and the suburban districts to participate. The key to the legislative and community support for the 220 program is the concept of choice: participation is voluntary both for the school district and for the students who transfer.

The Wisconsin 220 program is not a true voucher plan as that term is commonly understood, but it does have key similarities. It allows free choice of schools in the receiving districts, subject to racial composition constraints, and it uses financial incentives in the form of a voucher type of payment to both districts. Unlike a pure voucher program, however, it is designed solely for the purpose of desegregation; it is, in effect, an interdistrict M-to-M program.

Ironically, in spite of its clear purpose, this plan is now being challenged in a lawsuit brought by the Milwaukee city district against the state and all suburban districts. Among other things, the city district alleges that the 220 program violates the U.S. Constitution on two grounds: (a) not all suburban districts have agreed to participate, and (b) some participating suburbs have limited the number of minority students that can transfer to that district. Needless to say, a court ruling in favor of Milwaukee would undoubtedly discourage any further attempts to promote voluntary metropolitan desegregation. Legislatures are likely to adopt such plans only if they provide for the voluntary participation of suburbs, and yet, this is precisely the condition being used by the city to establish a constitutional violation.

EXPANDED-CHOICE PROGRAMS AND THE COURTS

This brings us to the key issue of the courts' role in future and possibly more radical innovations in metropolitan desegregation. As an illustration of the problem, consider the proposal for an "expanded-choice" program for metropolitan desegregation. This proposal expands the Wisconsin concept in several major ways in order to broaden its appeal. (The proposal here is similar to one made by Rossell and Hawley, 1982.)

The basic idea of an expanded-choice program is to offer a voucher type of payment to any student who transfers from a nondesegregated school to a desegregated school, including within-district transfers, between-district transfers, and transfers to private schools. A desegregated school would be defined in absolute terms (e.g., 15%–55% minority), with minor adjustments to reflect the racial and ethnic composition of a broad metropolitan region. Voucher payments would be proposed as well for minority sending schools, as in the Wisconsin plan, to improve the educational program for those students remaining at the sending school.

This expanded-choice plan has two key features that broaden its appeal. First, both minority and nonminority students would receive incentives for leaving segregated schools, including transfer options from a city to a suburban school district. Second, minority students would have increased opportunities to attend private schools, which are beyond the economic means of many minority families at the present time. Equally important, private schools would have an incentive to become integrated.

A voucher type of desegregation plan would be most feasible in those states where public education is financed primarily by state funds, because school district lines have lost much of their original meaning. By a combination of per capita funds from both state and federal sources (the federal component going only to those students meeting the economic means test), a voucher should be sufficient to meet most of the tuition fees charged by private schools. Obviously, those private schools receiving state funds through a voucher desegregation plan would have to meet state guidelines for curriculum and staffing.

As for the Wisconsin plan, another key requirement for success is voluntary participation by any private school or public school district. Any attempt to make the program mandatory, through legislative or court action, would render the program politically untenable.

Clearly, a voucher desegregation program cannot succeed without approval by the courts, particularly of those features allowing transfers of nonminority students and transfers to private schools. Yet, without such features, it is unlikely that a voucher desegregation program would gain the necessary political support for passage.

Ultimately, the courts and all policy makers must come to grips with one overwhelming fact. In the case of large city districts that are predominantly minority, most white students will be found only in suburban districts and in private schools. Unless flexible and realistic voluntary programs are devised to allow access to these groups, there will be no solution at all to the growing segregation in our metropolitan areas.

REFERENCES

Armor, D. J. (1978). White flight, demographic transition, and the future of school desegregation (R-5931). Santa Monica, CA: Rand Corp.

Armor, D. J. (1979). Exhibits prepared for Crawford v. Los Angeles Board of Education. Unpublish court document.

Armor, D. J. (1980). White flight and the future of school desegregation. In W. G. Stephan & J. R. Faegin (Eds.), Desegregation: Past, present, and future. New York: Plenum Press.

Armor, D. J., & Ross, J. M. (1981). Analysis of alternative student assignment strategies for the Chicago school desegregation plan (Report for the Board of Education) Illinois: City of Chicago.

Armour v. Nix, Atlanta (N.D. Ga, Sept. 24, 1984).

Bradley v. School Board of Richmond, Va, 462 F. 2d (1972).

Bronson v. Board of Education of Cincinatti, 578 F. Supp. 1091 (1984).

Brown v. Board of Education of Topeka, 347 U.S. 483 (1954).

Brown v. Board of Education of Topeka, 349 U.S. 294 (1955).

Coleman, J. S., Kelly, S. D., & Moore, J. A. (1975). Trends in school segregation, 1968–1973 (Paper No. 722-03-01). Washington, DC: Urban Institute.

Evans v. Buchanan, Wilmington, 393 F. Supp. 428 (1975).

Farley, R. (1975). Racial integration in public schools, 1967–1972: Assessing the effect of governmental policies. Sociological Focus, 8, 3–26.

Farley, R. (1976). Can Governmental policies integrate public schools? Paper presented at the 1976 annual meeting of the American Sociological Association, New York.

Goldsboro Board of Education v. Wayne County Board of Education, 745 F. 2d 324 (1984).

Green v. School Board of New Kent County, 391 U.S. 430 (1968).

Jenkins v. State of Missouri, Kansas City (W.D. Mo, June 5, 1984).

Keyes v. School District No. 1, Denver, 413 U.S. 189 (1973).

Keyes v. School District N. 1, Denver (Colo, June 3, 1985).

Little Rock School District v. Pulaski County Special School District, 584 F. Supp. 328 (1984).

Little Rock School District v. Pulaski County Special School District (8th Circuit, Nov. 7, 1985).

McClendon, J. J. (1985). Racism, rational choice, and white opposition to racial change: A case study of busing. Public Opinion Quarterly, 49, 214–233.

Milliken v. Bradley, Detroit, 418 U.S. 717 (1974).

Pride, R., & Woodard, J. D. (1985). The burden of busing. Knoxville: University of Tennessee Press.

Riddick v. School Board of Norfolk (E.D. Va, July 9, 1984).

Riddick v. School Board of Norfolk (4th Circuit, February 6, 1986).

Ross, J. M. (1983). Effectiveness of alternative desegregation strategies: The issue of voluntary versus mandatory policies in Los Angeles. Unpublished manuscript, Washington, DC.

Rossell, C. H. (1975). School desegregation and white flight. Political Science Quarterly, 92, 675–696.

Rossell, C. H. (1978). Assessing the unintended impacts of public policy: School desegregation and resegregation. Report for the National Institute of Education, Washington, DC.

Rossell, C. H. (1983). Applied social science research: What does it say about the effectiveness of school desegregation plans? Journal of Legal Studies, 12, 69–107.

Rossell, C. H. (1985). Estimating the net benefit of school desegregation reassignments. Educational Evaluation and Policy Analysis, 7, 217–227.

Rossell, C. H. (1986). Is it the distance or is it the blacks? Unpublished manuscript, Boston University, Department of Political Science.

Rossell, C. H., & Hawley, W. (1982). Policy Alternatives for Minimizing White Flight. Educational Evaluation and Policy Analysis, 4, 205–222.

Rossell, C. H., & Ross, J. M. (1979). The long-term effect of court-ordered desegregation on student enrollment in central city public school systems: The case of Boston, 1974–1979. Report prepared for the Boston School Department.

Smylie, J. A. (1983). Reducing racial isolation in large school districts. *Urban Education, 17*, 477–502.

Swann v. Charlotte-Mecklenburg Board of Education, 318 F. Supp. 786 (1970).

Swann v. Charlotte-Mecklenburg Board of Education, 402 U.S. 1 (1971).

U.S. Commission on Civil Rights. (1967). *Racial isolation in The public schools.* Washington, DC: U.S. Government Printing Office.

United States v. School Commissioners of Indianapolis, 541 F. 2d 1211 (1976).

Wilson, F. D. (1985). The impact of school desegregation programs on white public-school enrollment, 1968–1976. *Sociology of Education, 58*, 137–153.

Wolf, E. P. (1981). *Trial and error: The Detroit school segregation case.* Detroit: Wayne State University Press.

14

The Contribution of School Desegregation to Academic Achievement and Racial Integration

Willis D. Hawley and Mark A. Smylie

INTRODUCTION

It seems reasonable to assert that, in the last 30 years, no social policy has been as divisive as school desegregation. And few would argue that the numbers of minority and white leaders actively pursuing the goal of desegregation has declined from a decade or more ago. But the issue will not go away, and advocacy persists for at least two general reasons. First, on balance, and even though both massive and passive resistance have been more common than genuine efforts to make it work, school desegregation has benefited most of those who have experienced it. Second, the problems that school desegregation was meant to address are still with us in many communities, and social policies likely to be more effective in remediating them are not in evidence.

Given that the mention of school desegregation is often a conversation stopper in polite social discourse, it seems important to be clear about some meanings. School desegregation is a conscious effort—authoritatively prescribed by judicial, legislative, or administrative mandates—to eliminate or to substantially reduce the racial isolation of children in biracial or multiracial school systems. Few Americans oppose voluntary school desegregation, but few school systems engage in comprehensive desegregation voluntarily. Legal mandates requiring desegregation are almost always premised on findings of past or present racial discrimination.

Current laws and court opinions requiring remedies for the effects of segregation are premised on assumptions that such remedies will alleviate the educational and social disadvantages imposed on minorities by legally sanctioned discrimination. Thus, we think it is reasonable to stipulate that the justice and efficacy of remedies for segregation

WILLIS D. HAWLEY • Office of the Dean of Education, Peabody College, Vanderbilt University, Nashville, Tennessee 37203. MARK A. SMYLIE • School of Education, University of Illinois, Chicago, Illinois 60680.

and discrimination can be judged by their contribution to the attainment of at least two broad goals:

1. Increasing what students learn in school, especially as this learning is measured by academic achievement.
2. Preparing children to live and achieve in an integrated society.

In this chapter, we examine the degree to which school desegregation affects the attainment of these two goals. The approach we take is fundamentally pragmatic. Philosophical arguments about the use of force or the moral imperative of racial desegregation are not dealt with here. We are concerned with outcomes for children and communities.

We also identify several potential costs of desegregation and how these costs may affect the efficacy of desegregation as an educational and social policy. Because many school systems are becoming increasingly nonwhite, and because the results of desegregation often do not match the high hopes of its advocates, there has been increasing advocacy of what we will call racially *separate but enriched* education as both a supplement to and a substitute for desegregation. We will therefore explore how this alternative compares to desegregation as a way of increasing opportunities for academic learning and preparing children, especially minority children, for successful lives in an integrated society. In short, this discussion focuses on whether the above-mentioned goals can best be achieved in racially desegregated or racially isolated learning environments.

We will demonstrate that, on balance, desegregated schools afford greater opportunities than segregated schools to remedy discrimination and to attain the goals of increasing student academic achievement and of preparing children to live in an integrated society. School desegregation is not without costs. Our analysis will show, however, that these costs and the degree to which they restrict the attainment of educational and social outcomes are often exaggerated. Although separate but enriched education may theoretically enhance the academic learning of students in segregated settings, this option provides little potential for students to reap the affective and postschool opportunities provided by desegregation. Further, we contend that the potential academic benefits of separate but enriched education are likely to be undermined over time by political pressures that would limit the resources necessary to remedy the disadvantaged status of most minority children in segregated settings.

If ending the racial isolation of students could be achieved by facilitating parent and student choices of racially integrated schools, there would be little controversy over desegregation. Almost all of the costs—economic, educational, and political—attributed to desegregation derive from the use of mandatory reassignment of students to schools for the primary purpose of achieving what is called (often euphemistically) racial balance. Thus, we begin our analysis by examining whether mandatory desegregation is necessary to bring about substantial reductions in government-imposed racial isolation of children in schools.

REDUCING RACIAL ISOLATION

One cannot hope to significantly reduce racial isolation in most school systems in which desegregation is controversial without relying, at least in some substantial measure, on mandatory student reassignments and busing. Wishful thinking to the contrary and occasional anecdotes notwithstanding, wholly voluntary strategies are only partially successful in reducing racial isolation.

These conclusions are supported by virtually every study that has examined the relative effectiveness of desegregation plans based on mandatory student reassignments and those based primarily on voluntary strategies (e.g., Blank, Dentler, Blatzell, & Chabotar, 1983; Foster, 1973; Morgan & England, 1981; Rossell, 1979, 1983b; Royster, Blatzell, & Simmons, 1979; Smylie, 1983). This research shows that voluntary plans may effectively desegregate some schools, such as those designated as magnets, but in general, these plans have a limited impact on the levels of racial isolation throughout the system, particularly in districts with substantial proportions of minority students. Voluntary strategies implemented as components of mandatory reassignment plans have been relatively successful, but as Royster and his colleagues (1979) concluded in their reference to magnet programs, most of the reductions in racial isolation in systems implementing such combinations of strategies are attributable to the mandatory components of the plan.

Rossell and Clarke's (1987) recent longitudinal analysis of mandatory and voluntary desegregation strategies contradicts many of these findings. Their data suggest that voluntary plans based primarily on magnet schools lead to greater reductions in racial isolation and interracial interaction than mandatory plans over time. At the same time, Rossell and Clarke conclude that mandatory plans, on the average, have made significant contributions toward system-level desegregation.

The advantage this study gives to magnet-voluntary plans seems to rest on several important considerations. The first is that the magnet-voluntary plans included in this study's sample are comprehensive, that is, they all have as their goal to desegregate the entire school district by voluntary means. They may also be considered comprehensive in terms of the significant average proportion of schools designated as magnets in the sample of districts (⅓ of all schools). These plans are distinguished from those not included in this study that have a limited number of magnet schools and those that rely primarily on voluntary strategies other than magnet schools (e.g., open enrollment and/or majority–minority transfer programs). They do not include plans that do not specify an overall goal of achieving or maintaining "a racially balanced school system" (p. 25). These strategies in and of themselves, the study acknowledges, are ineffective.

The second consideration is that while none of the districts with voluntary plans analyzed in this study had an explicit mandatory backup, all used some additional mandatory techniques such as selected school closings and contiguous rezoning, particularly at the secondary level. Although Rossell and Clarke consider these mandatory techniques minimal, it has not been established what contributions these mandatory components have made toward the reduction of racial isolation relative to the voluntary strategies. Nor has sufficient attention been paid in this or any other study to the contribution of implicit "threats" in court-ordered voluntary plans of mandatory backup plans toward the success of voluntary strategies.

Finally, this study as well as others comparing the relative effectiveness of mandatory and voluntary plans have not considered the critical issue of the degree to which school districts adjust their plans to address problems of demographic change or resegregation over time. It is very unlikely that districts employing any type of plan can maintain the gains they achieve in reducing racial isolation in the face of demographic change without making corrective adjustments. To a certain extent, voluntary plans may be considered self-adjusting if they incorporate majority–minority transfer policies and/or guidelines for the racial compositions of magnet schools. Mandatory plans, on their face, seem more difficult to change but they are not unalterable. There is virtually no evidence to date that chronicles planned adjustments in desegregation plans nor the relationship between such adjustments (or lack thereof) and levels of desegregation over time.

Although mandatory student-reassignment plans are clearly the most effective way

of substantially reducing racial isolation systemwide, these plans have several consequences that critics contend compromise their ability to achieve their social and educational goals. Our analysis of the costs of desegregation will focus on two general assertions made by those who oppose desegregation:

1. The economic costs of busing and the time students spend on buses significantly
   diminish resources that could promote student learning.
2. Mandatory desegregation induces white and middle-class flight, which (a) reduces the resources available to the schools and (b) reduces opportunities for
   interracial contact in the long run.

Although the courts have not explicitly legitimized either of these two propositions, it is
clear enough from court records and from legislative actions that these propositions
shape public policy.

We think that the evidence indicates, however, that school desegregation can make
significant contributions to student learning and to the possibilities that our children will
live in a more fully integrated society. But we do not want to be understood as arguing
that mandatory school desegregation should be pursued at all costs. Indeed, it is precisely our point that desegregation should be seen as a *remedy* to the consequences of
governmentally imposed segregation, and that its efficacy must be weighed against the
efficacy of other remedies. It follows, then, that a wide variety of strategies might be
employed within the same school district to achieve the goals of eliminating the effects of
segregation. These strategies, for example, could result in some schools' being racially
isolated while others are desegregated by combinations of mandatory and voluntary
pupil reassignments.

The mix of strategies that one might recommend to remedy the effects of segregation
would depend on the conclusion one would reach about the point at which the benefits of
desegregation are exceeded by the costs. Such estimates will be shaped by the situation,
but the assumptions that guide specific analyses should rest on evidence accumulated
from the nation's experience rather than on intuition or myths, or on partial consideration
of the factors that influence the outcomes of desegregation. We turn, then, to a discussion
of that evidence.

INCREASING ACADEMIC ACHIEVEMENT

BENEFITS OF DESEGREGATION

Does school desegregation enhance or impede student learning of so-called academic
subjects? Some desegregation advocates would argue that this question is diversionary
and does not speak to the central question: How do we eliminate the isolation of racial
and ethnic minorities? But if students were educationally disadvantaged by desegregation, the game would be over—and probably should be.

During the 1970s, evidence on the effects of desegregation on academic achievement
increased significantly. The data come primarily from three types of studies: (a) longitudinal comparisons of test scores aggregated at the regional level; (b) so-called input–output
analyses, which use the racial composition of a school as a predictor of average student
performance; and (c) syntheses of case studies of school desegregation. Regardless of the
type of evidence one examines, the conclusion is the same. Desegregation is generally
associated with moderate gains in the achievement of black students and the achievement of white students is typically unaffected (Crain & Mahard, 1978). There is very little

evidence relating to other racial or ethnic groups, but there is reason to believe that Hispanic students also benefit in desegregated settings (Mahard & Crain, 1980).

This simple summary masks considerable controversy over the magnitude of the positive effect on black children. But the most comprehensive synthesis of case studies, which includes 93 inquiries and used the statistical techniques employed by the most sophisticated researchers on this topic, concluded that the effect is significant (Mahard & Crain, 1983). For example, of 20 studies comparing the academic achievement of blacks who had experienced desegregation since kindergarten or first grade to the achievement of blacks who had never experienced desegregation, 16 showed significantly positive effects of desegregation, and only two showed negative effects (Crain, 1983). Of those 20 studies that used randomized experiments, all showed relatively large treatment effects. Among these most rigorous studies, the median treatment-effect size was a standard deviation of .34. (Crain, 1983).

The average performance of students in a wide range of schools, some committed to effective desegregation and many adamantly opposed, seems a conservative estimate of the potential impact of desegregation on student achievement. Recent research permits one to identify how the positive effects of desegregation could be increased (Hawley, Crain, Rossell, Smylie, Fernandez, Schofield, Tompkins, Trent, & Zlotnik, 1983; Hawley & Rosenholtz, 1986).

The credibility of the finding of positive achievement effects of desegregation for minority students probably depends less on the elegance of the research than it does on whether the reasons for such effects make sense. After all, the justification for desegregation is that segregation results in the denial of equal educational opportunity. How could sending white children to previously segregated minority schools, and sending disadvantaged minority students to previously all white schools, result in a net gain in student achievement?

Unfortunately, the research provides no definitive answer to this question. However, there appear to be several reasons that desegregation generally results in improvements in academic achievement for minority students without negative consequences for whites: (a) the availability of peers who achieve at different levels provides a resource for students and teachers; (b) teacher expectations increase; (c) teacher training often accompanies desegregation; (d) community pressures for school performance are more intense; and (e) more financial resources have often been available.

It can be argued that the last four of these sources of student achievement can be secured in separate but enriched schools. We agree with this argument, but the special effort that must be made to maintain high teacher expectations, to renew teacher capabilities, and to increase and maintain the resources and community interest in schools serving minority children may be easier to sustain when minority children attend schools with white children. In a sense, this is something of a paradox. But as long as racial differences in achievement and opportunities exist, and as long as desegregation results in parental and community anxiety, the presence of minority and white students in the same classrooms will result in the recognition of inequalities and tensions that can most productively be resolved through positive educational programs. Moreover, when minority and white children attend the same schools in political systems dominated by whites, the whites have more reason to address the needs of the minority students. The fact that an increasing number of school systems are governed by minorities does not alter the salience of this last point because state governments increasingly shape local school policies and finance local educational services. Nonetheless, let us focus on the relationship between diversity in student performance levels and the academic achievement of individuals.

The Logic of Heterogeneous Instructional Settings

In addition to what might be thought of as the consciousness-raising and political functions of school desegregation, the primary contribution that school desegregation makes to academic achievement is derived from the increased diversity in the levels of performance of students in the school, which is the outcome of efforts to reduce or eliminate racial isolation. In most school systems, this learning resource cannot be gained in any other acceptable way.

Why are heterogeneous classrooms a potential learning resource? One answer to this question is that schools in which students manifest a relatively narrow range of achievement do not provide opportunities for lower achievers to learn from higher achievers. Teachers can "use" the performance of higher achievers as a benchmark and thus avoid the tendency to ask too little of lower-achieving youngsters. The diversity of students in a classroom seems to increase the teacher's awareness of individual differences that transcend racial and social differences.

The evidence on the effects of tracking and inflexible homogeneous-ability grouping shows that lower-achieving students usually do less well in these settings than they do in heterogeneous classrooms and groups (Leinhardt & Pallay, 1982; Oakes, 1982; Rosenbaum, 1980). There are exceptions, of course. The key seems to be how teachers organize instruction and cope with diversity (for a review of this research, see Hawley & Rosenholtz, 1986). Heterogeneous learning environments *cause* nothing, but they do seem to allow for learning opportunities from which the majority of children can benefit.

Of course, increasing the diversity of students also requires that teachers respond to a broader variety of individual student needs. A danger of multiability classrooms is that lower achievers will develop low self-esteem if they do not achieve at the levels of their higher-achieving peers. This phenomenon can have the same consequence as tracking or inflexible ability grouping. But this potential problem can be mitigated, and the benefits of diverse classrooms can be increased, by helping teachers to learn and implement a number of practices that have been shown to increase student learning in classrooms with a broad range of student abilities:

- Effective classroom management (Brophy, 1983; Evertson, Sanford, & Emmer, 1981; Evertson & Smylie, 1987).
- Cooperative learning (Sharan, 1980; Slavin, 1980; Slavin & Karweit, 1985).
- Peer tutoring (Cohen, Kulik, & Kulik, 1982; Gerber & Kauffman, 1981).
- Emphasis on multitask learning structures (Nelson-Le Gall & Glor-Scheib, 1983).
- Noncompetitive assessment of and rewards for student performance (Ames, 1981; Nicholls 1979).
- Communication to students of the importance of different abilities in achieving tasks (Rosenholtz, 1985; Tammivaara, 1982) and the importance of respecting each other's strengths (Cohen, 1982).

There seems little doubt that lower- and middle-achieving youngsters do better in more heterogeneous learning environments. But if higher-achieving youngsters are learning resources for others, does their education suffer in heterogeneous situations? Although the evidence on this point is mixed, there is reason to believe that higher-achieving youngsters who experience conventional instructional strategies do better in homogeneous groups of higher achievers (Kulik & Kulik, 1982). But this does not need to happen. When teachers make competent use of instructional strategies designed with student differences in mind, such as cooperative team learning and peer tutoring, both high- and low-ability students typically benefit from heterogeneous settings. Moreover, there is no reason that students should not be grouped by ability for some learning tasks.

The problems associated with homogeneous grouping derive from the stability of these arrangements over time and the tendency of both teachers and students to stereotype lower achievers.

POTENTIAL COSTS OF DESEGREGATION THAT COULD AFFECT STUDENT ACHIEVEMENT

There appear to be four possible sources of costs in implementing desegregation that might negatively affect student achievement: (a) the time and energy lost while riding the bus to a school other than the one nearest one's home; (b) busing's drain on financial resources; (c) the loss of parental involvement in and support for the schools; and (d) slower rates of economic growth and the loss of public support for the schools.

Riding the Bus and Student Achievement. The available evidence indicates that how students get to school does not seem to affect their attitudes toward school or their academic achievement. Students do not seem to be affected by whether they walk to school, ride the bus, or arrive by car (see Davis, 1973; Natkin, 1980; Zoloth, 1976). Of course, excessively long rides—say, of an hour or so each way—could well affect energy and interest in school. However, few courts have required rides of such duration. For example, between 1968 and 1978, when most desegregation plans were implemented and schools were being consolidated, the proportion of students riding the bus more than 30 minutes to school remained the same, at about 15% (U.S. Bureau of Census, 1979).

Doesn't busing detract from student learning time? Theoretically, perhaps; practically, no. Walking to school takes time (and is less safe than riding the bus), as does the fooling around that typically occurs along the way. Busing does not subtract time from the school day, so its costs in learning time, if any, must be from homework. Riding the bus for purposes of desegregation may reduce out-of-school learning time by less than 30–40 minutes. There are at least 8 nonschool hours in each child's waking day. On average, American students spend less than an hour a day on homework (Coleman, Hoffer, & Kilgore, 1983).

The Financial Costs of Busing. In terms of raw dollars spent, busing for desegregation is costly.[1] However, in terms of proportions of total school budgets spent, the costs are relatively small. The costs of transportation for the purpose of school desegregation are very difficult to calculate. There is no research on what proportions of predesegregation transportation budgets were usually reallocated for desegregation purposes. There are no reliable data to show what future transportation costs might be in the absence of desegregation in school districts experiencing demographic shifts in student populations within them. And it is difficult to determine how the costs of transportation for mandatory student reassignments compare to the costs of transportation offered under open enrollment or other districtwide voluntary plans, where busing costs per student are typically very high.[2] The most widely cited estimate of increases in transportation costs indicates

---

[1]It may be relevant to provide some perspective on how many children across the country are, indeed, bused. In the nation as a whole, more children ride the bus to school than walk (U.S. Census Bureau, 1979), and the number of children who ride the bus under a school desegregation order is actually quite small. Although no one knows for certain what percentage of the nation's students ride the bus for desegregation who would not otherwise ride the bus to school, the number is probably between 3% and 5% (Moody & Ross, 1980). The extent to which busing has become a symbol of opposition to desegregation itself is suggested by the fact that the proportion of students in Los Angeles involved in court-ordered busing between 1978 and 1981, the period of most intense conflict, was about 4%.

[2]The difference between the costs of busing to achieve voluntary desegregation and those to achieve

that the district expenditure on transportation, on the average, is no more than two percentage points higher (in constant dollars) after desegregation than before (Moody & Ross, 1980). Of course, the cost of busing for desegregation is contingent on numerous factors, including the number of students requiring transportation, the distances between homes and schools, the number of additional buses that must be purchased, and variations in fuel and maintenance costs. Even though the economic costs of busing are difficult to generalize about, it may be useful to examine briefly the financial implications, at the district level, of various types of school improvement efforts to increase student achievement.

There are a host of things that school systems can do, if they are not already doing them, to improve student achievement, the costs of which, aside from initial training, are relatively modest (cf. Hawley & Rosenholtz, 1984):

- Classroom management strategies that maximize academic learning time.
- The use by teachers of so-called interactive teaching methods.
- More effective facilitation of good teaching by school administrators.
- The development within the school of a climate that emphasizes the importance of self-discipline, orderly conduct, and academic achievement.
- High expectations of students among teachers and administrators.
- The direct involvement of parents in the education of their own children.

On the other hand, one can identify a number of research-based strategies for improving student achievement that are fairly costly:

- Early-childhood intervention programs.
- Greater use of computer-based and computer-managed instruction.
- Reductions in class size, at least for younger children with achievement deficiencies.
- Provision to teachers of significantly richer information than they typically have about student learning, which, in turn, is linked to the development of opportunities for professional growth that can increase teachers' effectiveness.

We note, as we did earlier, that the opportunity to expend funds for some programs other than desegregation-related busing does not mean that the opportunities will be taken and, even if initiated, that they will be sustained. This seems obvious on its face, but those who advocate separate but enriched schools in lieu of desegregation do not explain why enrichment efforts had not been initiated in the absence of desegregation. One reason is the failure of school systems to respond to minority children. Another reason, however, is manifest in the absence of such programs in many predominantly white school systems. School systems do not make profits or run surpluses that they can carry over. Increasing the quality of the services available to students usually requires an increase in taxes or the reallocation of resources from other public services. Neither source of funding is readily tapped.

The Effect of Pupil Reassignment on Parental Involvement. One potential cost of desegregation is the likelihood that the assignment of students to schools that are not the schools closest to students' homes makes it more difficult to involve parents in the education of their children. Sadly, perhaps, most parents have minimal contact with their children's

---

mandatory desegregation obviously depends on the plans involved but the costs per student of voluntary plans are usually greater because routing is inefficient and the number of students carried per bus is usually lower (this lower number is dealt with by the use of smaller vehicles, but they are more expensive per student).

teachers and do not participate in any meaningful way in school activities regardless of the physical distance between home and school. But this statement begs the question.

How does parental involvement affect student achievement? As far as one can tell from research, parents' involvement in the education of their own children, rather than parents' involvement in PTA, fund raising, and other support activities, is what matters. Indeed, one of the best-kept secrets of the current educational reform movement is the impressive array of evidence that active efforts on the part of teachers and principals to involve parents directly in the educational process that their children experience is a powerful strategy for improving student achievement (e.g., Gordon, Olmsted, Rubin, & True, 1978; Hawley & Rosenholtz, 1984; Walberg, 1979, 1984). The key here is that school systems must take the initiative (cf. Epstein, 1985). This means, if necessary, that teachers must go to parents in person and on the phone. It means that teachers must be clear about course objectives and how parents can help. And more. Such initiatives may be somewhat more complicated to implement when students live far from the school. For example, teacher–parent consultations might take place in a community center or the school nearest to home rather than in the school the child attends. But there are many desegregated schools in which parents are as involved in their children's education as is the case in many so-called neighborhood schools.

Financial Support for Public School Systems. Critics argue that desegregation often results in a loss of public support because of white flight and a decline in the tax base due to the loss or nonlocation of industry and business in desegregated school systems. We discuss the white flight issue in the next section of this chapter. There is no existing research that would allow one to determine whether desegregation inhibits the economic growth of a community. There are numerous cities that have desegregated and that have used busing heavily to achieve "racial balance" whose economic vitality is strong (e.g. Nashville, Tampa, and Charlotte). And there are contrary cases.

A second related issue is whether desegregation reduces the proclivity of communities to support public education financially. Again, there is little evidence on this question. One recent study of school districts in five southern states reveals a pattern of general continuity and stability in public school finance during the 1970s (Wirt, 1986). This study shows that changes in school district finance were largely independent of trends in school desegregation. In addition, the research on electoral behavior after the implementation of desegregation plans suggests that voter protest is generally short-lived (Rossell, 1983a).

Summary

The available research indicates not only that minorities often benefit academically from desegregation and that whites seldom lose, but that the overall effects could be improved if certain instructional and organizational practices were widely used. There are several possible explanations for the generally positive effects of desegregation on student achievement. Hypothetically, at least, some of these could be obtained in minority schools if the necessary levels of support and responsiveness were provided. Many of the alleged costs of desegregation turn out, on critical examination, to be inconsequential or relatively easy to mitigate. If one were thinking in cost-effectiveness terms and measuring effectiveness in terms of test performance, the choice between desegregation and separate but enriched schools might come down to the educational gains to be achieved through more heterogeneous schools and classrooms, as compared with the gains that could be achieved by programs purchased at the economic costs of desegregation-related busing. There is no way we know about to conduct such an analysis because the data available on the effectiveness of alternative educational strategies almost never identify the costs per student.

ACHIEVING A RACIALLY INTEGRATED SOCIETY

Segregation was clearly intended to eliminate the possibilities that whites and non-whites would be friends, would live in the same neighborhood, would have access to the same governmental services and jobs, or would otherwise live in an integrated society. Racial isolation, whether imposed by the state or not, tends to foster further racial isolation. Racial isolation fosters prejudice, limited access to information about opportunities for residential and occupational mobility, ignorance about how to relate to people of other races, and lack of confidence about interpersonal relationships across racial lines. In the last few years, as more and more children who have experienced desegregation throughout their school years graduate from high school, clear evidence is emerging that school desegregation promotes the racial integration of the society. Children who have attended desegregated schools tend to have more friends who are of another race, to work in higher-status jobs, to attend and graduate from multiracial colleges and universities (Braddock, 1980; Braddock, Crain, & McPartland, 1984; Braddock & McPartland, 1982; Crain and Strauss, 1985; Green, 1981; McPartland and Braddock, 1981), and to live in integrated neighborhoods (Orfield, 1981; Pearce, 1980; Pearce, Crain, & Farley, 1984).

Could the goals of a racially integrated society be achieved as effectively without school desegregation as with it? Fair housing and fair employment laws exist, of course, but the former appear to have had little impact. Pearce *et al.* (1984) examined changes between 1970 and 1980 in the racial integration of neighborhoods in 25 central cities. They found that virtually all of the reductions in the segregation index (which measures racial isolation) occurred in cities with school desegregation plans.

Fair employment laws have been more successful than fair housing statutes because they are easier to enforce and job opportunities are not as income-dependent as are residential options. But it is clear that, even when fair employment laws are in place, minority job-seekers who attended desegregated schools are more likely to pursue and to be hired into jobs not traditionally held by minority persons (Crain & Strauss, 1985).

CONDITIONS THAT FOSTER INTEGRATION

Two prerequisites to racial integration throughout our society are (a) the reduction of racial prejudice and (b) the development of self-confidence and capabilities that foster successful interracial interaction. The strategy that appears to be far and away the most productive with respect to both of these conditions is interracial contact among young people (cf. Schofield & Sagar, 1983).

Certain conditions in schools enhance the positive effects of interracial contact on racial tolerance (see Hawley *et al.*, 1983; McConahay, 1981; Schofield & Sagar, 1983).:

1. Cooperative interracial contact is provided for, both in classrooms and in extracurricular activities.
2. Human relations programs are integrated with the rest of the curriculum and are continuous.
3. School and district officials make their support for positive race relations clear and known to teachers, students, and parents.

It seems reasonable to assume that similar conditions would enhance the willingness of people to seek out and be effective in their relationships with persons of other races.

We do know that black students who experience school desegregation are more likely than those who do not to feel confident in their dealings with whites (Braddock *et al.*, 1984; Braddock & McPartland, 1983; Crain, 1984; Green, 1981, 1982) and, in general, to feel that they have control over their own fate (cf. Beady, 1983).

As we implied above, steps used to improve relationships among races when students are racially separated are not likely to be very effective. Even in racially mixed school districts, the resources available to one-race schools—"multiethnic curricula," for example—have considerably less influence on student attitudes than do opportunities for interracial contact, even when such resources are carefully planned and purposefully structured (Slavin & Madden, 1979).

DESEGREGATION AND RACIAL CONFLICT

Some opponents of desegregation argue that forcing interracial interaction actually increases racial conflict and thus reduces the chances for achieving racial integration. There is, of course, never any interracial conflict in segregated schools, and it is clear that, under certain conditions, interracial contact can lead to increased intergroup hostility and conflict (Gottfredson & Daiger, 1979). Overall, however, the disruption and disorder related to desegregation are usually short-lived. Despite the attention the media have given to the occasional violence accompanying the desegregation process, the massive *Safe Schools Study* found:

> A school's being under court order to desegregate is associated with only a slight increase in the amount of student violence when other factors are taken into account. . . . [The statistical analysis] shows further that there is no consistent association between the *number of* students bused and school violence, controlling for other factors. Finally, there is a weak association between student violence and the *recentness* of initial desegregation efforts at a school. Together these findings suggest that some violence may be due to the initiation of mandatory desegregation, but that as time goes on, and larger numbers of students are bused to achieve racial balance, the desegregation process ceases to be a factor. (National Institute of Education, 1978, p. 123)

The lesson of the research and of our experience with desegregation is that interracial hostility and violence are not the usual result of school desegregation. Improved race relations are. Obviously, simply mixing white and minority students together in schools will not do much to improve race relations. However, when schools adopt programs to this end, the desired improvement is likely to occur (System Development Corporation, 1980). We do not underestimate the difficulties involved in bringing about significant and positive interracial contact in desegregated schools, especially when minority and white students of the same age tend to be achieving at different levels. This issue was addressed at some length in our discussion of academic achievement.

WHITE FLIGHT AND LONG-TERM PROSPECTS FOR INTERRACIAL INTERACTION

If one is to judge from the record of federal court cases or debates in the Congress over antibusing legislation, the most powerful argument made by the opponents of desegregation is that mandatory pupil reassignment results in white flight. Not only, it is argued, does white flight lead to a loss of revenues to school systems (a claim not thus far demonstrated empirically), but it reduces students' opportunity for interracial interaction in the long run.

School desegregation is one cause of white flight. The magnitude of flight related to desegregation, however, depends on the situation (Rossell, 1983b; Rossell & Clarke, 1987). White flight was generally greater when mandatory student reassignment plans were implemented than when voluntary desegregation strategies were used, at least in the early years of desegregation and at least where minority students comprised more than one third of the school population. White flight was greater in central-city school districts than in countywide and metropolitan school systems. And it was greater in districts with large proportions of minority students and in districts where large proportions of white students were reassigned by mandate to previously minority schools (see also Rossell, 1983a; Welch & Ligur, 1986).

The long-term relationship between school desegregation and white flight is not as clear. The research shows that white flight has usually been greatest in the year before and in the first two to three years after a student reassignment plan has been implemented (Armor, 1980; Clotfelter, 1979; Farley, Wurdock, & Richards, 1980; Rossell, 1978a). After the initial implementation period, the rate of decline in white enrollment usually decreases, sometimes to preimplementation rates, but it is almost always lower than on the initial implementation-year rates (Rossell, 1983b; Rossell & Clarke, 1987; Smylie, 1983).

It is difficult to predict with certainty the amount of white flight that will result from desegregation. To attribute declines in white enrollment entirely to desegregation ignores many possible reasons that parents may choose to leave a school system. It is a risky business to predict or estimate white flight from linear projections based on past demographic and enrollment figures and on projections that do not account for changes in income, job and residential mobility, and measures of dissatisfaction with aspects of the school system other than desegregation.

Parents' choices of schools for their children involve a very complicated decision-making process. We know very little about this process and the way in which different parents identify and weigh the various costs and benefits of their choices. But it is obvious that educational options are viable primarily to the extent that they can be afforded. Parents' decisions to remain in or leave school systems may be influenced by various characteristics of desegregation plans and the strategies that the school systems implement to reduce the likelihood of flight. For example, white flight is related to the proportions of white students reassigned under a desegregation plan, to the racial composition and the perceived quality of the schools to which white students are reassigned, to whether desegregation plans are phased in or implemented *in toto*, to the grade level of the students, to the busing distances, to the support of, or resistance to, desegregation by the city's leadership, and to the role of the media in publicizing protest (Rossell, 1983b; Rossell & Clarke, 1987). How school systems deal with these factors has much to do with the amount of white flight they experience (cf. Hawley *et al.*, 1983; Rossell & Hawley, 1982). To date, few studies of white flight have taken into account specific local variations in school desegregation plans and the specific strategies that school systems can implement to reduce white flight.

Several studies of school systems that have implemented mandatory desegregation plans identify strategies that have helped reduce parental and community opposition to desegregation, protest, and flight. These strategies have sought to prepare communities for desegregation, to build grass-roots support for and ownership of desegregation efforts, and to dispel rumors and misinformation that have a negative impact on public perception and opinion. These strategies are:

- Providing opportunities for community involvement in planning for desegregation (McDonnell & Zellman, 1978; Willie & Greenblatt, 1981).
- Establishing communitywide multiethnic citizen–parent–student committees to monitor the implementation of desegregation plans (Smith, Downs, & Lachman, 1973; U.S. Commission on Civil Rights, 1976).

- Building support for desegregation among community leaders (Rossell, 1978b; U.S. Commission on Civil Rights, 1976).
- Providing opportunities for parent and student visits to newly assigned schools before the implementation of the desegregation plan (U.S. Commission on Civil Rights, 1976).
- Encouraging comprehensive media coverage of schools and desegregation that acknowledges the problems but also tells of the successes (Levinsohn, 1976; Rossell, 1978b; Stuart, 1973; Weinberg & Martin, 1976).
- Establishing information and rumor-control centers (U.S. Commission on Civil Rights, 1976).

It is difficult to influence public opinion about issues as divisive as school desegregation. However, these studies strongly suggest that school systems can reduce levels of protest and flight if they take steps to build grass-roots support for desegregation before implementation and to maintain and expand that support once the plans are in effect.

If mandatory student reassignment results in lost opportunities for interracial interaction, will some alternative remedy to segregation be more effective over time and ensure greater opportunities for integrative contact? Obviously, separate but enriched programs will not do this. But it is often argued that voluntary desegregation strategies will provide greater opportunities for interracial interaction in the long run and thus are the strategies of choice. The most compelling evidence to date to support this claim is the recent study by Rossell and Clarke (1987). As we argued earlier, the findings of this study rest on several important considerations and issues that have not been resolved in the literature. Their conclusions contradict more than a decade of research and their data will no doubt be reanalyzed in the future to test those conclusions. Still, to assume that white parents and students who would flee mandatory student reassignments and have refused to participate in voluntary desegregation programs would at some future date opt to attend desegregated schools or predominantly minority schools is to assume improbable changes in attitudes and behavior. In short, even if voluntary desegregation results in less white flight, it may not result in greater opportunities to foster better race relations than does more comprehensive pupil reassignment unless these changes occur.

SUMMARY

Fostering positive interracial contact among children is the best way we know to bring about a racially integrated society. Racially separate schools, regardless of the programs in them, fail to address the issue. Unfortunately, perhaps, the schools are the only social institution in which substantial interracial contact can occur among children. Families, neighborhoods, churches, and social organizations are usually not interracial. In short, when we relinquish the opportunity to desegregate our schools, we reduce the prospects of living in a society in which one's race does not determine one's chances to maximize one's potential.

CONCLUSION

One of the major impediments to effective school desegregation is the widely perpetuated myth that desegregation has reduced the quality of education in the nation's schools and has had little, if any, positive impact on racial tolerance. We have cited evidence that school desegregation usually contributes to the academic achievement of minority youngsters without slowing the progress of white children, and that it seems to significantly increase the prospects that, someday, racial prejudice and discrimination will cease to play a major role in American life.

To say that desegregation has generally had positive consequences and that we have the knowledge necessary to enhance its benefits is not to argue that desegregation is without costs. And in some school systems, comprehensive desegregation is not feasible. Thus, a variety of strategies for remediating the vestiges of segregation are appropriate. The issue, as we see it, is the priority given to desegregation, compared to what we have called separate but enriched strategies.

Our analysis leads us to give considerable emphasis to desegregation. If we hope to make significant progress in eliminating racial prejudice, the best way to do it is through structured interracial contact when children are young. Separate but enriched programs obviously do not offer this opportunity, nor does any other social policy. Moreover, racial discrimination devalues the benefits of academic achievement. Unless racial prejudice ceases to play a substantial role in decisions regarding employment, occupational advancement, housing, and political behavior, whites will benefit more from their education than will nonwhites of similar academic achievement.

One cannot know from the available research how the cost-effectiveness of desegregation as a source of student achievement compares with the potential for increased academic achievement presented by enrichment strategies. But it is clear that the instructional opportunities provided by more heterogeneous classrooms cannot be purchased with any amount of money. Enrichment strategies, on the other hand, can be purchased. In other words, forgoing desegregation in favor of enrichment *de facto* eliminates some educational options. The obverse holds only under conditions of absolute constraints on fiscal resources.

The argument for separate but enriched minority-dominant schools rests on the assumption that the states and localities will pay the costs of enrichment. That assumption deserves to be met with considerable skepticism. Desegregation is a response to intentional segregation. A main problem that it seeks to address is racial prejudice. And the major obstacles to effective desegregation are rooted in the sources of discrimination. Given this context, one who expects the white-dominated policymaking processes of the federal government, the states, and the localities to be responsive to demands by the advocates of enriched education for minorities that will make higher expenditures per pupil for minority than for white students is whistling Dixie.

Financial resources are not the only kind of support needed for enriched schools serving minority youngsters. They also need to attract the best teachers, administrators, concerned parents, and public confidence. Racism reduces the access of minority youngsters to these resources as well.

It seems important to note that many of the strongest opponents of desegregation have never experienced it, nor have their children. On the other hand, recent college entrants, from whose ranks the nation will draw its leaders, and who, as a group, are the first generation of high-school graduates who have grown up with desegregation, not only increasingly support desegregation but, by a clear majority, support mandatory busing as a strategy for achieving an end to the racial isolation of minority students (Meyer & Evans, 1986). It is instructive of both the generally positive response to desegregation of those who have directly experienced its consequences, and of the power of the negative myths, that black and white parents of children who have been bused to school for purposes of desegregation, by the extraordinary ratio of 5 or 6 to 1, reported that they felt good about their children's school experiences (Harris, 1981, 1983). That many parents do not talk about their positive feelings in public and that our political leaders more often than not echo the voices of fear and ignorance may be the most powerful testimony that can be offered in support of the notion that serious efforts should continue to be made to desegregate the nation's schools. And why is it that most Americans can see how racial separation in South Africa is an unjust but effective strategy for keeping nonwhites from achieving their potential but view the increasing racial isolation of the nonwhite poor in this country, who are growing in number, with dispassion?

REFERENCES

Ames, C. (1981). Competitive versus cooperative structures: The influence of individual and group performance factors on achievement attributions and affect. *American Educational Research Journal, 18*, 273–287.

Armor, D. J. (1980). White flight and the future of school desegregation. In W. G. Stephan & J. R. Feagan (Eds.), *School desegregation: Past, present, and future*. New York: Plenum Press.

Beady, C. H., Jr. (1983, April). *Race and futility: Toward a program of research for reducing and achievement and income inequity*. Paper presented at the annual meeting of the American Educational Research Association, Montreal.

Blank, R. K., Dentler, R. A., Blatzell, D. C., & Chabotar, K. (1983, September). *Survey of magnet schools: Analyzing a model for quality integrated education*. Chicago: James H. Lowry.

Braddock, J. H. (1980). The perpetuation of segregation across levels of education: A behavioral assessment of the contact hypothesis. *Sociology of Education, 53*, 178–186.

Braddock, J. H., & McPartland, J. M. (1982). Assessing school desegregation effects: New directions in research. In R. Corwin (Ed.), *Research in sociology of education and socialization*. Greenwich, CT: JAI.

Braddock, J. H., & McPartland, J. M. (1983). *More evidence on social-psychological processes that perpetuate minority segregation: The relationship of school desegregation and employment segregation* (Report No. 338). Baltimore: Johns Hopkins University, Center for Social Organization of Schools.

Braddock, J. H., Crain, R. L., & McPartland, J. M. (1984). A long-term view of school desegregation: Some recent studies of graduates as adults. *Phi Delta Kappan, 66*, 259–264.

Brophy, J. E. (1983). Classroom organization and management. *Elementary School Journal, 83*, 265–286.

Clotfelter, C. T. (1979). Urban school desegregation and declines in white enrollment: A reexamination. *Journal of Urban Economics, 6*, 352–370.

Cohen, E. G. (1982). Expectation states and interracial interaction in school settings. *Annual Review of Sociology, 8*, 209–235.

Cohen, P. A., Kulik, J. A., & Kulik, C. C. (1982). Educational outcomes of tutoring: A meta-analysis of findings. *American Educational Research Journal, 19*, 237–248.

Coleman, J. S., Hoffer, T., & Kilgore, S. (1983). *Public and private schools*. New York: Basic Books.

Crain, R. L. (1983). *Is nineteen really better than ninety-three?* Baltimore: Johns Hopkins University, Center for Social Organization of Schools.

Crain, R. L. (1984, April). *Desegregated schools and the non-academic side of college survival*. Paper presented at the annual meeting of the American Educational Research Association, New Orleans.

Crain, R. L., & Strauss, J. (1985). *School desegregation and black occupational attainment: Results from a long-term experiment*. Baltimore: Johns Hopkins University, Center for Social Organization of Schools.

Davis, J. (1973). Busing. In *Southern schools: An evaluation of the Emergency School Assistance Program and of desegregation*. Chicago: National Opinion Research Center.

Epstein, J. L. (1985). Home and school convictions in schools of the future: Implications of research on parent involvement. *Peabody Journal of Education, 62*(2), 18–41.

Evertson, C. M., & Smylie, M. A. (1987). Research on classroom processes: Views from two perspectives. In J. Glover & R. Ronning (Eds.), *History of educational psychology*. New York: Plenum Press.

Evertson, C. M., Sanford, J. P., & Emmer, E. T. (1981). Effects of class heterogeneity in junior high school. *American Educational Research Journal, 18*, 219–232.

Farley, R., Wurdock, C., & Richards, T. (1980). School desegregation and white flight: An investigation of competing models and their discrepant findings. *Sociology of Education, 53*, 123–139.

Foster, G. (1973). Desegregating urban schools: A review of techniques. *Harvard Educational Review, 43*, 5–36.

Gerber, M., & Kauffman, J. M. (1981). Peer tutoring in academic settings. In P. S. Strain (Ed.), *The utilization of classroom peers as behavior change agents*. New York: Plenum Press.

Gordon, I., Olmsted, P., Rubin, R., & True, J. (1978). *Continuity between home and school: Aspects of parent involvement in Follow Through.* Chapel Hill: University of North Carolina.

Gottfredson, G. S., & Daiger, D. C. (1979). *Disruption in six hundred schools* (Report No. 289). Baltimore: Johns Hopkins University, Center for Social Organization of Schools.

Green, K. (1981, April). *Integration and attainment: Preliminary results from a national longitudinal study of the impact of school desegregation.* Paper presented at the annual meeting of the American Educational Research Association, Los Angeles.

Green, K. (1982). *The impact of neighborhood and secondary school integration on educational achievement and occupational attainment of college-bound blacks.* Doctoral dissertation, University of California–Los Angeles.

Harris, L. (1981, March 26). *Majority of parents report school busing has been satisfactory experience.* Chicago: Chicago Tribune-New York News Syndicate.

Harris, L. (1983, July 21). *Black voting the key to outcome in 1984.* Chicago: Chicago Tribune-New York News Syndicate.

Hawley, W. D., & Rosenholtz, S. J. (1984). Good schools: What research says about improving student achievement. *Peabody Journal of Education, 61*(4), 1–178.

Hawley, W. D., & Rosenholtz, S. J. (1986). *Achieving quality integrated education.* Washington, DC: National Education Association.

Hawley, W. D., Crain, R. L., Rossell, C. H., Smylie, M. A., Fernandez, R. R., Schofield, J. W., Tompkins, R., Trent, W. T., & Zlotnik, M. S. (1983). *Strategies for effective desegregation: Lessons from research.* Lexington, MA: Lexington Books.

Kulik, C. C., & Kulik, J. A. (1982). Effects of ability grouping on secondary school students: A meta-analysis of evaluation findings. *Journal of Educational Research, 75,* 133–138.

Leinhardt, G., & Pallay, A. (1982). Restrictive educational settings: Exile or haven? *Review of Educational Research, 52,* 557–578.

Levinsohn, F. H. (1976). TV's deadly inadvertant bias. In F. H. Levinsohn & B. D. Wright (Eds.), *School desegregation: Shadow and substance.* Chicago: University of Chicago Press.

Mahard, R. E., & Crain, R. L. (1980). *The influence of high school racial composition on the academic achievement and college attendance of Hispanics.* Paper presented at the annual meeting of the American Sociological Association, New York.

Mahard, R. E., & Crain, R. L. (1983). Research on minority achievement in desegregated schools. In C. H. Rossell & W. D. Hawley (Eds.), *The consequences of school desegregation.* Philadelphia: Temple University Press.

McConahay, J. B. (1981). Reducing racial prejudice in desegregated schools. In W. D. Hawley (Ed.), *Effective school desegregation: Equity, quality and feasibility.* Beverly Hills, CA: Sage.

McDonnell, L. M. & Zellman, G. L. (1978, August–September). *The role of community groups facilitating school desegregation.* Paper presented at the annual meeting of the American Political Science Association, New York.

McPartland, J. M., & Braddock, J. H. (1981). Going to college and getting a good job: The impact of desegregation. In W. D. Hawley (Ed.), *Effective school desegregation: Equity, quality, and feasibility.* Beverly Hills, CA: Sage.

Meyer, T. J., & Evans, G. (1986, January 15). Most of this year's freshmen hold liberal views, study finds. *Chronicle of Higher Education,* pp. 34–35.

Moody, C. D., & Ross, J. D. (1980). *Costs of implementing court-ordered desegregation.* Ann Arbor: University of Michigan, School of Education, Program for Educational Opportunity.

Morgan, D. R., & England, R. E. (1981). *Assessing the progress of large city school desegregation: A case survey method.* Norman: University of Oklahoma, Bureau of Government Research.

National Institute of Education (1978). *Violent schools—Safe schools: The safe school study report to the Congress* (Vol. 1). Washington, DC: U.S. Government Printing Office.

Natkin, G. L. (1980, April). *The effects of busing on second grade students' achievement test scores (Jefferson County, Kentucky).* Paper presented at the annual meeting of the American Educational Research Association, Boston.

Nelson-Le Gall, S., & Glor-Scheib, S. (1983, April). *Help-seeking in elementary classrooms: An observational study.* Paper presented at the annual meeting of the American Educational Research Association, Montreal.

Nicholls, J. G. (1979). Development of perception of own attainment and casual attributions for success and failure in reading. *Journal of Educational Psychology, 71,* 94–99.

Oakes, J. (1982). Classroom social relationships: Exploring the Bowles and Gintis hypothesis. *Sociology of Education, 55,* 197–212.

Orfield, G. (1981, December). *Toward a strategy for urban integration: Lessons in school and housing policy from twelve cities.* New York: Ford Foundation.

Pearce, D. M. (1980, November). *Breaking down the barriers: New evidence on the impact of metropolitan school desegregation on housing patterns*. Washington, DC: National Institute of Education.

Pearce, D. M., Crain, R. L., & Farley, R. (1984, April). *Lessons not lost: The effect of school desegregation on the rate of residential desegregation in large central cities.* Paper presented at the annual meeting of the American Educational Research Association, New Orleans.

Rosenbaum, J. E. (1980). Social implications of educational grouping. In D. Berliner (Ed.), *Review of Research in Education, 8,* 361–401.

Rosenholtz, S. J. (1985). Modifying status organizing process of the traditional classroom. In J. Berger & M. Zelditch, Jr. (Ed.), *Status, attributions, and justice.* San Francisco: Jossey-Bass.

Rossell, C. H. (1978a). *Assessing the unintended impacts of public policy: School desegregation and resegregation.* Washington, DC: National Institute of Education.

Rossell, C. H. (1978b). The effect of community leadership and the mass media on public behavior. *Theory into Practice, 17,* 131–139.

Rossell, C. H. (1983a). Applied social science research: What does it say about the effectiveness of school desegregation plans? *Journal of Legal Studies, 12,* 69–107.

Rossell, C. H. (1983b). Desegregation plans, racial isolation, white flight, and community response. In C. H. Rossell & W. D. Hawley (Eds.), *The consequences of school desegregation.* Philadelphia: Temple University Press.

Rossell, C. H., & Clarke, R. C. (1987,). *The carrot or the stick in school desegregation policy?* (Report to the National Institute of Education, Grant NIE-G-83-0019) Boston: Boston University.

Rossell, C. H., & Hawley, W. D. (1982). Policy alternatives for minimizing white flight. *Educational Evaluation and Policy Analysis, 4,* 205–222.

Royster, E. C., Blatzell, D. C., & Simmons, F. C. (1979). *Study of the Emergency School Aid Act Magnet School Program.* Cambridge, MA: ABT Associates.

Schofield, J. W., & Sagar, H. A. (1983). Desegregation, school practices, and student race relations. In C. H. Rossell & W. D. Hawley (Eds.), *The consequences of school desegregation.* Philadelphia: Temple University Press.

Sharan, S. (1980). Cooperative learning in small groups: Research methods and effects on achievement, attitudes, and ethnic relations. *Review of Educational Research, 50,* 241–272.

Slavin, R. E. (1980). Cooperative learning. *Review of Educational Research, 50,* 315–342.

Slavin, R. E., & Karweit, N. L. (1985). Effects of whole class, ability grouped, and individualized instruction on mathematics achievement. *American Educational Research Journal, 22,* 351–368.

Slavin, R. E., & Madden, N. (1979). School practices that improve race relations, *American Educational Research Journal, 16,* 169–180.

Smith, A. D., Downs, A., & Lachman, M. L. (1973). *Achieving effective desegregation.* Lexington, MA: Lexington Books, D. C. Heath.

Smylie, M. A. (1983). Reducing racial isolation in large school districts: The comparative effectiveness of mandatory and voluntary desegregation strategies. *Urban Education, 17,* 477–502.

Stuart, R. (1973). Busing and the media in Nashville. *New South, 28,* 79–87.

System Development Corporation. (1980). *Human relations study: Investigations of effective human relations strategies* (Technical Report, Vol. 2). Santa Monica, CA: System Development Corporation.

Tammivaara, J. S. (1982). The effects of task structure on beliefs about competence and participation in small groups. *Sociology of Education, 55,* 212–222.

U.S. Bureau of the Census. (1979). *Travel to school: October 1978.* (*Current population reports,* Series P-20, No. 342). Washington, DC: U.S. Government Printing Office.

U.S. Commission on Civil Rights (1976, August). *Fulfilling the letter and spirit of the law: Desegregation of the nation's public schools.* Washington, DC: U.S. Government Printing Office.

Walberg, H. J. (Ed.) (1979). *Educational environments and effects: Evaluation, policy, and productivity.* Berkeley, CA: McCutchan.

Walberg, H. J. (1984). Families as partners in educational productivity. *Phi Delta Kappan, 65,* 397–400.

Weinberg, M., & Martin, G. (Eds.). (1976). *Covering the desegregation story: Current experiences and issues.* Evanston, IL: Center for Equal Education.

Welch, F., & Light, A. (1986). *New evidence on school desegregation.* Los Angeles: Unicon Research Corporation.

Willie, C. V., & Greenblatt, S. (1981). *Community politics and educational change: Ten school systems under court-order.* New York: Longman.

Wirt, F. (1986). *School finance and school desegregation: Ten-year effects in southern school districts.* Urbana: Department of Political Science, University of Illinois–Urbana.

Zoloth, B. (1976). The impact of busing on student achievement: A reanalysis. *Growth and change, 7*(7), 43–52.

C. Intergroup Conflict

15

Desegregation, Jigsaw, and the Mexican-American Experience

Elliot Aronson and Alex Gonzalez

In 1954, when the U.S. Supreme Court outlawed school segregation, hopes ran high that we might be on our way to a better society. At that time, many of us believed that, if only youngsters from various ethnic and racial backgrounds could share the same classroom, negative stereotypes would fade and cross-ethnic friendships would develop under the glow of contact. Ultimately, it was believed, these young people would grow into adults who would be largely free of the racial and ethnic prejudice that had plagued our society since its inception.

The case that brought about the court's landmark decision was that of *Oliver Brown v. The Board of Education of Topeka, Kansas*; the decision reversed a 1896 ruling (in *Plessy v. Ferguson*), which held that it was permissible to segregate racially, as long as equal facilities were provided for both races. In the *Brown* case, the court held that, psychologically, there could be no such thing as "separate but equal" because the forced separation, in and of itself, implied to the minority group in question that its members were inferior to those of the majority. To quote from the *Brown* decision:

> Does segregation of children in public schools solely on the basis of race, even though the physical facilities and other "tangible" factors may be equal, deprive the children of the minority group of equal educational opportunities? We believe that it does . . . to separate Negro school children from others of similar age and qualifications solely because of their race generates a feeling of inferiority as to their status in the community that may affect their hearts and minds in a way unlikely ever to be undone. . . . We conclude that in the field of public education the doctrine "separate but equal" has no place. Separate educational facilities are inherently unequal.

As Stephan (1978) spelled out, the language of the court in the *Brown* decision shows the influence of a group of distinguished social psychologists, led by Kenneth Clark, Stuart Cook and Isidor Chein, who testified as "friends of the court" in this case, as well

ELLIOT ARONSON • Adlai E. Stevenson College, University of California, Santa Cruz, California 95064.   ALEX GONZALEZ • Department of Psychology, California State University, Cedar at Shay, Fresno, California 93740.

as in previous cases in state supreme courts. The social psychologists testified to the effect that, in segregated schools, black children "learn the inferior status to which they are assigned" and the black child wonders "whether his group and he himself are worthy of no more respect than they receive. This conflict and confusion leads to self-hate." The implication of the *Brown* decision was that, because segregation lowers self-esteem, desegregation would eventually produce an increase in the self-esteem of minority students. Furthermore, because segregation was depriving minority group members of equal educational opportunities, the implication was that desegregation would lead to improved education for these students. Thus, the *Brown* decision was not only a humane interpretation of the U.S. Constitution, it was also the beginning of a profound and exciting social experiment with three clear hypotheses, that desegregation would (a) reduce prejudice; (b) raise the self-esteem of minority students; and (c) improve the classroom performance of minority students.

THE EFFECTS OF DESEGREGATION

More than three decades have passed since the *Brown* decision, and it appears that some of us may have been overly optimistic. Things did not work out exactly as we had hoped they would. For example, in a longitudinal study in Riverside, California, Gerard and Miller (1975) found that, long after the schools had been desegregated, black, white, and Mexican-American children tended not to integrate; rather, they hung out in their own ethnic clusters. Moreover, anxiety among the ethnic minorities had increased and remained high long after desegregation had occurred. These trends were echoed in several other studies. Indeed, the most careful scholarly reviews of the research show few, if any, benefits (see St. John, 1975; Stephan, 1978). For example, according to Stephan's review, there isn't a single nonexperimental study that shows a significant increase in the self-esteem of minority children following desegregation; in fact, in fully 25% of the studies, desegregation was followed by a significant decrease in the self-esteem of young minority children. Stephan also reported that desegregation reduced the prejudice of whites toward blacks in only 13% of the school systems studied; moreover, the prejudice of blacks toward whites increased in about as many cases as it decreased. Similarly, studies of the effects of desegregation on the academic performance of minority children present a mixed and highly variable picture.

What went wrong? First of all, it is important to note that the social psychologists who testified in these cases were sophisticated and properly cautious: they neither stated nor implied that the predicted benefits would occur automatically. Certain preconditions would have to be met. These preconditions were most articulately stated by Gordon Allport in *The Nature of Prejudice* (1954), published the same year as the Supreme Court decision:

> Prejudice . . . may be reduced by equal status contact between majority and minority groups in the pursuit of common goals. The effect is greatly enhanced if this contact is sanctioned by institutional supports (i.e., by law, custom or local atmosphere), and provided it is of a sort that leads to the perception of common interests and common humanity between members of the two groups. (p. 281)

Thus, according to Allport, desegregation will produce beneficial effects if, and only if, it occurs in the context of equal-status contact in pursuit of common goals, sanctioned by authority. It is our contention that very few of the studies reviewed by Stephan and by St. John involved a school situation in which all three of these prerequisites had been met. Let us look at each of these three factors separately.

SANCTION BY AUTHORITY

In some school districts, there was clear acceptance and enforcement of the ruling by responsible authority. In others, the acceptance was not as clear. In still others (especially in the early years), local authorities were in open defiance of the law. As early as 1961, Tom Pettigrew demonstrated that desegregation proceeded more smoothly and with less violence in those localities where local authorities sanctioned integration. But such variables as self-esteem and the reduction of prejudice do not necessarily change for the better even where authority clearly sanctions desegregation. Although sanction by authority may be necessary, it is clearly not a sufficient condition.

EQUAL-STATUS CONTACT

The definition of *equal status* has never been made clear in the context of desegregation. For example, one might claim that there is equal status on the grounds that all children in, say, the fifth grade have the same "occupational" status; that is, they are all fifth-grade students. On the other hand, if the teacher is prejudiced against minority children, he or she may treat them unfairly, thus lowering their perceived status in the classroom (see Gerard & Miller, 1975). Moreover, if, because of an inferior education (before desegregation) or because of language difficulties, black or Mexican-American students perform poorly in the classroom, this poor performance could also lower their status among their peers.

An important insight by Cohen (1972) pointed to a more subtle complication. Although Allport (1954) predicted that positive interactions would result if cooperative equal status were achieved, expectation theory, as developed by Cohen, holds that even in such an environment, biased expectations by both white Anglos and minorities may lead to sustained white dominance and concomitantly lower status for minority children. Cohen reasoned that both of these groups have accepted the premise that the majority group's competence results in dominance and superior achievement. She suggested that alternatives be created to reverse these often unconscious expectations. According to Cohen, at least a temporary exchange of majority and minority roles is required as a prelude to equal status. In one study (Cohen & Roper, 1972), black children were instructed in building radios and in how to teach this skill to others. Then, a group of white children and the newly trained black children viewed a film of themselves building the radios. This film was followed by some of the black children's teaching the whites how to construct radios while others taught a black administrator. Then, all the children came together in small groups. Equal-status interactions were found in the groups where the black children had taught whites how to construct the radios. The other group, however, demonstrated the usual white dominance. We will return to this point in a moment.

IN PURSUIT OF COMMON GOALS

If there is one statement that we can make unequivocally about the typical American classroom, it is that children are almost never engaged in the pursuit of common goals. During the past several years, we and our colleagues have systematically observed scores of classrooms at all levels. We have found that, in the vast majority of these cases, the process of education is highly competitive. Children vie with one another for good grades and for the respect of the teacher. This occurs not only during quizzes and exams, but also in the informal give and take of the classroom, where children typically learn to raise their hands (often frantically) in response to questions from the teacher, groan when someone else is called on, and revel in the failure of their classmates. The pervasive competitive atmosphere unwittingly leads children to view one another as foes to be heckled and vanquished. In a newly desegregated school, all other things being equal, this atmosphere could exacerbate whatever prejudice existed before desegregation.

A dramatic example of dysfunctional competition was demonstrated by Sherif, Harvey, White, Hood, and Sherif (1961) in the classic "robber's cave" experiment. In this field experiment, the investigators encouraged intergroup competition between two teams of boys at a summer camp; this created fertile ground for anger and hostility even in previously benign, noncompetitive circumstances, like watching a movie. Positive relations between the groups were ultimately achieved only after both groups had been required to work cooperatively to solve a common problem.

It is our contention that the competitive process interacts with "equal-status con- tact." That is to say, any differences in ability that existed between minority children and white children before desegregation are emphasized by the competitive structure of the learning environment; furthermore, because segregated school facilities are rarely equal, minority children frequently enter the newly desegregated school at a distinct disadvan- tage, which is made more salient by the competitive atmosphere.

THE JIGSAW METHOD

It was this reasoning that first led us to develop the hypothesis that interdependent learning environments would establish the conditions necessary for the increase in self- esteem and performance and the decrease in prejudice that were (perhaps naively) ex- pected to occur as a function of desegregation (Aronson, Blaney, Sikes, Stephan, & Snapp, 1975; Aronson, Stephan, Sikes, Blaney, & Snapp, 1978). To this end, we devel- oped a highly structured method of interdependent learning and systematically tested its effects in a number of elementary- and secondary-school classrooms. The aim of this research program was not merely to compare the effects of cooperation and competition in a classroom setting. Such a comparison had been ably made by other investigators dating to as far back as 1949 and Deutsch's classic experiment. Rather, our intent was to devise a cooperative classroom structure that could be used easily by teachers on a long- term, sustained basis, and to evaluate the effects of this intervention via a well-controlled series of field experiments. In short, this project was an action research program aimed at developing and evaluating a classroom atmosphere that can be sustained by the class- room teachers long after the researchers have packed up their questionnaires and re- turned to the more cozy environment of the social-psychological laboratory. We dubbed our invention the *jigsaw method* for reasons that will become clear in the next paragraph.

The method is described in detail elsewhere (Aronson, 1984; Aronson & Goode, 1980; Aronson & Yates, 1983; Aronson et al., 1978). Briefly, students are placed in six- person learning groups. The day's lesson is divided into six paragraphs, so that each student has one segment of the written material. Each student owns a unique and vital part of the information, which, like the pieces of a jigsaw puzzle, must be put with the others before any of the students can learn the whole picture. The individual must learn her or his own section and teach it to the other members of the group. The reader will note that, in this method, every student spends part of her or his time in the role of expert. Thus, the method incorporates Cohen's findings (previously discussed) within the context of an equal-status contact situation. The most important aspect of this method (and one that makes it unique among cooperative techniques) is that, in jigsaw, each student has a special, vital gift for the other group members—a gift that is unattainable elsewhere.

An example will clarify: In our initial experiment, we entered a fifth-grade classroom in a newly desegregated school. In this classroom, the children were studying the biographies of famous Americans. The next lesson happened to be a biography of Joseph Pulitzer, the famous publisher. First, we constructed a biography of Pulitzer consisting of six paragraphs. Paragraph 1 was about his ancestors and how they came to this country; Paragraph 2 was about Pulitzer as a little boy and how he grew up; Paragraph 3 described him as a young man, his education, and his early employment; Paragraph 4 was about his middle age and how he founded his newspaper; and so on. Each major aspect of Joseph Pulitzer's life was contained in a separate paragraph.

We mimeographed our biography of Pulitzer, cut each copy of the biography into six one-paragraph sections, and gave every child in each of the six-person learning groups one paragraph about Joseph Pulitzer's life. Thus, each learning group had within it the entire biography of Joseph Pulitzer, but each individual child had no more than one sixth of the story. Each child had one piece of the "jigsaw" puzzle, and each child was dependent on the other children in the group for the completion of the big picture. In order to learn the biography, each child had to master a paragraph, teach it to the others and listen carefully while each of his or her group-mates recited.

The Expert Group

Each student took his or her paragraph and went off to master it. The child then consulted with "fellow experts" from the other learning groups. That is, if Bill had been dealt Joseph Pulitzer as a young man, he would then consult with Nancy, Carlos, and Samantha, who were in different jigsaw groups and had also been dealt Joseph Pulitzer as a young man. In the expert groups, the children used one another as consultants, to rehearse and clarify for themselves the important aspects of that phase of Joseph Pulitzer's life.

This part of the process is of great importance in that it provides time, space, and practice for the less articulate and less skillful students to learn the material and affords them an opportunity to make use of the more adept students as models for organizing and presenting their report. Without the mediation of this expert group, the jigsaw experience might backfire. That is, as Brown (1986) pointed out, the jigsaw classroom can be a little like baseball: if the boy playing right field keeps dropping fly balls, it hurts your team and you might begin to resent him. Thus, if you must depend on the performance of a Mexican-American child who is less than perfectly articulate in English, you might resent him—unless he had a clear idea of how to present the material. Thus, the practice in the "expert" groups was crucial to the success of the enterprise. Even so, things rarely went as smoothly in practice as on the drawing board—as we shall see.

The Jigsaw Group

After spending from 10 to 15 minutes with their fellow experts, the students met again with their original six-person groups, and the teacher informed them that they had a specified amount of time (usually from 20 to 30 minutes) to communicate their knowledge to one another. They were also informed that, at the end of the time (or soon after), they would be tested on their knowledge.

When thrown on their own resources, the children eventually learned to teach and to listen to one another. The children gradually learned that none of them could do well without the aid of each person in the group—and that each member had a unique and essential contribution to make. Suppose you and I are children in the same group. You've been dealt Joseph Pulitzer as a young man; I've been dealt Pulitzer as an old man. The only way I can learn about Joseph Pulitzer as a young man is to pay close attention to what you are saying. You are a very important resource for me. I do well if I pay attention to my peers; I do poorly if I don't. I no longer get rewarded for trying to please the teacher at your expense. It's a whole new ball game.

But cooperative behavior doesn't happen all at once. Typically, children require several days to learn to use this technique effectively. Old habits die hard. The students in our experimental group had grown accustomed to competing during all of their years in school. For the first few days, most of the youngsters tried to compete—even though competitiveness was dysfunctional.

Let us illustrate with an actual example, typical of the way the children stumbled toward the learning of the cooperative process. In one of our groups, there was a Mexican-American boy, whom we will call Carlos. Carlos was not very articulate in English, his second language. He had learned over the years how to keep quiet in class because frequently, when he had spoken up in the past, he had been ridiculed. In the jigsaw group, initially, he had a little trouble communicating his paragraph to the other children; he was very uncomfortable about it. This is not surprising because, in the system we introduced, Carlos was forced to speak, whereas before he had always been able to deindividuate himself and keep a low profile in the classroom. But the situation was even more complex than that; it might even be said that, long before jigsaw had been introduced, the teacher and Carlos had entered into a conspiracy. Carlos was perfectly willing to be quiet. In the past, when the teacher had occasionally called on him, he would stumble, stammer, and fall into an embarrassed silence. Several of his peers would make fun of him. The teacher had learned not to call on him anymore. The decision probably came from the purest of intentions: the teacher simply did not want to humiliate him. But by ignoring him, she had written him off. The implication was that he was not worth bothering with; at least, the other students in the classroom got that message. They believed there was one good reason that the teacher wasn't calling on Carlos: he was stupid. Indeed, even Carlos began to draw this conclusion. This is part of the dynamic of how desegregation, when coupled with a competitive process, can produce unequal-status contact and can result in even greater enmity between ethnic groups and a loss of self-esteem for the members of disadvantaged ethnic minorities.

Let us go back to our six-person group. Carlos, who had to report on oseph Pulitzer's young manhood, was having a hard time. Although he had learned the material quite well in the expert group, when it was his turn to recite in his jigsaw group he grew very nervous. He stammered, hesitated, and fidgeted. The other youngsters in the circle were not very helpful. They had grown accustomed to a competitive process, and they responded out of this old, overlearned habit. They knew what to do when a fellow student stumbles—especially a student whom they believed to be stupid. They ridiculed him, put him down, and teased him. During our experiment, it was Mary who was observed to say, "Aw, you don't know it, you're dumb, you're stupid. You don't know what you're doing." In our initial experiment, the groups were loosely monitored by a research assistant who floated from group to group. When this incident occurred, our assistant made one brief intervention: "OK, you can do that if you want to. It might be fun for you, but it's not going to help you learn about Joseph Pulitzer's young manhood—and the exam will take place in an hour." Notice how the reinforcement contingencies have shifted. No longer does Mary gain much from putting Carlos down; in fact, she now stands to lose a great deal. After a few days and several similar experiences, it became increasingly clear to the students in Carlos's group that the only way they could learn about his part of the jigsaw was by paying attention to what Carlos had to say.

Moreover, they began to develop into pretty good interviewers. Instead of ignoring or ridiculing Carlos when he was having a little trouble communicating what he knew, they began asking friendly, probing questions—the kind of questions that made it easier for Carlos to communicate what was in his head. Carlos began to respond to this treatment by becoming more relaxed; with increased relaxation came an improvement in his ability to communicate. After a couple of weeks, the other students concluded that Carlos was a lot smarter than they had thought he was. They began to see things in him they had never seen before. They began to like him. Carlos began to enjoy school more and began to see the Anglo students in his group not as tormentors but as helpful and responsible people. Moreover, as he began to feel increasingly comfortable in class and started to gain more conidence in himself, his academic performance began to improve. The vicious circle had been reversed; the elements that had been causing a downward spiral had been changed, and the spiral now began to move upward.

Working with the jigsaw technique, children gradually learn that the old competitive behavior is no longer appropriate. Rather, in order to learn all of the material (and thus to perform well on a quiz), each student must begin to listen to the others, to ask appropriate questions, and to contribute in other ways to the group. The process makes it possible for children to pay attention to one another and to begin to appreciate one another as potentially valuable resources. It is important to emphasize that the motivation of the students is not altruistic; rather, it is primarily self-interest, which, in this case, happens also to produce outcomes that are beneficial to others.

Each group remained intact for approximately six weeks. The groups were were then dissolved and reformed. This procedure was followed to increase the diversity of experience that each youngster could have, that is, so that each youngster could have an opportunity to interact with a great many of his or her fellow students of various ethnic groups.

EXPERIMENTS IN THE CLASSROOM

Since the mid-1970s, systematic experiments in the classroom have produced consistently positive results. Typical of the research on jigsaw is an early field experiment that we conducted in Austin, Texas (Blaney, Stephan, Rosenfield, Aronson, & Sikes, 1977). The recent desegregation of the Austin schools had produced a great deal of tension and even some interracial skirmishes throughout the school system. In this tense atmosphere, we introduced the jigsaw technique in 10 fifth-grade classrooms in seven elementary schools. Three classes from among the same schools were also used as controls. The control classes were taught by teachers who, although using traditional techniques, were rated very highly by their peers. The experimental classes met in jigsaw groups for about 45 minutes a day, 3 days a week for 6 weeks. The curriculum was basically the same for the experimental and control classes.

SELF-ESTEEM, LIKING SCHOOL, AND LIKING ONE ANOTHER

Students in the jigsaw groups showed significant increases in their liking for their group-mates both within and across ethnic boundaries. Moreover, the children in jigsaw groups showed a significantly greater increase in self-esteem than the children in the control classrooms. This was true for Anglo children as well as for ethnic minorities. Most children in the jigsaw classrooms also showed relatively greater liking for school than those in traditional classrooms.

The major results were replicated and refined in several experiments in school districts throughout the country. For example, Geffner (1978) introduced jigsaw in Watsonville, California. As a further control (for the possibility of a Hawthorne effect), Geffner compared the behavior of children in classrooms using the jigsaw technique with that of children in highly innovative (but not interdependent) classroom environments, as well as with traditional classrooms. Geffner found consistent and significant gains only in the cooperative classrooms. Specifically, the children in these classes showed increases in self-esteem as well as increases in liking for school. Negative ethnic stereotypes were also diminished. That is, the children increased their positive general attitudes toward their own ethnic group as well as toward members of other ethnic groups to a far greater extent than did children in the traditional and innovative classrooms.

ACADEMIC PERFORMANCE

Conventional wisdom has long held that, if one designed a classroom structure that increased the joy of education or led students to appreciate themselves and each other better, this would occur at the expense of fundamental learning. Thus, when the public is periodically made aware of the fact that our children are not learning as much in school as they might, there is usually an outcry to eliminate the "frills" and "get back to basics." Research on the jigsaw classroom and other cooperative techniques has proved this general wisdom to be bankrupt.

We made our first systematic attempt to assess the effects of jigsaw learning on academic performance in Austin, Texas (Lucker, Rosenfield, Sikes, & Aronson, 1977). The subjects were 303 fifth- and sixth-grade students from five elementary schools. Six classrooms were taught in the jigsaw manner, and five classrooms were taught traditionally by highly competent teachers. For 2 weeks, the children were taught a unit on colonial America taken from a fifth-grade textbook. All the children were then given the same standardized test. The Anglo students performed just as well in jigsaw as they did in traditional classes (means = 66.6 and 67.3, respectively); the minority children performed significantly better in jigsaw classes than in traditional classes (means = 56.6 and 49.7, respectively). The difference for minority students was highly significant. Only two weeks of jigsaw activity had succeeded in narrowing the performance gap between Anglos and minorities from more than 17 percentage points to about 10 percentage points. Interestingly enough, the jigsaw method apparently does not work a special hardship on high-ability students: the students in the highest quartile in reading ability benefited just as much as the students in the lowest quartile.

Since that experiment, a number of experiments have been done on academic performance, comparing jigsaw (as well as other cooperative methods) with learning in the usual competitive classroom. In an analysis of the literature, Robert Slavin (1983) found striking support for cooperative classroom structures. Of the 46 studies that Slavin designated as methodologically sound, 63% showed significantly higher academic performance in cooperative classrooms, whereas only 4% favored competitive classrooms. The remaining studies were insignificant. So much for conventional wisdom!

SOME MECHANISMS UNDERLYING JIGSAW

DISSONANCE REDUCTION

What is there about cooperative learning that produces these highly desirable effects? One underlying mechanism is cognitive dissonance. Several years ago, Jecker and Landy (1969) demonstrated that doing a favor for a person increases our liking for that person. Specifically, if we exert effort to help another, anything about that person that we don't like produces dissonance. In order to reduce dissonance, we emphasize the recipient's positive qualities and deemphasize his or her negative qualities. Because the jigsaw method allows people ample opportunity for favor-doing, all other things being equal, it should lead to greater liking among the participants. Moreover, because it feels good to be liked, this could also increase feelings of self-esteem, which would, in turn lead to better performance, greater liking for school, and so on.

EMPATHIC ROLE-TAKING

We believe that people working together interdependently increase their ability to take one another's perspective. For example, suppose that Jane and Carlos are in a jigsaw group. Carlos is reporting and Jane is having difficulty following him. She doesn't quite understand because his style of presentation is different from what she is accustomed to. Not only must she pay close attention, but in addition, she must find a way to ask questions that Carlos will understand and that will elicit the additional information she needs. In order to accomplish this, she must get to know Carlos, put herself in his shoes, empathize.

This notion was systematically tested by Diane Bridgeman (1981). She reasoned that, if taking one another's perspective is required and practiced in jigsaw learning, the more experience students have with the jigsaw process, the greater will their role-taking abilities become. In her experiment, Bridgeman administered a revised version of Chandler's role-taking cartoon series (1973) to 120 fifth-grade students. Roughly half of the students spent eight weeks in a jigsaw learning environment, and the others were taught in either traditional or innovative small-group classrooms. Each of the cartoons in the Chandler test depicts a central character caught up in a chain of psychological cause and effect, so that the character's subsequent behavior is shaped by and fully comprehensible only in terms of the preceding events. In one of the sequences, for example, a boy who has been saddened by seeing his father off at the airport begins to cry when he later receives a gift of a toy airplane similar to the one that had carried his father away. Midway into each sequence, a second character is introduced in the role of a late-arriving bystander who witnesses the resultant behaviors of the principal character but is not privy to the causal events. Thus, the subject is in a privileged position relative to the story character, whose role the subject is later asked to assume. The cartoon series measures the degree to which the subject is able to set aside facts known only to himself or herself and to adopt a perspective measurably different from his or her own. For example, although the subject knows why the child in the above sequence cries when he receives the toy airplane, the postal worker who delivered the toy is not privy to this knowledge. What happens when the subject is asked to take the postal worker's perspective?

After 8 weeks, students in the jigsaw classrooms were better able to put themselves in the bystander's place than students in the control classrooms. For example, when the postal worker delivered the toy airplane to the little boy, the students in the control classrooms tended to assume that the postal worker knew the boy would cry; that is, they behaved as if they believed that the postal worker knew that the boy's father had recently left town on an airplane—simply because they (the subjects) had this information. On the other hand, the students who had participated in a jigsaw group were much more successful in taking the postal worker's role, realizing that he could not possibly understand why the boy would cry on receiving a toy airplane.

PEER REWARDS AND INCREASED PARTICIPATION

The jigsaw method also provides ample opportunity for students to reward one another for good performance, an action that tends to raise performance as well as self-esteem. The method also requires people to participate more actively; this active participation probably improves performance and reduces boredom. In addition, as implied above, children pay closer attention to one another; the result is not only increased empathy (as mentioned above) but increased self-esteem and self-confidence as well.

ATTRIBUTION OF SUCCESS AND FAILURE

Working together in the pursuit of common goals changes the "observer's" attributional patterns. There is some evidence in support of the notion that cooperation increases the tendency for individuals to make the same kind of attribution for success and failure to their partners as they do to themselves. In one of our experiments (Stephan, Presser, Kennedy, & Aronson, 1978), we found that, when people succeed at a task, they attribute their success dispositionally (e.g., they attribute their success to skill), but when they fail, they tend to make a situational attribution (e.g., to luck). We went on to demonstrate that individuals engaged in an interdependent task make the same kinds of attributions to their partner's performance as they do to their own. This was not the case in competitive interactions.

INTERACTION AMONG OUTCOMES

As implied above, it is reasonable to assume that the various consequences of jigsaw learning become antecedents for one another. Just as low self-esteem can work to inhibit a child from performing well, anything that increases self-esteem is likely to produce an increase in performance among underachievers. Conversely, as Franks and Marolla (1976) indicated, increases in performance should bring about increases in self-esteem. Similarly, being treated with increased attention and respect by one's peers (as almost inevitably happens in jigsaw groups) is another important antecedent of self-esteem, according to Franks and Marolla. There is ample evidence of a two-way causal connection between performance and self-esteem (see Covington & Beery, 1976; Purkey, 1970).

THE GENERALIZATION OF POSITIVE ATTITUDES

In their interesting and provocative chapter, Brewer and Miller (Chapter 16) suggest that, although cooperative interactions (like jigsaw) have been successful in reducing negative stereotypes attributed to particular members of another group, they are unlikely to lead to generalization outside the specific encounter. That is, to the extent that counterstereotypical experiences with outside group members become personalized, individuals are likely to drop their prejudiced attitude against the specific person they have encountered but are unlikely to generalize this positive interaction to the group as a whole. Nevertheless, Brewer and Miller argue that such interactions stand a good chance of reducing intergroup conflict in the long run because "frequent individualization of outgroup members results in a loss in the meaning and utility of the broader category distinction."

We agree with Brewer and Miller; it is important that cooperative experiences with outgroup members include a continually changing cast of characters. Indeed, it was with this in mind that we set up the the jigsaw technique so that jigsaw groups would be dissolved and reformed at regular intervals—thus ensuring that positive experiences with an out-group member would not be narrowly attributed to specific nonstereotypical aspects of that particular person. In our experience, students initially resisted the dissolution of their group ("just when we're beginning to feel comfortable") but quickly learned that their new partners could be just as interesting and helpful.

SOCIALIZATION IN THE MEXICAN-AMERICAN FAMILY

In describing the jigsaw method, we used a fifth-grade student named Carlos as an exemplifying case. This was not an arbitrary choice. Recent evidence indicates that Mexican-American children, in particular, are not being well served by our public school system. For example, only 15% of Hispanics graduating from high school in California are eligible for admission to California's state colleges, compared with 33% of Anglos and a whopping 49% of Asians. If anything, this is an overestimate of Mexican-American eligibility because the high-school dropout rate for Hispanics is far higher than for Anglos and Asians.

We believe that the jigsaw technique may be of special benefit to Mexican-American children because of the special dynamics that exist within the typical Mexican-American family. Unlike families in mainstream American culture, Mexican-American socialization stresses mutual dependence, cooperation, and achievement for the group rather than individual achievement (Ramirez & Castaneda, 1974). In addition, Hispanic children are taught very early about mutual respect, support for family members, and the importance of status (Diaz-Guerrero, 1975).

Let us first look at cooperation. Since 1971, Spencer Kagan and his colleagues have been conducting research with Mexican, Mexican-American, and Anglo-American children aimed at identifying the social motives of these groups. He has used a paradigm that has children select from different alternatives (ranging from cooperative to competitive) on a choice card. Specifically, the children have a choice of assigning themselves and another child various numbers of trinkets. The absolute and relative amounts they give themselves and the other child over a series of trials yield a measure of cooperation or competition.

Not surprisingly, Kagan's findings indicate that Anglo-Americans are highly competitive. Indeed, their competitiveness exceeds absolute self-interest: they prefer a smaller, absolute outcome for themselves as long as they end up with more than the other child. In contrast, children of Mexican descent show a clear preference for equity, altruism, and cooperation. Moreover, the stronger the cultural bond, the more cooperative the individuals. For example, rural Mexican children are more cooperative than urban Mexican-Americans (Kagan, 1971; Kagan & Madsen, 1972). In addition, Knight and Kagan (1977) found that such prosocial behavior decreased for Mexican-Americans for each succeeding generation, a finding suggesting a trend toward the assimilation of the values of the dominant cultural group.

These behavioral differences between Anglo-Americans and Mexican-Americans are also reflected in measures of motivation. Thus, Ramirez and Price-Williams (1976a,b) compared Mexican-American and Anglo-American fourth-graders on need for affiliation and need for achievement and found that Anglos scored higher on need for achievement, whereas Mexican-Americans scored higher on need for affiliation. Kagan and his colleagues (Sanders, Scholz, & Kagan, 1976) found similar results with fifth- and sixth-graders.

When viewed as a whole, these results indicate strongly that the typical American classroom puts Mexican-American students in a terribly disadvantageous position. Not only must many Hispanic children struggle linguistically (as in the case of Carlos), but they are also expected to perform in a manner that goes against the grain of their family socialization and cultural tradition. Thus, the jigsaw technique is especially important for Mexican-Americans because it provides them with a situation in which, for a few hours a week, they can use to their advantage their higher need for cooperation and affiliation.

In a recent study, Wong-Fillmore and McLaughlin (1985), compared Chinese- and Spanish-speaking children in their ability to learn English as a second language. Consistent with the findings reported above, these investigators found that Hispanic children profited much more than Chinese children from the opportunity to interact with peers who spoke English well; Chinese children profited more from learning directly from the teacher. This finding provides us with additional encouragement in our belief that the jigsaw method is an ideal strategy for aiding underachieving linguistic minorities.

One must use great sensitivity in applying this method. For example, we noted earlier that "status" is an important value in Hispanic socialization. We can speculate that one way of losing status is to be the only member of a group who is having difficulty with the English language. In our early experiments with jigsaw, we noticed that several of our Mexican-American students seemed inordinately anxious. With hindsight, we now realize that these students were weak in English and were in groups where they were the only Mexican-American members. We speculated that this anxiety might have been reduced if the Mexican-American children had been in a situation in which it was not embarrassing to be more articulate in Spanish than in English. Thus, Geffner (1978), working in a situation in which both the residential and the school population was approximately 50% Spanish-speaking, found that Mexican-American children showed no such anxiety—and showed the kinds of gains in self-esteem, academic performance, and prosocial behavior that we had come to expect. These results were subsequently confirmed by Gonzalez (1979), who systematically varied the proportion of Anglos and Hispanics in his jigsaw groups and found that the positive effects of the jigsaw method were most pronounced when the group consisted of equal numbers of Hispanics and Anglos. He also found that Mexican-American students shifted their locus of control from external toward internal as the proportion of their membership in the group approached parity.

CONCLUSION

Our results offer substantial evidence supporting the value of the jigsaw method in raising self-esteem and academic performance, in reducing intergroup enmity, and in increasing the attractiveness of school. We have also shown why this structure is particularly beneficial to underachieving linguistic minorities, such as Mexican-Americans. Moreover, we hasten to add that the jigsaw technique is merely one of several cooperative strategies developed more-or-less independently by Robert Slavin and his colleagues at Johns Hopkins, Stuart Cook and his colleagues at the University of Colorado, David Johnson and his colleagues at the University of Minnesota, Shlomo Sharan and his colleagues in Israel, and others. Although each of these techniques has its own unique flavor and its own special advantages and disadvantages, they all essentially involve a far higher degree of student interdependence than in the traditional classroom. And all produce results similar to those discussed here.

It should be clear that we are not suggesting that jigsaw learning or any other cooperative method constitutes the solution to our interethnic problems. What we have shown is that highly desirable results occur when children spend at least a portion of their time in the pursuit of common goals. These effects are in accordance with predictions made by social scientists in their testimony favoring desegregating schools over 30 years ago.

It is also worth emphasizing the fact that the jigsaw method has proved effective even when it is used for as little as 20% of a child's time in the classroom. Moreover, it has been shown that cooperative techniques have produced beneficial results even when accompanied by competitive activities (Slavin, 1980). Thus, the data do not support either attempting to eliminate classroom competition or interfering with individually guided education. Cooperative learning can and does coexist easily with almost any other method used by teachers in the classroom.

ACKNOWLEDGMENTS

For this report, we have shamelessly cannibalized a few sections of previous articles written by the senior author in collaboration with several of his former students. We especially wish to thank Diane Bridgeman, Robert Geffner, and Neal Osherow for their earlier contributions.

REFERENCES

Allport, G. W. (1954). *The nature of prejudice.* Reading, MA: Addison-Wesley.

Aronson, E. (1984). Modifying the environment of the desegregated classroom. In A. J. Stewart (Ed.), *Motivation and society.* San Francisco: Jossey-Bass.

Aronson, E., & Goode, E. (1980). Training teachers to implement jigsaw learning: A manual for teachers. In S. Sharan, P. Hare, C. Webb, & R. Hertz-Lazarowitz (Eds.), *Cooperation in education.* Provo, UT: Brigham Young University Press.

Aronson, E., & Yates, S. (1983). Cooperation in the classroom: The impact of the jigsaw method on inter-ethnic relations, classroom performance and self-esteem. In H. Blumberg & P. Hare (Eds.), *Small groups.* London: Wiley.

Aronson, E., Blaney, N., Sikes, J., Stephan, C., & Snapp, M. (1975, February). Busing and racial tension. *Psychology Today,* pp. 43–50.

Aronson, E., Stephan, C., Sikes, J., Blaney, N., & Snapp, M. (1978). *The Jigsaw Classroom.* Beverly Hills, CA: Sage.

Blaney, N. T., Stephan, C., Rosenfield, D., Aronson, E., & Sikes, J. (1977). Interdependence in the classroom: A field study. *Journal of Educational Psychology, 69,* 139–146.

Bridgeman, D. L. (1981). Enhanced role taking through cooperative interdependence: A field study. *Child Development, 52,* 1231–1238.

Brown, R. (1986). *Social psychology* (2nd ed.). New York: Free Press.

Chandler, M. J. (1973). Egocentrism and antisocial behavior: The assessment and training of social perspective-taking skills. *Developmental Psychology, 9,* 326–332.

Cohen, E. (1972). Interracial interaction disability. *Human Relations, 25*(1), 9–24.

Cohen, E., & Roper, S. (1972). Modification of interracial interaction disability: An application of status characteristics theory. *American Sociological Review, 6,* 643–657.

Covington, M. V., & Beery, R. G. (1976). *Self-worth and school learning.* New York: Holt, Rinehart & Winston.

Deutsch, M. (1949). An experimental study of the effects of cooperation and competition upon group process. *Human Relations, 2,* 199–231.

Diaz-Guerrero, R. (1975). *Psychology of the Mexican: Culture and personality.* Austin: University of Texas Press.

Franks, D. D., & Marolla, J. (1976). Efficacious action and social approval as interacting dimensions of self-esteem: A tentative formulation through construct validation. *Sociometry, 39,* 324–341.

Geffner, R. A. (1978). *The effects of interdependent learning on self-esteem, inter-ethnic relations, and intra-ethnic attitudes of elementary school children: A field experiment.* Unpublished doctoral thesis, University of California, Santa Cruz.

Gerard H., & Miller, N. (1975). *School desegregation.* New York: Plenum Press.

Gonzalez, A. (1979). *Classroom cooperation and ethnic balance.* Unpublished doctoral dissertation, University of California, Santa Cruz.

Jecker, J., & Landy, D. (1969). Liking a person as a function of doing him a favor. *Human Relations, 22,* 371–378.

Kagan, S. (1971). Cooperation and competition of Mexican, Mexican-American, and Anglo-American children of two ages under four instructional sets. *Developmental Psychology, 5,* 32–39.

Kagan, S., & Madsen, M. C. (1972). Experimental analyses of cooperation and competition of Anglo-American and Mexican children. *Developmental Psychology, 6,* 49–59.

Knight, G. P., & Kagan, S. (1977). Acculturation of prosocial and competitive behaviors among second- and third-generation Mexican-American children. *Journal of Cross-Cultural Psychology*, *8*(3), 273–284.

Lucker, G. W., Rosenfield, D., Sikes, J., & Aronson, E. (1977). Performance in the interdependent classroom: A field study. *American Educational Research Journal, 13*, 115–123.

Pettigrew, T. (1961). Social psychology and desegregation research. *American Psychologist, 15*, 61–71.

Purkey, W. W. (1970). *Self-concept and school achievement*. Englewood Cliffs, NJ: Prentice-Hall.

Ramirez, M., & Price-Williams, D. R. (1976a). Achievement motivation in children of three ethnic groups in the United States. *Journal of Cross-Cultural Psychology, 7*, 49–60.

Ramirez, M., & Price-Williams, D. R. (1976b). *Need affiliation and need guidance in three ethnic groups in the United States.* Unpublished manuscript.

Ramirez, M., III, & Castaneda, A. (1974). *Cultural democracy, bicognitive development and education.* New York: Academic Press.

St. John, N. (1975). *School desegregation: Outcomes for children.* New York: Wiley.

Sanders, M., Scholz, J. & Kagan, S. (1976). Three social motives and field independence-dependence in Anglo-American and Mexican-American children. *Journal of Cross-Cultural Psychology, 7*(4), 353–359.

Sherif, M., Harvey, O. J., White, J., Hood, W., & Sherif, C. (1961). *Intergroup conflict and cooperation: The robber's cave experiment.* Norman: University of Oklahoma Institute of Intergroup Relations.

Slavin, R. (1980). Student team learning. In S. Sharan, P. Hare, C. Webb, & R. Hertz-Lazarowitz (Eds.), *Cooperation in education.* Provo, UT: Brigham Young University Press.

Slavin, R. (1983). When does cooperative learning increase student achievement? *Psychological Bulletin, 94*, 429–445.

Stephan, C., Presser, N. R., Kennedy, J. C., & Aronson, E. (1978). Attributions to success and failure in cooperative, competitive and interdependent interactions. *European Journal of Social Psychology, 8*, 269–274.

Stephan, W. G. (1978). School desegregation: An evaluation of predictions made in *Brown v. Board of Education. Psychological Bulletin, 85*, 217–238.

Wong-Fillmore, L., & McLaughlin, B. (1985). *Effects of instructional practices on learning English among Hispanic and Chinese immigrant children.* Unpublished manuscript.

16

Contact and Cooperation
When Do They Work?

Marilynn B. Brewer and Norman Miller

Although the social-science-based justification for the *Brown* decision of 1954 was framed primarily in terms of its effect on the achievement and self-esteem of minority children, it is generally agreed that a major societal goal of desegregation is improved intergroup relations (Stephan, 1978). Presumably, what we mean by this is not simply that we can create conditions in which members of different ethnic groups coexist temporarily without conflict. What most of us have in mind when we think of improving intergroup relations is that any positive effects of contact will extend beyond the contact situation to reduce intergroup conflict and prejudice in general.

Despite the practical importance of generalization effects, relatively little research on desegregation has focused on this aspect of the contact hypothesis. Interventions (such as the cooperative learning technique described by Aronson and Gonzales Chapter 15) have been directed toward improving intergroup acceptance within the desegregated setting. Whether the positive effects observed within the treated classrooms will persist in time or will generalize to other settings and/or children remains an open question. Ironically, it may be the case that some of the factors that most effectively promote positive intergroup behavior within a given situation actually *reduce* the probability of generalization to other times and places. A closer look at the nature of generalization effects and the processes underlying them will clarify why this may be true.

TYPES OF GENERALIZATION

What does it mean for the effects of a particular experience with intergroup contact to generalize to the group as a whole? We distinguish among three different types of generalization effects:

MARILYNN B. BREWER • Department of Psychology, University of California, Los Angeles, California 90024.   NORMAN MILLER • Department of Psychology, University of Southern California, Los Angeles, California 90007.

1. *Change in attitudes toward the social category.* This is the most direct form of generalization, where positive experiences with individual members of a broad social category lead to alterations in the affect and stereotypes associated with the group as a whole.

2. *Increased complexity of intergroup perceptions.* This form of generalization involves a change in the perceived heterogeneity of category structure. Instead of perceiving the out-group category as a relatively homogeneous social group, the individual comes to recognize variability among category members. Attitudes toward the category as a whole may not be altered, but affect and stereotypes are differentiated among various "subtypes" of the general category.

3. *Decategorization.* In this form of generalization, the meaningfulness of the social category itself is undermined. Based on the frequency or intensity of exposure to individual members of a social group, the utility of category membership as a basis for identifying or classifying new individuals is reduced.

These three forms of generalization correspond to the distinction drawn by Brewer and Miller (1984) among three different levels of intergroup interaction: (a) category-based; (b) differentiated; and (c) personalized. Each of these implies different cognitive processes occurring at the time of intergroup contact. Considering each in turn, we will illustrate how different conditions of contact may promote or inhibit different types of generalization.

Category-Based Generalization

In his programmatic research on the contact hypothesis, Cook (1984, 1985) was particularly interested in testing whether positive contact experiences would generalize to intergroup attitudes. Consistent with the specifications of the contact hypothesis, he found that intensive, equal-status interaction in cooperative groups could succeed in promoting cross-ethnic liking and respect within such groups, even among persons who were highly prejudiced at the outset. In most cases, however, these effects did not extend to measures of racial prejudice in general. Such findings led Cook (1984) to speculate that

> attitude change will result from cooperative interracial contact only when such contact
> is accompanied by a *supplementary* influence that promotes the process of generalization from favorable contact with individuals to positive attitudes toward the group
> from which the individual comes. (p. 163; italics added)

In the absence of such special influence, there is apparently a strong tendency for individuals to isolate the contact experience from other cognitions, and to regard the individuals they come to know and like as special exceptions rather than representatives of their social group.

In Cook's experiments, the "supplementary influence" that helped promote generalized attitude change was one in which group norms supporting racial equality and nondiscrimination were *explicitly* articulated in association with pleasant experiences with members of the out-group. At least two problems can be noted in this solution to the problem of generalization. First, it requires that the contact situation be engineered in such a way as to ensure that the interpersonal experience will be uniformly pleasant, so that any generalized attitude change will be in the desired direction. Such conditions are not easily achieved, at least not in ways that permit interactions that are not highly constrained or superficial.

Second, this mode of enhancing generalization depends on category-based information-processing. The out-group member in the interaction must be perceived as representative of his or her social category if attitudes developed toward that individual are to be generalized to the group as a whole. In a laboratory experiment on contact effects, for instance, Wilder (1984) found that pleasant interaction with a *typical* student of another college resulted in more positive attitudes toward the out-group college in general, but interaction with an *atypical* (i.e., counterstereotypical) member produced no generalization. This was true even though the atypical student was liked better than the typical student.

Thus, categorical generalization of contact experiences occurs only when the superordinate category membership of the out-group individual is salient in the contact situation. As a consequence, the distinctiveness of the social category itself may be reinforced during the course of the interaction. In the long run, such maintenance of in-group–out-group category distinctions may undermine any immediate positive effects on intergroup attitudes.

DIFFERENTIATION AND COMPLEXITY

In general, it is unlikely that firmly established category stereotypes will be substantially altered on the basis of a few interactions with category members that disconfirm stereotypical expectancies. Instead, individuals appear to handle such discrepant experiences through a process of *subtyping:* the creation of a new, counterstereotypical subcategory that is differentiated from the category as a whole (Weber & Crocker, 1983). As Rothbart and John (1985) put it:

> Contact and familiarity permit a more differentiated encoding of the stimulus person, and this very process of individuation serves to insulate the attributes associated with the category from those of the individual. This process leads to the unhappy prediction that inferences from the individual to the group should decline with increasing familiarity with that individual, particularly when the individual is perceived as generally atypical of the group. (p. 94)

Such subtyping processes may not alter stereotypes about characteristics of the group as a whole, but they may enhance perceived diversity or variability among category members. This provides another way in which individual contact experiences may generalize to perceptions of the group as a whole. Following contact with out-group members who do not conform to category stereotypes, the individual may not necessarily develop a more favorable perception of the group as a whole but may view that group as more complex or differentiated than previously.

Quattrone (1986) pointed out that the perception of variability within a group can take at least two forms. *Dimensional variability* refers to the extent to which individual differences are perceived to exist with respect to a particular trait characteristic. Even though a specific trait may be considered "typical" of a social group, group members may vary in the extent to which they possess that trait. Perceptions of such variability can range from the idea that "all" group members are essentially the same on this dimension to a recognition that individuals within the group are distributed across all points on the dimension. Group stereotypes may also be characterized by *taxonomic variability*. This term refers to the extent to which the category is differentiated into distinctive subtypes, each subtype being represented by a unique configuration of characteristic traits.

Both dimensional variability and taxonomic variability are measures of the complexity of the cognitive representation of a social category, and both are likely to be increased by contact with diverse category members. It is important to note, however, that exposure to diversity alone is not sufficient to ensure greater differentiation of category representations. It is also necessary that the perceiver *pay attention* to information that distinguishes one category member from another. Thus, the generalization of contact experiences to an increase in category complexity requires conditions in which individual differences are made salient and participants are motivated to encode and remember such individuating information.

There is some reason to believe that changes in the complexity of intergroup perception may lead to changes in the evaluation of the group as a whole. A series of studies by Linville (1982; Linville & Jones, 1980) demonstrated that category complexity is associated with reduced polarization of affect toward category members. Individuals with more complex (differentiated) representations of a social category were less extreme in their positive or negative evaluations of a category member than were individuals with less complex representations. Further, Wilder (1978) found that the presence of a dissenter (i.e., an individuated member) in an otherwise homogeneous out-group increased reward allocations to all out-group members, compared to a condition in which no dissenter was present. It should be noted, however, that the generalization of category complexity effects depends on the perceiver's being *aware of* category diversity at the time a judgment about an out-group person is made. If no cuing of category subtypes is present, the individual may fall back on generalized attitudes toward the superordinate category when making evaluations of individuals in new situations.

PERSONALIZATION AND DECATEGORIZATION

Both of the processes of generalization discussed thus far rely on some type of categorization effect for their effectiveness. The contact experience generalizes to new situations if it modifies the individual's cognitive representation of the out-group category—either the representation of what is typical of the category or the representation of category variability. Another way to look at the effects of intergroup contact is to consider the extent to which interpersonal interaction reduces awareness of category distinctions or group membership—what Brewer and Miller (1984) referred to as "decategorization."

Decategorization occurs to the extent that interrelations in the contact situation are personalized rather than category-based. Personalized interactions are ones in which category identity is replaced as the basis for classifying other individuals in favor of information that is self-relevant and not necessarily correlated with category membership. Such interactions are characterized by information processing that is "piecemeal" rather than category-based (Fiske & Pavelchak, 1985). In piecemeal processing, impressions are abstracted from incoming information about the individual rather than being derived from preexisting category stereotypes.

Differentiation is a necessary but not sufficient condition for personalization and decategorization. Obviously, before information can be personalized, individual differences must first be recognized. However, categories may be differentiated into subtypes or distinct individual members without eliminating superordinate category identity. (For instance, one may learn to discriminate accurately among different presidents of the United States but still classify all of them as occupants of a specialized role in terms of their relationship to oneself.)

With personalization, category identity becomes subordinate to individual identity rather than vice versa. To illustrate this distinction, consider the statement "Janet is a nurse." This description can be psychologically represented in one of two ways. It could mean that Janet is subordinate to (i.e., a specific instance of) the general category of nurses. Or it could mean that being a nurse is subordinate to (i.e., a particular characteristic of) the concept of Janet. The former interpretation is an example of category-based individuation, and the latter is an example of personalization. In this sense, personalized contact is the polar opposite of category-based interaction, and the conditions that promote decategorization are antithetical to the categorical generalization of contact effects.

REDUCTION OF CATEGORY-BASED INTERACTION

Interpersonal contact will be category-based to the extent that the category membership of the participants is made salient in the contact situation. Physical distinctiveness is one basis for category salience but not its sole determinant. (A person wearing a green shirt in a room full of people with pink shirts is physically distinct, but it is unlikely that such an individual would be placed in a category of "green shirt wearers.") Categorization is more likely to occur when categories are characterized by what Brewer and Campbell (1976) called "convergent boundaries," in which group identities based on many different distinctions—for example, religious, economic, and political—all coincide. When social category membership is so multiply determined, the probability is high that at least one cue to category identity will be relevant in almost any social situation.

Tajfel (1978) gave particular emphasis to the structure of intergroup relations at the societal level as a critical determinant of category salience. Of most relevance is the presence of intense conflict of interest between groups (as in the relation between two rival football teams) or the existence of a fairly rigid system of social stratification within the society that establishes differences in status between the social categories. According to Tajfel, an individual's feelings of positive social identity are deeply affected by the prevailing differences in status between social groups. For those who belong to categories with superior status, the importance of maintaining category distinctiveness will depend on how secure the established status relationship is. When high status is secure, one's own category identity will not be particularly salient in most social situations. However, if status differentials are perceived to be insecure or threatened, the need to preserve category distinctiveness may be high for members of both high- and low-status groups.

Group structure within the contact situation is also an important factor in category salience, particularly the relative proportion of members of the different social categories that are represented. In general, in fairly large social groupings, a relatively equal representation of two social categories makes category distinctions less salient, whereas the presence of a clear minority enhances awareness of category identity (see Aronson & Gonzales, Chapter 15). The so-called solo effect (Taylor, Fiske, Etcoff, & Ruderman, 1978) illustrates the extent to which the category identity of a single member of a distinctive social group is made salient when embedded in an otherwise homogeneous social environment. The effects of minority–majority representation also interact with differences in group status to determine the extent to which category differentiation is important to the members of the respective groups. Majority groups with an insecure or negative self-image and minority groups with a positive self-image have been found to display the greatest degree of discrimination against out-groups, whereas majority groups with a secure positive self-image and minority groups with a negative self-image show relatively little discrimination (Espinoza & Garza, 1985; Moscovici & Paicheler, 1978).

The effects of category size and group composition are more complex in situations in which more than two distinguishable social categories are present. Based on perceptual factors alone, we hypothesize that the salience of particular category distinctions will vary as a function of the ratio of category size to total group size. If a fairly large group is divided into several categories of relatively equal size, those categories will provide a useful way of "chunking" the social environment, and category differentiation will be highly salient (each category, in effect, being treated as a distinctive minority). When several different social categories are equally represented in a much smaller social group, however, category salience should be substantially lowered. When the representation of any one social category is small relative to that of other categories, the distinctiveness of that category may be highly salient, whereas distinctions among the other categories will be less apparent.

The conditions that characterize desegregation in a variety of social settings typically have a number of features conducive to category-based social interaction. First of all, the groups involved are usually social categories that are differentiated by convergent boundaries, including distinctions in cultural, economic, linguistic, and physical features. In addition, these objective group differences tend to be confounded with status in the larger social system, often under conditions in which the existing status structure is under threat. Moreover, desegregation frequently occurs within a political context that affects groups differentially and brings individuals into the situation as representatives of their respective social categories. Finally, the immediate social structure tends to be one of disproportional (majority–minority) representation of the different groups and thereby makes category identity perceptually salient as well as emotionally significant.

If personalized rather than category-based interactions are the goal of desegregation, then the contact situation must be designed to eliminate or overcome the features that promote category salience. In effect, the situation must reduce information processing that is category-based and must promote, instead, attention to personal or individual information that is not correlated with category membership. In our view, many of the cooperative interventions designed for implementation in classroom settings are not adequate to achieve this goal. A cooperative task structure by itself is not sufficient to guarantee personalized interaction within heterogeneous groups or to ensure that such interactions will generalize to new situations. In general, we hypothesize (Brewer & Miller, 1984) that the effects of categorization on social interaction will be reduced most successfully when (a) the nature of the interaction in the contact situation promotes an interpersonal rather than a task-oriented approach to fellow participants, and (b) the basis for the assignment of roles, status, social functions, and subgroup composition in the situation is perceived to be category-independent rather than category-related.

The paradox in all of this is that successful decategorization, by its very nature, reduces the possibility of category-based generalization, in either form. To the extent that relationships with individual members of an out-group are highly personalized, they are also insulated from category-based prejudices and stereotypes. Cook's experiments (1984) provide an illustrative case of conditions that promote personalized interactions that did not extend to attitudes toward the group as a whole. Nevertheless, in our view, such interactions have the most promise for reducing intergroup conflict in the long run. Frequent individualization of out-group members results in a loss of meaning and utility of the broader category distinction. Note, however, that such effects cannot be expected to follow from single contact experiences. Generalized decategorization depends both on personalization within contact situations and replication across situations.

GENERALIZATION OF COOPERATIVE INTERACTION

As Aronson and Gonzales discuss in Chapter 15, cooperative learning programs create many of the factors that enhance positive intergroup exchanges within a desegregated setting. The structure of cooperative learning tasks promotes equal-status contact in pursuit of common goals and the experience of helping and being helped by out-group members. There is by now an extensive literature documenting the positive effects of cooperative learning on improved interethnic acceptance within desegregated classrooms (Johnson, Johnson, & Maruyama, 1984; Slavin, 1985). The question remains, however, how much these effects generalize to new situations and other out-group members. According to the preceding analysis, the answer depends on the conditions of category salience that prevail in the cooperative setting.

Unfortunately, large-scale implementations of intervention programs in field settings rarely permit the kind of fine-grained analysis of the effects of various conditions of implementation that our theoretical analysis suggests may be of importance. For that reason, we have been working with a laboratory analogue of the desegregation situation that allows for experimental variations in the conditions of interest (Brewer & Miller, 1984; Miller, Brewer, & Edwards, 1985).

In skeletal form, the laboratory analogue includes three components: (a) the creation of two distinct categories subdividing an otherwise homogeneous group of subjects; (b) the provision of opportunity for members of the two categories to interact for some specified time in isolation from each other; and (c) the creation of a new task environment in which representatives of the two categories come into contact under conditions of cooperative interdependence. These elements of the experimental paradigm are intended to capture the basic features of any intergroup desegregation situation: the presence of distinct category identifiers (made visually salient in our situation by colored name tags or uniforms), a period of isolation between groups, and a contact situation in which either category-based or personalized interactions are possible. Given these initial conditions, the characteristics of the contact situation can then be varied so that their effect can be determined on intergroup acceptance within the contact setting and on its generalization to other category members beyond that setting.

In our experimental paradigm, generalization is assessed by having subjects view a videotape of an interaction between in-group and out-group category members. Following their own experience with a cooperative problem-solving task in which in-group and out-group members work together, the subjects are asked to evaluate a taped discussion of a four-person team, ostensibly from another experimental session, that is engaged in the same problem-solving exercise. Persons shown on the videotape are clearly identifiable as to category membership. After viewing the tape, the subjects are asked to make ratings of the video team members so that we can determine the extent of category-based bias that remains toward strangers with whom the subjects have had no direct contact.

It should be acknowledged that, even with a number of embellishments, the laboratory analogue remains a "stripped-down" representation of intergroup contact situations in the real world. It would be virtually impossible to capture in the lab the sense of historical and cultural tradition that marks intergroup distinctions in the larger society. Nonetheless, experience with the analogue paradigm indicates that it can engage—at least, temporarily—much of the emotional significance attached to other social category identification. During the initial period of category segregation, members of the two subgroups do establish a strong sense of "in-group–out-group" differentiation, express evaluative biases in favor of their own category, and exhibit apprehension about future interaction with members of the other category. Further, some of the factors that have significant effects on generalization in our laboratory setting have also been demonstrated to be important in field research settings. For illustrative purposes, we will discuss two of these factors: interteam competition and preexisting status differences.

EFFECTS OF INTERTEAM COMPETITION

Variations on cooperative learning techniques differ in the extent to which they engage interteam competition as a method of enhancing team spirit and cooperation. Aronson's "jigsaw" technique, for instance, relies primarily on cooperative efforts toward reaching individualistic goals, whereas in DeVries and Edwards's Teams-Games-Tournament procedures (DeVries, Slavin, Fennessey, Edwards, & Lombardo, 1980), learning teams compete against each other. In our analysis, the latter techniques may enhance intrateam cohesiveness, but they also promote high task orientation and depersonalized interactions within teams that may reduce generalization effects in the long run.

Our first analogue experiment (Rogers, 1982) examined the effects of cooperative versus competitive interteam reward contingencies, crossed with an instructional manipulation designed to focus attention on task versus interpersonal aspects of team performance. Each experimental session enlisted eight female subjects whose judgments on a series of dot-estimation problems provided the ostensible basis for division into two (equal-sized) categories, designated respectively as "underestimators" and "overestimators." The members of the two categories were differentiated by large yellow or purple badges labeled **Under** or **Over** (in bold letters), followed by a unique identifying number for each category member by which she could be individually designated.

Following a period in which the subjects interacted with their own category members, they were randomly reassigned to two heterogeneous teams, each consisting of two underestimators and two overestimators. The teams were located in separate rooms and were then introduced to a problem-solving task that consisted of two subparts. In the first part, each individual team member worked separately to generate a list of four or five of her own personality characteristics that she believed would be important qualifications for space travel. After producing these individual lists, the team convened as a whole to discuss them and to arrive at a selection of five traits representing the team's consensus about the most important characteristics needed for space travel. The components of this task set the stage for our manipulation of interaction focus during the problem-solving effort. In the *interpersonal focus* condition, team members were told that successful task performance required that they form accurate impressions of what their fellow team members were really like. In the *task focus* condition, they were told that it would be important to make an accurate assessment of the quality of each member's list as a contribution to the team product. Further, in the *cooperative* condition, the subjects were told that the problem solutions of the two teams would be evaluated jointly for a determination of their joint eligibility for a monetary reward. In the *competitive* condition, the subjects were told that the two team solutions would be compared and that the team with the better product would be eligible for a reward.

Following these task instructions, both teams worked on the assigned problem and submitted a final list to the experimenter at the end of a set time period. At this point (without knowing the outcome of the evaluation of their products), the participants were asked to make a series of ratings of their own and the other team product, followed by ratings of the individual team members, designated by category label and identification number. After the completion of these team ratings, generalization was assessed via evaluations of a videotaped team consisting of in-group and out-group category members.

In all versions of the cooperative task structure, in-group bias in evaluations of own-team members was relatively low; that is, the subjects evaluated the members of their own team relatively favorably regardless of category identity. (Out-group evaluations were somewhat more positive under conditions of personal focus and interteam cooperation than under task focus and interteam competition, but own-team positivity was high in all conditions.) Our primary interest, however, was on the generalization of these effects to the in-group and out-group participants on the videotaped team. For these ratings, both orientation and interteam reward structure had large and significant effects on the degree of in-group favoritism. As indicated in Table 1, the mean evaluation of in-group category members on the video team relative to that of out-group category members was significantly more biased when the subjects had been in the task focus condition rather than in the personal focus condition and under conditions of interteam competition rather than under cooperation.

Our findings with respect to the relative effects of interteam cooperation and competition were replicated in a field experiment in desegregated classrooms conducted by Warring, Johnson, Maruyama, and Johnson (1985). Students in the experimental classes

TABLE 1. In-Group Bias in Evaluative Ratings of Category Members of Videoteam[a]

Instructional Focus	Interteam reward structure	
	Cooperation	Competition
Personal	0.65	1.52
Task	2.01	2.87

[a] Mean evaluative rating of in-group team members minus rating of out-group team members.

participated in mixed-ethnic cooperative learning groups for 55 minutes a day across 10 class days. In the intergroup cooperation condition, emphasis was placed on how well the entire class achieved, and rewards were allocated accordingly. In the intergroup competition condition, the emphasis was placed on which group achieved the highest, and prizes were allocated competitively. Results from a measure of interactive activity indicated that intergroup cooperation promoted more cross-ethnic relationships than did competition and that these relationships generalized into unstructured class, school, and home activities.

Differences in Group Status

For a number of reasons, equal status between members of different social groups at the structural level may not correspond to equal status at the psychological level. In a series of field experiments in racially desegregated schools, Cohen (1982, 1984) demonstrated that status differences existing outside the contact situation tend to carry over into the desegregated setting, even on tasks for which the basis of status differentials is irrelevant. Such carryover effects have also been demonstrated in a version of our laboratory analogue setting (Rabin, 1985).

In Rabin's experiment, category identity was again created by using a dot-estimation task for designating subjects as under- or overestimators. The subjects were then assigned to two problem-solving teams, composed of two "unders" and two "overs" each. Before working on the cooperative problem-solving task, the subjects were given some "background information" regarding underestimators and overestimators in the population at large. As a part of this descriptive material, all subjects were informed that underestimators were, in general, more accurate than overestimators in their estimations of the number of dots actually present in a stimulus display. This instruction constituted our manipulation of prior "status" differences between the two categories. (Two other manipulations of population structure and task outcome were included in the experimental design, but they did not interact with group status and will not be discussed here.)

Of interest here are the results of Rabin's experiment with respect to the subjects' ratings of in-group and out-group category members on a videotaped team, following their experience with the cooperative team task. The major outcome was a consistent tendency for the instructionally created difference between groups in dot-estimation accuracy to carry over onto an array of judgments about the unders and overs on the videotape. As shown in Table 2, both overestimators and underestimators gave more favorable ratings to the video team members who were labeled as "unders." This outcome resulted in a positive in-group bias on the part of underestimator subjects and a negative bias (out-group favorability) on the part of overestimators. Thus, ratings of the

TABLE 2. Ratings by Underestimators (U_s) and Overestimators (O_s) of Videotape Team Members

	In-group bias[a]		Out-group ratings[b]		In-group ratings[b]	
	U_s	O_s	U_s	O_s	U_s	O_s
Task attributions						
Influence	.38a	−.41b	6.04a	6.69b	6.42a	6.28a
Responsibility	.32a	−.35b	5.97a	6.55b	6.29a	6.20a
Ability	.31a	−.34b	6.17a	6.65b	6.48a	6.31a
Effort	.40a	−.44b	6.45a	6.71a	6.85a	6.27b
Affective ratings						
Liking	.32a	−.20b	5.50a	5.98b	5.82a	5.78a
Trust	.02a	.06a	5.69a	5.98b	5.71a	6.04a
Respect	.28a	−.20a	5.84a	6.32b	6.12a	6.12a

[a] Average rating of in-group targets minus rating of out-group targets.
[b] Positive scores are more favorable. Scores with different subscripts differ significantly by Newman-Kuhls test.

videotape participants were clearly caregory-based, despite the cooperative contact experience.

These outcomes attest to the persistent influence of external status characteristics on judgments about others, even when the status variable is unrelated to the task at hand or to any actual task-performances differences among team members. Even though dot-estimation accuracy was never linked either explicitly or implicitly to any other traits or task-relevant skills, category-based status differences intruded into judgments made of strangers identified according to category membership. These effects are perhaps even more striking in that they were essentially unmodified by the success or failure of one's own team on the cooperative problem-solving task.

CONCLUSIONS

Taken together, the results of these studies show that the transfer of the effects of positive cooperative experiences to out-group persons in other settings is sensitive to the instructional set and the structural arrangements under which the initial experience took place. Category-based responding is reduced only when the conditions of interaction promote attention to the personal characteristics of fellow team members and decrease the salience of category-related status differentials. Given the conditions under which cooperative learning programs are implemented in many classroom settings, understanding these effects of group formation and composition has immediate practical implications.

In the long run, cooperative programs that rely on interteam competition seem to be less effective than programs (such as jigsaw) that do not have a competitive element. It is our assumption that the effect of competition is to increase task focus during group interaction in a way that decreases attention to the personal characteristics of fellow team members. It is also possible that interteam competition enhances the threat of potential failure, which reduces positive identification with other members of one's own team.

Our theoretical analysis also suggests that, in the formation of cooperative learning teams, it is important to avoid implicit or explicit use of ethnic identity as a basis for assignment to teams. When classes are imbalanced with respect to the number of students in different social categories, an exact replication of whole-class proportions within every team will not only enhance category salience by creating a distinctive minority within each team but will also call attention to category representation as a rule for team formation. A better strategy is to establish teams that are numerically balanced in category representation even though, in imbalanced classrooms, this will result in a residual set of teams that are homogeneous with respect to ethnic composition. Such teams will have the effect of undermining any perception on the part of students that category membership is relevant to team formation. In combination with frequent rotation of team composition, this structural variation—relatively simple to implement—may prove to be quite powerful in promoting generalized decategorization.

REFERENCES

Brewer, M. B., & Campbell, D. T. (1976). *Ethnocentrism and intergroup attitudes: East African evidence.* New York: Halsted Press (Sage Publications).

Brewer, M. B., & Miller, N. (1984). Beyond the contact hypothesis: Theoretical perspectives on desegregation. In N. Miller & M. Brewer (Eds.), *Groups in contact: The psychology of desegregation.* New York: Academic Press.

Cohen, E. G. (1982). Expectation states and interracial interaction in school settings. *Annual Review of Sociology, 8,* 209–235.

Cohen, E. G. (1984). The desegregated school: Problems in status power and interethnic climate. In N. Miller & M. Brewer (Eds.), *Groups in contact: The psychology of desegregation.* New York: Academic Press.

Cook, S. W. (1984). Cooperative interaction in multiethnic contexts. In N. Miller & M. Brewer (Eds.), *Groups in contact: The psychology of desegregation.* New York: Academic Press.

Cook, S. W. (1985). Experimenting on social issues: The case of school desegregation. *American Psychologist, 40,* 452–460.

DeVries, D. L., Slavin, R. E., Fennessey, G. M., Edwards, K. J., & Lombardo, N. M. (1980). *Teams–games–tournament: The team learning approach.* Englewood Cliffs, NJ: Educational Technology Publications.

Espinoza, J. A., & Garza, R. T. (1985). Social group salience and interethnic cooperation. *Journal of Experimental Social Psychology, 21,* 380–392.

Fiske, S. T., & Pavelchak, M. A. (1985). Category-based versus piecemeal-based affective responses: Developments in schema-triggered affect. In R. Sorrentino & E. T. Higgins (Eds.), *The handbook of motivation and cognition: Foundations of social behavior.* New York: Guilford Press.

Johnson, D. W., Johnson, R., & Maruyama, G. (1984). Goal interdependence and interpersonal attraction in heterogeneous classrooms: A metanalysis. In N. Miller & M. Brewer (Eds.), *Groups in contact: The psychology of desegregation.* New York: Academic Press.

Linville, P. W. (1982). The complexity-extremity effect and age-based stereotyping. *Journal of Personality and Social Psychology, 42,* 193–211.

Linville, P. W., & Jones, E. E. (1980). Polarized appraisals of out-group members. *Journal of Personality and Social Psychology, 38,* 689–703.

Miller, N., Brewer, M. B., & Edwards, K. (1985). Cooperative interaction in desegregated settings: A laboratory analogue. *Journal of Social Issues, 41*(3), 63–79.

Moscovici, S., & Paicheler, G. (1978). Social comparison and social recognition: Two complementary processes of identification. In H. Tajfel (Ed.), *Differentiation between social groups.* London: Academic Press.

Quattrone, G. A. (1986). On the perception of a group's variability. In S. Worchel & W. Austin (Eds.), *Psychology of intergroup relations.* Chicago: Nelson-Hall.

Rabin, I. (1985). *The effect of external status characteristics on intergroup acceptance.* Unpublished dissertation, University of Southern California.

Rogers, M. (1982). *The effect of interteam reward structure on intragroup and intergroup perceptions and evaluative attitudes.* Unpublished dissertation, University of Southern California.

Rothbart, M., & John, O. (1985). Social categorization and behavioral episodes: A cognitive analysis of the effects of intergroup contact. *Journal of Social Issues, 41*(3), 81–104.

Slavin, R. E. (1985) Cooperative learning: Applying contact theory in desegregated schools. *Journal of Social Issues, 41*(3), 45–62.

Stephan, W. (1978). School desegregation: An evaluation of predictions made in Brown vs. Board of Education. *Psychological Bulletin, 85,* 217–238.

Tajfel, H. (1978). Social categorization, social identity and social comparison. In H. Tajfel (Ed.), *Differentiation between social groups.* London: Academic Press.

Taylor, S. E., Fiske, S. T., Etcoff, N. L., & Ruderman, A. J. (1978). Categorical and contextual bases of person memory and stereotyping. *Journal of Personality and Social Psychology, 36,* 778–793.

Warring, D., Johnson, D. W., Maruyama, G., & Johnson, R. (1985). Impact of different types of cooperative learning on cross-ethnic and cross-sex relationships. *Journal of Educational Psychology, 77,* 53–59.

Weber, R., & Crocker, J. (1983). Cognitive processes in the revision of stereotypic beliefs. *Journal of Personality and Social Psychology, 45,* 961–977.

Wilder, D. A. (1978). Reduction of intergroup discrimination through individuation of the outgroup. *Journal of Personality and Social Psychology, 36,* 1361–1374.

Wilder, D. A. (1984). Intergroup contact: The typical member and the exception to the rule. *Journal of Experimental Social Psychology, 20,* 177–194.

D. Affirmative Action

17

The Future of Preferential Affirmative Action

Nathan Glazer

WHAT IS AFFIRMATIVE ACTION?

In the autumn of 1985, the debate over affirmative action—which goes back at least 15 years—heated up again. The Reagan administration, it appeared from newspaper reports, was preparing to revise the executive order of 1965 that had been the basis of affirmative action, as well as the federal regulations that specified how federal contractors were to fulfill their affirmative-action requirements. A political uproar ensued in the wake of the newspaper reports, as could have been expected, and after some dispute within the administration about just what was to be done, a new quiet descended. Either revision had been abandoned, or a better control over leaks was being enforced.

The author has played a role in this debate in the past as a critic of one form of affirmative action (Glazer, 1976, 1983), but of course, no issue remains the same in public life, particularly if it spans a spell of more than 15 years and no less than four different presidential administrations. The debate over affirmative action in 1986 cannot be what it was in 1971. Too many things have changed, even though the major question to which it was addressed, the economic condition of blacks, is still with us and should be a major concern of scholarly investigation and public policy. But we now also have before us the experience of 15 years of affirmative action, and that must affect what we think of it.

Affirmative action refers both to a specific federal policy and to specific policies of states and cities that address the same ends, and to a general approach to overcoming the effects of past discrimination against blacks and other minorities and women, and to improving their present condition. The approach in question is that nondiscrimination alone is not sufficient to overcome the effects of discrimination and to improve the economic conditions of blacks, other minorities, and women. The argument is over what more is necessary. The federal policy has the force of law, and so do, in varying degrees, the policies of other subordinate units of government. But there are many other actions that may also be called affirmative action, in that they share with public policy the position that color blindness in hiring or promoting employees or in admitting applicants to selective admissions programs is not sufficient to overcome a heritage of discrimina-

NATHAN GLAZER • Graduate School of Education, Harvard University, Cambridge, Massachusetts 92138.

tion, and that more than a simple nondiscrimination is required. These policies are multifarious: hundreds if not thousands of educational institutions and bodies and employers, public and private, have such policies, which may consist of special advertising campaigns, assistance in taking tests, counseling, special tutoring, or many other things. These policies may be—most are—exceedingly race-conscious, choosing blacks or Hispanics or perhaps some others from groups that we know lag behind some average in educational attainment or income or employment or in getting good jobs.

This chapter does not deal with this enormously expanded meaning of *affirmative action*. Indeed, regarding most such programs there is no dispute, and thus no argument, over affirmative action. The argument over affirmative action concentrates specifically on one approach to affirmative action, which sets a statistical target for employers or educational institutions in hiring, promoting, and selecting. The argument becomes most heated over "goals and timetables" or, as their opponents sometimes call them, "quotas." The issue is: Should the federal contractors covered by Executive Order Number 11246, which requires them to be held to "affirmative action," undertake the very specific color-conscious and sex-conscious actions that the federal regulations that implement this order require? Is it legal, or constitutional, or right, to undertake, as federal regulations require,

> an analysis of areas within which the contractor is deficient in his utilization of minority groups and women, and further, [to set] goals and timetables to which the contractor's good faith efforts must be directed to correct the deficiencies and, thus, to increase materially the utilization of minorities and women. (*Code of Federal Regulations*)

To indicate the full grounds of the debate, we must point out that the Executive Order was issued in the wake of the Civil Rights Act of 1964, which banned discrimination in employment. This act also specified that "it shall not be an unlawful employment practice . . . for an employer to give and act upon the results of any professionally administered ability test . . . ," and that nothing in the act should be interpreted "to require any employer . . . to grant preferential treatment to any group because of the race, color, sex or national origin of such individual or group."

A potential conflict thus was created between the Civil Rights Act, with its specific demand for color blindness, its ban on racial preference, its approval of tests and of (in another section) seniority systems, and the executive order and its implementing regulations. Two different bodies were also created to enforce the requirements of the act and the order: the Equal Employment Opportunity Commission and the Office of Federal Contract Compliance Programs. The Civil Rights Act explicitly banned quotas. However, in case of findings of discrimination, a court could order remedial action: "such affirmative action as may be appropriate, which may include, but is not limited to, reinstatement or hiring of employees, with or without back pay, or any other equitable relief as the court deems appropriate." When discrimination is found under the Civil Rights Act of 1964, quotas are quite frequently required—and many police and firefighting forces operate under such quotas today. This is generally called affirmative action but is quite different in legal standing from the affirmative action required under the executive order. That affirmative action is not dependent on any finding of discrimination. All federal contractors are subject to it, depending on their reaching a minimum in the size of the federal contracts they hold (and through the operations of law, no college or university or hospital or sizable employer is not a "federal contractor").

The argument that exploded over federal affirmative action often took the form of a debate over words: Were the "goals and timetables" required by affirmative action "quotas"? If so, they were not only not required by the Civil Rights Act, but illegal under it. Some victims of "affirmative action"—denied jobs, they asserted, because of race or sex under the requirements of the executive order, as interpreted by employers—were able to gain redress from courts on the basis of the Civil Rights Act of 1964. Defenders of color-conscious affirmative action insisted that they were not requiring quotas—that "goals and timetables" were simply what the words said, that only a "good faith effort" to reach them was required, and thus they were not really "quotas." The critics of race-conscious affirmative action insisted that this was a quibble: when enforced by vigorous advocates with federal power, particularly in the early 1970s, it was impossible to see the difference between goals and timetables, and quotas.

And indeed, there were enough examples of practices by employers and colleges and universities that supported this interpretation (Glazer, 1983, pp. 160–167). My aim is not to rehearse the argument; it is to explain it. With hundreds of thousands of employing and promoting authorities, and with, in the Nixon and Carter administrations, federal officials committed to enforcing affirmative action requirements, it seems clear that, in many cases, goals and timetables did operate as quotas. It is also clear that this was more common in the early days, when employers and personnel authorities found it difficult to tread or define the fine line that separated goals and timetables from quotas. There were examples of university officials' requiring that departments hire only women or minorities (Glazer, 1976, pp. 60–61). But one suspects that, as institutions adapted to these requirements, as court cases warned them of what they could do and not do (among them in the *Bakke* case, in which an explicit quota for minority admissions to the medical school of the University of California at Davis was declared unconstitutional), one found less egregious examples of goals operating as quotas. Once a goal was set, a pressure, gentle or severe, it is true, existed to reach it, a pressure stemming from the federal affirmative action officers, or from the administration of the firm or college. But a distinction was maintained, or at least maintainable.

Indeed, the conflicts of the 1980s, it seems, revolve less about the "goals and timetables" requirement than around the explicit quotas required on the basis of discrimination, or in consent decrees accepted by firms or municipalities on the basis of a fear of a finding of discrimination. These quotas, involving the hiring of firefighters, or police officers, or teachers, and in particular those involving the question of who should be fired in case of cutbacks—and in the presence of union contracts requiring dismissal by seniority—now seem to be the front line of dispute over affirmative action. We call these affirmative action cases, but as I hope is clear from the above account, they do not arise under the executive order requiring affirmative action; and a change in the executive order would not necessarily affect the status of these disputes.

Why did affirmative action become so acrimonious an issue? Why did *goals* and *timetables* and *quotas* become fighting words? One reason, and a very important one, was because they truly determined in some cases who got a job, or a promotion, or was admitted to a law or medical school. On one side, we had groups, principally the blacks, that held, on average, jobs of low prestige and providing little security, income, or satisfaction. The groups had been subject to severe discrimination, official and unofficial. As President Johnson said in a famous speech, simply taking the shackles off someone who had long been bound and saying "Now run in the race," did not provide equal competition. On the other hand was a key principle that required, in the Constitution's Fourteenth Amendment, and in general opinion, that each individual be judged as an individual, independently of race or national origin or sex. That was the very principle that the advocates of civil rights who succeeded in 1964 were fighting for. When the meaning of true equality of opportunity moved from a color- and sex-blind judgment of the individual to policies that took race and sex into account in making judgments, a key aim of the civil rights struggle had been transgressed, in the view of many of those who had fought in it. In particular, Jewish groups active in the fight for civil rights refused to go along with race preference. They accepted affirmative action and even accepted goals and timetables, but they fought vigorously against erasing a line between the "good faith" efforts required by affirmative action and the quotas into which these often seemed to evolve. Thus, they were strong supporters of Bakke in his legal struggle against medical school quotas.

Thus, there were issues of interest: Who would get the job or the professional school opening? And there were also issues of principle: Should the individual be judged on the basis of his or her achievements, under a "veil of ignorance" as to group identification, so to speak, or should race or national origin or sex play a role in that judgment?

There were also issues of pragmatic judgment: Could the blacks make progress without goals and timetables and quotas? Was nondiscrimination enough? If they could not, did not social peace almost require a stronger effort than nondiscrimination alone called for? But on the other side of the pragmatic argument was the claim that discrimination was not the key constraint on black progress; it was qualification. Although in many jobs a significant degree of education or experience was not required, and one could well imagine that a quota for blacks would not affect the job to be done, in others it was crucial. How could one increase the number of black faculty members if very few blacks were preparing for doctorates in the arts and sciences? And in the course of the 1970s and 1980s, even that minuscule percentage dropped.

Finally, there were issues of conflicting visions of an ideal America. In one, any consideration of race or national origin in judging individuals was anathema. In the other, this consideration was essential, at least as a first step to overcoming racism. The first said we would never give up preferences once established and might have to extend them to more and more groups; the second said that if progress was made, the protected groups would be happy to give up preference (see Glazer, 1983, pp. 173–181, for the arguments for and against).

THE EFFECTS OF AFFIRMATIVE ACTION

In the campaigns of 1980 and 1984, the Republicans took a clear stand against quotas. We have already explained the different meanings of the terms in the disputes, and a stand against quotas did not necessarily mean a stand against goals and timetables; nor did a stand against quotas necessarily mean that the new administration could act against them through the Equal Employment Opportunity Commission (EEOC) or the Office for Federal Contract Compliance Programs (OFCCP); most quotas were imposed by the courts on the basis of findings of discrimination. And *these* findings were generally made on the basis of challenges to employment tests that blacks or women or other minorities failed disproportionately. Such tests could not easily qualify as nondiscriminatory on the basis of the stringent standards that the government civil-rights agencies had adopted for employment tests (Glazer, 1976, pp. 51–58; 1983, pp. 164–166).

Various routes to attacking the elements of affirmative action that required preferential hiring on the basis of race were available to the new administration: changing the regulations that were issued under the executive order, changing the definition of discriminatory tests, changing the composition of the civil rights enforcement agencies, and challenging the court decisions. The administration did not try to move on the first two fronts during its first term; it did change the top administration of the agencies, but how much that change affected the decisions or actions of employees lower down is arguable. Toward the end of the first term, it did begin to act against consent decrees requiring quotas, and in the second term, as we have seen, it undertook an effort to change either the Executive Order or the implementing regulations. Its greatest success to date has been the ruling in the U.S. Supreme Court on *Firefighters Local Union No. 1784 v. Stotts*, on

June 12, 1984, which upheld a union's seniority role on layoffs over the requirements of a consent decree. The case is complicated and it would not be useful to go into all its complexities here (see U.S. Commission on Civil Rights, 1985). Other cases will tell us just what the Supreme Court thinks are the legitimate limits of what has come to be known as affirmative action. From the point of view of social scientists interested in prejudice, discrimination, and race relations, the key questions lie elsewhere: Do we need affirmative action to achieve equality for blacks? What has been its record up to now? What follows if the administration seriously weakens the executive order or the enforcing regulations and, through its action in the courts, assists in a weakening of the legal structure that now requires quota hiring, in many cases, and supports goals and timetables? How can and do blacks and other minorities make progress?

As to the effects of affirmative action and what it has done for the employment of the target groups (blacks, other minorities, and women), the recent work of Jonathan S. Leonard (1984a,b, 1985) gives as good an answer as we have. He has distinguished between firms under preferential affirmative action (supervised by the Office of Federal Contract Compliance Programs, and with affirmative action plans) and those not in that position, and he has shown that affirmative action has increased the employment of black males and females substantially in this sector; of nonblack minority males less so, but also by a respectable percentage; and of white females much less. This is as good a measure of "hard" affirmative action as we can find. These findings are clear and can be taken to demonstrate the efficacy of preferential affirmative action, for blacks in particular. This gain holds true controlling for establishment size, industry, region, and other factors. This impact of affirmative action on nonminority males and white females is more mixed (Leonard, 1985, Abstract). The crude figures—econometricians, of course, refine them considerably—suggest that more black males were already employed in contractor firms in 1974 (5.8% vs. 5.3%), but that the increase was larger in contractor firms (to 6.7% against 5.9%).

In another analysis, Finis Welch (1985) pointed out that affirmative action seems to lead to a "proskill" bias in hiring blacks, understandable in view of the reduction of flexibility in firing and promotion that is imposed by antidiscrimination law and affirmative action requirements: "One would like to think that an affirmative action program would encourage risk-taking by employers; that actions which create expanded opportunities for productive workers would be subsidized rather than taxed" (p. 17). This is the argument on empirical grounds that Thomas Sowell (1981) made on theoretical grounds. It suggests that we must balance the gain for skilled blacks, on whom it is worth taking a chance, with the possible reduction of opportunity for the less skilled. It is generally felt that affirmative action has made few, if any, inroads into the problem of unemployed, and less skilled or unskilled, blacks.

I do not examine the situation of black women, where, in general, the gap in income or employment compared with those of white women is not as great as for males, and indeed, where some categories of black women earn better than similar categories of white women (Jencks, 1985). Nor do I examine here the situations of nonblack minority males and females, or of white females, which raise so many other considerations, some of which I discuss later.

Clearly, in the case of a program that raises such violent disagreements of principle, these results, although important, will be argued over, as is true of empirical findings in almost any area of disputed public policy. The rest of this chapter considers, in the light of this evidence and many other considerations, what would be the impact on the conditions of minorities and women of a change in federal policy weakening affirmative action requirements.

In order to make any judgment, we must have some sense not only of what these policies achieve, but of what other policies that would continue to exist in their absence would achieve. And we must make some judgment of where we, in general, stand in American society on the scale of racial prejudice and discrimination. Do we conceive of our society, its employers and its institutions, as irremediably racist, ready to spring back, on the basis of a change in coercive policy, to the practices of 1964 or 1969? Or do we think that most employers and most Americans want to be fair, and to judge potential employees, employees being considered for promotion, and applicants to selective programs on the basis of their qualities rather than on their race or national origin or sex? These judgments are hard to make, and we tend to diverge sharply in making them. Many who might agree that Americans are not irremediably racist refer to "institutional" racism, that is, the impact of tests, institutionalized procedures, expectations, and so on in reaching the same result as racism.

Rather than any argument on American opinion—one could show that it steadily becomes less racist—we should consider just what institutional supports exist that, in the weakening of affirmative action, would maintain nondiscrimination and, beyond that, preference for blacks. There are a great many. One policy that exists and would continue to exist, obviously, because it is law under congressional statute, is the law against discrimination in employment. And the agency that enforces it, the EEOC (whose budget is substantially larger than that of the OFCCP, the agency responsible for affirmative action by government contractors), would also continue to exist. If we were to ask what the future would be like without preferential affirmative action, then we would have to have a sense of what that act and that agency—and the cases brought under it by the Justice Department—achieve. It is my impression that they achieve a great deal. If we add to what they achieve the work of state and municipal agencies or orders that require preferential affirmative action, we can see that a good deal of such action would exist even if federal policy changed. Quotas imposed by the courts would continue. Newspapers are filled with news of settlements under the Civil Rights Act (which very often do involve "quotas") and of action by state agencies quite independent of federal requirements.[1]

Opponents of preferential affirmative action would want to move against this policy generally, and to eliminate it in state and local action, as well as in federal action, in private and nonpublic institutions where it exists voluntarily, and in contractor firms now required to have such policies. Nevertheless, I think it makes sense to think of policies in the packets in which they come in reality. A change in federal affirmative action regulations, seems, in view of the attitudes of the present administration and the relative ease legally of changing them, to be the most likely change. It is most reasonable to think of that change in considering the potential effects of a limitation of preferential affirmative action on the prospects of minority groups and women.

An exercise considering what the effects of a policy different from preferential affirmative action would be requires us to keep in place other elements that determine occupational choice and income. It would be an act of demagogy to assume that, if we do away with federal preferential affirmative action, everything else changes: that the Civil Rights Law is no longer in effect, that the EEOC is no longer funded or operative; that the courts shift 180 degrees in their interpretation of the Constitution and the laws and other

---

[1]For example, "Georgia Agrees to Hire 243 Blacks, Women," news of a settlement of a Department of Justice suit against Georgia (*Washington Post*, August 9, 1984). The news story noted that this was the second largest settlement (in terms of back pay) obtained by the U.S. government against a public agency, the first being the settlement of a suit against Fairfax County, Virginia, in 1982; or "Road Contractors Evading Bias Law—44 Barred by Jersey for Failure to Achieve Minority Goals," reporting an action by the State Transportation Department of New Jersey (*New York Times*, November 30, 1984).

federal regulations; that state and local antidiscrimination commissions, laws, and regulations become inoperative; that all the internal rules and regulations that create a degree of affirmative action within employing agencies, public, private, and voluntary, would become ineffective; and that the organizations of minorities and women that now press for fairness or preference would fall dumb and powerless. Perhaps a political philosopher can assume all this, or an econometrician. A policy analyst must deal with more realistic alternatives, and that is what I have chosen to do.

As I have already suggested from my accounting, itself not complete, of the forces that keep in place a system of employment and promotion that, on the whole, exercises a good deal of preference for minorities or women, not much would change. The fact is the procedures that require preference have, in large measure, been institutionalized. Affirmative action policies have helped institutionalize these procedures. And this institutionalized system would remain more-or-less in place, whatever the changes in federal regulations on affirmative action.

I agree with Robert J. Samuelson (1984), who analyzed what the effect of a reduction in strong enforcement would be:

> These pressures [the aggressive use of antidiscrimination laws, including affirmative action] have changed the way labor markets work. Many firms have overhauled personnel policies. Recruitment has been broadened. Tests unrelated to qualifications have been abandoned. Promotions are less informal. When positions become open, they are posted publicly so anyone (not just the boss's favorites) can apply. Formal evaluations have been strengthened so that, when a manager selects one candidate over another (say, a white man over a woman) there are objective criteria.
>
> Equally important, women and blacks increasingly are plugged into the informal information and lobbying networks that remain critical in hiring and promotion decisions.

Have these institutionalized procedures that were brought into existence in response to antidiscrimination law and affirmative action in the 1970s survived the 1980s? It would be revealing to uncover what the effects of 5 years of somewhat slackened enforcement—and more than that, expectation of slackened enforcement—have been. The reality of looser enforcement and the expectation of looser enforcement have, I assume, not been without effect, but they have been of much less effect than the supporters of strong enforcement believe. This conclusion is based on modest experience and, rather more, on some settled convictions about how institutions operate. The experience is primarily in the field of higher education, but it is an area in which preferential affirmative action has been very controversial (more controversial, in my judgment, than in industry or government generally). If slackened enforcement is to have effect, one would expect it there.

I have seen no change in the affirmative action procedures instituted in the 1970s. All posts must still be advertised. *The Chronicle of Higher Education* is fatter with advertising than ever as a result. In my institution, and in many others I know about, a special effort to find minority and female applicants for all posts is still required. Deans and other administrative officers still look more favorably on a proposed female or minority appointment than on a white male appointment. The pressure from women faculty, graduate students, and undergraduates, and from minority groups that helps maintain these policies has not changed. One hears less about pressures from regional offices of the OFCCP to prepare elaborate affirmative-action plans. But once the institutional forces are in place—and some of them exist, it is true, owing to the initial pressure to create affirmative action plans—the plans themselves hardly matter. The varied forces maintaining the pressure are not reduced by a reduction in the efforts of regional offices.

Admittedly, higher education is a rather special segment. Perhaps more liberal administrators and more liberal employees than are the norm elsewhere, and in addition the pressure of liberal students, a force which does not exist in private industry or in public employment, make things different. But in public and private employment, other and equivalent pressures come into play, for example, the role of political pressures and competition for the vote in affecting city and state employment policies. News accounts do not suggest any slackening in those states and cities with large minority populations and liberal traditions. In federal employment, almost every agency submits affirmative action plans, today, after 6 years of Reagan administration. (Only William Bennett resisted when he was director of the National Endowment for the Humanities; I would guess he does not maintain his obduracy as Secretary of Education.) In business, one expects, the personnel procedures institutionalized during the 1970s have not been abandoned. One has not heard of a mass firing of affirmative action officers, or of a mass return to tests that have been declared discriminatory. Institutions do not change that rapidly, and in the private sector, as in the academic and public sector, one must also contend with a body of law, enforced by energetic lawyers whose numbers and expertise in antidiscrimination law have increased apace. Consider the advice and warnings given to managers and entrepreneurs in the "Small Business" column of the *Wall Street Journal* on February 1984:

> What's wrong with asking a woman job applicant these questions: Who takes care of your children when you're at work? What if they get sick? How does your husband feel about your taking business trips? What would he say if a male employee went too?
>
> They may seem like reasonable questions. But in fact they could be construed as biased against women and could embroil the employer in charges of discriminating against female job applicants in violation of federal or state laws because male applicants aren't asked such questions.
>
> Don't ask if someone has ever been arrested. (Because blacks are arrested more than whites, a federal court has held, such a question can be discriminatory against blacks.) However, asking about criminal convictions is usually safe. And not hiring a convicted felon can be justified as a business necessity for such reasons as not being able to bond the person.
>
> Restrictive job requirements can get a company in trouble, too. It may be discriminatory to have an educational barrier to a position (only high school grads need apply) if it can't be justified as necessary to doing the job. (Jacobs, 1985, p. 25)

Four years after Reagan came to office, employers were thus advised to be more careful than ever not to trigger charges of discrimination. The basis for this advice was public law, public agencies, and private lawyers, and all these are in place and unchanged.

To show how strong institutional commitments can be, consider the recent case— from an area of affirmative action, university and college admissions, that is not under consideration here—from Harvard. Former Dean of the Faculty of Arts and Sciences Henry Rosovsky had commented on the rapid increase of Asian students at Harvard and elsewhere. Asian students, as is well known, are "represented" in institutions of higher education in numbers far greater than "expected" by their proportion in the population. Asian student representatives protested what they interpreted as a possibility they would be deprived of "minority status"—their term. One may properly be mystified about what their official recognition as a minority by Harvard gives them. Not, I believe, more financial aid, better grades, more tutoring, or anything else. Concretely, it appeared from their protests, the only thing they may get is special effort to recruit Asian students. In response to the protest, a dean assured the Asian students (or rather their organizational representatives) that their minority status would continue to be recognized. It is true that sillier things may happen on campuses than elsewhere, but when, for example, Asian Indian businessmen can get themselves recognized as a minority deserving special consideration in the awarding of contracts, who is to say Harvard is exceptional?

The first point to be made, then, in considering alternatives to preferential affirmative action is that the institutional structure, public and private, that now supports it would stay in place and is hardly likely to be dismantled. And a second and related point is that the social pressures to maintain preferential affirmative action would also remain in place, and indeed, one might expect that they would be intensified in response to a loosening of federal requirements for contractors. Minority organizations, women's rights organizations, and civil rights organizations are numerous, and experienced. In universities and colleges, one can be sure that student and faculty groups representing minority and women's interests would continue to exert pressure. In businesses, there is less of a tradition of employee organizations of this type, but many unions are committed to these goals and would press for them.

What may we expect in regard to the future of the major group beneficiaries of preferential affirmative action if this policy is abandoned? Preferential affirmative action is only partially and perhaps to a modest extent responsible for the enormous changes we have seen since the mid-1960s in the position of the black minority and of women. Some of these great changes have occurred in the absence of any governmental pressure for preferential affirmative action, for example, the huge increase in the percentage of women entering law and medical schools. There has been no governmental pressure in this area, and no voluntary affirmative action by law and medical schools to recruit larger numbers of women for law and medical schools. This change has occurred entirely as a result of the great change in women's desires about the occupations and professions they wish to pursue, assisted only marginally by the legal prohibition against discrimination.

Women have already vastly expanded their occupational and professional horizons. This expansion has been assisted by the fact that, where mental tests are involved (e.g., for entry into selective institutions of higher education, into law and medical schools, or into the legal and medical professions, and possibly—though here I am not sure—in the case of psychological tests designed to assess suitability for certain professions), women, on the whole, do as well as men, with minor differences. Preferential affirmative action for women has not been necessary to overcome gross differences in test achievement, except for physical tests (for fire and police employees and armed-forces specialties). Insofar as preferential affirmative action has sought too vigorously to overcome traditional tastes (e.g., for indoor as against outdoor work, as in the AT&T settlement), it has been expensive and a failure. There are complex issues involved in the rise of women in bureaucratic hierarchies, but they can be addressed through litigation under civil rights law as effectively as through statistical quotas under preferential affirmative action.

We are engaged in a revolution of expectations, by men and by women; some of us think that that revolution has ignored some differences that are significant and that must be taken account of in assessing suitability for certain roles (e.g., the armed forces and fire and police services). There is no way for preferential affirmative action as against nondiscrimination to make determinations on these matters. What is the base against which one decides there is "underutilization" of women? Who is to say that women in the armed forces or a police force should number 40% of the personnel (as they do for occupational roles generally), or 20% (as is often required for new hires in police and fire departments), or 10% (which is their present percentage in the armed forces)? These figures should result from a combination of the actual choices women make in the occupations they wish to follow and administrative decisions about how many may be accommodated without damage to the mission of the profession or occupation.

The abandonment of preferential affirmative action for women would mean no loss in terms of women's desires for equality. Bridgeheads have been established everywhere—and indeed, more than bridgeheads—and procedures other than federal administrative decisions about how many women should be employed for this or that job by this or that employer are unnecessary and, in some cases, harmful to effective functioning. For the armed forces, certainly, there are already grave questions.

When we come to racial-ethnic minority groups the matter is in some respects more simple, in other respects complex. The inclusion of Asians under preferential affirmative-action requirements—here and there being abandoned—is, in a word, silly. Without denying the existence of massive discrimination in the past and pockets of discrimination today, preferential affirmative action for Asians makes as little sense as preferential affirmative action for Jews. Asians' incomes tend to be above the average and their education well above the average, and Asians are very well represented in the areas of their occupational choice, for example, engineering, computer science, and architecture. That there are few in the humanities and not many in the social sciences should bother us as little as the fact that there are few Jews in forestry or agriculture: it is their choice, and it is no business of government to interfere. If government does interfere, we can be sure that various Asian groups will happily accept the advantage offered. They will argue that they are deprived and are worthy recipients of set-asides in government contracting. Asian Americans are not discriminated against today in any way that requires affirmative action. If one or another group (Korean, Filipino, Cambodian, or Laotian) is worse off than others, we can ascribe that condition quite properly to its recency of immigration, to the numbers with inadequate language skills or inadequate or inappropriate education, or to a different cultural orientation. Many need assistance with language, with education, and with adaptation to a new culture. None of these requires preferential affirmative action.

One of the chief weaknesses of preferential affirmative action is the amalgam it has created of Hispanic Americans. Cubans don't need it, most Latin Americans are happy to make their way as other immigrants have, and persons of Spanish descent are included only by accident. One could make a better argument for preferential affirmative action if it were limited to Mexican-Americans and Puerto Ricans, as putative victims of American imperialism and subjects of discrimination. But how can preferential affirmative action operate effectively for Mexican-Americans, in view of the large and indeterminate element that consists of illegal immigrants and is not fully counted, and the divisions one must make between very long-settled groups, some dating to the seventeenth century, and recent immigrants, who must undergo, as all immigrants do, the transition to a new language, a new educational system, and different occupations and occupational demands? What is a suitable base on which to compute the statistical measures that preferential affirmative action requires? Laws against discrimination offer sufficient protection against discrimination for Mexican-Americans. I would argue similarly for Puerto Ricans.

Blacks are the best claimants to preferential affirmative action: They have suffered the most from discrimination and are more victimized by discrimination than any other group. They show—along with Puerto Ricans—the most substantial gap in income when compared with other Americans. The very large differences in test scores of whites and blacks in tests for admission to institutions of higher education and for various occupations point to a very serious problem: We must expect that black participation in key professions such as law, medicine, and higher education, in teaching and the civil services, which tend to be test-based in various degrees—which rule out disproportionate numbers of blacks—will show a serious "underutilization," if preferential policies are not in effect.

And preferential affirmative action has substantially increased the numbers of black doctors, lawyers, professors, teachers, and so on above what they would have been had race-blind procedures not been in effect.

For the black group in particular, the consequences of a departure from preferential affirmative action could be quite serious. Undoubtedly, these policies have increased the representation of blacks in selective occupations, in skilled jobs, and in executive positions. They have also had negative consequences, which critics of these policies have pointed to, among them Thomas Sowell (1981), in encouraging a view of blacks as less competent—a view held not only by others but by many blacks—and by reducing incentives to high performance. One can assume such effects theoretically, but I know of no empirical research that gives direct support to such effects. Nor do I know by what metric we could balance gains against losses, as they are of such different types.

This analysis suggests the virtues of a policy that contracts the reach of preferential affirmative action, first for the groups that do best (Asian Americans and women) and then for groups of Hispanic Americans, restricting it to the groups that need it most. Even for such groups, a time limit on how long such policies operate would be desirable. Time limits can be extended almost indefinitely (as in the case of the Voting Rights Act, and in the case of preferential affirmative action in India). Nevertheless, the idea that preferential affirmative action is a policy for a limited time is a reasonable one to put into the public arena. It would protect blacks from the most radical effects of cold-turkey abandonment and yet signal to all that we expect ours to be a society in which a strict enforcement of fairness and nondiscrimination will satisfy all groups. The benefits of preferential affirmative action even for the black group are sufficiently ambiguous—particularly when we take into account that it is not at all effective in reaching the most disadvantaged and problem-ridden strata of the population—so that such a policy could be justified, even if it is utopian to expect that it will attain wide acceptance among blacks. Fears of what it might produce could be moderated if it were combined with vigorous attention to the elements in the education of blacks that lead to those test scores of all types that are at present a substantial barrier to black achievement in the absence of preferential affirmative action.

REFERENCES

Code of Federal Regulations, 41, 60-2.11.

Glazer, N. (1976). Affirmative discrimination: Ethnic inequality and public policy. New York: Basic Books.

Glazer, N. (1983). Ethnic dilemmas, 1964–1982. Cambridge: Harvard University Press.

Jacobs, S. L. (1985, February 5). Changes in employment laws can trap unwary companies. The Wall Street Journal, p. 25.

Jencks, C. S. (1985). Affirmative action for blacks: Past, present and future. American Behavioral Scientist, 28(6), 731–760.

Leonard, J. S. (1984a). The impact of affirmative action on employment (National Bureau of Economic Research, Working Paper No. 1310). Washington, DC.

Leonard, J. S. (1984b). What promises are worth: The impact of affirmative action goals (National Bureau of Economic Research, Working Paper No. 1346). Washington DC.

Leonard, J. S. (1985, February). What was affirmative action? Paper prepared for U.S. Commission on Civil Rights Panel on Affirmative Action as a Remedy for Discrimination.

Samuelson, R. J. (1984, July 11). Affirmative action's usefulness is passing. The Washington Post.

Sowell, T. (1981). Markets and minorities. New York: Basic Books.

U.S. Commission on Civil Rights. (1985, January). Towards an understanding of Stotts (Clearinghouse Publication 85). Washington, DC.

Welch, F. (1985, March 6–7). Affirmative action in employment: An overview and assessment of effects (Report #85-02-DoL). Paper prepared for U.S. Commission on Civil Rights Consultation on Affirmative Action in Employment.

18

Affirmative Action and the Legacy of Racial Injustice

Ira Glasser

INTRODUCTION: THE LOSS OF MORAL CONSENSUS

Over 40 years ago, Gunnar Myrdal, in his seminal book *An American Dilemma,* dissected the moral problem of American racism as it had never been dissected before. His key insight is by now a cliché: that a terrible tension existed in American society between its professed ideals of equality and fairness based on individual merit and the reality of brutal, suffocating oppression based on skin color. This tension was said to create a dissonance in the American psyche so sharp that it threatened to split us asunder, but if we came to grips with it and made genuine efforts to make reality conform to our ideals, it could be the source of our redemption.

Scarcely 10 years after Myrdal's book was published and 85 years after the states had been prohibited by the Fourteenth Amendment from denying individuals the equal protection of the laws, the U.S. Supreme Court ruled that requiring the separation of black and white children in schools was unconstitutional. The High Court had measured reality against our constitutional ideal and had found reality wanting.

Two years later, Rosa Parks sat down in the "wrong" seat on a public bus in Montgomery, Alabama, and a little-known 27-year old black Baptist minister named Martin Luther King, Jr., aroused the conscience of a nation by organizing a bus boycott in her support. The civil rights movement was under way.

In many respects, the movement was a laboratory for Myrdal's thesis. Its fundamental goals, as well as its strategy and tactics, were to expose America to the reality of racism, which its ideals did not permit. In those days, the issues were clear and uncomplicated, at least in the South. Blacks and whites were kept apart by law and by custom, in schools, on buses, in theaters; at luncheonettes, restaurants, hotels, and toilets; at drinking fountains, swimming pools, parks, and baseball games; at the ballot box and in the jury box (where blacks were effectively excluded altogether); and in the workplace, where blacks were pervasively denied equal opportunity. Moreover, such separation was not benign: "separate but equal" was a lie. Inferiority was institutionalized and enforced by the police power of the state and by tradition. If you were black, individual merit was irrelevant, even dangerous. As James Baldwin has told us, black parents often feared for

IRA GLASSER • American Civil Liberties Union, 132 West 43rd Street, New York, New York 10036.

their children when they showed ambition or revealed hope. Repression became internalized, the near-final solution of a racist society.

The civil rights movement confronted all of this, brought it into our homes on television, and forced us to choose between abandoning our ideals, and therefore ourselves, or working to change reality. The moral issue was unmistakable, and starkly visible. White liberals in the North, aroused by the massive insult of racial segregation in the South and the naked violence that periodically erupted to defend it, poured their money, and sometimes their bodies, into the fight. Eventually, it became unfashionable to defend and even to permit the cruder forms of racism. Driven by the moral urgency of the facts and shamed by the distance between those facts and its stated ideals, American society grudgingly, but surely, began to change.

Grievances were translated into laws; protest into politics. In less than a decade after Rosa Parks had refused to obey the law of segregation, major civil-rights legislation prohibiting discrimination in voting, housing, employment, and education was in place. The courts repeatedly struck down laws or practices that permitted racial separation, and regulatory agencies were established to enforce remedial legislation. By 1968, when Martin Luther King, Jr., was gunned down on the balcony of a Memphis motel, most of the important legal principles initially sought by the civil rights movement had been established.

But the gap between the reality of discrimination and the ideal of equality did not so quickly close, despite all the new legislation. The residual effects of centuries of slavery and legal discrimination could not be easily erased, and the removal of legal barriers to equal opportunity and the inclusion of blacks as full-fledged citizens of the American polity proved to be only the first stage in a longer, more painfully redemptive, struggle.

Three decades of litigation followed and established the legal principle that it is unconstitutional for the state to mandate or maintain racial separation and discrimination. Similarly, the legal principle that it is unlawful for private parties to discriminate on the basis of race in housing, employment, and public accommodations was clearly and firmly established by both Congress and the courts. Today, these principles are no longer in doubt, and no serious ideology or movement threatens them.

Yet, implementing these principles has turned out to be much more difficult and frustrating than anyone anticipated. Resistance has been strong, not any longer to the legal principles themselves, but to specific claims that these principles have been violated and, even more, to the remedies necessary to correct such violations. The facts of racial discrimination were clear and undisputed 30 years ago, and the remedies seemed clear. Today, claims of racial discrimination require careful analysis of facts that often prove to be murky, complicated, and deeply in dispute, even among those who share common goals. And even where it is possible to agree about the facts, there is great dispute over the appropriate remedies.

Racial exclusion from the benefits of society and the rights of citizenship is no longer nearly total, as it once was. But it is still disproportionate and it still limits the opportunities and stifles the hopes of many black Americans. In many counties of the old South, for example, blacks are still effectively excluded from the political system, even though the blunter instruments of intimidation and formal legal barriers to voting no longer exist. In many school systems, North and South, racially separate attendance patterns and exclusionary practices still exist, and black children are still disproportionately suspended and channeled into lower-ability tracks. In most metropolitan areas, there is still a firm division of the races between city and suburb—what a presidential study commission nearly two decades ago called "two separate Americas"—that cannot be traced to any explicitly racial law. Most ominously, unemployment rates for blacks remain disproportionately and explosively higher, especially for young males, than corresponding rates for whites. And racial stratification in employment, including public employment, is still widespread, especially in the South.

Are such starkly unequal results caused by racial discrimination? Many people no longer think so. "When we talk about discrimination today," Nathan Glazer wrote, "we really do not have in mind discrimination; we have in mind inferior economic status which is the effect of many causes, among which may be discrimination." And the black economist Thomas Sowell (1984) claimed that "skills, education and work habits" are the answer, not civil rights jaws or court-imposed remedies. To a limited degree, these critics have a point. Skills and hard work *are* important. And overt racial discrimination of the kind blacks faced 30 years ago has been greatly reduced and, in some cases, has all but vanished. On the other hand, writers like Glazer and Sowell have become part of the new "blame-the-victims" movement, in part because they seem to underestimate the impact and persistence of the less visible but still effective force of racism, and in part because they fail to credit the relationship between discrimination and ambition. The expectation of opportunity is part of what drives people to develop their skills and to work hard. When opportunity does not exist, or is extremely limited, or is perceived to be extremely limited, ambition is dampened and hope dies. It is all well and good to urge the oppressed to work harder. But skills will not be developed if there is little expectation of employment and mobility.

These are not simple issues, and that is partly why the moral consensus of 30 years ago has been lost. Today, we are faced not with clear and obvious moral issues, but with hotly disputed assertions of fact, difficult problems of proof, and even more difficult problems of remedy.

Among various remedies, none has proved to be more controversial than affirmative action. Not only has affirmative action failed to command the kind of moral consensus enjoyed by the civil rights movement 20 years ago, it is claimed by some who supported that movement to be itself a form of discrimination or racism. Ironically, at precisely the time when the popular moral consensus for affirmative action seems to have been lost, the institutions of society seem to have become committed to it. The U.S. Supreme Court has steadily affirmed affirmative action by permitting numerical goals and timetables, called quotas by some, and Congress has clearly refused to legislate against such remedies. Moreover, according to a recent survey in *Fortune* magazine, over 95% of major American corporations would continue to use numerical objectives in the hiring and promotion of minorities even if not required to do so. Thus, the institutions that were at first resistant to civil rights laws and remedies now seem to have grown used to them, even as popular support has waned and popular resistance has increased. That divergence cannot continue forever, which is precisely why it is important to come to grips with the concept of affirmative action as a moral issue rather than merely as a legal one.

The entire subject of affirmative action thus provides us with an opportunity to revisit the moral issue first posed over 40 years ago by Gunnar Myrdal. Is affirmative action fair? Is it moral? Is it consistent with American ideals, or is it opposed to them?

In the discussion that follows, I shall limit myself mostly to a discussion of affirmative action as it applies to and affects black Americans, in part because the issues are somewhat different with respect to other racial minorities and women, and in part because I wish to focus, in the limited space available, not on affirmative action in general, but on the somewhat narrower issue of discrimination against blacks and the remedies required to end this discrimination.

ORIGINS AND DEFINITIONS

Because affirmative action has become something of an undifferentiated code word, for both its advocates and its opponents, it is useful to define our terms. The concept of affirmative action, as distinct from the term, has two separate, though related, origins. Under one definition, affirmative action is a narrow, if drastic, *legal remedy*, temporarily imposed or approved by the courts in particular cases to redress the specific effects of past or current discrimination, where such discrimination has been proved. Under the second definition, affirmative action is a broad kind of moral reparation, a form of temporary *compensatory opportunity*, designed to make up generally for past injustices and to get things even again before allowing the race to continue on relatively equal terms. There is a third strain of thought as well, which defines affirmative action as an effort to achieve *fair and visible representation* for minorities for reasons of social or political effectiveness. Under this definition, for example, police forces in inner cities should reflect a fair proportion of blacks not only because that may be a remedy for specific discrimination or a compensation for prior exclusions, but also because we will have a better police force when blacks are included, especially if a large proportion of the community is black. This argument has also been applied to teachers and other employment categories. The argument has been made most forcefully with respect to political representation on governing bodies such as local legislatures and school boards.

People who make such arguments claim that such representation in leadership roles is not only a legitimate extension of the right of suffrage itself, but also a manifestation of full citizenship and a crucial indicator that, at last, historic racial exclusions from the rights of citizenship have ended. Moreover, some political scientists, notably Philip Green (1981), have argued that only the creation of leadership classes that forcefully demonstrate the capabilities inherent in the communities excluded can begin to erode the internalized belief on the part of many in the excluded group that somehow the fault is theirs.

Although this line of argument provides a compelling justification for affirmative action, it is not itself affirmative action, as no one argues that such representation should be mandated in the absence of discriminatory exclusion or independently of whatever standards of merit otherwise apply. In fact, therefore, affirmative action is usually understood to mean either a specific legal remedy to specific discriminatory exclusion or a more general, if temporary, compensatory opportunity for the members of a group that has long been disadvantaged relative to the dominant social group. Both of these definitions will be examined below.

Affirmative Action as Legal Remedy

The problem that most easily illustrates this concept is jury discrimination. Imagine a southern town with 40% of its adult population black, not one of whom has ever served on a jury. A civil rights suit is brought, and after a trial, the judge finds that the town has discriminated on the basis of race and that this discrimination is illegal. An order is issued requiring the town to stop discriminating.

A year later, the plaintiffs are back in court. Their complaint is that the town is still discriminating, despite the court order. The town defends itself by proving that 10 blacks have served or have been called to serve on juries during the past year. But the judge finds that 10 blacks amount to only one-tenth of 1% of the adult population. As all adults are qualified to serve and should be chosen at random, it is impossible to believe that so few blacks would be chosen unless racial discrimination was still being practiced. The town offers other explanations, but none is found to be persuasive. The judge rules that discrimination has continued and orders the town once again to stop, and to institute a new system for choosing jurors that will ensure nondiscrimination.

Six months later, everyone is back in court again. This time the plaintiffs seek an order requiring the town to meet a goal of 40% blacks in the jury pool within the next 3 months. The town again claims that it is no longer discriminating and says that it is trying as hard as it can to include blacks. But the facts show that only 10% of the jury pool is black—a vast improvement, but still far short of what one would expect if there were no discrimination. The judge closely examines the procedures used by the town as well as its explanations for why only 10% of the jury pool is black when 40% of the available qualified population is black and when the choice is supposed to be random. The judge also takes into consideration the history of entrenched racism in the town and the particular impact of that racism on jury selection. After the trial, the court finds that, despite significant improvement, the only explanation for the continued exclusion of blacks is discrimination. The town claims that it no longer intends to discriminate, but intent is hard to prove, and given the long history of purposeful discrimination, the court looks to the effect of the system for choosing jurors and finds that it continues to exclude disproportionate numbers of qualified blacks. As a result, the court now orders a more drastic remedy to rectify the continued exclusion: the town is ordered to adopt a system that results in approximately 40% blacks in the jury pool, plus or minus 3%, within 6 months. Moreover, an independent monitor is appointed by the court to review the town's progress and to report periodically to the court.

It is difficult to see why anyone would find this sort of specific remedy objectionable, under the circumstances described. Yet, all the elements of affirmative action to which people frequently object are present in this example. First of all, *the remedy is race-conscious, not color-blind*. It counts people based on race and measures the degree to which discrimination has stopped by comparing the percentage of blacks chosen to their percentage in the qualified pool. Second, *the remedy includes a numerical goal* (40%, plus or minus 3%) *and a timetable* (6 months, with periodic monitoring), or what would some would call a *quota*. The goal is established as a way of measuring whether discrimination has stopped; the timetable is set to put pressure on the town to stop dragging its heels.

Opponents of affirmative action regularly say that we should be color-blind, not race-conscious, and that goals and timetables are "reverse discrimination." They stigmatize such goals and timetables by calling them "quotas," in order to identify this sort of remedy with historical mechanisms that were used to place artificial ceilings on the inclusion of minorities. But in a case such as that described above, how can we fairly measure progress against the discriminatory exclusion of blacks except by counting blacks? And if 40% of the qualified population is black, why is it unreasonable to expect that something close to 40% would be included in the jury pool *if the choice were made fairly, and without discrimination?*

Jury discrimination is an easy case, of course. In cases of employment discrimination, the principles just established are much harder to apply. The reasons are fairly obvious. It is easy to tell who is qualified to be on a jury: anyone who has reached the age of majority. If 40% of the adult population is black, then 40% of the qualified population is black. The calculation is more complex and problematic in the area of employment. If 40% of the adult population is black, it does not necessarily follow that 40% of those qualified to teach high school, or to be firefighters, will be black. But it is possible to identify reasonable qualifications for these jobs and to assess the proportion of the qualified labor pool that is black. Suppose, for example, that careful studies showed that 20% of the population qualified to be firefighters was black, but no more than 3% were ever chosen. Wouldn't that present the same problem and justify the same remedy as the jury discrimination case?

Obviously, the determination of the proper percentage is much more difficult in the area of employment. Definitions of what constitute proper qualifications for given jobs differ. So do methods of measuring those qualifications. But so many "qualifications" in the past were not really bona fide qualifications related to job performance; rather, they were restrictions designed to exclude people for impermissible reasons. That's what literacy tests were in the area of voting, or college degree requirements for various manual labor jobs, or weight-lifting requirements that eliminated women even though such requirements were not related to the job.

The fact is that, traditionally, the definition of qualifications for particular jobs as well as the methods for evaluating the applicants have themselves often been reflections of discrimination rather than fair tests of job-related qualities. Affirmative action litigation has forced everyone to think more carefully and precisely about what qualifications are actually required for a given job, and to find better ways of measuring those qualifications. This process has undoubtedly reduced discrimination and made hiring fairer.

In any case, it is usually possible, for any job category, to determine, within a reasonable range, what percentage of the available qualified labor pool is black or female. Suppose, again taking our hypothetical town, that 20% of the population qualified to be firefighters was black, but no more than 3% blacks had ever been chosen. Assume that the figure of 20% is reasonably accurate, and that the town has a history of racial discrimination and persistently hires no more than 3% black firefighters. Why isn't that situation, in moral terms, exactly like the jury discrimination case?

Suppose, for example, that a number of blacks, who claim to be qualified for the job of firefighter but who were turned down, sue the town, claiming racial discrimination. Suppose further that, after trial, the court finds that the town has had a long history of racial discrimination in public employment and, in particular, in the hiring of firefighters. Finally, suppose the court finds that the tests currently being used by the town to qualify firefighters disproportionately exclude blacks and are not validly predictive of job performance. The court then prohibits the use of that test and orders the town to develop a method of evaluating job applicants that is nondiscriminatory.

As in the jury case, a year passes and the proportion of blacks hired as firefighters hardly increases and does not come close to approaching the estimate of 20%, which is the proportion of available qualified blacks in the labor force. The town defends itself by showing that it now uses nondiscriminatory tests and has engaged in vigorous recruiting of minorities. It therefore claims that its failure to hire more blacks is not evidence of discrimination and that, in fact, it has acted in good faith to recruit and hire on a nondiscriminatory basis.

If, after hearing both sides and examining the evidence as well as the testimony of experts, the court accepts the town's arguments, then the lawsuit will be dismissed. Good-faith efforts to hire on a nondiscriminatory basis are enough. If, on the other hand, the court finds the town's arguments specious and a cover for continued, if more subtle, discriminatory acts, or if the court finds that the town's current methods are not sufficient to overcome the effects of past discrimination, then the court may order the town to reach a goal of, say, 15% blacks in its firefighter force within 2 years. As in the jury case, this goal would be established based on the court's finding that, in the absence of discrimination, approximately 15% of the firefighters would be black. Although the actual percentage used may well be open to dispute, the fact that more blacks would have been hired but for discrimination is difficult to dispute. In the face of persistent discriminatory exclusion, why is it unreasonable, much less immoral, for a court to order the offending employer to stop discriminating and then to measure compliance with that order by establishing a reasonable goal?

The examples I have used are relatively simple. Cases can and do arise that are much more complex and make the remedy of goals and timetables much more difficult to apply fairly. But the principle remains the same: If qualified blacks are available but are not being hired as the result of past or current discrimination, then they should be hired. And the only way to measure whether they are being hired on a nondiscriminatory basis is to count them and compare the percentage hired with the percentage of qualified people in the available population. To deny this sort of remedy in cases where discrimination has been proved, and where racial exclusion remains persistent, is to say that even though fundamental rights have been violated, we will not act to remedy such violations. That result seems profoundly immoral.

AFFIRMATIVE ACTION AS COMPENSATORY OPPORTUNITY

Affirmative action as a specific remedy imposed in particular situations where discrimination has been proved is the easiest form of affirmative action to justify. More problematic is the broad provision of compensatory opportunities or entitlements, special advantages given on the basis of race in order to make up, in a general way, for disadvantages that were imposed on the basis of race. The earliest examples of such compensatory opportunities and entitlements occurred after the Civil War, when Congress established certain economic and educational programs to which only recently freed slaves and other blacks in the South were entitled. Whites were explicitly excluded (including poor whites), and some blacks were included who arguably had not personally been victims of discrimination. But the judgment was made that blacks as a group had suffered a special disadvantage—slavery—and therefore required certain special advantages to even things out. As it turned out, the special advantages weren't enough and hardly made up for the disadvantages, both past and continuing. But the principle seemed fair; indeed, it seemed the only moral stance.

In nonracial settings, the same principle has been applied without controversy. The GI bill and various other special benefits for war veterans following World War II did not require that each veteran prove personal disadvantage. Nor did these benefits allow nonveterans to apply on the basis of disadvantages they might have suffered as a result of the war. Rather, the society made a judgment that, because all veterans, as a group, had been taken out of the race, as it were, by being conscripted to fight in a foreign land, all veterans, as a group, were entitled to various economic and educational benefits to get them even.

These programs were generally perceived to be morally justified. Why shouldn't similar programs be similarly justified in behalf of blacks, who as a group certainly have been more deeply and pervasively disadvantaged by government action than returning veterans? But from the beginning, unlike special programs for veterans, special programs for blacks were not seen as morally justified—indeed, were often seen as immoral, as being a form of "reverse racism." If the problem is seen in this way, it is compelling to believe that the sharp difference in perception between affirmative action programs for veterans and affirmative action programs for blacks is itself a reflection of race discrimination.

As far back as 1963, at the height of the civil rights movement, this idea began to be discussed. Guichard Parris, an assistant to Whitney Young of the National Urban League, put it precisely:

> It's time to discriminate in the Negro's favor for five or ten years. . . . The veterans of World War II got a break—the G.I. bill and extra points in Civil Service examinations—because they were out of the mainstream of the economy for three or four years. Negroes have never been in that mainstream. (*Newsweek*, July 15, 1963, p. 69)

Martin Luther King, Jr., made much the same point on national television at about the same time:

> Temporary special provisions for Negroes are urgently needed to bring about a greater racial balance. . . . Discrimination in reverse [is] a good idea. ("Protestant Heritage," 1963).

The idea of compensatory opportunity was not being advocated only by black leaders. In an influential book published in 1963, John H. Fischer, then the president of Teachers College, Columbia University, said explicitly that equal opportunity was not enough. He pointed out that the idea of treating black children in a special way was nothing new: "The American Negro youngster," he wrote, "happens to be a member of a large and distinctive group that for a very long time has been the object of special political, legal and social action." These special actions, Fischer said, were deeply destructive over a long period of time. To act now "as though any child is suddenly separable from his history is indefensible. In terms of educational planning, it is also irresponsible." And although he was very careful to recognize that every child, including every black child, is entitled to be treated as an individual, he also insisted that "Every Negro child is the victim of the history of his race in this country. On the day he enters kindergarten, he carries a burden no white child can ever know." He ended his analysis by asking and answering the key question:

> Is it not a reasonable contention—and a just one—that to compensate for past injustice, we should offer these children educational services beyond the level of what might be called standard equality? Could it be that to achieve total equality of opportunity in America we may have to modify currently accepted ideas about equality of opportunity? . . . We may need to substitute for our traditional concept of equal educational opportunity a new concept of *compensatory opportunity*. (p. 295)

These early thoughts, and others, began to suggest that there had to be a temporary imbalance in favor of blacks if we meant to achieve true equality of opportunity. It is important to emphasize that all these people were talking about *temporary* programs, and all resisted any notion of permanent, institutionalized preferential systems. Indeed, they were deeply opposed to permanent preferences based on race and were working hard, in some cases laying their lives on the line, for a color-blind society where individuals would be judged on the basis of merit, not skin color. But they were beginning to see that the disadvantages that had been imposed on blacks as a group could not be overcome by pretending that the race was even or that everyone had started together. They were beginning to understand that, in a country that had been so destructively race-conscious for so long, the road to a color-blind society required a transition period of constructive race consciousness. They knew it had to be temporary and they were not wholly comfortable with the idea. Nor did they know specifically how the idea should be implemented. But the principle had begun to take hold and it seemed both moral and necessary.

Even at this earliest of stages, however, fissures appeared on the horizon. In an address to the U.S. Senate on June 27, 1963, Senator Abraham Ribicoff, an otherwise staunch supporter of the civil rights movement, announced his opposition to the idea:

> Those who claim that X number of jobs or Y percent of jobs must be set aside for Negroes are not favoring equality of opportunity. They are saying that opportunity doesn't matter, that merit doesn't matter, that only arbitrary numbers and percentages matter. That point of view will undermine the whole effort to achieve equality in this country.

But the idea persisted—and grew. By 1965, it had reached the White House. In a now-famous speech at Howard University, President Lyndon Johnson observed:

> Freedom is not enough. You do not wipe away the scars of centuries by saying: Now, you are free to go where you want, do as you desire, and choose the leaders you please. You do not take a man who for years has been hobbled by chains, liberate him, bring him to the starting line of a race, saying, "you are free to compete with all the

others," and still justly believe you have been completely fair. Thus it is not enough to
open the gates of opportunity.

But if it was not enough to open the gates of opportunity, no one knew exactly what
was enough. In 1965, Lyndon Johnson seemed to be talking mostly about a kind of
Marshall Plan for black families. For a variety of reasons, that Marshall Plan never got off
the ground. But the moral principle behind it was clear: Equal opportunity was not
enough. In 1965, that seemed to be a moral principle that American society was ready to
accept. Indeed, it seemed to be the next logical stage of the civil rights movement.

Today, that moral principle is under broad attack. William Bradford Reynolds, Assistant Attorney General of the United States, has said that "the use of racial preferences,
whether in the form of quotas, goals or any other numerical device [is] morally wrong"
(*New York Times,* January 30, 1986, p. B9). It behooves us to examine the basis of such
moral criticisms.

JUSTIFICATIONS AND CRITICISMS

MERIT

A major criticism of affirmative action is that it ignores merit in its relentless drive to
achieve the desired proportion of blacks. According to this line of criticism, individual
merit and only individual merit ought to be what determines whether a person gets a
particular job or is admitted to a particular school. At first glance, this would appear to be
an unobjectionable standard. Wasn't it the goal of the civil rights movement to achieve a
society in which individuals would be judged, as Martin Luther King, Jr., said, by the
content of their character and not by the color of their skin?

But "merit" is a tricky issue, hard to define and harder still to justify in terms of
traditional practices. In fact, determinations of who gets a particular job and who gets
admitted to a particular school have always been made, and continue to be made, on the
basis of criteria other than individual merit.

As we've already pointed out, veterans receive preference when they apply for
certain civil service jobs. This preference is bestowed on all veterans, whether they were
drafted or not, whether they saw combat or not, whether they specifically can be shown
to have been disadvantaged by their military service or not. Those who are not veterans
are discriminated against even if, as individuals, they may be more disadvantaged in
some way or arguably more qualified. This preferential system, which is not based strictly
on individual merit, has not been seen by American society as unfair or immoral. The
assumption was made that veterans were disadvantaged as a group and that fairness
therefore required us to give them special, if temporary, advantages as a group.

Other preferential systems do not even attempt to justify compensatory advantages
on the basis of fairness. Schools, for example, often prefer applicants who reside in the
state where the school is located, even if these applicants show less merit than out-of-
state applicants. Schools also frequently prefer the children of alumni, even if other
children show more merit as individuals. This sort of preference not only downgrades the
importance of individual merit; it also perpetuates past discriminatory advantages. If
prior patterns of admission to a particular school reflected discrimination, then a system
that prefers the children of alumni perpetuates such discrimination. Yet, such preferential systems have not caused a storm of protest among those who champion the merit
system, nor have such preferential systems been generally perceived by Americans as
unfair or immoral.

Seniority rights in employment provide another example. The length of service in a particular job determines certain benefits relating to promotion, protection against layoff, training programs, and so on. These benefits accrue regardless of individual merit simply as the result of length of service. This system may well be justified on several grounds, but individual merit is not one of them. Moreover, in a system that has discriminatorily excluded people on the basis of race in the past, the seniority system perpetuates the disadvantages of this discrimination and continues its effects into the future. Yet, often those—particularly labor union leaders—who talk most about merit when affirmative action programs are being discussed, manage to forget about merit when seniority systems are discussed.

Finally, those who oppose affirmative action on the ground that it is a diversion from the merit system must concede, if they have any respect for facts at all, that factors having nothing to do with merit have traditionally governed entry into many professions. Philip Green (1981) put it well:

> To make their case consistent, these opponents [of affirmative action] would also have to explain what "merit" has been possessed by those professionals who have enjoyed the rewards of restrictive rules of entry to their professions (e.g., lawyers and doctors); by businessmen, bankers and brokers who were privileged by virtue of coming from an acceptable social background; public employees who belonged to the right ethnic group in the right place at the right time; craftsmen whose acceptance by a trade union has been contingent on their recommendation by members of their own family; and academics who through most of their careers have engaged in neither productive scholarship nor innovative teaching but have rather been "good old boys," expertly mimicking the values of their superiors. (p. 79)

The fact is that, although everyone pays tribute to the idea of merit, factors extrinsic to merit often and routinely determine who gets particular jobs. "Only in the most technologically advanced and abstruse careers are factors extrinsic to any true ranking of skills totally discarded," Green concluded. "Most of the time, the question is not whether other facts . . . are going to be taken into account by us, but which ones" (p. 80).

People do discriminate. They take into account certain characteristics, which they believe are proxies for merit but which often are not. For many blacks, who have lived for generations knowing that, despite what individual merit they might possess, they would be passed over and others, less talented, would be chosen, the current concern by opponents of affirmative action about the idea of merit seems to be little more than an effort to change the rules in the middle of the game.

Closely related to the idea of merit is the phenomenon of the superblack. For years, blacks were not allowed to play major league baseball. When Jackie Robinson was hired by Branch Rickey to play for the Brooklyn Dodgers in 1947, he did not have to be as good as the average white player; he had to be the best. Moreover, for years after Robinson's breaking of the color line, only exceptional black ballplayers were hired. It was not until many years later that black baseball players in the major leagues displayed the same range of skills—from poor to mediocre to great—displayed by white players.

No responsible advocate of affirmative action opposes merit or argues that employers should be required to hire unqualified applicants, or that standards should be reduced in order to meet affirmative action goals. What we do argue is that the rules should be the same for blacks as they have always been for whites. Standards should not be raised to higher levels when measuring black applicants. Merit should not be invoked in a new way to make it harder to end discrimination. Nondiscrimination means applying the same standards to everyone regardless of race. If those standards are high, they should remain high. But they should not be made higher as a response to affirmative action.

If Jackie Robinson had hit .230 or fielded his position erratically, he would not have made it in the major leagues. Yet, at that very moment, white players hitting .230 or fielding their positions erratically were employed. Merit is important, but when higher standards exist for blacks than for whites, that's called discrimination.

Affirmative action is a method of ending such discrimination. It is not opposed to high standards, but it is opposed to double standards. And it does recognize that employers who have for years discriminated in their employment practices by using criteria extrinsic to merit cannot be expected suddenly to end such habits without a little push. Goals and timetables are such a push, and they are reasonable.

They are also dangerous, because, although they are intended to be temporary remedies to end the habits of discrimination, they can be transformed into permanent quotas that institutionalize discrimination. Responsible advocates of affirmative action recognize that danger and are alert to it. But the existence of that danger does not justify abandoning the remedy.

FAIRNESS

A major criticism of affirmative action—a criticism perceptually shared by many white workers—is that affirmative action requires employers to discriminate against better-qualified, or equally qualified, whites who themselves bear no responsibility for discrimination. This is what is sometimes called *reverse discrimination*. According to this criticism, if, in a given factory, there are 100 jobs, all held by whites, and the affirmative action goal requires 20% blacks, then ultimately 20 whites who would otherwise have been employed will not be employed, even though they, as individuals, were not responsible for the prior discrimination.

The issue of responsibility is an interesting one, but it does not come to grips with the fact that, even though such white workers were not themselves responsible for excluding blacks, they certainly benefited from that exclusion. Moreover, they benefited unjustly. Every discriminatory exclusion of a black worker unjustly benefited a white worker. The argument that such unjust benefits should be perpetuated is an argument for the continuation of discrimination against blacks, at least in a context where the number of jobs remains finite and smaller than the number of people seeking jobs.

For example, at the time Jackie Robinson broke the color line in baseball, there were approximately 400 major league jobs for baseball players. All were held by whites, because blacks were totally excluded. If blacks had been permitted, in a nondiscriminatory fashion, to compete for these jobs on the basis of merit, certainly some blacks would have proved to be better than some whites. If 100 blacks had won jobs, 100 whites would have been out of jobs. But those whites were employed only because blacks were excluded. Except for racial discrimination, they would not have been good enough to hold those jobs. The benefit of employment for those 100 white players was a direct result of discrimination. These jobs were unjustly awarded. Less-qualified whites were employed whereas more qualified blacks were not. Why, then, should it be considered reverse discrimination to remedy the situation by imposing a system of nondiscrimination?

In baseball, it happened without affirmative action goals and timetables. But what if, after the success of Jackie Robinson, the Brooklyn Dodgers had been the only team willing to hire blacks? What if several teams continued to refuse to hire blacks? Eventually, wouldn't it have been legitimate for black ballplayers to sue those teams and charge them with discrimination? And if discrimination were found, wouldn't it have been legitimate for a court to determine the percentage of black ballplayers in the available labor market and set that percentage, with a timetable for reaching it, as a goal to force the end of discriminatory hiring?

In baseball, although several teams did continue to resist hiring blacks for some time, the imposition of such a court-ordered remedy did not prove necessary. Discrimination was ended without it (at least with respect to players). But in many other employment contexts, discrimination was not ended. And that is why lawsuits were brought and, where discrimination was found, remedies were ordered.

To be sure, where the number of jobs is limited, fewer whites will be employed, just as fewer men will be employed if women are allowed to compete on a nondiscriminatory basis. But where there are too few jobs to go around, who gets those jobs cannot morally be determined on the basis of race or sex. The fact that the distribution of jobs was determined for so long on the basis of race and sex created an expectation among whites and males. The loss of that expectation may now seem unfair to them. But the expectation was not fair in the first instance. Fairness requires ending discrimination, not perpetuating it, and that includes ending the advantages that whites enjoyed as the result of discrimination against blacks.

But although individual whites were the beneficiaries of this discrimination, in many instances they did not, as individuals, cause it. The responsibility for employment discrimination lies with the employer, who may bear certain obligations, to both white workers and black, during the transition to a nondiscriminatory system.

For example, suppose a worker in a factory is unjustly fired. He contests the firing by grieving under his union contract. While the grievance proceeds, the employer hires a replacement. Six months pass. Finally, an impartial arbitrator hands down a decision in favor of the employee and orders him reinstated with back pay. The employer complies and lays off the replacement, who has now been working for 6 months. The employee who is now laid off was not responsible for the unjust firing of the original employee. But he was the beneficiary of it and now he has lost his job as a direct result of the remedy ordered by the arbitrator. Fairness triumphs, but the replacement employee is out of a job.

The first point to make is that no one would argue that the replacement employee was unjustly fired. He owed his job in the first instance to a vacancy created by illegally excluding the original employee. Now that the illegal exclusion has been rectified, he loses the benefit. Exactly the same moral analysis applies to racial discrimination lawsuits. Vacancies were created for white employees as the direct result of illegal exclusions of black workers. When those illegal exclusions are rectified, the benefits unjustly derived are ended.

Normally, the imposition of an affirmative action remedy does not result in white workers' getting fired.[1] The remedy is prospective. Thus, white workers will now have to compete with black workers for the available jobs. Moreover, as whites have for so long enjoyed an unfair advantage, blacks have a lot of catching up to do. The terms of the competition, biased for so long in favor of whites, will now be temporarily reversed. The employer is required to hire a certain number of blacks within a certain period in order to end discrimination within a reasonable time. During this temporary period, the terms of competition may not be even. Blacks may be given the edge. That does not mean, or should not mean, that unqualified blacks will be hired. It does mean that, where qualifications are met, and are roughly equal, blacks will be given preference, not only because it is the only way to break the employer's habit of favoring whites but also because it is

---

[1]The exception is in a layoff situation, where seniority systems may be overridden to permit the employer to lay off whites and blacks in a way designed to prevent the reinforcement of past discrimination, as reflected by seniority. In such instances, it may be proper to place the burden not on the white employees, but on the employer who has discriminated, and to require this employer to compensate those white employees who were laid off despite their expectations that their seniority would protect them. It is fair for such employees to argue that the rules have been changed for them, too, and that the responsibility should be borne by the employer who discriminated and not by the employees who unjustly benefited from such discrimination.

unfair to have maintained biased terms of competition for so long without reversing the bias for a period of time.

Reversing the bias, of course, is dangerous because it may institutionalize the legitimacy of bias and make it more difficult ultimately to achieve a color-blind, nondiscriminatory world. That is a danger that advocates of affirmative action must face up to and resolve to avoid. Affirmative action goals and timetables are a fair and moral remedy for institutionalized racism, but the remedy must be temporary and measured. Critics of affirmative action remedies perceive the danger but are insufficiently sensitive to the persistence of discrimination and its effects and to the need for drastic remedies. Chemotherapy is a drastic remedy for cancer. It has bad side effects. Used injudiciously, it can kill the patient. But used judiciously and with awareness of its side effects, it can stop cancer.

The cancer of racial discrimination is no less relentless. It has grown for a long time in the body politic. The danger of affirmative action remedies is real, but the argument that such remedies should be abandoned, and the cancer left alone before it is completely destroyed, is immoral.

Some critics of affirmative action remedies now argue that the time has come to abandon the temporary imposition of affirmative action goals and timetables because the procedures that require fairness have in large measure been institutionalized. In the view of these critics, not much would change if affirmative action remedies were ended now. As Robert J. Samuelson (1984) wrote:

> [The aggressive uses of antidiscrimination laws, including affirmative action,] have changed the way labor markets work. Many firms have overhauled personnel policies. Recruitment has been broadened. Tests unrelated to qualifications have been abandoned. Promotions are less informal. When positions become open, they are posted publicly so anyone (not just the boss's favorite) can apply. Formal evaluations have been strengthened so that, when a manager selects one candidate over another (say, a white man over a woman), there are objective criteria. Equally important, women and blacks increasingly are plugged into the informal information and lobbying networks that remain critical in hiring and promotion decisions. (p. 8)

Although this description is undoubtedly accurate in some instances, it does not justify a general abandonment of affirmative action remedies for two reasons.

First, the situation Samuelson described is idealized and does not describe every employer. Affirmative action remedies are never imposed except when discrimination has been proved and a court, or the parties to a dispute, agrees that such a remedy is necessary to end discrimination. In some few cases where nondiscriminatory hiring has been firmly institutionalized, it may be possible to begin to discuss relaxing the temporary remedy of affirmative action procedures. But that should be very carefully done and should be monitored, on a case by case basis.

Second, much of the situation that Samuelson described is the direct result of pressures imposed by affirmative action goals and timetables. It is too soon to believe that the habits of discrimination and preferential systems for the hiring and promotion of whites, nurtured and institutionalized for generations, would not reemerge, at least in part, if affirmative action pressures were removed. The reification of a color-blind culture of nondiscrimination has not yet been accomplished. The truth is that the strongest advocates of ending affirmative action remedies now are those who never supported them in the first instance. It is, perhaps, time to begin discussing Samuelson's claims in specific instances. It is not yet time to begin a general relaxation of the pressures that have only begun to break the habits of racial discrimination.

THE INTERNALIZATION OF INFERIORITY

The most ironic critics of affirmative action remedies argue that such remedies damage blacks themselves and retard their economic advancement. This line of argument takes several forms.

Charles Murray (1984), for example, argued that affirmative action remedies, or what he called "preferential treatment," perpetuate a feeling of inferiority among blacks. This feeling, he implied, derives from the suspicion by many blacks that they got their jobs not on their own merits but only because they were black, and also from the personal failures that resulted from being thrust into positions for which they were not qualified.

The latter argument is a straw man. Success surely breeds confidence, and failure, especially repeated failure, just as surely shatters confidence. But no one advocates placing people in positions for which they are not qualified. And no one wants to give people jobs they cannot do. If that is happening as a result of affirmative action, it should stop. But thrusting people into positions for which they are not qualified is not a necessary ingredient of affirmative action, nor is it a phenomenon limited to affirmative action.

Political patronage has forever been a mechanism for placing unqualified people in important jobs. So have family and business connections. When I was growing up, the phrase "It's not what you know, it's who you know" was an accepted cliché of life in the real world. This reality certainly troubled those who were thereby excluded from certain opportunities, but one never imagined that the beneficiaries of such connections spent many sleepless nights worrying about it.

It is true that, where affirmative action hiring goals are met in crude and mechanistic ways, the beneficiaries of those hiring goals may well wonder if they were hired on their own merits. Most often, however, minority applicants, like all of us, will assume that they are capable people who, if given a fair chance, will be able to perform satisfactorily. And they will perceive affirmative action goals as necessary to give them a fair chance, or, in Philip Green's phrase (1981), "to force their prospective employers to recognize and reward their abilities" (p. 80). After all, most blacks, like most whites, know full well that jobs often depend on who you know and on who you are rather than on innate abilities. In Green's telling words:

> Do all those corporate directors, bankers, etc., who got their jobs for extraneous reasons—first, because they were somebody's son, second, because they were male, third, because they were Protestant and fourth, because they were white—feel demeaned thereby? It would be interesting to ask them—or to ask the same question of those doctors who managed to get into good medical schools because there were quotas keeping out Jews, the skilled tradesmen who were admitted to the union because two members of their family recommended them and so on. Clearly implicit in this standard critique of affirmative action, is a notion that whereas it's never painful to be rewarded because you are in the majority or the established elite, it's always painful to be rewarded because you're in the minority, or a marginal group. (p. 79)

A second line of argument suggests that black economic progress cannot be legislated and that the effort to do so through the imposition of affirmative action goals actually reinforces the idea among blacks that skills and hard work aren't important and that their lack of progress is society's fault.

Thomas Sowell (1984), an economist who is himself black, has been predominantly identified with this position:

> Is it possible to din into the heads of a whole generation that their problems are all other people's fault; that the world owes them an enormous debt; that everything they have yet to achieve is an injustice; that violence is excusable when the world is flawed—and yet expect it all to have no effect on attitudes? Is the arduous process of acquiring skills and discipline supposed to be endured for years by people who are told, by word and deed, that skills are not the real issue? (sec. B, p. 4, col. 4)

Thomas Sowell is fond of chiding liberals for their failure to support their rhetorical claims with hard evidence, but he has cited no evidence to support his own rhetoric. No responsible advocates of affirmative action even suggest that skills and hard work are not important, nor is there any evidence of which I am aware that shows that blacks' willingness to devote themselves to "the arduous process of acquiring skills" has been eroded by affirmative action remedies. Indeed, I would argue that the opposite is true. By breaking down discriminatory barriers to employment, affirmative action remedies encourage the development of skills.

Sowell was right when he wrote that skills will not be developed by people who are told, by word and deed, that skills are not the real issue. That was what the reality of racial discrimination did. It told blacks, by word and deed, that no matter what skills they developed, no matter how hard they worked, opportunity would not be theirs and certain jobs would simply not be available. It was discrimination, not the effort to end discrimination, that suffocated ambition and destroyed hope. It was the guarantee of exclusion from employment, not the expectation of inclusion, that made hard work futile.

Affirmative action remedies should certainly not be implemented in a way that diminishes standards or the importance of skills. To the extent that some affirmative action plans have diminished the importance of skills, they deserve criticism. But the idea of affirmative action itself cannot be diminished by reference to those instances where it has not worked well, or where it has abandoned some of the principles that justified it in the first instance.

Affirmative action remedies, properly conceived and implemented, ought only to open up opportunities for the development of skills, opportunities previously closed either by overt racial discrimination or by the habits that flourished in a discriminatory culture.

Sowell also made much of the inability of affirmative action remedies to solve all of the economic problems of blacks. He argued that affirmative action has a poor record in opening up opportunities for the poorest black Americans and implied that it should for that reason be abandoned:

> The truly disadvantaged—those with little education or job experience, or from broken families—have fallen even further behind during the era of affirmative action. As in other countries, the benefits of preferential programs go disproportionately to those already more fortunate. It may help a black professor get an endowed chair, but it is counter-productive for the black teenager trying to get a job. . . .
> This is not unique to the United States. A number of studies of preferential programs for untouchables in India have concluded that little or no benefit actually accrues to these poverty-stricken people. Yet it is precisely the poor untouchable who suffers from the backlash against the great privileges he is thought to be enjoying. Violence against untouchables doubled in less than a decade during the 1970s, amid rising denunciations of preferential policies in their behalf. (sec. B, p. 4, col. 4)

But if affirmative action remedies cannot reach the problems of poor education and institutionalized poverty, that does not mean they should be abandoned. Indeed, no advocate of affirmative action has claimed that it is a panacea, or a cure for all the racial and economic ills we face. Affirmative action is merely a means of breaking through a reified system of discrimination and of giving people who have long been handicapped by that system a temporary leg up.

Moreover, to the extent that black children growing up need to know that opportunities are available and that hard work matters, it is crucial to have visible examples. To use the example of Jackie Robinson once more, the system of racial exclusion that existed in baseball before 1947 was enforced in part by internalized limitations: most black children growing up knew that, no matter what they did, they would not get an opportunity to play major league baseball. They could see that all the faces were white. Once Robinson broke that image and was followed by others, perceptions changed and possibilities opened up. It used to be argued by defenders of white baseball that blacks didn't apply for these jobs. Mostly, they were right. Why should they have applied when rejection was certain? But when opportunities were opened, and when the results of such opportunities became visible, ambition was fueled and hope nurtured.

It is hard to believe that the same isn't true of other jobs in other industries. Sowell put down the accomplishment of a black professor getting an appointment to an endowed chair as if that appointment had no relation to the dreams and hopes of poor black children and their parents. He was profoundly wrong. Affirmative action will not today open up opportunities for the poor and the uneducated and the unskilled. But it will change how they look at the world, and it will say, by word and deed, that hard work pays off and that skills matter. Affirmative action remedies may not quickly solve every problem. But without such remedies, the suffocating impact of discrimination will continue.

CONCLUSION: REGAINING A MORAL CONSENSUS

I have tried to demonstrate that there is a moral basis for the concept of affirmative action and that those who supported efforts to break down the legal barriers to racial justice a quarter century ago ought, for the same reasons, to support affirmative action remedies today. It is the same fight.

I have also conceded, and I think it is incumbent on advocates of affirmative action to concede, that such remedies must be temporary, must not result in diminishing the importance of skills, and must not be administered in a way that lowers standards or institutionalizes, however unintentionally, unfair practices. It is difficult for me to believe that a moral consensus behind these principles cannot be regained.

The residue of slavery and centuries of legal discrimination still stains our society and substantially limits the opportunities of many black children. Simple justice requires that those of us who do not suffer from the disadvantages caused by past and current racial discrimination—who, indeed, may have benefited from it—not abandon the fight to find reasonable remedies for those who do. Yet, white liberal support for such remedies, including affirmative action, has substantially dissolved since the height of the civil rights movement, now nearly two decades ago. Blacks stand in danger of being isolated again, and this remains a major moral issue in American life.

Affirmative action is not the only element of this moral issue, but it has become a polarizing symbol for it. Somehow, the moral issue must regain its consensus and its place high on our social agenda, until the color of our skins no longer determines where we work, where we live, where we go to school, and whether we are treated fairly. We have made much progress, but there is still a long way to go.

REFERENCES

Fischer, J. H. (1963). Educational problems of segregation and desegregation. In A. H. Passow (Ed.), *Education in depressed areas*. New York: Teachers College, Columbia University.
Green, P. (1981, March 30). The new individualism. *Christianity and Crisis, 41*, 79–80.
Johnson, L. B. (1965, June). Address, Howard University.
Kerner, O. (1968). *Report of the National Advisory Commission on Civil Disorders*. New York: Bantam Books.
King, M. L., Jr. (1963, June 30). *Protestant Heritage*, National Broadcasting Company.
Murray, C. (1984, December 31). Affirmative racism. *The New Republic*.

Myrdal, G. (1944). *An American Dilemma: The Negro problem and modern democracy.* New York: Harper.

Parris, G. (1963, July 15). *Newsweek*, p. 69.

Reynolds, W. B. (1986, January 30). *New York Times.*

Ribicoff, A. (1963, June 27). Address, United States Senate.

Samuelson, R. J. (1984, July 11). Affirmative action's usefulness is passing. *Washington Post*, sec. D, p. 8, col. 1.

Sowell, T. (1984, August 12). Black progress can't be legislated. *Washington Post Outlook*, sec. B, p. 4, cols. 3,4.

19

Conclusion

Dalmas A. Taylor and Phyllis A. Katz

> Under certain circumstances desegregation not only proceeds
> without major difficulties, but has been observed to lead to the
> emergence of more favorable attitudes and friendlier relations
> between races. . . . Much depends, however, on the
> circumstances under which members of previously segregated
> groups first come in contact with others in unsegregated
> situations. Available evidence suggests . . . the importance of
> consistent and firm enforcement of the new policy by those in
> authority. It indicates also the importance of such factors as: the
> absence of competition for a limited number of facilities or
> benefits: the possibility of contacts which permit individuals to
> learn about one another as individuals; the possibility of
> equivalence of positions and functions among all the participants
> within the segregated situation.
>
> *Minnesota Law Review*, 1953, pp. 437–438

The above quotation is part of a statement from social scientists submitted to the U.S. Supreme Court in the *Sweatt v. Painter* (1950) school desegregation case, a case that has had broad implications for the practice, study, and theory of intergroup relations since the mid-1950s. Because so many of the chapters in this book are intertwined with both the political and empirical aspects of desegregation, a closer look at its history seems in order.

The Court issued a major ruling in *Brown v. Board of Education* (1954) when it decreed that racially separate facilities were inherently unequal. The legal origins of this decree can be found in two earlier Supreme Court decisions. In tests made in 1938 and again in 1948, operating under the doctrine espoused in *Plessy v. Ferguson* (1896), school desegregation was ruled unconstitutional only when the facilities provided for blacks were determined to be unequal to those provided for whites. By 1950, however, the Court was

DALMAS A. TAYLOR • College of Liberal Arts, Wayne State University, Detroit, Michigan 48202.   PHYLLIS A. KATZ • Institute for Research on Social Problems, 520 Pearl Street, Boulder, Colorado 80302.

willing to expand on its criteria for equality. In *Sweatt v. Painter* (1950), for example, the University of Texas Law School was ordered to dismantle its black law school because it did not have "those qualities . . . which make for greatness in a law school" (Vinson, 1950). In *Sweatt v. Painter* (1950), the Court had not based its decision on the unequal physical facilities alone; it had examined the totality of the educational experience. Specifically, the Court stated:

> Segregation of white and colored children in public schools has a detrimental effect upon the colored children. The impact is greater when it has the sanction of the law; for the policy of separating the races is usually interpreted as denoting the inferiority of the Negro group. A sense of inferiority affects the motivation of a child to learn. Segregation with the sanction of law, therefore, has a tendency to retard the educational and mental development of Negro children and to deprive them of some of the benefits they would receive in a racially integrated school system. Whatever may have been the extent of psychological knowledge at the time of *Plessy v. Ferguson*, this finding is amply supported by modern authority.

Social scientists served as expert witnesses in both the *Sweatt v. Painter* and the *Brown* cases. The social science documentation for the 1954 ruling relied in part on the Clark and Clark (1947) doll study. That study found that young children (both black and white) associated more positive attributes with white dolls and chose the white doll to play with more frequently. Although some of these conclusions and the earlier interpretations were questioned by later investigators (see Banks, 1972; Hraba & Grant, 1970; Katz & Zalk, 1974; Stephan & Rosenfeld, 1978), this work was accepted in 1954 as indicating that black children had negative attitudes toward their own race.

The major theoretical context for the social scientists' statement and the *Brown* ruling was Allport's contact hypothesis (1954). The general hypothesis predicts that a favorable change in attitude and interpersonal attraction will occur when members of in-groups and out-groups are brought in contact with each other, if four necessary conditions are met:

1. The contact must occur in a situation in which the participants have equal status.
2. The contact should encourage a mutually interdependent relationship (i.e., cooperation in the achievement of common goals).
3. There must be institutional support for the contact arrangement.
4. The contact situation should make salient the values common to the two groups.

Allport's work generated studies of the effects of contact in a variety of settings. Based on Allport's work, later investigators (e.g., Amir, 1969; Stephan, 1978) made specific predictions regarding the positive effects of contact on black self-esteem and achievement. Differing methods have been used in contact studies. Early investigators used primarily survey methods (e.g., interviews, questionnaires). Others used field experiments that took advantage of desegregation as it occured in housing, education, and employment. Finally, a third group tested the contact hypothesis in the laboratory under better controlled conditions. This wide variety of methodologies has served as a safeguard against inappropriate generalizations of research findings. It has also, however, created interpretive problems, particularly in naturalistic settings, where the absence of controls compromises the ability to rule out extraneous influences or to make causal statements.

Additional factors added to the complexity of evaluating the contact hypothesis and the progress of racial integration. The Court's original *Brown* dictum "with all deliberate speed" was sufficiently vague to allow the passage of 10 years without noticeable changes in school desegregation. Additionally, entrenched residential segregation gave a benign appearance to the school system's complicity in frustrating the Court decree. The passage of the 1964 Civil Rights Act and its concomitant titles on affirmative action put new rigor into enforcement. Finally, by 1970, the Court's *Swann* decision had led to two controversial but enduring policies. The *Swann* decision permitted the lower courts to order mandatory busing away from neighborhood schools and to use racial balance formulas in the design of desegregation plans. Racial balance soon became synonymous with desegregation and, simultaneously, its criterion of success—and busing became a primary tool of implementation. The interplay between resistance and changing judicial policy has provided the backdrop for a good deal of the social science research and theory presented in the preceding chapters.

As indicated in the foreword, the organization of this book attempts to capture the proliferation of controversies surrounding the changing remedies designed to reduce or eliminate racist attitudes and behavior. As noted in Chapter 1, much has happened in the study of race relations since the mid-1970s, including a changing political climate, a slowing of momentum for civil rights, improving research strategies, the inclusion of more ethnic groups in studies, and conceptual innovations from people of color. These have all changed the context of research, and we have tried to represent this change by using a dialectical format in which pairs of authors elucidate differing views of an issue. The ensuing debates have not always disagreed about outcomes; rather, they have expressed differences on proposed strategies or policies and interpretations of data.

We began in Chapters 2 and 3 with a focus on the varying philosophical goals underlying the pursuit of racial justice. Harry Triandis and Tom Pettigrew have provided us with contrasting views of pluralism and varying degrees of cultural assimilation. This section of the book concludes with two chapters that debate opposing interpretations of current data on racial attitudes: symbolic racism (David Sears) and group conflict and prejudice (Lawrence Bobo).

Chapters 6–10 provide critiques of the potential generalizability of the dynamics of prejudice and discrimination against blacks to other ethnic populations (Hispanics, Asians, and Native Americans) and women. Until recently, most of the theory and research in this area has dealt principally with blacks. The growing number of investigators from different ethnic groups, as well as the federal and state legislation establishing "protective classes" that include groups other than blacks, has been responsible for a greater sensitivity to the similarities and differences between ethnic groups. There is now a sizable research literature to turn to for answers regarding generalizability. We will attempt to synthesize these views later.

Finally, the book concludes with eight chapters that explore the controversies associated with specific remedies: school desegregation, mandatory busing, intergroup contact (integration), and affirmative action. The arguments presented in these chapters represent the most current analyses of the complex conceptual and empirical approaches to the amelioration of prejudice and racism in our society.

THE PSYCHOLOGY OF DESEGREGATION

In 1975, Gerard and Miller published a lengthy account of their case study of desegregation in the Riverside, California, elementary school district. The study assessed 1,800 children over a period of 6 years as the district's one-way busing program (ethnic minority children bused into predominantly all-white schools) was initiated and established. Gerard and Miller's data revealed an absence of any overall effect of desegregation on measures of achievement motivation, anxiety, and self-worth. This experience seems to have formed the context of doubt expressed in Gerard's chapter (Chapter 11), "School Desegregation: The Social Science Role." In this chapter, Gerard criticizes the framers of the social science statement used in the *Brown* decision as naive and myopic. Specifically, he charges that the statement was vague about how desegregation would correct the harms of segregation, and that it was incorrect in its assumption that the conditions necessary for positive change (from Allport's contact hypothesis) could or would be met in the typical school situation.

Advancing what he considers a more sophisticated hypothesis—lateral transmission of values—Gerard, nonetheless, concludes that there is a lack of evidence that classroom contact between blacks and whites results in the transfer of achievement-related values. Instead, he concludes that we need better social engineering if we are to be successful in contributing to the attainment of equality of opportunity. The work of Aronson and his colleagues on cooperative learning strategies in the classroom (see Chapter 15) was cited by Gerard as an example of the direction we should take.

Stuart Cook's rebuttal (Chapter 12) accuses Gerard of "overgeneralizing his own results and failing to take account of those many similar studies" that have obtained positive findings. Cook further suggests that Gerard's chapter presents a misleading picture of the research outcomes of school desegation and the complex interpretations required for a proper understanding of this research.

The arguments presented by Cook are based on three sources: (a) an analysis of the social science statement itself; (b) the history of the Supreme Court's deliberations on constitutional guarantees against racial discrimination; and (c) recent research reviews (between 1970 and 1978) of empirical research on the contact hypothesis. Concerning the statement itself, Cook notes that it addressed the issue of what effects the absence of government-enforced segregation would have and *not* how to remedy the effect on children who had already experienced segregated schools. Thus, the social scientists focused on the prevention of future negative consequences of legalized segregation such as self-hatred, antisocial behavior, and decreased aspirations, rather than on the remediation of these effects. In contrast to Gerard's charge of myopia, Cook maintains that the statement did address the potential difficulties in carrying out a plan of desegregation.

In examining review studies of the effects of school desegregation on achievement, Cook notes a distinction between the findings of unplanned and those of planned studies. The large majority of unplanned desegregation studies have reported inconclusive or mixed findings, whereas a different pattern has emerged from reviews that concentrated on studies of planned desegregation. In the latter group, approximately 60% of the studies found greater achievement among black students after one year of desegregation. It was also encouraging that a number of reviews using meta-analysis (Crain & Mahard, 1978; Krol, 1978; Wortman & Bryant, 1985) have demonstrated that the achievement of black children was significantly greater under desegregation than under segregation.

The assessment of desegregation effects is a complex and difficult enterprise for a variety of reasons. Methodologically, for example, studies may use measures that are too global and/or too insensitive to changes. The expectation of immediate rather than long-term change is also a frequent reason for negative findings in evaluations of public policy interventions (Lewis, 1987). This has been the case in evaluations of Headstart programs and may be true of desegregation research as well. Hawley and Smylie (in Chapter 14) cite evidence of the positive effects of attending desegregated grade schools on black college students.

A second major problem source is that the conditions necessary for contact to elicit positive outcomes are simply not met. Aronson and Gonzalez (Chapter 15) call attention to how infrequently one essential feature of Allport's hypothesis—the pursuit of common goals—is found in the typical American classroom:

> We have found that, in the vast majority of these cases, the process of education is highly competitive. Children vie with one another for good grades and for the respect

of the teacher. This occurs not only during quizzes and exams, but also in the informal give and take of the classroom, where children typically learn to raise their hands (often frantically) in response to questions from the teacher, groan when someone else is called upon, and revel in the failure of their classmates. The pervasive competitive atmosphere unwittingly leads the children to view one another as foes to be heckled and vanquished. In a newly desegregated school, all other things being equal, this atmosphere could exacerbate whatever prejudice existed prior to desegregation.

The competitive dynamics of the classroom then intensify predesegregation group differences. In order to decrease these, Aronson and his colleagues experimented with small cross-ethnic, interdependent learning groups in which each student learns a unique part of the learning material, then teaches it to his or her fellow group members and, in turn, learns the remainder of the material from them. In 10 years of research, studies using jigsaw groups (as they are called) have found significantly greater increases in liking, greater increases in self-esteem, and better performance than in control (traditional) classrooms. The jigsaw method has proved effective even when it has been used for as little as 20% of classroom time. These experiments tell us more about the true effects of desegregation, perhaps, than most of the other programs of research discussed.

Brewer and Miller (Chapter 16), however, challenge the generalizability of the jigsaw effect. Their analysis of intergroup conflict places emphasis on individualization as the key to prejudice reduction. As in Triandis's concept of "additive multiculturalism," Brewer and Miller draw attention to the ameliorative outcomes associated with reducing group boundaries. Further, they emphasize that improving intergroup relations implies that the positive effects of contact should extend beyond the contact situation. Three types of generalization effects are discussed by these investigators: (a) *category-based* (changes in attitudes toward the social category itself); (b) *differentiated* (increased complexity of intergroup perceptions); and (c) *personalized* (decategorization of individuals). The type of effect desired is critical in the design of a desegregation situation. For example, cooperative interventions in the classroom and many other situations may themselves be category-based and, therefore, may preclude attention to personal or individual information. Personalized situations, on the other hand, are effective to the extent that contact minimizes features that promote category salience.

In general, the historical, cultural, and political dimensions of segregation in America have frustrated the ability of the behavioral scientist to offer ameliorative possibilities. Taken together, the studies on cooperative learning strategies have been most faithful to the tenets of Allport's hypothesis and offer the greatest promise to date in shaping public policy in this complicated arena.

The absence of common goals may not be the most important problems in desegregation studies. The conditions under which desegregation has been carried out range from rigid resistance and overt hostility to local initiatives with widespread community support. Additionally, a mixture of judicial decisions has produced shifting standards. Justice Thurgood Marshall of the Supreme Court has dissented from most school decisions in recent years, complaining that the Court is rendering the goal of compliance more and more difficult to achieve. Under these circumstances, few studies have been able to use appropriate experimental controls and to set up the conditions necessary for positive outcomes. Although we are encouraged by the increasing application of meta-analysis to this literature, we believe that the many methodological deficiencies found in the studies reviewed make interpretations difficult, if not impossible. Additionally, interpretations and conclusions drawn from studies that are methodologically deficient miscommunicate the state of our knowledge to the less sophisticated reader and lead to improper policy decisions. As a result, we believe that Gerard's death knell is premature.

The issue before the Court in 1954 was a constitutional one. The "separate but equal" interpretation prevailed in 17 states and the District of Columbia. In reversing *Plessey v.*

Ferguson (1896), the Court formally declared that separation of the races is bad or harmful when the separation is based solely on the criterion of race. *De jure* segregation is a violation of the most fundamental justice principle. The courts, however, have subsequently failed to remedy separate and unequal education. Social scientists have failed in assessing the efficacy of the decision. We have settled for inadequate methodological strategies in attempting to assess controversial remedies where experimental control has been difficult, impossible, or sacrificed. Exceptions are the classroom studies on cooperative learning strategies. The systemic issues of equity, equality, and need (see Deutsch, 1975) have received little or no attention in examining the educational programs of children of color. There is no more important question than how the fairness with which individuals are treated sets limits on how they will function.

The *Brown* decision (1954) had its origins in earlier black struggles for quality education. The Reverend Joseph Albert DeLaine, a South Carolina minister-teacher, rallied the black community of Clarendon County in 1949 to file suit against the racially segregated county public schools. Two years later, Reverend Oliver Leon Brown, another black minister, challenged an all-white school system in Topeka, Kansas. Today, Linda Brown Smith, daughter of the plaintiff Reverend Brown in the original *Brown* case, has joined a group of Topeka parents as plaintiff to urge the federal court there to take action to wipe out the persisting vestiges of segregation in education (see the Foreword). It is clear from this historical trail that blacks (as well as other ethnic groups) remain concerned about the quality of education for their offspring. We need new initiatives in social science and public policy to provide an appropriate resolution for inequities in the resource allocations to education for *all* children. The initiatives taken by Aronson and Gonzalez (Chapter 15) and Brewer and Miller (Chapter 16), combined with other new social science research (e.g., see research on justice principles in Brickman, Folger, Goode, & Schul, 1980), may ultimately provide a more effective gauge of the scientific efficacy of the *Brown* decision.

GENERALIZABILITY OF CULTURE AND RACISM

In Chapter 6, Jones postulates a bicultural model of racism with two components: (a) the reactionary and (b) the evolutionary. The former denotes the adaptive strategies pursued by blacks in "reacting" to a racist and oppressive society. The evolutionary view, on the other hand, represents an unfolding of culture with roots in an African past. Two aspects of this analysis are important in considering the chapters in this book. Jones was the first to make a distinction between the concepts *prejudice* and *racism* (Jones, 1972). He suggested that "there are three forms of racism, *individual, institutional,* and *cultural*" (p. 3). Despite the problems created for social psychology, with its strong emphasis on the individual, Jones has persisted in highlighting the importance of cultural racism as "subtle, insidious, and pervasive" and as a key to understanding blacks' adaptation to disadvantage and oppression. Second, the analysis presumes a generalizability of disadvantage based on the concept of *difference*. Specifically, Jones (1972) asserted that racism initially addressed to blacks has served as a "spawning ground for the evolution of a society in which normative values insure that *difference* defined in a variety of ways, will be associated with disadvantage" (p. 1). In this latter regard, Jones defined the generalizability of in-group bias in which disadvantage is associated with disability (handicappism), nonnormative sexual preference, the aged, ethnicity, and skin color.

The cultural context of Jones's analysis in Chapter 6 is revealed in five dimensions of human experience: *T*ime perspective, *R*hythm, *I*mprovisation, *O*ral Expression, and *S*pirituality (TRIOS). The concept of *TRIOS* depicts polar opposites in strategies for living.

How we experience and organize life, make decisions, and formulate beliefs, according to Jones, minimally represents two different dialectical and opposite cultural worlds: materialistic, future-oriented, individualistic, and hard-work versus spiritual, present-oriented, orally expressive, flexible, easy-going, and affectively driven. For people of color, these poles represent warring factions of life inside and outside the cultural mainstream, where adjustment is a function of a successful struggle against a pernicious system. Biculturalism is both a strategy and the cumulative effect of accomplishments resulting from struggle. Jones summarizes biculturalism in statistical terms: *central tendency* as melting pot and *variance* as ethnic pluralism.

In disagreement with Jones, Pettigrew (Chapter 2) highlights the distinctive nature of black subculture, shaped by unique experiences in the North American legacy of slavery and segregation and the absence of recognition as a culture by many whites. By contrast, he argues, other ethnic groups (e.g., Chicanos) enjoy a subculture that is widely recognized, although criticized for being "different." Although we have not specifically addressed religious prejudice in this book, phenomena such as anti-Semitism may also be based on preceptions of "difference." For Pettigrew, the uniqueness of black cultural status is epitomized in the integration-versus-pluralism arguments that he claims confuses assimilation with integration. Specifically, he argues that impediments to blacks' progress are manifest in impenetrable group boundaries unlike those experienced by other groups.

In Chapter 3, Triandis provides a contrasting point of view to the Pettigrew analysis of black culture. Using exchange theory, Triandis suggests that differences in subjective culture derive from resource availability—economic exploitation, denial, and oppression. Further, he challenges the notion that integration is an appropriate or effective remedy for achieving intergroup harmony. Instead, he argues that broadening the cultural experiences of all groups (additive multiculturalism) achieves optimal levels of group harmony through the discovery of superordinate goals and interdependence. Additive multiculturalism is likened to societal creativity, in which thesis and antithesis are openly joined in productive conflict. All groups with manifest differences would presumably gain by this arrangement. Thus, Triandis reinforces the generalizability suggested by Jones's analyses, whereas Pettigrew's thesis focuses on the uniqueness or nongeneralizability of cultural ethnicity.

Four authors were invited to comment, from their individual perspectives, on the generalizability of the racism analysis provided by Jones. In Chapters 7–10, Ramirez, Nakanishi, Trimble, and Reid address the issues of culture and racism as experienced by Hispanics, Asians, Indians, and black women, respectively. Do the experiences that blacks have confronted in dealing with racism have applicability to these groups? The answer appears to be yes—and no. As Isaacs (1975) indicated (in a quote by Nakanishi in Chapter 8), the

> crisis of "black" and "American" identity would by itself be crisis enough. But its effects in these years was to shake up all the other groups in the society located in various stations along the road from being "out" to being "in"." It brought on change in the perception and self-perception of the "group" that had always been seen by all the others as "in." . . . In other mostly nonwhite groups . . . something of the black pattern began to be reproduced. (p. 20)

Signs of this reproducibility can be seen in Ramirez's description of the pejorative labels ascribed to Hispanics and in Trimble's account of negative stereotypes used to describe Native Americans. The polarity in the characterization of Mexican-American values and Anglo-American values bears a striking resemblence to Jones's theory of TRIOS. Positive values are ascribed to the dominant Anglo culture and are justified as a basis for its virtually exclusive hold on wealth, power, and status.

Although Nakanishi acknowledges that the methodological and philosophical underpinnings of race research fail to reflect an adequate convergence of the many similar issues, he presents an intriguing analysis of the potential policy implications of such a convergence. Specifically, he explores the isomorphism between blacks during slavery and the racial victimization of the bombing of Hiroshima, as well as between the political resurrection of the internment of Japanese-Americans and the activism of blacks during the 1960s and 1970s. The heightened assertiveness and the search for redefinition of self by blacks provided a cultural context that facilitated the collective response to the dormant issue of internment among Japanese-Americans. Internment, claims Nakahishi, was symbolic of a test of character for second-generation Japanese-Americans. Additional parallels can be found between blacks and other groups in this country, which include oppressive and traumatic institutional treatment based on group membership. The Holocaust in Europe has served a similar historical function for Jews.

Blacks experienced the cruel sting of the brutality of slavery. Black women, however, not only endured slavery but were also constant victims of sexual abuse. In addressing the question of whether racism and sexism are parts of a generalized response, Reid argues that black women have dual identities and are oppressed under each. Further, she suggests that these processes may have an additive effect. She concludes, therefore, that what is needed is an interactive analysis of racism and sexism in which black women are compared with other gender–race groups within specific social contexts. Trimble also highlights unique or nonparallel aspects of being a Native American. Unlike many of the groups discussed, they were indigenous to America and wanted to retain their sovereign status.

The most pervasive institutional experience suffered by people of color and women, cited in almost every chapter, is segregation. The continued settlement of the United States following the War of Independence was essentially an extension of colonialism in which Euro-Americans controlled and dominated those groups that were culturally different. In one way or another, each of the gender–race groups discussed above has been victimized by this history. The particular context in which these processes occurred and the unique characteristics of each group differ, however. A more comprehensive understanding of this difference will require a diversity of methodologies and new conceptual approaches in future research.

THE NEW AMERICAN DILEMMA

Gunnar Myrdal (1944) was among the first to provide comprehensive documentation of the contradiction of America's promises of liberty and freedom and the denial of these rights to blacks. The Civil Rights Movement had as one of its objectives the highlighting of this very contradiction. The legacy of slavery died a slow death through the codification of "separate but equal." Despite the legal death of "separate but equal" and the admonishment to desegregate with "all deliberate speed," the gap between the reality of racism and the ideals embodied in the new legislative mandate did not close easily. As indicated by recent events in Howard Beach, New York, and Forsyth County, Georgia, racism remains alive and well, and thus, some aspects of the dilemma are still very much with us.

The arguments and analyses presented in this book highlight the new dimensions of this contradiction. As noted above, the differencies that have been presented here are not disagreements about goals. They are primarily disagreements over conceptualizations of the problem and/or the strategy being advocated as a solution to the problem.

A subtle shift in the major dimensions of race relations in America has occurred since the early 1970s. The "separate but equal" era was characterized by institutional norms and practices that granted privileged status and advantage to members of the dominant culture. Political and legislative attacks on this system were met with firm resistance by a large segment of the dominant culture. Frequently, the resistance designed to maintain the status quo was embodied in counterlegislative proposals. Occasionally, the resistance was expressed by physical aggression and other violent means. In general, the rationale for the resistance was predicated on claims of genetic superiority or the rightful entitle-ments of a priviledged class.

A new dynamic in American race relations was initiated by Martin Luther King, Jr. His activism and philosophy of nonviolent resistance heightened the saliency of the dilemma cited by Myrdal approximately a decade earlier. New Frontier politics, legisla-tive initiatives, and court-imposed remedies began the process of eroding the machinery that had perpetuated racial exclusion. The Civil Rights Movement, before King, produced the *Brown* decision and in part was changed by its many legal dimensions. Under King's leadership, the nation was challenged to a higher level of social and ethical criticism. Black youths added a staccato rhythm to this movement with the introduction of "body politics." Lunch counters, water fountains, and buses were invaded by a cadre of black youths who accepted jail when they refused to accept "no" to requests for service or accommodation.

In the context of an expanding economy, the nation soon moved to a social agenda in which it sought to repair the racial and gender inequities highlighted by the Civil Rights Movement. To help advance the social agenda, the government and the private sector formed a partnership. A series of presidential executive orders, coupled with new civil rights legislation, gave evidence of a federal commitment to solving the problem. Be-tween 1870 and 1970, there was only one major civil rights initiative (women's suffrage). In contrast, between 1957 and 1970, Congress created a Civil Rights Commission, a voting rights bill, and six other initiatives.

By the end of the 1970s, the social and political climate had shifted. The new eco-nomic realities of limited growth engendered a weakening commitment to the social agenda. Government programs designed to end racial and gender discrimination were called into question. Although there was massive public support for the general princi-ples of racial and gender equality, implementation was now being criticized as creating new inequities. Since 1977, the Supreme Court has been divided on the question of affirmative action remedies for women and people of color. David Sears (Chapter 4) labels this new posture "symbolic racism." It involves (a) antagonism toward blacks' pushing too hard (occasionally through violence); (b) resentment toward preferential treatment; and (c) the belief (or perception) that discrimination is a thing of the past. According to Sears, symbolic racism is a continuing political force or attitude that represents a desire to sustain the status quo by the dominant culture even when the individual's own interests are not directly affected (e.g., a person may be antibusing even if his or her children are already grown). Even with regard to recent theoretical characterizations, dissent seems to be the norm. Bobo (Chapter 5) takes exception to Sears's characterization, arguing that racial attitudes involve both group-interested ideology and irrational hostilities.

Contemporary discussions of racism are based on a recent historical development. As civil rights legislation moved from general principles to specific remedies, there was a heightening of conflict with other (traditional) values. Most remedies are now perceived by some as violating the rights of one class of citizens as they attempt to ameliorate the negative condition(s) of another class. Affirmative action, with its emphasis on preferen-tial treatment, goals, and timetables, has proved to be the most controversial (see Chap-ters 17 by Glazer and Chapter 18 by Glasser). This conflict or dilemma has been charac-terized as tension between two equal ideals: providing a remedy for victims of discrimination and racism, on the one hand, while honoring the Fourteenth Amendment principle that each person be judged as an individual irrespective of gender or race. These distinctions have been described elsewhere as a conflict between "microjustice" and "macrojustice" principles (Brickman *et al.*, 1980). Americans pride themselves on being rugged individuals who excel because of ability, drive, and hard work. This microjustice focus, traceable back to Aristotle's *Nichomachean Ethics*, is framed in the maxim "to each according to his or her ability." Affirmative action remedies are addressed to race and gender groups in recognition of the fact that, historically, individuals have been disadvantaged largely because of their group membership. The imbalance created by this history sensitizes us to the possibility that treating individuals fairly can produce what seems like an unfair effect on rewards to groups. Further, given the history of gender and race discrimination, it is unreasonable to evaluate women and people of color exclusively on individual qualities. Affirmative action programs, by and large, acknowledge this conflict. Most approaches are based on macrojustice principles that can be found in Plato's *Republic*.

The new American dilemma, then, involves the seemingly irreconcilable differences between these two approaches to justice. Securing protection for an individual against overt racial or gender discrimination in the future is clearly insufficient to ameliorate harm done in the past, but the courts (and society) seem unwilling to go beyond this remedy. As noted in Chapter 18 by Glasser, individuals can be partitioned into two camps—those who are ideologically or philosophically constrained from going beyond future protections against discrimination and those who find merit in the moral basis of affirmative action to ameliorate past wrongs.

Economist Thomas Sowell (1986) described two basic visions in human history that are relevant to this debate: the constrained and the unconstrained. The constrained vision, associated with conservative intellectuals such as Adam Smith, Thomas Hobbes, and Edmund Burke, characterizes people as hopelessly flawed and ill equipped to ameliorate the infirmities associated with individual differences. Adherents of this philosophical persuasion would clearly support equal opportunity but would take sharp exception to the causal attributions made to individual deficits by political liberals, as well as to most affirmative action remedies. The unconstrained vision, traceable to Jean-Jacques Rousseau, Thorsten Veblen, and John Kenneth Galbraith, rejects the notion of limits and sees people as capable of reforming society. They would be on the opposite side of the issue.

Sowell's thesis of dual and conflicting visions appears to epitomize the themes addressed in this book. There has been little disagreement about the evils of prejudice and racism. The basic disagreements—the new dilemma—center on an interpretation of the causal factors, in some instances, and on the proposed remedies, in others. Equality of result (macrojustice) and equality of process (microjustice) are dichotomies in search of reconciliation. Better integration of the social-psychological theories (e.g., equity, contact, and attribution theories) that address these themes will be a first step toward the resolution of this new dilemma.

REFERENCES

Allport, G. (1954). *The nature of prejudice*. Reading, MA: Addison-Wesley.
Amir, Y. (1969). Contact hypothesis in ethnic relations. *Psychological Bulletin, 71*, 319–342.
Banks, J. (1972). Racial prejudice and the black self-concept. In J. Banks & J. Grambs (Eds.), *Black self-concept*. New York: McGraw-Hill.
Brickman, P., Folger, R., Goode, E., & Schul, Y. (1980). Micro and macro justice. In M. J. Lerner (Ed.), *The justice motive in social behavior*. New York: Plenum Press.
Brown v. Board of Education of Topeka, 347 U.S. 483 (1954).

Clark, K. B., & Clark, M. (1947). Racial identification and preferences in Negro children. In T. M. Newcomb & E. L. Hartley (Eds.), *Readings in social psychology*. New York: Holt.

Crain, R. L., & Mahard, R. E. (1978). Desegregation and black achievement: A review of the research. *Law and Contemporary Problems, 42*(3), 17–56.

Deutsch, M. (1975). Equity, equality and need: What determines which value will be used as the basis of distributive justice? *Journal of Social Issues, 31*, 137–150.

Gerard, H. B., & Miller, N. (1975). *School desegregation*. New York: Plenum Press.

Hraba, J., & Grant, G. (1970). Black is beautiful: A reexamination of racial preference and identification. *Journal of Personality and Social Psychology, 16*, 398–402.

Isaacs, H. (1975). *Idols of the tribe*. New York: Harper & Row.

Jones, J. M. (1972). *Prejudice and racism*. Reading, MA: Addison Wesley.

Katz, P. A., & Zalk, S. R. (1974). Doll preferences: An index of racial attitudes? *Journal of Educational Psychology, 66*, 663–668.

Krol, R. A. (1978). A meta-analysis of comparative research on the effects of desegregation on academic achievement. *Dissertation Abstracts*.

Lewis, M. (1987). *Assessing social intervention: Scientific and social implication*. Institute for the Study of Child Development, Robert Wood Johnson Medical School, unpublished paper.

Minnesota Law Review. (1953). Pp. 437–438.

Myrdal, G. (1944). *An American dilemma: The Negro problem and modern democracy*. New York: Harper.

Plessy v. Ferguson, 163 U.S. 537 (1896).

Sowell, T. (1986). *A conflict of visions*. New York: William Morrow.

Stephan, W. G. (1978). School desegregation: An evaluation of predictions made in *Brown v. Board of Education*. *Psychological Bulletin, 85*, 217–238.

Stephan, W. G., & Rosenfield, D. (1978). Effects of desegregation on racial attitudes. *Journal of Personality and Social Psychology. 36*(8), 795–804.

Swann v. Charlotte-Mecklenburg Board of Education, 318 F. Supp. 786 (1970).

Sweatt v. Painter, 339 U.S. 629 (1950).

Sweatt v. Painter, 210 S.W. 2d442 (1947), 339 U.S. 629.

Wortman, P. M., & Bryant, F. B. (1985). School desegregation and black achievement: An integrative review. *Sociological Methods and Research, 13*(3), 289–324.

Author Index

Subject Index